Spain in the Liberal Age

5

History of Spain

Published

Forthcoming

Spain in the Liberal Age

From Constitution to Civil War,
1808–1939

Charles J. Esdaile

 BLACKWELL
Publishers

The right of Charles J. Esdaile to be identified as author of this work has been asserted in accordance with the Copyright, Designs and Patents Act 1988.

First published 2000

2 4 6 8 10 9 7 5 3 1

Blackwell Publishers Ltd
108 Cowley Road
Oxford OX4 1JF
UK

Blackwell Publishers Inc.
350 Main Street
Malden, Massachusetts 02148
USA

British Library Cataloguing in Publication Data

A CIP catalogue record for this book is available from the British Library.

Library of Congress Cataloging-in-Publication Data is available for this book.

ISBN 0 631 14988 0 (hbk)

Typeset in 10½ on 12 pt Sabon
by York House Typographic Ltd, London
Printed in Great Britain by TJ International, Padstow, Cornwall

This book is printed on acid-free paper

Contents

For my mother, Elizabeth Alice Ellen Esdaile, with much love.

Preface

As all hispanists would agree, there is today a great need for a new single-volume history of modern Spain covering the entire period from 1808 to 1939, the thirty-three years that have passed since the publication of Sir Raymond Carr's seminal *Spain, 1808–1939* having been marked by a positive flood of articles, monographs and partial studies which has for years been crying out for synthesis. The present work is designed to fulfil that need: within its pages will be found a clear and accessible account of 131 years of politics, warfare, and social and economic change. However, whilst chronicle and chronology are indispensable, on their own they are dry and unsatisfactory, the result being that the author has at every stage striven to blend analysis with narrative. As an early-nineteenth-century specialist, meanwhile, it is very much the author's hope that this work will provide a general sense of modern Spain that many anglophone undergraduates (and possibly some Spanish ones as well) have hitherto found difficult to acquire: too often the starting point for the subject has been 1936 rather than 1808. If the result is less than perfect – even 190,000 words are insufficient to address all that needs to be addressed – it is still to be hoped that it proves to be of service.

All that remains to be done, then, is for me to express my gratitude to all those who have assisted in the appearance of *Spain in the Liberal Age*. First and foremost, of course, comes the general editor of the current series, Professor John Lynch, who has been a model of patience and encouragement. Next to him, perhaps, comes Blackwell's Tessa Harvey, the latter having responded to the many problems thrown up in the past five years with much kindness and common sense. Beyond them I owe particular thanks to my good friends Rory Muir and Christopher Allmand, who lavished immense amounts of time and trouble on reading the manuscript, the latter also being owed my warmest thanks for his great understanding and generosity as my Head of Department. Also of considerable assistance at various times have been Ian Jackson and John Fisher of the University of Liverpool, Paul Preston of the University of

London, and Martin Blinkhorn of the University of Lancaster, whilst Anthony Grahame and his staff at G&G Editorial made an excellent job of the copy-editing.

Spain in the Liberal Age will for me always be indelibly associated with the very happy year that I spent in Spain with my family in 1994–5. Funded by the British Academy and the University of Liverpool, to both of whom I owe my sincere thanks, this most profitable sabbatical was marked by the immense help which I received from many Spanish sources. At the Universidad Complutense de Madrid, Emilio de Diego, Octavio Ruiz Manjón, Enrique Martínez Ruiz, Rosa María Martínez de Codes and Pazzis Pi y Corrales all afforded me considerable assistance, as did Agustín Guimera of the Consejo Superior de Investigaciones Científicas and Leopoldo Stampa of the Ministerio de Asuntos Exteriores. Too many for me to name here, all the staff of the Biblióteca Nacional were as efficient as they were welcoming, whilst, amongst my fellow researchers, Azucena Pedraz Marcos, Nuria Carmena Jiménez, Grahame Harrison, Susan Alonso and María Quevedo López-Varela were all kind enough to share insight and friendship alike. However, support came not just from academic circles, but from friends old and new. Marta Requena, Concha Bocos, Rafael Agasagasti, William and Sonia Chislett, Neville Britton, María Teresa Berruezo, Emilio and Dolores de Castro, Jo Klepka, Enrique Mardones, Francisco Díaz, Sarah Herbert, Fernando Fanjul, Antonia Rodríguez, Sharon Juden, Santiago Nistal, Maribel Piqueras, and Father Raymond Sullivant were amongst the many people who showered us with kindness, whilst a special word must also be put in for the many nameless citizens of Madrid who went out of their way to show kindness to my wife and children.

At the very last, I come to my family. As before, my dear wife, Alison, has continued to support me in everything, whilst loyally enduring the drawbacks of marriage to an academic, and, still worse, a historian. As for my children, Andrew, Helen and María-Isabel, they are, it seems, proud of Daddy's 'stories'. Be that as it may, I am certainly proud of them.

Charles Esdaile, Liverpool, 19 January 1999

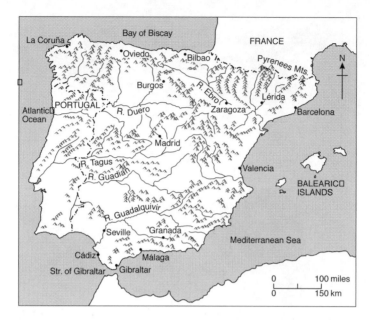

Spain (physical features), based on H. Thomas, *The Spanish Civil War* (London: Penguin, 1977), p. 12.

Spain (political regions), based on H. Thomas, *The Spanish Civil War* (London: Penguin, 1977), p. 15.

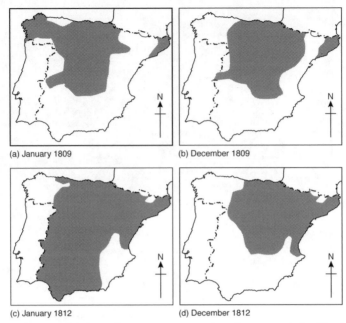

(a) January 1809 (b) December 1809

(c) January 1812 (d) December 1812

The Spanish War of Independence, 1808–1814, based on C. Esdaile, *The Spanish Army in the Peninsular War* (Manchester: Manchester University Press, 1988), p. 160.

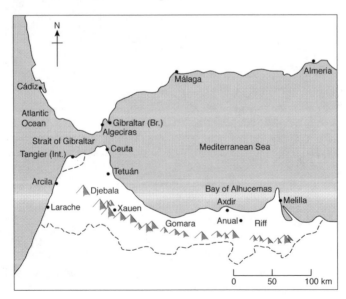

Spanish Morocco, based on S. Payne, *Politics and the Military in Modern Spain* (Stanford, California: Stanford University Press, 1967), p. 104.

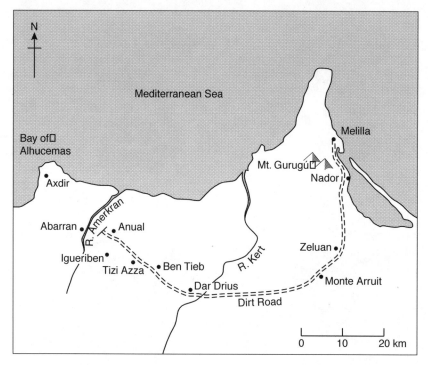

Melilla and the Riff, 1909–1923, based on S. Payne, *Politics and the Military in Modern Spain* (Stanford, California: Stanford University Press, 1967), p. 158.

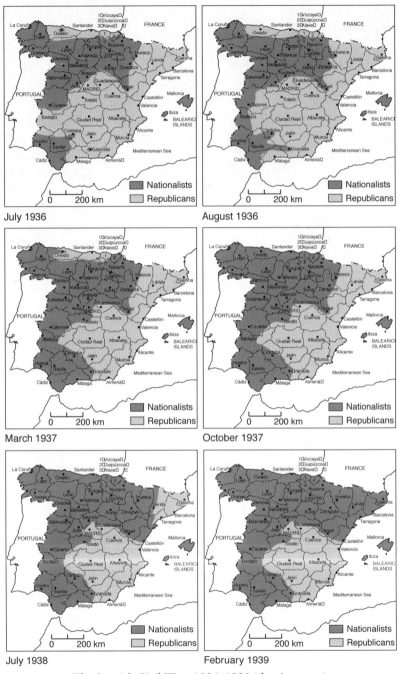

The Spanish Civil War, 1936–1939 (the six stages)

1

The Spanish Uprising

A Shot in the Dark

About midnight on the night of 17–18 March 1808 a single shot rang out in the *real sitio* of Aranjuez. Within moments its streets were filled with an angry crowd intent on lynching the hated royal favourite, Manuel de Godoy. Within two days a battered Godoy was under arrest, whilst Carlos IV was king no more, having been replaced by his eldest son as King Fernando VII. Watershed though they were, however, these events can only be understood in the context of the previous twenty years. On the death of Carlos III in 1788 Spain had been a flourishing imperial state with a growing transatlantic trade, a nascent cotton industry, an unrivalled supply of bullion, a colonial empire of vast proportions that a period of capable reform had opened to far more effective exploitation by the metropolis, and a navy that was amongst the most powerful in Europe. By 1808, however, all this was lost: Spain was bankrupt and exhausted, cut off from her colonies, bereft of her naval power, and in thrall to an ally both ruthless and dangerous.

The Emergence of Godoy

If there was one factor that played no part in Spain's misfortunes, it was the replacement of the vigorous Carlos III, by the supposedly half-witted Carlos IV. If the latter was hardly a very impressive monarch, it is doubtful whether even the most dynamic of rulers could have overcome the problems that were to beset his reign. Thus, the salient fact about the latter was that it coincided with the French Revolution. In March 1793 Spain – most unwillingly – found herself at war with France. A year-long invasion of Roussillon having been repulsed in 1794, by the summer of 1795 the French had occupied large parts of Catalonia and the Basque provinces. Forced to fight a war for which it was unprepared – ever since the Seven Years' War Madrid's foreign policy had been predicated on a permanent alliance with France – the army could do no more; the initial popular enthusiasm for the war had long since ebbed; a republican conspiracy had been unmasked in Madrid; and little help was forth-coming from Spain's allies, the result being that on 22 July 1795 peace was therefore signed at Basle.

For a brief moment Godoy was genuinely popular, whilst a grateful Carlos IV rewarded him with the title of Prince of the Peace, the peace terms having proved remarkably favourable. However, Spain's with-drawal from the war made it extremely likely that Britain would threaten the Spanish empire, and in April 1796 the then General Bonaparte invaded northern Italy and proceeded to sweep all before him, thereby threatening a number of important Spanish dynastic interests. In short, a fresh alliance with France was essential, the result being, first, the treaty of San Ildefonso of 18 August 1796, and, second, the outbreak of war with Britain on 9 October of the same year.

At this point we need to say a little more about Godoy's personal position. An obscure scion of the *extremeño* nobility, Godoy had first come to Madrid in 1787 as a private soldier in the royal bodyguard, and had quickly attracted the attention of Queen María Luisa on account of his manly bearing. Doted upon by king and queen alike, by 1792 Godoy held the rank of Captain General of the army, was a grandee of the first class, and had been appointed prime minister. Astonishing as this last appointment may appear, however, it was not the result of mere caprice. With his court the focus of a bitter struggle between the rival factions known as the *corbatas* and the *golillas*, Carlos had come to the conclu-sion that the safest course was to award power to a man whose loyalty was owed to him alone. Be this as it may, however, Godoy was clearly extremely vulnerable. Whether or not he was genuinely the queen's lover (and it is at least possible that he never was), the belief that he owed his position only to his prowess in her bedchamber could hardly be avoided. At the same time, too, his advancement could not but anger the grandees who dominated the court, and, in particular, that element of the nobility which had seen the Conde de Aranda's brief period as Secretary of State from March to November 1792 as an opportunity to reverse the creeping Bourbon erosion of their status. Lacking in any power-base, Godoy could only rely on continued royal favour and the influence of his own patronage, the problem with the first being that it could be withdrawn at any time, and the second that it was likely to win him as many enemies as it did friends.

If Godoy had actually been the idler of legend, it is possible that his position might have been much easier. In this respect, believing that France was not to be trusted in the slightest, his first target was the army, which he was determined should be given an adequate system of recruit-ment, a modern system of tactics and a better-trained officer corps, and be pruned of such costly encumberances as the royal guard. From 1796 onwards, he therefore became engaged in a spasmodic campaign to secure these goals, only to find that every effort that he made at fundamental reform was blocked by the protests of powerful vested interests within the military establishment, vetoed by the throne, or derailed by popular opposition. In the event little was achieved other than to tinker with a few details and pack the high command with the favourite's clients, Godoy earning the hatred of some officers, especially in the royal guard (whose strength he did succeed in cutting quite dramatically), the contempt of many others, and the loyalty of virtually none.

Nor was the army the only institution to be alienated by Godoy. Under great financial pressure, eager to win some credit with the strongly reformist bureaucracy, determined to create a clientele amongst the hierarchy, and much influenced by the thinking of such liberal economic theorists as Jovellanos, Godoy turned his attention to the Church. In consequence, the Church found that the severe regalist pressure of the past century was much intensified, especially with regard to ecclesiastical appointments. More dramatically, meanwhile, a start was also made on the expropriation of the Church's immense wealth, the fact being that by 1808 it had been stripped of something over fifteen per cent of its property. To suggest that the process turned the whole ecclesiastical establishment against Godoy would be an exaggeration, for the Church was locked in an increasingly bitter struggle between reform and tradition. For all that, however, much of the clergy did come to hate Godoy, reformists being angry at his failure to give them full support, traditionalists resentful of his depredations, and all shades of opinion united in their condemnation of his lifestyle, which was, beyond doubt, extremely scandalous. With many members of the lower clergy in a state of real want, Godoy was therefore unlikely to obtain much support from the pulpit.

Elite hostility to Godoy extended beyond Spain's institutions. With the cost of the war with England mounting and the government bonds that the regime had issued to finance the struggle perpetually depreciating, the need for fresh revenue was pressing. Yet the economic situation was extremely poor, and it therefore seemed unwise to pass the burden on to the mass of the population, and all the more so as there had already been fierce anti-taxation disorders in Galicia in 1791. If the era of Godoy was one of opportunity for men of property, it was also one of increased pressure. Thus, from 1798 onwards *los pudientes* were subjected to a series of forced loans, whilst new taxes were imposed on servants, horses, mules and carriages, on all rental income, and on the establishment of new *mayorazgos*. Meanwhile, particular members of the elite were alienated by various other aspects of Godoy's rule: for *ilustrados* such as Jovellanos, Godoy's licentiousness and venality killed their faith in his reformism; equally, for titled magnates such as the Duque del Infantado, Godoy remained an upstart who posed a dangerous threat to their privileges; finally, for wealthy merchants, such as the Valencian Bertrán de Lis, Godoy's foreign policy was little short of ruinous.

At the most exalted level of all, elite resentment of Godoy found a focus in the figure of the heir to the throne, Prince Fernando. Emotionally stunted and neglected by his parents, for whom he conceived a deep resentment, Fernando came to hate Godoy, whom he believed to have stolen the affection of *los reyes* and poisoned them against him. Such adolescent jealousy – in 1800 Fernando was sixteen – might have gone for nothing, had not he become surrounded by a number of figures with a grudge against Godoy, most notably the scheming cleric, Juan de Escoíquiz, the Duque del Infantado and the Conde de Montijo. Motivated by a mixture of jealousy and ambition, the magnates amongst them, at least, also stood for something else. Throughout the eighteenth century the old aristocracy had been increasingly under threat, whether it was from the growth of the bureaucracy, the creation of a new 'nobility of service', or the erosion of the link that had hitherto firmly linked the concept of nobility with that of martial prowess, and in 1794 Montijo had been sent into internal exile for protesting at these developments. The ignorant and cowardly Fernando being the perfect puppet king, Infantado and Montijo therefore decided to make use of him to put things to rights, to which end they convinced the prince that the favourite intended to oust him from the succession, matters being much helped in this respect by the prince's marriage in October 1802 to María Antonia of Naples, the princess detesting *los reyes*, Godoy and the French alliance in approximately equal measure.

War, Reform and Economic Crisis

Whilst factious grandees and a rebellious crown prince might provide sufficient explanation for a palace revolution, they cannot account for events of the magnitude of those which now followed. To understand the cataclysm that Spain was about to experience, we must move beyond the confines of the court to the burgeoning social crisis precipitated by the war with Britain.

Until 1795 Spain had escaped relatively unscathed from the Revolutionary Wars. With the conflict with Britain, however, the situation changed dramatically. Despite the strength of her navy, Spain was unable to prevent the blockade of her ports, whilst the length of her sea lanes rendered her particularly vulnerable to commerce raiding. Some trade still got through, of course, whilst the British even licensed the export of such products as they happened to need, but on the whole the impact was disastrous, Spanish seaborne trade being largely paralysed (by the same token, of course, the flow of bullion from the empire was also interrupted: hence the financial difficulties that helped precipitate Godoy's assault on the Church).

Had Spain remained the stagnant state of the early eighteenth century, this development need not have mattered. However, the reign of Carlos III had seen her exports increase dramatically. At the same time, in many areas of the country agriculture had switched to cash crops, whilst industry had experienced a certain modest growth. In Catalonia, for example, the peasantry had increasingly turned to the production of wine and brandy; meanwhile, an important cotton industry had grown up around Barcelona that by the late 1780s may have employed as many as 100,000 workers. In Valencia, boosted by the ready availability of the raw material, a silk industry existed that at its greatest extent had more than 3,000 looms. In the province of Granada there was another silk industry that employed some 2,000 looms in 1798 and a woollen industry with over seventy different manufacturers; at the same time, the fertile *huerta* surrounding the capital was increasingly given over to the hemp and flax demanded by the shipyards of Cartagena. In Seville, the famous tobacco factory employed over 1,500 people, whilst the colonial trade gave employment to at least 70,000 artisans in the vicinity of Cádiz. Around Santander the liberalization of commerce and establishment of several foundries and shipyards led to an economic boom based on flour, iron, leather, forestry, charcoal-making and basket-work. And finally, as well as developing as a major centre for the export of Castillian wool and grain, Bilbao was the centre of an important iron industry that in 1790 sent 4,000 tons of iron goods to the empire alone.

Of course, neither industry nor agriculture produced entirely for the empire or even for the export market in general. According to one recent estimate, in fact, only 50 per cent of Spanish exports went to the empire, whilst only 25 per cent actually consisted of Spanish products; as for the proportion of Spanish agricultural and industrial production that went abroad, a variety of factors suggest that this was gradually falling. Yet this should not allow us to minimize the war. By 1805, for example, cotton was only employing some 30,000 people in Catalonia. Elsewhere, meanwhile, the situation was even worse, the fact being that maritime transport was crucial to a very wide sector of the economy. Raw materials often came by sea, as did much of the imported grain on which whole areas of the country were more or less dependent. Meanwhile, the navy and merchant marine provided a market for a whole host of ancillary industries, whilst necessitating the employment of thousands of muleteers, woodcutters, stevedores and the like. With the British patrolling the seas more or less unmolested (for the showing of the under-funded Spanish navy was almost uniformly dismal), the war's impact was therefore catastrophic, and all the more as there was no room for manoeuvre: many Spanish industries were hopelessly archaic, for example, whilst the domestic market was increasingly impoverished, and a protectionist France positively hostile to Spanish exports.

In fairness to Godoy, it must be said that Spain's alliance with France was not the only cause of her difficulties. On the contrary, she was simultaneously assailed by an extraordinary crop of natural disasters that included unseasonal weather, floods, droughts, earthquakes and even plagues of grasshoppers. With considerable proportions of the harvest repeatedly lost and the population experiencing steady growth (between 1752 and 1797 it seems to have increased by approximately 10 per cent), the result was, first, a series of severe subsistence crises, and, second, a great acceleration of the price inflation that had been afflicting Spain since the 1780s. And, as if all this was not enough, large parts of Spain were swept by terrible epidemics of yellow fever.

All these disasters were inflicted on a country that was already in the grip of a severe social crisis. As might be expected, agricultural issues were well to the fore in this respect. In the Cantabrian mountains, for example, the problem was essentially one of access to the forests that cloaked the hillsides. Essential to the region's peasantry as a source of food and pasturage, this had for some time been under increasing threat. On the one hand, the industries that had sprung up along the coast were consuming ever greater quantities of timber (by the 1790s wood was having to be brought in from as far away as Burgos). On the other, particularly in the Basque country, the richer elements of the peasantry – indeed, the term is really a misnomer in this context – were steadily advancing their position at the expense of their poorer fellows. Thus, large amounts of land that had been used as common pasturage were cleared and brought under the plough, whilst many smallholders were forced to sell out. With many municipalities having been forced by fiscal pressure to embark on the sale of the common lands, by the first years of the nineteenth century a powerful group of middling and even large proprietors had therefore emerged who were quick to destroy the last vestiges of the Basques' traditional peasant democracy (in all the Basque provinces there survived the assemblies that had safeguarded their traditional privileges or *fueros*; supposed to represent that entire community, they were now entirely in the hands of the notables).

In other parts of the country the problem was rather financial. Throughout Spain the *campesinos* were obliged to pay the traditional dues of tithes and first fruits to the Church, the total in 1800 amounting to nearly 650,000,000 copper *reales*. In addition to the direct demands of the Church, meanwhile, there was also the question of the dues owed under the feudal system. Although the feudal lord – the *señor* – might be the monarch himself, an absentee grandee, a member of the petty provincial nobility, a monastery or convent, a bishopric, one of the four mediaeval military orders, or even a municipal corporation, a very great number of Spain's villages, towns and even cities were subjected to such obligations. The details varied from place to place, but in general the *señor* was owed as much as a quarter of all produce as rent for the land and a variety of other dues and fees; in addition, he enjoyed a series of monopolies on such activities as milling and baking, and controlled the administration of justice, thereby being enabled to exploit the commons for his own profit and burden his *vasallos* with rules and regulations that could impose a heavy cost on even the most basic of agricultural activities. Nor was it even just a case of the *señores* versus the rest. In most of Spain, agriculture, and with it local government, had become dominated by a powerful *rentier* class composed of officials, lawyers, merchants and others who rented the land of the *señores*, and then either sublet it at a great profit to peasant smallholders or alternatively farmed it directly with the help of armies of landless labourers. On top of all this, of course, there was the question of taxation. Far too complex an issue to discuss here (for one thing the system varied enormously), suffice to say that the population was subjected to a bewildering variety of taxes, levies and monopolies whose administration was unjust in the extreme, and whose weight was naturally augmented by the demands of the war.

To make matters worse, this great weight fell on an agrarian economy that was, with some exceptions – Catalonia and a few irrigated areas around such cities as Granada and Valencia – desperately poor. Soils were poor, rainfall low, irrigation minimal, holdings too small, labour superabundant, monoculture too general, capital lacking, transport costs enormous and technology backward. In the context of war and natural disaster, the poverty that was the constant lot of much of the population slipped very rapidly into complete destitution, the impact of the catastrophe being intensified by the damage done by disamortization to the Church's ability to dispense charity. Hospitals, poorhouses and orphanages were crammed to overflowing; the already substantial number of smallholders being forced into the ranks of the *jornaleros* or trapped by usury underwent a significant increase (in this respect Godoy's disamortization of the lands of the Church was particularly significant since a decree of 15 September 1803 effectively gave the new owners *carte blanche* to raise rents); desperate labourers and their families fled to the cities in search of work only to find that there was no choice but for them to swell the ever-growing crowds of beggars, thieves and prostitutes; dockers, muleteers, artisans and out-workers lost their employment by the thousand; and the countryside was terrorized by gangs of bandits and desperate *jornaleros* out to find work by any means available. Meanwhile, of course, the *pudientes* were able to extend their estates at bargain prices (in that they were able to buy Church land with depreciated government bonds), escape the worst effects of taxation, shrug off or evade the pressures of the state, and engage in wholesale rack-renting and grain speculation.

Thus far we have spoken of the crisis of the *antiguo régimen* very much in social and economic terms. Important though these were, it also had a political and ideological dimension. Let us take, for example, the question of the army. Neglected in favour of the navy though it may have been, this force had yet been prominent enough to make itself thoroughly detested. In the first place, and most obviously, it was the first line of defence against such activities as smuggling, banditry and riot, and, by the same token, the ally of the tax-collector, landlord and *señor*. In the second, it was an economic burden, the various dues that were imposed to cover its transport, subsistence and quarters amounting to an annual average of perhaps 40,000,000 *reales*. In the third, officers and men alike were notorious for the bullying manner which they adopted towards civilian society. And, in the fourth, it carried with it the constant threat of military service, although conscription was so unpopular that it was only employed in time of war (needless to say, the brunt of the burden was borne almost exclusively by the urban and rural poor). Such injustices aside, meanwhile, the common soldiery were poorly paid, miserably housed, subjected to a most brutal code of discipline, and seen as drunken, licentious brutes, further offence being caused by the presence in the army of large numbers of foreign mercenaries and deserters.

If the army was a constant source of irritation, even more was this the case with the regime's cultural policy. Crudely speaking, under Carlos III and Carlos IV alike this aimed at civilizing the masses. To combat Spanish backwardness what was needed was the encouragement of education and cleanliness, the spread of enlightenment, the elimination of vice, and the inculcation of a new work ethic, these aspirations engendering activities that ranged from the sublime to the downright ridiculous. Thus at one end of the spectrum one has the foundation of the Societies of Friends of the People, a growing interest in popular education, a fixed aversion to bullfighting, the construction of new cemeteries away from populated areas, and a determination to purify Spanish Catholicism of many of the popular traditions with which it was held to be adulterated. At the other one has the criticism of charity, denunciation of all forms of holiday and popular entertainment, desire to eradicate all manifestations of folk-culture (even traditional songs and carols were frowned upon), attempt to replace both *la zarzuela* and the classical drama of the Golden Age with a new 'enlightened' theatre, and interest in dress reform (the all-enveloping cloak typical of lower-class men was regarded as an ideal cover for bandit daggers). Underlying the whole was a terror of the common people – *el populacho* – that is almost palpable: ignorant, savage, brutal, irrational, and vicious, they had to be kept under control by a diet of constant labour and denied any outlet for their emotions.

Unpleasant in its connotations, this cultural reformism was also dangerously provocative. For a population such as that of eighteenth-century Spain, the various communal rituals and celebrations that were so hated by the *ilustrados* were the very stuff of life. Welcome interruptions in an otherwise unending round of drudgery and boredom, they were also vital manifestations of identity. Thus, for Carlos III and the various ecclesiastical reformers whom he patronized, such traditional ceremonies as the burial of the sardine in Murcia were examples of the darkest ignorance and superstition. However, for the towns involved they were the lifeblood of the community, and the source of much local pride. Still worse, take them away, and the community would be deprived of the supernatural help that was its only protection against misfortune, a fear that could only be intensified given the growing tendency of traditionalist preachers to argue that Spain's ills stemmed from divine punishment of Godoy. Allied to all this was the question of xenophobia, and, particularly, francophobia. In many parts of Spain, economic rivalry, the presence of a substantial French community, folk memories of the War of Spanish Succession, and, most recently, the anti-revolutionary propaganda associated with the war of 1793–5, had led to considerable anti-French feeling. Yet, with the *petimetre* – the fashionable young fop who affected French dress and French manners, and peppered his speech with gallicisms in order to curry favour with the authorities and demonstrate his own superiority – already becoming something of a stock figure, and the Enlightenment already being portrayed by traditionalist clerics as a satanic plot, in popular eyes for what did Bourbon cultural policy stand if not frenchification and the destruction of Spain's very identity? At all events it is clear that, just as early manifestations of Bourbon reformism had helped provoke serious disturbances in 1766, so Godoy was playing with fire in continuing to impose it in the Spain of the 1790s; indeed, of all his many actions there were probably none more unpopular than his prohibition of all bullfights in 1805.

Hardly surprisingly given the pressure that she was under, by 1800 Spain was in a state of ferment. In the first place we may observe a series of severe disorders, such as the peasant risings that occurred in Galicia and Asturias in 1790–1, Galicia in 1798, Valencia in 1801, and Bilbao in 1804, and the bread riots that took place in Segovia in 1802 and Madrid in 1804. In the second we can see a growing challenge to *señores* and

Church alike. With regard to the former, if acts of violence were relatively rare, in many parts of Spain *pueblos* attempted to mount a legal challenge against their *señores*. As for the demands of the Church, many peasants pretended that they had produced less than was actually the case, or circumvented the tithes altogether by introducing new crops which were not specifically subject to them. Meanwhile, there was also much resistance to many of the regime's political and social reforms. In the Basque provinces, for example, the dominant notables were outraged by Godoy's attempts to whittle away the *fueros* still further in accordance with the centralizing policies of Carlos III, and engaged in a fierce campaign of obstruction and propaganda. More humbly, meanwhile, all over Spain, townsfolk and peasants who had been forced to see their loved ones buried in new-fangled municipal cemeteries stole their bodies back at night and tried to restore them to the protection of the old resting places; more particularly, in Madrid the growing *afrancesamiento* of the court was met by the swaggering figures of the *majos* and *majas* – shopkeepers, artisans, taverners and labourers who, together with their women, dressed in exaggeratedly traditional style and took pleasure in picking fights with the representatives of the new order.

To return to national politics, it was the existence of this complex web of resentment, resistance, hunger and despair that enabled the anti-godoyist faction in the court to reach out to the people, and all the more so as the fashion which had emerged amongst the more adventurous spirits of the court nobility of mingling with the Madrid crowd in disguise gave the conspirators an ideal means of spreading scurrilous rumours. Thus it was that when María Antonia of Naples met an early death, stories spread that she had been poisoned; still worse, it was put about that Godoy was plotting to seize the throne, the conspirators also distributing a series of insulting cartoons which made much of his supposed relationship with the queen; the prince, meanwhile, was portrayed as an injured innocent who would rescue Spain from all her ills.

Effective though this propaganda was, there is no reason to suppose that at this stage Spain was heading for anything more serious than the riots of 1766 (when mob violence had toppled an equally unpopular chief minister). What changed the situation was Spain's ever more precarious international position. In this respect it cannot be denied that Godoy's aims in forming the alliance with France had gone disastrously astray. Far from being enabled to rebuild her strength under the protection of the French navy, and thus ultimately to reassert her independence as a great power, Spain found rather that she was seriously weakened. On the one hand, with the government deprived of much of the revenues of the American empire, there was little that Godoy could have done to strengthen the Spanish army, even had his plans encountered less opposition. On the other, even such strength as Spain had was dissipated with the Spanish fleet suffering a number of serious defeats, and Godoy being forced to mount a ruinously expensive expedition against Portugal in 1801. Following the French lead, peace was signed with Britain in March 1802 – the price was the loss of the colony of Trinidad – but in little more than a year Britain and France were at war again. Conscious of the dangers of a fresh conflict, Godoy made frantic efforts to stay clear of the new struggle, but in the event the best he could do was to secure Napoleon's agreement that Spain might redeem the pledges made in the treaty of San Ildefonso by a subsidy of six million *francs* per month. Onerous as this arrangement was (the government had to raise the necessary money by means of an extortionate loan on the Paris market), it did not even achieve its aims: arguing that in reality Spain remained allied to France, Britain went back to war with her in October 1804. The result, just over one year later, was the catastrophic defeat of Trafalgar of 21 October 1805, in which the bulk of Spain's remaining seapower was destroyed, and a renewal of the economic disasters which we have already detailed.

Mutiny at Aranjuez

All this would have been more bearable had there been the slightest sign that France was prepared to defend Spain's interests, or even simply to respect them. On the contrary, however, Napoleon snubbed Madrid at every turn. With the very *raison d'être* of the alliance scattering the seabed off Trafalgar, the empire now under direct threat (Britain was not only patronizing such revolutionaries as Francisco Miranda, but had occupied Montevideo and Buenos Aires), and his own popularity at a new low, Godoy began to cast around for some form of escape. Encouraged by friendly overtures from Russia, in the autumn of 1806 Godoy was presented with what seemed the perfect opportunity in the form of war between France and Prussia. Contemporary wisdom holding that the Prussian army was the best in Europe, Godoy immediately called Spain to arms. Great was the consternation in Madrid, therefore, when on 14 October 1806 Napoleon smashed the Prussians at the battles of Jena and Auerstädt. Desperate to escape the emperor's wrath, Godoy maintained that his ill-advised call to arms had been directed not against the French but the British, congratulated Napoleon upon his victories, and agreed both to join the newly-established Continental Blockade and to dispatch a division of 14,000 men for service with the *grande armée*. Conscious that in doing so, he was only fanning the flames of domestic unrest and political opposition, and that the health of Carlos IV was dangerously precarious, Godoy now embarked on a last-ditch attempt to save himself. Even before the *débâcle* of October 1806 he had been dreaming of conquering Portugal as a means both of satisfying his desire for martial glory – Godoy fancied himself a great general – and of securing an independent principality. Until now a mere pipe-dream, the establishment of the Continental Blockade seemed suddenly to put such a plan within his grasp, for Napoleon determined that an army should be sent to Portugal to force her to cut her links with Britain. Months of complex negotiations followed, but on 27 October 1807 Spain signed the treaty of Fontainebleau, this providing for a Franco-Spanish invasion of Portugal and the latter's partition into three petty statelets, one of which would be given to Godoy. Some ten days earlier the first French troops had marched into Spain, and by the end of November Lisbon was under military occupation.

The appearance of the French armies coincided with a dramatic deterioration in Godoy's situation. In addition to doing all that they could to blacken the favourite's reputation and ensure that the machinery of power could be immediately taken over by them should Carlos IV die, the *fernandino* conspirators had early in 1807 decided to guarantee the succession of their figurehead by marrying Fernando into the Bonaparte family (the fact that the only possible candidates were junior in the extreme did not deter them). In consequence, secret negotiations were opened with the French ambassador, in the process of which Fernando was persuaded to write a letter openly begging Napoleon's protection. However, for reasons which remain unclear, in a dramatic confrontation at the royal palace of El Escorial on 27 October, Carlos and María Luisa confined the prince to his quarters and ordered an investigation into his affairs. In so far as can be ascertained, Fernando's papers revealed little more than that he hated Godoy, had dreams of persuading his father to have him imprisoned, and had been in some sort of contact with Napoleon. Nonetheless the king and queen came to the conclusion that the prince had been plotting their overthrow. Bullied into admitting that this had indeed been his aim, Fernando was eventually pardoned, but those he named as his collaborators – Escoiquiz, Infantado, Montijo and various others – were arrested and sent into internal exile.

For Godoy, all this was a catastrophe, the general verdict being that the whole affair had been an audacious attempt to remove Fernando from the succession, the banishment of Escoiquiz *et al* therefore being viewed as a monstrous abuse of justice. Even more disastrously, meanwhile, the affair finally convinced Napoleon of the need for intervention. Whilst keeping his options open in so far as the future was concerned, at the end of January 1808 he therefore ordered the armies that he had by now massed in northern Spain to seize the fortresses of San Sebastián, Pamplona, Figueras and Barcelona and sent yet more troops across the frontier.

Lacking orders, in large part convinced, along with the rest of Spain, that the French had come to oust Godoy, and in some cases subjected to the most bare-faced trickery, the Spanish border garrisons submitted without a fight. In so far as the favourite was concerned, however, there was now no option but to go to war, to which end he frantically tried to concentrate such forces as he could around the royal family's current residence of Aranjuez whilst at the same time attempting to persuade the king and queen to flee to the safety of America. With Napoleon's response being on 9 March to order his supreme commander in Spain, Marshal Murat, to march on Madrid with 50,000 men, war seemed inevitable. For the *fernandinos*, however, such a development was unthinkable given, first, that they remained convinced that the emperor intended to place Fernando on the throne or, at least, to get rid of Godoy, and, second, that any provocation of Napoleon might well produce the overthrow of the dynasty. Terrified of what might occur, Fernando therefore summoned Montijo to Madrid, and ordered him to organize a rising that could present the emperor with a *fait accompli*.

In achieving this goal, there was little difficulty. At this stage virtually the only troops actually at Aranjuez were the royal guard, this being violently hostile to Godoy on account, first, of its aristocratic officer corps, and, second, of the fact that he had cut its size by half. Meanwhile, the population of Aranjuez was wholly dependent on the court for its prosperity, and was currently much swelled by the hordes of courtiers and retainers who travelled with *los reyes* on their seasonal migrations from one royal palace to the next. At the same time, many of the villages around Madrid happened to be *señorios* of the leading *fernandinos* and could thus be galvanized into action by economic means. Yet such economic means were probably barely needed. For all their discontent, the *populacho* retained a touching faith in the protection supposedly afforded them by the monarch, the news that *los reyes* intended to leave them to their fate therefore causing as much fear as the idea that Godoy might evade his doom caused fury.

Disguised as one *tío pepe*, Montijo had within a very few days succeeded in massing a large crowd around the palace at Aranjuez, and, in addition, in whipping the royal guard's hatred of Godoy to fever pitch. Initially it seems that the plan was for the revolt to be sparked off by the departure of the royal family, but, thanks to Carlos' vacillation, such an event stubbornly failed to materialize. Fernando and Montijo therefore took steps to precipitate matters themselves, but such was the tension that trouble started of its own accord in the form of an accidental clash between some of Godoy's hated personal bodyguard and a group of rebel soldiers late in the evening of 17 March. With the bulk of the royal guard in a state of rebellion and the favourite himself hiding in the attic of his palace, a terrified king quickly agreed to have Godoy arrested, but, under Montijo's orchestration, the disturbances continued unabated. Told by the commander of one of the rebel regiments that only Fernando would enjoy the loyalty of the troops, Carlos and María Luisa caved in, and on the morning of 19 March abdicated the crown into the hands of their son. Driven from his hiding place by thirst, meanwhile, Godoy narrowly escaped a lynching, and was placed under close arrest.

For all its popular aspect, we should be in no doubt as to what the so-called 'tumult of Aranjuez' represented. Inspired by elements from outside its ranks though it may have been, a section of the army – in this case the royal guard – had sought to impose its views upon the body politic by 'pronouncing' against the regime. Challenged by this call to arms, Godoy and his royal patrons found that they had few defenders. The officer corps as a whole was disgruntled by the failure of the favourite's reforms to make any difference in its situation, whilst there is some evidence that his orders to resist the French were already being widely disobeyed; much of the upper nobility and the Church was hostile; the *ilustrados* had long since lost all faith in Godoy's political credentials; and the common people were in a state of open revolt. Far from there being any attempt to defend Godoy, all over Spain his fall was greeted with general rejoicing, attacks on his known partisans and rioting against his property and the symbols of his rule. Meanwhile, when Fernando rode into Madrid in triumph on 24 March he was greeted by vast crowds who cheered his every move.

The Spanish National Uprising

Popular though the new king was, his security was far from assured. Murat had occupied the city only the day before, and, despite increasingly abject attempts to win France's favour, refused to recognize Fernando; still worse, indeed, Carlos IV was persuaded to protest against his abdication and appeal to Napoleon for assistance. With the two rivals openly craving his mediation, the emperor was placed in an ideal position to recast the situation as he wanted. Given that he believed that Fernando was popular enough to be able to offer spirited resistance to his immediate aims – free access for French commerce to the Spanish empire and the annexation of all Spanish territory north of the Ebro – his goal was now to place one of his brothers on the throne and thus to transform Spain into a mere satellite. Summoning his older brother, Joseph, from Naples, where he had been king since 1806, he in the meantime succeeded in persuading Carlos, María Luisa and Fernando alike to travel to meet him for a conference across the French border at Bayonne (as a sop to the former *reyes*, Godoy was rescued from captivity and whisked to safety in France). With all the protagonists in the drama united in his presence, Napoleon proceeded to explode the waiting bombshell: the rival kings were both to renounce all right to the throne and place it in the hands of the emperor. To this demand Carlos made no resistance – indeed, he positively ordered his son to give way – and on 5 May, after some days of unedifying squabbles, such feeble defiance as Fernando was willing to offer was also overcome, the throne now being formally signed over to Napoleon in exchange for generous pensions and guarantees of Spain's territorial and religious integrity.

However, the fall of the Bourbons was only the beginning of the turmoil that was to assail Spain in 1808. Ever since the seizure of the Spanish border fortresses, suspicion of the French had been growing, whilst the imperial forces' usual arrogance had also been giving great offence. Thus far the fiction had somehow been maintained that Napoleon was a friend, but on 29 April the council of regency left by Fernando to govern Spain in his absence received a smuggled letter from the prince which left no doubt that he was effectively a captive. Within twenty-four hours the whole capital was in uproar, but the regency, bewildered by the contradiction between hints that it should prepare for resistance and orders that it should do nothing that might jeopardize Fernando's safety, merely dispatched a deputation to Bayonne requesting further instructions. Indeed, far from resisting Murat, it agreed to his demands that the last members of the royal family remaining in Madrid should be sent off to Bayonne in their turn. The result, of course, was that it was overtaken by events. With the population in a ferment, a clash was inevitable, and on the morning of 2 May the crisis finally erupted: a large crowd having gathered outside the palace to protest against the departure of the royal party, scuffles broke out and the French sentries opened fire. As the news spread, the population took to the streets, and the few troops actually posted in the city were forced to withdraw. With 35,000 men at his immediate disposal, Murat had no difficulty in restoring order. Indeed, powerful columns of French troops were soon fighting their way back into the city, the only serious resistance being put up by a handful of soldiers who had seized the army's artillery depot. With the capital firmly back in French hands, the scenes that followed were a grim precursor of many that were to come, at least 200 *madrileños* being executed.

As a military event the Dos de Mayo, as it became known, can only be described as trifling, but in political terms it was pure dynamite. With refugees from Madrid spreading the most wildly exaggerated accounts of what had occurred, the authorities almost everywhere responded with appeals for calm. Given that the vast majority of the Captains General, military governors and intendants then in office were necessarily still nominees of Godoy, an opportunity suddenly emerged for their complete destruction. All over Spain, then, and seemingly quite independently of one another (in Valencia it even seems that there were two separate conspiracies afoot), conspiratorial groups emerged whose aim was to provoke a national revolt that could be exploited for political purposes. Well to the fore in these activities were men who were either representatives of the vested interests offended by the favourite, or who bore a personal grudge against him: good examples of the former include the Conde de Montijo, who was active in both Seville and Cádiz, and the leaders of the conspiracy in Zaragoza and Valencia, José Palafox and Juan Rico, who were respectively an aristocratic guards officer and a Franciscan friar. Of the latter, we might cite the *sevillano* leader, Nicolás Tap y Núñez, a merchant who had suffered imprisonment for some financial irregularity. But, whilst recognizing the importance of hostility to Godoy in the organization of the uprising, it is quite clear this was not the only issue involved. For the lower ranks of the officer corps, for example, an uprising was seized upon as a means of advancing their professional interests. With many officers – perhaps one-third – recruited from the rank and file and promotion dominated by the aristocracy, advancement was excruciatingly slow, whilst salaries had also been outstripped by thirty years of burgeoning inflation. For such men, an uprising offered an obvious solution to their problems, and it is therefore hardly surprising to find that in city after city subaltern officers were prominent. Amongst the lower clergy, too, so great were poverty and unrest that an uprising was an attractive proposition, if only as an antidote to the moral and spiritual degradation in which many ecclesiastics genuinely perceived Spain to be labouring.

For a generation of Spanish historians of more or less Marxian orientation, it is axiomatic that the mainspring of the revolution of 1808 was the bourgeoisie. In so far as this idea is concerned, it is easy to show that representatives of the bourgeoisie were frequently prominent in the leadership of the uprising. Tap y Núñez in Seville is one example that we have already seen, whilst others include Lorenzo Calvo de Rozas and Sinforiano López, who were prosperous entrepreneurs who figured in the risings at Zaragoza and La Coruña. What is much harder to show is that such men were moved by a coherent revolutionary ideology: Calvo de Rozas, for example, was at this time an acolyte of the aristocratic reaction headed by José Palafox. The presence of liberal ideas cannot be denied but there is little evidence to show that these had as yet spread very far beyond a relatively narrow circle of officials, students and intellectuals (it would, however, be fair to say that such social issues as the desire to acquire land and jealousy of the officer corps and its privileges could not but create a climate favourable to the growth of liberalism). As for the idea that liberalism immediately seized control of the uprising, the prominence of such liberal luminaries as Alvaro Flórez Estrada, the Conde de Toreno and Manuel Quintana in the Patriot camp cannot hide the fact that French intervention split Spanish liberalism from top to bottom with many of its supporters throwing their weight behind the cause of Joseph Bonaparte. As a result only in a few places – Cádiz, La Coruña, Oviedo and Valencia – may liberalism be said to have been predominant, the general pattern being that the leading role was played by bishops, cathedral chapters and old-established local oligarchies.

Though founded throughout on a *populacho* that was as radicalized as it was desperate, the uprising was therefore the product of a wide variety of forces linked for the most part only by a common desire to purge Spain of the partisans and creatures of Godoy (and sometimes, indeed, not even that: around Algeciras the prime mover of the revolt was the commander of the large regular army that was blockading Gibraltar, Francisco Javier Castaños). When revolt exploded, moreover, it did so in a most piece-meal and uncoordinated fashion. Thus, in some cities there was no leadership at all, the uprising being precipitated rather by the arrival of news of Fernando's abdication or of revolt elsewhere; in others the hands of the conspirators were forced by the population taking to the streets; and in others still rebellion was the work of conspiracy pure and simple. Nor was there any unity of timing: if Cartagena and Valencia rose on 23 May, Valladolid did not do so until 1 June.

Whatever the details, however, the end results were almost everywhere the same in that the Captains General and military governors who had occupied the apex of the local administration were either forced to join the uprising, or, as was usually the case, overthrown, and new organs of government established in the form of provincial juntas and, occasionally, dictatorships (one such example was Zaragoza where Palafox succeeded in seizing supreme power). Underlying the process was an inchoate current of popular unrest of frightening dimensions: in Valencia, for example, there were manifestations of peasant discontent that culminated in the massacre of a large part of the city's French community, and in a few instances land was occupied, whilst all over Spain mobs of angry soldiers and civilians murdered a variety of officers, officials and private individuals who had the misfortune to be associated with Godoy. Confronted with a serious problem of public order, the new authorities made repeated appeals for calm and in some cases executed the ring-leaders of popular disturbances. Having everywhere declared war on Napoleon, however, they had little need to make use of outright repression, the desperate need to form new armies providing them with the perfect means of channelling the energies of the crowd (it should be noted, however, that this militarization of the revolution did not take place without resistance, the new levies frequently opposing the imposition of military discipline and remaining notoriously unruly).

The situation in the aftermath of the national uprising was extremely complex. Militarily speaking, the whole Peninsula was on the brink of war (the uprising in Spain had immediately precipitated one in Portugal), with the French only in control of the ground that they actually occupied – in Spain, Toledo, Madrid, Lerma, Aranda de Duero, Burgos, Vitoria, San Sebastián, Pamplona, Barcelona and Figueras; in Portugal, Lisbon, Elvas and Almeida – but about to dispatch punitive columns in all directions. Politically speaking, although insurrections had occurred at virtually every point where the French were not physically present (the one exception, in a possible reflection of discontent at Bourbon centralization, was Vizcaya), the confusion was even worse. The Balearic Islands, Catalonia (albeit at Tarragona rather than Barcelona given the latter's occupation by the French), Valencia, Murcia, Granada, Jaén, Córdoba, Seville, Extremadura, Asturias and Santander all had juntas of government whose writ was basically unchallenged. In the Canary Islands and Galicia, Tenerife, Gran Canaria, Santiago and La Coruña continued to engage in their traditional rivalry through the establishment of competing juntas, although there, too, supreme juntas eventually emerged. In Old Castile, the extremely hard-bitten Captain General, Gregorio García de la Cuesta, was exercising a precarious dictatorship from Valladolid in defiance of the civilian juntas that had been formed in most of the main cities of the region. And in Aragón a combination of local family connections, careful stage management, and sheer demagogy was enabling José Palafox to govern without any form of junta at all. Meanwhile, whilst Cuesta and Palafox knew exactly what they wanted – in the case of the one the re-establishment of the legitimate Bourbon authorities, and in the case of the other the creation of an aristocratic regency that could pursue the noble revival championed by Infantado and Montijo – these authorities were often divided in themselves and bitterly at odds with one another. Nor is this situation surprising: the rising was a product of a wide variety of discontents and had been ignited by the wholly negative catalyst afforded by hatred of Godoy and Napoleonic intervention; to describe it as a 'bourgeois' revolution would therefore be distinctly *jejeune*.

The Crisis of the Antiguo Régimen

With Spain in arms against the French, we have now reached a convenient place at which to end this introductory survey. Quite clearly, the *antiguo régimen* was in a state of crisis by 1808. Thus, the deep divisions in the Spanish court that facilitated and ultimately sparked off French intervention were symptomatic of even deeper divisions in the ranks of the elite. By advancing the cause of enlightened reform Godoy had inevitably earned the opposition of considerable sections of the aristocracy, the army and the Church, whilst at the same time inflaming the hostility of a population already experiencing the most severe pressure. Yet, that said, the disasters brought about by his foreign policy, the failure of his reforms to deliver any tangible results, and the deficiencies of his own character and administration prevented him from developing any power base of his own even amongst those groups who might have been expected to support his cause. Desperate to ensure Spain's stability and security, he merely succeeded in undermining both, and in bringing the various tensions and contradictions inherent in the *antiguo régimen* to a head. Whether there would have been a revolution in Spain without French intervention is impossible to say, but what is certain is that Napoleon's decision to intervene in her affairs by means of armed force unleashed a reaction that had soon gone far beyond the aims of the tiny handful of conspirators who had given birth to it at Aranjuez. Impelled by popular unrest, the desire to further sectional or personal interest and a genuine sense of outraged patriotism, a variety of elements now seized power. Some of these forces were 'new', but this was by no means necessarily the case – not only can many examples be found of senior officers of the army and navy rallying wholeheartedly to the uprising, but even the provincial juntas were in large part drawn from well-established municipal, official and ecclesiastical hierarchies.

For all that, however, the importance of what had occurred cannot be gainsaid. In the first place, the military predominance that had characterized Bourbon Spain was completely swept away. Hitherto at provincial level presided over, if not actually controlled, by the armed forces (in that the Captain General of a province was the *ex officio* president of its *audiencia* or *chancilleria*, and, in effect, its *de facto* viceroy), the governance of Spain was now in the hands of authorities that were largely civilian, and the army firmly subordinate to their rule. Given that the generals had derived their authority from the throne, it was clear that there had been a genuine shift of power. Here we come to the most fundamental implication of the uprising of all. In abdicating their rights to the throne, Carlos and Fernando had acted entirely in accordance with the principles of absolutism: if sovereignty rested with the monarch, then, logically, he was perfectly entitled to do whatever he liked with the throne. Of its very nature, however, the Spanish rising challenged such a doctrine, for its only possible justification was that, whether acting under duress or not, the monarch did not have the right to make such a decision. With those authorities who attempted to maintain the Bourbons' right to do so swept away by the insurgents, and those who still attempted to base their power on the principles of legitimacy in the most fragile of positions (Cuesta, for example, was within a few months to find himself stripped of his Captain Generalcy), it can be seen that, in a few short days, the doctrine of the sovereignty of the people had acquired a *de facto* reality.

2

The War of Independence

The Birth of Modern Spain

Between 1808 and 1814 Spain experienced the most devastating struggle in her entire history. French, Spanish and Anglo-Portuguese armies marched and counter-marched across the face of the Peninsula. City after city was devastated by assaults and sieges. A savage guerrilla war and burgeoning social unrest reduced large parts of the country to anarchy. Revolution in Latin America shattered Spain's tottering finances. Famine and epidemic swept the country. However, amidst these horrors, a new Spain was born, the country experiencing a series of reforms that were to dominate political debate for much of the next half-century. So marked were the divisions that in consequence emerged that it has been argued that henceforth Spanish history was to be characterized by a struggle between two Spains. Such a vision is overly simplistic, but the War of Independence still acted as a catalyst whose effects would be felt well into the twentieth century.

Spain in Eclipse

In the previous chapter, we left Spain with French armies in control of parts of the Castiles, the Basque provinces, Navarre and Catalonia, and the rest of the country under the sway of a variety of authorities committed to fighting for Fernando VII. Ordered to suppress the uprising, within a matter of days the French were bearing down upon Valladolid, Valencia, Zaragoza, Seville, Gerona and Lérida. Initially all went well. The bulk of the army having been deployed against British raids, the areas most directly threatened had no other defenders than untrained levies. No match for the imperial forces in the open field, these were for the most part swept aside, and for a moment the uprising seemed doomed. Yet the French were both poorly trained and few in number, and an embarrassing defeat at the hands of the irregular Catalan home-guard known as the *somatén* at El Bruch was therefore followed by the failure of assaults on Zaragoza, Gerona and Valencia. Despite a substantial victory at Medina de Río Seco on 14 July which effectively cleared the whole of Old Castile, still worse was to follow. Having reached Córdoba, the 20,000 men sent against Seville learned that the garrison of Andalucía was closing in on them, and in consequence began to fall back, only to be surrounded and forced to surrender at Bailén. Horrified by the news of this defeat, Joseph Bonaparte quite unnecessarily abandoned the siege of Zaragoza and ordered the French forces in central Spain to retreat to the Ebro. With the French also in trouble in Catalonia, where they had been forced to withdraw to Barcelona and Figueras, the War of Independence could hardly have begun more auspiciously.

Wildly acclaimed and attributed willy-nilly to the heroism of the common people, these successes were shortlived. Highly anti-militaristic and lulled into a false sense of security, the Patriot camp sat upon its collective laurels. Meanwhile, shorn of a central government, Spain was in chaos. No ideological unity existed amongst the leadership of the insurrection. If many liberals had been prominent in the uprising, they were countered on the one hand by servants of enlightened absolutism such as the erstwhile ministers, Jovellanos and Floridablanca, and on the other by the representatives of ecclesiastical and aristocratic reaction such as the dictator of Zaragoza, José Palafox. The remnants of the old administration were making a determined attempt to regain their influence. Provinces such as Valencia and Catalonia which had seen their corporate rights suppressed by the Bourbons were eager to regain them, whilst those which still enjoyed them, such as Asturias, were determined to protect them. Traditional local rivalries caused much disruption. Long-standing hostility to the army and fears of collaboration led to much suspicion of the high command. And, finally, the events of the campaign had produced deep feuds amongst the *generalato*. In consequence, it was only with the utmost difficulty that a new government – the Junta Central – was established. As there was even then little agreement with regard to its precise status, many of the provincial juntas paid only lip service to its authority. Meanwhile, the appointment of a commander-in-chief proved altogether impossible. As a result, the war effort completely stagnated: the army's concentration on the Ebro was disrupted; the provincial juntas tried to reserve for themselves the copious supplies that had now begun to arrive from Britain (which had naturally leapt to support the Spanish revolt); and a series of complicated intrigues took place that saw Cuesta seeking to challenge the Junta Central by force of arms, and José Palafox and his supporters attempting to neutralize Castaños as a contender for their cherished regency.

Had the eclipse of the French really been due to the heroism of the Spanish people, none of this would have mattered. However, this was not the case. In certain circumstances the civilian population had indeed entered the struggle with unwonted ferocity: at Zaragoza, for example, the complete absence of regular troops had not deterred the inhabitants from defending the city house-by-house even after the French had stormed the walls. For all that, however, the people-in-arms had shown itself to be utterly incapable of meeting the French in the open field, whilst even the most desperately defended cities could not hold out for ever. Indeed, given sufficient numbers, the French could have overrun the entire country and then put down popular resistance at their leisure, their misfortunes having been in large part the result of their own errors. Meanwhile, if the efficacy of 'people's war' can be challenged, there is also some question as to its extent: voluntary recruitment to the new armies being raised by the juntas often did not prosper, whilst conscription engendered much desertion and in some cases outright resistance.

Discontent notwithstanding, it is quite clear that the only hope for Patriot Spain was the formation of a large and effective army. Much enraged, by the beginning of November Napoleon had concentrated an army of over 200,000 men around Vitoria and Logroño. Facing these troops, which were much better than their unfortunate predecessors, were fewer than 150,000 Spaniards deployed in a great semi-circle stretching from Vizcaya to Navarre. Caught at a hopeless disadvantage, the Spaniards were undermined still further by a variety of technical deficiencies. Many of the Patriot forces were composed of raw levies commanded by officers who owed their commissions solely to the patronage of the juntas, whilst both cavalry and artillery were in short supply, the former also being very badly mounted. When the French finally attacked, the result was therefore a foregone conclusion: within six weeks every Spanish army had been routed, Zaragoza besieged, Madrid reoccupied, and the Junta Central forced to flee to Seville.

Disastrous though all this was, the war did not come to an end. Large parts of the Spanish armies on the Ebro had escaped to the south and west, and the forces in Catalonia were untouched, whilst Zaragoza once again mounted a heroic defence. At the same time, a useful diversion was provided by the British army of Sir John Moore. Until now Britain's aid to Spain had been limited to money and *matériel*, her rather limited striking forces having been sent to expel the French from Portugal. However, by the end of August the French had been forced to surrender, the British being left free to intervene in Spain. Having concentrated his army at Salamanca, Moore resolved to create a diversion by striking eastwards at Napoleon's line of communications with France. Much alarmed, the emperor suspended operations against the Spaniards and sent the bulk of his forces to annihilate the British. However, in this he was unsuccessful – Moore's army escaped by sea – the end result merely being to add Galicia and much of León to France's conquests.

By the beginning of 1809, then, the French were in control of most of central and northern Spain. Only possessed of sufficient strength to mount a limited number of offensives, they initially concentrated on overcoming the isolated fortresses of Zaragoza and Gerona whilst at the same time making an attempt at the reconquest of Portugal from Galicia. All this provided the Junta Central, which was now receiving copious support not just from Britain but also Spain's American colonies, with a chance to build new armies and re-establish its authority. Given continued French military superiority, it ought to have remained on the defensive, but this was impossible. A fairly liberal body, the Junta faced the enmity of both legitimist forces who objected to the Spanish revolution *per se*, good examples being such generals as Cuesta and the Marqués de la Romana, and the champions of the aristocratic reaction personified by José Palafox (if the latter was now trapped in Zaragoza, he had become a veritable hero, whilst his cause was ably championed by his brother, Francisco, and the ever-scheming Conde de Montijo). Last but not least, many of the provincial juntas were still resentful of the Junta Central. For much of 1809 these forces did all that they could to obstruct the Junta, whilst in the meantime plotting against its rule. Despite the fact that their conspiracies invariably either failed or were uncovered, the Junta knew that it could not remain idle. Announcing that a *cortes* would meet on 1 March 1810, it issued a circular inviting views on reform, whilst in the meantime seeking both to remodel the central administration and increase the efficiency of its deliberations. However, none of this restored its prestige, which hostile propaganda, an irresponsible press and the loss of first Madrid and then, on 20 February 1809, Zaragoza, had reduced almost to nothing. In consequence, the Junta also embarked on a series of offensives in Extremadura, La Mancha and Aragón in the hope that these might bring a dramatic victory.

Whilst this decision was understandable, it was nonetheless disastrous. In the first place, the Spanish armies were no better than those of 1808; weakened by desertion to the growing numbers of guerrillas; scattered around the periphery of Spain; and faced by operations in countryside – the plains of the *meseta* – where the weakness of their cavalry placed them at an immediate disadvantage. In the second place, the political background was such that operations were invariably marked by the utmost confusion. And, in the third place, many provinces were in a state of complete turmoil and therefore unable to contribute to an offensive strategy. In Asturias, for example, in May 1809 the Marqués de la Romana overthrew the notoriously liberal Junta of Asturias in a military coup, whilst in Valencia La Romana's brother, José Caro, was engaged in a complicated series of intrigues that led to endless disorder.

All this ensured that an offensive strategy was bound to prove a failure. Advances in La Mancha, Catalonia, Extremadura and Aragón led only to defeats at Uclés, Valls, Ciudad Real, Medellín, María and Belchite. Things briefly looked a little more optimistic at the beginning of July when the British expeditionary force, which had regrouped at Lisbon under Wellington, entered Extremadura after having first expelled the French from northern Portugal. Plans were then laid for a concentric advance on Madrid from the west and south, only for this to be thwarted, albeit not without a major victory at Talavera, by quarrels between Wellington and Cuesta, the arrival of massive French reinforcements and the meddling of the Junta Central. After yet another Spanish defeat at Almonacid de Toledo, the whole affair fizzled out, with the British withdrawing to the Portuguese frontier and abandoning the Spaniards to their own devices. By now absolutely desperate, in the autumn the Junta Central attacked again, only for this to lead to yet more catastrophes at Alba de Tormes and, above all, Ocaña, where the biggest battle of the war saw 18,000 Spaniards killed, wounded or taken prisoner.

Both at the time and since, these battles elicited the response that they did not matter: however heavy her losses, Patriot Spain kept fighting. But they did matter. Because of the very open terrain in which they tended to be fought, the great French superiority in cavalry, the fact that fugitives could always find a haven with the guerrillas, and the undisciplined nature of the Spanish soldiery, defeat was invariably accompanied with enormous losses, with the result that on each occasion new armies had to be created from scratch. Not only were the Spaniards thereby denied any hope of remedying the weaknesses of their armies, but their finite resources were placed under intolerable strain. After Ocaña and Alba de Tormes, indeed, they had very little left, and the initiative therefore passed back to the French. Massing an army of 60,000 men, in January 1810 Joseph Bonaparte invaded the Patriot stronghold of Andalucía. Since Ocaña the Junta Central had been making frantic efforts to raise fresh troops and fortify the chief passes through the mountains, but resources were scanty and enthusiasm for military service weaker than ever. Within a matter of days, Bonaparte's troops had therefore broken through. Abandoning Seville, the hapless government fled to the safety of the island city of Cádiz. Though its enemies were in equal disarray – an attempt by partisans of the aristocratic faction headed by the Palafox family to organize a revolt in Seville had been scattered to the four winds – the Junta knew that it could not survive such a disaster. No sooner had it reached Cádiz, then, than it ceded power to a council of regency, albeit one of its own making.

The occupation of Andalucía, downfall of the Junta Central, installation of a regency and transfer of the capital to Cádiz (which was saved from conquest by virtue of its strong garrison and impregnable situation) together constitute an important moment. Never again would the Spaniards be able to mount offensive operations, the consequence being that they would now have to rely on Wellington. With the establishment of a regency, meanwhile, the vested interests that had opposed the Junta Central would inevitably be forced into the open for they could no longer hide their ambitions behind claims that the government was illegitimate. Equally importantly, defeat cleared the way for reform. Finally, as we shall see, in the Spanish colonies news of the French offensive provided the pretext for wholesale rebellion. In short, a mere eighteen months had transformed Spanish history.

The French Kingdom of Spain

Before going on to discuss the consequences of the invasion of Andalucía in greater detail, it is first necessary to say something about Napoleon's new satellite monarchy. Joseph Bonaparte was not the drunk of Patriot propaganda. A kindly man, whose chief vice was a strong predilection for women, he came to Spain determined that he would be a Spanish monarch, rather than a French one. No despot, he struggled to learn Spanish, emphasized his respect for Spanish culture, attended mass, patronized bullfights and other popular festivities and repeatedly clashed with his imperial brother. As we shall see, however, all his good intentions came to naught, French rule in Spain in the end proving an utter nullity.

The central object of Napoleon's intervention having been to transform Spain into an efficient and reliable satellite, she was immediately subjected to a programme of reform. Thus, in addition to accepting Joseph as king, an assembly of notables summoned to Bayonne had also acceded to a new constitution. Very similar to those introduced in the other satellite states, this provided for a cabinet, modern ministries, a council of state, and a bicameral *cortes* of very limited power, chosen in part by royal appointment and in part by indirect election. Also accepted were such fundamental principles as personal liberty, equality before the law and freedom of occupation. Much of this never materialized, but, for all that, French rule was far from inactive. On the contrary, when Napoleon reoccupied Madrid in December 1808, he immediately abolished feudalism, the Inquisition, the Council of Castile, and all internal customs barriers, suppressed two-thirds of Spain's convents and monasteries and prohibited the accumulation of *mayorazgos*. Thereafter, Joseph's Spanish ministers continued the work by dividing Spain into French-style departments, abolishing the Mesta, the Voto de Santiago, the military orders and most of the monopolies hitherto enjoyed by the state, suppressing such religious foundations as had been allowed to remain by Napoleon, expropriating known Patriots, selling off the various royal factories, establishing new systems of education and justice, and taking steps towards the introduction of the *Code Napoléon*.

By these means, Spain was in theory transformed. Enormous quantities of property were put up for sale, the privileges of the Church and aristocracy were abolished, the way was opened for the rise of the bourgeoisie and the emergence of a capitalist economy, the ideological unity that had underpinned absolute monarchy was undermined, the last provincial *fueros* disappeared, and Spain was given a modern administration and a single code of law. The only problem, of course, was that, so long as the war lasted, the impact of all this was minimal, many *josefino* reforms either never attaining concrete form or being hamstrung by such factors as the continued hostilities and want of money. In any case, except round Madrid, the real rulers of Napoleonic Spain were the military authorities. No great general, Joseph had been left with only vestigial control of the French armies when Napoleon left Spain in January 1809. In consequence, the generals ignored his pronouncements, snubbed his officials and starved him of revenue. In the spring of 1810, moreover, the problem was compounded: convinced that Joseph was not tough enough, Napoleon decreed that the whole of northern Spain should be divided into a number of military districts whose governors would be responsible to Paris. As a result the area concerned ceased to afford Joseph any revenue at all. The French generals having many fewer inhibitions than Joseph, the experience of occupation was uniformly unhappy. Thus, executions were frequent, enormous numbers of people were imprisoned or deported, heavy fines were imposed on communities or families whose members were known to be serving with the *partidas* or the Patriot armies, and numerous villages were burned in reprisal for guerrilla attacks. In one or two instances, there were also cases of wholesale massacre. Violence was meanwhile accompanied by extortion, those areas under French occupation being forced to supply the invaders with large quantities of money, food, fodder, clothing, horses, mules, oxen and carts. Added to all this was the pillaging of the imperial soldiery, large quantities of valuables simply disappearing into their knapsacks.

Despite these problems, Joseph received much indigenous support. The phenomenon of *afrancesamiento* is a complex one. In only a few cases – essentially the tiny group of committed liberals personified by such figures as the writers Marchena, Llorente, Fernández de Moratín, and Meléndez Valdés – are the motives for collaboration clear. When one turns to other groups – Bourbon ministers, officials and generals such as Cabarrus, O'Farrill, Urquijo and Azanza; prominent grandees such as the

Duque de Frías and the Conde de Orgaz; and bishops such as those of Burgos, Palencia, Valladolid and Madrid – the picture is less clear. For the representatives of Carolinianism, *josefino* reformism could be argued to represent the acme of their own aspirations. Such approval would obviously sit less well with grandees and churchmen, but in their case they could be moved by admiration of Napoleon, fear of unrest, honest conviction and simple opportunism. Meanwhile, too, the grandees were, as elsewhere in Europe, without any doubt swayed by the creation of a glittering 'family court'.

Collaboration, however, was not just a phenomenon of the prominent. Thanks to the involvement of large numbers of Spaniards at every level of society, the French were able to staff a full administrative and judicial apparatus, and organize a regular army, substantial civic guards, and even anti-guerrilla guerrillas. Largely undocumented as this phenomenon of rank-and-file *afrancesamiento* is, it is difficult to interpret. Marxian claims that it represents a positive identification on the part of the bourgeoisie with the Napoleonic revolution are impossible to substantiate, but not necessarily wrong: certainly, there were committed liberals amongst the more obscure collaborators. In practice, however, the reasons for collaboration were probably practical rather than ideological. Thus, support for the French was a vital means of securing long-standing family interests or pursuing ancient feuds. Above all, the French offered protection: if the social unrest which characterized the Patriot zone was alarming, the activities of the guerrillas were still more terrifying. Frequently a serious threat to the interests of property, they were in addition unable to offer any protection against the reprisals that they provoked. Finally, it should be noted that the experience of occupation was not necessarily unpleasant for families of substance, it being French policy to cultivate local elites and bring them within the orbit of the empire. In every garrison there was therefore a constant round of social events to which the local *pudientes* rallied in large numbers. An integral part of this policy was the formation of large numbers of the masonic lodges that were always associated with the French forces, although on the whole this seems to have been less successful, most of those involved in the lodges being Frenchmen. Meanwhile, the notables were frequently shielded from the more unpleasant aspects of occupation, the levies imposed by the invaders being frequently passed on to the lower classes, or even turned into a source of profit.

In the last resort, however, collaboration with the French was patently insubstantial. If it was generally not quite as transient as that exhibited by the many prisoners of war who volunteered for service in Joseph's army solely as a means of escape, it was frequently lacking in ideological commitment. Though the *cortes* of Cádiz instigated a rigorous persecution of the collaborators, there was little need to do so, the fact being that, even among his supporters, Joseph Bonaparte had struck few real chords.

Discussion of the French kingdom of Spain is inseparable from discussion of the guerrilla war that remains the best-known aspect of the War of Independence. Yet there are few aspects of the struggle that have been more misunderstood. According to the usual version of events, a mixture of traditionalist Catholicism, hostility to things foreign and devotion to Fernando VII, it is assumed to have had massive popular support and inflicted untold damage on the imperial war effort. However, almost every item in this creed is open to challenge, *la guerrilla* being a phenomenon that was extremely complex.

That said, it is impossible to dismiss the traditional picture out of hand. In the first place, there is no doubt that irregular resistance to the French was widespread. From as early as May 1808, isolated French soldiers were being murdered, whilst in Catalonia the existence of the *somatén* meant that the imperial forces quickly came under attack from bands of irregulars. What thrust guerrilla warfare into real prominence, however, was the French offensive that marked the winter of 1808: not only did many stragglers take to the hills in company with embittered members of the civilian population, but in February 1809 the whole of Galicia exploded in revolt. All this made life very difficult for the invaders. Large forces had to be left in garrison; reconnaissance, foraging and the collection of taxes and requisitions became very difficult; isolated strongpoints were liable to be starved into surrender; large numbers of soldiers were killed or wounded; and morale fell dramatically, much to the detriment of order and discipline. At the same time Patriot morale was boosted: however minor, the irregulars' successes served as a useful counterpoint to the regulars' failures, whilst in June 1809 it appeared as if popular resistance had gained a great victory, the French suddenly evacuating Galicia, never to return. Encouraged by French reprisals, promises of booty, and military patronage, meanwhile, the number of *partidas* grew dramatically until by the end of 1809 the French were being harassed on all sides.

Yet there are important qualifications to be made. In the first place, such success as the guerrillas achieved was due to the fact that the French were simultaneously fighting a conventional war: thus, Galicia would never have been abandoned had it not been for Wellington's decision to invade Spain. In the second, the guerrillas encouraged desertion, for the life of a freebooter had considerably more appeal than the life of a soldier. Questions must also be asked with regard to the guerrillas' motivation and aims. In 1808 the populace's actions had stemmed not just from blind loyalty to Fernando VII, but rather the belief that he personified the remedy to its many ills. Violence had therefore been directed not just against the French, but against all those who were identified with Godoy, in particular, and Boubon reformism in general. With the authorities in chaos, it was not long before other targets suggested themselves, not least the tithes and feudal dues. As the war progressed, such social tensions could only increase: on the one hand the population was impoverished by the rapacity of French, Spanish and British armies alike, whilst on the other the conflict accelerated tendencies towards disamortization. In particular, many municipalities were driven to sell land in order to meet French exactions, the resultant sales depriving the peasantry of access to pasturage, firewood, and windfall crops, whilst increasing the power of the *pudientes*. Hardly surprisingly, then, unrest continued unabated, the result being a variety of riots and other disturbances.

What conclusions may be drawn from this evidence with regard to the guerrilla struggle? According to Marxist observers, *la guerrilla* was based upon social discontent pure and simple, the *partidas* frequently being headed by men who had either been bandits or smugglers or had played a leading role in outbreaks of anti-feudal unrest. However, if we look at the province of Navarre – the seat of the most imposing guerrilla movement of the entire war – we find a picture that is very different from that which one might expect. Navarre is divided into two very different regions in the shape of the then largely Basque-speaking *montaña*, or 'mountain', to the north, and the Castillian-speaking *ribera*, or 'riverside', to the south, of which the former is dominated by small peasant properties and the latter by great estates. Of the two, it was the *ribera* which experienced more social tension: not only were the majority of the population artisans, landless labourers, or tenant farmers with insufficient land to support a family, but the war years saw a sustained attempt on the part of the *pudientes* to exploit their power. However, far from the *ribera* becoming a hotbed of resistance, we find that it remained comparatively quiet, the chief support of the guerrillas coming rather from the homogenous and relatively prosperous *montaña*.

If the evidence is contradictory, it is nonetheless clear that irregular resistance fed upon, and was fuelled by, poverty and despair; that it had a reputation for indiscriminate rapine; and that in many areas it was closely linked with traditional forms of social protest. The consequences of this situation were obviously very serious. Setting aside the fact that the guerrillas' hostility to the propertied classes encouraged *pudiente* collaboration, the regular army lost many recruits to their ranks, whilst the bands themselves frequently had other objectives besides operations against the French. Even when they were acting with the best of intentions, meanwhile, the *partidas* suffered frequent defeats, and all the more so as they were often at odds with one another. Not surprisingly, then, from the beginning the Patriot authorities made desperate efforts to subject them to some form of control, placing them under the command of regular officers and sending out regular troops to act as cadres. There thus began a creeping process of militarization whereby a number of the larger *partidas* evolved into brigades and divisions of the regular army, many of the guerrilla commanders being eager to aid and abet this process on the grounds that it brought with it a greater degree of prestige and authority. However, even by the end of the war it seems to have affected only a minority of the *partidas*, the result being that many of the evils that we have discussed continued unabated. At the same time, it should be noted that the guerrillas did nothing to halt the march of French conquest: impede the invaders though they did, they could neither hold territory nor liberate areas that had been occupied.

Constitution and Collapse, 1810–12

The years from 1810 to 1812 witnessed a dual process whose inter-connection has never really been appreciated. On the one hand, the Spanish revolution was given its definitive form, whilst on the other the Patriot cause experienced a series of disasters that led directly to the restoration of absolutism in 1814. Let us begin with the revolution. Within eight months of the Junta Central's downfall, a unicameral *cortes* was pursuing a liberal agenda at Cádiz. Few in numbers as committed liberals were, this might seem somewhat surprising, and it has often been suggested that the only reason that the liberals triumphed was that they were unfairly favoured by such factors as Cádiz's status as a stronghold of the bourgeoisie. However, this misses the point. As witness the response to the Junta Central's appeal for suggestions for the sort of programme that might be implemented by the *cortes*, the mood in the Patriot camp was strongly reformist. Meanwhile, the differences that marked out the liberals from their fellows were far from clear, and all the more so as the former were employing very much the same language as the traditionalists who were to become their most bitter opponents. A tight-knit group who had often known one another for many years, and were possessed of great oratorical talent and journalistic talent, the leading liberals were therefore able to command much wider support than might have been expected, whilst they could also count on the general approval of a variety of important interest groups amongst their fellows.

For a variety of reasons, then, the convocation of the new *cortes* was followed by a sweeping liberal victory. Yet at the very same time the death warrant of that victory was being signed in Spanish America. As more and more territory fell into the hands of the French, so the

American empire became ever more important to Spain's ability to continue the war. Yet, despite the strong support evinced in America for Fernando VII, all was not well in the relationship between Spain and her colonies. From the days of Carlos III the *criollo* community had come increasingly to resent Spanish rule, such feelings having been much sharpened by the extension of Godoy's disamortization to America, the evil reputation of the Spanish court, and the manner in which the war against Britain had both given the inhabitants a taste of the benefits of free trade and convinced them that they now had much less need of Spanish protection. Inspired by loathing of the French and fear that their influence might stir up the same sort of bloody racial revolts as those that had rocked the Caribbean in the 1790s, the *criollos* had initially joined the *peninsulares* in rallying to Fernando VII. Yet they remained restive: the 'provisional juntas' formed in most of the capitals of Spanish America in response to the news from Spain were dominated by *peninsulares*, whilst the Junta Central failed to make any attempt to address *criollo* grievances.

As early as the summer of 1809 revolts therefore broke out against the *peninsulares* in La Paz and Quito. These were suppressed, but the arrival a year later of news of the fall of Andalucía provoked the most dramatic reaction. As Spain, it seemed, had either fallen, or was about to do so, the *criollos* had no option but to look to themselves. As a result, between April and October 1810 modern-day Venezuela, Argentina, Colombia, Ecuador, Chile, Mexico, Bolivia, Paraguay and Uruguay all rose in revolt, the only areas of Spanish rule to remain loyal – Peru, Cuba, and central America – being those where racial fears were particularly intense. This was but the beginning of a long and complex story: in Mexico and Venezuela the spectre of social unrest led to the wholesale defection of the *criollos* and the restoration of the *status quo*; in Bolivia, Ecuador and Chile Peruvian expeditionary forces were able to crush the rebels; and in Colombia the disintegration of the uprising in civil war enabled the local loyalists to maintain a foothold. However, Argentina, Paraguay and Uruguay all remained independent, whilst such was the disruption caused by the fighting that financial support for Spain inevitably dwindled to a trickle.

Though Spanish rule was far from dead, its chances of survival were not helped by the response of Cádiz, where there was not only a wanton refusal to understand the colonists, but a tendency to deride the indigenous populations – European, mixed-race, Indian and negro alike – as, at best, degenerates and, at worst, downright savages. Notwithstanding the fact that it was the key to Spain's situation, consideration of the problem was therefore relegated to a secondary level. Repeated efforts were made by the American deputies, many of whom were anything but eager for a total rupture with metropolitan Spain, to introduce the *cortes*' genuine measures of reform, but these either foundered for lack of interest, or were brought down by the determination of merchants to protect their commercial interests, liberals to safeguard the principle of a unitary state, and traditionalists to defend the patrimony of Fernando VII. Even the political equality offered by the *cortes* on 14 October 1810 was hedged about with qualifications that effectively rendered it null and void, whilst many of its general reforms actually exacerbated American grievances. In short, the Spanish revolution can be seen to have offered the colonies almost nothing.

The total failure of the *cortes* of Cádiz with regard to Spanish America has been obscured by its dramatic record in other areas. In a series of measures of which the constitution promulgated on 19 March 1812 was but the most important, the *cortes* transformed the face of Spain. Although the monarchy was declared sacrosanct, the most severe restrictions were placed on the king, real power being placed in the hands of the *cortes*, the plan being for the latter to be elected by universal suffrage, meet each year for three months, and enjoy complete control of taxation. With their freedom further safeguarded by a proviso that no changes in the constitution would be permitted for at least eight years, Spaniards were to enjoy equality before the law, freedom of occupation, employment, and property, equal liability to taxation and military service, and all the basic civil liberties except that of religion. The corollary of this programme was manifold: all forms of privilege, whether it was the right of the Basque provinces to tax themselves, of army officers to be tried by military courts, or of the nobility to enjoy a monopoly on direct entry to the officer corps, were swept away; the power of the guilds and the Mesta was broken; internal customs barriers, torture, the military orders, the Inquisition, and *señorialismo* were all abolished; and a new system of progressive income tax was introduced, this being known as the *contribución única* or 'single contribution'. Meanwhile, Spain was declared a unitary state, her governance being completely remodelled. The king was to be aided by a council of state, and the network of councils that had stood at the apex of administration and justice replaced by seven new ministries. In contrast to the confusion that had characterized the *antiguo régimen*, plans were laid for Spain to be divided into a number of provinces of equal size, each of which would be administered by a governor – the *jefe político* – assisted by an intendant and an elected *diputación*. At a lower level, local government would henceforth be hands of elected *ayuntamientos* rather than hereditary ones. And, last but not least, Spain was also given a unitary system of law courts which envisaged a supreme court in Madrid, a district court in each province, and a stipendiary magistrate in every municipality.

Meanwhile, the *cortes* also applied itself to the problem of disamortization. Necessary from a financial point of view, this was given further impetus by the liberals' determination to reduce the power of the Church, create a free market in land, and stimulate Spanish agriculture. Already reeling from other liberal measures – the destruction of the feudal system, and the abolition of the Inquisition and such levies as the Voto de Santiago (which applied to only one part of the country and therefore fell foul of the principle of equality of taxation) – the Church now found that the *cortes* was as keen as Joseph Bonaparte to strip it of its patrimony. Thus a variety of properties were declared available for expropriation, whilst it is clear that only pressures of time prevented the *cortes* from acting upon proposals for a fundamental reform of the regular clergy that would have increased the Church' losses still further. However, disamortization was not directed at the Church alone: certain crown lands, the properties of those declared traitors, and half the municipal lands – the commons – were all put up for sale.

Dramatic though all this was, there are still numerous criticisms to be made of the *cortes*, there being, for example, no doubt that the constitution had serious technical deficiencies. Despite the liberals' populist rhetoric, meanwhile, little was done to resolve Spain's social problems, one form of privilege simply being replaced by another. Whilst the constitution cemented the power of the notables by denying the vote to such groups as domestic servants and setting up a complicated system of indirect elections, disamortization and the abolition of feudalism brought the peasantry few benefits. Not only were the *señores* confirmed in their property rights, but, the *bienes nacionales* were simply put up for sale to the highest bidder, whilst no steps were ever taken either to parcel out the commons in the manner that had been intended (it had been agreed that 50 per cent should be sold and the other 50 per cent distributed in small lots to ex-soldiers and landless labourers). As a result, wherever the Patriot cause held sway, existing proprietors consolidated their position and were joined by new investors, the peasantry in the meantime being subjected to rent rises, eviction and exclusion from the commons.

Not surprisingly, the *cortes*' measures greatly inflamed the already tense situation that pertained in those parts of Spain that remained in Patriot hands, the period 1811–12 therefore being marked by a fresh rash of rent strikes, land occupations and attacks on the symbols of feudalism. In view of the military situation, nothing could have been more unfortunate. In the course of 1809, Spain had been shielded from the wrath of Napoleon by the decision of Austria to resume hostilities. Decisively defeated at Wagram on 5–6 July, the Austrians were forced to make peace, however, the emperor thereby being enabled to send enormous reinforcements across the Pyrenees. In consequence, the French conquest of Andalucía was but the harbinger of a series of fresh offensives that the Spaniards were in no position to withstand. Initially, a large part of the renewed French effort was absorbed in an invasion of Portugal that by the beginning of the autumn had confined Wellington's Anglo-Portuguese army to the environs of Lisbon. Whilst it was safe enough there – Wellington had ordered Lisbon to be protected by a series of impregnable fortifications – for the whole of the rest of 1810 and the first part of 1811 it was effectively out of action. Although forced to retreat in March 1811, the French still for the time being succeeded in keeping Wellington penned up behind the Portuguese frontier. For the best part of two years, then, the Spaniards were left to fight alone, the result being a catalogue of disaster. Astorga, Ciudad Rodrigo, Lérida and Oviedo fell in 1810; Badajoz, Tortosa and Tarragona in 1811; and Valencia in January 1812, these territorial losses being accompanied by a litany of lost battles.

The importance of these events cannot be exaggerated. All but incalculable, the Spanish losses could not be replaced, all that was left to the Patriot cause now being the interior of Catalonia, the southern Levante, Cádiz, and populous but poverty-stricken Galicia. As for America, it had simply become a burden, *gaditano* pressure sending over 10,000 troops to the colonies between 1811 and 1813. In effect, the Patriot cause was paralysed: the guerrillas of the interior may have been growing in strength and, in some cases, organization, but they were incapable of liberating an inch of territory. However, until some territory was liberated, the regular army would remain completely impotent. In short, everything now depended on Wellington. For the time being the implications were not revealed in full, but, even so, the position was serious enough given the political situation that was now developing in Cádiz. Although the liberals continued to command a surprising amount of support, as time wore on opposition to their rule began to grow. The reforms of the liberals had always been opposed by a handful of conservative ecclesiastics, disgruntled *señores*, and displaced officials, but such protests had initially been swamped. As time went on, however, Spain's utter prostration allowed the liberals' enemies to accuse them of neglecting the national interest in favour of selfish political objectives. In consequence, the diehards who had always opposed the liberal revolution were now joined by increasing numbers of disillusioned centrists, the result being the emergence of a definite absolutist party, known scornfully by the liberals as the *serviles*.

As yet the challenge to the liberal system was not serious, but from 1812 onwards a number of developments combined to plunge Spain into a deepening political crisis. Ironically, the first factor in this development was an improvement in the military situation. If the guerrillas could not save Spain from disaster, they did at least ensure that her conquest required far more troops than would otherwise have been the case, the French being forced not only to maintain field armies that could neutralize Wellington and eradicate the remaining foci of resistance, but garrison every inch of their conquests. With casualties from combat and disease extremely high, the price of victory was an endless stream of reinforcements and replacements. Forthcoming until the end of 1811, Napoleon's impending war against Russia now suddenly cut this off, a small number of French troops even being withdrawn from the Peninsula. With the invaders in the process of conquering Valencia, they were thrown off balance, the consequence being that Wellington was at last enabled to break the stalemate on the Portuguese frontier, storming the crucial border fortresses of Ciudad Rodrigo and Badajoz, winning a great victory at Salamanca, and liberating Madrid.

Although the French were now forced to evacuate the whole of southern Spain, the Patriot cause gained little from these successes. Few of the *partidas* in the liberated areas showed the slightest sign of following up the French retreat, preferring rather to engage in pillage and highway robbery. Meanwhile, the authorities' troubles were increased by the swarms of men who were fleeing the starvation and misery that characterized the regular army. Despite their best efforts, the new *jefes políticos* simply did not have the strength to restore order, whilst revenue was in any case limited by two years of French occupation and the disastrous failure of the harvest of 1811. Nor was this an end to the matter. With the liberated territories for the first time exposed to the legislation of the *cortes*, the confusion was augmented by other factors. On the one hand, the many vested interests injured by the constitution began to stir up trouble, whilst on the other the peasantry were soon up in arms at the survival of the feudal dues and the sale of the commons. Needless to say, such unrest could only be fuelled by the pressures engendered by requisitioning, taxation and conscription. Last but not least, the establishment of the new *ayuntamientos* envisaged by the *cortes* led to an immense wave of faction fighting as rival local oligarchies struggled for supremacy in even the pettiest of *pueblos*.

Despite Wellington's victories, then, the Spanish armies remained barely capable of taking the field, the liberals therefore remaining as vulnerable as ever. Indeed, their situation was now to deteriorate still further in that they were laying themselves open to fresh attacks on the political front: not only did the *cortes*, which was, after all, a constituent assembly, remain sitting despite the fact that the constitution had now been proclaimed, but it now embarked upon the discussion of such matters as the abolition of the Inquisition and the reform of the regular clergy. The result was a veritable storm of controversy, the *serviles* growing steadily in strength and confidence. Very soon a plot was afoot to overturn the current regency and replace it with a new one headed by the violently absolutist wife of the Prince Regent of Portugal, who was the sister of Fernando VII. Desperate to forestall such a move, the liberals hit upon the notion of ensuring British favour by offering Wellington the command-in-chief of the Spanish army. However, this merely caused further confusion. When news of the event leaked out, a particularly ambitious general named Ballesteros 'pronounced' against the appointment at Granada. Meanwhile, when Wellington – who had, somewhat embarrassingly, been forced to abandon Madrid and flee for the safety of Portugal – announced that he would not accept the command unless he was given a wide range of political and administrative powers, many liberals turned against the appointment, being further alarmed by claims that the British were secretly favouring the cause of the rebels in Spanish America. As a result, for the first half of 1813 Wellington found his efforts to ready the Spanish army for battle impeded at every turn.

Though far fewer Spanish troops took part in the fighting than might otherwise have been the case, the army's continued eclipse was not just the result of the clash between Wellington and the liberals. The chaos in such of the liberated territories as remained in Patriot hands – essentially Asturias, Extremadura and Andalucía – was now worse than ever: furious quarrels were in train on all sides; traditionalist clerics were preaching rebellion; social unrest was raging unabated; and the erstwhile guerrillas were running amok. Meanwhile, the religious conflict mounted to a crescendo as the *cortes* moved closer to the abolition of the Inquisition. No opportunity was lost to compare the work of the liberals with that of the French Revolution, the constitution was denounced – the guerrilla leader, Espoz y Mina, is even supposed to have had a copy executed by firing squad – and repeated efforts were made to persuade Wellington to overthrow the liberals. Faced by these developments, the latter responded by reinforcing their control of the executive, dismissing a number of suspect generals, expelling the papal nuncio, attempting to build up a force of loyal troops in Cádiz, packing the administration, and delaying both the election of a new *cortes* and, once the matter had become an issue, the transfer of the capital to Madrid.

Despite the chaos in Patriot Spain, Wellington's retreat proved purely temporary. Anxious to raise a fresh army after his defeat in Russia in 1812, Napoleon had no troops to spare for Spain, and withdrew some of the forces he had left there. Meanwhile, the area remaining under French rule had been badly destabilized. A number of the *partidas* having by now evolved into 'flying-columns' of battle-hardened regular troops, they were able to wreak havoc on the over-stretched French garrisons. By the beginning of 1813 the situation in the Basque provinces and Navarre had become so serious that Napoleon ordered the dispatch of the bulk of the forces containing the Anglo-Portuguese to restore order, it being his belief that Wellington had been so badly beaten in the autumn of the previous year that he would not dare to intervene. This, however, was not the case. Wellington had been planning a renewed offensive, and in May 1813 he once again struck deep into Old Castile. Desperate to regroup their scattered forces, the French evacuated Madrid yet again, and fell back behind the Ebro, only to be overwhelmed by Wellington at Vitoria on 21 June. Defeat was total, and the French were forced to flee for the frontier, as well as to evacuate the Basque provinces, Navarre, Aragón and Valencia. Aside from a few besieged strongholds, in short, all that was left of the Bonaparte kingdom of Spain was now Catalonia.

Once again, however, military victory merely brought an extension of the political crisis. Fresh areas of the country were plunged into turmoil and the opposition to the liberals was swelled by such new recruits as the oligarchies that had hitherto monopolized the benefits conferred on the Basque provinces by their *fueros*. According to traditional accounts, the central problem was that the liberal revolution was an utterly isolated phenomenon which had no support outside a very narrow social and geographical section of the country. Such simplicities are not good enough. In the towns and cities the crowd was often sympathetic to the liberals, whilst much of the popular unrest of 1813–14 was directed not against the liberals but rather against representatives of the old order who wanted to reassert their *señorial* rights. Nevertheless, however much it might be suspected that the crowds involved were largely mercenary, numerous anti-liberal disorders did take place. At the same time, too, it cannot be denied that, when the ordinary *cortes* finally opened its sessions on 1 October 1813, it contained a far higher proportion of outright *serviles* than before.

Despite this increase in strength, on their own the *serviles* were unlikely to be able to overthrow the constitution, the stalemate only being broken by the fact that an increasingly desperate Napoleon decided to release Fernando VII in the hope of cutting his losses, *el rey deseado* duly crossing the front line in Catalonia on 24 March 1814. Fernando had been horrified by such news as he had heard from Spain, and he was quickly surrounded by a clique of aristocrats and churchmen whose dearest hope was to persuade him to overthrow the constitution. Encouraged by traditionalist gold, popular unrest was increasing in tempo, whilst there was genuine rejoicing at Fernando's return. Meanwhile, some evidence of the extent of opposition to the liberals in the *cortes* came to light when Fernando was presented with a manifesto signed by sixty-nine deputies demanding the restoration of absolutism. Cautious and timid as he was, Fernando was at first unwilling to precipitate an open break with the constitution. Arriving in Valencia on 16 April, however, he was met by the commander of the Second Army, General Elío, who placed his troops at Fernando's service and swore to uphold his rights against the liberals, the king in consequence resolving on a coup.

With the mass of the people at best indifferent to the constitution, the support of the army was crucial. Yet this was something that the liberals did not have. It was, of course, only to be expected that many generals, as nobles and *señores*, were *serviles*, but much had happened in the army since 1808. Although between 20 and 25 per cent of subalterns were commoners in 1800, the old officer corps had been dominated by the nobility. The war had changed all that, however, the noble monopoly on direct entry into the officer corps having collapsed even before the *cortes* had abolished the privileges of the nobility in this respect on 17 August 1811. In consequence, the officer corps had been transformed, one opinion being that the proportion of nobility in its ranks shrank to as little as 25 per cent (it should be noted, however, that this process only affected the lower ranks: of the 458 generals appointed during the war, at least 174 are known to have been officers in 1808, and only nine civilians or members of the rank and file).

In short, a constituency had been created within the army that had every reason to fear the return of absolutism. However, although numerous examples may be cited of liberal officers, a number of factors weakened the chances of liberalism taking hold in the army. Many of the new men who had become officers in the course of the war having in part done so to secure a share in the privileges of the officer corps, their abolition was extremely frustrating, whilst officers of every rank and origin could, with some justice, resent the juxtaposition of the attack on their status with the sufferings they had been enduring. In this respect, the government's continued inability to make good the army's needs did the liberals no favours at all. Still worse, the army found itself reduced to a secondary role in the fighting, whilst at the same time being forced to endure a torrent of anti-militarism, the liberals condemning it as a threat to liberty, glorifying the concept of the people-in-arms, forming a national guard, and promulgating a so-called 'military constitution'.

By the time that Fernando VII returned from France, various factors were therefore propelling many officers in the direction of *servilismo*. Yet this did not, of itself, make the army absolutist. Whilst the opposition of a few officers was clearly ideological, over and over again the concerns that came to the fore were explicitly professional, though this did not mean that the army was becoming any less politicized. As a succession of military pamphleteers began to argue, since the military estate was vital to the nation's independence and well-being, it followed that its needs should be satisfied and its members treated with respect; put another way, the interests of the army were synonymous with those of the nation. As the guardians of the national interest, it further followed that the army had the right – indeed, the duty – to intervene against any government that failed to meet these criteria.

With General Elío's *pronunciamiento* in Valencia, then, the liberals were doomed, and all the more so as the war was at last at an end, Napoleon having abdicated on 6 April. Absolutist forces were soon marching on Madrid, whilst city after city witnessed riots and disturbances. Although a few commanders were loyal to the liberals, they knew that they could not trust their subordinates and therefore attempted little in the way of resistance. Armed with a decree dissolving the *cortes* and annulling all its works, Elió's troops arrived in Madrid on 10 May 1814, and immediately proceeded to arrest dozens of liberals. All over Spain, meanwhile, crowds recruited by the supporters of absolutism toppled the constitutional authorities, the *ayuntamientos* of 1808 being restored and the local liberals seized or forced to flee. The revolution was dead.

The Two Spains?

Conventionally, the War of Independence of 1808–14 is regarded as one of the defining moments of modern Spanish history. Not only did the conflict with the French provide a myth that was to become a central feature of political debate for the entire period up till 1939, but from it there are supposed to have emerged two Spains – the one clerical, absolutist and reactionary, and the other secular, constitutional and progressive – whose mutual incompatibility was to plunge the country into a prolonged era of confrontation and civil war. Such a picture is far too simplistic, however, closer examination showing the 'two Spains' not to have been nearly so sharply defined. Ideologically speaking, the liberals may have more or less conformed to the conventional stereotype, but their opponents were rather divided into different positions of which one stood for the perpetuation of eighteenth-century enlightened absolutism, and the other a monarchy stripped of its Bourbon reformism that would only be absolute to the extent that it would allow the Church, aristocracy and other corporations the untrammelled enjoyment of their privileges.

It is not enough, however, to talk even of three Spains. Caught between these forces was an increasingly radicalized *populacho* that identified with no goals more complicated than peace, bread and access to the land, and was as hostile to the 'freedom' of the liberals as it was to the 'chains' of the *antiguo régimen*. Loyal to none of the contending tendencies, they were open to manipulation by all three of them, whilst at the same time pursuing a dimly perceived agenda of their own, the popular disturbances and cheering crowds that greeted the return of Fernando VII being at one and the same time the product of bribery and coercion, a vague belief that somehow *el rey deseado* would put all to rights, and a swelling mood of protest that was but little connected with the cause of absolutism.

To make matters still more complicated, meanwhile, the Revolutionary and Napoleonic Wars had also given Spain an army that was deeply politicized: in 1808 the royal guard had overthrown Godoy; in 1809 the Marqués de la Romana had overthrown the Junta of Asturias; in 1812 Francisco Ballesteros had revolted in protest at Wellington's appointment as commander-in-chief; and in 1814 Elío had brought down the liberal system. At the same time, of course, the army had also been imbued with a strong sense of mission: interests that were essentially sectional having in each case been dressed up in the guise of patriotism, it came to believe that its interests – order, political unity, military primacy – were coterminus with those of the nation – indeed, that they were those of the nation. Certain sections of the press having heaped much praise on generals such as Palafox and Ballesteros, they were transformed into the veritable embodiment of patriotic heroism; thus was born the concept of the military messiah.

Yet, as with the *populacho*, the army was in practice an operator that was separate from the liberals, the *serviles* and the enlightened absolutists. Thus, if sections of the army had risen in revolt in May 1814, they had done so in pursuit of essentially professional concerns whose satisfaction seemed most likely under the rule of an absolutist Fernando. Whether the new monarch would retain the army's support was very much a moot point, however: indeed, with much of the officer corps now a natural constituency of liberalism, it was hardly a likely prospect.

How these competing forces were to be reconciled was yet to be revealed. At this point suffice to say that Fernando presided over, not two Spains, but many, and, further, that the War of Independence had given birth to the violence and popular antagonism that were, along with military intervention in politics, to be nineteenth-century Spain's most pronounced characteristics.

3

Restoration and Revolution

Thesis and Antithesis

Few figures in Spanish history have attracted such odium as Fernando VII. Restored as absolute monarch in 1814, he was until the Civil War generally portrayed as having presided over a regime of the blackest hue that in 1820 was overthrown by a liberal movement composed of apostles of progress. Under Franco, a very different view prevailed, but the years since his death have witnessed a return to the demonization of the earlier era. The whole subject having become a riot of contradictions, the time is obviously ripe for a new synthesis.

The Return of the King

When Fernando VII returned to Madrid in May 1814, he was the subject of competing expectations. The nobility desired a reduction in the power of the throne and the restoration of its privileges. The Church desired the restoration of its economic and political fortunes. The old bureaucracy desired its restitution. The Basque notables desired the restoration of the *fueros*. The army desired reward. And, last but not least, the people desired the golden age epitomized by *el rey deseado*. However, Fernando VII inherited a ruined land. Trade and industry were at a low ebb; many cities had lost a considerable proportion of their population; and agriculture was in crisis, matters not being helped in this respect by a fresh round of natural disasters. And, above all, Argentina, Uruguay and Paraguay had all won their independence, whilst Venezuela, Colombia and Bolivia were in a state of open rebellion. With 184,000 men under arms in Spain alone, Fernando was bankrupt, whilst he himself was suspicious, fearful, ignorant and unimaginative. Meanwhile, local government was in chaos, and the restored administration ponderous and unrealistic.

Of one thing, however, Fernando was clear. Pressing though the *serviles* were for a programme centred on the abandonment of reform – both enlightened and liberal – and the restoration of order, even Fernando realized that the financial situation rendered any move in this direction out of the question, whilst he was in any case unwilling to relinquish the gains made by his predecessors. In consequence, the administration was filled with men who had been associated with enlightened absolutism, whilst the ministries established by Carlos III were retained, the *contribución única* only abandoned with the utmost reluctance, and the judicial attributes of the *señorios* kept in the hands of the state. In so far as the nobility were concerned, in fact, Fernando proved a grave disappointment, and all the more so given the effervescence that continued to grip the countryside. The result was numerous protests, but these met with no success whatsoever.

In so far as turning the clock back was concerned, the chief beneficiary was the Church, a string of decrees restoring those religious communities which had been dissolved, the Inquisition, and the Jesuits, the latter having been expelled by Carlos III. Yet here, too, there were limits, Fernando refusing to return the property sold off before 1814, and giving serious consideration to further expropriations. On this last issue he was forced to yield, but in other respects the Church's revenues continued to be plundered whilst a greater measure of regalism was imposed than ever. If much favour was shown to the more reactionary elements of the clergy, once again the policies of the eighteenth century remained in force.

Fernando therefore returned to Spain as anything but an apostle of mediaevalism. Though violently antipathetic towards the liberals, large numbers of whom were imprisoned, he had no more patience with the notion of a *cortes* of estates than he did with that of a *cortes* of deputies, and refused to overturn the achievements of either liberalism or 'ministerial despotism' in their entirety. In only one respect did Fernando make a clean break with the past. Thus, whereas Carlos IV had frequently been completely under the sway of his ministers, the new king was determined to be his own master. In consequence, the ministers of the restoration lived a difficult existence, the king repeatedly acting behind their backs and dismissing them without warning. Understandable though this might have been from Fernando's point of view, it rendered absolutism's response to the problems which Spain faced all the more ineffectual.

The Impossible Conundrum

If coherent government was essential, such was the scale of Spain's troubles that it is hard to see how they could have been overcome. At the heart of the problem was a single conundrum. Bankrupt and exhausted, Spain could only restore her situation through victory in America. However, precisely because Spain was bankrupt and exhausted, this was not a practical possibility. Progressive historians would argue that the answer lay in a fiscal reform, the creation of a national market, the expropriation of the Church and the nobility, and the emergence of a capitalist economy. Whether such a development would have made much difference is debatable, however. During the War of Independence, the Patriot authorities had found it almost impossible to raise an adequate supply of revenue from a radicalized countryside, and it is hard to see why the situation should have been any different after 1814.

Thus, the events of 1808–14 had gravely exacerbated the serious social crisis which had erupted in the last years of the eighteenth century. Many observers have believed that the root of this crisis was the blow dealt trade and industry by the combination of British competition, the American revolt and government mismanagement. Such views have, perhaps, been overstated, but even so in many parts of Spain industry did not recover for some time, not least because peace opened Spain to a flood of foreign goods. Even less doubtful is the fact that Spain continued to face a serious social crisis. Emigration – already important in parts of northern Spain – had been largely cut off by the American revolts. Disamortization had been accelerated. The *señores* had been confirmed in their property rights at the very time that many of them had been consorting with foreign invaders, and were now attempting to regain their jurisdictional ones as well. In addition, on 2 October 1814 Fernando restored the rights of the Mesta, thereby incurring bitter conflicts with villages desperate to extend their lands by ploughing up the *baldios*. Not surprisingly, the result was considerable resistance. In places this amounted to open revolt, but more commonly the response was a renewed upsurge in banditry.

Notwithstanding the use of the most draconian measures, the authorities were unable to restore order, the result being that revenue collection remained extremely difficult. At no time, however, had order been more necessary. Thus, 1814 had not brought peace to Spain. Setting aside the 'Hundred Days', which forced Spain to concentrate a large army in the Pyrenees, there was the question of America. Gestures at conciliation notwithstanding, Spain therefore remained at war. At first, some success was obtained. In February 1815, 10,000 men had sailed for America under the command of Pablo Morillo. Disembarking in Venezuela, Morillo found a country racked by civil war, the 'cowboys' of the interior having rebelled against the creole elite who had led the independence struggle. As a result, he had soon ended Venezuelan independence, after which he moved on to Colombia, driving all before him in the process. Yet resistance was not dead. In Venezuela and Colombia alike, the rebels retreated into the hinterland and formed new armies. These, however, Morillo was powerless to destroy: his forces were being decimated by tropical diseases; he received no more than a trickle of reinforcements from Spain; and his overbearing behaviour led to bitter disputes with the local *peninsulares*, whilst at the same time encouraging Patriot resistance.

Thus was revealed the bankruptcy of the military solution. Aided by the local loyalists, expeditionary armies could win great victories, but they could not hope to conquer the entire continent, the fact being that reconquest required resources that Fernando did not have. As early as May 1816, in fact, it was agreed that an army twice the size of Morillo's should be sent to Argentina, but such were the difficulties encountered in preparing this force that its departure was repeatedly postponed. In the meantime, all that could be done was to send the loyalists such reinforcements as Fernando's very limited means permitted. The number of men involved was by no means unimpressive, but such was the lack of shipping that the troops could only be dispatched in 'penny-packets', many of them then dying on the overcrowded and insanitary transports or falling into the hands of rebel warships (the Spanish navy, by contrast, was virtually unable to put to sea). For some time, the loyalist commanders managed to hold their positions, but in such circumstances nemesis could not be long postponed.

As early as January 1817, indeed, the Argentinian general, San Martín, led an army across the Andes to liberate Chile. For over a year, the fortunes of war tilted first one way and then the other, but on 5 April 1818 a decisive victory was obtained at Maipú. Far to the north, meanwhile, the Venezuelan leader, Bolivar, had been fighting Morillo. Inspired by the news from Chile, he hit upon the plan of invading Colombia, which had been left with only a minimal garrison. Defeating the main royalist army at Boyacá on 7 August 1819, he quickly declared Colombia's independence. With catastrophic stubbornness, however, Fernando fought on, and that despite the fact that he was by now courting disaster at home as well.

Pronunciamiento *and Rebellion*

The restoration of absolutism did not go unchallenged, Spain being rocked by a series of rebellions and conspiracies that culminated in the revolution of 1820. Thus, numerous elements of the propertied classes, and, in particular, the industrial and commercial bourgeoisie, quickly became increasingly disaffected. To show that this discontent existed, however, is not the same as demonstrating that revolt was primarily a civilian affair, the result being that we must necessarily focus on the army. In so far as this force was concerned, the basic problem was that Spain could not afford 184,000 men under arms. To make matters worse, the officer corps, which had been thrown open to all classes of society, had been grotesquely swollen by the prodigality of the provincial juntas, the creation of too many new regiments, and the demands of the guerrillas. Even as matters stood, many officers were effectively unemployed, but there now returned from France the 4,000 officers who had been held there as prisoners-of-war. In short, the regime faced a major crisis.

Severe as this crisis was, it was handled in a singularly unfortunate manner. As his first War Minister, Fernando appointed Francisco Eguía, a general possessed of an undistinguished war record and singularly old-fashioned aspect. With such a figure in charge, the chief casualties were inevitably the many officers who had been civilians in 1808, or who had gained vastly accelerated promotion on account of the war. Meanwhile, many of the army's senior appointments went to men who could be accused of having sat out the war in safety or, still worse, treason. At all events, much offence was caused, these developments being all the more galling in view of the imprisonment as liberals of such heroes of the struggle as Pedro Villacampa and Juan Díaz Porlier and the dissolution of many regiments formed during the war.

The effect of Eguía's measures was to undermine the anti-liberal consensus of 1814. Deprived of their commands, large numbers of officers were retired, attached to other units as supernumeraries, or placed on half pay. For such men, life was truly desperate, whilst, even for those who managed to remain on the active list, pay was insufficient and constantly in arrears. As for the army as a whole, meanwhile, the troops continued to go starving, shoeless and in rags. Desperate protests having gone unheard, it was not long before some officers began to rally to the cause of liberalism. Much weight has traditionally been accorded to masonry in this respect, it being argued that many of the prisoners who returned from France in 1814 – amongst whom were many prominent figures of the revolution of 1820 – had become masons whilst in captivity, and that masonry thereafter spread very rapidly through the officer corps. However, the reality was very different, masons being few and far between in army and society alike. In any case, opposition was professional rather than ideological.

Thus, trouble first began in Navarre, which had by 1814 become a virtual fief of the successful guerrilla commander, Francisco Espoz y Mina. His relations with the constitutional authorities having been anything but cordial, Mina had gladly rallied to the absolutist cause, only for him to become increasingly disillusioned. The local authorities refused to succour his men, who perforce began to return to their homes; the government refused to recognize his troops as regulars, with the result that they were threatened with immediate dissolution, all irregulars having been ordered to disband; and Fernando not only denied Mina the viceroyalty of Navarre, but publicly snubbed him when he travelled to Madrid to air his grievances. Thus rejected, Mina decided that the only way out was rebellion. On the night of 25 September 1814, he therefore attempted to seize Pamplona, only for his troops to refuse to follow him. Fleeing across the frontier, Mina proceeded to play the liberal, but in reality his only goal had been to secure his own position.

Rather more credibility attaches to the next revolt to break out against the restoration, for its leader, Juan Díaz Porlier, had been imprisoned in 1814. Yet, again, there is little to show that Porlier – another guerrilla commander – possessed progressive convictions, the only motive for his imprisonment being the fact that he happened to be connected to the prominent liberal, Toreno. Like Mina, too, he had been out of favour with the constitutional authorities, and there seems no reason to suppose that he would have revolted had he been treated differently. As it was, however, imprisoned in La Coruña, Porlier resolved on a coup. Getting in touch with disaffected elements of the garrison, which had become much alarmed by rumours that it might be sent to America, he succeeded in instigating a rising on 19 September 1815. Released in triumph, Porlier issued a proclamation bemoaning the ills that had befallen Spain since 1814, and demanding the immediate convocation of a new *cortes*. However, things soon began to go wrong. Despite the economic problems the city was experiencing, the population as a whole remained quiet, whilst few representatives even of the merchant community offered Porlier any support. Beyond La Coruña, meanwhile, the only response to the general's proclamations came from El Ferrol, whose garrison made haste to join him. Mustering his few soldiers, Porlier tried to seize Santiago, only for a group of sergeants suborned by loyalist agents to surprise him in his quarters and take him back to La Coruña where he was executed soon after.

Initially, then, the military opposition to Fernando VII consisted of little more than individual malcontents motivated by a variety of personal grievances. As witness the next conspiracy, however, it gradually became more politicized whilst at the same time developing closer links with civilian liberalism. Once again, the focus was a single individual, in this case General Lacy. Relatively young, Lacy had commanded the Spanish army in Catalonia during the war, and was therefore much disappointed with the relatively minor post in the garrison of Barcelona that he was given in 1814. Always liberal in sympathy, he now fell in with a particularly ambitious and turbulent irregular named Francisco Milans del Bosch. Soon resolving on a coup, the two officers quickly won over considerable elements of the Barcelona garrison, whilst also making contact with certain members of the bourgeoisie. On 4 April 1817 Lacy and Milans duly 'pronounced' at the latter's estate near Mataró, but in the event few of the troops who were supposed to support them did so, the result being that they had to flee. Milans escaped across the frontier to France, but Lacy was captured and shot.

The extent of civilian support for Lacy's revolt is in some respects open to doubt, for the general was not a popular man in Catalonia, having not only constantly sought to regularize the *somatenes*, but also killed hundreds of people in a botched attempt to retake Lérida by exploding a large mine. It is nonetheless clear that the discontent of the military was beginning to fuse with that of the liberals. In 1816 a group of guerrillas and *madrileño* liberals had hatched a plot to waylay Fernando and force him to accept the constitution of 1812, whilst the period from 1817 to 1819 was marked by the discovery of a series of conspiracies that brought together not only army officers, but also a variety of priests, functionaries, artisans and men of business. Obviously, then, opposition to Fernando VII was not just a military affair. If prominent members of the bourgeoisie became involved in conspiracy, however, they did so in relatively small numbers, whilst it is further clear that such representatives of the crowd who followed their lead were frequently their dependants. If one adds to this the very clear evidence that liberal mobs could be hired as easily as servile ones, it is difficult to accept claims that political unrest was an overwhelmingly popular phenomenon.

Until January 1820 Fernando had more or less been holding his own. Within three months the picture had changed dramatically, however. Although the ships that were needed to transport the large army that Fernando had ordered to subdue Buenos Aires could never be found, the troops themselves were duly concentrated in the vicinity of Cádiz and left to fall prey to boredom, hunger and disease, not to mention the blandishments of agents sent from Argentina with the express purpose of fomenting discontent. In Cádiz, meanwhile, support for the restoration had always been minimal, and by 1817 a number of prominent merchants led by Francisco Javier Istúriz had got into contact with the expeditionary army. After a variety of *contretemps*, on 1 January 1820 the situation finally came to a head. At the small town of Cabezas de San Juan some forty miles north of Cádiz Lieutenant-Colonel Rafael del Riego proclaimed the constitution of 1812. Swayed by promises of land, money and demobilization, the troops followed Riego's lead – it helped that he had been provided with considerable funds by one Juan Alvarez Mendizábal, who was the local agent of the leading Valencian liberal, Vicente Bertrán de Lis – and the army was soon concentrated before the walls of Cádiz. Again, however, things began to go wrong. Most of the conspirators' agents in the garrison having just fallen prey to an epidemic of yellow fever, Cádiz not only failed to rise but beat off the attacks of the rebels. With little support forthcoming from the local population, meanwhile, the soldiers were deserting in large numbers. With loyal forces beginning to close in, it seemed that the rebels would soon themselves be surrounded. In a desperate effort to raise a more general revolt, Riego therefore led a small column of troops back into the hinterland. No support was forthcoming, however, and on 11 March Riego was cornered at the remote village of Bienvenida. Realizing that the game was up – he had less than 100 men left – he ordered his followers to disperse, and himself embarked on a desperate race for the sea.

Emerging from the wilderness, Riego found that he was not a fugitive but a hero. His march through Andalucía may have awoken few echoes, but elsewhere the situation was very different. From 21 February onwards Spain had been gripped by a succession of revolts inspired by Riego's efforts in Andalucía, the towns affected including La Coruña, Vigo, El Ferrol, Pontevedra, Murcia and Zaragoza. In Madrid, the bulk of Fernando's advisers were by now pressing for some sort of retreat, and on 3 March the king had duly issued a vague promise of reform. Realizing that this was not enough, however, both the Conde del Abisbal and General Ballesteros – respectively Captain General of Andalucía and military governor of Madrid – turned on the monarch, whilst riots now broke out in the capital itself, on 7 March the king finally agreeing to restore the constitution of 1812.

So much, in outline, for the downfall of the first restoration, though it should be noted that the next few days saw Barcelona, Pamplona, Valencia, Cádiz and many other places all erupt in revolution in their turn. In so far as the nature of these events is concerned, the most important role in events was everywhere taken by the army, such civilian foundation as the revolution possessed lying in sections of the propertied classes. A large part of the urban masses either being dependent upon such men for employment or custom, or happy to play the part of mercenaries, the revolution certainly gained an appearance of popular support. In reality, however, the order of the day was rather indifference, whilst Riego had obtained hardly a single recruit, the crowds being interested in little more than pillage.

None of this is to say that the populace was happy, however. Setting aside the attempts of the Church and the nobility to enforce the payment of tithes and feudal dues and the social and economic difficulties that continued to beset large parts of the Spanish countryside, the war in America had left the regime with no option but to increase its demands. After three years free of conscription, from 1817 onwards annual levies of 17,500 men were imposed on the populace, whose reaction may be judged by the issue in 1818 of draconian new measures against desertion. By 1816, meanwhile, Fernando had become increasingly aware that the fiscal structure of the *antiguo régimen* was simply incapable of meeting

Spain's changed circumstances, and was therefore more and more inclined to listen to the numerous servants of Caroline absolutism who had survived from 1808. As a result, in December 1816 one of their number – a senior treasury official named Martín de Garay, who had served as secretary of the Junta Central – was appointed Minister of Finance. For such men, it was axiomatic, first, that taxation should be rationalized, and, second, that greater pressure should be exerted on the Church and nobility. In brief, Garay's solution to the problem was to reintroduce a modified form of the system of taxation introduced by the *cortes* of Cádiz. Thus, the most important element of the new system was an income tax known as the *contribución general*, or 'general contribution'. Meanwhile, the various indirect taxes paid by the municipalities were unified into a single category known as the *derechas de puertas*. With large parts of the country thereby immediately subjected to much heavier financial pressure, and the population as a whole everywhere exposed to the efforts of the notables to minimize their contributions, the result was immense unrest.

Logically, then, Riego's *pronunciamiento* might have been expected to precipitate a full-scale popular revolt. All too obviously, however, this failed to occur. Although Riego's actions won the support of significant sections of the army and the educated classes, claims that the constitution was restored by the people seem dubious in the extreme. All the more can this be seen to be the case given the fact that the *cortes* of Cádiz had in practice offered very little to the populace, the future of the revolution that was now in train being very largely dependent on whether its successors could do any better.

The Revolution of 1820

If recent Spanish writing on the constitutional *trienio* has been dominated by one idea, it is that the supposedly popular revolution of 1820 was effectively hijacked by elements of the propertied classes, being stripped in the process of many of its central aspirations. Unwilling to pursue the aims espoused by the crowd, the new authorities inevitably finished by temporizing with the forces of absolutism, which were therefore enabled to stir up opposition to the revolution, and ultimately to provoke a crisis that resulted in a French army once again marching across the Pyrenees. Between 1808 and 1814, foreign invasion had been met by a redoubtable resistance movement founded upon the belief that feudalism was to be swept away, but in 1823 there was no chance of a fresh *guerrilla*, the hopes of the people having been dashed over the previous three years by the counter-revolutionary behaviour of the liberal leadership.

At the heart of this theory lies a simple assertion. In brief, the revolution was the work not of the bourgeoisie but the people. According to this view, the risings of 1820 were followed by a concerted effort to bring them under control. Thus, in Madrid the rising was followed by the emergence of a provisional government – the Junta Provisional de Gobierno – dominated by General Ballesteros. A loyal servant of absolutism, Ballesteros secured the replacement of the new *ayuntamiento* that had been established by acclaim in the immediate aftermath of the revolution by one which had been properly elected, whilst at the same time ensuring that the king appointed only the most moderate men as ministers. All over Spain, meanwhile, control of the revolution (in terms, for example, of the control of the *ayuntamientos, diputaciónes*, militias and patriotic societies that were formed in the wake of the uprising) was seized by the propertied classes. Thus entrenched, the latter proceeded to quash all attempts to give the revolution a genuinely popular base, whilst at the same time showing little interest in anything other than the advancement of their own families. All over Spain the result was that the forces of the *antiguo régimen* were allowed to regroup unmolested.

Yet to argue that the leaders of the revolution were from the very beginning engaged in its subversion is dangerously facile. Fernando, certainly, was almost undoubtedly determined on the constitution's overthrow, but to doubt the liberal convictions of the *doceañistas* who were summoned to form the new government is to fly in the face of reality. Much has been made of the fact that the War Ministry was placed in the hands of the aristocratic Pedro Agustín Girón, but, even if it can be shown that Girón was a decided enemy of the constitution, his appointment was the work not of the revolutionary authorities but of the king. Nor can anyone deny that during its brief life the Junta Provisional de Gobierno sought to consolidate the revolution. Thus, all the institutions and positions established by the constitution of 1812 were reconstituted and, as far as possible, manned by the same personnel as in 1814; all the legislation of the *cortes* of Cádiz was declared once more to be in force; measures were taken to facilitate the introduction of measures which the first constitutional regime had discussed but never implemented; the administration was purged of *serviles*; many opponents of liberalism were placed under arrest; and a number of measures were taken to block attempts at constitutional reform. Beyond the level of government, meanwhile, there was a general rush to establish patriotic clubs whose aim was in part to ensure that the authorities remained loyal to the revolution and in part to galvanize support for the new regime. With regard to the latter aim, in particular, no effort was spared, for the next three years Spanish political life being characterized by the wholesale use of political propaganda.

Notwithstanding the survival of numerous representatives of the *anti-*

guo régimen, there was, then, a genuinely revolutionary atmosphere in the spring and summer of 1820. Within a very short space of time this was confirmed by election of a new *cortes* that was almost entirely devoid of *serviles*. Having opened its sessions on 9 July, moreover, this body proceeded to press on with the programme of 1810–14, the measures that it decreed including the suppression of the Jesuits, the secularization of most of the religious orders, and the abolition of all restrictions on external commerce. Already, however, all was far from well. Unlike in 1812, the supporters of liberalism could look back to a period of constitutional government, and amongst some of them at least the belief began to emerge that the disaster of 1814 had primarily stemmed from a failure to obtain the support of the people. If the revolution of 1820 was to survive, it followed that it should adopt a far more radical line. Thus, political power was to be decentralized, the people freed from the burdens of taxation, conscription, the tithe and feudal dues, and given access to the national militia and the lands of the Church, nobility and municipalities. Underlying these matters was also a generational problem. Thus, many men who had been too young to take part in the events of 1812–14 resented the dominance of the *doceañistas*. Though often from precisely the same sort of background as their elders, they still had to make their way in the world. Meanwhile, they had in effect been excluded from the *cortes*: not only did the electoral law stipulate that deputies had to be at least twenty-five, but the ballot had frequently been manipulated by the local establishment. Anxious both to gain access to the spoils of victory and generally to cut a dash in the political world, such men had no option but to try to outbid their rivals. Gradually, then, there emerged a separate faction amongst the revolutionary ranks whose enthusiastic radicalism gained it the name of the *exaltados*. Flocking to the political clubs, the latter also became prominent in the militia. Thus it was that a deep rift began to open in the ranks of the revolution.

Whilst they were on the whole no less devoted to the cause of liberalism, the circles that dominated the government, the *cortes*, the *ayuntamientos* and, to the extent that it was of any importance, Spanish freemasonry, had other concerns. Commerce, the administration, the universities and the law were recruited from a relatively small number of powerful, successful and well-established families that were frequently of noble origin and possessed of considerable landed wealth. Given that the revolution guaranteed them renewed access to the lands of the Church, promised to resolve a number of the difficulties under which many merchants were labouring, and seemed likely to secure many of the bureaucracy's traditional aims, such men were by no means hostile. What they were not interested in, however, was a social revolution. Disamortization was to be pursued, certainly, but it was to be pursued in accordance with the interests of the propertied elite. Also of importance, at least for the commercial classes, was the creation of a unified internal market and the establishment of a national customs frontier, whilst there was general agreement on the need to abolish the privileges of the Church, the nobility and the officer corps, and put an end to the pretensions of the army. All this, of course, could only be secured in the context of a constitutional regime, but, beyond that, the aims of the *moderados*, as they became known, were strictly limited. The rights of property were to be protected, and order maintained at all costs, whilst there could be no retreat from the rigid centralization that had marked the constitution of 1812. As for ideas of democratization, these were sheer anathema: power was to be in the hands of men of property and education, whose responsibility was guaranteed by the stake which they possessed in society.

The extent to which these divisions were underpinned by social class is a moot point, some historians having suggested that the *moderados* were essentially the representatives of finance and the land, and the *exaltados* the representatives of commerce and the professions. Attractive though they are, such ideas have no basis in fact. In so far as there was any difference at all, it was really one of age, reputation and success. Thus, the *moderados* were drawn almost exclusively from men who were already well-established on the social scale thanks to a combination of a prosperous family background and the pursuit of successful careers in the army, the administration, the professions or big business. Whilst often sharing the same background, the *exaltados* were by contrast men who had yet to establish themselves, who had not risen above the second rank of liberal politics in 1808–14, or who had found themselves excluded from the orgy of patronage that had followed the revolution. In short, they were the first of the *pretendientes* – the office-seekers whose desperate search for preferment and security was to help to fuel political change in Spain throughout the nineteenth century.

Such were the divisions that existed in the liberal camp that they could not long be suppressed. Following the revolution it had been resolved that the moment was propitious for the American rebels to be offered a ceasefire and the possibility of negotiations. Reinforcements would still be sent to the loyalists, but these were to come entirely from volunteers recruited specifically for the purpose. As for the expedition to Buenos Aires, this was to be suspended indefinitely. The army that had rebelled at Cabezas de San Juan having thereby been rendered redundant, the government resolved on its dissolution. The result was uproar. In fact the fruit of financial pressures, the attack on the so-called Army of Overseas was interpreted by the *exaltados* as an attempt to stifle the forces of radicalism, their argument being that the relatively junior officers who had headed the coup of January 1820 were the heart and soul of the revolution. Meanwhile, the heads of many of the officers concerned had been turned by a combination of frustrated ambition and public adulation. Despite the fact that they had generally been offered tempting new appointments – Riego was to be Captain General of Galicia, for example – a number of the officers concerned refused to accept the decision and threatened a fresh revolt. Dissuaded from such a step, Riego instead travelled to Madrid to plead his case, having been further mollified by the replacement of Girón as Minister of War by one of the very few senior commanders actively to have opposed the coup of 1814. Such was the tension provoked by the news that the Army of Overseas was to be abolished, however, that trouble was inevitable, and on 3 September an act of homage organized by an *exaltado* club degenerated into an angry demonstration. Thus provoked, the government immediately stripped Riego of his new Captain Generalcy and banished him from Madrid, whilst also purging a number of his leading supporters. Several days of disorder followed, whereupon the *cortes* curbed the liberty of the press and banned all political clubs.

Within a very short time a series of fresh troubles caused the moderates to repent of this clamp-down, which was in any case distinctly ineffective. In brief, shortly after the *cortes* closed on 9 November, Fernando initiated a major crisis by appointing a noted opponent of the constitution to be Archbishop of Valencia. When this choice was rejected, the king picked an equally noted absolutist, José María Carvajal, to be Captain General of New Castile. Setting aside these attempts to test the will of the *cortes*, meanwhile, from all round the country reports were coming in of *servil* agitation. As yet open resistance was very limited, but all the same the government became much alarmed, and in consequence decided that it had no option but to patch up its relations with the *exaltados*. When news arrived of Fernando's *démarché*, it therefore immediately rehabilitated Riego and his colleagues and ended the ban on the political clubs, the king being left with no option but to back down.

As the increase in absolutist activity had the effect of encouraging the *exaltados* in their demands, reconciliation proved ephemeral. Thus, the government once again moved against the political clubs, the response of the *exaltados* being the formation of a nation-wide secret society known as the *comuneros* (the name refers to the sixteenth-century rebels who rose against Carlos I in defence of the privileges of the towns of Castile). The first organized political movement in Spanish history, this is alleged to have had branches in at least fifty different towns and cities. At all events the determination of the *exaltados* was now further highlighted by the Vinuesa affair. On 21 January 1821 an honorary royal chaplain named Agustín Vinuesa was arrested in Madrid on suspicion of conspiracy. The case against him is difficult to take seriously, but such was the growing paranoia that the affair occasioned a fresh series of popular demonstrations, the general excitement being fuelled by the fact that Madrid was celebrating *carnaval*. On 6 February Fernando's daily carriage drive was disrupted by clashes between the crowds and the king's escort of Guardias de Corps, the royal palace then being blockaded by the crowd. Offered peace in exchange for the dissolution of the Guardias de Corps, on 8 February Fernando surrendered, those of his soldiers who did not manage to escape immediately being imprisoned.

Disintegration and Conquest, 1821–3

The conflict of February 1821 had important consequences. Furious at the treatment accorded to the Guardias de Corps, Fernando added an unauthorized paragraph to the speech that he delivered during the opening ceremony of the parliamentary session of 1821 in which he complained bitterly of the failure of the constitutional authorities to uphold his dignity. The next day, moreover, Fernando dismissed the entire government in favour of a new ministry headed by Eusebio de Bardají. Though the *cortes* continued to implement reforms of all sorts – most notably the elaboration of new ordinances for the army – *exaltado* unrest was therefore likely to continue.

Had the revolution been secure, radical discontent might have remained at a low level. From as early as the autumn of 1820, however, news had been coming in of the formation of guerrilla bands and insurgent juntas, and in April 1821 there were serious disturbances in Alava and parts of Old Castile. Meanwhile, the countryside remained as desperate as ever, the situation being made still worse by a further series of natural disasters. To be fair to the *moderados*, not all of them were blind to the social problem. In the wake of the revolution much indirect taxation had been abolished, and in March 1821 the *cortes* decreed that the tithes should be reduced by 50 per cent. Also of importance in this respect were decrees that the burden of proof as to whether particular seigneurial dues were jurisdictional or contractual should rest with the *señor* rather than the *pueblo* (a crucial distinction: contractual dues had still to be paid as rent), and that the lands of the municipalities should be parcelled out in small lots. However, in the event, these measures proved absolutely nugatory, the situation of the populace actually deteriorating dramatically. In part the blame for this situation lay at home – the decree concerning the *señorios*, for example, was blocked by royal veto until May 1823, whilst that concerning the commons was largely ignored – but the chief culprit was rather the war in America, all hope of a compromise peace soon being shattered. In Venezuela a thoroughly disgusted Morillo obeyed the orders that he received from Spain to sign an armistice with Bolivar, only for negotiations to break down and the latter to gain a decisive victory at Carabobo on 24 June 1821. Turning south, Bolivar next sent his troops against loyalist Ecuador, whilst San Martín invaded Peru and captured Lima. For many of the dominant groups in the few areas still loyal to Spain, meanwhile, news of the restoration of liberalism was an unparalleled disaster. In consequence, in January 1821 Mexico's *criollos* and *peninsulares* alike joined the last remnants of the rebels of 1810 in a great national revolt under the leadership of General Agustín de Iturbide, independence also being declared in such areas as Guatemala and Panama.

By the middle of 1821, then, the Spanish position was desperate, the implications for the future of the revolution being severe in the extreme. Thus, the treasury was placed under greater strain than ever, in part because of the demands of the war itself, and in part because attempts to secure substantial loans from abroad were undermined by the heavy blow that had been dealt to Spain's financial credibility. With the national debt now standing at 14,219,000,000 *reales*, the only way out was to maximize revenue at home. Most of the dues that had been abolished in March 1820 were therefore restored at a higher rate than ever. The tithes having been paid in kind, and therefore declining in value, the benefits derived from their reduction was wiped out, and all the more so as the fall in agricultural prices that had been in train since 1814 forced the peasantry to market an ever greater share of their produce. Yet how this increase in sales was to be achieved was a moot point, for the continuing war in America meant that many of the economic activities which had absorbed such crops as grapes and flax remained at a very low ebb. As for the sale of lands of the Church, this now proved an outright disaster. Financial necessity decreeing both that the properties concerned should be offered for sale in large lots to the highest bidder, and that payment should primarily be in titles to the national debt, the bulk of the population were almost entirely excluded from the process, whilst the notables were able to secure huge estates for a fraction of their real value. Having acquired these properties, moreover, the purchasers generally proceeded everywhere to force up rents, thereby exposing the peasantry to still more misery.

As the difficulties experienced by the peasantry continued to mount, so more and more of the inhabitants began to rally either to the guerrilla bands being organized by absolutist clerics and notables or to the bandit gangs that were becoming inextricably linked with them. By the winter of 1821, in fact, such bands were active in large parts of Catalonia, Valencia and the Basque provinces, whilst other areas witnessed repeated outbreaks of disorder, of which the most famous is the outbreak of Luddism that occurred at Alcoy. With the aid of hindsight it is possible to see that Spain was in no sense in the grip of counter-revolution, the number of insurgents at this stage remaining relatively small, and their motivation primarily social and economic. However, at the time this was by no means apparent, the *exaltados*, who were also much alarmed by the suppression of the various revolutions that had broken out in Italy, in consequence being presented with fresh grounds for protest. Many clubs therefore became more and more excited; on 5 May 1821 an angry mob murdered the unfortunate Vinuesa in his prison cell; and from Barcelona there came reports of a republican plot. Much alarmed, the government made some concessions to the *exaltados* – most importantly, the deportation of a number of leading *serviles* and the authorization of trial by court martial – but it remained determined not to submit to their agenda, placing the clubs under close observation and appointing the hard-bitten Morillo, who had returned to Spain early in 1821, Captain General of Madrid. As another general suspected of *servil* inclinations was at the same time appointed *jefe político*, the *exaltados* were furious.

With matters in this state, a crisis could not long be avoided. When it came, the central figure was once again Rafael del Riego. Following his rehabilitation the previous November, Riego had been made Captain General of Aragón, where he had since been fraternizing not only with the local *exaltados*, but also with a number of French exiles. Some of the latter being involved in conspiracies against Louis XVIII, the *jefe político* of Zaragoza complained to Madrid. Already incensed by Riego's encouragement of the *exaltados*, the government promptly dismissed him, only to provoke a fresh wave of unrest. Noisy street demonstrations in Madrid were dispersed on 18 September, but over the next few months Cádiz, Seville, Cartagena, Murcia, Valencia and La Coruña all experienced full-scale popular revolts, disturbances of a more minor nature occurring in Córdoba, Cuenca, Zaragoza, Granada, Badajoz and Pamplona. Where they were thus brought to power, the *exaltados* of these cities proceeded to take vigorous action against the local *serviles*, to broaden recruitment to the militia, and to implement a number of measures designed to assist the poor. Dramatic though these events were, however, the rebels had little idea of what to do next, the whole affair fizzling out in a series of bloodless surrenders.

Tame though the outcome of all this was, the *exaltado* revolution had a number of important effects. In the first place, it undoubtedly pushed many erstwhile *moderados* into support for counter-revolution. In the second, it deepened divisions within the liberal camp, a new secret society being formed whose members, the so-called *añilleros*, or 'ring bearers', were in their entirety prosperous *doceañistas* determined to secure the establishment of a second chamber representing the interests of property. In the third, the various instances of popular anti-clericalism to which it gave rise provided much useful ammunition for absolutist agitators. And, in the fourth, and perhaps most importantly, it led to fresh popular unrest. Whilst in the vast majority as yet unwilling to join the absolutist *partidas*, the rural populace had been becoming increasingly alienated by the arrogant behaviour of the troops sent out to hunt them down. In this respect, injury was added to insult by the restoration of conscription. Desperate to assuage *exaltado* discontent, in September 1821 the government had agreed to the convocation of an extraordinary sitting of the *cortes*, the latter decreeing a *quinta* of some 16,000 men.

No action could have caused more damage. Hostility to conscription having been a constant feature in Spanish society since the eighteenth century, the result was a massive upsurge in resistance. Notwithstanding a series of attempts to raise guerrilla bands from amongst its inhabitants, the province of Santander, for example, had until now remained relatively quiet, but news of the impending *sorteo* caused hundreds of men to flee to the rebel leaders operating in the Cantabrian mountains. In Catalonia, meanwhile, absolutist elements who had fled into exile in France succeeded in raising most of the Segre valley in revolt and in establishing a rebel junta at Seo de Urgel. In the Levante there was a large uprising at Orihuela on 14 July 1822. And in Navarre, where once again partisan activity had hitherto been relatively insignificant, the local liberals had soon been blockaded in such towns as Pamplona, Tudela and Estella.

The nature and extent of resistance to the constitutional regime has been a subject of considerable debate. However, whatever conclusions are reached in this respect, there is no doubt that its effects were very serious. Although the new general elections due in 1822 had produced an *exaltado* majority, Fernando insisted on appointing another *moderado* government under the leadership of the writer, Francisco Martínez de la Rosa. Needless to say, the *exaltados* were furious, the result being fresh riots that culminated in serious clashes between the militia and the various battalions of guard infantry stationed in the capital. Provided with just the pretext that he needed, Fernando promptly ordered the guard to assault the city, only for his men to be forestalled by the militia and driven back into the royal palace.

Triumph though the *exaltados* most certainly had – Fernando was left with no option but to appoint an *exaltado* government under the leading *veintista*, Evaristo de San Miguel – their victory made little difference to the nature of the Spanish revolution. In social terms, the *cortes* had changed but little in the elections of 1822 – indeed, the number of landed proprietors amongst the deputies had increased from forty-five to sixty-one – and there was no sign of the radical change in agrarian policy that was the only hope of restoring order in the countryside. Symbolic of this situation were the new regulations agreed for the militia just prior to the rising of the royal guard: whilst these ended the requirement that all recruits should have to pay for their own equipment and made service compulsory rather than voluntary, numerous exemptions ensured that the lower classes would remain outside its ranks. This is not to say that the *exaltados* were counter-revolutionary: the militia grew enormously in size; on 8 June a fresh *quinta* was decreed; and every effort was made to foment support for the constitution and boost the morale of the populace. Furthermore, on 15 September the government convoked a further extraordinary session of the *cortes*, which then sat continuously until 19 February 1823, in the process calling up nearly 60,000 fresh troops, authorizing a fresh loan of 348,000,000 *reales*, and introducing a new municipal law which gave more autonomy to the *diputaciones provinciales* and *ayuntamientos*. At the same time, vigorous action was taken against the absolutist rebels: a number of the monasteries that had thus far been allowed to remain open were suppressed; *jefes políticos* who had failed to take a strong enough line against the rebels were replaced; severe measures were taken against a number of prominent *serviles*; and a large army was concentrated in Catalonia under Mina, who proceeded to retake Seo de Urgel.

To argue that the liberal authorities were somehow counter-revolutionary is therefore facile. That said, however, they were deeply unrealistic. Ignoring the evidence that America could never be reconquered, the *cortes* of 1822 rejected a plan for a transatlantic federation that represented the last hope of a compromise peace. Meanwhile, despite the fact that the general misery ensured that there was no shortage of recruits for such units as the companies of 'constitutional chasseurs' raised by many *ayuntamientos* from June 1822 onwards, the *cortes* also voted for fresh *sorteos*. With the ranks of the guerrillas thereby swelled still further, the civil war continued unabated, this in turn encouraging further outbreaks of violence amongst those sectors of the populace who favoured the liberals. Themselves the victims of economic collapse and natural catastrophe – Barcelona, for example, was struck by a particularly virulent outbreak of yellow fever – they lashed out in fury. Needless to say, the Church was a prime target. Thus, a number of monasteries and churches were burned, and several members of the clergy murdered. Particularly in Catalonia, such excesses were encouraged by the authorities, who executed at least fifty clerics, and made little attempt to restrain the militia's propensity to engage in acts of anti-clerical violence. With some of the more excited radicals using language that recalled the most extreme period of the French Revolution, the impression naturally began to get about that Spain was in the grip of a Jacobin revolution.

More than anything else, it was this that sealed the fate of the revolution of 1820. Though guerrilla resistance gripped large parts of Spain, it was quite clear that there was little hope of the liberals being overthrown, Fernando having in consequence for some time been seeking help from abroad. Initially reluctant to become involved, the powers now decided to act, and on 7 April 1823 the first of 60,000 French troops marched across the frontier. Meanwhile, not even the threat of invasion had been enough to inject the revolution with a dose of reality, the winter of 1822–3 being marked by a bitter power struggle in the ranks of the *exaltados*. Eager to profit from the manner in which the latter were trying to outbid one another, when it was proposed that king, government and *cortes* alike should evacuate Madrid for the safety of Seville or Cádiz, Fernando appointed a new administration chosen from the most radical section of the *exaltados*. As this group had been demanding that the capital be defended to the death, the king's motives are not hard to divine, but in the event an angry mob forced him to reinstate the San Miguel government and set out for Seville.

There remains but little to tell. Despite much wild rhetoric, the two Spanish armies in the Pyrenees were too ragged, starving and unpaid to put up much of a fight, and were soon in full retreat. Decimated by desertion, that in the west disintegrated altogether, but, still headed by Mina, that in the east barricaded itself in Barcelona, which it defended for the next few months against a French blockade. Its example was followed by a few other garrisons, but elsewhere the Spanish commanders, most of whom were not *veintistas*, but rather *moderados* such as Morillo, Abisbal and Ballesteros, either surrendered or defected. As for popular resistance, there was none. In Seville, meanwhile, the San Miguel administration having resigned in despair, a new government had taken power under Calatrava, and early in June this decided that it was time to head for Cádiz. Refusing to go, Fernando was declared insane and taken along anyway. By 23 June Cádiz was again under siege. For a brief time, all was optimism, the liberal press deluding itself with fantastic stories of heroic resistance and foreign aid, but on 1 October the city finally surrendered. Most of the other liberal redoubts having also fallen – the very last place to give up was Alicante, where resistance continued till 5 November – the way was clear for the second restoration.

The End of Doceañismo

The fall of Cádiz marked the end of an era. Notwithstanding the loyalty of a handful of die-hard *exaltados*, the constitution of 1812 was a dead letter that was never to be revived. Given its numerous practical defects, its demise was hardly to be lamented, and yet its departure from the scene was to cement a development that the *trienio* of 1820–3 had made all too apparent. Thus, far from being a creed that was set to overthrow the established social order, Spanish liberalism was rather a tool of the narrow landed elite that had for generations monopolized commerce, the administration, the professions and local government. Committed to political revolution though they were – for the experience of 1814–20 showed very clearly that their interests were not served by the survival of absolutism – these *pudientes* were yet determined to preserve the social order and monopolize the fruits of revolution, and in consequence adopted policies that left the bulk of the populace excluded from the political process, subject to many feudal dues, exposed to rack-renting, and denied access to the lands of the Church.

In this respect, those critics who contend that the whole *trienio* was an exercise in the repression of the populace are quite right. However, when they contend that the regime that ruled Spain between 1820 and 1823 was somehow counter-revolutionary, they are less convincing. Given the series of reforms that the liberals either inherited from the *cortes* of Cádiz or proceeded to introduce on their own account, to argue in this fashion is simply perverse. Nor is it clear that a more radical social policy would have made much difference to the fate of the revolution. The abolition of feudalism, a reduction in the demands of Church and state, and greater access to the land were all causes that were dear to the hearts of large sections of the populace. It is therefore entirely possible that a greater measure of social justice might have prevented the *serviles* from attaining much of a following. That said, however, it is arguable that a foreign invasion would thereby have been rendered even more likely. In this respect, one should remember, too, that the invasion of 1823 did not just stem from a desire to smash Jacobinism. Also important were such factors as the desire of significant elements in the French army and government to restore France's prestige; of Alexander I to secure some compensation for Russia's climb-down over the Eastern Question in 1821; and of Metternich to obviate a Franco-Russian combination that would have undermined Austrian influence in Italy. Indeed, Britain being most unlikely to threaten war in defence of Spain, intervention was a near certainty.

Dazzled by the myths of 1808–14, revisionist observers have been inclined to argue that a progressive Spain would have had little to fear from such a prospect. Nothing, however, could be further from the truth. Sooner or later, Spanish resistance must inevitably have been overcome, but even this is not an end to the matter. Liberal policy may well have been inequitable in a number of respects, but such was Spain's financial situation that it is difficult to see the possibility of any alternative. Surrender in America would doubtless have eased the problem, but such were the consequences of the loss of empire that the treasury would still have been in immense difficulties. Hence the need for the disposal of the *bienes nacionales* in such a manner as to maximize the gains that were made upon them; hence, too, Spain's acquisition of a social problem whose consequences were to dog her history right up till the Civil War. Of more immediate concern, perhaps, was the complicated political situation bequeathed by the *trienio*. Even before 1820 serious divisions had come to light in the absolutist camp. Between 1820 and 1823, however, equally serious divisions emerged amongst the liberals. If the decade that beckoned has been called 'ominous', it was not without reason.

4

The Coming of Liberal Spain

Transformation Muted

Between 1823 and 1840 Spain witnessed further oscillations in her political development. At first plunged into a further period of absolutism, following the death of Fernando VII she acquired a new constitution modelled on the French *charte* of 1814. By that time, however, she was once again at war, the clique who surrounded Fernando's brother, Don Carlos, instigating a massive insurrection. Precisely for this reason, however, the 'royal statute' had no chance of survival: making use of the rhetoric of 1810–14 and 1820–3, the more radical elements of Spanish liberalism rose in revolt, and imposed their own agenda. With Carlism now clearly doomed, the triumph of liberalism seemed assured. Spanish liberalism being deeply divided, however, it took six years of further turmoil to give the new Spain its definitive form, and even then all was far from settled.

The Ominous Decade

Although the decade following 1823 has a dark reputation, how far this is merited is debatable. Let us begin with the repression that accompanied the defeat of liberalism. This was without doubt very sharp. To the accompaniment of much mob violence, a network of military tribunals was established to deal with the personnel of the *trienio*; several prominent figures were executed (examples include Riego and the erstwhile guerrilla leader, El Empecinado); the Church, the bureaucracy, the administration and the judiciary were all purged; the *ayuntamientos* of 1820 were restored; the bulk of the army was disbanded; and much property was confiscated.

Ferocious though it was whilst it lasted, the terror was mitigated by a number of factors. Thus, many French and Spanish officers did what they could to urge moderation. Meanwhile, even the most rabid *apostólico* was aware of the drawbacks of mob violence, the peasant rebels of 1822–3 hastily being incorporated into a new militia known as the

Voluntarios Reales. And, most important of all, growing doubts filled the mind of Fernando himself, the king being desperate to acquire the revenue that he needed to reconquer America. With foreign loans unobtainable except at the most exhorbitant rates, the only solution was an alliance with the technocrats of 1814–20, not to mention the trickle of *afrancesados* who had started to return to Spain. As a result, Fernando adopted a middle course, vetoing the re-establishment of the Inquisition, and issuing a partial amnesty. Thus encouraged, the proponents of enlightened absolutism on the whole proved willing to cooperate, Fernando's most important ally in this respect proving to be Luis López Ballesteros, a senior treasury official who became Minister of Finance in 1824.

Rewarded with important positions though many of them were, the *apostólicos* were deeply offended. Bombarding Fernando with protests, they therefore repeatedly clashed with the advocates of moderation, and established a number of secret societies. Much alarmed, the king in turn decided that he could no longer trust his defence to a soon-to-be-withdrawn foreign garrison, a force of disgruntled peasant volunteers and the handful of guard units that was all that remained of the regular army. In consequence, a fresh *quinta* was ordered in the course of 1824, and large numbers of officers recalled to the colours. As little attempt was made to vet the officers concerned, the loyalists of 1821–3 were incensed, and all the more so as their forces were reduced in size and placed under tighter control, and they themselves demoted, dismissed, or even executed.

Furious at these developments, the *apostólicos* began to look to Fernando's notoriously pious younger brother, Don Carlos, whom the king's continued childlessness was making an increasingly likely heir to the throne. Before looking at what followed, however, we should first consider the situation in America. Although Fernando was still dreaming of reconquest, matters had been going from bad to worse. Mexico and Central America were now free, whilst the situation further south was beyond redemption: having liberated Venezuela and Colombia, Bolivar had gone on to free Ecuador in 1823, before smashing the loyalist armies that still dominated the interior of Peru at Ayacucho. All that was left was Bolivia, which Bolivar was easily able to mop up early in 1825. Here and there isolated forces clung on until January 1826, but, Cuba and Puerto Rico aside, the American empire was finished.

In itself, the loss of America had little impact in Spain. The rebellions and civil wars that bedevilled Spain's erstwhile colonies for years to come gave the impression that the loyalist cause was still alive, whilst the economy adjusted to the situation remarkably well. Only with regard to finance was the picture any different. Realizing that the wealth of the

Indies was gone for good, Ballesteros implemented a series of reforms, which streamlined the machinery of taxation, introduced a series of new taxes and attempted to reduce the national debt.

For all its reputation for obscurantist reaction, in short, Fernando's government was moving in the direction of political modernization. The result was conspiracy and rebellion. With much of the countryside in as great a state of misery as ever, it was relatively easy for the *apostólicos* to gain a following, and all the more so in those areas where they had managed to put down firm roots during the *trienio*. Thus, in Catalonia the spring of 1827 saw the outbreak of wholesale rebellion in the south. Despite attempts to stir up rebellion elsewhere, however, the insurgents gained little support, whilst they had little chance of seizing such strongholds as Tarragona or Barcelona. As a result the dispatch of fresh troops soon restored order. Nevertheless, *apostólico* discontent continued to smoulder unabated, whilst it also began to spread to other parts of the country: by 1830, for example, thanks to a series of bad harvests, a plague of grasshoppers, and a serious earthquake, the southern Levante had been particularly radicalized.

Apostólico unrest was strong in this latter region for other reasons. In 1823, the garrison of Alicante had incurred much hatred, whilst from 1823 onwards the Levante once again found itself exposed to the vagaries of liberalism in arms. Though often bitterly divided and at odds with one another, the many liberals who had fled to England had immediately thrown themselves into a series of attempts at invasion. The result, however, was disaster. Landing after landing was scattered without producing the slightest sign of the general rising of which the conspirators dreamed. The last gasp came on 2 December 1831 when José María Torrijos disembarked at Fuengirola with sixty men, only to be captured and executed.

Despite this record of failure, change was still on the way. The *apostólico* revolt, the liberal raids, and a foolhardy attempt to invade Mexico in 1829, had combined with the imperfect success of Ballesteros' reforms to provoke a major financial crisis. Concessions to the Carlists, as we may now begin to call them, therefore being out of the question, Fernando therefore had to make some provision for the future. His third wife having recently died, he now took a fourth in the person of his own niece, María Cristina of Naples, and, when she became pregnant, this effectively excluded Carlos from the succession altogether. Needless to say, the result was uproar. Basing their argument on a variety of points of which most important was that, as the baby was a girl – Isabel – it could not inherit the throne, they sought desperately to have Carlos reinstated, whilst at the same time building up a strong party in the army and the court. For a brief moment in September 1832 it seemed that they might have succeeded, but in the event the cause of Isabel prevailed, the 'events of La Granja', as this crisis became known, making civil war all but inevitable.

To secure their ascendancy, the so-called *isabelinos* knew that they needed the support of the generals who had backed Fernando against the *apostólicos*, not to mention the enlightened reformers who had provided the mainstay of his regime, a mildly reformist government therefore being formed under the leadership of Francisco Cea Bermúdez. Meanwhile, Carlos was banished to Portugal; the universities, which had been closed in the course of the troubles of 1830, reopened; the liberals amnestied; the army purged; and the *Voluntarios Reales* almost entirely disbanded. Meanwhile, particularly in the military, the new government also made much use of patronage to cement its rule, finding employment for deserving officers, rehabilitating generals who had previously fallen from favour, and showering titles, decorations and promotions on all and sundry.

None of this amounted in any sense to a liberal revolution: Cea and his fellow ministers were opposed to the idea of a constitution on pragmatic grounds, whilst María Cristina was an outright absolutist who was deeply jealous of her position as regent (Fernando was now very ill, eventually succumbing on 29 September 1833). All this mattered not a jot, however, for around Spain the period 1832–3 was marked by the outbreak of a new civil war that was to overwhelm the forces of reaction, and with them the whole *antiguo regimen*.

The Outbreak of War

Though undoubtedly a complex phenomenon, Carlism is not one that is open to much debate. Whilst conservative Spanish historians continue to claim that the rebels of 1833 were above all motivated by a determination to maintain the rights of Don Carlos and the Catholic Church, such arguments are unconvincing. Amongst leaders, and rank and file alike, support for Don Carlos was primarily a protest against social and economic change.

Let us look first of all at Spain's elites. In so far as these were concerned, there were numerous groups that had every reason to fear the re-emergence of reform. Though few bishops supported the rebellion, the Church's finances were so weak that the prospect of further disamortization could only cause serious alarm. For many sections of the propertied classes, whether noble or otherwise, meanwhile, a move in the direction of liberalism was equally worrying. Let us take, for example, the *foreros* of Galicia. Essentially the tenants of the great magnates and religious foundations that owned the land, the *foreros* paid very low rents and had hitherto enjoyed both *de facto* security of tenure and the right to sublet their holdings to unlimited numbers of tenants on whatever terms they chose. For such men, liberalism – and, above all, disamortization – represented a serious threat for it would not only require them to buy their holdings, but also to stave off outside competition – hence the fact that Galicia had been notorious as a hotbed of reaction from the War of Independence onwards. In the same way, in Navarre and the Basque provinces at stake were the *fueros*, the many notables who had in one way or another profited from them therefore being strongly Carlist. And, last but not least, throughout Spain the nobility were under threat, the great danger being that the abolition of *señorialismo* might be settled in their disfavour.

Whilst the participation of landed, propertied or educated elites in the Carlist insurrection was of very considerable importance, the heart of Carlism was always the support that it could count upon amongst the lower classes. Already oppressed enough, the *populacho* had since the late eighteenth century been assailed by soaring taxation, crop failure, deindustrialization, natural disaster, epidemic, invasion, conscription, and a series of blatantly discriminatory agrarian reforms. In many regions of Spain, meanwhile, this general crisis was exacerbated by more local issues such as over-population, de-forestation, the erosion of the commons, or the transition to a market economy. Having already exploded thrice, these tensions were now exploited by Carlist agitators who whipped up the same sort of millenarian hopes occasioned by the overthrow of Godoy. What we see is therefore not the legitimist crusade of legend, but rather a massive revolt against pauperization, considerable elements of the lower classes finding in the Carlist cause both leadership and succour.

This is not to say, however, that images of the 'real' people of Spain rising up to fight godless liberalism and freemasonry can be accepted: in Orihuela, for example, the Carlist sympathies of the populace did not prevent it from engaging in a general refusal to pay its tithes. Had the situation been otherwise, the Carlists might have won the war, but as it was they were faced by insuperable difficulties. In Navarre and the Basque provinces, the backing of traditional elites, the existence of both alternative organs of government and significant stockpiles of arms (for the area was not only self-governing, but also supposed to provide for its own defence), inspired leadership, and, above all, the comparative absence of regular troops, allowed the establishment of a substantial army that was able to bottle the *cristinos* up in such strongholds as Bilbao and Pamplona. Elsewhere, however, the revolt never amounted to more than a guerrilla war. Harried unmercifully though the *cristinos* were, only Catalonia and Aragón saw the establishment of other bastions, the

Basques and Navarrese being unable to launch the sort of general offensive that was the only hope of winning the war whilst *cristino* garrisons continued to hold out in their very midst. As these could not be expunged, the war became a stalemate.

Towards a New Spain

This very stalemate would prove decisive in the history of Spain, for the inability of the *cristinos* to win a quick victory brought with it the definitive triumph of Spanish liberalism. In large part the transformation which now occurred can be interpreted in terms of traditional rivalries in the corridors of power. Being a bureaucrat in the Caroline tradition, Cea Bermúdez disliked the manner in which the army had come to occupy a central role in the governance of Spain, and in consequence wanted to remedy the many weaknesses that had allowed this to happen. In a number of areas reform was therefore accelerated. On 30 November 1833, for example, Spain was finally divided into her current system of provinces, whilst a new Ministry of Economic Development was created whose officials assumed many tasks that had hitherto been handled by the Captain Generalcies. In proceeding in this fashion, however, Cea could not but antagonize the leading generals. Unable to retain the confidence of the queen as a result, in January 1834 Cea was forced to resign, being replaced by the erstwhile *doceañista*, Francisco Martínez de la Rosa.

Important though offended military vanity may have been in the fall of Cea, it was certainly not the only issue at stake. Even the generals believed that a real measure of political change was necessary to avoid a liberal revolution, whilst many civilian officials were only too well aware that Spain's financial problems were such that the only hope lay in liberal reform. Last but not least, liberals of all sorts were naturally restive, as were merchants, bankers and the cotton manufacturers of Barcelona, whilst many even of the court aristocracy were sufficiently alarmed by the threat of peasant revolution to favour anything that promised a quick end to the war.

In this manner, then, the winter of 1833–4 witnessed the emergence of an unlikely coalition in support of some move in the direction of constitutionalism, the likelihood of which was increased by the fact that Cea had been forced to re-establish the militia, albeit in a form in which recruitment was limited strictly to men of property and education. Unable to delay matters any further, Martínez de la Rosa therefore offered Spain a 'royal statute' (the Estatuto Real) modelled very much on the French *charte* of 1814. In brief, this established a two-chamber assembly with the power to petition the throne and approve legislation.

All archbishops, bishops, grandees of Spain and *titulados* of Castile were automatically members of the upper chamber whilst their ranks were augmented by an unlimited number of royal appointees drawn from prominent figures with an annual income of at least 60,000 *reales*. Little more democratic was the lower chamber, which was elected by all men over thirty years of age who possessed an annual income of at least 12,000 *reales*.

Whatever the regime may have hoped, the Estatuto Real had no chance of survival. In the first place, it was accompanied by a wide range of other measures – greater press freedom, an amnesty that allowed even the most radical *exaltados* to return home, and an ever greater relaxation in the recruitment to the militia – that encouraged the re-emergence of radicalism as a political force. In the second, the woeful performance of the army produced demands for a less conservative policy. And in the third the arrival of the first of the great cholera epidemics which assailed nineteenth-century Europe led to serious social disorder. From the moment that the new *cortes* opened on 25 July 1834, the lower chamber therefore adopted a posture that was as aggressive as it was critical. As a result, the government was quickly forced on to the defensive, and this despite its decision to send an army to aid the constitutionalist side in the quasi-Carlist civil war that had broken out in Portugal in 1832.

As 1834 wore on into 1835, the government did secure one victory of great significance. The Estatuto Real had said nothing about local government, and the old *ayuntamientos* had therefore continued to function. Realizing that reform would alienate many of his natural supporters, Martínez de la Rosa for a long time evaded the issue. Finally pressurized into taking action, he managed to outmanoeuvre the radicals by asking for a vote of confidence that would permit the government to legislate on the issue by decree. Unable to oppose such a move, the *progresistas* – the heirs of the *exaltados* – were therefore forced to stand by whilst Martínez de la Rosa settled matters to the benefit of *moderantismo*. The result was the decree of 23 July 1835, this abolishing the *regidores perpetuos* and opening all seats to election, whilst at the same time imposing strict limits on both the franchise and the right to stand for election, making the vote obligatory, written and public, and subjecting *ayuntamientos* to a greater level of state control. As an instrument of revolutionary change, in short, the *ayuntamientos* were largely nullified.

Despite this success, Martínez de la Rosa had by now completely lost the confidence of María Cristina, and on 6 June 1835 he was forced to resign. His replacement was the Conde de Toreno, a one-time radical who had long since been won over to *moderantismo*. This change only made things worse, however, for Toreno appeared a mere creature of the palace. With the cholera epidemic still raging and parts of the country gripped by further natural disasters, the new municipal law came as the last straw, and all the more so as the elites whose position it guaranteed proceeded to exploit it to the full. The beginning of the year had already witnessed an abortive attempt at an *exaltado* coup in Madrid, whilst serious radical disturbances had taken place in Málaga, Zaragoza, Murcia and Huesca. However, unrest now became revolution, July being marked by full-scale popular revolts in Zaragoza and Barcelona. In both instances many priests and religious were killed, but in Barcelona a new element entered the fray, the numerous cotton workers also turning their attention to the large-scale factories that had recently begun to wreak havoc with the traditional putting-out system. Led by the militia, meanwhile, the insurrection spread to Madrid and other cities. Events varied from place to place, but common elements included the proclamation of the constitution of 1812, the massacre of Carlist prisoners, anti-clerical riots, the formation of revolutionary juntas, and demands for a more active prosecution of the war and the suppression of the monasteries.

Faced by this situation, Toreno was helpless. Though he succeeded in facing down the revolt in Madrid, by the beginning of September it was clear that many even of his closest collaborators were advocating some form of compromise. Chief amongst these conciliators was Riego's ally, Juan Alvarez Mendizábal, who had just added to the laurels of 1820 by providing financial assistance to the liberal side in the Portuguese civil war. Extremely unwillingly, on 13 September 1835 Toreno therefore resigned. Firmly opposed to any move towards radicalism, the queen at first attempted to retain his services, but Mendizábal was rapidly assuming the role of the only man who could bring the crisis under control, and on 15 September María Cristina agreed that he should become prime minister.

With the appointment of Mendizábal, Spain had in theory come to be ruled by the *exaltados*. Despite the concerns of María Cristina, in some respects this mattered very little. Their leaders were becoming more and more conservative, and they certainly had no intention of restoring the constitution of 1812, seeking rather merely to amend the Estatuto Real whilst effectively buying off the popular revolution that had brought them to power (hence Mendizábal's flattery of the militia and co-option of the revolutionary leadership). Yet, for all that, radical change remained on the agenda, the dynamic and experienced Mendizábal being convinced that only this could win the war: otherwise there would be neither men nor money but only endless disorder.

In the short term, however, the priority was simply to intensify the struggle, in which respect Mendizábal was helped by sheer good fortune. Thus, Britain, France, Spain and Portugal having since April 1834 been united in the pro-liberal Quadruple Alliance, there now arrived substantial forces of British and Portuguese volunteers who had been raised specifically for service in Spain, together with a contingent of the French Foreign Legion. With his credit much reinforced, the new prime minister was able to increase the pressure still further. The *quinta* had been in annual operation in Spain since 1830, but only 20,000–25,000 men had been called up each year. Determined to gain more men, on 23 October Mendizábal ordered the call-up of 100,000 men. Sustaining such forces was a considerable problem, but here, too, Mendizábal displayed considerable virtuosity, the national debt being secretly reorganized so as to reduce the amount of interest which the government had hitherto been funding. Meanwhile, conscription itself was made a source of revenue, Mendizábal abandoning the egalitarianism of 1812 in favour of a system of redemption that in a few months had brought in no fewer than 46,000,000 *reales*.

As a result of all this, by the time that the *cortes* reopened on 16 November, the situation was much more stable. However, Mendizábal was by no means finished. Spain being burdened by debt, the prime minister resolved to despoil the Church of all that remained of its landed property, to which end he demanded a vote of confidence giving him the authority to rule by decree. This he obtained without difficulty, the *moderados* having been so shaken by the events of the summer that they were prepared to accept almost anything. Thus it was that Spain embarked upon the consummation of the liberal revolution. In reality, this was already underway, the Cea Bermúdez, Martínez de la Rosa and Toreno governments having issued a series of decrees that legalized all previous purchases of ecclesiastical and municipal property, suppressed the Jesuits, and closed a large number of religious houses, whilst many other *conventos* had been suppressed in the course of the fighting or the risings of July–August 1835. What Mendizábal now did went far beyond anything that had gone before, however, for by a series of fresh decrees culminating in that of 8 March 1836 he ordered the suppression of all but a tiny handful of the male religious orders and the expropriation and sale of their property.

The impact of this definitive wave of ecclesiastical disamortization was mixed. It has often been claimed that the land was valued too cheaply, that the desperate need to raise money led to the acceptance of bids that were far too low, and that the titles to the national debt that were offered in payment were accepted at full value, however depreciated. However, much of this has now been shown to be unfair: though the problem of depreciated bonds remains (only 11 per cent of the 4,500,000,000 *reales* involved was paid in cash), the land was valued at the going rate and sold at prices that were generally considerably higher. More to the point are the facts that payment was authorized over a period of several years, that the war went on longer than Mendizábal had expected, and that the expenditure which the whole process generated was enormous, whether as the result of the immense bureaucracy which it created or the pensions which had to be paid to the clergy who were thereby secularized. At all events, the results were the same in that the process was of far less financial benefit than had been expected. In social terms, meanwhile, the exercise proved a disaster. As a doctrinaire liberal, Mendizábal was utterly opposed to any notion of government intervention in the defence of social justice, and would therefore have rebuffed radical pleas that the land be rented or sold off in small lots even had they not clashed with the obvious financial imperatives. As the land was generally sold off in accordance with its normal usage, there were plenty of areas where the lots were relatively small, but, even so, the result was inevitable: in town and countryside alike the bulk of the spoils went to a small minority of the purchasers.

This is not the place to discuss the long-term economic effects of disamortization, if only because it was a process that took many years. As for its more immediate effects, Mendizábal's government was not in existence long enough to experience them. Although the *cristino* commander on the northern front, Luis Fernández de Córdoba, now headed an army of 120,000 men, he proved quite incapable of winning a decisive victory. Still worse, Mendizábal's policies merely added fuel to the fire, bringing the Carlists large numbers of new recruits, inflaming clerical resistance and giving rise to many outbreaks of agrarian unrest.

Hardly surprisingly, Mendizábal's failure to secure the victories that he had promised provoked fresh popular disturbances, these in turn increasing conservative concerns which had been growing apace ever since Mendizábal had received his vote of confidence. Many *moderados* were unhappy at the attack on the Church, believing that, if Britain, France and Portugal could be persuaded to intervene in force, the Carlists could be defeated without further ado. If they were prepared to let this pass, they were not prepared to tolerate the assault on their political power that now seemed to be in the making. Thus, confronted by a *cortes* in which his supporters were in a minority, Mendizábal announced his intention of framing a new electoral law. Maintaining that this would provide a more accurate guide to public opinion, he proposed to replace the system of universal, indirect suffrage that had been inherited from the *cortes* of Cádiz with one of limited, direct suffrage, and in addition to make the constituency the district rather than the province. The potential effect of this being quite clear – in effect to strengthen the urban vote and to limit seriously the power of local notables – the *moderados* stood firm, being joined in their opposition by the ambitious and unscrupulous Francisco Javier Istúriz. A sometime *exaltado* and intimate of Mendizábal, Istúriz had been seduced by worldly success and was now concerned primarily to ensure that the liberal revolution drifted no further to the left. Deeply jealous of the prime minister, he had become increasingly attractive to María Cristina as a possible alternative, and by January 1836 was in close contact with the palace. Getting wind of his activities, Mendizábal realized that the game was up, and, after first abandoning his plans for electoral reform, hastily convoked new elections.

The contest that followed was without doubt 'made' by the government, the *progresistas* obtaining a sweeping victory. The *cortes* that opened its doors on 22 March 1836 was therefore a much more radical body than its predecessor. Mendizábal having always shown a strong inclination to conciliate the *moderados*, he was in consequence placed in a very difficult position. Certainly the new electoral law was now passed without difficulty, but, backed up by fresh disturbances in such cities as Barcelona, the *exaltados* began to demand such measures as the exile of a number of suspect bishops and a purge of the generals. Forced to pursue at least the latter part of this programme, Mendizábal promptly ran into problems with the palace. Already alarmed by the *progresista* victory, María Cristina was now seeking the prime minister's downfall. Had the *progresistas* remained united, the government might yet have survived, but Istúriz was now more disaffected than ever. Knowing that Istúriz would therefore have no hesitation in acting as a 'trojan horse', the queen duly rejected Mendizábal's demands for the removal of certain absolutist generals, the great *desamortizador* in consequence being left with no option but to resign.

With the fall of Mendizábal, the government was placed in the hands of Istúriz, only for the latter immediately to be defeated in a no-confidence motion. Promptly calling new elections, the new prime minister promised a revision of the Estatuto Real, in the meantime issuing a far more generous electoral law. Held in July, the fresh contest was marked by heavy government intervention and produced a chamber dominated by a combination of *isturiztas* and *moderados*. Such a situation had no chance of surviving, however. The strength of provincial radicalism had already been demonstrated by the events of the summer of 1835, and feelings were now running higher than ever. Not only was cholera continuing to rage unchecked, but the harvest had failed for two years in succession. As for the war, the army was still destitute, whilst two Carlist 'expeditions' were running amok in the *cristino* heartlands. With it by now perfectly clear that disamortization was not going to be connected with any increase in social justice, Istúriz's conduct of the elections therefore came as the last straw. An outbreak of rioting in Madrid on 19–20 July was suppressed, but on 25 July 1836 Málaga proclaimed the constitution of 1812. On 28 July Cádiz followed suit, and by mid-August the movement had spread to Extremadura, Valencia, Murcia and Catalonia. In the midst of the turmoil Istúriz at first tried to cling on to power, but it soon become clear that large parts of the army were unwilling to fight for the regime, whilst on 12 August part of the royal guard mutinied at La Granja, whereupon María Cristina agreed to the restoration of the constitution of 1812 until such time as the *cortes* had decided upon a definitive solution.

Thus ended the revolution of 1836. Istúriz fled abroad, and a new government was formed under the presidency of the respected *doceañista*, José María Calatrava. Determined to carry through the abortive revolution of 1835, the new administration, which included Mendizábal as Minister of Development, adopted a vigorous posture. The cautious Fernández de Córdoba was replaced by General Espartero, a tough ex-ranker who had risen to prominence through the American wars; a *quinta* of 50,000 men was imposed, together with a forced loan of 200,000,000 *reales*; the provincial juntas that had headed the revolution were institutionalized as juntas of armament and defence; a pay cut was imposed on the bureaucracy; and elections were called for a constituent assembly. Meanwhile, much of the legislation of 1812–14 and 1820–3 was restored, the sale of Church property accelerated, those bishops who had joined the Carlists or otherwise absented themselves dismissed, and the tithe finally abolished. Initially, at least, all this was sufficient to reassure the radicals who had 'made' the revolution, but in fact they were already being betrayed. Whether veterans of the *cortes* of Cádiz, or younger men such as Joaquín María López and Salustiano Olózaga, the leaders of *progresismo* were prepared to use the urban poor and national militia to seize power, but beyond that their radicalism was tempered by a subconscious belief that the object of the revolution was ultimately to gain access to the fruits of office. At the same time, they were also mesmerized by a naive vision of revolutionary unity that led them to make great efforts to reconcile the *moderados*. Hardly revolutionary even as it was, the constitution of 1812 was therefore quickly abandoned in favour of a new document of a far more conservative cast. Thus, more power was given to the monarch, the existence of a second chamber was confirmed, universal suffrage was abolished, and the liberty of the subject made conditional upon future 'regulation', the new constitution finally being adopted on 17 June 1837. In social terms, too, the *progresistas* also proved remarkably circumspect. Not only was no effort made to alter the direction that disamortization was taking, but the laws of 1811 and 1823 relating to the abolition of feudalism were interpreted in a manner guaranteed to allow the *señores* the continued enjoyment of their perquisites, a most repressive attitude also being adopted with regard to law and order. All this, moreover, was hardly surprising. Thus, the *progresista* ministers and deputies sprang from precisely the same social groups as their *moderado* opponents, whilst the constituent *cortes* of 1836 was little different in its composition from its predecessors, except, perhaps, for some diminution in the number of ecclesiastics. On the ground, meanwhile, the revolution had meant even less, dominant local families having little difficulty in maintaining their supremacy.

The betrayal of the radicals did not go unnoticed. Under the leadership of Fermín Caballero, Pascual Madoz and Mateo Ayllón, many of the younger deputies put up a spirited fight against the conciliatory attitude of Calatrava. In the provinces, meanwhile, the secret society began once again to emerge in the form of such shadowy groups as 'Los Unitarios', the relatively democratic nature of the municipal law of 1823 also allowing the *exaltados* to acquire a certain degree of influence. Nor is it any coincidence that it was at this time that the first sprouts of proto-socialism began to appear in Spain. All this was reflected in considerable tension, but no new revolts occurred, the march of conservatism therefore continuing unabated.

Indeed, so far as the radicals were concerned, the situation took a turn for the worse. An old-guard *exaltado*, Calatrava had in some senses represented a guarantee of their interests, but in August 1837 even he was swept away. Ever since the *progresistas* had returned to power, their relations with the army had become increasingly frosty. Many officers had never liked the revolution of 1836, either because they were *moderados* or because they were alarmed by the implications of the mutiny of La Granja. However, the concerns of these men soon came to be shared even by the *progresistas*' numerous partisans and clients. If the determination of the revolutionary juntas to have a say in the direction of the war was bad enough, the behaviour of the government caused outrage. Thus, the generals remained short of money and supplies, and yet they were subjected to a barrage of demands for total victory, the Minister of War, General Rodil, eventually being dismissed as a scapegoat. Such a move was foolish in the extreme, however. By no means a bad general, Rodil had used his position to further the interests of the men who had served under him in America, where he had been the mainstay of loyalist resistance in Peru. These officers – the so-called *ayacuchos* – were naturally enraged by his dismissal, and it was not long before they avenged themselves upon the government. Madrid having been threatened by a new Carlist expedition that had set off from Navarre, the *ayacucho* Espartero had been forced to march to its defence. Presented with the perfect opportunity, the general instigated a mutiny amongst his own men. Informed that the army would not fight unless the government resigned, Calatrava promptly went, and a new ministry was formed under the *moderado*, Bardají.

For the radicals there was worse to come. The constituent *cortes* having completed its labours, new elections were convoked for September 1837. These were conducted on the new restricted franchise, which gave the vote to all men over 25 who paid over 200 *reales* in direct taxation or had an annual income of over 1,500. At the same time the editor of one of the chief *moderado* newspapers, Andrés Borrego, set up a central committee to run the campaign, published a manual for party activists, publicized the names of *moderado* candidates, and established a rudimentary party organization in the provinces. As a result the *moderados* triumphed, gaining some 150 seats to the *progresistas'* ninety-seven. Radicalism, in short, was clearly in retreat.

The Emergence of Praetorianism

Significant though the elections of 1837 undoubtedly were, there yet remained the Carlist War. In some respects, the Carlist cause seemed stronger than ever: the various foreign expeditionary forces were in a state of complete dissolution; Navarre, the Basque provinces and the interior of Catalonia remained as impregnable as ever; a new liberated area had been established in southern Aragón; large parts of the country were in the grip of incessant guerrilla warfare; and the various expeditions had consistently outmarched and outfought their lumbering opponents in a series of campaigns that had taken them across the length and breadth of the Peninsula. Yet the reality was that Carlism was in a most precarious position. Thus, its forces were as incapable as ever of winning a decisive victory; its heartlands increasingly war-weary; and its leadership increasingly disunited. As 1838 wore on, moreover, so the fundamental problems facing the Carlists became ever more apparent. One by one the *partidas* of La Mancha, Old Castile, Galicia and elsewhere were hunted down and exterminated, whilst on the crucial northern front the balance was tipping ever more heavily against the exhausted Carlist forces. Convinced that the end was near, disgusted with the ineffectual Don Carlos, and hopeful that he could secure reasonable terms, on 17 February 1839 the commander-in-chief of the Carlist forces in the north, General Maroto, therefore launched a sudden coup. Summarily executing five die-hard generals, he forced the dismissal of the *apostólico* ministers who monopolized the Carlist government, and set about securing such terms as he could from the *cristinos*, these proving to be remarkably generous (the rank and file were to be allowed to return to their homes, and the officers to enlist with the *cristinos*, Espartero also agreeing to attempt to protect the *fueros*). Completely satisfied, on 29 August 1839 Maroto finally laid down his arms at Vergara. Although Don Carlos escaped to France, the end could not be long delayed. By the summer of 1840 Espartero had crushed the remaining Carlist bastions in Aragón and Catalonia, and on 6 July the last rebel troops filed into France. The war was over.

The prominence attained by Espartero in the dying campaigns of the Carlist War was not just the fruit of military success, but also a reflection of the political situation. Despite Borrego's attempts at party organization, the *moderados* lacked the cohesion necessary to exploit their majority. As a result, it was only with some difficulty that a new government was formed under the Conde de Ofalia, whilst an attempt to waive the oath of loyalty that had to be sworn by the deputies – a reflection of the fact that a number of the *moderados* had Carlist sympathies – was blocked by the *progresistas*. Fierce opposition, too, was occasioned by the government's programme, this centring on, first, a reconciliation with the Church, and, second, the reform of local government. After extensive debate it was eventually agreed that the Church should be compensated for the loss of its land by the restoration of a portion of the tithes, but the new municipal law was another matter. In brief, the intention had been both to reduce the autonomy of local government and to limit the electorate by means of a property franchise. Realizing that these measures threatened them with political extinction – the *ayuntamientos* were, after all, their only real power base – the *progresistas* put up such a fight that the measure had to be abandoned.

By the spring of 1838, then, it was clear that neither *progresismo* nor *moderantismo* were strong enough to carry the day. In this situation, political power could not but gravitate to the one force that had the ability to tip the balance. This was, of course, the army, and, in particular, the figure of the *caudillo* – the general-cum-saviour who could either make and unmake governments at will or head the administration himself, whilst at the same time using his power to ensure that he never lacked for a powerbase in the officer corps. In this respect, everything now revolved around the figure of Baldomero Espartero, the reality of the situation soon being made all too clear. Thus, desperate to reduce the general's influence, which was all the more intolerable because of his growing association with *progresismo* – intensely vain as he was, Espartero revelled in popular adulation and was much inclined to court the urban crowd – Ofalia decided to remove him from command. The events that followed are too arcane to enter into here in any depth, but in brief September 1838 saw the fall not of Espartero but the government. A certain amount of jealousy amongst the rest of the *generalato* notwithstanding, Espartero was left as the effective arbiter of Spanish politics. Thus he was able to impose a cabinet headed of his own making headed by, first, the Duque de Frias, and, second, the *veintista* prime minister, Evaristo Pérez de Castro, while at the same time extending his control over the army through ensuring the advancement of his numerous henchmen.

It will be noted here that Espartero made no attempt to establish a *progresista* government. Whilst counting many veterans of *exaltado* revolts amongst his allies, the general was a man of order who was deeply loyal to María Cristina. Much interested in winning the war, he also disliked the *progresistas'* anti-militarism. Indeed, when the new *cortes* elected in the fresh general elections held in the summer of 1839 showed signs of being overly susceptible to *progresista* influence, he forced its dissolution, heavy government pressure ensuring that the chamber that was elected in its place was firmly dominated by the *moderados*. In acting in this fashion, however, Espartero found that he had gone too far. Believing, perhaps, that the general was in their pocket, the *moderados* announced that they intended to force through not only Ofalia's munici-pal law, but also a variety of other measures including a new press law, a reduction in the franchise, and a bill to re-establish a council of state. Overawing the *progresistas* by the threat of force, they were also per-suaded by Espartero's deadly rival, General Narváez, to set about restricting the influence of the *ayacuchos*.

The *dénouement* was not long in coming. No sooner had the *cortes* passed the new municipal law on 4 June 1840, than the *progresistas* erupted in a storm of protest. Fearing a fresh rebellion, María Cristina promptly travelled to Espartero's headquarters in Catalonia – at this stage, of course, the general was supervising the last stages of the Carlist war – in the hope that she could win him over. In this, however, she had miscalculated, for, though no lover of *progresismo*, Espartero was con-cerned at the impact that counter-revolution would have on his own popularity. At the same time, meanwhile, he was all too well aware that Narváez was bitterly jealous of his glory (as *cristino* commander in the south the latter had been denied the opportunity of major victory). Far from supporting the queen, Espartero therefore placed himself at the head of the revolt that her actions had immediately precipitated in Barcelona. Determined to defeat *progresismo* once and for all – she was, of course, wholly in approval of the *moderados* – the queen fled to Valencia in the hope of rallying support. By now, however, all Spain was on the brink of revolt, whilst the government had resigned in despair. On 1 September the *progresistas* who controlled the *ayuntamiento* and militia of Madrid proclaimed the capital to be in a state of rebellion. Within a week this example had been followed by many other cities, including not only such veterans of revolution as Cádiz and Málaga, but also many of the far more tranquil cities of Old Castile. At Valencia, the Captain General, Leopoldo O'Donnell, remained loyal, but the vast majority of the generals agreed to swear allegiance to the provisional government that had by now been proclaimed in Madrid, the fact being that few officers were prepared to risk opposing Espartero. Recognizing the inevitable, María Cristina now agreed to the formation of a new government under Espartero, and took ship for Marseilles, leaving behind her the eleven-year old Isabel II in the care of Espartero as *ministro-regente*.

The Regency of Espartero

What, then, had occurred between 1837 and 1840? One development of prime importance was that the Spanish army had been drawn into politics more overtly than ever before. Apologists for the military tradition have always tried to argue that this situation came about through the weakness of the politicians. Within limits these arguments can be seen to have some foundation, for the vagaries of Spanish politics left politicians of all persuasions no option but to appeal to one faction or another of the officer corps. However, this is hardly the end of the story. At least as important were the ambitions and rivalries of the generals themselves, the latter being all too eager to establish friendly relations with the politicians. But, above all, the generals needed governments that could govern, Espartero's views in large part being the fruit of a belief that the *moderados* could not maintain their position in the face of the pressure for change building up amongst rank-and-file *progresistas*. Hand in hand with all this, of course, went a preoccupation with order that was to become all-consuming, revolution being associated with indisciplined militias, supply failures, attacks on the generals, and visionary notions of people's war.

At all events, Spain was now ruled by a *caudillo*. However, Espartero was not a dictator: *moderados* and republicans alike – 1840 had seen the emergence of the first small republican groups – were allowed a reasonable degree of freedom of operation, whilst the structure of government remained unchanged. What is the case, however, is that it was the *progresistas* who were now in control. For the latter the revolution of 1840 had in theory represented a great triumph, but in practice the regency of Espartero was to prove a disaster, the story of the next three years being that of the disintegration of *progresismo*. The first problem that emerged was the nature of the government and regency. Headed by Joaquín María López and Fermín Caballero, the radical wing of the *progresistas* had envisaged that the task of government would be taken over by a central junta drawn from the various provincial juntas that had emerged in the course of the revolution, and further that the regency should henceforth be composed of at least three people. However, neither aim was achieved. The central junta was effectively prevented from meeting, whilst the new *cortes* that met after the fresh elections held in February 1841 rejected every attempt to secure a council of regency, *progresista* moderates such as Olózaga having absolutely no intention of alienating Espartero. Still worse, the government was remodelled by Espartero in such a manner that not a single important *progresista* was included; a modified version of the municipal law of 1840 was introduced; and the hated monopolies on salt and tobacco were retained, these having been farmed out to the rich financiers whose support was the key to financial survival. Equally, if sales of Church land were speeded up, the efforts of such radicals as Spain's first ever republican deputies, Manuel García Uzal and Pedro Méndez Vigo, to secure some protection for the poor were swept aside, far too many of the *progresista* leaders having an interest in the system prevailing hitherto for them to have any chance of success.

If the *progresistas* were deeply divided, the radicals' disgruntlement did not immediately translate into open opposition. On the contrary, when María Cristina in October 1841 launched a bid to overthrow Espartero, the radicals rallied to the defence of the regime, forming local 'commissions of public vigilance' and taking an enthusiastic part in the mobilization of the militia. How far their actions were important is another matter, for the coup proved distinctly unimpressive. At all events, Espartero does not seem to have been impressed, for as soon as the danger was over he ordered the suppression of the vigilance commissions. This, however, only served to provoke further trouble, especially in Barcelona, where the local commission had won much approval by imposing heavy levies on many prominent members of the bourgeoisie (it should be noted that the *ciudad condal* had recently witnessed the formation of Spain's first trade unions). Refusing to dissolve itself, the commission defiantly set about the demolition of the great citadel that dominated the city, only for Espartero to move in and dissolve both junta and trade unions.

Thanks in large part to the struggle that now broke out over the question of free trade, the general air of division and crisis now grew still worse. Spain's coastline was so long, and her badly paid customs guard so easy to bribe, that she was especially vulnerable to smuggling, much of it British. The need to do something to remedy the situation having become essential, in 1840 Espartero had set up a commission of enquiry. Voted through by the *cortes* in July 1841, the scheme that this proposed did not win universal approval, for there were numerous interests which it threatened. That said, there was no reason why the storm should not ultimately have blown itself out had not an innocuous remark in the British parliament given rise to a rumour that Spain was to be opened to unrestricted free trade. The cotton industry being in the grip of a severe depression, November 1842 therefore witnessed a furious rebellion in Barcelona. Retribution being swift and brutal – the city was subjected to indiscriminate bombardment – the regent's credit with the *progresista* left was completely exhausted.

If urban radicalism had now been driven into a position of outright hostility to Espartero, the unity of the *progresistas* had been irrevocably broken. However, the regent had not been able either to assuage the hostility of the *moderados* or to retain his hold on moderate *progresismo*, many of whose leaders had been inveigled into a *de facto* alliance with their erstwhile opponents. Nor was the situation much better within the army. Although the *ayacuchos* were loyal, Narváez had been secretly plotting against the regency, whilst many officers were deeply resentful of their continued economic problems, the manner in which Espartero openly favoured his former American comrades, and the various measures of demobilization that had followed the end of the war. Conscious of his growing isolation, the regent dissolved the *cortes* and called fresh elections in April 1843, but so eroded was his prestige that the best efforts of the administration to pack the chamber with his supporters produced no more than seventy deputies.

Faced by a situation that was near impossible, the general at first sought a way out by forming a radical ministry under López in the cynical hope that whilst this would satisfy the left, the new prime minister's extremist rhetoric would be tempered by the fruits of office. However, prime minister and regent soon fell out, whereupon López promptly resigned. Unable to find a replacement, Espartero called new elections, only to find that even the centrist *progresistas* would no longer back him, instead joining with both right and left of the party to call for rebellion, whilst at the same time inviting the *moderado* diaspora to intervene in defence of constitutional liberty (since the autumn of 1841 Espartero had been becoming more and more repressive, restricting the freedom of the press and arresting a wide range of dissidents).

Watching from afar, María Cristina and her supporters needed no further urging, Narváez and several other generals sailing to Valencia, where fear of lower-class unrest quickly persuaded the *ayacucho* Captain General to throw in his lot with the rebellion. Even before Narváez had landed on 27 June, meanwhile, military rebellions had taken place in Málaga, Alicante, Seville, Granada, Teruel, Reus, Barcelona and Zaragoza. Sufficient of the *ayacuchos* remained loyal for the direct roads to Madrid from the east and south blocked by loyal troops, but Narváez nevertheless managed to get a small column of troops to the outskirts of the capital. For a while he was checked by the local militia, for whom in the last resort fear of *moderantismo* seems to have outweighed disillusionment with Espartero, and enough time was gained for the arrival of a relief force. On 22 July, however, Narváez won a crucial victory at Torrejón de Ardoz, whereupon Madrid had no option but to surrender. Realizing that all was lost, Espartero fled to Cádiz, where he got aboard a British warship, leaving behind him a Spain that had simply exchanged one *caudillo* for another.

The Die is Cast

Curiously enough, the fall of Espartero did not lead to the immediate formation of a *moderado* cabinet, Narváez rather bringing back López. However, in reality the latter was little more than a cypher kept on to placate the *progresistas*. Real power was exercised by Narváez who proceeded to force the government to purge the *ayacuchos*, dismiss numerous *diputaciones provinciales* and *ayuntamientos*, surround the Princess Isabel with conservative councillors, and order the dissolution of the militia. The only resistance came from the rank and file of *progresismo*, which took to the streets yet again in Zaragoza, Segovia, Badajoz, Seville, Córdoba, Almería, and Barcelona. Meanwhile, a number of terrorist incidents took place in Madrid, in one of which Narváez narrowly escaped death. Significantly, however, the rebellion failed. In contrast to what had happened in 1840 and 1843, most officers stayed loyal, Narváez's violent anti-radicalism naturally being attractive to men who had for years been subject to a barrage of threat, insubordination and insult. Faced by soldiers who shot them down without mercy, the radical mobs for the most part simply dissolved, and, if they secured control of Barcelona, it was only because this was the only city in Spain where the garrison went over to them. Fight bravely enough though Barcelona did – the city held out for two months under intense bombardment – the fact was that radicalism simply lacked the fighting power necessary to prevail.

Well aware that he was being rendered irrelevant, López was eventually driven to make a stand, only to find himself betrayed by his own supporters, most leading *progresistas* being above all opportunists who had little desire to challenge the social and political order and had over and over again shown themselves to be willing to compromise on matters of principle. Since the early autumn, the right wing of the party had been collaborating with Narváez in plans for the formation of a new ministry from which López and his supporters would be excluded, and, when the prime minister responded to *moderado* aggression in the new *cortes* elected in the course of the autumn by ordering the restoration of the militia and the convocation of fresh municipal elections, it refused point-blank to support him. Thus betrayed, López resigned, his place being taken by Salustiano Olózaga. Without doubt, the latter was perceived by

Narváez as a 'useful fool', but in this they had misjudged him. Whilst more conservative than López, Olózaga had primarily been driven by a determination to seize office for himself, and, to the astonishment of his some-time allies, not only refused to appoint any *moderado* ministers, but also secured a new dissolution of the *cortes*. What Olózaga believed he could achieve by this is unclear, but such independence was nevertheless utterly unacceptable. In consequence, Isabel II (who was now formally queen of Spain, having been proclaimed of age – at the age of thirteen – by the *moderados* on 8 November) was prevailed upon by Narváez to rescind the decree of dissolution, an utterly mendacious story being put about to the effect that Olózaga had secured this by force. Had the *progresistas* stood firm, they might have yet have survived, but once again they played straight into the hands of their opponents. Having overthrown López to secure his own advancement, Olózaga now found himself sold in his turn. If he controlled one of the major factions within the party, another had grown up around the equally ambitious and opportunistic Luis González Bravo. Realizing that Narváez was very much the man of the moment, Bravo decided that the general was his best prospect, and in consequence offered the *moderados* the support of his fifty-odd deputies. Completely out-manoeuvred, on 1 December 1843 Olózaga resigned, leaving Bravo to form a new ministry (at this stage it suited Narváez and the *moderados* to remain in the background, the last thing that they wanted being to risk uniting all the *progresistas* against them).

The downfall of Olózaga was not quite the end of *progresista* government, González Bravo remaining in power until 2 May 1844. However, for all practical purposes it marked the end of twenty years of turmoil. Superficially, the most important change that had resulted from innumerable risings, coups and civil wars was Spain's emergence as a liberal state, but this had long since been a foregone conclusion. The vital issue was not whether Spain would turn to liberalism, but rather the form in which it would do so. From 1820 onwards, Spanish liberalism had been deeply divided. Violent though the conflicts that resulted from this division undoubtedly were, there was at heart little disagreement as to the form that the new Spain should actually take. For Martínez de la Rosa as much as Riego, for Toreno as much as Mendizábal, and for Narváez as much as Espartero, the ideal was a Spain that would be dominated by the oligarchy that had in fact already dominated her since the early eighteenth century. Social change was not an issue, still less democracy, the object being rather to re-order Spain in such a manner as, first, to take account of the financial and economic realities which she faced, and, second, to allow the *pudientes* to maintain their position, if not to improve upon it. In order to secure these aims, most of the factions into which the liberal world was divided were prepared to call upon the *populacho* as demonstrators, rioters or members of the national militia, just as *serviles*, *apostólicos*, *agraviados*, and Carlists had been prepared to call it forth as rioters, guerrillas or *requetés*. Once nirvana had been attained, however, the *populacho* were superfluous to requirements, the chief goal thereafter being the restoration of order.

The *populacho*, however, were not mere pawns to be moved around at the whim of one faction or other of the elite. If they proved easy to mobilize, it was because they were suffering a veritable holocaust. War, epidemic, natural disaster, harvest failure, economic change, over-population, fiscal pressure, and rack-renting combined to flay the populace to the bone, in the meantime precipitating a social conflict that formed a constant backdrop to the evolution of national politics. Recognizing this, a handful of the political elite came gradually to the conclusion that the future of Spanish constitutionalism could not be secured unless political and social emancipation went hand in hand, pressure therefore mounting for such measures as greater equity in the implementation of disamortization. Themselves often drawn from marginal elements, they increasingly moved outside the scope of mainstream politics, through successive secret societies becoming the champions of a democratic, and, ultimately, republican, tradition that repeatedly sought to hijack the political process, but was in practice never able to do so.

What was at issue in the period 1823–43, then, was not so much a clash between constitutionalism and absolutism, as between liberalism and, as it were, 'liberalism with a human face'. Notwithstanding romantic marxian dreams of 'the people' being the decisive force in the revolution, in this latter conflict there could be but one winner, Spain as a result being burdened with a social structure that perpetuated the crisis of the early nineteenth century. If Spain had in 1823 been facing the 'ominous decade', she was now facing the 'ominous century'.

5

The Moderate Decade

The Triumph of Moderantismo

If the basic characteristics of the new Spain were established in the period 1833–43, the succeeding years witnessed their consummation. Thus power and authority were concentrated in the hands of a narrow elite who proceeded to govern Spain in their own interests. Under their aegis, meanwhile, Spain underwent a rapid process of modernization whose most important feature was considerable development in the infrastructure of the state. So powerful, indeed, did the state become that the radicals found that they were completely impotent. Yet *moderantismo* was nevertheless unable to maintain its hegemony. With the *moderados* dependent from the beginning on the ruthless and uncompromising Ramón Narváez, the combination of military unrest and internal division led in 1854 to the restoration of *progresismo*. In ten short years, in fact, the defects of the Spanish revolution were cruelly revealed.

Counter-Revolution and Modernization

Following the fall of Espartero, Spanish politics revolved around Ramón Narváez. Six years younger than his predecessor – he was born in 1799 in the Andalusian town of Loja – he shared his concern for order, scorn for civilian politicians, simplistic worldview, and love of wealth and ostentation. If the two generals were enemies, the reasons were entirely personal. Never having served in America, Narváez detested Espartero's advancement of the *ayacuchos* and bitterly resented the manner in which his rival had secured most of the credit for the defeat of Carlism. Brooding and vindictive, he had therefore rallied to the cause of *moderantismo* as a matter of course, and thus it was that he now stood at the head of the counter-revolution.

As might have been expected, Narváez's first priority was the restoration of order. Although he did not enter the González Bravo cabinet himself, he assumed the captain generalcy of Madrid, whilst securing the War Ministry for one of his clients, a series of last-ditch radical uprisings therefore being suppressed with the utmost savagery. Meanwhile, in the hope that he could ultimately secure a *moderado–progresista* reconciliation, Bravo sanctioned the return of María Cristina, purged the administration and judiciary, allowed the *moderados* free rein in the *cortes*, suspended disamortization, ordered new local elections, restored the municipal law of 1840, disarmed the militia, and ordered the formation of a new gendarmerie known as the Guardia Civil. However, this policy proved futile: whilst alienating many *progresistas*, Bravo completely failed to conciliate the *moderados*. As he had planned all along, meanwhile, Narváez now put himself forward as the guarantor of constitutional legality, in which guise he took over the government himself on 4 May 1844.

The way was now open for the creation of a new political system. Central to this process, of course, was the 'making' of a new assembly, Narváez convoking elections which duly produced an overwhelming victory for the *moderados*. With the necessary preliminaries thus completed, work began on a new constitution. Prepared by a committee consisting of Narváez and a variety of *moderado* worthies, this deemed sovereignty to rest not with the people, but with the monarch and the *cortes*; increased the power of the throne; proclaimed Spain to be Catholic; declared civil liberties to be subject to 'regulation'; and deleted all reference to the militia. Passed on 23 May 1845, it was quickly supplemented by a new electoral law that restricted the franchise still further whilst increasing the influence of the local notables. Also quick to make its appearance was a new municipal law which further limited the right to vote, amalgamated many authorities in such a way as to counterbalance known haunts of radicalism with bastions of *caciquismo*, and restricted the autonomy of the *ayuntamientos* to the absolute minimum. At provincial level, meanwhile, the power of the *diputaciones* was similarly reduced and that of the *jefe político* (now renamed the civil governor) greatly increased.

With Narváez at the helm, a certain degree of regression in the field of civil–military relations was also inevitable. Under the Bourbons, the army had come to acquire a position of very considerable predominance in both local government and the judiciary. Completely unacceptable to Spain's first generation of liberals, this situation had been drastically revised by the constitution of 1812, the anti-militarism which this embodied having been inherited by the *progresistas*. In consequence, the period 1837–43 had been marked by a number of reforms designed to reduce the role of the military. For Narváez, of course, such changes were anathema. Reversing the changes made to the powers of the military authorities, he therefore introduced a variety of measures that were designed to lend them greater weight, whilst at the same time effectively transforming the newly created Guardia Civil into a branch of the army.

In the last resort these reforms were designed to put an end to any possibility of a radical administration. Rather less partisan were the changes that the Narváez administration introduced in the fiscal system, these having been seen as a major landmark in the modernization of the treasury. Thus, the fiscal structure was simplified still further, the whole of Spain at last being subjected to a uniform system of taxation. Revenue was still insufficient – indeed, the deficit increased remorselessly – but by the mid-1850s the receipts from taxation had nonetheless risen to 1,500,000,000 *reales* per year in comparison to the miserably inadequate 770,000,000 of the period 1835–9. At the same time, too, the government's enormous debt was centralized in the hands of the Bank of San Fernando and converted into bonds made payable at a standard rate.

Also important in this context are the major developments that took place at this time in the system of banking. Created in 1829, the Bank of San Fernando was the effective precursor of the Bank of Spain, and as such was essentially a bank of issue with only the most limited facilities for depositing and lending. At the time that the *moderados* came to power, then, the only source of credit available to entrepreneurs within Spain was the great commercial families who dominated the money market. Such a situation was grossly inadequate: extensive though they often were, the resources of these families were not sufficient to meet more than a limited increase in demand, whilst investment was inhibited by the lack of capital in circulation and the absence of any clear guarantee that loans could be collected. With the restoration of order, however, sufficient confidence was generated for a group of businessmen headed by the leading tycoon, José de Salamanca, to establish a new lending bank entitled the Bank of Isabel II. This example was followed by various other consortia, and by 1846 at least three similar institutions were in operation, the Bank of San Fernando having also been forced to move into the private market. The edifice thus erected was anything but stable, but one of the major barriers to Spain's modernization was clearly being levelled.

The *moderado* triumph was therefore followed by a series of reforms that consolidated the gains made from the expropriation of the Church and opened the way for a new stage in Spain's development. Certainly, the 1840s were the moment when she began to industrialize. Taking Catalan cotton as an example, it was at this point that it began to take on the appearance of a modern industrial complex based around factories, machines, and steam power. For the next twenty years, indeed, tariff protection, increased stability, the abolition of the British ban on the export of machinery, and the inability of the traditional textile industries of the interior to compete, gave rise to rapid growth. The result of a massive advance in mechanization, all this was accompanied by a rapid process of concentration that saw the elimination of many small firms and the establishment of ever larger units of production.

As yet cotton was king, but the 1840s and 1850s also saw promising developments in other sectors. Still in Catalonia, Sabadell developed a factory-based woollen industry of considerable size, whilst in Valencia the first steps were taken in the mechanization of the silk industry. In Andalucía, Asturias and Vizcaya alike, there were sustained attempts to establish a modern metallurgical industry, whilst in Bilbao construction began of the first steam ships to be built in Spain. Above all, the 1840s witnessed the beginnings of railway construction, though by 1850 only one line – that from Barcelona to Mataró – was actually open, and two others (Madrid–Aranjuez and Langreo–Gijón) under construction.

None of this constituted an industrial revolution, but important changes were clearly nevertheless under way. At the same time there were major developments in urban physiognomy. Strongly influenced by French models, the dominant elite were no longer prepared to tolerate dark and stinking streets and spartan tenements. Armed with money, opportunity, and, in some cases, genuine vision, they proceeded to embark upon a dramatic programme of urban renewal. Broad boulevards lined with modern shops, banks and apartments were driven through quarters that had hitherto been a warren of alleyways; numerous *conventos* were torn down to make way for public gardens or imposing public buildings; and whole new districts were constructed in which the elite could live in style and comfort. Meanwhile, public services also improved, with the provision of better drains, better lighting, and better water supplies.

The Survival of Instability

If the great *moderado* construction boom suggests that the political era radiated stability, nothing could have been further from the truth. Quite simply, the *partido moderado* was not a real party at all, but rather a heterogeneous collection of interests that had coalesced round a handful of more or less egotistical parliamentarians. At the heart of this development was a measure of ideological unity, certainly, but at no stage did the party ever develop a coherent statement of binding principles, whilst it was recruited from a bewildering array of *doceañistas*, *exaltados*, *afrancesados*, enlightened absolutists and even Carlists. At the same time, too, for many of its militants politics was in any case not so much a matter of ideas, but rather of the personal advancement that was all the more pressing in view of the high costs of living in the new society.

All this ensured that different tendencies could not but emerge within *moderantismo*. Most important of these groups were the *doctrinarios*. Enjoying the support of many of the most powerful figures in party and army alike, this faction believed that Spain had reached a social and political ideal in which a balanced constitution guaranteed property and order whilst establishing the basic conditions for progress and prosperity. Determined to defend this ideal at all costs, the *doctrinarios* were in the meantime bent on enjoying the fruits of victory to the full, their ranks therefore encompassing a wide range of sub-groups centred on one prominent worthy or another. With *narvaístas*, *monistas*, *pidalistas* and *polacos* engaged in an endless struggle for influence, division and intrigue became ever more the norm.

If the *doctrinarios* on the whole maintained their hegemony, it was only because their opponents had rather less to offer. Thus, on the left of the party were to be found the so-called *puritanos*. Headed by Joaquín Francisco Pacheco and Nicomedes Pastor Díaz, this faction yielded to no one in their social conservatism. Unlike the *doctrinarios*, however, they were convinced that power could not be maintained by means of illegality and subterfuge. Instead, both constitution and spirit of the revolution had strictly to be respected. Disliking Narváez intensely and suspicious of military influence, they were inclined very much to seek a reconciliation with the right wing of *progresismo* in the hope that proscription might thus be restricted only to those groups which refused to accept liberalism's basic structures. Underpinning these ideas was an abiding obsession with liberal unity, but, failing this, Pacheco and his friends were willing to accept periodic spells of *progresista* government as the only means of maintaining stability and keeping the army out of politics. On the other wing of the party, meanwhile, there stood the so-called neo-absolutists. Headed by Narváez's initial choice of Foreign Minister, the Marqués de Viluma, this faction desired a return to the statute of 1834, an end to disamortization, the inclusion of at least some representatives of Carlism in the government, and the marriage of Isabel II and the son of Don Carlos, the Conde de Montemolín.

From the beginning, then, *moderado* rule promised to be dangerously unstable, its disunity being made all too apparent when a storm of protest forced Viluma to resign after he had somewhat incautiously given voice to his views. These divisions were sharpened by Narváez's moves to revise the constitution. Thus, whilst the *puritanos* demanded the constitution of 1837, the *vilumistas* called for the Estatuto Real. Too weak to carry the day and further alienated by the arrangements made for the support of the Church, in January 1845 they resigned their seats in the *cortes*, thereby provoking a species of mini-election, which they contested – almost entirely unsuccessfully – under the title of Unión Nacional. Much alarmed, the *puritanos* swallowed their growing doubts, but it was not long before their loyalty was again under threat.

Notwithstanding the revolution of 1843, there had as yet been little change in ecclesiastical policy, sales of Church land having continued unabated. Eager though the *moderados* were to increase their gains, however, a belief had begun to grow that matters had gone too far. Catholic and conservative, they were most unwilling to see the Church destroyed altogether. Yet this now seemed a real possibility. In serious financial difficulty, the Church had been stripped of its chief instruments of popular evangelization, and had nothing to put in their place, the parish clergy being utterly unequal to the task. It was therefore time to redress the balance, the hope being that this might also undercut support for Carlism. Ofalia and González Bravo had already restored the tithes and ordered all harassment of the clergy to cease, but reconciliation now accelerated. Several prominent ecclesiastical exiles were allowed to return to Spain; an emissary was sent to Rome; steps were taken to ensure that the parish clergy received their proper stipend; and disamortization was suspended, that portion of the Church's property that still remained unsold being formally restored to it in April 1846. Last but not least, in the new constitution the government not only recognized Catholicism as the sole religion of Spain, but formally promised financial support.

To all this, the Church responded with guarded favour. In the course of the Espartero regency her relations with the Spanish state had reached a nadir, Pope Gregory XVI having publically denounced the whole gamut of liberal ecclesiastical policy. However, the defeat of Carlism had destroyed all hope of reversing the momentous changes of the past few years. Moreover, if there was no evidence of any real drift away from Catholicism, many churchmen were genuinely convinced that Spain's social and cultural mores were under threat. Reconciliation with the regime being essential, the hierarchy therefore recognized Isabel II. None of this was much to the taste of the *puritanos*, but their fears were again overcome, this time by a startling *démarché* from the exiled Carlist court. In May 1845 Don Carlos abdicated in favour of his son, the Conde de Montemolín, who surprised the political world by hinting that he would be prepared to grant a constitution. Alarmed by the threat that this represented, the *puritanos* once again curbed their anger, but by the end of the year their growing disquiet had finally driven them into open opposition.

Within a very short space of time, then, the unity of the *moderados* had irrevocably broken down. Increasingly alarmed, Narváez in consequence delayed the opening of the next session of the *cortes* until by-elections had been held to replace forty-five deputies who had been appointed to various posts in the administration, whilst at the same time clamping down on the press. By these means Narváez was able more or less to remain in control, but on 11 February 1846 he suddenly resigned, ostensibly for reasons of health, but in reality on account of the growing differences that were marring his relations with the royal palace. At the heart of this problem was the question of the marriage of the queen and her younger sister, Luisa Fernanda. Ostensibly inconsequential, the matter was actually one of considerable importance, the queen being so ignorant and immature that her consort would be certain to exert a considerable influence over her. The result, of course, was that every faction had soon acquired its own candidate. One could dilate upon the various positions at length, but the most significant were those of Narváez and María Cristina. Of these the former wanted the Duc de Montpensier, who was the younger son of Louis Phillippe of France, and the latter either Prince Leopold of Saxe Coburg or her own brother, the Conde de Trapani, it being his inability to get his way that led the general to resign.

There followed several months of the utmost confusion. Narváez was replaced by the Marqués de Miraflores, but on 16 March 1846 María Cristina's obduracy caused him to go as well. The general was then brought back, only to be driven to resign again after a mere nineteen days, this time going into exile. There now reappeared the more pliable Istúriz, the fact that a variety of diplomatic considerations forced María Cristina to adopt the compromise candidate represented by Isabel's cousin, the Duque de Cádiz, allowing him for the time being to remain in office. On 10 October 1846, meanwhile, Isabel duly married Cádiz, her younger sister, Luisa Fernanda, on the same day becoming the wife of Montpensier.

Wedding or no wedding, order remained unrestored, Isabel's marriage in reality proving a disaster. A young woman possessed of a powerful sexual drive, the queen found Cádiz a distinctly sorry figure, and proceeded to take refuge in a series of lovers, of whom the first was General Francisco Serrano, who had been War Minister in the government of González Bravo. Always deeply devout, she also became more and more inclined to seek solace in religion, falling under the influence in the process of the nun known as Sister (Sor) Patrocinio who had achieved much fame by proclaiming that she had received the stigmata. Welcomed into the bosom of the court on account of her piety, she succeeded in instilling Isabel II with both a marked clericalism and a fixed hatred of the *progresistas*. With the *populacho* all this was not too great a problem – to the end of her reign Isabel remained extraordinarily popular – but amongst the political classes the prestige of the court was certainly diminished very badly, even the *doctrinarios* feeling ill at ease with Sor Patrocinio's blatant clericalism.

Meanwhile, Isabel's unfortunate marriage was producing extreme confusion in the corridors of power, the *doctrinarios* having been left badly split. Deprived of the iron hand of General Narváez, the government therefore suffered a major upset in the fresh general elections that were called in the autumn of 1846. The *progresistas* and *puritanos* obtaining far more seats than might otherwise have been the case, Istúriz was forced to resign. Such were the divisions and intrigue in the *doctrinario* camp that it was only with the greatest difficulty that a new prime minister was found in the person of the Duque de Sotomayor. However, the *doctrinario–puritano* coalition that he formed did not last very long, for Spain was now experiencing a serious economic crisis, the resultant popular discontent being further inflamed by the *quinta* of 50,000 men that the government was forced to summon on account of the new civil war that had broken out in Catalonia (see below). At this point, the scandals that were transpiring in the court led to a serious crisis. Outraged by the growing prominence of Serrano, Cádiz separated from his wife. Desperate to avoid a scandal, and, at the same time, get rid of Serrano, who was suspected of intriguing with the *progresistas*, Sotomayor appointed him Captain General of Navarre. To this the queen's response was as swift as it was irresponsible: Sotomayor was summarily dismissed, and Pacheco summoned to take office in his place. Forming a largely *puritano* ministry, Pacheco attempted a policy of reconciliation based on rigorous respect for the constitution, reductions in indirect taxation, the resumption of a limited measure of disamortization, and the rehabilitation of such figures as Olózaga. However, this satisfied no one. Attacked on all sides, Pacheco dissolved the *cortes* on 5 May 1847, but by September his ministry was in a state of complete dissolution. Next to be tried was a 'government of concord' which brought together *doctrinarios*, *puritanos*, and *progresistas* alike, but the more conservative elements were outraged by such concessions as the decision to allow Espartero to return from exile and take up a seat in the senate. Matters, it was felt, had gone far enough. Narváez had, in fact, already been asked to return from exile to save the situation, and, after first assuring himself that he had the support of the army, large parts of which had been dismayed by a decree which attempted to strengthen the civil authorities *vis à vis* their military counterparts, on 5 October 1847 the general simply presented himself at the cabinet meeting scheduled for that day and ordered the ministers to go home.

Conspiracy and Insurrection

With the return of Narváez, stability was restored. Chastened by the manner in which their disunity had prevented them from maintaining control, most *moderados* sank their differences and rallied behind their saviour, the so-called *gran gobierno de Narváez* (great Narváez government) therefore being able to remain in office for a record period. However, despite the fact that the Istúriz government had passed a Public Order Law that effectively gave the civil authorities the power to call out the army and declare martial law whenever it suited them, this does not mean that Spain experienced any increase in tranquillity. Almost from its very inception the dominance of the *moderados* had been coming under attack from both left and right. Before looking at the *pronunciamientos* and revolts that resulted, however, we must examine the institution on whose loyalty the regime depended.

To understand the position taken by the army in the course of the period 1844–8, we must return to the policies followed by Narváez in the wake of the fall of Espartero. In the aftermath of the Carlist Wars and the successive revolutions of 1835–43, the Spanish army was desperately in need of reform. Whilst not in itself very large – in 1844 it numbered some 100,000 men – its officer corps had been rendered increasingly top-heavy by a combination of the Carlist Wars and wave upon wave of politically motivated promotions. What was required was therefore a considerable reduction in the number of officers. However, whilst spending on the army was steadily cut, economies were rather achieved through re-organization, sleight of hand, and downright parsimony, the officer corps actually continuing to grow. Knowing that he could not afford to alienate its messes, Narváez in effect chose bribery. Having already created a considerable following through hostility to the *ayacuchos* and the judicious use of promotion, the general ensured that the officers were regularly paid, that they got their first pay rise since 1820, and that the large numbers who were not on the active list received some form of alternative employment (in this respect, of course, the creation of the Guardia Civil was an absolute godsend). For some officers, too, there was the possibility of posts in the administration or seats in the *cortes* or the senate. Continuing the practice of the Carlist Wars (from which he had emerged as the Duque de Valencia), Narváez also made good use of his connections with the palace, many other generals also becoming counts or dukes. However, if this was the carrot, Narváez was also prepared to make much use of the stick, officers who took part in revolts being shot without mercy.

Absent from the control of affairs in 1846–7 though Narváez may have been, the nine cabinets that filled the intervening period did nothing to reverse his basic policies. If anything, indeed, they rather consolidated them: the royal weddings, for example, were accompanied by a positive blizzard of promotions. Yet the progressive neutralization of the army does not mean that revolt was out of the question. Setting aside the serious social and economic dislocation which large parts of the populace continued to experience, the exclusion of the *progresistas* was a recipe for disaster. Given that the bulk of the populace was utterly lacking in political consciousness, it might be thought that this would have had little resonance at street level. However, such a view would be short-sighted. Thus, the Municipal Law of 1845 had handed the administration of local elections entirely to the mayors. No longer elected, but rather appointed, these men – prominent local notables – were able to arrange matters virtually as they saw fit. The electoral register would therefore be tampered with, and then only published at so late a date that challenges were rendered all but impossible; constituencies would be gerrymandered; and the electorate subjected to many kinds of pressure and intimidation. On the actual day of the elections, meanwhile, known troublemakers would find themselves excluded from the ballot; the Guardia Civil occupy the streets; and ballot boxes mysteriously disappear or simply be 'stuffed'. And, if all this was not enough, results could be concocted or annulled more or less at will. To the victors, meanwhile, went the spoils. Taxation, conscription, the administration of the common lands, municipal employment, public works, all became means by which opponents could be persecuted, friends favoured, votes bought and the *populacho* coerced. Buttressed by the Guardia Civil, the oligarchy could also rely entirely upon the local magistrates, who were invariably notables themselves.

For large parts of the populace, then, *moderado* rule coupled increased poverty with greater subjugation. In consequence, trouble was only to be expected. Initially, the opposition to *moderantismo* rested on the two opposing poles of Carlism and *progresismo*. Taking the former first of all, the *cristino* victory in the war of 1833–40 had in itself solved nothing, many Carlists having escaped to France. For some time the hope that Montemolín might wed Isabel II kept things quiet, but, no sooner had the queen got married, than revolt broke out afresh. By the end of 1846, indeed, the interior of Catalonia was in turmoil. Though no more than 10,000 rebels were under arms at any one time, large areas of the hinterland were soon in the hands of the insurgents. Impressive though these achievements were, however, the Carlists soon realized that they had little hope of carrying the war to the rest of Spain. Fighting continued into 1848, but in effect the war had once again been lost.

By 1848, however, the regime had been confronted by another crisis. To understand this development, we must return to *progresismo*.

Though split by the events of 1844 – González Bravo and his followers were soon swallowed up amidst the ranks of *moderantismo* – the *progresistas* remained loyal to the principles of the revolution of 1836. Denied access to the all-important fruits of office, they responded by arguing that, if a government betrayed the ideals of the revolution, sovereignty reverted to the people, who were in consequence justified in taking power by force. The problem with this position, however, was that by helping to crush provincial radicalism in 1843, the *progresistas* had alienated their popular backing, whilst they were themselves so alarmed at the growing social unrest that they were unwilling to call for barricades. Within Spain and without, such figures as Olózaga and Mendizábal established conspiratorial juntas, but the bulk of their attention was therefore directed at the barracks. Thanks to Narváez's shrewd management, however, their calls fell largely on deaf ears: when General Zurbano was finally persuaded to initiate a revolt in November 1844, he was quickly captured and shot. This failure hardly made a *pronunciamiento* an attractive prospect, but by early 1846 growing resentment of Narváez had produced a more favourable climate. On 2 April 1846 a Comandante Solís therefore pronounced in Lugo, only to find that he, too, was betrayed and left to face the firing squad. Thoroughly disillusioned, the *progresistas* were in consequence only too happy to seize upon the thaw occasioned by the fall of Narváez to return to constitutional politics, seeking especially to secure the royal favour through the influence of Serrano.

If the *progresistas* were distinctly lukewarm in their pursuit of revolution, the same cannot be said of the *exaltados*. With republican and proto-socialist ideas increasing amongst the radical wing of *progresismo* since at least the mid-1830s, the period 1840–3 had witnessed the first steps towards its political differentiation. In its wake, meanwhile, this process could not but intensify. Whilst a number of Catalan republicans seized on the teachings of the French communist, Etienne Cabet, as a means of winning the populace over to their cause, the small Fourierist *tertulia* that had been established in Cádiz in the late 1830s embarked on a campaign of proseletization in Madrid. In September 1847, meanwhile, a group of radicals established the makings of a new political party that was to become known as the Democrats, whilst there were also attempts to assassinate both Isabel II and Narváez.

Given that the 1840s witnessed the first stirrings of labour organization in Spain, the radicals' efforts were not without success. Indeed, Barcelona, Alicante, Alcoy and Málaga all witnessed abortive popular risings. Yet the radical movement remained very weak. Hence the fact that the Spanish 1848 proved a damp squib. Radicalized by a combination of the effects of the great slump that affected Europe in 1846–7, the return of Narváez, and the news of the downfall of Louis Phillippe, the *progresistas* and the forces to their left sprang to arms. In Madrid, especially, for a brief moment matters looked quite serious – on 26 March an armed crowd seized a large part of the city centre and were only put down at the cost of a pitched battle – but, with the exception of Catalonia, where a handful of insurgents took to the hills as guerrillas, order was soon restored. Narváez's response to the rising being extremely sharp – individual liberties were suspended; liberal use made of courts martial; many suspects, including men as prominent as Salustiano Oló-zaga, imprisoned or deported without trial; and strict controls imposed on the press – all that was achieved was a further clutch of martyrs.

Unimpressive though they were, these events served to rebuild the ranks of *moderantismo*. Narváez, in particular, gained immense prestige from the manner in which he had withstood the crisis, and his popularity was further boosted by a number of measures which he took to strengthen the criminal law and restore stability to the financial market. Meanwhile, the sense of stability was increased still further by the collapse of the revolution in France, and the recognition of Isabel II by the papacy, Austria, Prussia and Piedmont on account of the dispatch of a force of Spanish troops to help crush the Roman republic. When the *cortes* reopened in 1849, it was therefore docility itself.

This period of peace did not last long, however. To the complete astonishment of the political world, on 18 October 1849 Narváez and his entire government was suddenly replaced by a new administration under the neo-absolutist Conde de Clonard (a grandee general with strong links with the court). Explanations for the change differ, but, in brief, it appears that Isabel had taken exception to a series of steps that Narváez had been taking to restore order to the court. Berated for her stupidity by her mother and ridiculed by the entire political world (for Clonard was generally regarded as a laughable nonentity), the queen was forced to bring back Narváez after a mere thirty-seven hours, but the fact was that Isabel had once again dismissed a prime minister for no better reason than the fact that he had interfered with her personal life.

Unimportant though this incident was, it can yet be seen as the beginning of the end for Narváez. As the spectre of 1848 receded, so concern once again began to grow amongst the *doctrinarios* at his arrogance, amongst the *puritanos* at his contempt for constitutional procedure, and amongst the generals at his arbitrary behaviour. Encouraged by the revelation that the queen might in certain circumstances be persuaded to sacrifice her champion, opinion became less and less docile. Amongst civilian critics of the general, the issue seized upon was government corruption, the extent of which led even the general's long-term friend and ally, Donoso Cortes, to denounce the regime as the enemy of morality. Amongst the generals, meanwhile, Generals Pavía and Fernández de San Román, both of whom bore personal grievances towards Narváez, seized upon a proposal for the creation of a reserve as a pretext for attacking his entire administration. Predictably enough, the general overreacted – in violation of his constitutional immunities, Pavía was stripped of his seat in the senate and exiled to Cádiz – only to find that such actions created martyrs to whom other dissidents were drawn, amongst them such other dissatisfied generals as Fernández de Córdoba, Ros de Olano, Roncali and Prim. All this in turn led to a revival of *progresismo*, a number of leading generals – Prim, Serrano and Alaix – now openly coming out in its support. Had he possessed the support of the palace or a more reliable party base, he might yet have hung on, but in the last resort Narváez knew that neither Isabel nor the *doctrinarios* were to be relied upon. Indeed, in so far as the latter were concerned, he was by now being deserted by even his closest collaborators, a particularly damaging loss in this respect being the Minister of Finance, Juan Bravo Murillo. Muttering darkly about being shot in the back, on 10 January 1851 Narváez therefore resigned.

The Revolution of 1854

The fall of Narváez presaged a new political upheaval that was far more dramatic than anything which Spain had witnessed in 1848. In so far as its origins are concerned, we may begin with the interesting figure of Bravo Murillo. A successful lawyer from Extremadura, Murillo had entered politics relatively late in life, and in consequence viewed it as something of an outsider. As such, he was distinctly unimpressed by what he saw: parties characterized by factionalism and intrigue; parliamentary debates whose chief features were grandiloquent oratory, personal insult and lack of order; elections that were openly rigged and gerrymandered; a civil service dominated by corruption and nepotism; a constitution that was ignored at every turn; and a political order that was dominated by the military. If Spain was to enjoy stability – which Murillo identified not just with the protection of order but also economic progress – it was therefore essential that the situation should be cleaned up. In concrete terms, what this meant was the revision of the constitution so as to curb the powers of the *cortes*, curtail public debate, and reduce the electorate almost to nothing, and the introduction of major administrative and fiscal reforms (in particular, Murillo wanted a reduction in the budget, and the establishment of a professional civil service whose functionaries would not be hanging on every change of regime). In putting forward these views, Bravo Murillo was moved primarily by a mixture of honesty and common sense – the current system was clearly in a state of disarray, and not only bore only the most slender relationship to its theoretical principles, but was disrupting the work of government and holding back the development of Spain. However, what he was proposing was essentially a return to a modified form of Caroline absolutism in which a reformist monarch would govern in accordance with the rule of law with the aid of a government of technocrats and an elected council of state.

Worthy though many of Murillo's ideas were, they were hardly founded in political realism. Under his guidance, many steps were taken to accelerate the programme of development that had been launched in the previous decade: it was at this time that work began on the canalization of the Ebro and the construction of a modern system of water supply for the capital, whilst Murillo was also responsible for the re-establishment of the old Ministry of Development and the creation of a General Railways Plan whose aim was the construction of a network of trunk lines radiating from Madrid. Although the link with Murillo was purely incidental, negotiations on the subject having been dragging on ever since 1845, he in addition happened to preside over the signing of a new *concordat* with the Church.

Despite these achievements, however, Murillo received little support. Matters were not helped by the fact that the unilateral repudiation of part of the national debt that was the chief feature of his financial policy had serious implications for many investors, but, even had this not been the case, Murillo's enemies would still have been numerous. Thus, the *doctrinarios* were alienated by the censorious view that he took of *moderado* politics; the *puritanos* disliked the terms of the settlement with the Church (which had admittedly got a very good deal: guaranteed generous state subventions and the *de facto* control of education, she was also allowed to re-establish many religious orders); and the *narvaístas* in particular regarded him as a traitor. In response to the difficulties that inevitably resulted, Murillo dissolved the *cortes* and simply pressed on regardless, not only introducing a decree that made entrance into the bureaucracy dependent on examinations and outlawed favouritism in its ranks, but also publishing his plans for constitutional reform.

The result was a storm of indignation: aside from a handful of *vilumistas* and neo-Carlists, the political world was united in its determination to stand by the basic principles of the system that had emerged over the course of the past fifteen years. Still worse, meanwhile, discontent spread to the army. Determined to reduce the influence of the military, Murillo had originally attempted to form a wholly civilian government and sent Narváez into exile, the result being that most factions of the *generalato* were angry and suspicious. Firmly ensconced in the upper house, many generals in consequence turned increasingly to outright opposition. Magnificently defiant, Murillo fought on regardless, but he continued to ignore the practicalities of Spanish politics in that his determination to root out corruption led to much unease in the palace (María Cristina, in particular, had amassed a vast fortune as a speculator). Warned on all sides that the throne stood on the brink, Isabel therefore informed Murillo that he no longer had her confidence, the latter having no option but to go.

For all Murillo's lack of political realism, his plans probably represented the only means whereby the *moderado* system could have been made to function effectively. At all events the next year was one of paralysis and confusion. In the apparent belief that she could still govern above party, Isabel replaced Murillo, not with the obvious choice of some powerful *moderado*, but rather with the pliant General Roncali, who had served as War Minister in the ultra-loyal Miraflores government of 1846. Faced by massive opposition from the new *cortes* – at the behest of Murillo fresh elections had been held in February 1853 – he suspended the session, but was nevertheless forced to resign. Still refusing to learn her lesson, Isabel replaced him with the equally uninspiring General Lersundi, only to dismiss him five months later. Lersundi's sin having been to threaten to expose the part played by the queen's latest favourite, José María Ruiz de Arana, in a questionable railway deal, Isabel now turned to the most unscrupulous figure that the *moderados* had to offer. Thus, the new prime minister was the notoriously opportunistic Luis Sartorius, an ambitious journalist who had served as Minister of the Interior in the third Narváez government, and was now the head of a faction known, from Sartorius' Polish origins, as the *polacos*, or Poles.

Hungry for office as he was, Sartorius was suitably compliant, but his appointment only deepened the crisis. Unpopular with all and sundry though he may have been, Murillo's denunciation of corruption had struck a chord with *puritanos*, *progresistas* and *demócratas* alike. Ministers, generals, and prominent members of the royal family had all been amassing huge fortunes from the boom in railway construction on which Spain had now embarked, but the palace was especially implicated in the problem on account of the fact that contracts to build new railways were invariably granted by royal decree. As the months went by, then, the boom attracted ever greater criticism, whilst at the same time providing dissidents of all sorts with a useful rallying cry. In consequence, the appointment of Sartorius was a blunder of the first order, and all the more so as he was himself an avid investor. To avoid disaster, the new prime minister adopted a policy of conciliation. Whilst allowing Narváez to return from exile, he recalled the *cortes*, and promised in future to abide by the constitution if it would in return abandon its criticism of the railway boom. However, this manoeuvre did not work. Sensing that they had an opportunity once and for all to end the meddling of the court, the opposition remained adamant, and on 9 December 1853 the *cortes* duly rejected his proposals by a majority of nearly two to one.

This gesture of defiance Sartorius would not tolerate. The *cortes* was again closed, and numerous newspapers were shut down, whilst all those members of the 'payroll vote' who had voted against the government were dismissed. However, as the men concerned included a number of senior generals, the prime minister had gravely misjudged the situation. The *generalato* was not especially interested in ruling Spain, but it did expect to be treated with due consideration. Meanwhile, military discontent was once more on the increase. Part of the problem related to the question of promotions. Three successive waves of mass promotion had occurred over the past ten years – after the fall of Espartero in 1843, the marriage of Isabel II in 1846, and the birth of Isabel's first child, Isabel Francisca, in 1852 – but these had been very partial, benefiting in the first case only those men who had declared against Espartero, and in the second two only officers above the rank of captain. If this situation affected all sections of the officer corps, particular interest groups within it had been increasingly upset by a series of organizational reforms that had been set in train by Bravo Murillo in the hope of reducing the military budget.

Military unrest was further stimulated by a growing fear of revolution: trade was at a low ebb; prices were on the increase; Galicia was being ravaged by a severe potato famine; and Barcelona was in the grip of growing unrest. Convinced that the only remedy was the establishment of a more progressive government, a number of generals – the three Gutiérrez de la Concha brothers, Facundo Infante, Leopoldo O'Donnell, Esteban León and Francisco Serrano – therefore turned once again to conspiracy. It was not just the military who were becoming rebellious, however. Amongst *doctrinarios* and *puritanos* alike, there were many men who shared the reasoning of the Conchas and their fellows, and on 13 January 1854 no fewer than 200 *moderado* deputies and senators formulated a petition calling for the re-opening of the *cortes*. This, of course, met with no response, and in consequence the cause of revolution acquired the support of such figures as the much respected jurist and parliamentarian, Antonio de Ríos Rosas. The left, meanwhile, was equally restive. Hitherto essentially a pressure group within *progresismo* whose organization was confined to a variety of secret societies, Spanish radicalism had undergone considerable changes since 1848. Formally organized into the new Democratic Party since 6 April 1849, it had won considerable support amongst the more politicized elements of the urban lower classes through its espousal of such causes as cheaper bread, a fairer system of taxation, the democratization of local government and the formation of labour associations. With their confidence boosted by a growing number of defectors from the *progresistas*, the radicals now began to organize a revolt of their own.

Far from blind to what was going on, Sartorius did his best to hamstring conspiracy in the army, whilst arresting virtually the entire *demócrata* leadership. However, defying orders which would have packed him off to the Canaries, General O'Donnell went into hiding in Madrid, and continued to work for an insurrection. However, without the active involvement of Narváez or Espartero, both of whom were cannily waiting on events, success proved difficult, matters not being made any easier by a premature attempt at a *pronunciamiento* in Zaragoza. It was therefore only with the greatest difficulty that some troops were got together at Alcalá de Henares. Placing himself at their head, on 28 June 1854 O'Donnell came out into the open and declared himself to be in a state of revolt.

At first the results were not very impressive. The rest of the army did not move, whilst the radicals were deterred from supporting O'Donnell by the fact that he very clearly had no interest in radicalizing the political system. In the absence of a popular rising his only hope was that Sartorius or the queen might be bluffed into surrender, but the prime minister was able to mount a convincing show of strength, and, when O'Donnell tried to march on the capital, he was blocked by 5,000 troops at Vicálvaro. Forced to turn away, he headed for Andalucía in the hope that something might yet be done to rouse the forces of the provincial radicalism that had made so impressive a showing in the 1830s. At Manzanares, however, he was joined by General Serrano and told that the south was at best apathetic. Already under pressure from contacts among the *puritanos* – and especially a relatively unknown placeman of Salamanca's called Antonio Cánovas del Castillo – to give some political content to his revolt, O'Donnell somewhat reluctantly issued a proclamation in which he made a number of rather vague promises of reform.

A few dissident voices aside, there seems little doubt that this proclamation was decisive. Thus, no sooner had it been issued than strikes broke out amongst the textile workers of Barcelona, the commotion becoming so great that the Captain General was left with no option but to declare his support for O'Donnell and Serrano. With the tide of popular risings showing signs of spreading, most of the other regional commanders quickly followed suit. Faced by the complete disintegration of his power base, on 17 July Sartorius resigned, whereupon Isabel ordered the still loyal Director-General of Infantry, Fernando Fernández de Córdoba, to form a new government. Although he was able to gain the support, not just of various prominent *moderados*, but also of Ríos Rosas and several other *progresistas*, Fernández de Córdoba's efforts went for nothing. On 17 July large crowds assembled for a bullfight were persuaded by radical agitators to march on the centre of the city. By midnight the crowds were in complete control, and the houses of María Cristina, Sartorius and Salamanca were in flames, a revolutionary junta having been in the meantime formed in the town hall under the aged Evaristo de San Miguel. Besieged in the royal palace, Isabel and Fernández de Córdoba at first attempted to essay a policy of conciliation. During the night, however, fighting broke out and for most of the next day a confused battle raged across much of the city. With the situation becoming ever more threatening – not only were there shouts of 'Long live the Republic!', but a rival junta appeared in the *barrios bajos* – the leaders of the insurrection became increasingly eager to come to some agreement with the palace. Fernández de Córdoba's 3,000 men having proved unable to restore order, by the end of the day the queen was only too eager to come to terms. Hastily dismissing the unfortunate general, she announced that she now wished Espartero, who had still taken no part in the movement, to form a *progresista* government. Until such time as he might arrive, she further agreed that power should be transferred to San Miguel. In short, the *década moderada* was over.

Stability Squandered

The period from 1844 to 1854 encapsulates a great irony. If there is one characteristic that marks out the moderate decade, it is an advance in the power of the state. A modern police force was established, the bureaucracy was professionalized, the fiscal system was rationalized, the autonomy of local government was swept away, the powers of the state to defend public order were systematized, the Church was secured as an ally of the establishment and the forces of revolution were disarmed. Despite this, however, government remained as unstable as ever, Isabel II being served by no fewer than fourteen different prime ministers. The reason for this was simple. In securing a monopoly of power, the *moderados* had destroyed the only link that bound them together. In part, the differences concerned rested on matters of principle, but the sub-groups which resulted were extremely fluid, their members being governed by personal interest. Thus, what really mattered was the question of clientage. With politics now more than ever a game in which the stakes were the advancement of self, family and friends, the *moderados* degenerated into a collection of factions whose rivalry made stable government impossible.

To be fair to the *moderados*, the situation would probably have remained unstable even had they not followed so self-destructive a course. We come here to the influence of the court and the army. Thus, the attempts of the palace to defend its interests were distinctly heavy-handed, the situation being rendered still worse by the fact that the voice of the royal household was by no means united. Meanwhile, the contribution of the army was even worse. Emerging from the Carlist War loaded with titles and rewards, the generals saw themselves as the architects of victory and the saviours of the state and were thus imbued with a sense of self-importance that the *moderados* did nothing to reduce: not only did the latter maintain the tradition that the Minister of War should be a general and that the Captains General should take precedence over the civil authorities, but they entrenched the *generalato* in both the Senate and the civil administration (many *jefes políticos* were generals, whilst martial law remained in force in Barcelona throughout the 1840s). Having in many cases acquired extensive land and business interests, the generals were an integral part of the milieu from which *moderantismo* was recruited, and would therefore have been players on the political stage even had this not been guaranteed by their own ambitions.

In conditions such as these, stability was not to be achieved. Needless to say, however, its absence was crucial. For all its sound and fury, the cause of popular radicalism was in decline in the 1840s. Failure may have been heroic, but it was also repeated, the utter inability of the revolutionary left to make progress in isolation being demonstrated beyond dispute by the events of 1848. This is not to say, of course, that poverty and despair did not continue to instil a mood of rebellion amongst urban and rural masses alike, but the state was now better placed to overcome unrest, whilst the abolition of the militia deprived the *populacho* of their most effective weapon.

As was to occur again in 1868, in fact, the escalating disputes in the ranks of *moderantismo* opened the way for a popular revolution that would not otherwise have occurred, the *sine qua non* of radical success in the streets of Barcelona, Valencia and Madrid being the fact that on the whole the army had swung behind O'Donnell and Serrano. And, in so far as these gentlemen were concerned, there was no question of a genuine revolution, the limit of their ambition being to revenge themselves upon Sartorius. For all the excitement of 18 July 1854, in fact, the cause of radicalism remained as weak as ever.

6

Revolution, Reconciliation and Relapse

Spain between Revolutions

In so far as Spanish radicalism was concerned, the revolution of 1854 proved to be extremely disappointing. As might have been expected, the revolutionary coalition proved to be distinctly unstable, and by 1856 *moderantismo* was once more effectively in the saddle. Indeed, far from democratizing Spain, the revolution actually strengthened the establishment, which proceeded to embark upon a determined effort to construct a new force that united the less intransigent elements of *moderantismo* and *progresismo* alike. For some time this combination did well, but for all that it could not bring stability. Beneath the surface as factional as ever, it was undermined by Isabel II's continued meddling and was eventually brought to its knees. Whilst these manoeuvres secured the queen's interests in the short term, the results were disastrous, for the *progresistas* were driven increasingly to reject the isabelline system. Meanwhile, Spain was assailed by a grievous economic crisis that brought to the fore the tensions that had been building up ever since the beginning of the nineteenth century. Much alarmed, many generals and other erstwhile *moderados* were propelled into overthrowing Isabel II. In some respects, however, the issue had been decided long before. If the dynasty had fallen, it was largely because it was incapable of governing a Spain devoid of social justice. The revolution of 1854 having in effect afforded the last hope that something might yet be done to redress the balance between *cacique* and *campesino*, the re-emergence of conservative rule rendered a new crisis all but inevitable.

The Downfall of Progresismo

In retrospect, the failure of the revolution of 1854 to effect any significant change in the social and economic development of Spain is unsurprising. Thus, O'Donnell and Serrano had only issued the proclamation of Manzanares as an unwilling ploy, whilst O'Donnell in particular was notorious for his devotion to the queen. Espartero was rather more promising, perhaps, but his fear of the *populacho*, regard for the royal family and dependence on O'Donnell all tied his hands. Meanwhile, the various politicians who had assumed the political leadership of the uprising were distinctly ambivalent in their attitude towards social reform: composed of prominent local notables, the revolutionary authorities devoted the bulk of their attention to restoring order. Finally, the *demócratas* were few in numbers and, in so far as the leadership was concerned, much concerned to gain access to the fruits of office, whilst their followers could not afford to stay away from work for very long and had in consequence no option but to abandon their barricades.

In short, the popular revolution simply evaporated, the result being that it gained very little. The queen was allowed to remain on the throne, for example, whilst the cabinet that Espartero assembled was devoid even of left-wing *progresistas*, let alone out-and-out democrats, and included not only O'Donnell, who was able to insist on being given the Ministry of War, but also the erstwhile *puritano* premier, Pacheco. Meanwhile, if the new government restored the militia, recalled the town councils of 1843, ordered a return to the municipal government law of 1823 and decreed the election of a constituent *cortes* under the relatively generous electoral law of 1837, it also dissolved the revolutionary juntas, ruled out an immediate reform of taxation, and banned the *cortes* from debating the question of a republic.

The implications of all this were not lost on radical opinion, but the issue that brought matters to a head was the question of María Cristina. Loathed by the crowd thanks to her ostentation and corruption, she was an obvious target, but Espartero was not the man to hound the woman under whom he had made his name, the result being that María Cristina was allowed to travel into exile, escaping with no worse punishment than the confiscation of her estates. Absolutely furious, on 28 August the radicals once again staged a major popular demonstration in Madrid. Within a matter of hours, however, peace had been restored, the bulk of the demonstrators simply melting away. With reaction around the country generally equally flacid, it was clear that the power of the streets was at an end.

The defeat of popular revolution by no means brought a return to tranquillity, the next few months rather seeing serious unrest in many parts of Spain. As a result the general elections were held in an atmosphere of crisis that could not but produce an overwhelming *progresista* victory. The victors having in the meantime been shifted a long way to the right by an influx of erstwhile *moderados*, the fact was that little was now to be expected from the *cortes*. Indeed, no sooner had it begun its formal business on 28 November than a motion declaring that the monarchy of Isabel II should be the basis of the new constitution was carried by 194 votes to nineteen. Refusing to be cowed, the left continued to fight on, proposing such reforms as the abolition of the *consumos* and the *quinta*, but in almost every case their efforts were turned aside (one of the few exceptions related to the *consumos* which were effectively abandoned). Nor were they successful in the debate that took place with regard to the principles that should govern the new constitution, the twenty-seven 'bases' that were eventually passed excluding the left's every proposal.

Given this situation, reform was likely to take one direction only. Whilst there were compelling short-term reasons for such a strategy – above all, a growing financial crisis – an acceleration of disamortization was all but inevitable, and all the more so as it allowed the *progresistas* to claim that they were addressing the radicals' agenda. Under the direction of the Minister of Finance, Pascual Madoz, 1 May 1855 therefore saw the authorization of fresh expropriations. Even more ambitious than the efforts of Mendizábal, the new act declared the confiscation of almost all of what remained of the patrimony of the Church, together with the endowments of schools, hospitals, universities and other charitable institutions and public corporations of all sorts, and the 80 per cent or so of the commons let out in small lots to peasant farmers. Financially, the measure was a huge success, but pious hopes that the land would be distributed on a fairer basis than before were scotched by the fact that 10 per cent of the value of each lot had to be paid immediately as a deposit. As purchasers were given fourteen years to make good the remainder, the lower classes did not even obtain the benefits that might have accrued to them in employment terms had investors been driven to realize very high short-term profits. In social terms, in fact, the whole exercise was a disaster.

As will be discussed, other measures were also passed by the *cortes*. In so far as the immediate situation was concerned, however, these were all but irrelevant. The result was that the *progresistas* continued to be undermined by incessant disorder. Always a time of penury in the countryside due to the cessation of much agricultural activity, the winter had brought even greater suffering than normal due in part to the heavy exports of wheat occasioned by the outbreak of the Crimean War, and in part to the greatly reduced ability of many *ayuntamientos* to provide relief work for the destitute. Already on the increase due to the poor harvests of 1852 and 1853, food prices soared, whilst cholera continued to ravage much of eastern Spain. As a result, bread riots, land seizures and other disorders affected many parts of the country; in Aragón and Catalonia there were Carlist stirrings; in Madrid the militia showed signs of mutiny; and in Barcelona the growing labour movement brought the cotton industry to a halt in a ten-day general strike.

To deal with this unrest, the government could either move in the direction of genuine concessions, or adopt a policy of reaction. Of these, however, the former was at best unlikely: the *demócratas* and left-wing *progresistas* (or *puros*) were too weak to impose their views upon the *cortes*, whilst republican *demócratas* such as Pi y Margall were in any case beginning to fall out with erstwhile *progresistas* such as Nicolás Rivero; Espartero was unwilling to break with O'Donnell; the centre and right of *progresismo* was driven by its fear of social disorder to remain on good terms with its *moderado* allies; and many radicals were more interested in political than social reform. To all intents and purposes, the result was that the initiative lay with conservatism.

As foretaste of what was to come, in April 1855 the *cortes* passed a bill outlawing political discussion amongst the militia. Admittedly, the government did take energetic steps to counter clerical resistance, expelling the bishops of Barcelona and Osma, removing many parish priests, and placing those areas of the country affected by the renewed Carlist guerrilla under martial law. However, in fact these measures proved a double-edged sword – the decree of martial law, for example, was used as a means of repressing the workers of Barcelona – whilst they were accompanied by an attempt, albeit unsuccessful, to impose property qualifications on recruitment to the militia. Much alarmed, on 5 June Madoz therefore resigned, the result being that the cabinet tipped still further to the right.

By the time that the *cortes* ended its first session on 17 July 1855, it could therefore be argued that the revolution was already moribund. Unfazed by revelations that Isabel had been intriguing with the Conde de Montemolín, the right now further consolidated its position by means of a sustained attempt to restore unity to *moderantismo* (the court's flirtation with Carlism, however, did lead to a decision that the chief posts in the royal household should be in the gift of the cabinet). As a result the session of the *cortes* which began on 1 October was marked by further defeats for the left in the form of an army law which retained not only the *quinta*, but also the wholly inequitable principle of substitution, and a labour law that severely curtailed the right of association. Outside the *cortes*, meanwhile, the country was in the grip of a renewed social crisis. Although the harvest of 1855 had been relatively good, the demand occasioned by the Crimean War meant that food prices continued to rise. The cotton industry, meanwhile, remained in a state of depression, whilst large parts of the country were struck by months of heavy rain that brought all work to a halt. Not surprisingly there were therefore further tumults in Zaragoza, Madrid, Alcoy, Tarragona, Málaga and Valencia which in some cases amounted to full-scale republican revolts.

However much exaggerated they were by *moderado* newspapers, these disorders undermined the efforts of the *demócratas* and left-wing *progresistas* to secure a change in the general direction that had been taken by events. Much frustrated, elements on the left of the *demócratas* represented, in particular, by the quasi-blanquist journalist and militia officer, Sisto Sáenz de la Cámara, responded with calls for a revolutionary terror. Beyond frightening the right still further, however, all this did was to exacerbate the already serious divisions in the left-wing camp, with the left-*progresistas* being alienated from the *demócratas*, and the moderate wing of the latter condemning Cámara and advocating closer links with *progresismo*.

By the late spring of 1856, then, the revolutionary regime was clearly in a state of crisis, its inability to prevent the drift to the right being underlined by the *de facto* reinstatement of the *consumos*, and the passage of new laws that placed strict restrictions on the right of journalists to criticize the crown, the Church and the *cortes*, and made enlistment in the militia dependent on certain property qualifications. Meanwhile, far from providing the leadership which the radicals expected of him – for Espartero's image as the 'people's general' had proved extraordinarily durable – the premier approved the brutal measures which had been taken in response to the popular unrest, and actually helped force through the *moderado* counter-revolution. With matters in this state, the regime ought to have been reasonably safe, for its nominal *progresismo* was a threat to nobody. However, the Church was still waxing furious in its denunciation of disamortization; Espartero's wholly undeserved reputation as a revolutionary was a constant spur to the paranoia of the propertied classes; the *moderados* were eager to oust the *progresistas* from power; and large parts of the officer corps were increasingly restive. Also of note was the fact that the regime of Napoleon III was increasingly dissatisfied with the situation in Spain, the inference being that a *pronunciamiento* could count on at least a measure of international approbation.

It was not long before the crisis came to a head. First of all, in early June the press reported the existence of a plot against the life of the queen. Fabricated though the story probably was, Isabel was nevertheless frightened enough to decide that Espartero, at least, must be removed. Still more dramatically, two weeks later a fresh series of disorders exploded in town and countryside, the area affected this time being the hitherto tranquil interior of Old Castile. Almost wholly spontaneous and in large part little more than a traditional bread riot, these new disturbances were attributed by the *moderado* and *progresista* press alike to socialism or even 'communism'. With this analysis the government agreed, being more than willing to accede to the harsh measures of repression engaged in by the military authorities, but in fact the fate of the regime was sealed, a genuinely horrified O'Donnell being egged on by the palace to provoke a crisis.

The *dénouement* was not long in coming. Increasingly aware of just how dangerous the situation had become, on 11 July 1856 the Minister of the Interior, Vicente Escosura, presented his colleagues with the draft of a decree designed to muzzle the *moderado* press in the belief that it had been deliberately stirring up popular unrest. In response O'Donnell demanded his resignation on pain of going himself. Two days of confusion followed as Espartero sought frantically to find a compromise, but eventually it became clear that Isabel would never accept the loss of O'Donnell. At this Espartero seems finally to have realized that he could squander his credit no more – he had, after all, for two years been bending to the conservative agenda almost without protest – and tendered his resignation himself, the result being that by dawn on 14 July Spain not only had a new government under Leopoldo O'Donnell but had been declared to be in a state of siege.

Though Espartero himself refused to fight, the drama was not yet over. Aided by the militia, which took over the centre of Madrid, Escosura barricaded himself in the Ministry of the Interior and ordered the provinces to resist, whilst the *demócrata* and left-*progresista* deputies hurried to the *cortes* in the hope of forcing an emergency session (since 1 July it had been in recess). Sure that the army would support him (as War Minister, O'Donnell had been solicitous of the welfare of the whole of the officer corps rather than just the *vicalvaristas*), the new premier refused to back down and on the morning of 15 July attacked the rebel forces. Although they fought bravely, the militiamen were gradually forced back, and by the end of the day the parliament building had had to be abandoned by its occupants. The struggle was not quite over – parts of the *barrios bajos* held out for most of 16 July – but the *progresista* cause was clearly doomed. Away from Madrid there were risings at Jaén, Málaga, Alicante, Zaragoza and Barcelona, but the hopelessness of their position soon persuaded most of the insurgents to disperse without a fight. Only in Barcelona were matters different, but even there four days of fierce fighting sufficed to restore order. Once again, in short, the progressive cause had been snuffed out.

Unión Liberal

To understand the events of the next seven years, we must turn to the figure of Leopoldo O'Donnell. A member of a military dynasty which had taken a leading role in the War of Independence, the new prime minister had from an early age acquired a strong belief in the right of the army to act as the arbiter of Spain's destinies. Beyond that, his political views were dominated entirely by a doctrinaire *moderantismo* – he had, for example, taken part in both the attempted coup of 1841 and the successful military rebellion of 1843. Rewarded with the captain generalcy of Cuba, he returned to Spain in 1848, whereupon he rapidly became a favourite of the queen, whom he appears genuinely to have worshipped. Thus far, O'Donnell might simply come over as another Narváez, but in fact a number of saving graces distinguished him from the bulk of his colleagues. Thus, not only had he refrained from the worst of their financial excesses, but no sooner had he arrived back in Spain than he came to the conclusion that the exclusive factionalism of the *moderados* was hardly a stable basis for the monarchy of his beloved queen. Although the idea was hardly a new one, having been shared by the *puritanos*, thus emerged the genesis of the scheme that would dominate the rest of his life – the formation of a political force that would end the schism that divided Spanish liberalism and broaden the basis of the constitutional regime sufficiently to render it safe from all further turmoil. Though powerless in other respects, as Inspector General of Infantry between 1848 and 1851 he had sought to put at least his main principles – above all, the idea that men should not be ostracized or passed over simply on account of association with the wrong political faction – into practice, only to fall foul of Bravo Murillo, for the next three years using his position in the senate to champion the cause of the opposition.

Nothing could be further from the truth than to portray O'Donnell as an altruistic constitutionalist: inherent in his world view, for example, was the clear belief that the army had the right not only to be free of civilian control but to overthrow any regime that betrayed its interests. Nor were his political ideas very advanced, his initial plans centring on little more than the belief that the constitution of 1845 should somehow be rendered workable. As for his character, it was marked by considerable vanity: hence the series of foreign adventures of the period 1859–63. That said, however, he was not a mere *caudillo*. Thus, whereas Narváez and Espartero had ruled as generals and had no qualms about the use of force, O'Donnell came to see himself primarily as a civilian politician and always sought to observe the rules of the political game.

In the immediate aftermath of the events of July 1856, O'Donnell's behaviour was certainly not that of a Narváez. Spain remained under martial law; the press was rigorously censored; those *ayuntamientos* that had declared against the new cabinet were dismissed; the *cortes* was dissolved; the militia was disbanded; and the constitution of 1845 was restored. However, the government remained a coalition of *puritanos* and right-wing *progresistas*; some of the more obnoxious features of the constitution were amended; none of the leading *puros* or *democratas* were arrested; there were almost no executions; the administration was left untouched; the military authorities were enjoined to be sparing in their use of their emergency powers; the new town councillors who were required were selected from men of no party as well as *moderado* trusties; and few curbs were placed upon disamortization.

Such moderation was not acceptable, however. Isabel was as pious in her views as ever, whilst she had been coming under increasing pressure from Pope Pius IX to end the expropriation of the Church's property. At the same time, too, the court *camarilla*, the Duque de Cádiz, and the exiled María Cristina were strongly absolutist in their sympathies, and therefore eager to exploit disamortization as a means of getting rid of the temporizing O'Donnell. Last but not least, Narváez had been eagerly proffering his services as an alternative prime minister. As a result it was not long before Isabel was demanding the complete annulment of the law of 1855. Well aware that this was a nonsense, on 10 October O'Donnell resigned, to be replaced by the far grimmer Narváez.

What followed was entirely to the satisfaction of queen, *camarilla*, and Church alike. The new government was perhaps the most reactionary of the entire liberal era, its Minister of the Interior being Cándido Nocedal, a devout Catholic who was drifting in the direction of Carlism, and its Minister of War, the one-time Carlist general, Antonio de Urbiztondo. In consequence, the amendments to the constitution of 1845 were jettisoned; the municipal law of 1845 was reinstated; the royal household was filled with men more amenable to Isabel and Cádiz; all measures that were held to breach the Concordat were nullified; María Cristina's estates were reinstated; disamortization was suspended; and the *consumos* and *derechos de puertas* were restored. To be fair, Narváez did issue a general amnesty, end the state of siege and convoke new parliamentary elections, but, when the latter were held in February 1857, they were marked by heavy government intervention and produced an almost wholly *moderado* assembly that effectively outlawed criticism of the government, gave the Church extensive rights with regard to the supervision of state education and voted a 33 per cent rise in the size of the army. Nor had Narváez lost his taste for brutality, an agrarian rising in the Andalusian town of Arahal being repressed with much cruelty and used as an excuse to arrest large numbers of *demócratas* and *progresistas*.

Reactionary though this programme was, it by no means satisfied the more extreme elements of the *camarilla*. However, Narváez was enough of a realist to realize that the full aims of the *camarilla* – dynastic fusion with the Carlists, a return to the statute of 1834 and the restoration of the Church's entire patrimony – was simply not a possibility. Having further angered Isabel by refusing to sanction accelerated promotion for her latest officer favourite, Enrique Puigmoltó, on 15 October 1857 he was therefore dismissed. However, if the intention was to appoint a prime minister who could launch some sort of neo-Carlist counter-revolution, then the plot miscarried: as Isabel quickly found out, there was simply no one who could possibly have implemented such a policy. After a prolonged hiatus, the queen was therefore forced to turn once more to *moderantismo*, and appointed a new government under General Joaquín Armero. This body, however, proved short-lived, being brought down in January 1858 by a fresh outbreak of intrigue in the ranks of the *doctrinarios*. A further premier was then found in the ageing *doceañista*, Istúriz, but he did not last long either: the *puritanos* had rallied en masse to the figure of O'Donnell, who was violently denouncing the *doctrinarios*, whilst at the same organizing the alliance of right-wing *progresistas* and left-wing *moderados* that was to become known as the Unión Liberal. Amongst the converts that he gained was none other than Istúriz's own Minister of the Interior, José Posada Herrera. Having first arranged matters with O'Donnell, the latter suddenly provoked a cabinet crisis that, as intended, secured the fall of Istúriz. For some days Isabel procrastinated, only to have her hand forced by Posada who now got up a riot in Madrid and sent her a wholly mendacious warning that revolution was at hand, the result being that on 30 June 1858 O'Donnell was again sworn in as premier.

Having thus secured power, O'Donnell lost no time in restoring conciliation. Thus, disamortization was resumed, whilst new elections were convoked on the basis of a revised electoral register, the resultant *cortes* being allowed to serve its full term. At the same time, so long as they accepted the central premises of the system – broadly speaking, Isabel II; the constitution, slightly modified perhaps, of 1845; and the defence of the existing social order – *doctrinarios*, *puritanos*, *progresistas*, and even *demócratas*, were welcomed into Unión Liberal and rewarded with the spoils of office. In short, doctrinal demands were kept to a minimum, and past history elided. Whilst this was certainly an improvement on Narváez, however, O'Donnell's aims remained highly regressive. The Church, for example, was allowed to establish many new religious communities and even to reoccupy a number of its old monasteries, whilst its demands for the suppression of dissent were on the whole heeded by the authorities; meanwhile, it continued to benefit from the 1857 Law of Public Instruction. Nor was O'Donnell's Spain especially permissive, the newspapers continuing to experience much censorship. Equally, the elections of 1858 were anything but free of government intervention, whilst it was during this period that the *cacique* system of electoral management acquired its classic characteristics. Last but not least, although the Unión Liberal manifesto had promised new press, electoral and municipal laws, in reality progress was absolutely non-existent.

Whilst O'Donnell's regime was by contemporary standards both legal and moderate, there is therefore much substance in the charge that Unión Liberal was little more than an exercise in pork-barrel politics whose chief object was to block reform. Whilst it was popular enough amongst its own clientele, the regime therefore felt driven to augment its prestige. We come here to the series of dramatic adventures that O'Donnell proceeded to embark upon in foreign policy. Thus, between 1858 and 1862 the army was engaged in Annam, Morocco, Mexico and Santo Domingo, and the navy against Chile and Peru. It would be unfair to say that all this was motivated by mere lust for glory – in each case there was a convincing argument for intervention – but the fact remains that Spain gained almost nothing.

If O'Donnell's adventures abroad were both futile and costly, the expense which they represented was not even supported by a period of major economic growth. In this respect, the foundations of the problems faced by Spain had been laid in the *bienio progresista*. Thus, as has already been mentioned, on 3 June 1855 the *cortes* had passed a general railway law which exempted railway construction from the restrictions the legislation of 1848 had put in the way of the formation of joint-stock companies, and in addition offered such enticements as guaranteed returns, the free importation of locomotives, rolling stock, rails and other equipment, and the possibility of major government subsidies. Meanwhile, on 26 January 1856 new laws came into force regarding the operations of banks and credit companies, the effect of which was to transform the old Banco de San Fernando into the Bank of Spain, regulate the conduct of financial operations and facilitate the establishment of new banking and credit institutions.

Thanks to these developments, the mood of confidence engendered by the return to openly conservative government was accompanied by a period of dramatic economic activity, of which perhaps the most striking aspect was the widespread construction of new railway lines. At the end of the *bienio progresista*, Spain's railways were limited to a few short lines in the vicinity of Madrid, Valencia, Cádiz, Gijón and Barcelona. Over the next ten years, thanks largely to government assistance, there was a period of massive expansion which saw the construction of the basis of the modern Spanish railway system. In all, the period 1856–68 saw the construction of 4,898 kilometres of railway compared to a mere 456 kilometres in the period 1848–56. As for the control of these lines, there emerged two giant companies, both of them very largely foreign-controlled and, in part, funded – the Norte, which ran the line from Madrid to Irun and its many subsidiaries; and the Madrid–Zaragoza–Alicante, which dominated Catalonia, the Levante and Andalucía.

In so far as any plan other than that of getting rich quickly lay behind the law of 1855, it was that railway construction should stimulate the rest of the economy. However, although it is true that many of Spain's problems were the result of poor communications and the absence of a national market, as it stood the Spanish economy simply could not sustain a railway network of the size and complexity of that which was now inaugurated. In the short term the railways therefore did not have the desired effect even in terms of the bank balances of their investors. This is not to say that there were no industrial advances at all. Thus, Catalonia continued to develop, whilst it was at this time, too, that the areas around Bilbao and Oviedo emerged as centres of heavy industry. Yet, when all this has been taken into account the fact remains not only that there was no industrial revolution, but also that even such progress as was made was actually very shaky.

Why was this the case? In brief, if one sets aside certain specific problems – cotton, for example, was badly affected by the outbreak of the American Civil War – the fact of the matter was that the relatively limited amount of capital available for investment was seriously mis-directed. With regard to Spanish capital, the prime culprit here was above all disamortization. Still worse, perhaps, the heavy investment in the land which this produced took place in conditions which ensured that the amount of capital which it generated for further investment was extremely limited. There was considerable expansion in the area under cultivation and a steady rise in grain production, but yields were very low, as much of the new land that was brought under the plough was of pretty marginal quality. So long, meanwhile, as labour remained cheap and cereal prices protected, there was no incentive to invest in better methods of production. And, so long as there was no improvement in methods, huge armies of landless labourers who might otherwise have moved to industry remained imprisoned in hopeless poverty on the great estates, a further effect of all this being that agriculture naturally consti-tuted a very poor market for Spanish industry.

Disamortization, however, should not take the full blame for the absence of a Spanish industrial revolution. The aims of the law of 1855 notwithstanding, the railway boom also proved a disaster. Thanks to the preferential conditions offered by the law's provisions, something like fifteen times the amount of capital, both domestic and foreign, was invested in the railways than in industry in the period 1856–64. Moreo-ver, except in the coal industry, which did experience a significant rise in demand, the railways did not have the sort of multiplier that was expected of them: because of the exemption of railway equipment from excise duty, it was infinitely cheaper to bring in rails, locomotives and rolling stock from abroad than to buy them in Spain. Meanwhile, construction costs were artificially high, thanks, first, to Spain's many mountains, and, second, to the adoption of a broader gauge than that which was increasingly standard elsewhere in the belief that the topography was such as to require much larger engines. Nor, of course, could the finished product generate much in the way of capital for new investment, the returns that it offered proving to be very low. All too evidently, moreover, the railway network was left saddled with serious technical deficiencies: a desire to cut construction costs and stick to the more populated areas of the country caused several important trunk routes to adopt courses that were improbably circuitous, whilst even main lines possessed only a single track. With track, engines and rolling stock alike poorly maintained for want of funds, the result was that the whole system was notoriously slow and inefficient.

Some of the details of this thesis are open to question: Spanish iron was so costly that it would have been unlikely to take off even without the extra competition; the foreign capital involved would probably not have been invested in Spain at all but for the railway law; and Spanish investors simply did not have the resources to have made much difference even had they looked to industry. However, the fact remains that O'Donnell no more brought prosperity than he did order. Thus, the countryside remained as disturbed as ever: in 1861 Seville, Huelva, Cádiz and Córdoba witnessed no fewer than 495 incidents of field burning, whilst in June of the same year there was a full-scale agrarian rising at Loja. At the same time it might also be pointed out that the combination of the railway boom with the rapid expansion of banking made corruption, and with it the risk of a serious failure of business confidence, all but endemic.

If the social and economic problems inherent in liberal Spain continued to rumble on, so did her political difficulties, the relative tranquillity of the first few years of O'Donnell's rule quickly being shattered by the unification of Italy. For *progresistas* of all shades it was axiomatic that the new state should be recognized forthwith, but this O'Donnell would not do, knowing that such a step would completely alienate Isabel II. Those *progresistas* who had rallied to the Unión Liberal – the so-called *resellados* – therefore started to become increasingly restive, a number of them – Ríos Rosas, Posada Herrera and Manuel Alonso Martínez – eventually being driven to break with the regime. Revolt, meanwhile, was not just confined to the *progresista* elements of Unión Liberal. The commander of the Spanish expeditionary force that had been sent to Mexico, General Juan Prim, had family ties with the country, and therefore quickly realized that the intervention was unlikely to be successful, in consequence withdrawing his forces to Cuba. Increasingly committed to establishing a satellite state in Mexico, Napoleon III was furious, as were the *moderado* unionists, the centrepiece of *moderado* foreign policy having always been friendship with France. Not best pleased himself, O'Donnell ordered Prim to be court martialled, only to find that he was blocked by Isabel, who had fallen out with Napoleon III over the question of who should be appointed to the new throne that had been established in Mexico, and was in consequence delighted with Prim's actions. The commander of the expeditionary force was therefore allowed to escape scot-free, the result being that O'Donnell's *moderado* allies became still more angry. Attributing the prime minister's lenience to the fact that Prim happened to be a *resellado*, indeed, many of them now broke with O'Donnell in their turn.

Much alarmed by all this, O'Donnell tried hard to conciliate the rival factions in his party by means of a major reshuffle, but it was increasingly clear that the Unión Liberal was in a state of near terminal decomposition. Moreover, it was simply impossible to contain such personal rivalries as that which divided the *progresista* Prim from the *moderado* Serrano, the only effect of concessions in one direction being to increase difficulties in another. By the end of January 1863 the new ministry was already in a state of collapse and the *cortes* virtually out of control. On 7 February O'Donnell therefore decided to seek a dissolution. By now, however, he had also lost the support of the crown, for Isabel resented a number of his ministerial changes, not to mention his refusal to tolerate the idea, which had recently resurfaced, that María Cristina should be allowed to return from exile. In consequence, she only agreed to the dissolution on conditions to which she knew O'Donnell could never accede. Exhausted and depressed, on 27 February the general resigned, his experiment in liberal union thereby being brought to an end.

Disintegration and Downfall

Given the proclivities of Isabel and her *camarilla*, only one course of action was likely in the wake of the fall of O'Donnell. Thus, not only did the queen once more invite the *moderados* to form a government, but she also selected as premier not even a *puritano*, but the *doctrinario* Marqués de Miraflores, who immediately made it clear that he intended to 'make' a more amenable *cortes* by means of fresh elections. Rightly suspecting that the contest would be conducted in conditions of extreme partiality, the *progresistas* responded by walking out. When this failed to have the desired effect of persuading the crown to abandon its opposition to a *progresista* government – although the Miraflores administration proved short-lived, it was succeeded by three further *doctrinario* cabinets under Lorenzo Arrazola, Alejandro Mon and, last but not least, Narváez – Prim and other elements began preparations for a *pronunciamiento*. That said, however, considerable elements of the party remained distinctly unhappy, whilst it should be noted that it had hardly become a revolutionary force. Prim, for example, had helped to overthrow Espartero in 1843 and even now remained very much a man of order, his rupture with the regime stemming largely from personal pique. Similarly, if Olózaga – now the 'grand old man' of the party – turned to revolt, it was because he was above all eager to supplant Espartero as hero of the masses.

Not surprisingly, similar contradictions are visible in the case of the *demócratas*. Although the years from 1856 to 1863 had been marked by a considerable degree of persecution, the party was hampered in its reaction by the serious divisions that existed in its ranks. Thus, like most of his more established colleagues, the leader of the party, Nicolás Rivero, accepted the monarchy and believed that the way forward lay in a closer relationship with the *progresistas*. However, he was increasingly being challenged by the far more radical Francisco Pi y Margall who combined support for a federal republic with a deep-rooted opposition to liberal social policy. Also inclined to republicanism was the other rising star of the party, Emilio Castelar, but, unlike Pi, he believed that the way forward was not to win the support of the masses, but rather to attract that of the *progresistas*. Unsurprisingly, the two were soon engaged in a bitter polemic. Having defeated one rival (Pi and his supporters were quickly driven from their positions), Castelar then turned on Rivero and overthrew him as leader of the party, which he then led into a revolutionary alliance with the *progresistas*. Unwilling to accept his defeat, however, Rivero launched a counterattack that had soon stripped Castelar of his victory. In short, as susceptible to intrigue as any other party, *democratismo* was temporarily out of action.

Disunited and ambivalent, the *progresistas* and *demócratas* did not represent much of a threat. Despite this, however, the queen was soon becoming increasingly alarmed. Thus, Spain was now experiencing major economic difficulties. The causes of the crisis were twofold. On the one hand, it was becoming all too clear that the railways were not going to pay anything like the dividend expected, the result being a series of banking failures and a serious run on the stock market. On the other, it was also becoming apparent that there was a hole in the government's finances: faced with the need to fund not only railway expansion, but also military adventure at a time when disamortization was being seriously curtailed, O'Donnell had been forced to rely very heavily on increased borrowing both at home and abroad. As a result the national debt rose from 13,778,000 *reales* in 1859 to 15,828,000 in 1864, the impact that this had upon the Bank of Spain being such that it was forced considerably to reduce its loans to the private sector.

Desperate to increase revenue, Narváez sought to push a forced loan through the new *cortes*, only for this twice to be rejected. Much irritated, Isabel responded by stepping in with a solution of her own in the form of a proposal for the sale of the royal patrimony, three-quarters of the proceeds of which were to go to the state and the remaining quarter to the crown. The result was uproar, much of the opposition maintaining that the queen's proposal was intended to do no more than line her own coffers. Having been particularly vociferous in his criticisms, Castelar became the target of government demands that he should be dismissed from the chair he occupied at the University of Madrid, only for these to provoke not only the resignation of the university's rector, but the outbreak of serious student disturbances. Although the Guardia Civil proved more than equal to the situation, Isabel's confidence suffered a further blow, her disquiet being redoubled when Prim, who had gone into exile, launched the first of a series of unsuccessful *pronunciamientos*. With share prices still dropping, the queen therefore once more turned to O'Donnell.

Installed as premier on 21 June 1865, O'Donnell immediately introduced a series of measures designed to conciliate the opposition. Many of those who had split from the Unión Liberal in the period 1860–3 were invited to join the government or otherwise mollified; Castelar and his supporters were amnestied and reinstated; civil-service tenure was strengthened as a protection against political appointments and dismissals; a new electoral law was introduced that tripled the number of electors by reducing the property qualification; and Italy was finally recognized as an independent state. Sincere though these efforts were, they were not enough. In the first place, the *progresistas* remained intransigent. Whilst most of the party's notables were now strongly in favour of re-entering the *cortes*, the rank and file had become thoroughly enthused with the idea of revolution (it did not help that they were being egged on by Olózaga, who was determined on the one hand to avenge the events of 1843 and on the other to counteract Prim's growing ascendancy). Meanwhile, there was a growing conviction amongst some of the party's younger leaders that backing down was simply impossible if the *progresistas* were to retain their credibility as a political movement. On 29 October a noisy meeting of the party therefore voted to continue the boycott.

Meanwhile, Spain was sliding into an economic and financial crisis that was growing ever deeper. The whole of Europe having been gripped by a slump, both foreign investment and the prices of the primary products that formed the basis of Spain's exports were badly affected. After levelling off somewhat in the summer of 1865, the fall in share prices rapidly intensified. At the same time, of course, the government's deficit grew still further, the result being a general recession. Railway construction was paralysed, many banks and credit societies were forced to close their doors, and industrial production slumped, the trouble being especially severe in those areas of the economy – Andalucian iron, for example – that had already been experiencing contraction. Meanwhile, 1866 had also seen the start of a serious drought that ruined the next two harvests, increased the price of wheat by some 45 per cent, and plunged large parts of the country into an old-fashioned subsistence crisis. The palliatives adopted by the authorities being quite insufficient to resolve the problem, there was a massive upsurge in banditry and other acts of disorder.

Some historians insist that the impact of the crisis has been exaggerated, but all that can really be said is that it was not the chief trigger in the downfall of the regime: not only had Prim been committed to a rising for some time, but the two attempts at a *pronunciamiento* that were made in 1866 received little in the way of popular support. Of these the first was a classic officer revolt engineered by Prim, but the second – the revolt that broke out in the San Gil barracks in Madrid on 22 June – was not only centred on the rank and file but also organized by the *demócratas*, and might have been expected to have awoken a much greater echo than was actually the case.

For all that, the regime did nothing to help itself by its management of affairs. Bitterly resentful of O'Donnell's 'treason', Isabel had for some time been exploring the possibility of getting rid of him, and in consequence allowed herself to be persuaded that the San Gil rising was entirely the general's fault. When O'Donnell presented her with a list of new senators for her approval a few days later, she therefore turned it down, this public snub leaving him no option but once again to resign, and all the more so as the new appointments had been designed to smooth the way for proposals that he had just put forward to the effect that civil liberties should be temporarily suspended to allow the government to deal with the political and economic crisis more effectively.

To replace O'Donnell, the queen once again had recourse to Narváez, only for the latter to behave in a fashion that was little short of suicidal. In the first place he immediately embarked on a policy of persecution that not only forced most of the leaders of the *progresistas* and *demócratas* to flee abroad, but persuaded the latter to restore the alliance engineered by Castelar (also instrumental here was the fact that the failure of the San Gil revolt persuaded the *demócratas* that success would depend on the support of the generals). Meanwhile, the *cortes* was prorogued; the electorate slashed; the municipalities purged; the press subjected to fiercer restrictions than ever; and the army subjected to numerous changes of personnel. As for the rump of Unión Liberal, its leaders were banished from Madrid – O'Donnell himself had gone into exile in

Biarritz – and the party punished by fresh elections that were marked by extreme levels of chicanery and government intervention. Finally, as if all this was not enough, Narváez succeeded in alienating many of the *moderados'* own supporters by doubling the land tax in a further attempt to increase revenue.

The end came on 5 November 1867. Thus far, O'Donnell had been steadfastly refusing to join the conspiracy, but on that date he died of typhus. With his passing there was nothing to stop his increasingly angry followers, of whom the most important were such generals as Serrano, Dulce and Ros de Olano, from joining the ranks of the conspiracy. Increasingly isolated, on 23 April 1868 Isabel lost even the support of Narváez who had fallen ill with double pneumonia and now followed O'Donnell to the grave. Nothing could now stop the onset of revolution, and especially not the appointment of the much distrusted Luis González Bravo as the old general's replacement (the new prime minister had begun his career as a radical, but in 1843 had betrayed the *progresistas* by acting as a 'stalking horse' for Narváez). Almost unbelievably, the new premier actually succeeded in adding to the queen's list of enemies: not only did a number of particularly maladroit promotions increase the number of malcontents in the army, but cuts in the naval budget angered many admirals as well. Even worse was the ineptitude shown by González Bravo with regard to the *unionista* generals. Given that they could be safely assumed to be conspiring against the regime, to have them all suddenly arrested in the early morning of 7 July 1868 was one thing, but to dispatch them to the Canary Islands, from which it would be relatively easy for them to join the opposition, quite another.

Things were now moving inexorably in favour of Prim and the more moderate *progresistas*, and all the more so as they now had less need to call on the services of the lower classes: indeed, Rivero, Pi, Castelar and the rest of the *demócrata* leadership were completely excluded from what was going on. Satisfied that he could count on the support of the generals who had been sent to the Canaries and assured that preparations for revolt were well under way, on 12 September Prim set sail from London to join the commander of the frigate *Zaragoza*. On 18 September the two pronounced at Cádiz, being joined the next day by the bulk of the *unionista* generals. In Madrid, meanwhile, González Bravo resigned and went into exile in France, whereupon a new cabinet was formed under the still loyal General José Gutiérrez de la Concha. Though city after city and garrison after garrison were declaring against the queen, the issue was decided on the battlefield: marching north from Cádiz under General Serrano, on 28 September such forces as the rebels had been able to muster collided with their loyalist counterparts at Alcolea and secured a decisive victory. The next day Isabel fled to France, whilst on 3 October the capital was entered by the victorious Serrano. The Bourbons, or so it seemed, were no more.

The Revolution of the Oligarchy

What, then, had brought down Isabel II? At the most simple level, of course, the answer is that, thanks in large part to her own wilfulness and stupidity, the queen had squandered her inheritance. Influenced by a *camarilla* whose nature could not but be a cause of serious provocation to even the most moderate liberals, she had earned the fixed enmity of the *progresistas* and *demócratas* alike by a determination to exclude them from office that quite ignored the fact that many of their members were more than open to integration with the regime. Still worse, perhaps, she had constantly intrigued behind the back of her most loyal servants, the result being that they were gradually filled with a conviction that Isabel's survival on the throne was simply incompatible with the solution of the immense difficulties that Spain faced by the late 1860s.

However, if many of Isabel's problems were the fruit of her own shortcomings, to regard her as the root of all evil would be superficial. If the queen certainly made matters infinitely worse than might otherwise have been the case, she cannot be blamed for the basic faults of the political system that she inherited. Mere collections of notables with little in the way of a clear ideology, neither of the two main parties had the cohesion to rule Spain in isolation for any length of time, and yet neither would willingly surrender power to the other. Moreover, given the fact that the chief goal of any Spanish politician was essentially to secure office for his own sake, it was never likely that attempts at liberal union would be any more successful in achieving the stability that was required, for, whichever factions were rewarded, there were always others who were left feeling resentful and disgruntled.

Riddled with faults and contradictions though it was, however, the Isabelline regime was far stronger than it seemed. By the 1860s it was confronted with what at first sight seemed a formidable opposition in the form of a well-established democratic party, a radical press and an incipient labour movement, whilst successive waves of disamortization had transformed large areas of Spain into a veritable tinderbox. Appearances, however, were deceptive. Formidable a force though the radical movement could be, it was bitterly divided and unable to secure power. If the Isabelline regime was eventually overthrown, then, it was not because of pressure from without, but rather disintegration from within.

In this process, of course, the army played a crucial role. Elevated to the status of power-brokers, generals such as Espartero, Narváez, O'Donnell, Serrano and Prim became major players on the political scene, whilst at the same time constantly vying for influence amongst themselves. In itself a source of further factionalism, this development also provided the means of political change, for the *progresistas* and *moderados* were no more capable of securing a change of regime than the radicals. Hence the difference between the fortunes of Isabel II in 1854 and 1868: whereas in the former year virtually no general could be found who wished to see her overthrown, in the latter there were all too many.

The revolution of 1868 – *la gloriosa*, as it became known – was above all a movement designed to secure the removal of a liability from the throne. That said, there was no agreement amongst the rebels as to what should replace Isabel. Some of the *demócratas*, certainly, wanted a republic, but in this, as in everything else, they were divided, whilst the fact was that both they and the crowd were but bit players in the drama unleashed by Prim and his fellow generals. For the rest, whilst there was general agreement that there should be a constitutional monarchy, some favoured Isabel's sister, Luisa Fernanda, and others a foreign prince. In so far as the planning of *la gloriosa* was concerned, all this was carefully elided, it being promised only that the definitive settlement would be left to a constituent assembly elected by universal manhood suffrage. Given the manifest divisions within the revolutionary movement, in short, whatever else happened, Spain was unlikely to be entering a period of either concord or stability.

7

The Revolutionary *Sexenio*

The Madhouse

Shortly before his abdication, Amadeo of Savoy, the young Italian prince eventually brought in to replace Isabel II, is supposed to have remarked that Spain had become a madhouse. A monarch who prided himself on his constitutionalism, his despair is entirely understandable. Thus, the coalition that had overthrown Isabel had almost immediately disintegrated, leaving the revolution with no basis for stable government. With matters gravely complicated by the outbreak of a major revolt in Cuba and the proclamation of a republic in Spain herself, still worse was to follow in that the country descended into not one but two civil wars. Not surprisingly, the result was renewed military intervention, and the restoration of the Bourbon dynasty in the person of Isabel's son, Alfonso XII. In less than six years, then, the wheel had come full circle. Nevertheless, the period from 1868 to 1874 was of immense importance. Possessed at last of mass support, Spanish radicalism sought to challenge the liberal system head on, only to find itself unable to carry the day. As a result, the heirs to *moderantismo* and *progresismo* were left to define Spain in their own image, the iniquitous effects of disamortization in consequence being left to fester *ad infinitum*. In short, the *sexenio* was the last hope of palliating the liberal revolution, and, by extension, the pivotal moment in the history of modern Spain.

The Balance of Forces

Before discussing the *sexenio*, we must examine the forces that stood behind the overthrow of Isabel II. For erstwhile *unionistas* such as General Serrano, the goals of the revolution had effectively been secured with the departure of Isabel. Slow to join the conspiracy, they wished only for a moderate regime based on the constitution of 1845, and were inclined to look no further for a replacement for Isabel II than her ten-year-old son, Alfonso, her sister, Luisa Fernanda, or her brother-in-law, the Duque de Montpensier. Rather more committed to some form of political reform were General Prim and the *progresistas*. Here too, however, there was little pressure for fundamental change, the manifesto that Prim had issued at the start of the revolution having done little more than demand an end to corruption and greater respect for civil liberty. On the right, then, of the revolutionary coalition were two parties whose slogan of 'Spain with honour' amounted to little more than a figleaf for the perpetuation of a slightly modified version of the existing political system. For a commitment to root-and-branch transformation, it is necessary to look to the *demócratas*, and, more particularly, their off-shoots, the republicans. Thus, in brief, the two groups were clamouring for a thorough-going revolution. Setting aside the question of the mon-archy, on which they were divided, this would have seen a programme of reform that met the grievances of the *populacho* in full. Yet here, too, there were many problems. As opportunist as any *progresista*, Rivero was to prove only too willing to compromise with the forces of reaction. As for the republicans, they were deeply divided between the followers of Castelar and Pi y Margall, the only mitigating factor being that years of argument over the form that a republic should take had been settled in favour of those who wanted a federal state.

To understand the situation that pertained within the ranks of repub-licanism, it is necessary to examine the figures of Francisco Pi y Margall and Emilio Castelar. A Catalan of humble origin born in 1824, Pi had come under the influence of Hegel and Proudhon, rejected Catholicism, and in 1847 embarked on a career in the capital as a literary critic. Rapidly becoming involved in radical journalism, by 1854 he had become an influential voice in the radical camp. As such, however, he was hardly a comfortable presence. A stark and austere man who was utterly indifferent to luxury and personal advancement, he regarded the person-alism and corruption of the Spanish political system with total contempt. Becoming increasingly concerned that the *demócratas* would inevitably be sucked into its maw, he therefore began to agitate for a rupture of the party's alliance with the *progresistas*. By the early 1860s, meanwhile, his ideas had coalesced around certain fundamental principles of which the most important was that Spain would experience neither freedom nor social justice until the state had been replaced by a federation of regional communities (it was no coincidence in this respect that Pi was himself a Catalan). Castelar was for the time being prepared to go along with this, but for all that there were some issues on which he and Pi remained deeply divided. Whilst he was much inclined to sentimentalize the com-mon people and envisage a republic as a veritable heaven upon earth, for example, as a product of the bourgeoisie Castelar continued to conceive of society in essentially elitist terms, and was therefore deeply hostile to Pi's programme of social reform. Wedded to the concept of *laissez faire*, meanwhile, he at heart remained not only an unreconstructed Spanish nationalist, but a centralist whose ideal was a unitary republic.

In 1868, then, the *demócrata* camp was in a distinctly precarious position. This, however, is hardly the impression that is obtained from a superficial consideration of the events of *la gloriosa*. Thus, ever since their formation, the *demócratas* had been seeking to reach out to the urban and rural populace through the publication of a series of more or less ephemeral newspapers which sought to popularize the ideas of proto-socialism. Through a variety of secret societies, cultural institutes and workers' associations, meanwhile, attempts were made to give the *demócratas* the potential to raise a popular revolt. Whilst it is difficult to quantify the effects of this activity, by the 1860s Spain therefore had an incipient labour movement that was finding expression in a mixture of trade-union organization, agrarian unrest and urban radicalism. Thanks to the events of the 1860s, moreover, this process of politicization was taken a step further. Following the San Gil rising, Narváez had abolished the right of association and imposed a blanket ban on all strikes and demonstrations. In the context of the crisis of 1866–8, however, the impact of such measures was extremely serious. With the result a further boost for the *demócratas*, Prim's revolt led to a series of popular insurrections. This process having been accompanied by the formation of revolutionary juntas, these bodies proceeded to order the closure or demolition of many churches, the immediate abolition of the *consumos* and *derechas de puertas*, and the formation of popular militias. All this, meanwhile, took place amidst triumphant demonstrations, acts of anti-clericalism, and land occupations. Far from being solely a military affair of the sort envisaged by General Prim, *la gloriosa* therefore also encompassed a vigorous popular movement, the key question being whether this could succeed in imposing its agenda upon the revolution as a whole.

Aftermath of Revolution

The immediate aftermath of the revolution was one of much confusion, but already trouble was brewing. In Madrid two juntas had actually been formed in the wake of the battle of Alcolea, the one composed solely of *progresistas* and *unionistas*, and the other solely of *demócratas*. Following the arrival of the victorious Serrano, it was agreed that a new body should be elected by universal suffrage, only for the radicals to find that they only won a quarter of the seats. With the radicals also excluded from the new government established by Serrano, a clash could not be long delayed. Matters eventually came to a head in three mass meetings held between 11 and 25 October. Attended by as many as 10,000 militants, these essentially resolved that the *demócratas* should declare for the cause of a federal republic and elected a new central committee from which the increasingly distrusted Rivero was excluded. Much angered, the latter promptly declared for the principle of constitutional monarchy and opened negotiations with the *unionistas* and *progresistas* for the formation of a new party that would draw all the monarchist elements of the revolutionary coalition together, the result being the emergence of the Partido Monárquico–Democrático. Within a mere two months, in short, the revolutionary coalition had fractured beyond repair.

As the autumn wore on, these splits deepened. On the one hand, the government formally accepted large parts of the revolutionary programme – religious freedom, for example, was guaranteed, whilst a series of decrees expelled the Jesuits, dissolved all religious communities established since 1837, and prohibited even those which were legally tolerated from owning property. On the other, however, it seemed determined to curb the revolution. Thus, although the pill was sweetened by the incorporation of many of their members into the new *ayuntamientos* and *diputaciones* that had been put together in the wake of the uprising, the juntas were dissolved and many of their measures revoked, whilst a concerted attempt was made to disarm the militia. Much to the detriment of the radicals, the voting age was made twenty-five rather than twenty, whilst their ability to foment mob action was dissipated by the enforced return to their *pueblos* of the large numbers of destitute *campesinos* who had flocked to the cities in search of work. Also alarming here was the virtual monopoly handed to the *progresistas* and *unionistas* when it came to the appointment of the revolution's civil governors and captains general. Meanwhile, many items in the popular programme were watered down or allowed to remain a dead letter: not only was there no attempt to separate Church and state, but the demolition of *conventos* – an important source of work for the unemployed – was curtailed, whilst the salt and tobacco monopolies were restored, and the *consumos* replaced by a new poll tax payable by all those over the age of fourteen.

As efforts to assist the population were very limited, the republicans quickly acquired a considerable degree of mass support. Given that in many areas the concept of a federal republic was connected not just with social discontent but also other issues – in Barcelona, for example, it appealed to the Catalan revivalists who had been starting to become active since the late 1850s – the municipal elections that were held on 18 December brought a series of dramatic republican victories: in Seville, for example, the republican vote outnumbered its monarchist counterpart by seven to one. Despite considerable reluctance on the part of their leadership, the radicals did not confine themselves to political agitation alone. A variety of factors having particularly radicalized the lower classes in Cádiz and Málaga, the suppression of the militia provoked major revolts that were only suppressed at the cost of several days of fierce fighting. Meanwhile, towns and cities as disparate as Barcelona, Valencia, Marbella, Seville, Aranjuez, Granada, Almadén, Carmona, Salamanca and Astorga witnessed serious strikes, whilst much of the country continued to experience a variety of agrarian disturbances. As the response of the authorities was almost invariably one of repression, the situation was polarized still further.

To make matters worse, meanwhile, the crisis had by now spread to the island of Cuba. Largest and most valuable of Spain's remaining colonial possessions, Cuba had in the years since Latin American independence emerged as the greatest producer of sugar in the world. As such, she had become dominated by a narrow stratum of planters and merchants, the rest of the population being composed of a mixture of poor whites, mulattos and negros. Of the coloured population, meanwhile, nearly a third were still slaves. Despite its wealth, however, the plantocracy had no political power, Cuba being ruled through the person of an all-powerful Captain General. Unrest had therefore started to grow amongst the planters, but racial fears had led them to confine themselves to a mild reformism. For much of the population, and especially the farmers of the eastern half of the island, who were both poorer and often of mixed race, this was not enough, however. When it became clear that Madrid was obdurate, preparations therefore began for revolt. For a moment it seemed that *la gloriosa* might save the day, for Prim and Serrano were both known to favour a policy of conciliation, but, in a fashion that was to be typical of events to come, the Captain General adopted so belligerent a position that by October 1868 war had begun.

For *la gloriosa*, the Cuban revolt, which plunged the colony into a savage war that was to last for the next ten years, was little short of cataclysmic. Initially, however, the impact was limited, attention being centred on the constituent elections convoked for January 1869. Despite considerable government intervention, the federalists did relatively well, winning some sixty-nine seats, the bulk of which were concentrated in the traditional radical strongholds of the east and south. However, the *progresistas* and *unionistas* between them gained 228 seats, the result being that Spain was given a statute that retained the principles of a constitutional monarchy, an established Church, and an army recruited by compulsory military service, whilst failing to restore such radical shibboleths as the national militia. Much had been obtained – the constitution included such major advances as full religious freedom, and the extension of the vote to all males over the age of twenty-five – but neither the republicans nor their sympathizers could possibly regard it with much pleasure.

By the time that the constitution was approved, however, Castelar and Pi had been presented with an even more potent weapon. As we have seen, opposition to conscription had been a central part of the *demócrata* programme, and there is no doubt that it had played a major part in the popularization of radical politics that had occurred since *la gloriosa*. Hence the importance of the Cuban revolution. Thus, the situation in the colony had been going from bad to worse. Initially, Prim had sought a negotiated settlement, only to be frustrated by the plantocracy who now organized a revolt of their own with the aid of the 30,000-strong volunteer militia which they had raised to fight the rebels. Forced to agree to a military solution, the Spaniards found the task quite beyond them: not only were the loyalist forces insufficient to subdue the rebels' rugged heartlands, but so savage were the activities of the loyalists that the rebels were driven into a war to the death. Besieged with demands from cotton interests that he should restore order, on 25 March 1869 Prim was forced to decree a *quinta* of some 25,000 men.

For the radicals this was the final betrayal. Placed in a difficult situation – apart from anything else, the autumn of 1868 had, as we shall see, seen the first stirrings of a revolutionary movement that was wholly opposed to any involvement in bourgeois politics – the republicans' only hope was to embark on the course of popular insurrection. Neither Pi nor Castelar being prepared to consider such a course, they therefore began to lose control, the summer of 1869 witnessing the emergence of the so-called 'pactist movement'. Essentially a series of regional alliances dedicated to defending the revolution's 'content' by force of arms, 'pactism' had the effect of handing the initiative to a variety of lesser figures for whom revolt was the only means of securing their personal aims, whether they were simple personal advancement, the imposition of a more radical agenda, or the wholesale conquest of republicanism in the name of socialism. Thus, the ringleaders of the earlier revolts in Cádiz and Málaga included José Paul y Angulo, a wealthy *jerezano* client of General Prim, who believed that he had not been sufficiently rewarded; Fernando Garrido, a writer and journalist who had for many years been the *demócratas'* most radical thinker on social issues; and the leading anar-chist 'apostle', Fermín Salvochea. Under the leadership of such men, in the course of the early autumn Barcelona, Tarragona, Valencia, Zar-agoza and a variety of smaller places scattered across Catalonia, Andalucía and the Levant experienced popular risings, only for the rebels in each case to be quickly suppressed.

Whilst it is difficult to generalize, the rather pathetic showing made by these risings suggests that federalism was beginning to lose its grip. In part this was the result of marginally better economic conditions, but it also reflected the influence of Bakuninism. Following the arrival of an Italian bakuninist named Giuseppe Fanelli, in December 1868 a branch of the International had been constituted at a meeting in Madrid, and in the course of 1869 further branches of the movement were established in such towns and cities as Barcelona, Cádiz, Valladolid and Jérez de la Frontera. In June 1870 a general congress was held in Barcelona, and from this in turn there emerged a national organization – the Federación Regional Española de la Asociación Internacional Trabajadora (FRE). At the same time, meanwhile, thanks in large part to the fact that the *internacionalistas* were dominated by disciples of Bakunin, the congress also voted that the FRE should not participate in politics. Whilst many supporters of the FRE – a movement which in any case never represented more than a fraction of the populace – ignored the resolution, the fact remains that disillusion was spreading.

If the risings of the autumn of 1869 prompted ever deeper divisions on the left of Spanish politics, on the right they concentrated minds on the need to find a new monarch. In this respect, matters were greatly complicated by the fact that both the *unionistas* and the *progresistas* had their own candidates in the persons of Isabel II's brothers-in-law, the Duque de Montpensier and the Duque de Sevilla. However, the two dukes soon cancelled one another out – in fact, they fought a duel in which Sevilla was shot dead – whereupon Prim was left to find the foreign prince whom he had always felt it was advisable to place upon the throne. This proved to be much harder than Prim expected, whilst his efforts also had the quite unexpected effect of sparking off the Franco-Prussian war of 1870–1, but a suitable candidate was eventually found in the person of the twenty-five-year-old Duke of Aosta. A younger son of King Vittorio Emmanuele of Italy, on 16 November 1870 he was duly proclaimed Amadeo I by the *cortes* by a majority of ninety-two.

Amadeo the Brief

Prim having provided Spain with a new king, it seemed that stability might now be restored, and all the more so as Amadeo was a conscientious young man who was determined to be the very model of a constitutional monarch. However, in reality all was far from well, the precarious nature of Amadeo's situation being graphically underlined by the fact that he was greeted by the appalling news that Prim had just been mortally wounded by a group of unknown assassins (though his guilt was never proved, the culprit appears to have been the ambitious and resentful Paul y Angulo). If this was not bad enough, Amadeo also found himself threatened on a new front. Relatively quiescent since its defeat in 1849, Carlism once again raised its head. Montemolín having died in 1861, his claim to the throne had passed to his nephew, who had assumed the title 'Carlos VII'. Calculating that the revolution would produce such chaos that he would ultimately be offered the throne, the latter had since 1868 been cultivating a moderate image, whilst ordering his followers to engage in the electoral process. Organized as the Asociación Católica-Monárquica, they had obtained twenty seats in the *cortes* and won over a number of right-wing *moderados*. However, the road of legality had always been a difficult one to follow, whilst the accession of Amadeo made it virtually inevitable that Carlos VII would turn to revolt, the only thing that still held him back being the need to gather arms and money. As well as the revolt in Cuba, in short, Spain was about to be confronted by civil war.

Needless to say, the Carlists were not Amadeo's only enemies on the right, for another claimant to the throne existed in the person of Isabel II's thirteen-year-old son, Alfonso. Initially the Bourbon cause was possessed of the loyalty only of certain elements of the court aristocracy and the army. However, it was soon swelled by a variety of reinforcements including Catholics outraged by the choice of an Italian monarch, Catalan industrialists eager to maintain the link with Cuba, and representatives of the Cuban plantocracy. As a result there emerged a vigorous alfonsist movement known as the Liga Nacional which married ferocious hostility to compromise in Cuba with a series of plots and conspiracies.

In the short term, however, the most immediate problem faced by Amadeo was the tension that was increasingly disrupting the government. Thus, Prim's veto of the Montpensier candidature had combined with his manipulation of promotions within the officer corps to alienate the *unionistas*. In consequence, much to the fury of Serrano, the latter's representation in the government had been steadily reduced and that of the *demócratas* increased. With Prim out of the way, the pendulum began to swing back in the opposite direction, for there was no choice but to appoint Serrano prime minister. Yet, for all that, the latter had still to include both the *progresistas* and the *demócratas* in his government, whilst the former gained an easy triumph in the elections called by Serrano in March 1871. No longer in any need of *unionismo*, the *progresista* leader, Ruiz Zorrilla, precipitated a breach with the general, and on 10 July 1871 succeeded in replacing him as prime minister.

However, at this point serious splits developed in the ranks of the *progresistas*. Ruiz Zorrilla had for some time been under threat from the rising figure of Práxedes Sagasta, an erstwhile radical who had won a reputation as an unscrupulous political manager. Inherent in the clash that now developed was an intense degree of personal rivalry, but at the same time there were also serious differences of analysis. Thus, Ruiz Zorrilla believed in an alliance with the *demócratas*, and Sagasta in an alliance with the *unionistas*; meanwhile, much influenced by years of mistrust of the court, Ruiz Zorrilla wanted the monarch to be kept on the sidelines, whilst the more pragmatic Sagasta believed that he should rather be brought to the forefront as a bastion of order and authority. With the parties' deputies flocking to join one camp or the other, the result was that the *progresistas* divided into two factions known as the *calamares* and the *radicales*. Meanwhile, the confusion also spread to the *unionistas* and the *demócratas*: in the ranks of the former, tension developed between the *puros*, who wanted to remain an independent conservative party, and the *fronterizos*, who believed that it would be better to join Sagasta; meanwhile, amongst the *demócratas*, opinion was divided between a moderate faction willing to cooperate with Ruiz Zorrilla – the *riveristas* – and a more radical one – the *cimbrios* – who were inclined to look towards the republicans.

Within a year of his arrival, then, the coalition that had crowned Amadeo had completely disintegrated. In theory, of course, this should have left the new dynasty at the mercy of its opponents, but, gain some success in the elections of 1871 though it had, the left, at least, was in no position to exploit the situation. Thus, already divided over matters of social policy and their response to the coming of Amadeo I, the republicans were thrown into confusion by the news that on 18 March Paris had risen in revolt and declared itself to be a self-governing 'commune'. For many republicans, of course, the idea of Paris in the grip of a radical revolution was extremely exciting, but for men such as Castelar the idea was anathema. At the same time the eventual failure of the Parisian revolt placed Spanish republicanism in a difficult position in that it had always held that success was only attainable in the context of the establishment of federal republics in France, Portugal and Italy. The result was that republicanism, too, began to fragment. Thus, whilst the left of the party – the so-called *intransigentes* – held out against any accommodation with the monarchy and loudly demanded an immediate revolt, Castelar headed a rival faction – the *benévolos* – which advocated an alliance with the *radicales* in the hope that they might ultimately be won over to republicanism. Implicit in this programme was first of all a tacit acceptance of the monarchy; secondly, the elimination of all traces of social radicalism from the republican programme; and, thirdly, the eclipse of Pi, of whom Castelar remained bitterly jealous. Whilst steadily growing in influence, meanwhile, Spanish socialism was still hostile to participation in the political process, the emergence of the *benévolos* and repression of the *communards* having if anything increased its suspicions of the republicans. Even had the FRE's response been more favourable, moreover, it was in no position to be of much help as it was not only experiencing increasing police harassment, but also suffering from divisions of its own. Thus, tensions had arisen over the question of strike action, whilst the Bakuninists were coming under attack from Marxist emissaries who had been sent to Spain to counteract their influence. Very soon yet another bitter controversy was raging, this time between the Marxist *autoritarios* and the Bakuninist *anti-autoritarios*, the fact being that the FRE was out of the fight (not that this stopped the *cortes* from making it illegal).

With the republicans and socialists in chaos, and the Carlists not yet ready for open revolt, Amadeo was relatively safe from open attack, but it was not long before his situation had deteriorated still further. Thus, in October 1871 Ruiz Zorrilla was forced to resign following humiliation in the *cortes* at the hands of Sagasta. Forming a new ministry in alliance with the *fronterizos*, the latter then convoked new elections. However, all that these did was to discredit Amadeo and alienate the *radicales* and *demócratas*, Sagasta having secured a solid majority of *fronterizos* and *calamares* by means of the most blatant intervention in the electoral process. Seizing on the election results as a pretext, meanwhile, the Carlists rose in revolt. Nor was Sagasta even able to maintain his position: accused of peculation a few days after the opening of the new *cortes*, he was deserted by the *fronterizos* and forced to resign. Power now went to Serrano, but the latter overplayed his hand by demanding a suspension of constitutional guarantees. This being more than Amadeo was prepared to concede, Serrano went the way of Sagasta, the king now being left no option but to summon Ruiz Zorrilla, who was in addition granted the decree of dissolution necessary to 'make' a new *cortes*.

With the government majority of 236 *unionistas* and *calamares* of the previous *cortes* replaced by a new one of 224 *radicales*, it again seemed that order might now be restored. However, in reality the administration was more isolated than ever, Zorrilla proceeding to make matters still worse by embarking on a programme of radical reform designed to outbid the *demócratas* and republicans alike. Thus, he cut the subsidy paid to the Church, revivified the militia, and set about the abolition of slavery. In the army, meanwhile, a series of openly political promotions and appointments bid fair to place it firmly under *progresista* control. In this respect, however, Ruiz Zorrilla went too far. Amongst the men selected for prominent commands was one Baltasar Hidalgo de Quintana, an artillery officer who six years earlier had been implicated in the San Gil uprising. Whipped up by *alfonsino*, *unionista* and colonialist opponents of the government, his fellow gunners engaged in a series of protests against this decision. Threatened by divisions in his own government, and determined to break the independence of the artillery (unlike in the rest of the army, promotion in its ranks was entirely dependent on seniority, and therefore immune to political manipulation), Zorrilla dismissed its entire officer corps.

All this was too much for Amadeo. With the country in the grip of insurrection and civil war, the army increasingly disaffected, every political party split asunder, and constitutional government impossible, he abdicated in disgust and left for home. This was something that Zorrilla had neither wanted nor anticipated, and in consequence he immediately resigned. Desperate to save something from the wreckage, the *radicales*, *riveristas* and *cimbrios* all abandoned their monarchist loyalties, the result being that by 11 February 1873, Spain had become a republic.

The First Spanish Republic

Whilst republicans greeted the dramatic events of 8–11 February 1873 with delight, the latter plunged Spain into a period of anarchy from which republicanism was to take generations to recover. Thus, the problems faced by the new regime can only be described as calamitous. Apart from anything else Spain was now engaged in two major wars. In Cuba a succession of generals had succeeded in obtaining a considerable degree of success against the rebels, but at least 10,000 guerrillas were still at large. In Spain herself, meanwhile, the Carlists had quickly taken control of large parts of Navarre and the Basque provinces. All this could not but place a heavy strain upon the treasury, but this was already burdened by a debt of 106,000,000 *pesetas* (the *peseta* – a coin worth four *reales* – had replaced the latter as the basic monetary unit on 1 July 1870), whilst revenue was simply not rising fast enough to make good the shortfall. Indeed, so heavy was the interest on the national debt that it absorbed more than half the budget. Even then the government fell more and more behind, but this only made the fresh borrowing that was essential still more expensive. And, last but not least, the harvest of 1872 having failed, there was a fresh wave of social unrest.

If the military, financial and economic circumstances which the republic inherited were extremely difficult, her political situation was little better. Thus, the republicans had been taken completely unawares by the fall of Amadeo, and were clearly no longer the force they had once been. At the same time, both old and new antagonisms rent the party: hostility between *benévolos* and *intransigentes* continued to smoulder; meanwhile, the leadership wanted to postpone all changes of personnel until the election of a constituent *cortes* whereas the grassroots wanted the preferment which they considered to be their due straightaway. Moreover, they also faced the hostility of the *radicales* and *demócratas*, who wanted at least to ensure that the republic was a unitary one.

If disunity was guaranteed, lurking in the wings were forces that were irredeemably hostile to the republic, including, most obviously, the *calamares*, *unionistas*, and *moderados*, not to mention the powerful colonial interest (one of the few things that united Spanish republicanism was a determination to abolish slavery and grant autonomy to Cuba and Puerto Rico). Conspiracy was therefore inevitable, whilst the danger which this posed was greatly increased by the fact that there was also much enmity to the republic in the Church and the army. Whilst the former had been maintaining a low profile, it was unlikely to remain inert in the face of the threat to separate Church and state. As for the army, meanwhile, whatever their political views, few officers could be happy at the prospect of losing the *quinta*.

Within a few days the dangers of the situation had become all too apparent. Thus, placed in the hands of a lack-lustre compromise candidate in the person of Estanislao Figueras, the government found itself faced by an impossible dilemma, in that it could either invite counter-revolution by pandering to the *populacho*, or squander all hope of mass support by seeking to conciliate the centre and right. Not surprisingly, it was the latter option which was chosen: whilst the voting age was lowered from twenty-five to twenty-one, everything possible was done to maintain the strictest order, and no attempt was made to satisfy radical demands for the local authorities to be remodelled.

If this measured programme accommodated one set of political realities, it took no account of another. Thus, the news of the abdication had been greeted in many places with rioting and demonstrations, the imposition of republican *ayuntamientos*, and the creation of revolutionary juntas. Confronted by the threat of social revolution, the government responded with a mixture of repression and demagoguery. Thus, whilst the new organs of power that had sprung up in the wake of 11 February were immediately suppressed, a series of decrees abolished the *quinta*, restored the militia, ordered the formation of eighty battalions of volunteers and suspended the army's code of discipline. Accompanying all this was a fresh wave of politically motivated promotions and appointments and the removal of no fewer than 400 officers on suspicion of *alfonsismo*. Had all this produced a dramatic shift in the fortunes of the Carlist War, it might just have been acceptable, but in fact the result was chaos: there proved to be too few rifles to arm the militia; few recruits could be found for the new volunteer battalions; and the news that the *quinta* was to go sparked off widespread indiscipline amongst those conscripts who were not immediately allowed to go home. At the front, in short, things went from bad to worse, whilst the bulk of the officer corps was deeply alienated, many of its members effectively going on strike and starting to plot against the republic.

It was not just the army that turned to revolt. Much alarmed by their lack of influence – they had only two seats in the cabinet – the *radicales* decided that they stood little chance in the elections to a constituent *cortes* that had immediately been announced, and in consequence turned to conspiracy themselves. Already possessed of a number of military supporters – by far the most valuable was the Captain General of New Castile, Manuel Pavía – they also won over Serrano by hinting that they would make him president of a unitary republic. With everything in place, on 23 April they therefore mobilized such battalions of the Madrid militia as they could and seized control of the capital's bullring. However, the result was failure, the government taking such decisive action against the rebellion that Serrano and Pavía decided to do nothing, the rebels quickly being forced to surrender.

Serrano, Sagasta, Rivero and many other figures on the centre and right now deciding either to flee into exile or to withdraw from politics, the republicans obtained a great triumph in the elections to the constituent *cortes*, winning 348 out of the 377 seats on offer and gaining four times as many votes as they had ever gained in the past. However, in almost every way these results were misleading – not only did a turnout of only 25 per cent seriously call into question the real popularity of federalism, but the increase in its vote was due largely to the reduction in the voting age. Furthermore, the republicans were even more deeply split than before. Thus, on the right was a group headed by Castelar that opposed both federalism and social revolution. On the left, the rump of the old *intransigentes* were demanding the immediate establishment of a federal republic. In between the two, meanwhile, were Pi and a loose and ill-defined centre in whom sympathy for federalism and social reform vied with opportunism and a desire for a strong central government that could defeat Carlism.

If this is a reasonable picture of the general position which confronted the Figueras government when the *cortes* met on 1 June 1873, it would be wrong to over-systematize the situation. Thus, whilst many deputies cast their votes on an issue-by-issue basis, the extreme heat and high cost of living in Madrid ensured that many only attended the sessions on a sporadic basis (despite the coming of the republic, deputies were still unpaid). Meanwhile, there were many issues that cut across party lines, many of the *intransigentes*, for example, having suddenly lost interest in the social reform they had espoused as a means of gaining power. With personal rivalries of all sorts also endemic, the result was a picture of even greater confusion than the basic pattern suggests. At all events, virtually the only thing that the *cortes* could agree upon was the principle that Spain should be a federal republic, whilst it proved all but impossible even to form a government, the stalemate only being broken when the *intransigentes* threatened a coup.

Pi being the most obvious compromise candidate, it was he who on 13 June delivered the equivalent of the old speech from the throne. In outline, the programme he suggested was sensible enough: the defeat of the Carlists, the restoration of the army's discipline and morale, the reconstruction of the government's finances, the formulation of a constitution, the separation of Church and state, the abolition of slavery, Cuban autonomy, and the introduction of a programme of social reform were all obvious priorities. However, it soon became clear that unity remained unlikely. Most of Pi's ministers were either complete nonentities or men regarded as traitors by one faction or other, whilst the president himself was not only a poor speaker but also too aloof and puritanical to flourish in the bohemian *demi-monde* of republican politics. However, no administration could have tackled the task with which Pi was faced. Thus, the right were averse even to the mild measures of social reform which Pi proposed – in brief, the introduction of mixed juries to settle labour disputes, and the reform of disamortization so as to ensure that land could henceforward be acquired by the poor – whilst the *intransigentes* objected to his plans to strengthen the army. Nor was there any way in which an acceptable compromise could be found with regard to the need to increase revenue and reduce expenditure. Meanwhile, the Carlists were running amok in the Basque country, Navarre and Catalonia alike; serious disturbances were shaking parts of Andalucía; and certain provincial *intransigentes* were attempting to precipitate cantonalist uprisings.

All this put the government under intolerable pressure, and on 21 June it collapsed. In trying to form a replacement, however, Pi was driven further right, for the *intransigentes* were openly hostile, whilst much of the centre was increasingly concerned at his continued attempts to conciliate the extremes of the party. As a result, when the new government was finally formed, it drew so heavily upon Castelar's sympathizers that it almost appeared to be in his pocket. Nor was this all: increasingly desperate to end the Carlist war, on 30 June Pi requested permission to suspend all constitutional guarantees, only for the *intransigentes* to interpret this as a sign that the president was planning to crush all those forces which opposed him, and walk out of the *cortes*.

The events of 24 April had already shown the dangers of excluding one faction or another from power, and they were now to be replicated, albeit on a much grander scale and with the *intransigentes* cast in the role of the *radicales*. With Spain still embroiled in civil war and social unrest – the period between the end of June and the middle of July witnessed serious internationalist uprisings at San Lucar de Barrameda and Alcoy, a dramatic Carlist victory in Catalonia, and a general strike in Barcelona – a widespread cantonalist revolt now erupted. Some historians have represented this movement as a desperate attempt to secure a genuine revolution, and all the more so as the revolt coincided with the decision of an exhausted and disillusioned Pi to resign in favour of the more conservative Nicolás Salmerón. Yet to adopt such a position is to dignify the movement far more than it deserves, *intransigencia* having long since demonstrated that it was little more than a collection of 'outs' whose radicalism varied in inverse proportion to their own advancement. In short, the great cantonalist revolt was the fruit above all of the refusal of successive republican governments to replace the existing *ayuntamientos* with new ones controlled by the *intransigentes*. Crucial because of the horde of officials and functionaries of all sorts employed by the municipalities, this question had become all the more pressing because of the failure of the *intransigentes* to do well in the municipal elections that had been held on 12 July. Rest though it did on the poverty and anger of the lower classes, whether cantonalism stood for anything other than personal ambition is therefore unclear.

What is certainly the case is that the leaders of the movement had absolutely no intention of letting their followers get out of hand. Thus, if cantonalism was generally strongly anti-clerical, considerable efforts were made to ensure that the mob was kept under control. As for the social question, meanwhile, if some cantons recognized the right to work, established the eight-hour day, reduced rents by half, increased the taxation of the propertied classes, abolished the *consumos*, and sought to introduce schemes of universal education, this was only in those few cases where internationalists took a leading role in the insurrection (the policy of the FRE was very much that its militants should boycott bourgeois politics and form an insurrectionary movement of their own). As a social revolution, in short, the cantonalist revolt was distinctly lacking.

Notwithstanding these many caveats, the rebellion had within a few days spread not only to cities such as Seville, Cádiz, Salamanca, Cartagena, Málaga, Granada and Valencia, but also to provincial towns such as Castellón, Algeciras, Almansa, Bailén and Andújar, and even to obscure backwaters such as Tarifa, Torrevieja and Fuenteovejuna. In every case the pattern was the same, the towns and cities concerned declaring their independence and establishing committees of public safety. From the very beginning, however, it was apparent that the revolt was a very flimsy affair. Given the victories recently obtained by the Catalan Carlists, Barcelona refused to take part in the rebellion at all, whilst it was notable that most of the towns and cities in which cantonalism triumphed had been only minimally garrisoned, the Carlist War having led to much of Spain being stripped of regular troops. In the few exceptions the rank and file might have gone over to the cantonalists, but it was all too obvious that their prime concern was generally simply to return home as quickly as possible. As for popular support, this was by no means as impressive as might have been expected, the situation being so bad in one or two cases that the new authorities dissolved themselves almost immediately. With most of the cantons protected by nothing more than crowds of militamen, the only hope was unity, but almost immediately a whole range of disputes broke out that in a few instances went as far as armed conflict. Small though the forces available to the government may have been, they were therefore easily able to restore order, canton after canton collapsing after only minimal resistance. By 12 August, in fact, all that was left was Málaga and Cartagena, both of which were placed under siege. Although the former held out till 19 September and the latter, which was protected by powerful fortifications, till 11 January 1874, *intransigencia* was a spent force.

Mixture of cynicism and farce though it was, the cantonalist revolt shattered what little popular credibility the republic retained. In theory, the pace of reform actually picked up with the months of July and August witnessing the presentation in the *cortes* of bills giving tenant farmers the chance to buy their lands outright, restoring a portion of the common lands to the municipalities, limiting child labour, restricting working hours in industry, and setting up mixed arbitration boards to settle industrial disputes and regulate working conditions. In reality, however, this meant very little. In the areas affected by the rebellion the juntas that were formed to take over the civil administration frequently contained men who were openly monarchist, whilst the generals who had been charged with the restoration of order had ensured that retribution was brutal in the extreme. As a result, wages were generally forced down, large numbers of militants arrested, and the International in particular subjected to considerable harassment, the propertied classes in the meantime being allowed to form a *de facto* private army. Happy enough though he was to go along with all this, Salmerón found that it was not enough to satisfy the generals, who were demanding the death penalty (abolished in 1870) and martial law. Aware that submission would precipitate a crisis in Madrid, on 6 September the president therefore resigned. Desperate to arrest the drift to the right, Pi stood for election in his place, but he was heavily defeated, the nomination instead going to the overtly conservative Castelar.

With Castelar came reaction. Convinced that the only hope was a reconciliation with the *radicales* and even the *unionistas*, Castelar set about taming the revolution still further, having first adjourned the *cortes* until 2 January 1874 and secured the power to rule by decree. Never very happy about federalism, he now preached the unity of Spain whilst conciliating the army, the Church and the interests of property alike by a raft of measures that included the restoration of the *status quo ante* in the artillery, the dissolution of the militia, the restitution of good relations with the Vatican, the imposition of press censorship, and the suspension of civil liberty. As for the radical new constitution that had been under discussion since the *cortes* met in June, this was quietly shelved.

Not surprisingly, Castelar's policies united the vast majority of the *cortes* in opposition to his rule, the only deputies willing to support him, other than a handful of his own clients, being the tiny rump now constituted by the monarchists of various persuasions. With it becoming increasingly clear that the president was unlikely to survive 2 January 1874, the conservative generals who continued to dominate the army decided that the only way out was for him to overthrow the *cortes*. This, however, Castelar was not prepared to do, the result being that Serrano, Pavía and a number of other leading generals came to the conclusion that the only solution was a *pronunciamiento*. Thus, when Castelar was defeated in a vote of confidence on the very day the *cortes* resumed its sessions, they were ready for action: no sooner had the result of the vote been announced than Pavía surrounded the parliament building and ejected the deputies from the chamber so as make way for the formation of a new administration under Serrano.

The fall of Castelar was not quite the end of the First Republic, for neither Pavía nor Serrano were by any means committed to the cause of the monarchy. Thus, Pavía's actions had been motivated almost entirely by a fear of what would happen to the army, whose discipline had been much restored under Castelar; meanwhile, Serrano not only harboured dreams of becoming head of state, but had been much affronted by the numerous snubs which he had received at the hands of the aristocracy on account of his 'betrayal' of Isabel II. However, with the most conservative elements of the old revolutionary coalition firmly in the saddle, it was quite clear that Spain no longer stood the slightest hope of being democratized. Indeed, the coup of 3 January 1874 was followed by a period of intense repression. Not only were all political organizations hostile to the government driven underground, but civil liberties were again suspended, the *cortes* left in abeyance, the press subjected to a rigid censorship, the militia dissolved, and public order placed under the jurisdiction of the military. Meanwhile, the Internationalists – incidentally the only elements in Spain actively to oppose the coup – were subjected to particularly heavy pressure and forced to go underground. By contrast, of course, the republic's attack on the Church was abandoned, the new administration proclaiming that it could be relied on to defend the latter's interests.

If the general outlines of the sort of Spain for which Pavía and Serrano stood were all too clear, the ability of the new regime to govern in a coherent fashion was much less obvious. Serrano was both indolent and vacillating, as well as married to an ambitious wife who used her position to sell favours and honours of all sorts. Meanwhile, the government was deeply divided, thanks not only to the squabbles that had inevitably broken out over the fruits of victory, but also to the longstanding rivalries of its various components. As a result, although agreement was reached that Spain should be governed in accordance with the constitution of 1869, 1874 was marked by a series of ministerial reshuffles, whose most significant aspect was the return to office of Sagasta (whereas Figueras, Pi, Salmerón and Castelar had combined the posts of president and prime minister, Serrano had separated them once more).

With the republic clearly in a state of drift, it is now time to turn to the camp of its monarchist opponents. For the first two years of the *sexenio*, the cause of Bourbon restoration had continued to centre on the rival claims of Isabel II, the Duque de Montpensier and Luisa Fernanda. Continuing, as they did, to enjoy much loyalty, the result had been much intrigue. Nothing, however, had borne fruit, and in June 1870 Isabel had therefore been persuaded to abdicate in favour of her twelve-year-old son, Alfonso. Important though this was – for the young prince was not only free of the taint of the long years that had preceded the revolution, but also a figurehead behind whom all supporters of the monarchy could rally – it was not in itself enough to secure a restoration. Despite the fact that the political leader of the monarchist movement – O'Donnell's erstwhile confidant, Antonio Cánovas del Castillo – was determined that Alfonso should be brought to the throne by political means, there was no chance of this so long as Serrano remained in power, the fact being that the general seemed determined to enjoy the perquisites of office *ad infinitum*. With no likelihood that the monarchists would be victorious at the polls, the decision once again lay with the army.

Realizing the importance of the army, the government had sought to conciliate its more conservative elements by appointing the notorious *isabelino*, Manuel Gutiérrez de la Concha, to the command of Army of the North – the mainstay of the war against the Carlists – and ordering him to take the offensive. Unfortunately for Serrano, however, the military situation actually took a turn for the worse, for Concha was defeated and killed. In consequence, preparations for a *pronunciamiento* were soon under way, and on 28 December General Arsenio Martínez Campos duly proclaimed Alfonso XII at Sagunto. Seconded as the coup was by most of the army's senior commanders, the *sexenio* was over.

An End and a Beginning

The six years between 1868 and 1874 are a crucial watershed in the history of modern Spain. In essence, what had occurred was the consolidation of a social and political system that had been in the process of elaboration ever since the death of Fernando VII in 1833, if not the inauguration of the *cortes* of Cádiz in 1810. Spain was confirmed as a constitutional monarchy governed by the principle of equality before the law – in the manifesto which he had issued from his exile in England on the urging of Cánovas on 1 December 1874, Alfonso XII promised that the future of Spain would be decided by a constituent *cortes* – but at the same time she was confirmed as a profoundly inegalitarian society in which political and economic power were monopolized by a propertied oligarchy. With varying degrees of sincerity, successive generations of radicals had been battling to secure a greater degree of justice ever since the 1840s, but it had now been shown beyond any doubt that all attempts to conquer the system from within were utterly futile. If the crushing legacy of disamortization was to be challenged, the way forward was not through bourgeois politics, but rather through the embryonic labour movement that had been seen to flex its muscles in the course of the *sexenio*. By the same token, if Spain was to be anything other than a rigidly centralized state governed from Madrid, the torch would have to be taken up by forces working from outside the system, be they elements of that self-same labour movement or regionalist movements rooted in cultural differences.

With this development, however, there came a sea change in the structure of Spanish politics. Hitherto postulated very largely on a struggle for patronage and influence within a system whose outlines were, in practice if not in theory, generally accepted, they were now increasingly to be dominated by a clash between 'order' and 'revolution'. For one Spanish institution in particular, the implications could not have been more far reaching. Until now, whilst on the whole subscribing to a common code of values and beliefs, army officers had on the whole felt free to choose between a range of political positions ranging from neo-absolutism to federalism. In the wake of 1873, however, revolutionary politics had a very different meaning: indeed, it is not without significance that the only new regime that was not inaugurated by some form of military intervention in the whole period from 1814 to 1874 was the First Republic. Whereas officers who became involved in politics had previously essentially been playing for limited stakes, the risks involved were now so high that they could no longer sit at the table – and were, indeed, inclined to kick it over altogether. Thus, henceforward the *pronunciamiento* was to become a wholly reactionary process whose aim was not to further political change, but rather to prevent it or even roll it back. Under the strain of the first thirty years of the twentieth century, the mould was to be broken once again, but, until then, revolution was out of the question.

But had revolution ever been a real possibility? To judge from the events of the *sexenio*, the answer must be 'no'. In large part, the revolutionary coalition of 1868 had simply not been revolutionary, the interests of the *unionistas*, the *progresistas*, and, to a very large extent, the *demócratas*, boiling down to little more than a desire for a share in the patronage and preferment that was the essence of the Spanish political system. The result was that the politics of the revolution slid very rapidly into chaos as the parties, which were little more than loose clienteles, one after another split into warring factions – hence the short-lived nature of the reign of the unfortunate Amadeo I. Of course, not all the members of the revolutionary coalition were so self-seeking: nobody, for example, could possibly doubt the fervour and integrity of Francisco Pi y Margall. But, although the failure of *la gloriosa* to deliver real change produced a genuine revolutionary movement, even here the picture was very far from rosy. Not only was the republican movement hopelessly divided, but both leaders and followers were intent on little else than their own advancement. Lacking any sense of the need for a genuine social pro-gramme, federalism was also increasingly undercut by an internationalism that was at best ambivalent about participation in its struggles. At the same time, however, internationalism, too, was ever more deeply divided between the followers of Marx and Bakunin, the result being that, even had it had the strength to do so, its ability to lead a true revolution must be seriously open to question.

What killed the possibility of revolution, however, was not in the long run the failures and deficiencies of its leadership. As the endless unrest and cantonalist insurrection showed, amongst certain elements of the populace there existed a real willingness to do battle with the system that ruled their lives (though whether such resentment could ever be mobi-lized effectively was a moot point). Against the army and the Guardia Civil, however, popular rebellion stood little hope of success. Remove those forces, of course, and the situation might have been very different, but federalism came to power at a moment when acting against the forces of order was simply out of the question. With the Carlists threatening Bilbao, Pamplona and Vitoria and making short work of every expedi-tion sent against their northern redoubts, the army was indispensable.

In short, the revolutionary *sexenio* did not just mark the end of an era in the history of Spain, but also prefigured the future. On the one hand, the *paviada* foreshadowed the new form of coup that was to be the future hallmark of military intervention in Spanish politics in that the interests with which the Spanish army had identified itself for the past sixty years now became associated with the cause of political reaction. On the other, the cantonalist revolt foreshadowed the fate of the revolution of 1936–7, it being conclusively demonstrated that social revolution was incompatible with civil war. From the *sexenio*, too, meanwhile, there sprang the chief contenders in the struggles that were to beset Spain in the new era, whether they were the alliance of power and privilege that came to constitute the modern Right, the rival movements that together made up the modern Left, or the new and influential force of regional nationalism. To conclude, just as the six years from 1808 to 1814 set the scene for the first half of this work, so the six years from 1868 to 1874 set the scene for the second.

8

The Restoration Monarchy

Pax Canovana

The thought that an entire era of Spanish history had been brought to an end by the coup of 29 December 1874 would have pleased no man more than the Andalusian writer who had become the Bourbons' greatest champion. For Antonio Cánovas del Castillo, one consideration was paramount. Revolution having at all costs to be contained, such ruptures in the governing classes as those of 1840, 1854 and 1868 could simply no longer be permitted. What was required, in short, was a new political system that, by allowing rival factions within the establishment fair turns at the trough, would dissuade them from summoning one ambitious general or another to elbow their opponents out of the way (a change that was all the sweeter given that it would end the overweening influence of the *generalato*).

Thanks to the willingness of the political establishment to play the same game as Cánovas, of the generals to adopt a more retiring profile, and of the palace to act with common sense, it proved possible to establish such a system. Implicit in this success, however, was wholesale electoral manipulation. In addition to high politics, we must therefore turn our attention to society. All the more is this the case, meanwhile, given that Cánovas' objective was not just to procure stability, but also to defend the basis of Spanish society as it existed in 1874. However, we are not just speaking of any social system. If the population could be so easily manipulated, it was because much of it lived in a state of dire poverty, the result being that the *pax canovana* proved no *pax* at all.

The Restoration of Order

Whatever problems lay ahead, for the propertied classes the Restoration Monarchy seemed a fresh dawn. Cánovas was possessed of talent, experience and vision. Arriving in Madrid in 1845, he had managed to insinuate himself into the confidences of both Joaquín Pacheco and Leopoldo O'Donnell, and had therefore become involved in the revolution of 1854. Thereafter employed in a variety of official posts, in 1864 he entered the cabinet as, first, Minister of the Interior and, second, Minister for the Colonies, and had therefore long since established a record as a skilful political operator, and one, moreover, who was convinced that politics should be inclusive rather than exclusive and that violence was a recipé for disaster. Add to these views a strong degree of traditionalism, and one is left with a monarchist and man of order who was yet realistic enough to realize that Spain could not go on being governed in the manner of Isabel II.

Though not involved in the *pronunciamiento* at Sagunto, Cánovas was universally recognized as the only possible premier, and on 30 December 1874 the *alfonsino* leader therefore duly assembled his first cabinet from a mixture of *moderados*, *unionistas* and *progresistas*. Thereafter action was fast and furious. Thus, the bureaucracy, the judiciary, the officer corps, local government and the universities were all subjected to a brutal purge; school and university courses were inspected to establish their religious and political orthodoxy; the republicans and socialists experienced greater repression than ever; two new police forces – the Cuerpo de Seguridad and the Cuerpo de Investigación y Vigilancia – were established; even tighter restrictions were imposed on the press; opposition meetings were prohibited; and the new local authorities were ordered to restore respect for property and hierarchy.

Repression, however, was not Cánovas' only concern. Thus, whilst attempting to conciliate moderate opinion – he frequently reprimanded officials who were too open in their harassment of protestants and free thinkers, and sought in particular to protect the Ateneo (the club-cum-library which to this day is a cornerstone of Madrid's intellectual life) – the new prime minister immediately set about the task of restoring constitutional government. In this respect he found that he had the full support of Alfonso XII whose clerico-military upbringing did not prevent him from seeing that Cánovas' programme was the only one that offered any hope. In consequence, Spain soon had a new constitution, this proving to be an *amalgame* of those of 1845 and 1869. Thus, sovereignty was declared to reside co-equally in the king and the *cortes*; the *cortes* re-established on the basis of an elected lower house and a senate that was in part elected, in part *ex officio*, and in part appointed by the king; ministers stipulated as being nominated by the king, but owing responsibility to the *cortes*; the king given wide-ranging prerogative powers; and the freedoms of person, occupation, residence, property, expression, education, assembly and association explicitly recognized (freedom of conscience was excepted, true, but even then the practise of faiths other than Catholicism was now to be permitted in private).

Though the new document borrowed from two traditions, its real leanings were wholly regressive. Indeed, the constitution was clearly utterly deficient as the fundamental document of a parliamentary monarchy. Taking the case of the individual freedoms retained from the *sexenio*, for example, these were all deemed to be open to 'regulation', and yet no attempt at all was made to place precise limits on the power of the throne. In short, what Spain was effectively given was a sham that was designed to reconcile a parliamentary facade with the defence of order and privilege. This, certainly, was the pattern established by the *cortes* which Cánovas proceeded to summon to ratify his draft constitution. Thus, in theory elected by universal manhood suffrage, the deputies were in practice the product of a campaign characterized by the most blatant corruption and intimidation, the result being that nearly 90 per cent of the new *cortes* consisted either of his own Partido Liberal Conservador – better known as the Conservatives – or of Alonso Martínez's Partido Centralista, of which the former was a coalition of *unionistas*, *moderados* and *progresistas* who had rallied to Cánovas, and the latter a group of *progresistas* who had decided to accept the constitution of 1876 whilst at the same time retaining their independence. Ignoring the solitary figure of Castelar, who was allowed a seat in the *cortes* in recognition of his conduct in 1874, the opposition consisted of just twenty-seven *progresistas* and twelve *moderados*. In consequence the new constitution enjoyed an easy passage, as did a series of measures that restored the government's powers to intervene in local government, ended universal suffrage, organized the boundaries of *cortes* constituencies in such a way as to neutralize the influence of the provincial capitals, and placed tight controls on the freedom of the press.

By 1877, then, the institutional outlines of the Restoration Monarchy had been clearly established. In the Spain of 1875, however, it was not enough just to make life safe for the propertied classes. Also clearly essential was the need to bring an end to the wars that were raging in Cuba and the north of Spain. Given the obvious danger of *moderado* disaffection, by far the most important was the Carlist rebellion. However, command an army of 70,000 men though Carlos VII did – he had returned to Spain in July 1873 – all was far from well with his cause. Bilbao, Vitoria and other major towns continued to defy his forces; the ramshackle administration which the Carlists had established was unable to meet the demands which were placed upon it; the guerrillas who ranged across wide reaches of Catalonia, Aragón and Old Castile were as likely to alienate potential supporters as they were to win them over; the rapid process of 'republicanization' that was currently in train in France was cutting off the support that had initially been forthcoming from across the Pyrenees; and the rather limited resources of Navarre and the Basque provinces were insufficient to sustain a war of attrition. In addition to these strategic problems, the very nature of the Carlist cause militated against success. Thus, if considerable elements of the populace had been prepared to take up arms, it was not so that they could fight for Don Carlos, but so that they could revenge themselves upon the liberal state and its beneficiaries. With matters made still worse by the puritanical character of Carlist rule, it was not long before the subjects of Carlos VII were deeply unhappy.

As the Carlist leaders were as factious as ever, it was soon evident that Carlos VII was doomed: indeed, by the end of 1874 his cause had largely been suppressed except in Navarre and the Basque provinces. Fierce fighting continued for another year – there is, indeed, some evidence that victory was delayed by a variety of efforts on the part of Cánovas to ensure that no general was given the chance of making use of triumph on the battlefield as a springboard for another coup – but early in 1876 the last Carlist field army was decisively defeated at Montejurra and Carlos forced to flee into exile. With Carlism out of the way, meanwhile, there was nothing to stand in the way of a Spanish victory in Cuba, and in December 1876 Martínez Campos – whom Cánovas was only too delighted to get rid of – was dispatched to Havana with a new army of 25,000 men. The new arrival proceeding to combine constant military pressure with a series of amnesties, pardons and promises of reform, the rebel cause was soon tottering, and on 11 February 1878 its leaders finally signed an armistice at Zanjón. Angered by the refusal of the Spanish authorities to concede an end to slavery, a few radicals fought on, but within a few months even they had been forced to surrender. Assisted by Martínez Campos, Cánovas then implemented a series of reforms that gave Cuba a measure of representation in the *cortes* and ended the dictatorial rule of the Captain General. However, many issues remained unresolved, the fact being that another war could virtually be guaranteed.

España caciquista

With the defeat first of the Carlists and then of the Cubans, the Canovine restoration may be said to have been completed. However, the broad outlines of the political system which it established are hardly a sufficient basis for an understanding of its workings. In consequence, the Restoration Monarchy must therefore be examined under another guise, and all the more so as the pivotal nature of the *sexenio* renders the return of Alfonso XII an ideal moment to take a step back from the march of politics.

Without any doubt, the heart of the Restoration Monarchy was the system of political and electoral management known as *caciquismo*. As we have seen, central to Cánovas' concerns was the fear that the establishment would once again implode in the style of 1854 and 1868. To avoid this, it was necessary to ensure, first, that politicians would still be guaranteed a niche in the system even when they were out of power; and, second, that the dynastic parties could alternate in power without having to call in the army. From this it followed that there should not only be regular elections, but also some means of deciding them in advance, not to mention of excluding those forces whose politics threatened the whole basis of the monarchy. Whilst limiting the electorate to men of property and education and driving genuine opposition underground were important steps in this respect, what was needed was a means by which elections could be 'made' so as to generate the correct result.

The basic pattern of what was to become known as the *turno pacífico* was established by the elections of January 1876. Thus, having decided that there should be an election, Cánovas contacted Sagasta to discuss which should party gain each seat. As election followed election, this system became increasingly formalized, the convention being, first, that constituencies should be categorized as being either permanent fiefs of one party or the other or negotiable properties that could be allowed to change hands, and, second, that the opposition should be granted between a quarter and a third of the available seats. Once agreement had been reached between the party leaders, the latter would then set about deciding how their seats should be apportioned amongst their supporters, this in turn occasioning a further process of negotiation with the local notables – the *caciques* – who gave their name to the system as a whole. Being the bedrock of the entire scheme, these men could not be ignored: it was, for example, most unwise to strip a prominent *cacique* of a seat he had traditionally controlled in favour of one of the young hopefuls who hung around Madrid in the hope of preferment. However, in a situation in which the outgoing party regularly lost two-thirds of its seats to the new administration, it was not possible to keep them all happy. Given that the benefits of participation in the political process were potentially enormous, the result was that no election was ever entirely lacking in excitement. To the very end, however, large numbers of seats remained uncontested, the fact being that the oligarchy had far too great an interest in the system to risk seeing it being rendered unworkable.

The result having been determined, it then had to be realized, the first task being to ensure that the administration of the elections was in trustworthy hands by embarking on a wholesale purge of local government and the judiciary, the number of officials, magistrates and local councillors affected often running into many thousands. There would then follow a campaign whose object was simply to ensure the support of the *caciques*, and elections characterized by wholesale fraud. Electoral rolls were falsified; electors bribed, brow-beaten, beaten up, impersonated or arrested; polling stations shut early or switched to inaccessible venues; and ballot boxes lost or stuffed. Generally speaking, such methods were more than sufficient to obtain the correct result – the only hope that dissidents usually had was to storm polling stations in the hope of engaging in a bit of ballot-rigging themselves – the few failures being easy to rectify by returning false results, or annulling the contests concerned and holding them again. As the years went on, moreover, various factors – the restoration of universal manhood suffrage, greater tolerance of opposition candidates, and the growing fragmentation of the dynastic parties – made things still worse, the whole process in fact slipping ever deeper into the realms of charade.

Yet, for all that, violence was hardly ever needed – indeed, it was regarded as bad form. Given the structure of Spanish society, however, this was hardly surprising. Thus, in most of the country political and economic power was monopolized by a propertied oligarchy who manipulated the system in such a way as to render their position ever more impregnable, whether it was by establishing political dynasties, acquiring titles of nobility, securing favourable treatment at the hands of magistrates and tax inspectors, enriching themselves from the public purse, or advancing family interests in the bureaucracy or officer corps. As for the rest of the population, meanwhile, it had been reduced to a state of dependence that was in some cases near total, the *caciques* controlling its every means of existence.

If this was so, it was in large part because of the situation of the peasants and landless labourers who together made up some 70 per cent of the Spanish population (in 1900 the figure still amounted to 60 per cent, whilst in 1930 it may at last have declined to about one half of the total population). With some exceptions, the whole of this sector lived in poverty. Central to this situation was the question of the land. Thus, as we have already seen, disamortization had made little or no difference to the structure of landed property in Spain. In some areas of the country, certainly, the land in question had been sold in small lots, but, even where this was the case, the results were hardly dramatic, whilst those *campesinos* who did manage to buy a little land sometimes found that their plots were so small that they later had no option but to sell up. The vast majority of the disentailed lands, then, passed into the hands either of the existing oligarchy or of new landowners drawn from the ranks of politics, the army, commerce and the professions.

Such imbalances notwithstanding, there were parts of the rural population whose conditions were reasonable. In the Valencian *huerta*, for example, the land was rented out to the peasantry in small lots on semi-permanent leases, whilst the latter's position was further eased by not only the growing importance of the district's export crops, but also the survival of a variety of traditional water rights. In the Basque provinces, Navarre and northern Aragón, all of which were blessed by a relatively favourable climate and reasonable soil, meanwhile, the land was either owned by the peasantry outright or rented out on the most reasonable terms, as well as generally being divided into smallholdings that were large enough to support a family. And, finally, in Catalonia, for whose cash crops of cork and grapes there was once again a heavy demand, leases were either based on the highly favourable Valencian model, or alternatively on the life of the vines themselves, the average in this case being around fifty years.

But for most of the agricultural populace matters were far less rosy, and all the more so as the 15,455,000 Spaniards of 1857 had increased to 18,109,000 in 1887. Let us first look at the position of the small tenant farmer. In Asturias, for example, many families had originally possessed smallholdings of their own, but these had become so subdivided on account of the inheritance laws in operation that most peasants also had to rent land as share-croppers on terms that were generally extremely onerous. Meanwhile, share-cropping was also the predominant form of peasant tenure in central and southern Aragón, La Mancha, Andalucía and Extremadura. Elsewhere, however – in Old Castile, Galicia, and the *huertas* of Granada and Murcia – rents were generally payable in money. In most cases plots were sufficient to support a family, but leases were very short and rents very high, the result being that the peasantry was constantly vulnerable to both eviction and usury. In Galicia, by contrast, though leases – *foros* – were generally semi-permanent, rents had risen dramatically, whilst, as in Asturias, each family's plot of land had been divided many times over. With yields very low and agricultural land in short supply – Galicia is a mountainous region of poor granite soils – the poverty of the inhabitants was extreme.

As if all this was not bad enough, the return of Alfonso XII coincided with the onset of the so-called 'great depression'. Experienced by the whole of western and central Europe, in Spain it seems probable that it was shorter and less acute than elsewhere – it helped that Spanish wine gained a massive market in France following the onset of the phylloxera disease – but even so its effects were severe enough. Space is insufficient to discuss the problem here in any detail, but, in brief, the arrival in Europe of large quantities of American and Canadian grain rendered much of the agricultural expansion that had taken place since 1814 valueless, and all the more so as it had often involved land of marginal quality. To make matters worse, meanwhile, the reduction in tariffs that had taken place in 1869 meant that the foreign grain began to arrive in

Spain herself. Needless to say, the response of the landowners was to take land out of production, large numbers of peasants being evicted in favour of pastoral farming. Meanwhile, in the late 1880s phylloxera spread to Spain as well with the result that the cereal growers of Castile were joined in their misery by the *rabassaires* of Catalonia.

If the conditions of the peasant farmer were desperate, those of the landless labourers were even worse, such men being concentrated in areas – above all, parts of Andalucía and Extremadura – where lack of rain and other problems rendered large-scale monoculture the only sensible option. Augmented by new *latifundia* as a result of disamortization, the great estates now amounted to an array that was imposing indeed. Thus, taking Andalucía and Extremadura as examples, estates of over 250 hectares accounted for 45 per cent of the area of the former and 36 per cent of the area of the latter. For the inhabitants of such areas, life was miserable indeed, matters not being helped by the facts, first, that the largely illiterate populace was growing at a disproportionate rate and, second, that alternative employment was extremely scarce. *Ayuntamientos* would customarily employ a few clerks, door-keepers, night-watchmen and street-sweepers, and the railways a number of porters, guards and ticket collectors, whilst there were also a number of areas where there were significant mining interests. Commerce and domestic service were also obvious alternatives, but the vast majority of shops were run solely by the owner and his family, whilst the tendency of richer families to live in the big cities ensured that footmen, chambermaids and the like were in less demand than might have been expected. As for industry, this was minimal. Every town had a variety of bakeries, oil presses, and other minor manufactories, but these businesses employed almost nobody and were in any case coming under increasing factory competition. As for the long-established textile and metallurgical industries that had operated in the hinterland of central, southern and eastern Spain, these were all in a state of terminal decline.

For large numbers of the inhabitants, then, nothing was left but the *latifundios*, and yet the latter for most of the year required very few workers. Setting aside the large parts of them given over to scrub pasturage (in the absence of large-scale irrigation schemes, there was often little else to be done), geography and climate ensured that they were universally characterised by the cultivation of wheat, vines or olives, all of which require very little labour for most of the year. To make matters worse, meanwhile, thanks to the lack of modern fertilizers, much of the wheat land could only be sown every third year. Every estate needed a nucleus of permanent staff – foremen, gamekeepers, craftsmen, grooms and domestics – but the number concerned was tiny by comparison. For the rest employment was strictly temporary, whilst hours were long, discipline strict and pay absolutely minimal. And, at the same time, of course, there were inevitably long periods of unemployment. In the first place the tasks available were increasingly restricted given the fact that, to reduce costs, many landowners were cutting back on such traditional practices as the hoeing of standing crops and the ploughing of land left fallow; and in the second the labourers generally found themselves competing with swarms of migrants from Galicia, Portugal and elsewhere. As a result, work was rarely available for more than 200 days a year. Still worse, population growth and sliding prices ensured that wages were being driven steadily downwards, it having been calculated that by 1900 they were 20 per cent lower than they had been a century before.

In consequence, life was grim in the extreme. Home was likely to be a desperately overcrowded cottage or tenement in a miserable slum characterized only by filth and decay. Amidst these conditions families of anything up to twelve children would eke out a miserable existence, whilst their menfolk were exposed to a hiring system that exposed them to constant ritual humiliation. Having been chosen for work, the men would have to labour from dawn to dusk in the full heat of the Spanish sun. Needless to say, the result was appalling levels of tuberculosis, typhus, malaria and malnutrition, and, in consequence, a further twist in the downward spiral, many labourers frequently being prevented even from offering their services in the market place.

Nor was illness the only catastrophe that could befall the unfortunate *braceros*. Spanish agriculture was particularly vulnerable to natural catastrophes of all sorts, and the result was very often to bring activity to a complete standstill. Whenever the harvest failed, however, the prices of basic foodstuffs soared dramatically, this problem being greatly worsened by the fact that there was a gradual retreat from the free-trade ideals of *la gloriosa*, the need to increase government revenue combining with the growing clamour for protection to produce a steady increase in tariffs. As wheat prices could rise by as much as 50 or 60 per cent, the *braceros* could therefore find themselves in a crushing double bind.

Poor though the countryside was, there was little chance of escape. We come here, of course, to the relative failure of the industrial revolution. Industrial growth, of course, was not altogether absent from Restoration Spain. In Catalonia the textile and engineering industries continued to thrive, whilst Vizcaya developed into a major centre of iron, steel and shipbuilding. Mining, too, increased dramatically with Spain's important mineral deposits all being exploited on a far more intense basis than ever before, albeit largely at the hands of foreign companies. Yet things were by no means as roseate as this picture might suggest. Cotton and shipbuilding alike, for example, were very heavily underpinned by the

Spanish colonies, whilst in general terms progress remained extremely slow. Assessing the responsibility for this situation has given rise to much disagreement – factors involved include the depressed state of the domestic market, the evil influence exerted by protectionism and railway construction, the overweening dominance of Catalonia, and the faults of the bourgeoisie themselves – but, whatever answer is arrived at, the fact is that Spanish industry was simply not equal to the task of absorbing the surplus labour that was vegetating in the countryside.

So where, then, did this leave the rural populace? Whilst some migration took place to the cities and industrial areas – the populations of Barcelona and Bilbao both more than doubled between 1877 and 1900 – on the whole internal resettlement was a twentieth-century phenomenon. Far more significant as a means of escape was emigration overseas. Thus, between 1882 and 1914 something over 2,000,000 Spaniards fled to Cuba or Latin America, whilst perhaps another million migrated to France, Italy or Algeria. However, these movements of population were at their greatest in such relatively favoured areas as the northern coastal littoral and the Levante, Andalucían and Extremaduran *braceros* proving slow to leave their homes.

How then did the *braceros* and their families survive? Babies were frequently abandoned, given up to foundling institutions, or simply killed; crime was common; and banditry, in particular, remained a celebrated feature of Andalucian life into the twentieth century. An alternative way out, at least in the popular imagination, was to become a bullfighter. Otherwise in times of unemployment *braceros* would seek to make some sort of living by weaving baskets from esparto grass, rag-picking, doing odd jobs, or trying to establish themselves as itinerant peddlers. Women, too, played an important role, whether it was by taking in laundry, acting as wet-nurses, seeking jobs as domestic servants or engaging in prostitution. Scavenging was also common, the more generous estate owners allowing the inhabitants to gather such plants as wild artichokes. Needless to say, such activities rarely brought in enough to make ends meet, however, and there were therefore few families which did not periodically resort to begging or otherwise seeking charity.

In this situation of general poverty, it is easy to see how the propertied classes maintained their control. First of all, of course, there was always a strong element of terror and intimidation, which was naturally facilitated by the fact that the local magistrates were themselves recruited from the propertied classes. Thus assured that the treatment of their enemies would be severe, landowners also had little hesitation in resorting to extra-official violence: amongst the poor were always toughs who were willing to sell their services for a few *pesetas*, whilst the *fijos* of their estates were generally only too eager to display their loyalty. Meanwhile, the state was also willing to sanction the employment of armed guards or the transformation of such traditional home-guards as the Catalan *somatén* into propertied militias. At the side of the oligarchy, too, of course, there was always the comforting presence of the Guardia Civil, which had now grown to a strength of over 15,000 men and had in 1878 been made an integral part of the army (with the effect that virtually any act of public disorder could be dealt with according to the terms of military justice). Notorious for their brutality, which went completely unchecked, the members of this force were never allowed to serve in their own localities, whilst they were housed with their families in fortified barracks and forbidden to socialize in any way with the local populace. Nor is it any coincidence that the force grew more rapidly at this time than at virtually any other in its history. Small wonder, then, that a grateful oligarchy christened it the *benemérita*, or 'well deserving'.

Given that they were officered entirely from its ranks, mention of the *civiles* brings us to the army. Whilst it would be wrong, as we shall see, to regard the officer corps as a preserve of the aristocracy, a wholly loyal ally of the Canovine system, or even a homogeneous force at all, it was nonetheless strongly inclined in the direction of repression. Thus, the cost of attending military academy ensured that most recruits were drawn from the propertied classes. At the same time, the more officers rose through the ranks – a process that was often closely linked with social status – the more they were able to profit from their position. Thus, if captains and lieutenants were relatively poorly paid, the more substantial salaries that accrued to their superiors had allowed many of the latter to benefit from disamortization. In recognition, meanwhile, of their political importance, many generals were appointed as company directors, whilst others found that they had no difficulty in marrying the most eligible heiresses. As a result, by 1875 the senior ranks of the officer corps were therefore deeply intertwined with those of the oligarchy – indeed, in some cases they had literally become *caciques* themselves.

It was not, however, just social class that turned officers into allies of repression. All officers were imbued with a view of history that saw disorder as the worst of evils. In large part a folk memory of the War of Independence – it should be remembered that at least 40 per cent of army officers were actually the sons of army officers – this sense of revulsion had been constantly reinforced by the struggle against brigandage that had been inherent to the Carlist Wars, whilst the experience of the *sexenio* had naturally strengthened it still further. Mixed up with all this was devotion to the unity of Spain – a concept that could not but come into conflict with the regionalist movements that were starting to make their appearance – loyalty to a monarch who was constantly portrayed as a soldier-king, and the dual conviction, first, that the interests of the army were synonymous with those of the nation, and, second, that the army was in fact the latter's saviour. Given the increasing isolation of the officer corps, meanwhile – the product of military families, officers were also educated separately, and inclined to marry girls from other military families, to find their friends amongst their fellow officers, and to read only military newspapers – the whole edifice was reinforced with every passing year. Such were conditions in the officer corps that disaffection was never entirely eradicated, but the fact was that only a minority of its members were willing to align themselves with the cause of popular revolution.

To return to the question of political control, overt terror was but a small part in the armoury of *caciquismo*. Away from the big cities, a variety of devices allowed acquiescence to be bought wholesale. At the very lowest level, the desperate *bracero* or tenant farmer could be bribed by gifts of money, food, wine or tobacco, or the offer of permanent employment, a plot of land or preferential treatment in the labour market. By the same token, of course, tenants could always be evicted and *fijos* and council employees threatened with dismissal, whilst *braceros* who stepped out of line knew that they risked being permanently blacklisted. However, such pressures were not just confined to the *populacho*. With their clientele desperately restricted by the masses' lack of purchasing power, the owners of the few up-market shops and cafés boasted by even quite substantial provincial towns knew full well that their continued well-being depended on political conformity, whilst such men as clerks and teachers were as liable to dismissal from their posts as any *bracero*. More positively, meanwhile, members of the provincial middle classes might also be flattered by the offer of a seat on the local council or a post in the office either of the mayor or of the agent of some absentee landlord.

Important though all these methods were as a means of maintaining control in the *campo*, however, they were less important than might have been expected. Ignorant and – until 1890 – disenfranchised, the bulk of the population remained utterly uninterested in the political process. Also influential here, of course, was the fact that the dissemination of information was initially largely in the hands of the oligarchy. In so far as the press was concerned, for example, large parts of the population never had access to anything other than local papers owned by prominent notables of the districts in which they lived. Also important in this respect was education, the fact that all Spanish children had since 1857 been supposed to receive free schooling up to the age of nine giving *caciquismo* access to another means of indoctrination. Thus, constantly drilled in the historic unity of Spain – Catalan, Galician and Basque, for example, were all effectively banished from the schoolroom – children were subjected to a programme of compulsory religious instruction, immersion in such national myths as the reconquest of Spain from the Moors, and lectures on the dangers of protestantism, republicanism and socialism. Outside the schoolroom, meanwhile, the message was reinforced by a variety of cultural events of all sorts, such as the celebrations occasioned by the four-hundredth anniversary of the death of Saint Teresa of Avila in 1882.

At least as important a factor in the Canovine struggle to keep the mass of the populace safely depoliticized was the *de facto* alliance that the regime had forged with the Church. Thus, if most clergy detested liberalism, their leadership recognized that Cánovas had been prepared to make substantial concessions. After all, moves in the direction of religious liberty had been kept to a minimum, whilst the Church was now guaranteed political representation – through the provision of a number of *ex officio* seats in the senate – the full payment of the dues of *clero y culto*, the right to establish its own schools, and much latitude with regard to the religious orders (in 1867 the number of monks in Spain was only 1,500, but by 1910 it had risen almost fifteenfold). Moreover, the state's determination to suppress republicanism and socialism, uphold the basic precepts of the Catholic religion, and repress popular anticlericalism was welcome indeed. Whilst pressing for further concessions of all sorts, the hierarchy in practice therefore lined up with the Restoration. Thus, the message to the faithful was invariably that the existing social order was divinely ordained, that any ideologies or intellectual developments that challenged it were incompatible with Catholicism, and that it was the duty of the poor to accept their lot and pray for eternal salvation. To be fair to the Church, it did make genuine efforts in the field of welfare, whilst the clergy remained both poorly paid and lowly in origin. Yet the bulk of its energy was always directed towards the energetic re-christianization of society, the result being that it was incapable of challenging the dominant pattern of social relations.

The extent to which all this indoctrination worked is naturally open to debate. Relatively prosperous as they were, Navarre and the Basque provinces were confirmed as strongholds of reaction. Much the same was true of large parts of Old Castile, where peasant indebtedness and vulnerability was countered by an increasingly vigorous programme of Catholic social action and the continued strength of Catholicism as a cultural phenomenon. However, elsewhere, Church, government and *caciques* were unable to prevent the emergence of a variety of forms of protest. As for the cities and provincial capitals, the extraordinary gerrymandering to which they were subjected suggests that they were regarded as a lost cause from the start. The fact is, however, that throughout the Restoration era, political participation remained extremely low, those instances that can be found of high turnouts almost invariably being the result of *caciquista* pressure. Explain this as a reflection of political maturity though we might, the reality is that large parts of the population remained untouched by politics of any sort.

The electoral foundation of *caciquismo*, this apathy was also a central pillar of its mentality, it being argued that the rural populace was a mass of simple yokels devoted to their priests and landlords. Mixed in with this, however, was not only another view of the *populacho* that saw it as a mob of savages who were as ignorant as they were violent, but also a belief that Spaniards as a whole were both lazy and ungovernable. From this it followed that the authorities had to shelter the people from the corrupting influence of such foreign doctrines as republicanism, anarchism and socialism, rule with a rod of iron, resist any amelioration in living and working conditions, and limit charity to the most worthy of cases. In short, economic interest was constantly reinforced by fear and self-delusion.

Reconstructing the Restoration: the Era of Sagasta

Whilst the main outlines of the system that were to govern Spain until 1923 were fashioned by Cánovas, it should not be thought that they remained wholly unadjusted. On the contrary the 1880s saw a series of major reforms that moved the 1876 constitution far closer to its 1869 predecessor, all this being the work of the erstwhile *progresistas*. Yet in practice little changed: despite an appearance of conflict that was sometimes ferocious in the extreme, the ethos of the new Liberal Party was exactly the same as that of the Conservatives.

It will be remembered that we left the evolution of Spanish politics in the year 1876. At this point relations between the Conservatives and the *progresistas* were certainly anything but 'pacific'. Thus, the latter were enraged by the ruthless nature of the general elections, the failure of the constitution explicitly to recognize the gains of *la gloriosa*, the refusal of many authorities and institutions even to pay lip-service to the principle of religious liberty, the impact of press censorship, the favourable treatment afforded to the *moderados*, and the publication in 1877 of a list of life senators from which they were almost completely excluded. The promise of thirty extra seats in the senate quickly persuaded Sagasta to tone down his language, but even so tension continued to mount: indeed, the *progresistas* even flirted with the idea of insurrection.

Meanwhile, all was not well in the government camp. Thus, the bullying ways of the Minister of the Interior, Francisco Romero Robledo, had produced considerable disaffection in the ranks of the Conservatives;

there was a growing feeling that greater concessions ought to be made to Sagasta; the king was discovered to be suffering from tuberculosis; and the loyalty of certain generals continued to give cause for concern. Following the peace of Zanjón of February 1878, moreover, a serious dispute had erupted with the victorious Martínez Campos in that the general not only put forward a series of proposals for reform that went far beyond anything that the government was prepared to tolerate, but also threatened to resign if they were not accepted. Faced by this crisis, the king intimated that he thought a change of ministry necessary, and on 3 March 1879 Cánovas therefore resigned, having in the meantime ensured that the new cabinet would be headed by Martínez Campos (whom he seems to have hoped to hoist with his own petard).

Exactly as Cánovas had hoped, the general did not last long. Lacking a personal following, he was unable to build up a party in the *cortes*, the 293 Conservative deputies that resulted from the new elections that he called being overwhelmingly canovine in their sympathies. Still worse, the infighting in the government's ranks produced the election of sixty-three *progresistas* and *centralistas* and no fewer than twenty-three republicans. With Cánovas deliberately whipping up Conservative disaffection in his rear, on 7 December the general was therefore forced to resign, the reins of government once again being placed in the hands of his predecessor.

Masterly a politician though Cánovas was, however, in this instance his judgement had deserted him. In the first place, Martínez Campos' reformism had possessed the support of many leading generals, whilst his attempts to build a party in the officer corps ensured that there were now many commanders who feared for their appointments. The prime minister having also repeatedly announced himself the enemy of military influence, it was therefore not long before the king's growing resentment of his mentor was being inflamed by the military men with whom he was surrounded; at the same time, in the spring of 1880 a furious Martínez Campos announced that he was leaving the Conservatives and going into opposition. If he did not actually leave the party, meanwhile, disaffection also surfaced in the person of Francisco Silvela, a leading supporter of Cánovas who had fallen out with Romero Robledo over the question of electoral management. All this, meanwhile, produced a radical change of mood amongst the followers of Sagasta and Alonso Martínez. Sensing that the king might be prepared to turn to them if only they could sink their differences, in May 1880 they came together to form the new Partido Liberal Fusionista, or, to give it its more common name, the Liberals. Joined by Martínez Campos, and a number of other Conservative dissidents, they had soon won the favour of a Alfonso XII who was now determined to rid himself of Cánovas rather than risk another

1868 (setting aside the political turmoil, 1880 also saw a series of labour and agrarian disturbances). Well aware of what was happening, Cánovas threw down the gauntlet by sending the king a decree whose preamble referred to the need to maintain the Conservatives in power. Needless to say, the royal signature was not forthcoming, and on 8 February 1881 Sagasta was at last sworn in as prime minister.

What did the advent of a Sagasta government mean for the Restoration Monarchy? In brief, far less than was believed at the time. Though there were many who regarded the Liberal leader as a dangerous revolutionary, nothing could have been further from the truth, the fact being that his rule was to be marked only by the appearance of change. At first, of course, things looked very different. Not only did the government issue a general amnesty, but politics was thrown open to republicans and other democrats. Meanwhile, press censorship was eased, the many university professors who had been dismissed in the purges of 1875 reinstated, and the Cardinal Archbishop of Toledo, Juan Moreno, sharply reprimanded after he had issued a pastoral letter denouncing the Italian government. Furthermore, having presided over fresh elections that produced an overwhelming Liberal majority, Sagasta introduced the first of a series of measures that were designed to restore the conquests of 1868–9. Amongst the first casualties of his rule, for example, were the old salt tax, the *consumos* and the *derechos de puertas*, whilst there were also moves in the direction of jury trials, free trade and a reduction in the length of military service. Above all, however, in the teeth of ferocious Conservative and clerical opposition, on 26 July 1883 Sagasta introduced a new press law that abolished the restrictions imposed on newspapers by Cánovas.

Yet in practice all this meant very little. In recognition for his help in bringing the Liberals to power, for example, Alfonso XII was given much more room to intervene in the day-to-day business of government, allowed to bring back his mother, and granted the restoration of the highly ornamental palace guard known as the Cuerpo de Alabarderos that had disappeared in 1868. At the same time *caciquismo* was accorded greater latitude than ever. Setting aside the fact that the advent of Sagasta was followed by a frenzied outbreak of office-seeking and municipal and parliamentary elections that plumbed the depths of fraud and chicanery, many of the reforms introduced by the Liberals were distinctly curious in their effects. Thus, the new tax structure reduced the taxation of landed property, whilst hitting such groups as small shopkeepers very heavily, just as the legal reforms actually reinforced the capacity of *caciques* to arrange matters entirely as they wished. As for local government, the right of the Ministry of the Interior to intervene was strongly reaffirmed. And, last but not least, popular movements of all sorts continued to be repressed without mercy, as witness the savage punishments meted out to sixteen inhabitants of Jérez de la Frontera who were put on trial in June 1883 for their involvement in the supposed anarchist secret society known as the 'Mano Negra' or 'Black Hand' (in all, more than 5,000 people were arrested in connection with this affair, many of them being badly tortured).

If Sagasta's style of government was even more disreputable than that of Cánovas, it was also far less capable of delivering stability. Thus, although Cánovas had twice been forced to resign, he had always commanded the loyalty of his party. In the Liberals, by contrast, everything was soon in a state of turmoil. From the very beginning there were incessant quarrels over the booty which had fallen into the party's hands, but it was not long before ideological factors had been added to the turmoil. The liberalization of politics to which the new prime minister's rule had given rise had allowed the more moderate wing of the *demócratas* to return to the political arena. Goaded by the criticism of these elements, many of Sagasta's followers began to feel increasingly uncomfortable, whilst the pot was further stirred by the return of General Serrano from exile. As vain and ambitious as ever, Serrano had been deeply angered by Sagasta's failure to include him in his cabinet (to add insult to injury, the Ministry of War had been given to Martínez Campos). Determined both to gain his revenge and supplant Sagasta as Liberal leader, Serrano therefore lambasted the government for failing to live up to the principles enshrined in the constitution of 1869. As he had hoped, this stance quickly secured him the support of a number of dissidents, and in November 1882 there duly emerged the new party known as the Dynastic Left.

Challenged by faction, then, Sagasta was also vulnerable to more altruistic elements. Whilst many republicans – the so-called *posibilistas* – had followed the lead of Castelar in believing that they could somehow democratize the monarchy, Ruiz Zorrilla remained in the exile into which he had fled in 1875 and was convinced that the only way forward was a military coup. Profiting both from the low wages, poor prospects and miserable conditions endured by many subaltern officers and from the growing realization that the army was barely fit to take the field, Zorrilla's Republican Progressive Party succeeded in setting up a secret society known as the Asociación Republicana Militar that by 1883 had some 3,000 members. Preparations were soon in train for a general revolt, but in the event the whole affair miscarried: though Badajoz was seized on 5 August 1883, the Asociación as a whole failed to move. Bitterly disappointed, Ruiz Zorrilla continued his conspiratorial activities – there were further risings in 1884 and 1886 – but his organization had suffered a fatal blow, the vigorous purge that Sagasta launched in response to the events of 1883 ensuring that the Asociación Republican Militar was effectively a dead letter.

Having weathered the crisis of August 1883, Sagasta appeared to be in a reasonable position, and all the more so as Serrano had not only been discredited by a major scandal relating to his son's marriage but was also ageing and unwell – he died in 1885. However, Alfonso XII was not a happy man: coming as it did on the eve of an important visit to Austria and Germany, the rising had caused him serious embarrassment, whilst he was also increasingly dismayed at the Liberals' failure to make any difference to the atmosphere of corruption and immorality that characterized Spanish politics. Eager to sack Sagasta, he was spared the necessity of having to provoke a crisis by developments in the government camp. Trouble having continued unabated in his party, in October 1883 Sagasta in consequence decided to resign in the hope that the consequences of such a move would establish his indispensability once and for all.

With his hands thus freed, Alfonso appointed a new ministry drawn from the Dynastic Left under the leadership of the erstwhile *unionista*, José Posada Herrera. For the next four months the new prime minister struggled to force through the programme of reform desired by the king, but his party was not big enough to afford him any chance of success. All the more was this the case as Sagasta refused pointblank to tolerate any talk of conciliation for fear that the price of re-unification would be his own head. The end came on 18 January 1884 when plans for the restoration of universal manhood suffrage were defeated. Had the Liberals and the Dynastic Left been prepared to join forces, Alfonso might yet have granted them a dissolution, for he remained convinced that reform was essential and retained bitter memories of the thrall in which he had been kept by Cánovas. However, the two remained hopelessly divided, and the result was that the architect of the Restoration was not only once again asked to form a ministry but also granted the general elections that he needed to create a majority.

Little time need be wasted on the elections that followed. Much aided by the fact that the Conservatives had now been joined by the vast majority of those *moderados* who had at first held out against the Restoration, Cánovas was able to ensure the election of 318 Conservatives as opposed to thirty-nine Liberals, thirty radicals and four Republicans (there were also a handful of independents and die-hard Carlists). Nor is there much to be said about the government which presided over them, Cánovas' one goal being to quell dissent and stifle reform. Behind the scenes, however, the Conservatives were in serious disarray, thanks in part to divergences between Cánovas' original supporters and the latter-day converts from *moderantismo*, and in part to the growing rivalry that divided Silvela and Romero Robledo. In the first half of 1885, meanwhile, the country was swept by a series of natural disasters that provoked a fresh wave of social unrest. Nor was Cánovas' morale improved when the growing tension in his party allowed the Liberals and Republicans to take control of the *ayuntamiento* of Madrid in the municipal elections of 1885. The regime was therefore gripped by a growing sense of crisis even before news broke that Alfonso XII was dying, the circumstances being such that even Cánovas lost his nerve. Summoning Sagasta to a conference, he offered him the premiership as the only means of forestalling revolution, the death of Alfonso on 25 November therefore being followed by a second period of Liberal rule.

With the death of Alfonso XII, Spain once again became a regency. This time, however, she was relatively fortunate. Thus, the widowed queen – Alfonso's second wife, María Cristina of Austria – was an austere, prudent and intelligent woman whose concern for the position of her unborn child – at the time of Alfonso's death she was two months pregnant – was quite enough to persuade her to play the political game. In April 1886 the Liberals were therefore allowed to hold new elections which duly returned an overwhelming majority whilst at the same time inaugurating a positive torrent of reform. To summarize, on 30 June 1887 the right of freedom of association was decreed; on 20 June 1888 the principle of trial by jury was re-established; on 1 May 1889 a new civil code was introduced that finally swept away all vestiges of the foral jurisdiction that had characterized Navarre and the Basque provinces; and on 5 March 1890 universal manhood suffrage was restored for municipal, provincial and national elections alike. Also worth mentioning here are the proposals put forward by Sagasta's second Minister of War, General Manuel Cassola, for a reorganization of the army that would have put conscription on a fairer basis, done away with 'political' promotions, ended the numerous privileges held by the artillery and engineers and alleviated the miserable economic status of the lower ranks of the officer corps.

The Failure of the Restoration

In theory, the passage of the electoral law of 1890 can be argued to have marked the high-water mark of Restoration Spain, Sagasta having apparently succeeded in remodelling the regime in such a way as to attract the support of all but the very fringes of Spanish politics. However, claims that Spain had become the most democratic monarchy in Europe were hopelessly adrift of the reality. Violently opposed to the principle of universal suffrage, for example, Sagasta had only consented to its restoration as a means, first, of maintaining his increasingly precarious position within his party; second, of staving off urban discontent at the workings of *caciquismo*; and, third, of spiking the criticisms of such respected figures as the noted professor of law, Gumersindo de Azcárate. Furthermore, it is difficult not to surmise that Sagasta realized that he need have no qualms in the matter: in the years since 1885 a series of measures concerned with taxation and local government had actually increased the possibilities for administrative corruption whilst the techniques of *caciquismo* had even gained a foothold in Madrid and Barcelona. Meanwhile, nothing changed: the 1886 elections were conducted amidst the usual scenes of fraud and disorder; scandal was rife; trial by jury became a farce characterized by benches that were bribed, packed or intimidated; the right of freedom of association was in practice severely restricted by a circular of 10 August 1885 reiterating the prohibition of demonstrations and meetings of protest of all sorts; and there was no let up in the brutality affected by the forces of order. Nor, indeed, did all of the reforms promised by the Sagasta regime even reach the statute book, notable casualties being the bill of rights that formed one of the chief planks in the Liberal programme and Cassola's plans for the reform of the army.

In consequence of all these deficiencies, it is richly symbolic that within a very few months of the passage of the new electoral law, Sagasta himself was toppled on account of his incrimination in a major railway scandal. At the same time, too, it is also worth pointing out that even the sincerely reformist General Cassola was a noted Murcian *cacique* who had secured a seat in the elections of 1881 by, amongst other things, invading a polling station at the head of an armed gang. Even before Sagasta fell from power, meanwhile, the fundamental weaknesses of the Canovine system were being revealed in another respect. Thus, exactly as had occurred prior to 1868, politics revolved around not ideology but the pursuit of influence, whilst it had at the same time been clearly demonstrated that the mere possession of a *cortes* majority was anything but a guarantee that power would be retained for the full five years of a legislature's potential duration. Nor, of course, was establishing a new political party particularly difficult: in the absence of mass politics, all that was needed was a handful of friends and a certain degree of credibility. Initially, at least, memories of 1873 had combined with mutual fear and suspicion to ensure a basic willingness to unite behind the figures of Cánovas and Sagasta, and all the more so as both of them were such self-evident masters of the political scene. By the late 1880s, however, these restraints were being increasingly dissipated: 1873 was receding into the past, the Republicans were no longer much of a threat, and it was becoming clear to Liberals and Conservatives alike that they were in practice prepared to operate within common parameters.

Always a likely characteristic of the Canovine system, factionalism therefore yet again emerged as a major factor in Spanish politics. Thus, furious at Cánovas' decision to relinquish power on the death of Alfonso XII, in 1886 Romero Robledo broke with his erstwhile master and established an independent group of his own known as the *reformistas*. In the ranks of the Liberals, meanwhile, things were even worse. As a deputy for the wheat-dependent area of Valladolid, for example, Sagasta's first choice as Minister for the Colonies, Germán Gamazo, soon identified protectionism as a means of advancing his own interests (Sagasta, it should be pointed out, was a confirmed free trader). Forced to resign from the cabinet in October 1886, by 1890 he was the effective leader of a powerful protectionist pressure group known as the Liga Agraria, as well as a 'loose cannon' in the ranks of the party. Also a source of trouble were the followers of the now-dead Serrano; the more altruistic elements of the old Dynastic Left such as Segismundo Moret and Eugenio Montero Ríos; and the growing number of defectors who had come over to the Liberals from the republicans, of whom the most significant was the erstwhile *demócrata*, Cristino Martos. As a result the period from 1885 to 1890 was marked by a seemingly endless series of cabinet crises which Sagasta only rode out with the greatest difficulty.

As ever, then, the auguries for the future were anything but favourable. As we shall see in the next chapter, meanwhile, new forces were emerging to challenge the system, whilst Spain was to all intents and purposes locked into a pattern of economic development that relied on the continued impoverishment of a large proportion of the population. Inherently unstable as this situation was, Cánovas' legacy ensured that the Restoration Monarchy would find it extremely difficult to cope with the pressures which it would face. Composed of ever more antagonistic factions whose leaders were constantly vying for the support of the local notables who formed the bedrock of the system, neither of the two main parties could ever hope to muster the unity and determination needed to force through a genuine programme of reform. Meanwhile, precisely because they were outside the charmed circle of *turno* politics, it would be impossible for alternative reformist movements to secure the sort of support that would have been needed to establish them in government (indeed, given the interests of the *caciques*, had they ever done so they would undoubtedly have been very quickly stripped of all traces of their original dynamism). As a result, the system was bound to stagnate, and the forces seeking to challenge it to become ever more menacing. Far in the future though the moment remained, the time would therefore come when the edifice erected by Cánovas would become uninhabitable even in the eyes of its most favoured inhabitants.

9

The Gathering Storm

The Challenge

The Restoration Monarchy, as we have seen, was a regime that both depended on, and existed to defend, a political, social and economic situation that was characterized by a complete absence of change. Rigidly centralized and strongly Catholic, Spain was to be governed by, and in favour of, the narrow landowning oligarchy that dominated politics, big business, finance, the professions, the army and the administration alike. As for the populace, it was to be reduced to the status of a pawn in the periodic exercises in fraudulence and manipulation that went under the name of elections. Yet this *pax canovana* was unlikely to survive. Within the establishment there were numerous points of friction, whilst there also emerged a variety of protest movements both new and old. Society, too, was changing with the result that the Canovine system was further undermined. That said, *fin-de-siglo* Spain was not even remotely on the brink of revolution, but it is nevertheless clear that the situation was distinctly unstable. In consequence, when Spain was assailed by the major crisis of 1898, a chain-reaction was unleashed that was eventually to damage the Restoration Monarchy beyond repair.

The March of the Little Man

However bleak the outlook may have been for the Restoration Monarchy, the forces of revolution were initially in headlong retreat. Particularly hard hit were the republicans. Whilst republicanism continued to command considerable support in some parts of the country, it was forced to remain underground until the formation of the first Sagasta government in 1881, and even then was confronted by impossible odds. Nor were matters helped by the fact that the republican movement itself was deeply divided. Thus, setting aside a few erstwhile *demócratas* who had effectively abandoned republicanism altogether, by 1880 the movement had split into several different camps. At the simplest level, these differences reflected attitudes to the regime in that, whilst the nationalistic Castelar had elected to participate in the Restoration system as a 'possibilist', Pi y Margall, Salmerón and Ruiz Zorrilla all remained loyal to both federalism and revolution. That said, however, rejectionism was anything but a united force, since Pi and Salmerón were bitterly at odds over the relationship between state and region, and Zorrilla inclined to seek salvation in not the people but the army (hence the plots of the early 1880s). Deeply opposed to one another, the three rejectionist parties were incapable of forging even the electoral alliances which were their only hope of making any sort of impact, whilst their effectiveness was further reduced by internal intrigue. At all events, all four tendencies were a picture of utter failure, the rejectionists losing ground to anarchism and Catalan nationalism and the possibilists eventually abandoning the struggle altogether (on 7 February 1888 Castelar finally recognized the monarchy, the bulk of his followers thereafter being absorbed into the Liberals).

The eclipse of republicanism did not, of course, mean that all criticism of the Restoration Monarchy was hushed. Thus, as deeply disillusioned by the shabby politics of the *sexenio* as they were by Canovine repression, many intellectuals became increasingly interested in the idea that Spain might be saved through means that were primarily educational and cultural. Chief product of this development was the formation of Francisco Giner de los Ríos' Institución Libre de la Enseñanza, or Free Institute of Education, in Madrid in 1876. A leading disciple of Sanz del Río, Giner de los Ríos had originally conceived this as an independent university which could propagate the principles of modern science and philosophy, and form the new elite that was needed for the modernization of Spain. In the event, however, this plan foundered, and the Institución were instead forced to move into the area of primary and secondary education, establishing a number of secular schools which were characterized not by brutality, rote-learning and traditionalism, but personal encouragement, modern teaching methods and a modern syllabus. Connived at by Cánovas, the movement survived long enough to enjoy the benefits of the more tolerant atmosphere of the period after 1885, the patronage of successive Liberal governments thereafter ensuring that the movement did eventually penetrate the world of higher education.

Nor was the Institución Libre de Enseñanza the only milieu that was conducive to the emergence of criticism. Thus, in the 1870s such authors as Bénito Pérez Galdos and Juan Valera published a spate of novels in which the Catholic Church and the ruling oligarchy alike were overtly criticized. Protected by an illogical Cánovas, meanwhile, the Ateneo remained an oasis of free and wide-ranging debate in which most of the great currents of contemporary thought were expounded to an enthusiastic audience. Also worth mentioning here is the controversial subject of freemasonry. Though certainly not the source of all evil portrayed in the demonology of the Spanish Right, masonry had flourished in Spain for most of the liberal era, attracting the participation of much of the educated elite. Popularized still further by the events of the *sexenio*, its lodges now served as a means of bringing together men of a variety of progressive ideas, whilst they at the same time assisted with the foundation of new secular schools, and even in some cases established such institutions themselves.

In many ways, then, the repression associated with the early years of the Restoration masked a period of considerable ferment, the result of which was that criticism could not be entirely stifled. In this respect a leading role was taken by Gumersindo de Azcárate, a professor of law who had been dismissed from his post at the University of Madrid by Cánovas in 1876. A founding father of the Institución Libre de Enseñanza, in 1877 he published a stinging denunciation of the Restoration settlement. The first systematic analysis of *canovismo* to have appeared in Spain, the chief premise of this work was that the constitution of 1876 had established not a parliamentary monarchy, but rather a form of caesarism, matters being worsened still further by the fact that civil liberties were at every turn sacrificed in favour of the interests of property. As a convinced liberal, Azcárate had no quarrel with the idea of a parliamentary regime, but from the early 1880s onwards voices began to be raised that were rather more ambivalent. Though other examples can be cited, we come here above all to the figure of Joaquín Costa. Some thirty years old in 1876, Costa came from a humble Aragonese peasant family, but had nonetheless succeeded in securing a post at the University of Madrid in the course of the *sexenio*. Purged by Cánovas, he had then become a full-time employee of the Institución Libre de Enseñanza, in which capacity he embarked on a long career as a publicist.

Unlike Azcárate, however, Costa was neither forward-looking, nor sympathetic to the doctrines of Spanish liberalism. Underlying his views, indeed, was the conviction that Spain should return to its roots in the shape of the self-governing commune of peasants and artisans, this being a position that might have been shared by many Carlists. Thus, his attack on the system began with a study of customary law in Aragón that argued that such codes had been a far more satisfactory bastion of liberty than the artificial confections imposed on Spain by successive liberal regimes, whilst he went on to praise the various organs of village self-government and popular cooperation that had survived in various parts of northern Spain until swept away by doctrinaire liberals offended at the manner in which they impinged on the freedoms of property and occupation. What was required, then, was a return to the principles of communal liberty and village democracy, the agent needed for such a change being a 'revolution from above' headed by an 'iron surgeon'.

The immense corpus of writing that flowed from Costa's pen in the period from 1876 to 1898 is susceptible of many different interpretations and marked by numerous contradictions. That said, however, he may be defined as a moving spirit in the movement of peasant and lower-middle-class protest that was to be characteristic of the late nineteenth and early twentieth centuries. Thus, at the heart of Costa's concerns was, first, an appreciation of the problems of the 'little men' – the small owner-occupiers, tenants, artisans and tradesmen – who made up the bulk of the population in the non-latifundist parts of the country; second, an innate hostility to the manner in which one part of Spain after another had been stripped of its traditional rights and privileges; and, third, a general dislike of the modern state. Until the 1870s such resentments had found expression in either Carlism or federalism, but both were now in a state of complete eclipse. As a result, a vacuum began to appear in popular politics. Filled in Catalonia by the emergence of regional nationalism, elsewhere the need was supplied by a species of populism which sought to mobilize the 'little man'.

Thus, Costa was soon moving more and more towards direct partici-pation in Spanish politics, the consequence being that in 1891 he formed the Cámara Agrícola del Alto Aragón, the aim of this being to mobilize the masses who were excluded by *caciquismo*. Campaigning on a pro-gramme of increased investment in irrigation, transport and education; opposition to any further sale of the commons; municipal autonomy; a reduction in the national budget; and the restitution of Aragonese cus-tomary law, he stood for parliament in the elections of 1896, only to be roundly defeated. Had Costa been alone in his criticism, the movement that he headed might soon have faded into relative obscurity, but in fact such unrest was becoming increasingly widespread. In Galicia, for exam-ple, the problem of the *minifundia*, old traditions of resistance to *señorialismo*, hatred of the *foristas*, rising land values, a soaring popula-tion, and the onset of the phylloxera disease had together produced a dramatic wave of agrarian agitation. Often erupting in violence, this was increasingly characterized by the formation of peasant societies whose aim was to oust the local oligarchy from their control of the *ayunta-mientos*. By 1885, meanwhile, under the influence of the *vallesoletano* Liberal, Germán Gamazo, most parts of Old Castile were resounding to peasant demands for tariff reform, an end to *caciquismo*, and greater government support.

Away from the field of regenerationism, or in Gamazo's case, pseudo-regenerationism (whipped up by his agents, the unrest in Old Castile was little more than a manoeuvre designed to embarrass Sagasta), mention should also be made of Carlism. Thus, the Carlist movement had since 1876 (when Carlos VII had gone into exile) undergone a major reorganization at the hands of a pretender convinced that he had no option but to shed his association with obscurantism. Although the cost was a serious schism – in July 1888 a group of fanatics revolted against Carlos VII and organized a separate Integrist party dedicated to establishing a Catholic theocracy – the result was that Carlism acquired a new capacity to voice peasant resentment. Thus, under the influence of the gifted Asturian writer, Juan Vázquez de Mella, it re-established the structures that it had put in place at the time of the *sexenio*, and for the first time began to address modern social problems, Mella arguing that the state should allow the people a greater measure of self-government and offer more support to the smallholder. Electoral success was limited – the number of Carlist deputies very rarely rose above ten – but in Navarre and parts of the Basque country Carlism yet became a force to be reckoned with.

Despite its *de facto* alliance with the regime, the Catholic Church also played a part in the mobilization of the peasantry. Published in 1891, the famous encyclical on the social question known as *Rerum Novarum* provided a way forward for those Spanish Catholics who were convinced that the spread of 'irreligion' would have to be combated by other means than simply extirpating impious doctrines, enforcing Christian morality, and encouraging popular devotion. Under the leadership of the lay organization known as Acción Católica, a major effort was made to reach out to the still largely Catholic peasantry of northern Spain through such activities as the formation of peasant cooperatives. As this was combined with the constant denunciation of the evils of liberalism, the result was that discontent with *caciquismo* was increased still further.

By 1898, then, much of northern Spain was gripped by various varieties of anti-liberal protest. That said, however, this development was much less impressive than it seemed, the angry smallholders whom it mobilized being in many cases little better than tools of the Catholic Church or the landed elite. Yet the peasantism which Costa, Gamazo, Vázquez de Mella and Acción Católica all sought to whip up cannot simply be dismissed in that it began slowly to undermine the ignorance and apathy on which the Canovine system ultimately depended for its salvation. Nor can it be viewed in isolation: if disillusioned Carlists turned to peasantism in Aragón, Old Castile and Galicia, in Catalonia and the Basque country, as we shall now see, a rival force began to emerge that tapped many of the same emotions.

The Coming of Regionalism

The political vacuum left by the simultaneous collapse of both federalism and Carlism was not only filled by agrarian protest, but also regional nationalism, of which the first examples were to be found in Catalonia and the Basque country, both of which were not only linguistically and culturally distinct from the rest of Spain, but also possessed of a long tradition of independence. Thus, originally a powerful feudal state – the County of Barcelona – that had forged a dynastic union with the neighbouring Kingdom of Aragón and established a considerable trading empire in the western Mediterranean, Catalonia had only submitted to rule from Madrid after a long and bitter struggle, and even now retained a separate code of law. As for the Basques, the four separate units that made up their homeland – the Kingdom of Navarre and the *señorios* of Vizcaya, Guipúzcoa and Alava – had all continued to enjoy a variety of privileges until well into the nineteenth century although these *fueros* had now been reduced to little more than a special agreement that limited taxation in the area to a figure that was only about half what it was in the rest of Spain.

For a variety of reasons, it was always likely that the standard of revolt would first be raised by the Catalans. Deficient though Catalan industrialization may have been, it yet gave birth to a myth that, whereas Catalans were thrifty, industrious and intelligent, Castilians were feckless, lazy and ignorant. To this sense of superiority was added resentment, for the rest of Spain was perceived as draining Catalonia of her resources, holding back her development, and stifling her cultural traditions, matters not being made any better by the fact that few Catalans succeeded in making their way as army officers or bureaucrats. Argue though one might that this was in part a reflection of the fact that educated Catalans had often shunned such employment, the machinery of the Spanish state had therefore evolved in a manner that virtually excluded Catalan participation.

If these were the general grievances that began to separate Catalan from Castillian in the first half of the nineteenth century, it should not be thought that Catalanist feeling was in origin a movement of the bourgeoisie. As in Navarre and the Basque provinces, regionalism was at first a primarily mediaevalist phenomenon – indeed, a protest at the coming of capitalism – that was adumbrated through the medium of Carlism. Such was certainly the character of the cultural revival known as the *renaixença*, or 'renaissance', which was its first real manifestation. Thus, alongside numerous epic poems, a series of historical works appeared that were designed above all to glorify Catalonia's traditions of self-government, not to mention the great success which she had enjoyed

under such figures as Jaume the Conqueror (1213–76). Further weight
was given to this mediaevalism by the Church, whose local representatives seized upon it as a means of reinforcing their war against liberalism,
and in 1859 it reached its apogee with the resurrection of the traditional
literary festival known as the *jocs florals*, or 'floral games'.

By the 1860s, then, Catalan nationalism was a reality. That said,
however, it was anything but a mass movement: there was as yet no
Catalan press; the *haute bourgeoisie* were mostly inclined to pursue their
interests through the medium of the main national parties; much of the
peasantry remained deeply influenced by Carlism; and the urban masses
were attracted either to the *demócratas* or to the teachings of proto-
socialism. In sum, the great strength which federalism acquired in
Catalonia cannot be portrayed as evidence of national feeling. On the
contrary, it is clear that the *sexenio* in reality gave rise to deep rifts in the
Catalan community. Although Catalans were prominent in the leadership of federalism, the upper classes were horrified by the threat of free
trade, Cuban autonomy, and social revolution alike, and in consequence
turned against it *en masse*.

To argue, then, that Catalan nationalism was a product of the frustrations of the industrial bourgeoisie is clearly untenable. Indeed, until 1898
business interests rallied wholeheartedly to the Restoration whilst yet
pressing for a move away from higher tariffs and a better deal for Spanish
exporters (perhaps surprisingly, the remnants of the empire were anything but a captive market, Spanish exports having to compete in them
with the much cheaper products emanating from Britain, France and the
United States). In these objectives they were largely successful – their
economic aspirations were met by the series of concessions which culminated in Cánovas' erection of a virtual 'tariff wall' around Cuba and
Puerto Rico in 1891 – whilst they were at the same time assured of a
reasonable degree of political representation in the two dynastic parties,
control of the *somatén*, and the support of the forces of order.

The origins of modern Catalan nationalism, then, are to be found not
amongst Catalonia's industrialists, but rather amongst their enemies, the
federalists. At first the smattering of Catalanist federalists sought fulfi-
lment in a general movement of decentralization, but a variety of factors
– a growing belief that Catalonia was a special case; disillusionment with
the revolutionary movement; and the acquisition of a more modern
aspect on the part of the *renaixença* – forced such men to reconsider their
position. Thus it was that in 1879 one of Pi y Margall's leading Catalan
disciples, Valentí Almirall, established the first Catalan-language daily.
By 1882, moreover, Almirall had broken with federalism to establish the
first specifically Catalanist political movement in history in the form of
the Centre Català.

Initially, it seemed that Almirall's initiative was going to startle the Catalan *haute bourgeoisie* out of its comfortable relationship with Madrid, for he succeeded in gaining its support for a proposal that Catalonia should present Alfonso XII with a statement of her grievances. Known as the *memorial de greuges*, or memorandum of grievance, the resultant petition constituted one of the classic formulations of Catalan nationalism, but it demanded too little to satisfy the more radical elements of the *renaixença*. Still worse, it became clear, too, that the industrial and commercial bourgeoisie simply regarded it as one more means of putting pressure on Madrid, their interest dying away after it was announced that Barcelona would host a great industrial exhibition in 1888. Some success was obtained with regard to the new civil code that was the same year promulgated by the Sagasta government – in brief, Catalonia was allowed to retain her own law – but within a short time the Centre Català had therefore fallen apart.

Despite these difficulties, the political movement that Almirall had tried to found was not dead. Thus, under the leadership of Almirall's lieutenant, Enric Prat de la Riba, a new force emerged in the early 1890s in the form of the Unió Catalanista. In 1892, meanwhile, the second annual congress of the Unió saw it stake Catalonia's claim to a separate parliament, fiscal system, judiciary, police force, and code of law, the recognition of Catalan as its official language, and liberation from the hated burden of conscription, Catalonia in the meantime being defined as a nation which happened to be a constituent part of the Spanish state. If the doctrines of Almirall and Prat de la Riba certainly awoke a powerful echo in Catalonia, the Catalan nationalism of the 1890s was not much of a threat. Challenged by mediaevalists who had strong links with Carlism, Prat de la Riba insisted that he was not a separatist, pretended that he was interested in little more than reviving Catalonia's old privileges, and sought to base Catalan nationalism in the countryside rather than in Barcelona and her industrial satellites. Nor did he receive much in the way of support from the industrialists and landowners who dominated Catalan politics, the 1890s, as we have seen, witnessing the satisfaction of many of their basic grievances.

If nationalism was weak in Catalonia, even more was this the case in the Basque country. In this respect, the key figure was Sabino de Arana y Goiri, the second son of a Bilbao shipbuilder who had been one of the chief supporters of Vizcayan Carlism in the war of 1872–6 and brought up his family in an atmosphere of Catholic and foralist traditionalism. Initially a Carlist, Arana became convinced Carlism was not part of the solution but rather part of the problem in that it did not recognize the Basques' separate identity. In many ways, however, it was clear that some such recognition was essential: increasingly only spoken in country districts of Guipúzcoa and Vizcaya, Euzkeran had long since been deserted by educated circles, whilst the number of immigrants from other parts of Spain was starting to become so great that Basque culture was in danger of being swamped altogether. Further stimulated by a period of residence in Barcelona, Arana therefore dedicated himself to the establishment of a new national movement, and, more immediately, the elaboration, first, of a modern Euzkeran grammar, and, second, of a highly romanticized version of Basque history. Announcing his intention of working for full independence, he invented a Basque flag, founded a bi-weekly nationalist newspaper, and established a new cultural institute in Bilbao. Finally in July 1895 there appeared the Bizkai-Buru-Batzar (Provincial Council of Vizcaya), a political movement whose tenets were essentially that Vizcaya should be an independent state organized and governed in accordance with its ancient traditions, confederated with the other Basque provinces, and dominated not just by native Basques, but by native Basque *speakers* (unlike Catalan, which had flourished, Euzkeran, which was to be the sole language of government, was now spoken only by the rural populace). As for the 'foreigners' who had been flooding into the Basque country, they were to be excluded from citizenship, and strongly discouraged from marrying 'true' Basques.

Before going any further, it is perhaps here worth pointing out the extent to which Basque nationalism was initially both Catholic and conservative. Extremely devout and violently anti-liberal, Arana was utterly horrified at what he saw as the dehumanizing and de-christianizing impact of urbanization, and, by contrast, clung to the Church as the central pillar of an ordered and hierarchical society, the consequence being that he was determined that his Basque confederation should above all be a theocracy. Aided by the fact that the Church's situation was much better in the Basque countryside than it was in the rest of Spain – owning relatively little land there, it had been able to maintain close links with the population – Arana was welcomed with open arms by the local clergy. Much less willing than many of their fellows to compromise with the Restoration, and for the most part originating from the very sorts of village which were later to be the bastions of Basque nationalism, they regarded him as a natural ally and increasingly rallied to his standard.

By the mid-1890s, then, Vizcaya, at least, possessed an embryonic nationalist movement. That said, however, Arana's impact was less than that of his Catalan fellows. Forced to struggle with a Carlist presence that drew as much strength as nationalism did from the revival of interest in Basque history and traditions, not to mention a foralist movement that rejected his separatism, Arana could make little headway even amongst the Euzkeran-speaking peasantry, let alone the increasingly anti-clerical and socialistic immigrants of Bilbao. Meanwhile, he was also hampered by his refusal (on the grounds that to have done so would have been to infringe the autonomy of the other Basque provinces) to extend his operations beyond the frontiers of Vizcaya. As for educated society, meanwhile, the situation was even worse. Thus, the industrialists of Bilbao were on the whole content, having been showered with titles, given a prominent role in local politics, and afforded a degree of tariff protection that was increased dramatically at the very time that Arana was attempting to launch a nationalist movement. Nor was the situation any better amongst intellectuals, such Basque luminaries as Miguel de Unamuno being as alienated by Arana's rejection of Castilian as they were by his clericalism. And, last but not least, if the parish clergy were supportive of Arana, their superiors were not, the bishops of such sees as Vitoria for a long time refusing even to sanction the use of the Basque version of Spanish Christian names. Even in Vizcaya, then, Basque nationalism remained extremely weak until 1898 and beyond, whilst in the rest of the Basque provinces it failed to gather any momentum at all.

Whilst Catalan and Basque cultural revivals were well under way by the 1890s (a development that was by now also being mirrored in Galicia), in political terms they had little impact. Apocalyptic though their implications were for the Restoration Monarchy, some catalyst was needed for their full impact to be felt upon its structures. That catalyst, of course, was to be provided by the events of 1898. However, before the effects of the loss of the colonies can be examined, it is first necessary to examine the socialism – Marxist and non-Marxist alike – that was to join regional nationalism in the eventual destabilization of the Canovine settlement.

Arousing the Starvelings

The history of Spanish socialism has not thus far been taken much beyond the period 1872–4. Emerging from the ranks of federalism and the pre-1868 trade-union movement, and much stimulated by the handful of 'apostles' sent to Spain by Mikhail Bakunin, internationalism, as it was first known, had by 1870 emerged as a major force, its chief manifestation being the Federación Regional Española de la Asociación Internacional Trabajadora. However, outlawed in November 1871, it had from then on been subjected to a period of more or less ferocious persecution, the effects of which were compounded by a variety of other problems of which the most notable was the internal disputes that beset the first International. Well enough known for them not to have to be recounted here in any detail, the issue round which these conflicts revolved was essentially the rift that had opened between Marx and Bakunin. At heart a dispute founded on personal and ethnic rivalry, the clash was expressed through rival theories of political organization and action. Thus, Bakunin, who drew heavily on the earlier ideas of Pierre-Joseph Proudhon, wanted a violent revolution that would destroy the state and replace it with loose associations of self-governing collectives, the only political organization that was needed being a network of secret societies that would labour, in the words of the *Internationale*, to rouse the starvelings from their slumbers. Meanwhile, Marx believed that the state should not be overthrown, but rather conquered for the benefit of the working classes, to which end the International had to engage in politics and, by extension, transform its national sections into a series of disciplined political parties.

Utterly opposed to one another, these rival conceptions of the International simply could not be conciliated, the result being a major split. As we have already seen, this dispute had not passed unnoticed in Spain. From the earliest days of its foundation, the FRE had contained within its ranks a number of men who were inclined to sympathize with Marx's views. Centred on the *madrileño* newspaper, *La Emancipación*, this group was in large part drawn from the leadership of a typesetters' union – the Asociación General del Arte de Imprimir – that had been established in 1871 under the leadership of one Pablo Iglesias. Quickly establishing a certain degree of influence, the *emancipacionistas*, as they became known, succeeded in a matter of months not only in persuading the FRE to adopt a rigidly centralized model of political organization, but also in infiltrating its leadership and securing permission for its members to engage in overt political activity. At the end of 1871, meanwhile, they were reinforced by the arrival from France of Marx's son-in-law, Paul Lafargue, who had come to Madrid with the specific brief of eradicating Spanish Bakuninism.

Though a superficial harmony was maintained, in practice the FRE split into two rival camps known as the *autoritarios* and *anti-autoritarios*. At length, in June 1872 the *autoritarios* were expelled from the FRE, a move to which they retaliated by establishing their own Nueva Federación Española. If Lafargue, Iglesias and their fellows had hoped that the FRE would simply follow their leadership, however, they were sadly mistaken. Determined to remain loyal to Bakunin, who had now formed a rival International of his own, the *anti-autoritarios* convoked a fresh congress of the FRE at Córdoba in December 1872, the fifty-four delegates who were present voting to retain the movement's decentralized and apolitical principles, and jettison the marxian structure that had been imposed upon it the previous year. As for the *autoritarios*, meanwhile, they were left with hardly any followers, the result being that both their new national federation and *La Emancipación* had soon folded.

Given the initial failure of marxian socialism, it is logical at this point to concentrate upon the anarchism that it had so signally failed to defeat. In spite of those who are inclined to argue that Spanish anarchism owed everything to the arrival of the magnetic figure of Giuseppe Fanelli, it is worth pointing out that its existence was also linked to influences that considerably pre-dated that of Mikhail Bakunin. Pride of place here must probably be given to the ideas of Proudhon. A self-educated printer from the Jura, Proudhon had coupled calls for the replacement of the state by a federation of autonomous units composed of associations of small owner-occupiers or artisans with the most visceral hatred of organized religion. Described by Proudhon as 'anarchy', the state of affairs that he envisaged found its first Spanish exponent in the person of an academic from Santiago de Compostela named Ramón de la Sagra, whilst it was also much commented upon by Pi y Margall, who developed Proudhon's ideas at some length.

Together with the widespread formation of workers' societies in the 1850s and 1860s, the views of Proudhon and Pi without doubt paved the way for the rapid success which Giuseppe Fanelli obtained in the course of his brief visit to Spain. Matters were further improved, meanwhile, by the fact that Bakunin advocated the violent revolution that was specifically rejected by Proudhon and Pi. However, if anarchism was a rational response to a particular set of social and economic conditions, its penetration of Spanish society is a subject of some complexity, it being fairly clear that its implantation was by no means as general as its many enthusiasts have been inclined to argue. Thus, far from embracing anarchism as a new religion, the *braceros* were inclined to rally to its standard only at times of acute crisis, the only reliable support that it obtained coming from such groups as small-holders, shopkeepers and skilled workers. Even within Andalucía support was patchy – anarchism made little headway in Huelva and Granada, for example – whilst beyond its frontiers it was concentrated in a few urban strongholds of which the most important were Barcelona and Zaragoza. Finding an explanation for this situation is one of the greatest problems of modern Spanish history, however. Taking the question of the *braceros*, for example, why should they have flocked to anarchism in Andalucía, but not in equally desperate Extremadura? In so far as industry is concerned, moreover, if it can be assumed that anarchism took root in Zaragoza and Barcelona on account of the influence of federalism, why did it not also do so in Cartagena and Valencia? In some cases the cause was purely accidental – initially Marxist, Gijón turned anarchist when a massive general strike that gripped the port in the early months of 1901 was given no support by the Socialist leadership; equally, Cádiz's pronounced libertarianism had much to do with the presence of one or two particularly magnetic personalities – but there is no doubt that much work remains to be carried out on the subject.

What there is little doubt about, however, is the nature of anarchism as an ideology. At the root of everything was the belief that man was created equal, good and social. From this, of course, it followed that the state was anathema, for of its very nature the state was an instrument for the exercise of authority, and the exercise of authority a perversion, the only reason why it was ever attempted being to keep one group of men subordinated to another. As even a workers' state would inevitably generate a new elite of its own that would end up by oppressing its progenitors, it followed that it had to be destroyed, and with it belief in God, for what was the concept of a deity but one more means of keeping men enslaved? From all this, there stemmed a compound of ideas that embraced not just a philosophical commitment to anarchism, but anti-clericalism, anti-parliamentarianism, and anti-militarism, as well as hatred of the police, the judiciary and the penal system. Meanwhile, being, in Proudhon's famous words, 'theft', private property was to be abolished, though until the popularization of the views of Peter Kropotkin in the late 1880s there was no suggestion of actual collectivization: the land was rather to be parcelled out for small-scale cultivation. However, as society was currently constructed, man was not only a slave to the bourgeois state and the institutions which propped up its rule, but also to his own baser instincts, whether it was greed for material possessions, addiction to products that were both harmful and unnecessary, a taste for luxury or even simple lust. As a result, anarchism displayed not only a deep interest in self-improvement – rational and scientific education was particularly prized – but also a strong commitment to the most moral and puritanical of lifestyles. Thus, the true anarchist was enjoined to live as simply as possible, to eschew alcohol and tobacco, to bring up his children in an atmosphere free of violence and bullying, and to forge stable and monogamous relationships with suitable female partners, who were, needless to say, to be treated as the absolute equals of their menfolk.

Confused and naive though many of these ideas were, they were nevertheless powerful enough to keep anarchism alive in the years of persecution that followed the collapse of the first republic. Indeed, the sheer scale of the repression was in some ways a blessing as it increased internationalism's popular renown, generated many 'apostles of the idea', and encouraged various forms of resistance, including terrorist actions of the sort that saw an attempt on the life of Alfonso XII in October 1878. As a result tension grew steadily in the countryside of

Andalucía and Extremadura, the last years of the decade being marked by an ever-growing wave of assaults and crop burnings. Nor was resistance confined to the south, there also being a number of strikes in Catalonia.

Edifying though all these activities may have been, they cannot camouflage the simple fact that by 1880 Spanish anarchism was in a state of real crisis. Setting aside the fact that the anarchist international that had been founded by Bakunin had collapsed after only five years, the leadership of the FRE was increasingly split between the syndicalists who, believing that the way forward lay in the revolutionary general strike, had initially dominated its proceedings, and a more violent group who had come to believe that the only hope lay in the direct action known as propaganda by the deed. Given the conditions that prevailed in Spain, it was the latter group which came to the fore, but this merely heightened tensions within the movement, for the reprisals provoked in Barcelona by the attempt on the life of Alfonso XII dealt its workers' societies a heavy blow, the result being that many workers began to desert the movement. Nor can that much comfort even be taken from the upsurge of violence in the southwest, for the forms of resistance which it took were typical of the agrarian unrest that had been endemic in the region for centuries and therefore did not necessarily testify to widespread politicization.

The consequence of all this was that the more moderate attitude adopted by the authorities after 1881 came as an absolute godsend. Thus, not only did it prove possible to re-establish the old FRE as the Federación de Trabajadores de la Región Española, but the 3,000 members of 1881 had within a year increased nearly twentyfold. Yet all this settled nothing. Whilst the commitment to revolution was reaffirmed, the trade-union leaders of Catalonia were determined in practice to confine the movement's efforts to achieving improvements in wages and conditions. For the *braceros* of the south-west, however, strike action represented the weakest of weapons, whilst the leadership was also challenged by those elements of the movement that remained committed to anarchism rather than syndicalism. As a result, anarchist violence continued unabated, and all the more so as fresh harvest failures had produced a period of great misery. One upshot of this development was the famous 'Mano Negra' affair (see above). Desperate to prevent a fresh prohibition, the leadership of the FTRE swore that the Mano Negra had nothing to do with them, but this only led considerable elements of the rank and file to form a rival movement entitled 'Los Desheredados' (the Disinherited), whilst doing nothing to appease the authorities who seized upon the affair as a pretext for smashing as many of its branches as they could manage.

Such was the pressure that by 1884 the Andalusian sections of the FTRE were in a state of collapse. However, this was not the end of the movement's woes, because it was from the mid-1880s onwards gripped by a major ideological schism in that its radical wing seized upon the new teachings currently being put forward by the exiled Russian theoretician, Peter Kropotkin, as a means of reviving the FTRE's faltering momentum. The gist of Kropotkin's argument being that the worker should be rewarded according to the product of his need rather than his labour, that trade-union action was incorrigibly reformist, and that anarchist movements should consist of federations not of workers' societies but militant cells, the inference was only too clear: the FTRE should embrace collectivization and abandon economic activity in favour of revolution. Needless to say, the result was that the FTRE was immediately plunged into crisis, so severe being the disputes that all this occasioned that in September 1888 its battered remnants voted themselves out of existence.

The demise of the FTRE did not put an end to the anarchist movement. Though split into insurrectionary and syndicalist wings, the movement continued to make its presence felt throughout the 1890s. Taking the syndicalists first of all, they mounted repeated general strikes, whilst at the same time becoming involved in a vigorous campaign for the institution of the eight-hour day. In common with the insurrectionists, meanwhile, they also made considerable efforts to energize the working classes through the foundation of cafés, clubs, cultural centres and night schools, the publication of newspapers, pamphlets and works of literature, and the celebration not only of May Day, but also of the anniversary of such events as the Paris Commune. If they were involved in these activities, however, the insurrectionists also had other concerns. Convinced of the value of propaganda by the deed, they threw themselves into the task of instigating an immediate revolution – hence the series of bomb attacks and assassination attempts that took place in Barcelona and elsewhere in the period 1893–7 (of these, the most prominent victim was Cánovas del Castillo, who was shot dead by an obscure Italian *émigré* on 8 August 1897).

What, however, did all this achieve? Other than the creation of numerous martyrs – in 1897, in particular, an attack on a religious procession in Barcelona led to the torture of large numbers of activists in the fortress of Monjuich – in the short term, the answer must be very little. Only one attempt at insurrection took place – at Jérez on 8 January 1892 – and even that has now been accepted as little more than an attempt to secure the release of a few locals who had just been arrested. With the authorities nevertheless afforded every pretext to wreak havoc, until 1898 and beyond the situation remained fundamentally bleak, the anarchist movement failing to build up a solid nucleus of support in more than a handful of localities.

Unfortunately for the cause of the Spanish labour movement, not much more could be said of the Marxist tendency that had been the other product of the splits of 1872. It will be recalled that by the middle of 1873 all that was left to Pablo Iglesias and his fellow *autoritarios* had been the printing union known as the Asociación General del Arte de Imprimir. Becoming president in 1874, Iglesias succeeded in keeping the society alive in the difficult years that followed the Restoration. However, no longer was it to be merely a trade union, for Iglesias had fallen under the influence of a fellow printer named José Mesa who had emigrated to France in search of work and become a friend of the leading French Marxist, Jules Guesde. Prominent amongst the latter's ideas was the belief, inherited from Marx himself, that the workers should engage in independent political action, and to this end on 2 May 1879 Iglesias secured the establishment of a group entitled the Grupo Socialista Madrileño. Following the elaboration of a party programme, which was supposedly passed by Mesa to Marx and Engels for their sanction and revision, two months later there emerged the Partido Socialista Obrero Español.

Initially the party was very small, but even so it was not long before it began to have some impact on proletarian politics. Thus, in 1882 Iglesias organized a highly effective strike amongst the typesetters of Madrid in 1882, whilst in 1886 there appeared the daily newspaper, *El Socialista*. As a result, by the time that the party held its first congress in 1888 it had no fewer than twenty-eight different branches. Further publicity accrued to the movement through the formation of a trade-union federation – the Unión General de Trabajadores – in 1888, the celebration from 1889 of May Day, the role played by the Socialists in the labour unrest that gripped the iron ore mines around Bilbao in 1890 and 1891, the participation of the PSOE in all parliamentary elections subsequent to that of 1891, and the absolute hostility with which Iglesias and his followers greeted the new wars of the 1890s. As a result the votes won by the party increased from approximately 4,000 in 1891 to 20,000 in 1898, whilst it also secured its first town councillors.

Despite all this, however, all was not well in the Socialist movement, the PSOE in many areas either failing to get off the ground at all, or only doing so with the greatest difficulty. One explanation that has been offered for this failure is that Pablo Iglesias and his colleagues failed to remain loyal to the ideas of Marx and Engels and instead allowed themselves to be influenced by the ideas of Jules Guesde. However, whilst Jules Guesde was neither a very profound thinker nor free of such influences as proudhonism, this is not especially satisfying. The Guesdist insistence that only genuine workers could be Socialists, and, further, that Socialist parties should never cooperate with representatives of the bourgeoisie may have driven away such intellectuals as Miguel de

Unamuno, prevented an alliance with the Republicans, and delayed the election of the first PSOE deputies, but there is no evidence to suggest that the influence of Guesdism damaged recruitment amongst the PSOE's natural constituency – indeed, if anything, the survival of many elements of proudhonist collectivism and bakuninite federalism ought rather to have boosted its appeal.

Whatever the truth may be, the fact is that the advances made by Spanish socialism in the period prior to 1898 were extremely disappointing, this being all the more surprising given that the conditions endured by the proletariat were just as bad as anything suffered by their counterparts elsewhere. In many mining districts, for example, the workforce were paid in truck and forced to reside in isolated settlements in which they were often subjected to severe economic exploitation, having no option but to shop, for example, in establishments owned by the company. Meanwhile, similar arrangements existed in Catalonia, where the middle years of the century had seen many owners attempt to escape the turmoil of Barcelona by setting up new industrial colonies in the upper valleys of such rivers as the Llobregat. Such conditions, perhaps, were atypical, but even in more established towns the situation was frequently appalling. Thus, rents were high, overcrowding widespread, and sanitation non-existent. Assailed in consequence by frequent epidemics, meanwhile, the populace had to work a ten-hour day for wages that were totally insufficient to support a family, and which, moreover, were further undercut by the employment of large numbers of women and children.

Aside from these conditions, it may also be noted that the anti-socialist bulwark that might have been constituted by the Catholic Church was at the very least being seriously undermined. With the growth of such cities as Madrid, Barcelona and Bilbao, the Church's parish structure was becoming increasing deficient, but this was only the beginning of the problem, for indifference was as much a feature of life in many rural areas as it was in the larger cities. Religious practice remained strong in the Basque country, Navarre, parts of Catalonia and Aragón, and much of Old Castile, but in much of Extremadura, New Castile, and Andalucía mass attendance was in steady decline. Much the same was true of vocations, the Church's priests increasingly coming only from the more practising parts of the country. As the periodic outbreaks of violence that took place against the Church showed, however, indifference was rapidly being supplanted by hostility.

For much of this situation, the Church had only itself to blame. Having chosen to side with the forces of, first, *moderantismo* and, second, the Restoration, it had unequivocally placed itself in the camp of landed property, and, indeed, the very forces that had benefited from disamortization, whilst the loss of its estates had in any case forced it to become heavily involved in big business (it should be noted that the destruction of the religious orders also deprived the Church of one of its chief means of popular evangelization). Nor, of course, were matters helped in this respect by the Church's promotion of 'yellow' trade unions, not to mention the fact that in the company towns established by some employers it maintained a strict watch over the workers' morals. In consequence it became identified as an integral part of the forces of repression, and all the more so given the tendency of many of its leaders to condemn any movement of protest out of hand. As many observers have noted, the result was a deep sense of betrayal that encouraged not just hatred of the Church but a desire to achieve its complete destruction. Also at issue, however, were more immediate problems. Given the slow progress that had been made in establishing a secular system of education, the lower classes were in large part dependent on the Church for schooling, just as the lack of any system of social security rendered them dependent upon it for assistance in times of dearth, infirmity and old age. Indeed, even work could fall within its purview given that an employer might easily insist on a certificate of good conduct from a worker's parish priest. Meanwhile, the Church's charity was frequently dependent on religious conformity, its education obscurantist, and its clergy harsh and authoritarian. And, last but not least, the Church was also a source of economic competition in that its institutions frequently engaged in activities that undercut the efforts made by the poor themselves to make ends meet.

In many ways, then, the situation ought to have been ripe for an explosion of anarchism and socialism alike, and yet this failed to occur. Why this should have been the case is not entirely clear, but conditions on the ground were evidently at least as important as the supposed deficiencies in revolutionary theory. Thus, in most industrial and mining areas the workforce was deeply divided and therefore slow to develop a common purpose, let alone a uniform identity. In Barcelona, for example, the native Catalan workforce hated, and were hated by, the *murcianos* who were beginning to arrive from the south, just as in the Basque country and Asturias the minority of miners who hailed from the immediate area hated, and were hated by, the Castilians and Galicians who had flocked to the area in search of work (in the same way, and for the same reasons, as the Irish in Britain, Galicians were particularly loathed wherever they went). Bitter competition, too, was fostered by the manner in which the mining industry, especially, was structured, whilst many workers were only 'part-time proletarians' who retained strong links with their native *pueblos*. In Madrid, indeed, many members of the so-called proletariat were not even proletarians at all, the structure of commerce and industry being such that a very large proportion of the workforce to all intents and purposes worked only for itself. Even more importantly, perhaps, to become a member of a trade union or vote for a PSOE candidate was to invite immediate retribution. Notwithstanding the decline in conventional religious practice, moreover, the workforce also remained far less hostile to religion than might at first sight have appeared, its growing failure to attend mass or go to confession remaining to some extent countered by its continued participation in traditional religious festivals. Add to this the very low cultural and educational standards that characterized the Spanish working classes and it will be seen that the obstacles to socialism were great indeed.

Setting aside structural issues that were operative across the board, it can be seen that anarchism and socialism both had to contend with problems that were particular to them alone. Thus, in so far as the former was concerned, revolutionary uprisings, terrorist atrocities and general strikes alike for the most part served only to bring down the wrath of the authorities and encourage desertion amongst the rank and file. As for the Socialists, meanwhile, it was almost equally hard for a movement that became more and more reformist in its tendencies, and which, moreover, placed its faith in a tactic whose only hope of success was to secure the support of a group whom its leadership went out of its way to alienate, to generate much faith amongst the working classes. Here, at least, attempts to pin the blame on the Socialists themselves are justified. Even ignoring the vexed question of Pablo Iglesias' understanding of Marxist theory, the fact is that he was a dessicated and lonely individual enmeshed in questions of bureaucracy who was quite incapable of providing the movement with charismatic leadership.

Whatever the precise reasons may have been, neither anarchism nor socialism made much progress in Spain prior to the disaster of 1898. All that can be said was that enough was achieved for many members of the establishment to become seriously alarmed. In this respect, however, its effect was destabilizing indeed. Already deeply hostile to what it saw as the secularizing tendencies of the Restoration, the Church, for example, was propelled further into such ultimately counter-productive campaigns as the one which aimed to consecrate Spain to the Sacred Heart of Jesus, Catholicism in consequence being made to look both aggressive and ridiculous.

Almost equally unfortunate, meanwhile, was the impact that the revolutionary left had upon the army. Even as it was, this force was increasingly disgruntled. Thus, the *sexenio* having increasingly receded into the past, many officers were becoming angered by the slow speed of promotion and the desperate shortcomings characteristic of the army's armament and equipment. As these problems showed no signs of being remedied – Cassola's reform programme, as we have seen, had had to be abandoned, whilst 1892 saw the third Sagasta government introduce a 'peace budget' which reduced military expenditure by some 5 per cent – many officers therefore began to complain of the selfishness and corruption endemic in the political system. Amidst all this the left's anti-militarism came as the last straw, and all the more so as the army itself came under physical attack – in 1891 a group of anarchists attacked a barracks in Barcelona, whilst in 1893 General Martínez Campos was severely wounded in a bomb attack. Against the revolutionary threat the authorities seemed to have little answer except from time to time to call in the troops (when, that is, they were prepared to do anything at all: the liberty afforded to the press was a constant source of outrage to many officers), but all that this achieved, so their commanders claimed, was to alienate the people still further. What was needed, then, was a new policy in the form of a campaign of indoctrination and repression that would eradicate anarchism and socialism once and for all (another target, of course, was the equally anathematical regionalism of Catalonia and the Basque country). From this it followed that the army would have to break one of the fundamental rules of the Canovine system and intervene in politics, for it was all too clear that neither the Liberals nor the Conservatives would be willing to do the job themselves. Opinions differed as to how this should be achieved, but at all events the army would save Spain.

The Eve of Disaster

We therefore end this chapter on a grimly prophetic note, for the Spain of the 1890s already contained within it the outlines of the 'two Spains' that were to fight the Civil War of the 1930s. Thus, on the one hand, many elements of the Church and the army, in particular, were developing clear signs of a messiah complex that eroded not only their own loyalty, but also that of the increasingly frightened landowners and entrepreneurs who dominated society and economy alike. On the other, there was a growing wave of popular unrest that, if prone to manipulation, badly led, and by no means united, foreshadowed the general revolutionary movement that in 1931 produced the Second Republic, and bade fair to ring the deathknell of *caciquismo*. In 1898, of course, this was still alive and well – for all the ferment of the previous years large sections of the population continued to remain utterly apathetic – whilst amongst the small shopkeepers, petty entrepreneurs, bank clerks, and minor officials who ought to have been the bedrock of republicanism the pull of the forces of traditionalism was still very strong. Quite clearly, however, the *pax canovana* was no peace at all, even if the full danger of the situation was not to be revealed until Spain was afflicted by the stunning events with which we must deal in the next chapter.

10

End of Empire

An End and a Beginning

It is a curious coincidence, but the three most striking dates in the history of nineteenth-century Spain all end in an 'eight'. Thus, 1808 saw the uprising against Napoleon, 1868 the *gloriosa*, and 1898 the loss of the last remnants of empire: defeated in a hopeless war against the United States, she was revealed for the second-class European power that was all that she could really claim to be. Dates, however, are no longer fashionable as historical commodities, and in this respect 1898 is no exception, it having been argued, first, that *el desastre* unleashed few new tendencies in political life, and, second, that the very word 'disaster' is a misnomer in that the colonies had for many years held back the development of Spanish industry and encouraged attitudes that perpetuated economic stagnation. To argue in this fashion seems shortsighted, however. Whilst the disaster failed to produce the sort of political cataclysm which many observers predicted, it is nonetheless the case that the Cuban war inflamed many of the tensions that had already begun to sap the Canovine system, accelerated the awakening of a public opinion whose very existence was incompatible with the *turno pacífico*, and shattered the faith of an establishment stripped of one of the central pillars of its propaganda in the very system which it had created. Though nothing happened in the short term, the result was that political change – and probably violent political change – became inevitable.

The Onset of Disintegration

By the beginning of the 1890s it was clear to any sentient observer that Spain's overseas empire was doomed. Thus, a new phase was dawning in the history of imperialism. With most of the world now conquered, it was very likely that the dominant powers would begin to cast a covetous eye on the possessions of their weaker fellows. In consequence, the Spanish empire was therefore very much at risk, and all the more so as it lay directly in the path of a United States that was increasingly bent on political and economic expansion.

However, Spain was not at all well placed to cope with such a threat. Thus, the navy was in a sorry state, many of its ships being either outmoded or unfit for service. For much of the time confined to port for want of coal, the fleet was also short of both target practice and sea-going experience, its officer corps having been so swelled by successive waves of promotions that the bulk of an already inadequate naval budget was swallowed up by salaries. A further problem was the lack of strategic bases, neither Cuba, nor Puerto Rico, nor the Philippines having either adequate reserves of coal or dockyards capable of dealing with the requirements of a modern fleet. Nor was the situation of the army much better. Here, too, the repeated wars and *prononciamientos* of the nineteenth century had had the effect of increasing the numbers in the officer corps to quite unmanageable limits, the result being a salary and pensions bill that absorbed at least one-third of the military budget. From this followed little money for new weapons or general manoeuvres, and, still worse, appalling conditions for the rank and file.

Spain's only real hope was therefore that she could somehow secure powerful foreign support, but this was not forthcoming. Ever since 1875 her chief goal had been to secure the friendship of Germany and Austria, who were identified as the powers most akin to Spain, and in May 1887 Spain was duly admitted to the Triple Alliance. Thus protected, Cánovas had felt no hesitation in offending Britain and France by raising tariffs, but, in reality, the Austro-German alliance offered Spain almost nothing, the fact being that she was simply too weak to have any hope of attracting real support. With even her friends ready to turn upon her – in 1885, for example, a major dispute had erupted with Germany over the Caroline Islands – it was all too clear that Spain was on her own.

Singularly depressing though Spain's naval, military and diplomatic situation was, her politicians seemed to have eyes for little else than the workings of *caciquismo*. Already evident in the so-called 'peace budget', this complacency was not even shattered by the difficulties which the Spaniards encountered in overawing the Moors in the course of a brief conflict that erupted on the periphery of the Spanish enclave of Melilla in 1893. Rather more concern was expressed by the generals, true, the military press being filled with criticism of the regime's neglect of the army. However, the only practical effect was to reinforce Madrid's determination to be intransigent elsewhere for fear that otherwise the result would be a *pronunciamiento*, and that despite the fact that the affair also highlighted the weaknesses of the navy: on 11 March 1895 one of the best ships in the fleet sank with all hands when it was caught by a violent storm in the Straits of Gibraltar.

Typically enough, this loss was not even thought worthy of an enquiry by the government, the latter being absorbed in yet another political crisis. To understand the situation, it is necessary to return to the moment when Sagasta resigned as prime minister in July 1890. As was to be expected, he was immediately replaced by Cánovas, but the new administration was soon thrown into complete confusion. For the past ten years one of the chief centres of disaffection within the ranks of the Conservatives had been constituted by the person of Francisco Silvela. Despite the fact that he was a typical product of the political system, Silvela had become increasingly alarmed at the corruption and instability inherent in *caciquismo*, and was therefore arguing that electoral management should be done away with; the political parties rebuilt as mass movements; and local government rescued from the constant intervention of the state. None of this, of course, was much to the taste of Cánovas, who was firmly convinced that any move in the direction of Silvela's views would destabilize his entire creation. However, in view of the continuing dissidence of Romero Robledo, the exclusion of Silvela was impossible, whilst it seems, too, that Cánovas was inclined not to take him too seriously (after all, Germán Gamazo had for the past few years been trumpeting similar views when in reality his sole aim was to cement his personal power base). As a result, Silvela was appointed to the crucial post of Minister of the Interior.

Immediately, however, things went wrong. To Cánovas' horror, Silvela attempted to translate his words into reality, the elections that were ordered for February 1891 witnessing a considerable reduction in government intervention, and, by extension, a great improvement in the fortunes of such groups as the republicans. That said, there was still much evidence of fraud and other malpractice, the result being that in July 1891 Silvela introduced a bill for the establishment of a new network of regional councils, the intention being that these would neutralize the influence of the *caciques*, shield local government from interference on the part of Madrid, and have the power to intervene in the affairs of any province or municipality where there was evidence of serious corruption. In doing so, however, Silvela only alienated Cánovas still further, the result being that the prime minister began openly to undermine his position, the Minister of the Interior eventually being left with no option but to resign in favour of Romero Robledo. The exchange, however, did not prove a very profitable one in that Romero's conduct aroused such a storm of protest that the Queen Regent was driven to announce that she had lost all confidence in the cabinet, the upshot being the formation of another Sagasta government on 7 December 1892.

The travails that broke the Cánovas government of 1890–2 were the first intimation of a tendency towards fragmentation that was to become ever more serious. Meanwhile, though the torch had passed to the Liberals, nothing was done to act on Silvela's ideas, the ferocious hostility exhibited towards the new government by a Conservative Party furious at the manner in which it had been overthrown hardly being calculated to encourage an interest in reform. As a result, the elections which followed Sagasta's appointment witnessed little improvement, whilst the municipal polls that were supposed to have been held in 1893 were postponed. However, Cánovas' anger did help to maintain the unity of the government, whilst the Liberals also gave some signs of pursuing reforms in other areas: setting aside the 'peace budget' and other measures designed to reduce expenditure, as Minister of Finance, Gamazo initiated a major campaign against tax evasion; the Minister of Commerce, Segismundo Moret, sought to limit the effects of protectionism by a trade agreement with Germany; and the Minister of Overseas, an up-and-coming Mallorcan named Antonio Maura, embarked on a serious attempt to provide Cuba with a degree of devolution. However, it was not long before the strains of office began to tell. The pressure for financial cutbacks soon cost the resignation of a number of ministers; Gamazo's attempts to increase revenue upset many of the Liberals' own supporters; and Maura's colonial reforms were undermined by fears of encouraging regionalism at home. As a result, reshuffle followed reshuffle until the Liberals were utterly discredited. When Sagasta tendered his resignation in protest at the army's refusal to discipline a group of officers who had sacked the offices of a number of newspapers which had offended them, the Queen Regent therefore allowed him to go, the consequence being that on 21 March 1895 Cánovas found himself in office yet again.

What, then, did all this show? In brief, it had become clear that both the Conservatives and the Liberals were little more than collections of warring factions unable to agree on any of the fundamental measures that were needed to address Spain's problems. Whilst Cánovas and Sagasta had not yet been challenged, the emergence of a second rank of ambitious politicians had rendered their position ever more difficult. At risk, therefore, was the whole structure of the Canovine system.

Loss of Empire

On 24 February 1895 bands of insurgents loyal to the outlawed Partido Cubano Revolucionario raised the flag of independence in various parts of Cuba, thereby precipitating a storm that had hardly been difficult to predict. Thus, the victory of 1878 had not been accompanied by a programme of political pacification of the sort that might have reconciled the former revolutionaries to the prospect of continued Spanish rule. On the contrary, whilst the constitution of 1876 was extended to Cuba and the island awarded forty *cortes* deputies, nothing was done to address the question of equality between *peninsulares* and *criollos*, whilst it became all too clear that Spain's sole aim was the colony's continued exploitation.

All this would have been very well had not Cuban society been undergoing a far-reaching process of change. First and foremost, in 1888 slavery had at last been ended, the result being that the Spanish presence was deprived of one of its chief *raisons d'être*. Meanwhile, benefit though it did from emancipation, the plantocracy was in other respects hard hit, for many of its estates and sugar mills had been devastated by the war, whilst the 1880s also witnessed the rapid development of a sugar-beet industry in metropolitan Spain. In consequence, many of Spain's greatest supporters were ruined whilst others only survived by renting out their estates to tenant farmers. Cuba, in short, was no longer the thriving island of days gone by, whilst continued Spanish rule was doing nothing to redress the balance: the poverty of the mass of the population was all too obvious, public services hopelessly insufficient, food prices very high, and corruption widespread. To make matters worse, in 1894 the United States – an increasingly important Cuban market – suddenly imposed a 40 per cent duty on raw sugar, Spain being quite unable to absorb the sudden glut that resulted.

Even now judicious concessions might have saved the day: the bulk of the opposition was concentrated in the extremely moderate Partido Liberal-Autonomista, whilst the rising was at first a dismal failure. However, never backward in his nationalism, Cánovas had been emboldened by the Melilla conflict, whilst he was afraid that a conciliatory policy would undermine his position in Madrid, where the uprising had sparked off a great wave of anger and indignation in establishment circles. Proclaiming his determination to make no concessions at all until the rebellion had been defeated, he immediately dispatched substantial reinforcements, imposed a blockade of the Cuban coast, and sent out Martínez Campos to take charge of operations in the hope that he might repeat the victory of 1878.

No such success was achieved, however. Although the independence movement lost its greatest leader, José Martí, in a skirmish, the onset of the rainy season made offensive operations extremely difficult for the Spaniards. All the more was this the case given the difficult terrain of the eastern half of the island – the revolt's heartland – and the guerrilla tactics engaged in by the rebels. Also crucial was the issue of disease and the diminished popularity of the unionist cause: by the end of 1895 no fewer than 50,000 of the 120,000 Spanish troops in Cuba had fallen sick, whilst the supply of Cuban volunteers was much smaller than it had been in the Ten-Years' War. Many Spanish troops being tied down in static garrisons, the rebels were therefore able both to establish a provisional government, and to consolidate their political influence, the consequence of this being that Martínez Campos' attempts to undermine the insurrection through offers of amnesty and negotiation fell on deaf ears. With the rebels beginning to penetrate many areas that had hitherto remained quiet and Cuban loyalism under ever greater strain, on 16 January 1896 Martínez Campos therefore resigned in despair.

Despite Cánovas' rhetoric, Spanish policy had thus far essentially revolved around hopes of another peace of Zanjón. The prospect of such a compromise now seeming very remote, the general chosen to replace Martínez Campos was the toughest and most competent commander in the entire Spanish army. Known from earlier campaigns as a 'hard man' and assisted by large numbers of fresh troops, Valeriano Weyler certainly brought real ruthlessness to the struggle. Thus, whilst the insurgents were harassed through the adoption of better tactics and the construction of a series of coast-to-coast defensive barriers, the population was herded into concentration camps and subjected to savage reprisals, the result being that Weyler had soon restored a semblance of order in the western part of the colony.

A semblance of order was not victory, however, whilst the cost of the war continued to soar alarmingly. Still worse, Weyler's tactics were alienating the civilian population, large numbers of whom inevitably fell prey to starvation and disease, whilst providing the insurgents with excellent propaganda and increasing the risk of American intervention. In this situation, Cánovas inevitably began to waver. Whilst the Church, the army, the shippers and the cotton industry were all inclined to press for total victory, in early 1897 the rebels were therefore again offered a compromise peace. Though the concessions involved were by no means insubstantial, this approach was rejected, however, Cánovas' difficulties being further increased by fresh domestic political problems. At first the government had enjoyed the support of the Liberals, the Republicans and the Unión Constitucional (a dissident movement formed by Silvela in 1894). However, this support was increasingly jeopardized by the character of the administration, for Romero Robledo had not only been restored to the cabinet, but brought with him a number of *protégés* who had a particularly notorious record of corruption. As a result it was not long before the government had become immersed in a series of scandals, and in May 1897 the Liberals, *silvelistas* and Republicans all walked out of the *cortes* in disgust.

What would have happened had matters pursued their natural course is difficult to predict, for Cánovas was now in serious trouble. In particular, there was much discontent amongst the officer corps. Thus, growing frustration at the army's inadequate equipment was coupled with intense resentment at the growing denunciations of Weyler's brutality, the general feeling being that the military had been placed in an impossible position. Yet another bone of contention was the growing opposition to the war, it being all too clear that the bulk of the population were at best indifferent to the struggle. Whilst over-excited journalists might wax ferocious and cheering crowds turn out to send off the unfortunate conscripts, such enthusiasm was all too obviously confined to groups that did not have to fight. Enabled to buy exemption from conscription for 1,200 *pesetas* by the army law of 1877, everybody who had any chance of doing so took advantage of this escape route. As a result service in Cuba was quite rightly perceived as an unfair burden, the consequence being at best a mood of sullen resignation and at worst periodic outbreaks of disorder, all this being further encouraged by the condemnation of the war emanating from the Socialists, the anarchists, the Catalan and Basque nationalists, and a handful of Republicans.

With military discontent growing, a *prononciamiento* did not seem impossible, and all the more so as angry officers now acquired a striking figurehead in the person of General Polavieja. Hitherto governor of the Philippines, Polavieja had established a considerable reputation in circles favourable to the colonial interest by the summary fashion in which he had put down a revolt that had broken out in May 1896. Recalled to Madrid on account of quarrels with the government, he was greeted as a hero and incited to overthrow Cánovas. On 8 August, however, the prime minister was assassinated by an Italian anarchist funded and egged on by Cuban exiles. A coup now being clearly unacceptable, the Conservatives were therefore left to reconstitute their ministry. However, the task was beyond them, and on 2 October Sagasta had to be summoned yet again.

Ever since the beginning of the year the Liberals had been arguing for a change of policy in Cuba, for they were convinced that the insurrection could only be ended through the offer of substantial concessions, and, further, that these were the only way of staving off American intervention. In rapid succession, then, Sagasta promised the Cubans full autonomy, suspended offensive operations against the insurgents, replaced the pugnacious Weyler with the emollient Ramón Blanco y Erenas and announced an amnesty for all political prisoners. In January 1898, moreover, an island government was established under the leadership of the *autonomista*, José María Gálvez. However, all this achieved very little: the rebel leaders were actually encouraged to fight on, whilst Sagasta rather spoiled things by ordering the dispatch of a further 20,000 troops. Sufficient had been done, however, for the *peninsulares* to feel that they were being betrayed, and on 12 January Havana witnessed a group of outraged army officers attack the offices of an *autonomista* newspaper which had offended their sensibilities.

There followed a fateful chain of events. Gulled by its consul in Havana – a strong supporter of intervention who exaggerated the riots out of all proportion – the American government dispatched the battleship, *Maine*, to protect the American colony in the city. On 15 February, however, the *Maine* blew up at its berth, killing two-thirds of its crew. The cause remains unknown to this day, but American opinion was outraged, President McKinley being left with no option but to demand that Spain declare an armistice and accept the principle of Cuban independence. This, however, was something that the Spanish government could not do, there being genuine fears that any such concession would lead to revolution: not only would the army have been outraged, but the colonial lobby was whipping up noisy anti-American demonstrations on all sides, whilst the Carlists had also been doing what they could to exploit the situation. To fight the United States, the more sentient ministers, admirals and generals privately admitted, could only be disastrous, but it did at least offer the hope of preserving the regime. Desperate efforts to escape notwithstanding, by 21 April 1898 the United States and Spain were therefore formally at war.

The events that followed need not detain us here. It is, however, worth pointing out that the war was not quite the walkover that has sometimes been depicted. If the navy was in a difficult situation, it nonetheless had the capacity to make life hard for the Americans, whilst the army was actually better armed than its opponents as well as being much more used to the climate and terrain. Possessed though they were of a host of strategic and economic advantages, meanwhile, the Americans had neither adequate land forces nor any recent experience of conducting large-scale operations.

If the Spanish government expected to be defeated, then, it was certainly not thinking in terms of the disaster which actually occurred. However, in the event, the Spaniards played such cards as they had with a distinct lack of skill. In the Philippines Admiral Montojo chivalrously moved his fleet away from the protection of the big guns of Manila in the hope of ensuring that the populace would not be caught in the crossfire, and was in consequence blown out of the water as soon as the American squadron that had been dispatched to the archipelago arrived there on 1 May. Meanwhile, in Cuba the Spanish Atlantic fleet had by the beginning of June allowed itself to be bottled up in the most inadequate refuge of Santiago, whilst the Spaniards made no attempt to contest the disembarkation of the American expeditionary force, withdrew all the troops in the immediate vicinity into a cramped and ill-planned defensive perimeter around Santiago, and failed to concentrate the remainder of their forces in the eastern half of the island into a field army that might have operated against the Americans' communications. Admittedly they fought very well when Santiago was finally attacked on 1 July, but even so a number of key hilltop positions were lost, the result being that the fleet of Admiral Cervera was forced to break out on pain of being sunk at its moorings. On 3 July his ships therefore put to sea, but, forced to do so under the very guns of a far superior force, they were one by one reduced to blazing wrecks. To all intents and purposes the war was over: deprived of all hope of succour and desperately short of food, Santiago capitulated on 16 July, whilst both Puerto Rico and the Philippines were invaded by substantial American armies. Having clearly done all that could be expected of it, the Spanish government sued for peace, the price being Cuba, Puerto Rico and the Philippines.

Aftermath

Whether or not the events of 1898 really constituted a *desastre*, there can be no doubt of the shattering effect that they had on the Spanish establishment, whose more irresponsible elements had been prophesying victory and hurling defiance at the Americans to the very end. Given the importance of the army in the events that were to follow, in this respect it might be particularly worthwhile to glance at the military press. On 16 April, for example, *El Heraldo del Ejército* had carried a long article denying that victory always went to the side with the greater numbers, and claiming that the hardened veterans of the Cuban garrison would easily defeat the untrained masses of the United States, whilst eight days later it anathematized the *yankis* as 'a bastard people without religion or fatherland' whose army was composed of 'mercenary hordes that do not even merit the name of militias'. On the very day that the Spanish Philippines squadron was being beaten so conclusively in Manila Bay, meanwhile, the same paper was praying for a decisive battle on 2 May – the ninetieth anniversary of the Spanish uprising against Napoleon – 'because on that day victory must be ours'. Much excited by the gallant Spanish resistance outside Santiago – an affair of which *La Correspondencia Militar* claimed 'morally speaking, to have the inestimable value of a most beautiful victory' – the reaction of such papers to the loss of one Spanish squadron after another was to engage in still greater flights of fancy. Spain, it seemed, did not need a fleet to fight a war in Cuba, Puerto Rico and the Philippines, and the navy's gallant self-sacrifice was not a catastrophe but rather an example of heroism that could only spur the nation to fresh efforts. Indeed, all was well, for the war effort was now entirely in the hands of the army, and the army would never surrender. News that the government was seeking a peace settlement was therefore greeted with howls of protest, it being pointed out that the bulk of the Spanish forces in Cuba remained undefeated and – so it was claimed – ready to fight to the last man. Meanwhile, though rather more realistic views were entertained elsewhere, there was nonetheless a deep sense of despair: utterly humiliated, Spain had lost not just her empire, but also the jealously guarded pretence that she was a great power inhabited by a people of unequalled heroism and virtue.

Plunged into turmoil, Spain for a brief time seemed threatened by a coup of the very sort that the war had been fought to avoid. Thus, many officers were furious at the manner in which the military authorities were being blamed for the disaster by parts of the press, and all the more so as the officer corps was convinced that the defeat ought rather to be blamed on the politicians, and, indeed, civilian society as a whole. Whipped up by the Carlists, who were seriously considering an uprising, there were therefore many angry protests and much talk of the need to establish a military government. However, all this came to nothing: no generals were actually prepared to move, whilst Carlos VII soon decided that a rising stood no chance, the episode's only real significance being that it marked the beginning of a *rapprochement* between the Carlists and the army – hitherto irreconcilable enemies – that was to bear much fruit in the 1930s.

If 1898 could not provoke a revolt on the Right, it certainly could not do so on the Left. One of the reasons that Sagasta had gone to war was that he had believed that public opinion would not tolerate capitulation without a fight. In this, however, he was utterly deceived. Whilst the wars of 1895–8 had certainly occasioned many patriotic demonstrations, such events were essentially the fruit of contrivance. Nor, of course, does the fact that the Liberals obtained the usual government majority in the elections of 1898 mean very much. Much more representative of the state of public opinion were the increasing difficulty that was found in obtaining substitutes, the desperate attempts of the populace to evade military service, and the bread riots that spread across most of Spain in May 1898. Notwithstanding the violent bellicosity adopted by many Republicans in the hope of winning over the army, there was therefore no chance of revolution.

All the more was this the case given that the war failed to produce the expected economic crisis. Whilst Spanish exports to the colonies had certainly been hit by the war, the sheer longevity of the latter's links with Spain and the preference of many of their inhabitants for Spanish styles ensured that they picked up again for long enough to allow industrialists to readjust to the new situation. At the same time, too, because the *peseta* had fallen in value as a result of the fighting, exports elsewhere were boosted. Finally, large quantities of capital were being repatriated from the colonies; the returning soldiery were crying out for civilian clothes; and domestic demand had been swollen by an excellent harvest. Some sectors of the economy, true, were hit very hard, but the overall result was not depression but rather lower inflation and higher growth.

This is not, however, to say that 1898 did not stimulate protest politics. In the first place the desperate efforts made to whip up support for the war had done much to awaken public opinion from its slumbers. In the second, defeat had tended to revive old grudges. Thus, hatred of military service was reinforced by the repatriation of the Cuban army: shipped home in terrible conditions, many soldiers died *en route*, whilst the survivors received the minimum of assistance. Equally, popular anti-clericalism was stirred up by the Church's support for the war (in this respect it did not help that many vociferous members of the colonial lobby were also prominent in Catholic circles). Though other factors were also of importance, it is therefore no coincidence that the years after the war were marked by numerous outbreaks of anti-clerical violence.

If popular hostility to the regime was strengthened, the opposition was much galvanized. Let us first examine the Republicans. However marginal he had now become, Emilio Castelar abandoned his earlier endorsement of the Liberals and placed all the blame for the defeat on the establishment, whilst younger figures such as the increasingly prominent journalist, Alejandro Lerroux – a raffish figure who had made his reputation by publicizing the torture of imprisoned anarchists – waxed furious in their denunciation of the regime, Lerroux going on to embark on a ferocious campaign to win over the workers of Barcelona. Meanwhile, the passage of the years was also coming to the aid of the deeply divided republican movement, for Ruiz Zorrilla had died in 1895, being followed to the grave by Castelar in 1899 and Pi y Margall in 1901. The only surviving leader from the first Republic being Nicolás Salmerón, it was therefore possible to restore the unity of the Republican movement through the formation of a single party known as Unión Republicana.

If these factors led to a modest revival in the republican camp, both socialism and anarchism were boosted by the war. Thanks to its fervent anti-bellicosity, the PSOE increased its official vote from 14,000 in 1896 to 20,000 in 1898, 23,000 in 1899 and 25,000 in 1901, and might well have obtained several *cortes* seats had it not been for the wholesale fraud of which it was invariably the victim. By 1901, meanwhile, it had secured representatives in no fewer than twenty municipalities, whilst the strength of the UGT had risen from 6,154 members in 1896 to 26,088 in 1900. With regard to anarchism the picture is again one of increased activity. Thus, in Andalucía, the libertarian movement sprang to life again. Many new anarchist unions appeared, whilst others awoke after years of dormancy; an attempt was made to impose a degree of organization; and there were numerous strikes amongst workers and agricultural labourers alike. In Barcelona, too, the immediate post-war period witnessed a considerable increase in union membership, the vast majority of it anarchist, whilst the number of days' labour lost through strike action soared from 169,176 in 1899 to 379,145 in 1903. Thereafter, thanks to a variety of factors – changing economic circumstances, the failure of most strikes, vicious reprisals and the growing influence of Lerroux – militancy fell off once again, but the image of Barcelona as a bastion of anarchism had nonetheless been firmly established.

If anarchism and socialism were both given a fillip by the events of 1898, this is even more true of the 'regenerationist' movement of Costa and his ilk. Thus, with the sort of criticism of the system which he had espoused redoubled in the wake of the war, in November 1898 Costa organized a general conference of Spain's chambers of commerce in Zaragoza in the hope that this would establish a new democratic party. No such decision was forthcoming, however – the congress resolved only to petition the Queen Regent – and Costa therefore proceeded to summon a similar conference of the chambers of agriculture. However, this gathering was just as much a failure as the first: unmoved by Costa's impassioned and highly nationalistic rhetoric, it was riven by divisions of all sorts and in the end agreed only to the formation of a new 'league of producers' whose task it would be to campaign for a moderate programme of administrative, fiscal and political reform.

Although Costa's failure to impose his agenda on the chambers of agriculture and commerce ensured that it was doomed to remain an irrelevance, the regenerationist movement survived. Not only had a number of figures within the two main parties – aside from Silvela, obvious examples include Antonio Maura, Santiago Alba and José Canalejas – become increasingly inspired by its modernizing ideals, but it was also firmly established as an intellectual current, the resultant 'generation of 1898' including such luminaries as Miguel de Unamuno, Ramón María Valle Inclán, Pío Baroja, Ramiro de Maeztu, Antonio Machado and Santiago Ramón y Cajal.

Setting aside the 'generation of 1898', the second Zaragoza assembly had not been long over before the regenerationist cause received a much-needed injection of support. In brief, although the Liberals had weathered the loss of the war, the growing differences in their ranks soon provoked a cabinet crisis. Unity having in the meantime been restored under the leadership of Silvela, the Conservatives were therefore able to demand that the Queen Regent should restore them to power, which she duly did on 4 March 1899. Silvela, of course, had been associated with the cause of regenerationism for most of the past ten years, whilst he had since the end of the war been loud in his claims that the Canovine system had enervated the nation. As he brought into the Cabinet not only a noted Catalanist, but also General Polavieja, who had over the past few months erected himself as a champion of both Catalan nationalism and regenerationism, the hopes that his accession aroused were considerable.

To be fair to Silvela, his personal morality was unquestioned, the elections of April 1899 showing evidence of a desire to act with clean hands. At the same time, his government saw a real attempt to improve the position of the working classes, to free local government from state intervention, to reduce government expenditure, and to establish a fairer system of taxation. However, much to the credit of Silvela though all this was, the revolution from above which he had promised showed no signs of materializing, whilst in some ways the situation actually got even worse. Thus, Silvela's social legislation was widely ignored by employers, whilst his new tax system in practice increased the pressure on the lower classes whilst doing nothing to address the manner in which landed wealth paid almost nothing. Nor, indeed, did Catalonia benefit very much: although Polavieja accepted the need for the region to enjoy a special relationship with Madrid, Silvela did not, the consequence being that he refused to entertain the idea that it should be accorded a *concierto económico* akin to that of the Basque provinces (in this respect, Silvela and others like him argued that the way forward was in effect to extend decentralization to every part of Spain).

Not all of this was apparent at once, but even so the summer of 1899 was therefore one of considerable turmoil. Thus, there were serious outbreaks of rioting in Valencia, Zaragoza and Barcelona, whilst Catalonia was affected by a widespread taxpayers' strike whose chief characteristic was a refusal by most shopkeepers to open their businesses. The government's only response being to denigrate the protests, send in the troops, and declare a state of siege, the regenerationist movement was at last pushed into open participation in politics: in January 1900 the chambers of commerce met at Valladolid and announced the formation of a new political movement. Entitled the Unión Nacional, this was soon joined by Costa and his Liga Nacional de Productores, and for a brief time it seemed that the domination of the Liberals and Conservatives might actually be under real threat. In the event, however, nothing of the sort occurred. Denied any chance of fighting the government at the polls, the new organization had no option but to resort to continued tax-strikes. In doing so, however, it alienated many of its own supporters, large numbers of whom had been greatly alarmed by the violence of the previous year, whilst at the same time adopting a course that could not but lead to defeat (the government being more than ready to dispossess defaulters, most of them were certain to cave in). Subjected to constant harassment, weakened by numerous defections, scorned by the Catalanists and the Socialists, and hamstrung by the reluctance of its leadership to unleash a popular revolt, the Unión Nacional was therefore a complete failure. A handful of deputies succeeded in achieving election under its standard in the contest of 19 May 1901, but by then Costa himself had resigned in disgust, whilst the movement itself had become little more than a *neo-gamacista* pressure group.

If regenerationism failed to establish itself as a major force in the wake of 1898, the same was not the case of regional nationalism. Thus, in different ways Catalonia, the Basque provinces and Galicia had all been hit very hard by *el desastre* – the main industries of both Catalonia and Vizcaya had been heavily dependent on the colonies, whilst the latter had been a traditional destination for Galicia's many emigrants – with the result that their respective regionalist movements received a major fillip. It was at this time, for example, that Basque nationalism secured its first electoral victories in Vizcaya, and that the Catalanists at last attracted the support of the industrialists of Barcelona, the result of this latter development being the formation of a new political party – the Lliga Regionalista de Catalunya – that quickly established itself as a major force in local politics.

To return to the hapless Silvela, these various movements of protest all served to complicate his chances of success. Even as it was, however, it was soon apparent that his policy was an extremely fragile construct. Thus, attempts to reduce the military budget led to Polavieja's resignation as Minister of War, whilst the Catalanist Minister of Grace and Justice, Manuel Durán i Bas, soon followed him in protest at Silvela's brutal repression of the Catalan tax strikes. Behind the scenes, meanwhile, the prime minister's rival, Romero Robledo, was doing all that he could to sabotage his rule in the hope of avenging the manner in which Silvela had supplanted him as Cánovas' successor. Seven ministerial crises and three different cabinets later, Silvela resigned, and on 6 March 1901 the Queen Regent restored to office no less a person than the utterly discredited Práxedes Sagasta.

If nothing else, the next few months served to show how far the Liberal leader had lost touch with the realities of politics. Thus, whilst Sagasta mouthed the slogans of regeneration, the elections of 1901 displayed none of the scruples of their predecessors. Having since 1898 been engaged in a bitter feud with Germán Gamazo, the 'old shepherd', as he was known, seized upon the contest as a golden opportunity to smash the *gamacistas* once and for all. Still worse, the subsequent conduct of his administration showed that government was once more to rely on a combination of bribery and force. All this, meanwhile, was carried on behind a façade of reform. Thus, one of the brightest lights of the Liberal Party, José Canalejas, was appointed Minister of Agriculture, Industry,

Commerce and Public Works, and from then until his resignation in May 1902 – a move, be it said, prompted entirely by the equivocations of Sagasta – he threw himself into the organization of an Instituto del Trabajo, or Institute of Labour, whose aim it would be to draw up schemes of social reform. At the same time, the government also threw itself into a fresh campaign against the Catholic Church, which, it quite rightly argued, was flouting the terms of the Law of Associations of 1887, and assuming far too dominant a role in education.

Typically, however, Sagasta proved most reluctant to press matters to a conclusion (it was in fact this issue that led to Canalejas' resignation), but, even had he been prepared to do so, it was unlikely that his government could have survived for very long: given that the premier was clearly nearing the end of his life, various party barons were eyeing one another with regard to a future leadership contest, whilst Canalejas became so angered that by the autumn he was in open rebellion. With the ranks of the Conservatives in the meantime reinforced by the remnants of the *gamacistas*, Silvela's reformism having attracted the support of their new leader, Antonio Maura (Gamazo himself had died towards the end of 1901), the palace became increasingly alarmed. Determined to deal with Canalejas in the same way as he had dealt with Gamazo, Sagasta made the mistake of asking for a decree of dissolution, only to find that Alfonso XIII – the king had come of age in May 1902 – would not break the unwritten rule that neither of the two main parties should be granted two successive dissolutions in a row (heavily influenced by the rhetoric of regenerationism, Alfonso was in consequence inclined to look with much favour upon Silvela). At the beginning of December Sagasta therefore found himself resigning for what proved to be the very last time. A month later, moreover, he was dead: truly it was the end of an era.

The Failure of Regeneration

As we have seen, the departure from the scene of the two men who had most symbolized the politics of the Restoration Monarchy in the years since 1875 more or less coincided with the arrival of a new monarch in the person of King Alfonso XIII. Dapper and affable, Alfonso was hardly the ogre of legend, but he was not at all well suited to the position in which he was increasingly to find himself. To understand this situation, we should take a close look at the position of the Spanish monarch in the Canovine system. Given that elections to the *cortes* inevitably produced a government majority, this was, in fact, extremely difficult, for the throne was in effect rendered the sole arbiter of whether or not a government was 'exhausted', the result being that even the most prudent and careful of monarchs found it difficult to avoid giving offence. Still worse, of course, there was also a real danger that ministries might be made and unmade in accordance with personal prejudice or the influence of assorted courtiers and hangers-on. Under Cánovas and Sagasta, it had at least been obvious whom the king should summon to form a government, but even this was no longer the case, the Liberals and Conservatives not only lacking leaders of a similar stature but also becoming increasingly split.

With another monarch than Alfonso XIII, none of these problems need have been insuperable, his mother, for example, having on the whole coped with the deteriorating situation with commendable tact and skill. Alfonso, however, was different. Deeply shocked by *el desastre*, he was much interested in any project connected with modernization, whilst, aided and abetted by his English wife, Victoria Eugénie – a bright and sparkling young woman who caused much scandal by her defiance of the social conventions – he displayed a healthy disregard for court routine. On the other hand, however, there was also a darker side to Alfonso's personality. Surrounded from early youth by a clique of well-connected officers – like his father, he was very much a 'soldier king' – he became infected by a scorn for civilian politicians that was much reinforced by the army's tendency to blame the civilian government for *el desastre*. Added to this scorn, meanwhile, was a deep-seated resentment of the Restoration settlement *per se*, Alfonso being determined to recover the ground that the throne had been forced to cede to the politicians. Already encouraged by the workings of the political system to see himself as the arbiter of the national will – for every party leader who demanded the removal of an 'exhausted' government invariably claimed that its departure was the will of the people – his position as head of the armed forces pushed him still further in this direction, the army having consistently maintained that it was above party politics and the guardian of the essential values of state and nation. Obsessed from the start with fears of revolution, meanwhile, he was in addition convinced that the civilian politicians could not be trusted to handle the situation: as he himself put it, if he did not govern, he would eventually end up in exile. Last but not least, he was intolerably vain, and therefore became infected not only by a desire to regenerate Spain, but by a belief that only he could do so. In short, what emerges is a picture of a man who could not but intervene in politics, and who by the worst possible mischance came to power at a moment when the political process was becoming particularly susceptible to his influence.

With the fall of Sagasta, meanwhile, office had once again been handed to Silvela, who now proceeded to embark on a second attempt at regeneration. Almost inevitably, however, the result was failure. Let us take, for example, the elections that Silvela proceeded to hold in April 1903. Under the stewardship of Maura, who had been rewarded for his defection to the Conservatives with the post of Minister of the Interior, the contest was conducted with a minimum of government intervention. However, this did not produce the results that were expected. Much to the fury of Alfonso XIII, an abnormally large number of Republicans and other oppositionists was elected, but what Silvela had quite failed to see was that retreat on the part of the government simply gave more freedom to the *caciques*. In the countryside, then, the change had no effect whatsoever, the only difference being that fraud and coercion was now the work of the representatives of the parties rather than those of the state.

Implicit in this misapprehension was the central problem that dogged all attempts at restoration from above. Thus, no matter what the state did, regeneration simply could not be effected unless the regime was prepared to tackle the numerous injustices of Spanish society, and, by implication, to attack the vested interests of the oligarchy which domi-nated the country's affairs. This, of course, Silvela was neither willing nor able to do, and the numerous reforms that his administration sought to introduce were therefore all but meaningless. To take just one example, Canalejas' plans for an Institute of Labour eventually resulted in the creation of a more powerful body entitled the Institute of Social Reform. Admirable in theory – the Institute consisted of representatives of both capital and labour and was given an impressive range of functions – the idea was rendered almost meaningless by the fact that the fiscal system simply did not deliver enough revenue to allow the government to act on the plans which it produced, whilst the Institute's best efforts were in any case frequently obstructed by the vested interests which it threatened. Nor were matters helped by the fact that the most reformist element in the government – Maura's erstwhile *gamacistas* – had been handled most severely in the general elections, their new allies having for the most part been most unwilling to grant them any leeway. Even if this had not been the case, meanwhile, the government was deeply divided. Thus, whilst sincerely committed to the principle of reform, Silvela was also deter-mined to rebuild the armed forces. However, his Minister of Finance, Raimundo Fernández Villaverde, was obsessed with the need to reduce expenditure, and was in consequence driven to resign, whereupon he kept up a barrage of protest from the backbenches and so boosted his reputation that he was elected by the *cortes* as its president. Much embarrassed, Silvela had to go, and on 20 July the king appointed Villaverde in his place, only for Silvela suddenly to announce that he was retiring from politics and leaving the Conservative party in the hands of

Maura. Utterly humiliated, Fernández Villaverde was left with no option but to tender his resignation, the result being the accession to power of Antonio Maura.

Both the last hope for the Restoration Monarchy and a major factor in its downfall, Maura is so seminal a figure that we needs must turn aside to say something of his character and background. Born in 1853 in Palma de Mallorca, the new prime minister was the son of a tannery owner, and was brought up in an atmosphere of the most devout Catholicism. Sent to study in Madrid, he arrived in the capital in the very midst of the revolution of 1868, and was much disturbed both by the spectre of mob rule and the deficiencies in the political system that had opened the way for its emergence. With his interest in politics thus awoken, he decided to study law rather than the science that had been his original intention, and through pure happenstance was drawn into the circle of Germán Gamazo. Eventually marrying the latter's daughter, in 1881 he entered the *cortes* as one of the *vallesoletano* leader's placemen. A loyal follower of Gamazo until the latter's death in 1901, Maura differed from his patron in that he took the latter's critique of the system at face value. Thus, whilst Gamazo was using regenerationism as a means of building an empire in Old Castile, Maura was becoming more and more committed to the cause of reform for its own sake. A prime mover, as we have seen, in attempts to secure reform in Cuba, he was also a leading influence in *gamacismo*'s continuing radicalism: deeply affected by *el desastre*, he was ever more impressed by the arguments that were being advanced by Silvela, and by 1900 was pressing for a genuine transformation in the government of Spain.

The problem with Silvela, Cánovas once observed, was that he lacked self-confidence. Undoubtedly a factor in Silvela's failure, such a charge could not be made of Maura. From the moment that he assumed the premiership on 4 December 1903, he at all events left no one in any doubt as to his sincerity. Proclaiming his determination that the Conservatives should become a mass party, he immediately introduced a major plan for the reform of local government, which in brief envisaged the establishment of, first, supraprovincial units of administration known as *mancomunidades* that would be too large for any local *cacique* to overawe, and, second, special commissions elected in part on a corporate basis that would oversee the workings of the *ayuntamientos*. Meanwhile, social reform continued: Sunday, for example, was officially decreed a day of rest, whilst the first steps were taken towards the abolition of the *consumos*. Tough though he was, however, Maura was undermined by the fact that significant elements of his party were opposed to his leadership (many *silvelistas* would have preferred the leading reformist, Eduardo Dato, whilst the followers of Fernández Villaverde were for obvious reasons deeply resentful), matters not being helped by the persecution of the *gamacistas* in the elections of 1903.

Redoubtable a character as he was, it was also not long before Maura had fallen out with Alfonso XIII, whilst he stirred up further unrest by attempting to insist on the appointment of a particularly controversial candidate to the vacant archdiocese of Valencia. After months of intrigue and obstruction, Alfonso therefore proceeded to engineer Maura's resignation by appointing Polavieja to the post of Chief of the General Staff in defiance of the wishes of the Minister of War. With the Mallorcan politician, however, went his plans for reform, Maura being the only figure in the Conservative Party who was genuinely willing to go to war against the *caciques*. Led once again by Fernández Villaverde, the Conservatives survived in office for some months more, but it was quite clear that they were now as 'exhausted' as the Liberals had been two and a half year earlier. Villaverde being unable to carry the party with him in his renewed pressure for reductions in government expenditure, the king restored the Liberals to power.

Seven Years On

The fall of the Villaverde government in June 1905 marks the end of the first wave of the repercussions that emanated from the events of 1898. Discontent in the army seemed to have fallen quiet – far from siding with the militaristic young monarch, its champion, General Weyler, had actually sharply reproved Alfonso XIII when the latter had tried to claim that only the king had the right to make appointments to the military hierarchy. The regenerationist movement that had erupted under the leadership of Joaquín Costa had fallen apart in disarray, its chief figures having either drifted into alternative forms of protest, or succumbed to the lure of office. Socialist and anarchist activity was once again on the wane: membership of the UGT fell from 57,000 in 1904 to 36,500 in 1905, whilst the same period saw the number of days lost to strike action in Barcelona decline by 90 per cent. Regeneration from above seemed to have shot its bolt – as Maura remarked at the time of his resignation, he could do 'absolutely nothing'. Catalan nationalism had effectively been taken over by forces that would always have far more to gain from an alliance with the system than from an alliance with revolution. Finally, in the camp of the Republicans there also appeared to be little chance of movement, the fact being that Unión Republicana was coming under severe strain thanks to the growing impatience of the new generation typified by the fiery Alejandro Lerroux.

It might therefore be argued that the Restoration Monarchy had weathered the loss of Cuba, Puerto Rico and the Philippines remarkably well. However, whilst both the economy and the political system were certainly affected rather less than might have been expected, 1898 nevertheless had a massive impact on the history of Spain. In the first place, the disintegration of the two-party system that was the bedrock of the Restoration Monarchy was considerably accelerated by the desperate attempts of the Liberals and Conservatives alike to adapt to the task of post-war reconstruction. In the second, the army's return to politics was also speeded up: if angry talk of a military government had receded, the feelings which had given rise to it remained as acute as ever, whilst they were encouraged at every turn by Alfonso XIII. In the third place, the entire oligarchy had suffered a massive blow to its self-confidence, this in turn augmenting its determination to resist any change in the status quo. And in the fourth the basis of the status quo was put under greater threat than ever. To the extent that it can in consequence be said that it was from the waters of Santiago and Manila that there emerged the two Spains of 1936–9, 1898 was indeed a *desastre*.

11

The Failure of Reform

The Age of Giants

The history of Spain between 1905 and 1923 is essentially that of the disintegration of the Canovine system. Until at least 1913, however, there were few politicians who would have predicted that its end was close. Whilst there was a certain degree of alarm, fundamental change seemed inconceivable, and all the more so because the scene was dominated by the immensely reassuring Antonio Maura and José Canalejas; such was the faith that they induced that there seemed little question that Alfonso XIII and his descendants would remain upon the throne for a long time to come. In the winter of 1912–13, however, both statesmen were suddenly swept away, the cause of regeneration thereafter draining slowly but surely into the sand.

From Fusion to Fission

The vulnerability of Spain's political institutions in the first years of the twentieth century was first revealed by the deep crisis that affected the Liberal Party in the period 1903–7. Under Sagasta, this body had increasingly become a collection of factions headed by various regional power brokers. As well as the *gamacistas*, such groups included the followers of Manuel Alonso Martínez, Cristino Martos, Segismundo Moret, Eugenio Montero Ríos, José López Domínguez and the Marqués de Vega de Armijo. Some of the proconsuls involved were now dead, but their influence had generally been inherited by a variety of *protégés* who had very often married into their families. In contrast to republicanism, then, the passage of time served solely to perpetuate division, the only positive development being the decision of the *gamacistas* to quit the party for the Conservatives in 1902.

For all the Liberal Party's factionalism, Sagasta's death found only Montero Ríos and Moret as real contenders for the leadership (much disillusioned by the equivocations of his party in matters of reform,

Canalejas had in November 1902 established a new Partido Liberal Democrático). Both men being powerful *caciques* whose experience dated back to the *sexenio*, the party was therefore bitterly divided. A congress that was held in November 1903 to settle the issue failed to give either candidate a decisive majority, whilst opinion remained more or less evenly split, the fall of the Conservatives in June 1905 therefore presenting Alfonso XIII with a difficult task.

Montero Ríos having obtained a slim majority at the congress of 1903, it was he who was selected as prime minister. From the beginning the affairs of the new administration were dominated by the issue of anti-clericalism. Already an issue in the last Sagasta government, the matter had been given new urgency by Maura's activities as prime minister. A devout Catholic, Maura had quickly proved himself suspect in religious matters, whilst in June 1904 he had signed a new agreement with the Vatican that effectively recognized the manner in which the Church had systematically exploited certain loopholes in the Concordat of 1851. In this respect, it has to be recognized that the Church had indeed experienced an extraordinary recovery in its fortunes, tripling the number of regular clergy and making substantial inroads in the field of education. Less apparent but just as startling was the extent to which the Jesuits, in particular, had poured immense resources into the stock market. Maura having in effect given the Church *carte blanche* to continue in the same vein, it was hardly surprising that concern was growing, and all the more so given the fact that many members of the clergy continued to heap abuse upon the liberal system.

Hostility to the Church being a good means of reuniting the party, the Liberals therefore fought the elections of September 1905 on a programme of much closer regulation of the Church's activities. What would have happened had the march of events continued is unclear, but Montero Ríos had barely been in power for six months when a fresh crisis broke out. Though overt criticism of the political system had fallen off, feelings in the army had nevertheless continued to run very high. Thus, stringent cuts in government expenditure had effectively blocked any hope that the army might have gained something from *el desastre*. On the contrary, in fact, matters were more absurd than ever: there were only 80,000 men for nearly 25,000 officers, whilst there was no money even for proper training, let alone the acquisition of modern weapons. In large part the problem lay with officers themselves – no government could possibly have risked the sort of rationalization that was the only way forward – but that did not stop them from lashing out, whilst discontent was further inflamed by the fact that promotion was slow, inflation on the rise, and an officer's life quite expensive, few officers being possessed of substantial personal means.

The resentment engendered by this situation was not all directed at civilian society. For example, those officers who had fought in the colonies were bitterly resentful of those who had remained in Spain, whilst traditional rivalries continued to divide the privileged *cuerpos facultátivos* – the artillery and engineers – and the less privileged *armas generales* – the infantry and the cavalry; the cavalry and the infantry; career officers and ex-rankers; and the general staff and almost everybody. Nor was resentment of civilian society aimed at one particular target. Thus, the dynastic politicians were attacked for placing selfish party interests before those of the Fatherland, the regenerationists for placing infrastructural improvement before investment in new arms and equipment, the *caciques* for sucking the life out of the people, the Church for perpetuating backwardness, the factory owners for exploiting the proletariat, the socialists for teaching internationalism, and the anarchists for undermining law and order. Almost any of these issues could have triggered an explosion, but in the event the fuse was lit by Catalan nationalism.

For many reasons a *bête noire* of the officer corps, Catalan nationalism had since 1898 become one of its chief concerns. In view of the situation, the latter would have been well-advised to maintain a low profile, but they instead laid down an endless barrage of satire and invective, insult having been added to injury by the fact that in 1899 the Supreme Court had ruled that press attacks on the military could only be prosecuted in the civil courts. Goaded beyond endurance, on 25 November 1905 a large group of army officers therefore sacked the offices of the satirical review, *¡Cu-cut!*. Despite the fact that forty-seven people were injured, the authorities failed to take any action whatsoever and instead imposed a state of war, the effect of this being that the military were enabled to unleash a reign of terror against the entire Catalan press.

The *¡Cu-cut!* affair precipitated a major crisis. The rioters received wide-ranging support from the rest of the officer corps, whilst the government was swamped with demands for the immediate extension of military jurisdiction to all offences committed against the army, the suppression of all manifestations of Catalanism, an increase in military spending and the dissolution of the *cortes*. Meanwhile, Alfonso XIII made no attempt to restore order or correct the military press' claims that he supported the rebellious officers, and announced that he intended to compel the government to fall in with the army's demands. In this attitude, meanwhile, he was seconded by the Minister of War, General Weyler, whilst the Civil Guard announced that it would not defend the *cortes* against a coup. What all this amounted to was a fundamental challenge to not just the Canovine system, but also the very principle of constitutional government, and it therefore behoved Conservatives, Liberals, Republicans and Socialists alike to meet it with the most determined opposition.

Needless to say however, nothing of the sort occurred. Concerned to effect cuts in military expenditure though they might be, neither the Liberals nor the Conservatives were in any position to take on monarch and army, even had many of them not been inclined to identify with the military in any case. Some of the wiser figures – amongst them both Maura and Canalejas – certainly had grave misgivings, but they came to the conclusion that resistance was useless, the best course therefore being to go along with the army's demands in the hope that the concessions might be clawed back at a later date. As for the Republicans and Socialists, neither felt much affinity for the Catalanists in that the former still dreamed of winning power with the help of the army whilst the latter wanted nothing to do with bourgeois nationalists.

If the Catalans had done little to make themselves popular in the rest of Spain, what followed was the most shameful episode in the entire history of the Restoration Monarchy. Despite the fact that he had immediately suspended all constitutional guarantees, it was soon clear to Montero Ríos that he no longer possessed the support of the palace, and on 30 November he therefore resigned in favour of a delighted Moret. Having so unexpectedly gained power, the new prime minister had no intention of taking on an army that was as angry as it was threatening. Thus, conscription was increased by 20 per cent, the War Ministry went to a leading supporter of the Barcelona officers and a scheme was introduced that was designed to give the military courts the right to try all attacks on the army or navy. Realizing that more was at stake than just the interests of the Catalans, the Republicans and Socialists did eventually rally to their support, but the dynastic parties remained unshakeable in their determination, and on 20 March 1906 the bill was duly passed as the Law of Jurisdictions.

The new measure's impact was immediate. Even before it had gone through, the military authorities were using it to clamp down on a variety of organizations and publications. In one sense this made little difference – the frequent use of the state of siege ensured that the military had already been able to make much use of the powers now conferred on them – but the fact was that some of the Restoration Monarchy's most positive features had been placed in serious jeopardy. Set beside this situation, the new government's adoption of a more radical agenda is really of little consequence, not that it survived for very long in any case. Having backed the army as a means of overthrowing Montero Ríos, Moret found that Alfonso XIII would not sanction the general elections by which he intended to remake the Liberal Party in his own image. Much chagrined, he therefore resigned after a mere six months, whereupon

Alfonso XIII summoned a leading Liberal general, José López Domingúez, to form a new administration. With the encouragement of
Canalejas, who was increasingly edging back towards the Liberals, the
new prime minister pressed on with the anti-clerical programme
announced by Moret, the reforms that he introduced including total
freedom of religion; a new law of associations; the secularization of all
cemeteries; and easier civil marriage. All this called forth much resistance
on the part not only of the Catholic Church but of wide sectors of
conservative opinion, but all this was as nothing compared with events in
the Liberal Party. Furious at his downfall, Moret suddenly announced
that he could not support the government's programme in its present
form. Faced by certain defeat, López Domingúez promptly resigned,
whereupon Alfonso XIII, as Moret had expected, invited the latter to
form a new cabinet. Hardly surprisingly, this came to nothing – Moret's
own supporters aside, the Liberal Party was aghast at his actions – and a
compromise candidate had to be appointed in the form of Vega de
Armijo. Such was the turmoil, however, that he too survived for little
more than a month. With the Liberals clearly 'exhausted', on 25 January
1907 Maura was restored to power.

The Long Government

Split though the Liberal Party now was, the dynastic parties had rarely
been further apart, Maura having been so utterly opposed to the anti-
clericalism espoused by his opponents that he had even threatened civil
war. Shelve those parts of the Liberal programme that had not got
through the *cortes* – most notably, the new Law of Associations – though
he did, however, Maura was no knee-jerk reactionary. Thus, frustrated in
1903, he was still bent on his so-called revolution from above, and all the
more so as his old rival, Fernández Villaverde, was now dead. Also gone
were Silvela and Romero Robledo, the result being that there was simply
nobody left who was prominent enough to challenge his lead.

At all events, no sooner had Maura conducted the usual general
elections, than he picked up matters where he had left them in 1903.
Thus, measures were immediately introduced to reform the local magistracy, the electoral system, and the *ayuntamientos* and *diputaciones*.
Taken as a whole, the three bills amounted to a wholesale assault on
caciquismo, for the first aimed at ending the practice whereby each
general election saw the removal of large numbers of local magistrates in
favour of placemen of the government of the day – in effect the nominees
of its *caciques*; the second at depoliticizing the administration of general
elections; and the third at freeing local government from the tutelage of

the centre whilst also sanitizing its election, increasing its power, and opening the way for the creation of supramunicipal and/or provincial *mancomunidades*. Also promised were better education, further measures of social reform, and the stimulation of commerce and industry. At the heart of all this lay what Maura termed 'citizenship': politics was to be transformed in such a way that it would cease to be the preserve of a narrow oligarchy, the result of which being that the ranks of the disaffected would be lessened and the Canovine system assured of general loyalty.

At root, then, Maura remained a conservative. The structure of government and politics was to be transformed, certainly, but the object was to avoid further 1898s – it was no coincidence that he intended to strengthen both the army and the navy – whilst at the same time encouraging social harmony and drawing the teeth of anarchism, socialism and regionalism alike. What was not on offer was an authentic social revolution: some attempt might be made to help the proletariat and educate them in the acceptance of their lot, but those elements which remained intractable would be crushed, society in the meantime being left entirely unreformed.

To argue that Maura could ever have transformed the Restoration monarchy is therefore futile. That said, however, there can be no doubt as to his energy, the *cortes* being deluged with a legislative programme of unprecedented extent. Nor can it be denied that much was achieved. For example, the new electoral law was passed in its entirety in little more than two months (in brief, this made voting obligatory, handed the administration of elections over to an – in theory – independent review body, abolished the need for elections in constituencies whose seats were uncontested, and made the Supreme Court responsible for judging cases of coercion and fraud). This measure was soon followed onto the statute books by the Law of Municipal Justice as well as by a variety of measures of social reform. Thus, intensive efforts were made to improve public health; the intermittent struggle of successive reformist governments against the bullfight was resumed (the *corrida* having traditionally been regarded as a symbol of savagery and backwardness, the hope was that it might be supplanted by the more healthy sport of football); the social legislation passed prior to 1907 was expanded and reinforced; laws were passed to prevent the exploitation of transatlantic emigrants by shipping companies; the first timid steps were taken towards the settlement of landless labourers on land that was not being directly exploited by its owners; the *consumos* were reduced and in some cases abolished altogether; the right to strike was recognized; old-age pensions were introduced; and the first 'mixed juries' of employers and workers were established as a means of settling industrial disputes. Faithful to its economic objectives, meanwhile, the government also did what it could to encourage economic activity. Thus, Spanish shipyards were given orders for three 'dreadnought' battleships; the tariff laws were tightened up; a 'buy Spanish' policy was introduced; and two national councils were created to integrate industrialists and agriculturalists with the regime.

Regeneration was accompanied by repression. In response to continued bomb attacks, of which a spectacular assault on Alfonso's wedding procession was but the most sanguinary, a new law was introduced that effectively banned the anarchist movement altogether, and the security forces greatly strengthened, whilst energetic methods were employed to hunt down malefactors of all sorts. Underpinning much of this activity was a theme that is not immediately apparent. The populace's failure to engage with the political system was a worry certainly, but what was even more alarming was the gradual emergence of a refusal to engage not just with its procedures but also with its values. Slow though Spain's modernization was, the population of many towns and cities had already experienced considerable expansion. This development should not be exaggerated, but the fact remains that it was prominent enough to cause considerable concern, and all the more so as it was frequently accompanied by the most appalling levels of social degradation. Freed from the healthy influence of rural life – better, the control of priest and landowner – the growing urban populace was seen as being prey to a variety of corrupting influences which ran the gamut from republicanism, socialism and anarchism to drunkenness, prostitution and free love. To make matters worse, literacy was also slowly on the increase – by 1900 36.2 per cent of the population could read and write as opposed to 28 per cent in 1877 – whilst the appearance of the cinema had opened the way for new forms of popular culture. As for literature and art, meanwhile, these seemed to be moving in ever more dangerous directions, a good example being the erotic verse of Rubén Darío.

When all this is taken into account, Maura's preoccupations can be seen to have had a very different focus. Let us take, for example, the position of women. Although feministic periodicals had been appearing since as early as 1851, none had lasted for more than a few issues, whilst the first feminist groups had only just been formed at the time that Maura came to power. The gap between male and female illiteracy had been somewhat reduced, meanwhile, but few women received a secondary education, whilst there was little opportunity for those that did. A handful of figures had made a name for themselves as writers – outstanding examples are Concepción Arenal, who wrote extensively on prison reform, and Emilia Pardo Bazán, who in 1916 was to become the first female university professor in the history of Spain – or become doctors, but otherwise progress was almost non-existent: of the 1,300,000 women in paid employment, the vast majority worked in domestic service, sweatshops, or light industry, whilst it was usual for them to be paid less than men and give up their jobs on marriage. With even such few feminists as there were inclined very much to believe that women were fitted only for some areas of public life, and the cause of women possessed of few allies, Spain was hardly threatened by a gender revolution.

Despite the reality of the situation, the position of women was all too clearly becoming a matter of some concern. At the highest level, as we have seen, many eyebrows had been raised by the lively demeanour of the queen, such concerns being further reflected by complaints about matters like the extravagance of modern fashion. At the opposite end of the social scale, meanwhile, the large and traditionally almost entirely female workforce of Spain's ten tobacco factories was a frightening example of the sort of threat that women could pose to the established order: relatively well-paid, highly skilled, and, most unusually, likely to work throughout their adult lives, the cigarette makers were notorious for their militancy in home and factory alike, not to mention their affectation of habits that did not accord with traditional perceptions of their sex. In short, regulation was becoming a priority, the result being that the growing number of women's magazines were filled with injunctions concerning the duty of wife and mother, the proper education of young women, and the need to dress and act with due modesty, whilst the Church conducted a constant crusade against sexual liberation, discouraged higher education for females and stressed the subordination of married women to their husbands.

Anti-feminism was not a particular product of the Maura years, but it was nevertheless Maura that first took action to ensure that the traditional image of the woman was protected. Thus, under the direction of Maura's puritanical Minister of the Interior, Juan de la Cierva, the variety of municipal regulations that had been introduced over the preceding fifty years to control prostitution were in 1908 supplemented by a new national code that aimed to confine the problem to licensed brothels, and thereby reduce its growth and visibility alike. Meanwhile, official sponsorship was also given to intensive campaigns against pornography, whilst attempts were made to stamp out any form of improper conduct on the part of the female population.

The reactionary characteristics of Maura's reformism are not just visible with regard to women. Thus, the attempts that were made to restrict the opening hours of taverns and cabarets were designed both to produce a healthier workforce and to cut down crime. Similarly, the populace's morals – and, by extension, capacity to improve their lot (it was an act of faith amongst the propertied classes that poverty was the product of vice) – might be protected by campaigns against blasphemy, but the latter also served to defend Catholic religiosity. Even more overt were the implications of the campaigns that were waged against those aspects of popular culture that were deemed to be questionable or even dangerous. Thus, tacit support was given to attempts to organize boycotts of questionable publications or theatres, whilst many dissidents were actively persecuted. A good example here is the treatment that was meted out to Francisco Ferrer. An erstwhile *zorrillista* who had come to sympathize with anarchism in the wake of the failed military coup of 1886, Ferrer had established both a chain of schools which united experimental teaching methods with political indoctrination, and a publishing company producing cheap editions of key progressive texts. All this arousing much opprobrium, when it was discovered that the anarchist who had attacked Alfonso's wedding procession was one of his employees, Ferrer was therefore flung into prison.

What Maura was engaged in, then, was a struggle not just to regenerate Spain, but to reinforce the parameters laid down by Cánovas. That being the case, it was inevitable that he should have faced considerable opposition: setting aside the Republicans, Socialists and Anarchists, even those Liberals who had gone along with the Law of Jurisdictions could not tolerate the sort of wholesale assault which his activities seemed increasingly to presage. When Maura came to power, however, his opponents were still in a state of disarray. Thanks to the formation of Unión Republicana, and, in Barcelona, at least, the energetic leadership of Alejandro Lerroux, the Republicans had been doing reasonably well. Some ground was lost to the nationalist Lliga in the elections of 1905, but even so it was clear that Catalanism was unlikely to triumph against a local leader who consistently espoused the most populist views. However, the *¡Cu-cut!* incident completely transformed the situation. The Lliga's furious reaction immeasurably boosted its position, whilst the Republicans were thrown into confusion. Encouraged by Salmerón, who had belatedly come to realize the need for an alliance with the Catalanists, many Catalan republicans joined the movement known as Solidaritat Catalana formed by the Lliga to fight the Law of Jurisdictions, but, being Castilian, Lerroux accused them of betrayal, as did large numbers of Republican militants in other parts of Spain (in this respect it did not help that the Carlists had also rallied to the cause of Solidaritat). Deeply angered and always eager to advance his own interests, Lerroux decided to use the issue to oust Salmerón, but for once he had miscalculated: undeterred by the violent assaults launched by the *lerrouxistas* on their pro-Solidaritat opponents, most Republicans remained loyal. Expelled from Unión Republicana, in the 1907 elections Lerroux also lost his seat in the *cortes*, Solidaritat Catalana sweeping all before it to win forty-one of the forty-four Catalan seats.

Lerroux was not yet finished – in January 1908 he founded the new Partido Radical Republicano – but he had nevertheless greatly weakened the cause of republicanism. With the Liberals still in disarray, and Canalejas for the time being inclined to give Maura the benefit of the doubt, chief responsibility for opposing his reactionary tendencies therefore fell upon Solidaritat Catalana and its leader, Francesc Cambó. In this respect, however, the latter proved a broken reed. Born in 1876 into a prosperous Conservative family, Cambó was a most reluctant radical, having prior to 1905 always been anxious to conciliate Madrid. As devout a Catholic as Maura, meanwhile, he loathed the anti-clericalism of his Republican allies, whilst his conservative principles, life-long admiration of Cánovas, and horror of disorder rendered him incapable of competing with Lerroux for the loyalty of the streets. Having recently been the subject of an assassination attempt, he was if anything inclined to sympathize with Maura, and all the more so when the Conservative leader reintroduced his plan for the reform of local government. Offering as it did a means both of satisfying the Catalanist demand for self-government and of defusing the pressures that were building up in Barcelona, Cambó fell upon the measure with delight.

Within a matter of months, then, Solidaritat Catalana had fallen apart, the more left-wing Catalanists breaking away to join a number of Republican *solidaritistas* in a new bloc known as the Esquerra. Yet the defection of the Lliga did not free Maura from all opposition. On the contrary, the Liberals, too, had become increasingly alarmed at the direction which events were taking. Meanwhile, Unión Republicana having fallen into a state of utter confusion, a number of moderate Republicans headed by the Asturian university professor, Melquíades Alvarez, had come to the conclusion that the only way forward was an alliance with the Liberals. Moret being more than willing to welcome their advances – typically, he saw an alliance as a means both of destabilizing Maura and of outflanking Canalejas – there therefore appeared the so-called Bloque de Izquierdas, or 'Block of the Left'.

Vigorous though this new alliance was, it was too weak to achieve very much. Despite being invited to join its ranks, the PSOE remained aloof; the *lerrouxistas* refused to join on the grounds that it was a cynical manoeuvre designed to purge republicanism of all signs of radicalism; and Montero Ríos and many other Liberals were unable to bring themselves to join in an alliance with even moderate elements of the Left. Amongst the Bloque's supporters, meanwhile, the Liberals were inclined to see it as a means of overthrowing Maura, harassing the Catalanists and taming the Republicans, whilst the Republicans viewed it as a way of democratizing the Liberals, and, by extension, the monarchy. In short, all that had been achieved was a negative alliance, it being no coincidence that its only policy was a doctrinaire anti-clericalism.

Tragic Week

Dominant in the chamber and contemptuous of extra-parliamentary opposition, Maura was unlikely to be brought down by the Bloque de Izquierdas. Fall though he soon did, this was rather the work of events in Morocco. Thus, for centuries Spain had been in possession of the coastal towns of Ceuta and Melilla, but in 1909 a variety of factors sucked her forces into an attempt to occupy the mountainous hinterland. The results were dramatic. The 6,000 troops in the area soon being shown to be too few for the job, the government decided to send out reinforcements. On 11 July, therefore, a partial call-up of reservists was announced, the units selected for mobilization being in large part recruited from Catalonia. As certain ministers may well have desired, the result was a major conflagration. Tension had been rising in Barcelona over the past two years – the anarchists, socialists, left-wing Catalanists and *lerrouxistas* had alike been competing to win the support of the working classes; the textile industry had slid into a serious depression; and Maura's social policies had been engendering much resentment. Meanwhile, feelings were further whipped up by the angry rhetoric of the Left, the insensitive ceremonies that accompanied the call-up and the arrival of bad news from the front, a serious reverse having been suffered at Monte Gurugú. On 25 July a small group of anarchists therefore decided to organize a general strike. With few soldiers available to stop them – most of the troops actually serving with the garrison had been sent to Morocco – bands of workers had soon taken over the entire city, whereupon they proceeded to hurl themselves upon the Church. Although only three members of the clergy were actually killed, at least fifty religious buildings were sacked and set ablaze, many convent funeral vaults also being broken open in an attempt to verify the popular belief that nuns who refused to submit to the discipline of their orders were tortured or even murdered.

What did this upsurge of popular violence stand for? What is quite clear first of all is that there was little agreement amongst its *lerrouxista*, anarchist and socialist participants. To the extent that the rebels had any concrete notions at all – and many of them did not, there being elements in the crowd who seemed bent on little more than pillage – these therefore ranged from stopping the war, to overthrowing Maura and even launching a revolution. In the second place, it was very much a movement driven from below: the local leaders had no foreknowledge of what was to come, and in many cases sought to limit the violence or at least to guide it into channels that were relatively safe.

This point, in particular, provides us with an opportunity to say a little more about the position of the Radical Party. Much given though he was to the most violent and inflammatory oratory, Alejandro Lerroux was a rather more complex figure than at first sight appeared; at heart the Radical leader was very much a conventional Spanish patriot who craved integration into the Canovine system and eventually came to work for it as a double agent. Deeply admiring the army, indeed, he had actually applauded Spain's intervention in Morocco. At all events, it was never his intention that Barcelona should actually have risen in revolt, his reaction to events there being to take to his heels. His lieutenants being no more willing than he was to captain the mob, *lerrouxismo* was in effect shown up as an opportunistic sham.

To return to Barcelona, the rebellion was soon in trouble. Disturbances also broke out at a number of Catalan towns, whilst there was also trouble in Valencia and Alcoy, but a Socialist general strike proved ineffectual. Retribution was delayed by sporadic acts of sabotage on the railways, but the military were soon able to amass enough forces to launch a counter-attack. Armed with a few looted pistols, the insurgents fought back, but by 31 July it was all over. In all, eight members of the security forces and 150 civilians had been killed, the next few days seeing the arrest of over 2,500 people, of whom courts martial eventually had five executed and many others sentenced to terms of imprisonment.

Though this so-called 'tragic week' had dealt a heavy blow to the leftist movement in Catalonia – in addition to the arrest of hundreds of militants, large numbers of offices, clubs and schools were closed down – in many ways the Maura government had acted with more moderation than might have been expected. However, amongst the five victims of its firing squads was the anarchist propagandist, Francisco Ferrer, who had been quite unfairly branded as the leader of the revolt. Glad though the authorities were to see the back of him, his execution proved a disastrous miscalculation. Ferrer being one of the very few opposition figures who was at all well-known outside Spain, he immediately became a *cause célèbre* throughout Europe. The repercussions were dramatic. Whilst the prime minister in theory remained as much in control of his party as ever, in practice it was increasingly restive, many Conservative *caciques* being deeply concerned at Maura's talk of clean elections. With regard to the reform of local government in particular, meanwhile, further disquiet was aroused by the fact that Maura appeared to be playing straight into the hands of *catalanismo* – hence the succession of delays that had been experienced in forcing his plans through the *cortes*. Last but not least, much alarm had also been caused by the ever worsening relations with the Liberals, the company that they were now keeping suggesting that Maura's extremism was threatening the most basic principles of the *turno pacífico*. In short, Maura was in an increasingly vulnerable position which the Bloque de Izquierdas naturally hastened to exploit. Stiffened on the one hand by the growing demands of Alvarez and his followers that he should do more to defend the principles of democracy, and on the other by the knowledge that the government's repression of the labour movement was persuading Pablo Iglesias to move towards an alliance with the Republicans, Moret decided to launch an all-out assault. To the accompaniment of cries of '¡Maura, no!', he therefore accused the premier of rendering Spain ungovernable, whilst at the same time announcing that the Liberals intended to vote against the credits needed for the Moroccan campaign. Convention demanding that Maura should resign, this he duly did, albeit in the firm belief that the king would have to support him – by allying with the non-dynastic opposition and, still worse, the mob, Moret had broken all the rules of the game. To his complete astonishment, however, Alfonso accepted his offer (ostensibly because he did not think that Maura could survive, but in practice because he believed he was jeopardizing the monarchy), and on 21 October 1909 the 'long government' therefore came to an end.

For all Maura's pretensions, he had achieved very little. Of his measures of real substance, the bill reforming local government was lost, whilst the electoral law of 1907 in some respects actually made matters worse, a number of its provisions – most notably the ruling that uncontested seats could now simply be filled by declaration – was obviously open to serious abuse. With regard to the armed forces, too, Maura had done little good: millions of *pesetas* were spent on three battleships of a type that could not hope to take on the vessels that were currently being built elsewhere, whilst the army in practice remained as neglected as ever, and that with Spain engaged in a full-scale war. As for the political situation, it had deteriorated alarmingly, with the *turno* under threat and the Liberals in closer contact with the Left than they had ever been, Maura's extremism having ensured that their historic role of 'attracting' the forces of revolution had for the time being been stood on its head. If Alfonso XIII was glad to see the back of Maura, it is therefore hardly surprising.

The New Messiah

On 21 October 1909, then, Spain entered a new *turno*, the Liberals being immediately restored to power under Moret. Moreover, they seemed more united than they had for some years: outflanked on the left, Canalejas had had no option but to rejoin the party. That said, however, there was only the appearance of unity. Thus, Canalejas had made it clear that he would revolt if the party did not remain committed to a radical programme; Moret regarded the Bloque de Izquierdas as little more than a vehicle for his personal advancement; and the increasingly influential Conde de Romanones had been voicing growing alarm at the way in which the party was being pulled to the left. Reinforced by the 'tragic week', the worries of the Liberal right were further strengthened by the fact, first, that even such moderates as Alvarez had been radicalized by Maura's actions, and, second, that Pablo Iglesias' response to the repression of the labour movement had been an alliance with the Republicans.

In this situation Moret could not remain in office for very long. Thus, in December 1909 new local elections showed all too clearly that in many areas, far from respecting the sensibilities of the Liberals, the so-called Conjunción Republicano-Socialista wanted to fight against them. As this tactic proved a great success – the Republicans and Socialists increased their vote enormously and succeeded in taking control of no fewer than nine provincial capitals – pressure began to grow in the party for a new leader, and all the more so as there were growing suspicions of Moret's relations with Lerroux. Thus, having sat out the 'tragic week' in London, Lerroux was now capitalizing on the revolt by praising the rebels, insinuating that they had been inspired by his example, and denouncing the repression. Despite the bitter hostility of the socialists and anarchists alike, these tactics paid off magnificently, the Radicals proceeding to secure an absolute majority in the *ayuntamiento* of Barcelona. Meanwhile, it was becoming clear that Lerroux had set his sights on a career on the national stage, and, further, that Moret was flirting with the possibility of an alliance as a means of breaking the *conjunción*. Well aware of this discontent, which was strongly mirrored in the army, Alfonso therefore decided that Moret had to go. When the Liberal leader asked for the customary decree of dissolution, the king therefore refused, the result, as he had expected, being that Moret immediately resigned.

On 9 February 1910 there therefore came to power José Canalejas. Of all Alfonso XIII's prime ministers, the new leader was undoubtedly both the greatest, and the only one who had any real hope of saving the Restoration Monarchy. Indeed, the reason why he was chosen by the king in preference to such rivals as Romanones was precisely the fact that he promised far greater hopes of salvation. What, then, were Canalejas' political ideas? Born in El Ferrol in 1851 to a comfortable bourgeois household of progressive inclinations, Canalejas had originally been a follower of Emilio Castelar, but repeated frustrations in his attempt to pursue an academic career led him to moderate his position and by 1880 he had therefore switched his allegiance to the erstwhile *demócrata*,

Cristino Martos and become a committed monarchist. Monarchism, however, was not the same as reaction, Canalejas coming more and more to advocate democratization as the only means by which the throne could be saved, the aim being to clean up the electoral system and encourage the populace genuinely to participate in the life of the nation.

Thus far it might appear that Canalejas was little more than a carbon copy of Maura, but in fact nothing could be further from the case. For Maura the object was to block change, but for Canalejas it was rather to assimilate it with the monarchy. Taking the question of social reform, for example, Maura viewed the matter very much in terms of the state policing popular behaviour, and Canalejas in those of it intervening in the interests of social justice. Moving on to the question of the Church, Maura was determined to defend the *status quo*, and Canalejas to establish complete religious liberty, ensure that the religious authorities were subordinated to those of the state, and impose strict controls on Catholic education. In fact, for one the watchword was tradition whilst for the other it was modernization.

Whatever may have been his differences from Maura, Canalejas was certainly just as energetic. Having quelled all opposition, formed a government that united all factions of the Liberal Party, and held parliamentary elections that both returned the smallest government majority yet to have been seen and produced Spain's very first socialist deputy in the person of Pablo Iglesias, on 15 June 1910 the new prime minister formally unveiled his political programme. The list of measures included a new concordat with the Vatican, freedom of worship, a new Law of Associations, a fairer system of conscription, the abolition of the *consumos* and greater protection for the disadvantaged. Despite howls of protest on the part of the Church, the Carlists and many Conservatives, by the close of the year a two-year moratorium – the so-called 'padlock law' – had duly been imposed on the establishment of any further religious houses pending the passage of a definitive reform of the Law of Associations. In 1912, meanwhile, this was followed by a law of military service that at long last established the principle of universal liability to conscription, as well as a new system of local-government finance that abolished the *consumos* in favour of the taxation of urban property, and laws that limited the hours of work that could be expected of mine workers and banned the employment of women and children at night.

All, however, was not as it seemed. Let us take the question of Church–state relations. For all his sound and fury, in reality Canalejas 'pulled his punches' in this respect. Not at all hostile to Catholicism *per se*, within certain limits he was most anxious to come to some arrangement with the Vatican, privately assuring Rome that the Spanish government would continue to maintain the friendliest relations with the Church. Meanwhile, if the 'padlock law' temporarily restricted the growth of the religious orders, it in practice cemented the *status quo*: so furious was the controversy that it provoked that it was decided to abjure all other measures until the passage of a new Law of Associations.

Also worthy of note is the question of the army. If Canalejas opposed the Law of Jurisdictions, many Liberals were absolutely unconditional in their support for its activities, whilst he himself was no anti-militarist. When the *cortes* initiated a debate on Ferrer, Canalejas therefore sought hard to quell the passions raised by the subject and refused pointblank to revise either the Law of Jurisdictions or the code of military justice. Indeed, it was in part to divert attention from the issue that the bill to reform conscription was introduced when it was, Canalejas being further influenced by the fact that he was strongly in favour of a forward policy in Morocco (though this may in part have been the result of his need to retain the support of an increasingly *africanista* Alfonso XIII). Here the occupation of a semi-circle of territory around Melilla had temporarily brought operations to a halt, but Canalejas did nothing to impose a real measure of control on his commanders, the result being that, provoked by continued Moorish attacks, the latter began to move in the direction of a policy of total conquest that paid little attention to the realities of the situation. Meanwhile, all opposition to the war was crushed by means of liberal application of the Law of Jurisdictions, Canalejas openly support-ing the principle that all offences in this respect should be tried in accordance with military law.

With regard to the army as much as the Church, then, Canalejas' policy was distinctly flawed. As a consideration of the conscription reform shows, this was also the case with his efforts to ensure greater social justice. In theory a great advance in view of its abolition of substitution, the new army law was only passed thanks to the inclusion of a number of crucial amendments that in fact rendered the reform all but meaningless. Most Spaniards were to be liable for military service, certainly (there were in fact still a small number of exemptions, most of them relating to sole breadwinners), but no longer would those men actually conscripted all be treated in the same way. Thus, in exchange for a substantial fee, conscripts might limit their service to a mere five months; alternatively, they could immediately purchase the rank of sergeant, and, after a few months' training in privileged conditions, pass into a new reserve officer corps entitled the *oficialidad de complemento*.

If Canalejas was less than successful in attracting the support of the republicans and socialists, this was hardly surprising, his chances of doing so being rendered even smaller by the policy that he adopted towards social unrest. Angry at the government's opposition to discus-sion of the *caso Ferrer* in the *cortes*, by the spring of 1911 the Conjunción

Republicano-Socialista was engaging in a vibrant campaign against the government. Meanwhile, political unrest was further swelled by the much-denounced resumption of the fighting in Morocco. In the course of the summer this agitation was seconded by a fresh outburst of social unrest that saw a mutiny on board the cruiser, *Numancia*, and serious strikes in Bilbao, Asturias and Málaga. Meeting with no support from the leaders of the *conjunción* as it did, the movement might quickly have petered out. However, by coincidence the period 8–11 September had been chosen for the first congress of a new labour movement known as the Confederación Nacional del Trabajo. A league of anarchist unions that had broken away from an earlier alliance of Catalan unions (both anarchist and socialist) founded in 1907 known as Solidaridad Obrera, the aim of this movement was in brief to conquer the working classes for anarchosyndicalism – the belief that capitalism could be overthrown by a great general strike. Deciding that the moment was ripe for just such a strike, the CNT therefore ordered its troops to take action, on 16 September Zaragoza, Valencia, Seville, and a number of other cities all being gripped by various degrees of paralysis.

Faced by these events, Canalejas could not have reacted with more ferocity. Denouncing the strike movement as a revolution, the prime minister launched a general attack on the republicans, socialists and anarchists, suspended all constitutional guarantees, and declared a state of war. In doing so, however, Canalejas only succeeded in augmenting the ranks of his opponents: the Radicals, who had hitherto remained aloof from, and even hostile to, the Conjunción Republicano-Socialista, were driven into seeking the formation of a common front, whilst the right wing of the republican movement – the so-called 'governmental republicans' epitomized by Melquíades Alvarez – finally turned their backs on the Liberals and formed the new Grupo Republicano Reformista.

By the third year of his premiership, then, Canalejas' credentials were wearing distinctly thin. What might have happened had he remained in power is a moot point – a new Law of Associations was in preparation along with an attempt to resolve the Catalan question through the unification of the four Catalan provinces as a single *mancomunidad* – but the unrest which the latter measure stirred up in the ranks of a largely anti-Catalan Liberal Party suggests that it might never have actually reached the statute book. Even the cherished revision of the Law of Associations promised to be problematic, meanwhile, many Liberals being less than willing to make the issue a war to the death. As for the government's attitude to the social problem, a very mild scheme for the expropriation of land that was not properly exploited by its owners was allowed to sink without trace; a railway strike was broken by the mobilization of all the men involved who happened to be reservists; and certain limits were imposed on the right to strike.

Underlying much of this activity was a belief that could not but limit the extent to which Canalejas could achieve the ample degree of reform that offered the only hope of truly regenerating the Restoration Monarchy. Whereas the reality was that the two-party system would have to be shifted to the left, Canalejas could not bring himself to jettison the Conservatives, and that despite the fact that Maura was proclaiming that he would never again alternate in power with the Liberals. Desperate to bring Maura back into the fold, he therefore made concession after concession, only to find that his ability actually to change the system became ever more limited. It was therefore probably fortunate for his future reputation that on 12 November 1912 he was shot dead by a CNT militant, the greatest failure of the Restoration Monarchy therefore actually falling as a hero.

Regeneration Aborted

Whatever deficiencies may have marred the assassinated Liberal leader, his death was a seminal moment. Whilst his government was rapidly sliding into complete immobilism, his death deprived the Liberals of the one figure in their ranks who believed in reform as something other than a mere stratagem, and thus of the possibility that they might genuinely have been able to 'attract' the forces of the Left into the camp of the monarchy. Meanwhile, it also ensured that the Liberals would fall back into the factionalism of earlier years, Canalejas being the only one of the Liberal Party's various satraps who possessed the strength to hold its rival cliques together.

If the death of Canalejas finally broke the cause of regeneration in the Liberal Party, it plunged the Conservatives into chaos. Thus, given the isolation of the government – it was effectively at war with both Left and Right – not to mention the divisions in its ranks, it was arguable that it was time for a new *turno*. However, persuaded that it was important not to jeopardize either the *mancomunidad* or the important agreement that the government was on the brink of signing with France on the subject of Morocco, Alfonso XIII allowed the *turno* of 1909 to continue under the leadership of the Conde de Romanones. Needless to say, the proud and arrogant Maura was deeply angered, and all the more so as the king had also undermined his leadership. Thus, already badly shaken by the manner in which they felt the 'long government' had put at risk the security of the monarchy, the army and the established order in general, the Conservatives' more moderate elements now came to the conclusion that Maura had to go. Realizing that a coup was afoot, Maura in effect launched a pre-emptive strike that managed to force the party to confirm him in the leadership, only to overplay his hand by trying to blackmail Alfonso XIII into immediately recalling him as premier. Absolutely furious, the king refused to do so, the fact being that Maura had in effect committed political suicide.

What made the actions of the Mallorcan politician all the more foolish was the fact that Romanones proved unable to survive for very long. A skilful 'charm offensive' coupled with a few more measures of anti-clericalism persuaded Alvarez's Grupo Reformista Republicano to declare its support for the monarchy, but Romanones could not maintain the unity of his party. To some extent matters were rendered a little easier by the death of Moret early in 1913, but Montero Ríos was not only still alive but attempting to install his son-in-law, Manuel García Prieto, as leader, the new prime minister soon discovering that his every move was therefore sabotaged. A bitter opponent of Catalan autonomy, García Prieto made use of the continuing debates on the *mancomunidad* to undermine Romanones' control of the party, the general detestation of Catalanism being such that by midsummer much of it was in open revolt. On 21 October the rebels declared themselves to be a new party – the Partido Liberal Demócrata – whereupon Romanones resigned, Alfonso in consequence being left with no option but to recall the Conservatives to office. Needless to say, it was at this point that Maura learned the error of his ways, the man who was chosen to be premier being not the erstwhile prime minister but rather the more moderate Eduardo Dato. For the Conservatives as much as the Liberals, therefore, regeneration and unity alike were at an end.

The Eve of War

How, then, is one to rate Spain's situation on the eve of the First World War? In political terms one could argue that the death of Canalejas and self-destruction of Maura had brought to an end a major period of reform that might have resulted in the overthrow of *caciquismo* and the democratization of the Spanish political system. In practice, however, such arguments appear exceedingly naive. Maura's 'revolution from above' may have been designed to involve an ever greater proportion of the population in the political process, but it is abundantly clear that appearance of the 'neutral masses' was conceived of primarily in reactionary terms: Catholic and conservative, they were supposed to lend the monarchy, the Church and the interests of property their unstinting support, the state in the meantime making certain of their loyalty through what amounted to a programme of indoctrination. As for Canalejas, he, too, was concerned not with democratizing the monarchy *per se*, but merely with ensuring that it was sufficiently democratized to abort the onset of revolution. Men of vision though both may have been in a tactical sense, neither of them were capable of envisaging a Spain that was radically different to the Canovine model to which they ultimately owed their allegiance. At the same time, it must also be arguable whether they were really capable of achieving even the very limited targets that they in practice set themselves: both of them were the leaders of parties that were in reality little more than loose coalitions; both of them were undermined by periodic outbreaks of rebellion amongst their subordinates; and both of them were attempting to address political problems whose resolution could not but impact very heavily upon important elements of their own supporters.

Neither the Conservative nor the Liberal variant of the 'revolution from above' therefore being likely to have much impact upon the development of Restoration Spain, the events of 1912–13 actually made very little difference. Yet, if Maura and Canalejas can in retrospect be seen to have been singularly ineffectual figures, even more was it the case of the lesser men who now once more came to the fore. By no means devoid of good intentions – Romanones, García Prieto and Dato alike were genuinely convinced that the state had a duty to ensure a greater degree of social justice, whilst they could also agree on the need for clean elections, municipal autonomy and wider engagement in the political process – they were even more blinkered than their erstwhile leaders. Thus, whereas both Maura and Canalejas had appreciated the need for some sort of agrarian reform, the new generation of party leaders appear to have convinced themselves that state intervention was an instrument that was best suited to the urban working classes, their approach to the problems of the countryside being rather to look to such measures as irrigation, improved communications and better technical education. From time to time one leader or another might castigate the landowners for their selfishness and egotism, but in practice the latter's interests never ceased to be protected. As for the problem of *caciquismo*, this was in effect simply not addressed at all. Thus, whilst Romanones lamented the skeletal nature of the *turno* parties, he yet argued that attempts to resolve the problem by radical means would be counterproductive, and to the end remained convinced that the parliamentary system was genuinely representative of public opinion.

In short, whereas Maura and Canalejas had both made some sort of attempt to confront the fundamental problems of the Restoration Monarchy, their successors sought refuge in delusion and double-speak. Lacking their predecessors' authority and skill, meanwhile, they were even less able to place controversial policies upon a substantial footing.

Yet the problems that they faced were worse than ever. Let us first of all take the situation in Morocco. After years of bitter fighting, the military situation across the Straits of Gibraltar had temporarily quietened down, whilst in March 1912 France and Spain had formally divided the country into two protectorates. However, the form that was given to the administration of the Spanish zone left much to be desired in that it gave disproportionate influence to the commanders of the three military districts into which the territory involved was divided and minimized that of the civilian government (a great admirer of the army, Romanones had been unwilling to do anything that might undermine its prestige). The local representatives of the Spanish military being inclined for a variety of reasons to adopt a forward policy, the result was that fighting quickly flared up once again. To be fair to the army, the trouble was not entirely its own fault – also at issue was the resentment of a particularly ambitious Moroccan chieftain who had found himself passed over in the selection of the viceroy, or caliph, who was supposed to represent the interests of the Sultan of Morocco in the Spanish portion of his divided dominions – but the fact was that Madrid was thereafter never able to impose a real measure of control on what was happening in its new colony.

Much more might be said here about the disastrous legacy of Spanish expansion in Morocco in military terms, but this issue is better left for the next chapter. In the light of the 'tragic week', however, it must be pointed out that the Moroccan imbroglio could not but inflame the situation at home. In earlier years, perhaps, this need not have mattered, but the post-Maura era, in particular, had seen a significant improvement in the position of the labour movement. Whatever doubts may be entertained with regard to the sincerity of Lerroux, for example, there is no doubt that his rhetoric had politicized significant elements of the Spanish working classes. When disillusion set in at Lerroux's failure to continue his crusade against the Restoration system, moreover, the workers who had followed his lead found an alternative focus for their discontent in the anarchosyndicalist CNT. In the period 1910–13, perhaps, government repression ensured that the latter's fortunes were at a low ebb, but the mere fact of its existence gave the anarchist movement a degree of coordination and organizational solidity which had hitherto been entirely lacking. Meanwhile, its militants were able to gain a strong foothold in metal-working, construction, woodworking and textiles, and to exert an influence that bore no relation to their numbers. As for the Socialists, they, too, were undergoing a distinct improvement in their fortunes in that membership of the UGT trebled between 1910 and 1913 (the strength of the PSOE only rose by one quarter in the same period, but it was at this time that it began to make significant headway amongst the intelligentsia).

The increased labour militancy evident in the *turno* of Canalejas and Romanones does not, of course, mean that Spain was on the brink of proletarian revolution. Anarchosyndicalism, for example, had so dismal a record of success in terms of labour conflict that even its most dedicated militants began to back away from the concept of the revolutionary general strike, a number of CNT activists also defecting to the less radical UGT. As for the Socialists, their situation was marked by increasingly bitter ideological divisions in that Iglesias' decision to enter the Conjunción Republican-Socialista was coming under increasing criticism from a dissident group who argued that supplanting the monarchy with a republic was a distraction that could only serve to weaken the labour movement (however, few of the rebels as yet showed any signs of wanting to 'bolshevize' the party: some, indeed, were eventually to move in this direction, but the majority were as legalistic in their thinking as Iglesias, the limit of their ambition being to return the PSOE to the isolationism that had marked its conduct prior to 1909). Much of the country remained comparatively quiet, meanwhile – Andalucía, for example, was relatively tranquil – whilst matters were not helped by the fact that relations between the two wings of the labour movement had become ever more strained.

That said, however, the pace of change was clearly beginning to increase. Urbanization picked up – having only increased from 30 to 32 per cent of the population between 1887 and 1900, the number of people living in settlements of over 10,000 inhabitants rose from 32 to 35 per cent between 1900 and 1910 – and the first decade of the twentieth century also witnessed a significant drop in the percentage of the population employed in agriculture. Illiteracy, too, was on the retreat, whilst the number of newspapers in publication rose from 1,128 in 1887 to 1,347 in 1900 and 1,980 in 1913. Meanwhile, the spread of new technology made for greater print runs, just as it was justified by demand: founded in 1912, the *maurista* flagship, *La Tribuna*, had within two years achieved a circulation of 80,000. If the population was better informed, meanwhile, it was also more mobile: the bulk of the network having been completed by 1900, railway construction fell away, but this was compensated by greater road construction, and the arrival of the omnibus. And finally, in line with all this, new forces began to make their appearance on the political scene: in the course of 1908–9 the Radicals formed a flourishing woman's section in Barcelona, whilst in 1911 García Prieto actually mentioned the possibility of female suffrage.

Well, then, might Antonio Maura have been increasingly concerned by the Spain that he saw around him, for the chief pillars of the Restoration Monarchy were visibly beginning to crumble. As yet the process was a slow one – there were still many parts of Spain on which the hold of the

Canovine system was unshaken – but the very last thing that the oligarchy needed was the onset of a crisis of the magnitude that now broke upon them.

12

Spain and the Great War

A Futile Neutrality

When the First World War broke out in July 1914, Spain immediately proclaimed her neutrality. Despite that, however, the conflict was still to test the Restoration Monarchy to its limits. Not only did the war accelerate the process of change already gripping Spain, but it also deepened the differences in the dynastic parties, accentuated the clash between reaction and reform and heightened class conflict. Shaken to the core, in 1917 Spain erupted in a multiple crisis that left her in no state to cope with the fresh complications of the post-war era. Had the Restoration Monarchy taken part in the war, in short, its position could hardly have been any worse.

The Rule of the Idóneos

In July 1914 Spain was governed by the charming and affable Eduardo Dato. Born in La Coruña in 1856, he had made his name as the progenitor of Spain's first measures of social reform and was from the start determined to rebuild the old consensus politics – hence the scornful nickname bestowed on him by Maura of the *idóneo* or 'trimmer'. However, even had Dato wished to be another Maura, he was in no position to do so, as the elections consequent upon the new *turno* produced much greater success for the opposition – dynastic and non-dynastic alike – than was normal, and that despite widespread irregularity. Though in part the fruit of the increasing inability of *caciquismo* to control the larger cities, this result also stemmed from the fact that the Conservatives went into the elections in the grip of a major schism. Thus, although Maura had withdrawn into a disgruntled retirement, such were the hopes that he had encapsulated that Dato's appointment called into being a new political movement. Known as *maurismo*, this had its origins at a major rally that was organized in Bilbao on 30 November 1913 by the Mallorcan politician's disciple, Angel Ossorio y Gallardo, and proclaimed a programme based on

support for the Church, the monarchy and the armed forces; the revitalization of the political system; and the implementation of the doctrines of
Social Catholicism. Though Maura himself did not back the movement
until June 1914, a combination of intensive propaganda, mass mobilization, Catholic sympathy, and the affectation of dynamism had soon
brought the *mauristas* much support, the result being that many constituencies actually witnessed a contest between rival Conservatives.

What, however, was *maurismo*? In brief, the answer is Spain's variant
of the proto-fascism that had been raising its head in many European
countries. Though large sections of the middle classes – petty *entrepreneurs*, small shopkeepers, minor functionaries, or lesser members of the
professional classes – were effectively excluded from the political system,
they were yet much exercised by the growth of anti-clericalism, the
spectre of disorder and the decay of the provincial towns in which many
of them lived. Sharing their discontent, meanwhile, were both young men
from propertied backgrounds who had yet to make their way in the
world and *caciques* convinced that the Canovine system was no longer
capable of facing down the threat of revolution, both these groups being
impatient with the structures of the Restoration Monarchy. In *fin-de-
siglo* Spain as elsewhere, then, social protest rubbed shoulders with
political reaction, and, having already been radicalized by *costismo*, the
two were now brought together in an ultra-nationalist movement that
promised both moral and physical regeneration and a recasting of the
state in a more authoritarian style.

In 1914, and for a few years thereafter, *maurismo* made a brave show
of defiance. Yet all was not well. Not only was the leadership deeply
divided between Social Catholics such as Ossorio y Gallardo and authoritarian hawks such as the head of the *maurista* youth movement, Antonio
Goicoechea, but it soon became apparent that progress was unlikely
without the acquiescence of the *datistas*: the number of *maurista* deputies
actually fell from twenty-one to fifteen in the 1916 elections, and even
then five of the men concerned only triumphed because the *datistas* gave
them a free run. There was therefore little chance of *maurismo* revolu-
tionizing Spanish politics, the consequence being that Maura himself
soon began to seek a reconciliation with the *datistas*.

That said, however, the rebellion remained most unsettling, for, by
persistently denigrating the Canovine system, *maurismo* encouraged
hostility to parliamentarianism as a whole. In the short term, moreover,
it was a distinct threat to Dato who was quickly moved to reinforce his
position in the *cortes* by making a deal with the Lliga, the result being
that the law providing for the establishment of *mancomunidades* was
hastily rescued from the stagnation in which it had been languishing in
the *cortes* and promulgated by royal decree. As the subsequent elections

showed, the move was a shrewd one, the Lliga's opponents in Catalonia being utterly humiliated. When the new *cortes* assembled in April 1914, Dato was better off than might otherwise have been the case. It should not be thought, however, that the Catalan problem had been resolved. Whilst Catalonia's four *diputaciones* now sat as a single assembly and elected a permanent executive council, in practice Catalanists had little reason to be satisfied. Setting aside the fact that the state had the right to dissolve the *mancomunidad* at any time, the municipalities and provinces were not compelled to transfer their powers to the new body, and, in fact, frequently would not do so. For several years, then, the Catalan administration was forced to engage in a constant struggle to extend its authority. By the end of the First World War real progress was being made, but the conditional nature of autonomy, the limited powers of the *mancomunidad*, the grudging attitude of the government, and the miserable budget within which the Catalans were forced to operate all ensured that the problem did not go away.

Initially at least, however, Catalonia did not loom too large on the government's horizons, the last months of peace rather being a time of relative tranquillity. Whilst there were worries about the impact of the overthrow of the Portuguese monarchy in 1910 and considerable turmoil in the Conservative party – premier or no premier, Dato was not officially head of his party, and did not secure the position until July 1914 – social unrest was at a low ebb, and republicanism seemingly on the retreat. Needless to say, however, it was not long before the prognosis was as stormy as ever.

Impact of War

No sooner had war broken out, indeed, than there was a sharp intensification of political debate, the chief subject under discussion being whether or not Spain should join the fighting. Although the bulk of the populace remained apathetic, this was a conflict that affected both Left and Right. Thus, whilst the anarchists remained hostile on principle, most progressives saw intervention in favour of the Allies as a means of furthering their cause. Amongst the political establishment, enthusiasm for wholesale intervention was less common, the vast majority of Liberals and Conservatives alike being agreed on the need for neutrality, but even so opinion was split between those who believed that Spain should do everything she could to assist the Entente, and those who preferred an 'absolute' neutrality that would in practice have favoured the Central Powers. In large part the reflection of ideological proclivities, this debate undoubtedly had an unsettling effect that helped considerably to destabilize both of the dynastic parties.

For most Spaniards, however, the issue of intervention was greatly overshadowed by the war's economic impact, there being no doubt that this was enormous. The picture was initially by no means bright – cotton, brandy, wine and cork were all brought to a near standstill – but it was not long before new patterns of supply and demand had been established, most of which were highly favourable. Spain's mines and factories finding a ready market in Britain, France and other places, the war was marked by unprecedented economic growth. At all events, textiles, engineering, chemicals, shipbuilding, armaments, mining, and iron and steel all boomed, so imposing being the development of Vizcaya in particular that it actually outstripped Catalonia as Spain's strongest industrial area. And, last but not least, the war also brought the beginnings of modernization: soaring coal prices stimulating interest in hydro-electricity, the amount of power generated in this fashion more than tripling between 1913 and 1920.

Striking though it was, the wartime boom was hardly an industrial revolution – total energy consumption, for example, seems to have risen by no more than 25 per cent – whilst it did not even bring much in the way of prosperity. A small number of *entrepreneurs* and industrialists made large fortunes, certainly, but for the bulk of the populace things were by no means so rosy. With the inefficient railway system taxed beyond endurance and the production and import of consumer goods in retreat, many areas began to experience shortages of all kinds, whilst the war inevitably produced general price inflation. On the whole, wages also rose, but even the most favoured sections of the workforce managed to do no more than to keep pace with the cost of living, whilst matters were not helped in this respect by the fact that many basic commodities such as rice, chickpeas and wheat increased in price by far more than the general norm. Nor was inflation the only problem. In the industrial and mining districts expansion brought much overcrowding and discomfort whilst in the *campo* reductions in the import of fertilizer and cut-backs in consumption abroad led to falls in production, wage reductions and falling opportunities for employment. Things were at their worst in sectors specializing in export crops, but few areas were unaffected, the general effect of the war therefore being not to enrich but rather to impoverish.

In consequence, Spain once more entered a period of serious unrest. Effective action by the government might have reduced the tension, but this was not forthcoming, the result being numerous strikes, protests and other disturbances. Meanwhile, increasingly at odds with the Lliga, whose leaders were demanding a series of measures aimed at reducing the cost of imported raw material, the Dato government was in November 1915 forced to resign after a plan that it had put forward for reform of the army was sidelined by the *cortes*. As power was immediately restored to Romanones, it at first appeared that matters might improve: genuinely interested in social reform, and the concept of 'attracting' the Left, the count appointed the relatively radical Santiago Alba as his Minister of Finance. Reinforced in April 1916 by elections that produced 230 Liberal deputies to only 113 Conservatives (*mauristas* included), the new government's most striking proposal was a tax on wartime profits that could be used to fund new measures of social welfare. In reality relatively timid, the new levy aroused a storm of protest, the lead being taken by Cambó and the representatives of Catalan industry (it did not help in this respect that Alba was a notorious opponent of catalanism). To make matters worse, the Minister of Finance soon found that he could not count on the support of a Liberal party unwilling to attack the interests of property. After a long battle the measure was therefore lost, the fact being that once again the oligarchy had blocked all chance of a move in the direction of greater social justice.

Alba's defeat has been described as a turning point in the history of the Liberal Party. Thus, whilst it was deprived of its last chance of transforming itself into a genuine party of the masses, the party's many splits were considerably deepened. Whether even Alba could have won a real measure of popular support is a moot point, however. Not only was he himself only too ready to seek a compromise, but the anarchists and socialists were becoming increasingly belligerent, the early months of 1916 witnessing general strikes in both Barcelona and Valencia. Meanwhile, despite serious misgivings on both sides, the CNT and UGT also agreed to combine in a campaign to force the government to ease the populace's sufferings on pain of a revolutionary general strike. Months of agitation followed, of which the culmination was a twenty-four hour national stoppage on 18 December 1916. However, nothing was achieved but fair words, 1917 therefore threatening to be marked by considerable tension.

Revolution Manqué

By 1917 for belligerent and non-belligerent alike the strains of total war were becoming all too apparent. In Spain pressures were by no means so great as they were elsewhere, but even so revolution was soon to appear a real possibility. If the crisis' depth had yet to be revealed, the New Year still found the Romanones government in serious difficulties. Setting aside the demoralizing effects of the profits struggle, the premier was in addition troubled by the German submarines that were ravaging the Atlantic trade routes. Already a serious problem, on 31 January 1917 the issue was thrown into high relief by the German declaration of unrest-ricted submarine warfare. A number of Spanish vessels almost immediately being sunk in cold blood, this in turn revived the question of whether or not Spain should join the Allies. Always strongly sympathetic to the Allied cause, Romanones now judged that he had a perfect opportunity at the very least to break off relations with Germany and Austria-Hungary. However, revolution having just broken out in Russia, many Liberals who would hitherto have favoured such an action now regarded any move that would take Spain closer to war with the utmost terror. Realizing this, the cabinet refused to support the count, and on 19 April a much discomforted Romanones therefore resigned in favour of García Prieto.

On one level Romanones' downfall may be seen as presaging the general crisis of 1917. Thus, encouraged by the Russian Revolution, demands for Spain's democratization now came to the fore, and all the more so as the new government proceeded to declare a state of siege and suspend the *cortes*. Convinced, first, that Romanones had been brought down by pro-German feeling in the palace, and, second, that war would lead to revolution, the Socialists and Republicans launched a concerted campaign in favour of intervention. As for the UGT and CNT, mean-while, they agreed that they should now move to the revolutionary general strike with which they had been threatening the government since the previous summer.

Impressive though all this was, the real trigger for the crisis of 1917 came from quite another direction in that on 1 June a full-scale military revolt erupted in Barcelona. To understand this development, it is neces-sary to turn to the war in Morocco. Thus, in brief, the period between 1909 and 1914 had seen the emergence of new divisions in the officer corps. One of the many factors that had led to the army becoming so spectacularly overburdened with officers having been the widespread use of selective promotion, in 1899 it had been decided that all promotions would henceforth rest on the principle of seniority alone, as was already the case in the *cuerpos facultátivos*. However, this decision could not but be undermined by the Moroccan war, for those officers sent to the Protectorate naturally felt that they were entitled to greater rewards than those who stayed at home, matters being made still worse by the fact that the volunteers who stepped forward to command the growing number of native troops that were being organized by the military authorities were naturally drawn from most adventurous and ambitious officers in the entire Spanish service (included in their number was a diminutive sub-altern of steely determination named Francisco Franco y Bahamonde). At all events, thus emerged the so-called *africanistas*, the latter coming to constitute a pressure group whom it was difficult to overlook, and all the more so as they soon acquired the royal ear, Alfonso being not only inclined to see them as a means of manipulating the army as a whole, but also much excited by the whole Moroccan affair.

Of all the results of the Moroccan war, few were more pernicious than the emergence of the *africanistas*. Whilst cultivating an image based on extreme violence, blind obedience, suicidal courage, wholesale terror and the supremacy of military power, they succeeded in forcing the government to reintroduce the principle of selective promotion. Tied though this was to heroism on the battlefield, the result was inevitably to stir up hostility and resentment in the rest of the army, and all the more so as conditions in Spain were very poor and the military record of the *africanistas* distinctly unimpressive. Even before the First World War broke out, then, a large part of the Spanish army was increasingly angry and disaffected. As the conflict dragged on, meanwhile, such feelings were inflamed still further by the manner in which officers' salaries were rendered even more inadequate by the impact of inflation, not to mention the fact that the war led Liberals and Conservatives alike once more to examine the question of military reform. The Dato government falling before it could address the issue, the torch was in consequence handed to Romanones. The result was the preparation of a new army law, whose salient points were a reduction in the number of higher formations, a lower retirement age, a partial freeze on promotions, the general introduction of the principle of selective promotion and the subjection of promotions by seniority to aptitude tests. All this was supposed to create a surplus of 11,000,000 *pesetas*, the proceeds of which would be used to improve the army's training and armament and increase its size to 180,000 men.

For the thousands of officers who continued to vegetate in the garrisons of the Peninsula all this amounted to a future that was suddenly very uncertain. Sullen and resentful, many began to consider the possibility of resistance, the most obvious vehicle for their protests being the so-called *juntas de defensa*, or committees of defense, which most of the army's various arms of service had over the past thirty years established to defend their interests. Evolving as powerful pressure groups, these councils had had some success – the representatives of the artillery and engineers had, for example, been able to rebuff repeated attempts to impose selective promotion upon them – and the impending reforms naturally stimulated a revival in their activities. In the infantry, however, no such junta existed, and in the autumn of 1916 a group of infantry officers in the Barcelona garrison therefore set about remedying the want. Playing on the dislike that officers stationed in the provinces felt for those stationed in the more comfortable surroundings of Madrid, not to mention the clique of court generals who surrounded the king, they had soon obtained much support in Barcelona and beyond, whilst in addition drawing up a constitution that swore all members of the movement to secrecy and bound them to obey its decisions.

Much more tightly organized than its counterparts in the rest of the army, the infantry movement was clearly a major threat to the plans of the government, and the latter therefore ordered its dissolution, only for this to provoke the wholesale resistance. With the situation completely out of hand, the García Prieto government panicked, and placed the entire leadership of the infantry *junteros* under close arrest. All this, however, was to no account: large sections of the officer corps reacted with outrage, and on 1 June the deputy committee that had taken the place of the arrested Junta Superior issued a long manifesto that mixed language of stridently regenerationist nature with a call for military revolt. Much shaken, the government gave way and ordered the release of all its prisoners. Further than this, however, it would not go – amongst other things the *junteros* wanted an immediate pay rise, the dismissal of a number of leading generals, smaller cuts in the officer corps and the immediate recognition of the *juntas de defensa* and their statutes – the result being that on 9 June García Prieto resigned, the principle of civilian supremacy having in consequence once more been shown to be meaningless.

It cannot be stressed too strongly that, in its origins at least, the *juntero* revolt was an entirely apolitical event. That said, it nevertheless provided the catalyst for a genuine social and political crisis. Thus, the forces of the opposition were convinced that the *junteros* were as devoted as they were to the democratization of Spain. If this was a piece of self-delusion, the rebellion certainly shook the structure of the state to its foundations: as poorly paid and frustrated as the peninsular officer corps, public servants of all sorts began to establish their own *juntas de defensa* so as the better to resist Romanones' cuts (the new army law was in fact part of a much wider effort to reduce expenditure). Meanwhile, angered by the fact that the king had summoned Dato to replace the count, the Reformists, Republicans and Socialists formed a grand alliance aimed at forcing the government to reopen the *cortes* as a constituent assembly. Given that Dato's forces were very much in a minority, however, the *cortes* remained firmly shut, the three allies therefore agreeing to organize an armed rebellion. At the same time, meanwhile, the crisis acquired a new dimension. Thus, although Cambó had remained aloof from the revolutionary coalition, he was nonetheless committed to securing a degree of political change. Faced by the government's refusal to reopen the *cortes*, the Catalan leader decided that the only way forward was to convene an 'assembly of parliamentarians' that would divert the Reformists, Republicans and Socialists from more dangerous pursuits and thereby avoid frightening the *junteros* into the arms of the forces of reaction. Held in Barcelona on 19 July, this gathering saw all the non-dynastic parties agree a list of demands which included the restoration of full civil liberty, the appointment of a supra-party government, and the convocation of a constituent *cortes*.

If Cambó hoped that the assembly movement would confine the growing turmoil to political channels, he was to be disappointed. Thus, regarding the revolutionary general strike to which they were in theory committed with considerable alarm, the Socialists were inclined to support his tactics, but they were constantly in danger of being outflanked. Thus, even though the CNT had by 1917 split into a moderate group inclined to think that a democratic republic was a necessary precondition for the establishment of syndicalism, and a more radical one that believed that the workers could establish their utopia immediately, it was only with the greatest difficulty that it was restrained from launching a strike straight away.

Cambó's tactics, in short, were unlikely to be successful, and all the more so given the government's response. Eager to confront the labour movement, Dato seized upon a relatively minor railway dispute as a means of forcing the CNT and UGT to take action before they were ready, the strike finally being launched on 13 August. Exactly as the government had hoped, the result was disappointing in the extreme. Whilst there were stoppages in most of Spain's cities and industrial areas, mutual suspicion, inadequate planning and government repression all combined to ensure that the movement proved a damp squib. As for hopes that the army might join the strikers, these proved to be totally misplaced, the *junteros* restoring order with a ferocity that was rendered all the worse by the armed resistance put up by a few CNT *pistoleros*. By 18 August the strike was therefore almost everywhere at an end, the only exception being Asturias, where the strong and well-organized miners held out for over two weeks.

Alarming though these events had been, the long-planned revolutionary general strike had therefore been a failure. There remained both the *junteros* and the assembly movement, however. Crush the general strike though they had, the dissatisfaction of the former had risen to fresh heights, the return of Dato having given rise to fears of a return to 'business as usual'. Whilst the *junteros* had helped suppress the general strike, the ageing mediocrities who led them were dreaming of installing a regenerationist government and posing as the saviours of Spain. Emerging from the strike filled with the conviction that they were indispensable, the *junteros* were also deeply angered by the manner in which the army was being pilloried on account of the eighty workers who had been killed in the course of the repression (indeed, there were even claims that the decision to provoke the strike had been a devious manoeuvre designed to discredit the army in the eyes of the people). Whilst remaining determined to secure change in the army – their demands had now expanded to include a purge of the *generalato* and the complete abolition of selective promotion – the *junteros* therefore became more and more strident in their demands for regeneration: on 23 October, indeed, Alfonso XIII was given just seventy-two hours to form a national government.

To say that the government was in no fit state to respond to these pressures is an understatement. Thus far it had possessed the tacit support of the Liberals, but the general strike had so scared Cambó that he had effectively dumped the Left in favour of a deal with the latter. Persuaded that it was safe to start playing politics again, the Liberals had therefore started to advance the case for a new *turno*. Sensing a way out of the crisis – he was, of course, unwilling to take on the army – Alfonso therefore sacked Dato, the crisis eventually being resolved by the formation of a coalition government headed by García Prieto, of which the chief components were the Liberals, the Lliga, the *mauristas* and the followers of the maurist-leaning Conservative, Juan de la Cierva.

In the event, however, this was by no means the political cataclysm which it at first appeared. Despite the fact that a new meeting of the assembly of parliamentarians was at that very moment demanding a new constitution and the appointment of Melquíades Alvarez as prime minister, the auguries for change were distinctly unimpressive. Thus, it was agreed that fresh elections would be held amidst conditions of the strictest fairness and neutrality, to which end the post of Minister of the Interior was given to a noted jurist of no political allegiance; that the new cabinet would include two Catalanists (though not Cambó himself); and that the government would respect the constitution, and refrain from closing the *cortes* and interfering in local government. However, the War Minister was the deeply reactionary La Cierva, whilst the forces of reform had failed even to place the constitution on the agenda, let alone to secure control of the cabinet as a whole. As witness the rage and despair of the Reformists, republicans and socialists alike, the crisis of 1917 had come to a disappointing end.

Trienio Bolchevique

Installed as it was on 3 November 1917, the national government had immediately to contend with the fact that on 7 November Lenin and the Bolsheviks seized power in Russia. The impact was immediate. Whilst the leadership of the PSOE and UGT viewed the coup with immense disapproval – convinced that the revolution could only come after a long period of bourgeois government, they regarded the Bolsheviks as little more than a gang of wreckers – for many members of the rank and file, not to mention the militants of the CNT, the picture was very different. Whatever may have been the intentions of the leadership, the grass roots of the PSOE, UGT and CNT alike had in many cases gone into the August strike in a spirit of genuine revolutionary fervour. Its disappointing outcome having therefore been a bitter blow, the Bolshevik revolution seemed a new dawn, and all the more so as the situation in Russia was widely misunderstood (extraordinary as it may appear, the anarchists in particular viewed the Bolsheviks very much as co-religionists).

In the light of the general excitement, 1918 was hardly likely ever to have been marked by much in the way of tranquillity. However, neither the government nor the doctrinaire moderates who dominated the UGT and PSOE did anything to help matters. Thus, it soon became clear that progress in the direction of political reform was likely to be minimal. Central to the whole issue of democratization, for example, was the re-establishment of the principle of civilian supremacy. In this respect, the appointment of La Cierva as Minister of War was at first sight distinctly encouraging in that he was the first civilian to hold the position in the history of the Restoration Monarchy. Appearances, however, were deceptive: given that appointing a civilian meant that the political generals who dominated the high command were excluded from power, García Prieto was actually addressing one of the *junteros*' major grievances, whilst La Cierva was in any case much inclined to regard the discontent which they voiced as a springboard for his political ambitions. Whilst pretending to combat the *junteros*, he therefore spent much of his time trying to win their support, the most important step that he took in this respect being to announce a programme of military reform whose every clause represented a surrender to their demands. Thus, a variety of measures were taken to raise pay, increase the number of posts, speed up promotion, restore the principle of seniority, and reduce the perquisites of *africanismo*. Provision was also made for the establishment of an airforce and the implementation of a general programme of rearmament, but the means by which these goals were to be achieved was not made clear, the failure to do anything to reduce the size of the officer corps ensuring that they would probably never be made good. As for the *junteros* themselves, the fact that they were persuaded to scale down the hierarchy of juntas that had sprung up in every branch of the army meant nothing, their spirit being allowed to live on in a fashion that was more or less untrammelled.

If modernization had clearly been sacrificed to expediency, still worse was the manner in which La Cierva's proposals were introduced, the War Minister insisting that they be promulgated by royal decree. Faced by this demand, the two Catalanists promptly resigned, but the prime minister eventually agreed to back La Cierva, the so-called Ley de Bases eventually becoming law on 13 March. By this time fresh elections had been held. True to its word, the government made no effort to intervene in proceedings, whilst it also amnestied all those involved in the strike movement, a number of the latter's leaders thereby being enabled to stand for election. Yet in point of fact all this amounted to very little. As previous episodes of reformism had illustrated, the state was not the only agent of electoral malpractice: in rural areas the *caciques* continued to run things more or less as they wished, there being some evidence that matters were worse than ever. Thus, although the PSOE and the regionalists made substantial gains, these were balanced by heavy losses amongst the Republicans and Reformists, the vast majority of seats continuing to go to the Conservatives and Liberals even though these were each now divided into three different factions (in the case of the former, *datistas*, *ciervistas* and *mauristas*; and in that of the latter *garciaprietistas*, *romanonistas* and *albistas*). All that the decision to hold free elections ensured, in fact, was, first, that neither of the two main parties enjoyed the usual overwhelming majority, and, second, that factional differences were exacerbated still further.

The results of the 1918 elections were therefore hardly encouraging, whilst it also became clear that the government had no answer to Spain's worsening social and economic problems (the damage wrought by the German submarine campaign was now causing serious disruption, whilst the winter of 1917–18 was extremely harsh). Openly spoken of as an interim administration, the coalition was very soon revealed to be even weaker than had generally been assumed: unbridgeable differences quickly opening between the violently repressive La Cierva and his more moderate colleagues over the attitude that should be taken towards a strike that had paralysed the post and telegraph system, on 19 March the cabinet dissolved in chaos. Days of deadlock followed, none of the obvious candidates to replace the prime minister being prepared to take office in a situation in which they neither had a majority in the chamber nor could count upon the support of the army. Left with no other way out, Alfonso turned once again to Maura, and on 22 March 1918 Spain duly entered what seemed to be yet another period of regeneration.

If Maura's reappearance placated the *junteros*, and, indeed, much of the essentially *petit-bourgeois* constituency that had rallied to earlier protest movements, it could not but alienate the Left. Distrusted even by the new prime minister, La Cierva, certainly, was out of office, but Maura was as reactionary as ever, whilst Cambó's appointment as Minister of Development suggested that the voice of industry was likely to weigh heavily in its deliberations. Sympathetic to social reform though some ministers were – the new cabinet contained all the various factions into which the dynastic parties had become divided – the Maura government was therefore ill-placed to conciliate a labour movement that was experiencing a period of mounting excitement.

Nowhere was this excitement more obvious than amongst the Anarchists. Thus, intoxicated by the glorious visions emanating from Moscow, from early 1918 onwards the anarchist movement began to experience a great revival. Whilst leading militants harangued endless mass meetings, anarchist newspapers filled their pages with praise of Bolshevism and appeals to the workers to follow its example. Inspired by visions of land seizures on the Russian model (though theoretically in favour of collectivization, the CNT was at this point very careful to cloud the issue in ambiguity), the landless labourers flocked to the new syndicates that were being established, whilst in Catalonia there was a mood of growing violence and frustration. Whilst Barcelona witnessed the first stirrings of the terrorism that was so much to disrupt its life over the next few years, Andalucía experienced a wave of strikes that brought an increase in wages, a reduction in working hours, the recognition of anarchist unions as *de facto* labour exchanges, and the abolition of piecework. Less than 20,000 strong in 1917, by June 1918 the number of *cenetistas* had therefore risen to 75,000.

Although militancy was on the march even within the ranks of the strongly reformist PSOE and UGT, amongst whom the first stirrings were visible of a 'left-opposition' terrified that the party would be left behind, the government did little to address the situation. Thus, as Minister of Development, Cambó supported a programme centred on improvements in transport, greater use of irrigation and a further expansion of hydroelectric power. Radical enough in its own way, all this offered little in the way of immediate assistance to the workers, whilst the rest of the government were in any case instinctively opposed to the heavy burden of debt that Cambó's interventionism would inevitably have incurred. Whether the leader of the Lliga would ever have achieved his aims is therefore very unclear, but the national government was in reality so divided that it could not have lasted for very long in any case. Trouble could in fact have erupted along any one of a whole series of fault lines, but in the event it was Alba who precipitated the crisis. Already angered by the preferential treatment that Cambó's programme accorded Catalonia, he was convinced that the Allied victory that was now all but a *fait accompli* required the formation of an overtly democratic government. Seizing on a minor pretext, on 9 October he therefore resigned from the government in the hope that this would precipitate its collapse and leave the king no option but to form a more progressive cabinet. In the event Maura managed to keep the government afloat, but on 27 October Dato followed Alba's example on the grounds of ill-health, whilst it was also becoming apparent that many Conservatives were unlikely to accept the moderate increases in direct taxation that the government had decided to introduce as part of its programme of regeneration. Weary and exhausted, Maura could take no more, and on 6 November he therefore tendered his resignation.

The end of the First World War five days later did not bring any relief to Spain's tense situation. Although there was no immediate end to the wartime boom, the situation was quite bad enough even as it was, whilst Spain had also begun to experience the first ravages of the influenza epidemic that swept Europe at the end of the war. Given this situation, the labour movement could only go from strength to strength. Some 75,000 strong in June 1918, the anarchosyndicalists had by the end of the year increased their numbers by at least one-third. Meanwhile, the Socialists were on the move too. Thus, though still committed to electoralism, even the dominant *pablistas* were excited enough by the end of the war to engage in a bout of quasi-revolutionary rhetoric, whilst the rank and file could not but be stirred by the example of the CNT. Now that the war was safely won, too, there emerged a more conciliatory attitude to the Bolshevik Revolution on the part of the leadership, the combined result being that by November 1918 the Socialist movement was gripped by real fervour. At the same time, there was a further increase in membership. Thus, 32,000 strong in 1918, membership of the PSOE had by 1920 grown to 53,000, the corresponding figures for the UGT being 89,000 and 211,000.

All this was accompanied by a further increase in labour unrest. Thus, in the province of Córdoba the beginning of November witnessed the outbreak of a great general strike that involved no fewer than thirty-four different *pueblos* and united *braceros*, artisans, shopkeepers and domestic servants. Whether the government was in a position to cope with this agitation was a moot point, however. Following the fall of Maura, a wholly Liberal government had been formed under García Prieto on the grounds, first, that the Liberals had slightly more deputies than the Conservatives, and, second, that they had a far more acceptable image in the eyes of the Allies. However, it was soon all too clear that García Prieto was extremely vulnerable, quarrels over the response that was demanded by the excitement generated in Catalonia and the Basque country alike by the famous 'Fourteen Points' leading to the collapse of his administration after barely three weeks.

The fall of García Prieto on 3 December 1918 serving notice that the Catalan problem was becoming extremely urgent, the king's next move was to summon the Conde de Romanones, it being Romanones who had essentially been responsible for establishing the *mancomunidad* in the first place. However, the former being opposed to any concessions to the Catalans whatsoever and the latter inclined to make demands that no Madrid government could have tolerated, the new premier was unable to secure the support either of the *garciaprietistas* and *albistas*, or the Lliga. In short, the Romanones government was unlikely to have survived for any longer than its fellows even had it not been swamped by other troubles of a rather different character.

In the immediate aftermath of the war, the situation in Barcelona was particularly tense. Eager to avoid trouble, the civil governor had been trying to strengthen the position of the more moderate element of the local CNT leadership (personified by the general secretary of the Catalan branch of the CNT, Salvador Segui, these men represented a growing trade-unionist tendency whose aim was not the overthrow of capitalist society, but rather the betterment of the conditions of the working classes). Typically enough, however, he found his authority challenged by the far more rigid Captain General, Joaquín Milans del Bosch. Thus, Milans had become increasingly preoccupied with the growing excitement of the Catalanists. Not only had an overtly separatist organization – the Federació Democràtica Nacionalista – been established by an emotional and romantic demagogue named Francesc Macià, but officers were being abused in the streets. Absolutely furious, Milans had in consequence forced Romanones to suspend constitutional guarantees in Barcelona, the Captain General promptly seizing the opportunity to clamp down not only on the Catalanists but also the CNT, the latter eventually being provoked into launching a general strike. Eager to seek a confrontation with the 'Bolshevik menace' as soon as possible, this was precisely what both Milans and the employers had wanted, the most draconian methods promptly being deployed against the strikers. However, this only served to stimulate the workers' resistance still further, and Romanones, who had never been very happy about the attempt to break the workers in the first place, came to the conclusion that the only way out was conciliation. With commendable decision, the prime minister therefore replaced both the civil governor and the chief of police with men who could be trusted to come to an agreement with the strikers, the result being that within three days a series of major concessions had been offered to the workers.

As the workers accepted these conditions, the city might now have returned to normal, but in fact the deal was sabotaged by Milans, the Captain General tendering his resignation rather than implement his part in the peace deal (specifically, the release of all imprisoned *cenetistas*). Knowing that Milans enjoyed the support of the *junteros*, Romanones had no option but to allow him to continue in post, the peace deal in consequence falling by the wayside. When this provoked a restoration of the strike, moreover, the Captain General ran amok. Under the protection of martial law, thousands of troops, police and *somatenes* patrolled the streets, took over the running of the city's public services, intimidated the lower classes, and forced open the many small shops which had supported the strike. As for the unions, their premises were closed down, their leadership arrested, their archives seized, and their activities suspended, the strikers having as a result by early April been forced back to work. Humiliated by Milans, the government tried to redress the balance by decreeing the eight-hour day (a key part of the original peace deal), but the Captain General showed what he thought of such attempts at conciliation by expelling Romanones' nominees on the grounds that they were undermining his attempts to restore order.

Faced by an intolerable situation, on 15 April 1919 Romanones resigned. As he tacitly recognized, the army was now the effective ruler of Spain, in which capacity it proceeded to drive the situation to fresh extremes. Thus, for all the CNT's revolutionary rhetoric, its most important figures – Salvador Seguí and the editor of *Solidaridad Obrera*, Angel Pestaña – were in reality closet reformists who believed that the immediate task of the syndicalist movement was to build up its forces and work for the betterment of the conditions of its members. The syndicalism that they represented being particularly strong among the Catalan militants who made up two-thirds of the CNT, the fact was that there had been very little that was revolutionary about the events that had convulsed Barcelona. However, within the CNT there had always been a number of pure anarchists who remained wedded to the idea of the revolutionary general strike, whilst its ranks had also begun to be infiltrated by rootless young drifters who had come to Barcelona in search of work only to end up leading marginal existences on the fringes of the underworld. Inured to violence, such elements had played a key role in the events of 1909, whilst they were naturally attracted to the concept of revolutionary terrorism, associating this with regular pay, little work and lots of excitement. Despised and feared by such men as Seguí, they were until 1918 more or less kept in check, but the defeat of the general strike inevitably brought them to the fore, and all the more so as the repression that followed saw the blacklisting of many militants who were then left with no other means of employment than terrorism.

With the CNT being nudged more and more in the direction of revolution and terror, the military authorities contrived to make the situation even worse. Even before the First World War there had been a tendency on the part of the forces of order to employ terrorists of their own – drawn, incidentally, from the self-same groups as those who supplied the CNT's *pistoleros* – to act as *agents provocateurs*, discredit the labour movement and assassinate key labour activists. Milans and the employers being much attracted by such a policy, the early months of 1919 therefore saw the authorities establish a terrorist gang under the leadership of a police officer disgraced when the CNT had revealed that he had been running a German spy ring, there following a series of brutal murders.

Appalling though Barcelona's situation quickly became, the attention of the propertied classes was in 1919 rather more focused on events in Andalucía, for the agrarian disturbances of 1918 had burst forth with much greater violence than before, there even being some attempts at collectivization and the establishment of 'soviet republics'. Absolutely terrified, the landowners started to flee their estates for the safety of the towns and cities, whilst some even left the country altogether. With matters in this state, the obvious candidate to replace the count was the tough and uncompromising Maura, and all the more so as he was the only politician acceptable to the *junteros*. Initially it seems that Maura planned to reconstitute the national government of the previous year, but such were the divisions that now prevailed that this proved impossible, the result being that he was forced to form a cabinet composed only of *mauristas* and *ciervistas*. Whilst pursuing a vigorous policy of repression, he therefore obtained a decree of dissolution and called fresh elections. These, however, proved a disaster. Having always forbidden his followers to develop a formal organization of their own, Maura could hardly expect them to do well, the fact being that the Conservative Party's *caciques* had on the whole remained loyal to more mainstream figures. For the first time ever, then, a government failed to win a majority in a general election (the exact figures were 104 *mauristas* and *ciervistas*, ninety-three *datistas*, 133 Liberals, thirty Socialists, Reformists and Republicans, twenty-three regionalists and fifteen others). No sooner had the assembly reassembled, then, than Maura was forced to resign, though such were the differences that had begun to emerge amongst the *mauristas*, of whom one wing were broadly social catholic and the other wholly reactionary, that it is difficult to see how even electoral victory could have made much difference. At all events, what was needed was a compromise figure acceptable to all sides, to which end the king selected the widely respected *datista*, Joaquín Sánchez de Toca.

Physically ugly and a poor public speaker, Sánchez de Toca was nevertheless possessed of both talent and common sense. Rejecting both misty notions of a 'revolution from above' and the idea that the question of public order was one that could be solved by repression alone, he therefore embarked on a policy of conciliation. Thus, Barcelona was given a new civil governor who believed in the need for moderation and social reform whilst at the same time being impossible for Milans to reject, the new man being a prominent *juntero* who had for a long time been the editor of a leading military newspaper. Meanwhile, Sánchez de Toca also ended martial law, decreed a general amnesty, and established a special commission composed of representatives of government, industry and labour alike to examine the situation in Barcelona. For a brief moment, all this made a real difference: with Milans and the employers forced to back down, Seguí proved only too happy to enter negotiations and order all *cenetistas* to return to work.

The respite, however, was short-lived. Unwilling to abandon their careers of violence, the anarchist *pistoleros* were in no mood to compromise, whilst they were tacitly supported by the many militants who rejected the trade-unionism of Seguí (for the whole of 1919 conflict had been growing between the anarchist and syndicalist wings of the CNT). Whether syndicalism would have been able to retain control is a moot point, but all chance of their being able to do so was soon lost in that the Spanish economy at last began to sink into the recession that had been threatening ever since 1918 (the economic expansion brought by the conflict had often been achieved on the shakiest of foundations – in Asturias, for example, many of the wartime mines depended on the coal that they were producing fetching prices three times the pre-war norm). Determined in consequence to cut costs, the employers suddenly imposed a general lock-out that by the end of November had affected more than 200,000 workers. Absolutely outraged, the unions renewed their strike activity and walked out of the special commission, which had, in fact, just worked out an agreement that might have restored a real measure of stability to labour relations in Barcelona.

In consequence of these events, Catalonia was plunged into a purgatory from which it proved difficult to escape. Whilst strikes and lock-outs continued to disrupt Barcelona, both sides' gunmen engaged in a tit-for-tat spiral of murder that was to cost at least 1,500 lives, matters being rendered still worse by the fact that the CNT was soon being challenged by a rival union of Carlist origin known as the Sindicato Libre. Within a very short time, meanwhile, the apparatus of terror had got completely out of control. Not only did its masters come to realize all too well that curbing the gunmen was likely to lead to them being killed themselves, but amongst the CNT in particular there was great reluctance to do anything that might jeopardize a comrade. Thus protected, the *pistoleros* were enabled to extend their actions into areas whose legitimacy was more and more dubious. Protection rackets and blackmail flourished, whilst the gunmen increasingly funded themselves by robbing banks and extorting money from the workers, the only beneficiaries from the situation in consequence being the proponents of dictatorship.

With Barcelona once again out of control, Sánchez de Toca resigned at the first pretext. It was now 5 December 1919. Forced to search for a fourth government in the space of less than a year, Alfonso was once again placed in a position of extreme difficulty, and all the more so as the anarchists and socialists were becoming ever more excited. With Seguí in retreat and the CNT now 760,000 strong, on 10 December 1919 the Anarchists held a congress in Madrid at which they proclaimed their support for collectivization; rejected moves that had been afoot to merge the movement with the UGT; evinced huge enthusiasm for the Bolshevik Revolution; and voted to join the Russian-organized Third International. As for the PSOE and UGT, whilst the leadership remained as reformist as ever, the rank and file were being radicalized by a combination of economic distress, the enormous growth of the CNT, disappointment with the results of the First World War, and the advent of the Third International. At a conference held in Madrid at the same time as that of the Anarchists, the *pablistas* more or less held the line, but only at the cost of accepting that joining the Third International should definitely be debated in the near future.

One way or another, in short, it appeared that 1920 would prove to be even more fraught than before, and yet the new government was weaker than ever. A frail coalition of Liberal and Conservative opportunists headed by a *maurista* nonentity named Manuel Allendesalazar, its only aim was survival, the consequence being that it did nothing to solve the social problem whilst doing everything that it could to conciliate the *junteros*. So severe was the clampdown that resulted, however, even some of its members objected, and on 3 May 1920 the cabinet finally collapsed, leaving the torch in the hands of a rather unwilling Dato. Instinctively reformist in social matters, the new premier at first swung back towards a policy of conciliation, and for a time it once more seemed that substantial progress might be made: many militants were released from jail, for example, whilst a variety of decrees were promulgated that imposed rent controls on all Spain's larger cities, encouraged the provision of cheap housing, and tightened up the implementation of existing legislation concerning the compensation of workers involved in industrial accidents.

Dato's attempt at conciliation was to prove short-lived, however, the prime minister being increasingly mesmerized by the spectre of revolution. Spurred on by the fact that strikes and murders had continued unabated, he therefore replaced the reformists that he had appointed as Minister of the Interior and civil governor of Barcelona with noted reactionaries, the person chosen for the latter post being the notoriously brutal General Severiano Martínez Anido. Already military governor of the city, the general promptly secured the support of the Sindicato Libre, mobilized the *somatén*, and embarked on an attack on the CNT that was unprecedented in its ferocity. Needless to say, the anarchists did not remain inert in the face of these measures, the immediate result of Martínez Anido's actions being to provoke both a considerable increase in the number of terrorist attacks and a near-total general strike, but the fight could not go on forever, Barcelona's libertarian movement having within a year been effectively broken.

Whilst Martínez Anido was crushing the Catalan CNT, the *trienio bolchevique* was also on the wane elsewhere. Turning to the other main epicentre of anarchist unrest, repression had never been relaxed in the countryside (even the most progressive Conservative ministers were as unwilling as they were unable seriously to consider agrarian reform). Meanwhile, the steep fall in agricultural exports consequent on the slump inclined the landowners, who were now much better organized, to take a harsher line with strikes, force down wages and allow much land to go out of production. Subjected to unremitting repression, reprisal and impoverishment, the *campesinos* in consequence lost all faith in the anarchist movement. In the larger towns anarchism survived rather better, whilst the mining areas continued to be extremely combative, but the fact was that it was not only in Catalonia that anarchism was a spent force.

Conscious of the worsening situation, in December 1920 the CNT leadership made one last effort. As we have seen, Martínez Anido had been met by a general strike, and a desperate attempt was now made to extend this to the rest of the country by invoking the terms of an alliance that the growing climate of repression had persuaded the CNT to sign with the UGT three months before. However, the latter having only responded to its overtures in the hope that it might thereby lay the foundations for an eventual takeover, it therefore refused to second the CNT's calls for a strike, the result being that the movement almost immediately fell apart.

In many ways the last gasp of the *trienio bolchevique*, the abortive general strike of December 1920 is symbolic of the reasons why a genuine revolutionary crisis failed to develop in Spain at the end of the First World War. True though it is that the establishment never lost its ability to repress disorder, the left was in a state of utter disunity. Indeed, thanks to the emergence of Communism, matters were now worse than ever, both the anarchists and the socialists being bedevilled by growing demands that they should affiliate with the Third International (indeed, in April 1920 a small Partido Comunista de España had been formed by a group of dissidents in the socialist youth movement, the PSOE actually voting to join the International two months later). Not only was the workers' movement disunited, meanwhile, but it was also bereft of allies (the 1917 alliance with the Republicans had long since completely broken down), and dependent on a membership whose commitment was open to serious question. In short, the *trienio* had not been very *bolchevique* at all, revolution still being far away.

Anual

If the failure of the general strike of December 1920 marked the end of the *trienio bolchevique*, it did not bring any respite to the embattled Restoration Monarchy. In the first place, the post-war depression had now reached its lowest point, mining, textiles, engineering, and iron and steel all experiencing widespread lay-offs. With labour unrest still by no means defeated, the political system was therefore going to be hard put to convince an increasingly hysterical establishment that it could continue to protect its interests. That said, the system might yet have struggled on, but in July 1921 the Spanish forces in Morocco suffered a disaster on an unprecedented scale, the result being a crisis of such magnitude that constitutional government was finally brought to its knees.

Before going any further, it must first be pointed out that such danger as the Left had ever represented was in the course of 1921 dissipated still further, for the anarchists and socialists alike were now to suffer internal disputes on a scale that dwarfed those of previous years. Thus, 1920 the PSOE, CNT and PCE had all sent missions to Moscow to apply for admission to the Third International, but of these only the last had been happy with what it found: whilst the PSOE delegation returned home deeply split, its CNT counterpart did so shocked and upset, it being all too obvious not only that the Communist regime rested on terror and dictatorship, but also that it was bent on the complete destruction of syndicalism. In consequence, the stage was set for a series of ferocious disputes. Within the PSOE the matter was settled by a stormy, extraordinary congress in April 1921 which decided against affiliation to the Third International by a solid majority, albeit at the cost of a major split that led to the formation of a second Communist group known as the Partido Comunista Obrero Español. In the CNT, meanwhile, a small group of militants headed by Andrés Nin and Joaquín Maurín had adopted Leninist ideas and continued to press for affiliation to the Comintern. Courtesy of the arrest of so many leading *cenetistas*, they achieved a position of considerable influence within the movement and were thereby able to commit the CNT to joining the syndicalist international known as the Profintern that was also being organized in Moscow at this time. However, their efforts were badly undermined by the report that was received from the delegation that had been sent to Russia, the result being that no sooner had a full CNT congress been able to meet than it broke off all contacts with Moscow. Unwilling to accept this decision, Nin and

Maurín seceded to form an independent communist–syndicalist movement. Also eclipsed at this meeting were the more anarchistic elements of
the CNT, the congress voting to move decisively in the direction of
seguismo, but the ideological unity that had at last been established was
all but meaningless, the CNT no longer being in any position to benefit
(at the same time, too, small groups of militants continued to intrigue
against the leadership in the hope that they could win back the movement
for the cause of revolution).

As a result of all this, the early 1920s found the labour movement in a
state of total disarray. The two Communist parties merged in November
1921, but they were completely unable to win the support of the socialist
and anarchist rank and file, the only result of their emergence therefore
being to spread dissension and mistrust, much to the detriment, of
course, of the efforts of the UGT and CNT to resist the employers'
attempts to force down wages and close down uneconomic enterprises.
With membership generally in decline, the fact was that the labour
movement was in full retreat. As early as the general elections that Dato
had held in December 1920 as the price of continuing in office, indeed,
the Socialist vote had declined dramatically. As was only to be expected,
meanwhile, Dato increased the number of his supporters from ninety-
three to 179. His triumph, however, was short-lived: on 8 March 1921 a
group of anarchist *pistoleros* ambushed his car and shot him dead. Other
than to provide the authorities with a further pretext for persecuting the
Left, his death made little difference, however: working though Dato was
to restore the unity of the Conservative Party, Spain was about to be
engulfed by events of a sort that could not but have swamped his best
efforts.

This being the case, it is now time to return to Morocco, where the First
World War had for a variety of reasons been a period of deceptive
tranquillity. In reality, however, the situation was anything but stable.
Extremely poor and still largely unconquered, the Spanish protectorate
was racked by repeated famines which the colonial administration did
little to ameliorate, the resultant effervescence being worsened by the
latter's pursuit of a policy of divide and rule that made many enemies for
the Spaniards whilst gaining them very little in the way of reliable
support. Though trouble was therefore a certainty, the Spanish forces
were little more impressive than before, the bulk of the garrison still
consisting of unwilling conscripts whose conditions remained as appalling as ever, the military administration being notoriously corrupt. In
every respect, then, it was imperative that conflict should be avoided, but
a variety of pressures – the colonialist enthusiasms of the Conde de
Romanones; pressure from the army in Morocco; and French demands
that the Spaniards end the raids that were constantly being launched

against their territory – led to offensive action being resumed in the spring of 1919.

For the first year of operations the fighting was mostly concentrated in the western part of the Protectorate, the Spaniards even obtaining some success. Under the command of the newly appointed governor of Ceuta, General Manuel Fernández Silvestre, direct communications were opened between the major bases of Ceuta, Tetuán and Larache, and a firm grip established on the Tangier peninsula. Moreover, success continued into 1920. Transferred to Melilla, Silvestre initiated offensive operations in the eastern zone as well, whilst in the west control was secured of the city of Xauen. With the Spanish forces reinforced both by extra Moorish auxiliaries and a new force of professional troops – the Foreign Legion – specifically recruited for service in the Protectorate and imbued with a spirit of the utmost ferocity, it seemed that 1921 could not fail to produce a triumphant advance into the Rif – the range of mountains between Xauen and Melilla that constituted the last heartland of tribal independence.

If things did not work out in this fashion, it was largely the fault of Silvestre. Whereas the overall commander in Morocco – the thoughtful and intelligent General Dámaso Berenguer – believed that every Spanish advance had to be preceded by a careful programme of political preparation designed to persuade the tribesmen concerned to accept Spanish rule, Silvestre was a deeply ambitious man who yearned for glory and progress. Still worse, he was a personal favourite of Alfonso XIII, the latter being known to be much excited by the prospect of a rapid conquest. Lionized by many newspapers and faced by resistance that was at best sporadic, Silvestre in consequence moved deep into the interior, the result being that by January 1921 he had established a line of outposts that stretched as far as the town of Anual. To make matters worse, meanwhile, he had none of the crack units of the Foreign Legion attached to his over-extended forces, to whose welfare he habitually paid little attention. Had the Moors of the Rif remained passive, none of this need have mattered, but by the winter of 1920–1 they had coalesced around the figure of Muhammed Abd al-Karim, a Spanish-educated chieftain who united considerable personal charisma with a high degree of intelligence. Large forces of Moors were therefore soon massing round Anual, but the general was now dreaming of advancing all the way to the important town of Alhucemas. Scorning Berenguer's increasingly worried attempts to check his operations, he therefore sent his troops still further forward to the villages of Sidi Dris, Abarran and Igueriben, only for Abd al-Karim to choose that very moment to launch an all-out offensive. Taken by surprise, the Spaniards were overwhelmed, and by 21 July it was clear that Anual was completely untenable. Many outlying positions had fallen, supplies were low, the Moorish auxiliaries were increasingly unreliable and the Spanish conscripts were utterly demoralized. Very reluctantly, Silvestre now gave the order to retreat, but such was the state of his forces that they disintegrated into a panic-stricken rabble. Encouraged by the certainty of plunder, large numbers of tribesmen who had hitherto remained neutral now joined in the attack, the result being that by the end of July the surviving Spanish forces were penned up in Melilla and a few isolated forts such as Monte Arruit. As their supplies ran out, the unfortunates who had taken refuge in the latter were forced to surrender, only for the most part to be massacred in cold blood, whilst Melilla itself would probably have fallen but for the hasty dispatch of several battalions of the Foreign Legion.

Anual was a shattering blow. Silvestre was missing; at least 10,000 men had been killed; and large quantities of weapons and other booty had fallen into the hands of the enemy, along with several hundred prisoners. Assailed by a storm of criticism, the government, which had since the assassination of Dato been headed by the stop-gap figure of Allendesalazar, resigned, its replacement being headed by the increasingly patriarchal Antonio Maura. Encouraged by renewed demands for a fundamental reform of the Restoration system, the Mallorcan statesman formed a new national government in the hope of at last securing his much-dreamed-of 'revolution from above'.

Initially all went well: every member of the cabinet could unite around the goal of restoring order in Morocco; the propertied classes threw themselves into an orgy of support for the war effort; and a series of counterattacks recovered a substantial amount of territory in the vicinity of Melilla. Once the immediate crisis was past, however, the government began to run into a web of contradictions. Thus, convinced that the defeat was in part due to the huge amounts of revenue that were absorbed by the salaries of the officer corps, Juan de la Cierva, who had once again been appointed War Minister, launched a sustained offensive against the juntas that stripped them of all independence. At the same time, meanwhile, he ensured that Berenguer was confirmed in the post of High Commissioner of Morocco, and exempted from the enquiries of the commission that had been established to investigate the disaster under General Juan Picasso, in the meantime doing everything that he could to flatter the *africanistas*. Yet in doing so he was not only providing much ammunition for the Republicans and Socialists – exempting Berenguer implied exempting the ministers to whom he had been responsible, not to mention Alfonso XIII – but jeopardizing the unity of the cabinet in that many of its members were opposed to the resumption of a forward policy and wanted the appointment of a civilian to the post of High Commissioner. Indeed, as Minister of Finance, Cambó was attempting to cut government expenditure in a manner that was incompatible with the *africanistas*' plans for total conquest. Nor did it help in this respect that he also forced through a new tariff that greatly increased the protection available to Catalan industry at the expense of the agrarian interests of Castile and Andalucía. Sooner or later, in short, collapse was inevitable.

It was not, however, the incompatibilities in its own make-up that broke the last Maura administration. Thus, almost from its very inception, it was enmeshed in the damaging question of 'responsibilities'. Not surprisingly, the defeat had provoked a storm of criticism amongst the Reformists, Republicans and Socialists, whilst the more progressive elements of the Liberal Party were unhappy at the prospect of having to support the government *tout court*, and all the more so when it became apparent that Berenguer was not even to be investigated. For those Liberals represented in the government – and for that matter the Lliga – the position therefore soon became increasingly uncomfortable. Within the Liberal Party, meanwhile, a growing *rapprochement* between Romanones and García Prieto seemed to offer the hope that the king would permit a new *turno*. On 7 March 1922 Romanones and García Prieto therefore ordered their placemen in the cabinet to resign, the result being that Maura was forced to surrender power for what proved to be the last time.

If Romanones and García Prieto had brought down Maura in the expectation of being appointed to power, then they had miscalculated, for Alfonso XIII was far too committed to the conquest of Morocco to be happy with the prospect of a Liberal government ruling in *de facto* alliance with the parliamentary Left. Much to the Liberals' chagrin, he therefore instead placed the premiership in the hands of Dato's replacement as Conservative leader, José Sánchez Guerra, the latter proceeding to form a coalition composed of the *datistas*, the *mauristas* and the Lliga. An intelligent *datista* from Córdoba, the new prime minister was above all a pragmatist, and therefore quickly saw that to continue in the traditions of his predecessor was impossible: indeed, it is not without significance in this respect that La Cierva had been excluded from the new government. Ignoring the fury of the *mauristas* and the Lliga, whose representatives proceeded to resign from the cabinet, he in consequence ended the suspension of constitutional guarantees that had been imposed as an initial response to Anual and attempted to back away from the compromise position that had eventually been adopted with regard to Morocco (in brief, it had been agreed that rather than either pulling back to the coast and attempting to control the Protectorate through indirect means, or going ahead with a policy of total conquest, the army should recover all the territory that had been lost at Anual and then consider the

position further). In this respect, moreover, a series of fortuitous developments enabled the new prime minister to go much further than he had
expected. Thus, in April 1922 the Picasso commission submitted its
report to the government which immediately proceeded to pass it on to
the army's highest judicial authority, the Supreme Council of War. The
senior generals of which the latter was composed being deeply jealous of
Berenguer, and in the case of its president, General Francisco Aguilera,
highly ambitious, this body voted to accept Picasso's recommendations.
Including as these did the proposal that Berenguer should be put on trial,
the High Commissioner immediately resigned, the result being that
Sánchez Guerra was able to replace him with the much more malleable
General Ricardo Burguete, the latter being instructed to make peace with
the Moors. Meanwhile, the post of High Commissioner was subordinated to the Foreign Ministry and the *cortes* persuaded to establish a
special all-party commission of enquiry.

Thus far it might appear that Sánchez Guerra was doing no more than
governing in alliance with the *junteros*. However, the prime minister also
restored the principle of promotion by merit, abolished the last vestiges
of *juntero* organization and dismissed Martínez Anido and his hench-
man, Miguel Arlegui, from the posts that they held as Governor and
Chief of Police of Barcelona. With Burguete's policy of conciliation
seemingly bearing fruit in Morocco – by the autumn, the chief opponent
of the Spaniards in the western part of the Protectorate had been
persuaded to accept a settlement that effectively transformed him into an
agent of the colonial administration – it really seemed that the post-war
crisis might at last be coming to an end.

In reality, however, nothing could have been further from the truth. In
the first place, Abd al-Karim refused to make peace, Burguete in consequence being drawn deeper and deeper into operations in the heart of
the Rif. On 1 November, meanwhile, a column dispatched in the direction of Anual ran into difficulties at a place called Tizi Azza, the relatively
large number of casualties that it suffered leading Sánchez Guerra to
prohibit any further forward movement. Yet by doing so, the prime
minister alienated many of his own supporters and created an indefen-
sible strategic situation that was in the long run to unsettle Spanish
politics at least as much as a resumption of a full-scale offensive would
have done. At the same time, his earlier handling of 'responsibilities' now
backfired dramatically in that the *cortes* commission of enquiry proved to
be incapable of fulfilling the role which had been expected of it, which
was effectively to limit the blame to Berenguer and Silvestre. Though no
fewer than seventy-seven officers had now been put on trial for their role
in affairs, it was soon apparent that the Allendesalazar government and
even the king might be vulnerable. The government's position having

become untenable – whilst those ministers who had actually been in office in the summer of 1921 were demanding that the prime minister defend them against attack, those who were not believed that some concessions would have to be made on the issue – on 5 December Sánchez Guerra was forced to submit his resignation. Left with no option, the king summoned the Liberals to power, the latter having recently sealed their right to office with a *de facto* pact of union.

In the Bleak Midwinter

With the collapse of the Sánchez Guerra government, the Canovine system had reached a nadir from which it was never to recover. More or less capable of governing the Spain of the period 1875–1914, it had shown itself to be utterly incapable of dealing with the problems thrown up by the First World War. Whether governing separately or together, the Liberals and Conservatives had repeatedly proved that they could not maintain even a minimum degree of cohesion, whilst such attempts as had been made to co-opt new forces had if anything made matters worse. If Spain had emerged from the immediate post-war crisis without undergoing a full-scale revolution, it was therefore hardly the fault of the politicians: what saved the system in this respect was rather the willingness of all factions of the army to set the defence of law and order above their many grievances, the ever more ferocious disputes that beset the socialists and anarchists and the distinctly flimsy character of the labour movement.

Grim though the period 1917–21 may have been, however, by the summer of the latter year it must have seemed that a corner had been turned in that the labour movement was clearly in retreat, and the Conservative party regaining its coherence: the government of Eduardo Dato had, after all, already lasted ten months when he was assassinated. In Morocco, however, years of mismanagement had created the proverbial disaster waiting to happen, and at Anual it duly did. Thus emerged the question that finally killed the Canovine system. Not only did the 'responsibilities' issue trigger a furious wave of in-fighting in the officer corps, but it intensified military – and, indeed, royal – discontent with the political system, and rendered government impossible. Sooner or later, the disaster was as bound to engulf the Liberals as much as it had already engulfed the Conservatives, the fact being that the new 'government of Liberal concentration' was likely to be as short-lived as that of Sánchez Guerra. Incapable of renovating itself – as we shall see, the hopes that were placed in the new administration soon proved to be illusory – the Canovine system was, in the words of its own terminology, 'exhausted'.

13

The Primo de Rivera Dictatorship

A Historical Parenthesis?

The dictatorship that ruled Spain from 1923 to 1930 has often been called a parenthesis in her development. Before 1923 Spain was a constitutional country, certainly, but one in which there were distinct limits upon not only popular sovereignty, but the extent to which politics was an affair of the people at all. After 1930, however, Spain entered a new era of mass politics in which ideology reigned supreme. Such an image of transition is further reinforced by the rhetoric of the dictator, Miguel Primo de Rivera, in that he presented his regime as an essay in modernization. In terms of political culture and institutions, there is much to commend such an argument, the differences between the Restoration Monarchy and the Second Republic being extremely marked. However, in other respects the dictatorship appears more as a continuum than a parenthesis. Thus, a bid by the propertied classes to perpetuate their dominance, it was also a fresh stage in the struggle between centre and periphery. This is not to say, of course, that Primo did not succeed in either mobilizing new forces or effecting a measure of infrastructural modernization, but to regard the dictatorship as somehow being separate from the Restoration Monarchy is misguided. Far from being a parenthesis, in short, it was rather a postscript.

The Road to 13 September

It is sometimes argued that the coup of 1923 frustrated the democratization of the Canovine system. By almost any token, however, this assertion is hard to credit. Composed not just of every faction of the Liberal party but also the Reformists, the new government established in December 1922 under García Prieto certainly gave the impression of being a strongly reformist force in that it promised changes in the position of the Church, the Senate, the army, and the electoral system, the pursuit of 'responsibilities', the adoption of a more pacific policy in Morocco and fresh measures of social reform. However, in reality all this made little difference. In the first place, its programme was in reality as vague as it was timid. In the second, the alliance on which it rested was in reality based more on a desire for office than a commitment to reform. And, in the third, from the very beginning the 'liberal concentration' was characterized not by unity but division. Thus, its programme had only been agreed with considerable difficulty, whilst the new ministry was riven by differences of all sorts. With García Prieto a lack-lustre figure who was unlikely to provide firm leadership, rebirth was therefore a long way off.

More than that, indeed, the 'liberal concentration' remained inextricably mired in the *turno pacífico*. Nowhere is this clearer than in the general elections which it convoked in April 1923. Despite promises that these would be cleaner than ever before, the need to satisfy every faction in the liberal coalition ensured that matters were but little changed. Having secured its majority, meanwhile, the government displayed little energy. Thus, the sort of fiscal and agrarian reforms advocated by its more radical elements were never introduced, whilst even the heart of its programme fell by the wayside. Even before the elections had been fought, for example, protests from Church and king had forced the abandonment of measures designed to limit the former's right to dispose of its property as it wished and abolish the last restrictions on the practice of faiths other than Catholicism. With regard to Anual, meanwhile, whilst the prosecution of large numbers of army officers continued, the question of whether or not the latter should be joined by representatives of the Dato and Allendesalazar governments was merely referred to a new *cortes* commission, the Conservatives having been offered a deal in exchange for giving the Liberals an easy ride in the elections.

Over Morocco, too, the government capitulated. Whilst it did secure the release of the 357 survivors of Anual still in Moorish hands by peaceful means, ensure that the Army of Africa maintained its current defensive posture, and appoint a civilian High Commissioner in the person of Luis Silvela, in reality it was begging the question. If the Moors were not to be conquered altogether, the only decision that made sense was evacuation, the military situation simply being too delicate to permit the sort of half-way house to which the ministers' fear and self-interest left them committed. The suspension of Burguete's offensive having left such posts as Tizi Azza dangerously exposed, whilst at the same time affording Abd al-Karim a chance to build up his forces, the spring of 1923 saw fresh Moorish offensives in east and west alike. Threatened by a second Anual, the government was plunged into the utmost confusion. Whilst the Minister of War, Alcalá Zamora, decided that what was needed was the resumption of a war of conquest, the rest of the cabinet vetoed such a course on the grounds that it could lead to revolution, whereupon Alcalá Zamora promptly resigned. Desperate to evade responsibility for the issue, the government turned the matter over to the general staff in the apparent belief that the *peninsulares* who filled its ranks would be certain to oppose the *africanistas*. To its horror, however, the staff recommended the adoption of the *africanista* obsession of an amphibious landing in the bay of Alhucemas followed by an advance on Abd al-Karim's capital of Ajdir. With the country in uproar and Málaga in the grip of a serious mutiny amongst conscripts awaiting shipment to Morocco, the cabinet therefore collapsed. Probably realizing that the game had been won, Alfonso asked García Prieto to form a new administration, to which request, astonishingly enough, the latter agreed. Adopt a conciliatory line with regard to the Málaga revolt though the government did, the Liberals' whole Moroccan policy had therefore been reduced to ruins.

If 'civilianization' was ineffectual in Morocco, the government was little more effective on the home front. In this respect, the loss of Alcalá Zamora – one of the Restoration's very few civilian War Ministers – had been a bitter blow, but matters were greatly worsened by the fact that García Prieto made no attempt at all to punish the many senior officers who were openly critical of the government and made no attempt to hide their scorn for all civilian politicians. Worst of all, however, was the situation in Barcelona, where the current Captain General, Miguel Primo de Rivera, was deliberately provoking a major confrontation with the workers in defiance of the cabinet's attempts to promote conciliation. Despite the fact that the result was a revival in terrorist violence and a series of strikes that brought the city to the brink of collapse, it was the general who received the government's backing, the fact being that it had once again failed to deliver.

Wherein, then, lies the basis for the argument that García Prieto was somehow transforming Spain? By the same token, however, wherein lies the basis of what has hitherto been the standard explanation for the coup of September 1923? If neither the king, nor the army, nor the Church, nor landed property, nor big business had any reason to fear the García Prieto government, why did the constitutional system have to be overthrown? The answer, of course, is that it no longer met the needs of its progenitors. Intended above all to sustain a social and political order characterized by the utmost inequality, *canovismo* was very clearly breaking down, the result being that it had necessarily to be swept away. Before going any further, it is but fair to point out that the concerns of the establishment were not entirely selfish. However the situation is looked at, Spain faced fundamental social, political and economic problems that the Canovine system had proved itself incapable of resolving, the miserable failure of the 'liberal concentration' having in the meantime shown beyond any doubt that hopes of change were futile. In consequence, by 1923 the idea that the circle could be squared by an act of force had become a common theme of discussion, such regenerationist thinking forming a major factor in the coup of 1923. Taking the figure of Alfonso XIII first of all, there is no doubt that he was genuinely committed to many aspects of modernization, as witness the great personal interest that he showed in such projects as the development of a Spanish car industry, the construction of the Madrid metro, and the establishment of a national airline. In the army, too, the growing contempt for party politics was the fruit not just of outraged corporativism, but, at least in some cases, of a belief that something really did have to be done. Thus, many erstwhile *junteros* had come to the conclusion that a military coup that could implement a programme of fundamental political reform was essential, such views naturally being boosted by the growing exasperation even of such respected figures as the intellectual, Ortega y Gasset.

However, such altruism should not be exaggerated. For example, if Alfonso XIII was interested in modernization, he was also a businessman whose considerable investments gave him a strong vested interest in the repression of social unrest. At the same time he was convinced that Spain was on the brink of revolution, that the constitutional system was incapable of confronting the revolutionary menace, and that the *turno pacífico* was betraying the interests of the army, and frustrating the will of the 'real' people of Spain. With regard to the Moroccan rebellion – the work, in his eyes, of Jews and Bolsheviks – in particular, Alfonso felt that all Spain's misfortunes were due to successive governments' mismanagement and parsimony, and, further, that the report of the *cortes'* new commission was likely to be extremely embarrassing. Though not directly in involved in conspiracy, in short, Alfonso had other interests than just regeneration.

Setting Alfonso aside, by the summer of 1923 the extent of military unrest knew no bounds. Obviously enough, the *africanistas* were furious at the attempt to curtail their operations and saddle them with all the blame for Anual. However, whereas until only a few months previously the officer corps had been deeply divided between *peninsulares* and *africanistas*, the gulf between the two was now much less, the *peninsulares* being as irritated as the *africanistas* at the direction which the 'responsibilities' debate had taken. Above all, however, the *junteros* were deeply concerned with regard to the questions of labour unrest and separatism. Exhausted and divided as the labour movement was, Spain was hardly on the brink of revolution. That said, however, 1923 undoubtedly witnessed an increase in tension. Thus, Barcelona, as we have seen, erupted in conflict; a sudden rise in the cost of living provoked strikes throughout the country; anarchist gunmen murdered the archbishop of Zaragoza and the governor of Bilbao; Socialist candidates did relatively well in the elections of April 1923 (at seven deputies the total was the highest that they had ever achieved); numerous demonstrations took place against the Moroccan war; and in August the Communists attempted a rising in Bilbao. As for the question of separatism, here, too, radicalism seemed on the increase: new groups – the Partido Nacionalista Vasco, Estat Catala and Acció Catala – were challenging the long-established parties and winning considerable support in the process, whilst the Basques, Galicians and Catalans had formed a supra-regional alliance known as 'Galeusca', and were even talking of links with the 'Republic of the Rif'.

Although the government had by no means lost control, at least two groups of officers – four Madrid-based *africanista* generals known as the 'quadrilateral', and a cabal of *junteros* ensconced in the garrison of Barcelona under a Colonel Nouvilas – now decided that enough was enough, and therefore embarked on preparations for a coup. Uncertain as to their ability to secure sufficient support, however, these officers soon swung behind yet another focus of revolt in the person of the Captain General of Barcelona, Miguel Primo de Rivera. Nephew of a general who had played an important role in the coup of 1874, Primo was a distinguished *africanista* who had come to the conclusion that the Moroccan war was both unnecessary and unwinnable. Twice dismissed from important posts on this account, his views gained more favour after Anual, and in March 1922 he was therefore appointed Captain General of Barcelona. No worse a position could have been chosen. Extremely opinionated and ambitious, Primo was imbued with a strong degree of anti-parliamentarianism, his new posting serving only to inflame his disaffection. Still worse, not only was the general placed in direct touch with one of the main foci of insurrection within the officer corps, but he became a prime target for the machinations of the Catalan bourgeoisie. For the past twenty years a mainstay of Catalan nationalism, this group was now as alarmed by the revolutionary menace as it was alienated by the regime's attempts to adopt a more conciliatory policy, the consequence being that Primo appeared a natural ally. At the same time, not only were there rumours that the *somatén* was to be abolished, but the government was backing away from the protectionism from which Catalan industry had previously benefited. Last but not least, under pressure from the left and excluded from government, the Lliga was clearly losing its influence. With Primo giving them full backing against the workers and adopting a notably conciliatory line in cultural questions, the Catalan bourgeoisie therefore hailed him as a saviour. Increasingly messianistic in his thinking, by June 1923 the Captain General had resolved on a coup, over the next two months winning over

Nouvilas' *junteros*, most of the senior officers of the garrison of Catalonia, the 'quadrilateral' – José Cavalcanti, Federico Berenguer, Leopoldo Saro and Antonio Dabán – and one or two other figures such as the *africanista* military governors of Madrid and Zaragoza. Meanwhile, both the War Minister, Aizpuru, and the Captain General of Madrid promised that they would at least do nothing to obstruct the coup's success. With the *cortes* due to reassemble very soon, and likely to debate Anual shortly afterwards, prompt action seemed essential, the date for revolt being set as 14 September.

Despite being well aware that something was afoot, García Prieto did nothing, his belief being that the storm would soon blow over. However, on 12 September the government received incontrovertible evidence that a coup was imminent. If ever there was a moment for prompt action, it was now, but Alfonso, who had been secretly briefed on what was afoot a few days before, effectively sabotaged the last hope that a coup might be averted by warning García Prieto that he feared the consequences of removing Primo. In consequence, all that was done was to have Aizpuru telephone the general in an attempt to get him to back down. Needless to say, his efforts were ineffectual: in the small hours of 13 September the garrison of Catalonia took to the streets, Primo in the mean time issuing a manifesto that both justified his revolt and made a series of vague promises of reform. Within a few hours the example of the Captain Generalcy of Barcelona had been followed by those of Zaragoza and Valencia, whilst in Madrid the 'quadrilateral' installed themselves in the War Ministry. The king refusing to accede to García Prieto's forlorn appeals for the removal of all the rebel commanders, the entire cabinet promptly resigned, whereupon Alfonso proclaimed the formation of a military directory under the presidency of Primo de Rivera.

What are we to make of these events? Looking at the government first of all, nothing could be clearer than its exhaustion and demoralization. Turning next to Alfonso, we see the utter speciousness of attempts to shield him from the taint of responsibility for the coup, the king having at the very least greatly facilitated its success. In later years the myth would be put about that he had thereby saved Spain from civil war, but how such a prospect could have become reality is difficult to see, the alienation of the officer corps from the regime being such that it had been left without any defenders. This is not to say that the armed forces were united behind Primo, however. On the contrary, the navy, the Guardia Civil and the vast majority of the army had either taken no part in the coup, or, as was the case of the artillery and the engineers, were actively hostile to it. The Communist 'August rising', the government's decision to commute the death sentence passed against the ringleader of the conscript rebellion at Málaga, and a particularly violent nationalist demonstration in Barcelona on the very eve of the *pronunciamiento*, may all have made it hard to mount effective resistance, but the fact remains that the bulk of the armed forces had hardly rallied to Primo's standard, the officer corps remaining as divided as ever. To obtain even the limited support that he succeeded in drumming up, Primo had had to make the most contradictory promises, telling the *peninsulares* that he would pursue responsibilities and scale down the war in Morocco, the 'quadrilateral' that he would end the witch-hunt and win the war, liberal constitutionalists that he would form a civilian government and introduce political reform, and extreme monarchists that he would give Alfonso dictatorial powers. For the most part, in fact, Primo enjoyed only negative support, whilst even his supporters were deeply divided. Given that the new dictator was possessed of the most simplistic ideas, the future was extremely problematic.

Iron Surgery

Despite these difficulties, the various contradictions that threatened the new regime were by no means immediately apparent. In one or two quarters doubt or concern was expressed, but such attitudes were very much in a minority. For much of the Church and the bourgeoisie, Primo de Rivera was little short of a saviour, as witness the delighted declarations of support offered by newspapers such as *El Debate* and *ABC*, Catholic organizations, employers' associations, the major banks, the *mauristas*, the Lliga and many members of the clergy. For politicians of the dynastic parties, meanwhile, the situation was obviously one of much greater ambiguity, but the fact that they were men of property inclined them to regard the situation with some complacency. As for the forces of progress, meanwhile, reaction to the coup was muted – whilst the Communists desperately attempted to organize a general strike, the CNT refused to act without the Socialists, whilst both the Socialists and the Republicans effectively declared their neutrality.

The complacency of the monarchist politicians was to some extent reinforced by the fact that there was at first no suggestion that the dictatorship was anything other than temporary, Primo maintaining that his aim was simply to restore law and order, purge the political system of corruption, find an honourable solution to the problem of Morocco and then hand over to a new government. Of the three concrete goals that he had set himself, the most pressing, at least in his own mind, was that of restoring order, in consequence of which the general promptly embarked on a period of the sharpest repression. Thus, Martínez Anido was immediately appointed to an important post in the Ministry of the Interior, and the *somatén* placed under the command of seconded army officers and extended to the whole of Spain. Meanwhile, thousands of left-wingers were arrested, Spain placed under martial law, the control of firearms greatly strengthened, the press subjected to considerable harassment and the Communists and CNT driven underground. Within a few months terrorism and strike action had therefore been virtually eradicated, but for Primo de Rivera 'order' had a definition that was political as well as social. On 18 September a decree therefore appeared prohibiting the use of any flag other than that of Spain and imposing heavy penalties on 'crimes against the unity and security of the Fatherland', this being followed by the suppression of the more radical elements of Catalan and Basque nationalism, the restriction of the use of all languages other than Castilian, and the elimination of all traces of regionalist culture from the schoolroom. For the time being the Mancomunidad survived, but its Lliga president was replaced by the leader of the tiny Catalan loyalist movement known as Unión Monárquica Nacional, whilst it was stripped of many of its nationalist representatives and packed with reliable *españolistas*. As for Republicanism, meanwhile, a number of activists were placed under surveillance and in some cases imprisoned or banished.

Order, however, was not just to be restored by repression, Primo also embarking on a wholesale ideological offensive. In brief, Spain was to be reconquered for the traditional values of 'God, King and Fatherland', Primo's first instinct in this respect being to reach out to the Catholic Church. Thus, Catholic schools were offered generous support, whilst state schools were purged of 'suspect' teachers, and forced to employ ultra-Catholic textbooks, and introduce both religious education and regular mass, benediction and confession. Meanwhile, the laws of blasphemy and Sunday observance were rigidly enforced, whilst much attention was paid by the authorities to such matters as pornography, and the behaviour of young women and courting couples; official support was given to organizations implementing Catholic social teaching or otherwise promoting Catholic interests; 'committees of citizens' were established for the defence of morality and religion, and permission was granted for the establishment of large numbers of new religious communities. At the same time, both the clergy and Catholic activists were given privileged access to the structures of the regime, members of the new association of Catholic journalists and intellectuals known as the ACNP, for example, figuring prominently among the new town councillors and civil governors appointed by Primo. Of almost equal importance in the struggle to re-establish Spanish traditionalism were the 'government delegates' appointed to each municipality. The primary objective of these officials, who were all army officers, was primarily to eradicate *caciquismo*, and, as such, they will be examined in greater detail below. Needless to say, however, this did not preclude them from taking an active part in the regime's ideological offensive, a similar role later being adopted by the political movement formed by Primo in 1924 known as Unión Patriótica.

If Primo's regime has thus far been analysed very much in terms of authoritarian conservatism, this should not disguise the fact that at least initially the dictator was prepared to turn his guns against the very oligarchy whom he was ostensibly protecting. The Canovine system in his eyes having degenerated into a game played out by a handful of corrupt and selfish cliques, it was necessary that it should be sanitized. From this there stemmed what was, on the surface at least, an attempt completely to recast Spanish politics. At national level, the *cortes* and the senate were immediately dissolved; all men in public life were excluded from the board of private companies; parliamentary immunity was suspended so as to allow erstwhile members of the *cortes* to be tried for their alleged crimes; a few officials were sacked *pour encourager les autres*; and the bureaucracy as a whole was subjected to constant demands that it work harder and behave with greater probity. It was, however, at provincial and local level that *saneamiento* was at its most acute. Thus, all the civil governors were supplanted by their military counterparts; the *diputaciones provinciales* and *ayuntamientos* were purged, subjected to rigorous inspections and in early 1924 replaced by new bodies hand-picked by the military authorities; a national Junta Inspectadora was set up to investigate the local magistracy; and new statutes were elaborated for both local and provincial government.

With these measures in force, Primo could hope that the body politic would soon be freed of the vices which he believed had corrupted it. Of his original goals, this left him only with the problem of Morocco. For some time, however, this remained as intractable as ever. Primo was prepared to throw the *africanistas* such sops as he could – most of the officers who had been imprisoned for their role in Anual were released, for example, whilst the remainder were either found not guilty or immediately amnestied – but he had come to power with the fixed intention of adopting a less belligerent posture in Morocco. Far from reversing García Prieto's policies, he therefore tried to buy off the Moorish leaders with generous offers of autonomy, abandoned a number of posts in the interior, slashed the *quinta* for 1924 by 13 per cent, and gave over 50,000 men an early discharge. Far from responding to Primo's olive branch, however, Abd al-Karim intensified his operations. Needless to say, the Army of Africa's reaction was one of fury. In an attempt to face down the growing unrest, in July 1924 Primo visited the protec-

THE PRIMO DE RIVERA DICTATORSHIP

torate, only to be openly threatened and insulted by officers of the Foreign Legion. Forced to abandon plans to pull back in the east to the city of Melilla, Primo was nonetheless by no means disposed to change his views *per se*. On the contrary, the difficulties of the Spanish position around Xauen induced him to order the evacuation of the whole of the interior of the western zone. With ever larger numbers of Moors taking the field, the operation ran into serious difficulties, Primo having to hasten to Tetuán to take charge. The forces affected by the evacuation soon being trapped in Xauen, a major relief operation had to be mounted, and, even though this was successful, the subsequent withdrawal turned into a nightmare. The road from Xauen to Tetuán was a tortuous track through rocky mountains, the weather was appalling, and the Spaniards had to fight a series of desperate battles before they finally struggled to safety, Primo being lucky extremely to avoid a major disaster.

Had matters been left to take their course, what would have happened next is hard to predict. The Spaniards were now in a rather better strategic position than they had been for some time, and were able to repel every assault that was mounted on their positions. However, victory was clearly unattainable, whilst Abd al-Karim showed no signs of interest in a compromise peace. Where Primo was likely to get his honourable solution to the conflict from is therefore difficult to see, the only bright spot in the situation being the fact that *africanista* resistance was temporarily in abeyance. In the event, what saved the situation was developments in the insurgent camp. With the Rif running short of food, Abd al-Karim began to cast his eyes on the fertile territory controlled by the French to the south, and in April 1925 he therefore launched an invasion that had soon inflicted over 3,000 French casualties.

For Primo this came as an act of deliverance. Having for years given the Spaniards little help, the French were forced to turn to Primo for assistance, it being agreed that they would attack the Moors from the south, whilst the Spaniards disembarked in the Bay of Alhucemas and marched on Axdir. Operations began on 29 August when the French attacked in the Uarga valley. Realizing what was in store for him, Abd al-Karim sought to throw the Spaniards off balance by attacking Tetuán, but Primo refused to be diverted, on 8 September 8,000 Spanish troops duly going ashore at Ixdain. The unfortunate defenders being pulverized by heavy naval bombardment and aerial bombing, a strong bridgehead had soon been established, and on 23 September the break-out began. Forced to fight a pitched battle against troops who were far better prepared than before (Primo had devoted the winter to a programme of intensive training and rearmament), the Moors were at a hopeless disadvantage. Resistance was initially fierce, but the defenders began to desert in droves and on 2 October the Spaniards took Axdir. The war was not yet over – pacification took a further year – but the Moroccan question had effectively been resolved.

The Structures of Dictatorship

With the Moors defeated and numerous measures in place to achieve his domestic goals, Primo's rhetoric demanded that he should now step down. Nothing of the sort occurred, however, it having long since become clear that he intended to remain in power for good. According to Primo himself, the reason was that the extirpation of *caciquismo* was proving extremely elusive, but such claims are disingenuous: the decision to institutionalize the regime was clearly taken as early as the winter of 1923 following the state visit which Primo and Alfonso paid to Italy shortly after the coup, the inference being that Mussolini had inspired them with a vision of an entirely new state.

In complaining of the *caciques*, however, Primo had spoken nothing but the truth. For all their orders to purge the structures of local government, in practice the military governors and government delegates had little room to manoeuvre. For its attack on the old order to be successful, the new regime had to have access to reservoirs of fresh talent that were both hostile to *caciquismo* and ready to come to Primo's aid. Scattered across the Spain of 1923 there were a considerable number of groups which seemed to fit the bill. On a national level, there existed the representatives of *maurismo* and political Catholicism. On a regional level an obvious candidate was the Lliga. On a purely provincial level, there were a number of small local parties which had been formed in recent years in protest at the neglect of local concerns and the imposition of placemen by the party leaders in Madrid. Yet in each of these categories there were serious problems. Since the retirement of Maura himself from active politics, *maurismo* had increasingly fallen under the influence of such figures as Antonio Goicoechea, whose interest in the movement was confined to the use that might be made of it in the defence of the existing social order. If political Catholicism was more genuine in its belief that *caciquismo* should be overthrown, its chief representative, the Partido Social Popular, had only been founded in December 1922, and was so seriously divided as to whether or not it should participate in the regime that it almost immediately collapsed in schism. Also genuinely regenerationist, the Lliga had been both discredited and alienated by Primo's anti-catalanism. Last but not least, the various local parties were in reality little more than emanations of *caciquista* networks that had either temporarily found themselves excluded from favour, or were too weak to obtain any leverage.

Whilst it was not always the case, the result was that the practical effects of 'iron surgery' were extremely limited. In many areas there being no men of education who were not in some way connected with the old system, it was often impossible to exclude its representatives. Meanwhile, the military authorities in any case frequently proved easy enough to buy off, matters being made still worse by the fact that the regime quickly became more interested in securing the *caciques*' support than in eradicating their influence. Thus, when Primo re-established the post of civil governor in April 1924, over 29 per cent of his original appointments came from the *turno* parties. Although the final figure fell to 8 per cent, the links with the old order remain all too obvious.

If Primo's *anti-caciquismo* ran into the sand, this was to a considerable extent related to the nature of the new political organizations over whose emergence he presided. Thus, in the immediate aftermath of the coup a large number of local movements sprang up which aimed at galvanizing support for the dictatorship. Notionally regenerationist, from the beginning these movements were filled with representatives of the old order, the latter going on to become equally prominent in the new national movement known as Unión Patriótica whose formation Primo ordered in April 1924. In some areas, certainly, the leadership of this force contained substantial elements that were drawn from beyond the ranks of *caciquismo*, whether they were representatives of political Catholicism or of the industrial, commercial and professional bourgeoisie. Indeed, in a considerable number of provinces such elements were even dominant. This, however, is not to say that there was any real political renovation. In at least fourteen provinces the UP's leadership was drawn entirely from the *turno* parties, whilst in several others it was dominated by forces that, if ostensibly separate from them, stood for the same interests. Moreover, even where the provincial leadership was composed of new men, at municipal level committees were often full of the same old faces as before. With such examples widespread, the fact is that the formation of the UP simply provided a means by which *caciquismo* could prosper in a new guise, and all the more so given the fact that the new party enjoyed a near monopoly of office.

From all this there flowed a number of consequences. In the first place, the regime became even more wedded to the defence of the established social order, whilst in the second the nature of local politics was altered not a whit. Certain *cacicatos* whose heads had for one reason or another earned the particular wrath of Primo disappeared or were broken up, but, for every *cacique* who was humbled, another sprang up in his place. In consequence, nepotism, corruption, arbitrariness and incompetence all remained extremely common. Meanwhile, even the mobilization of opinion that UP was supposed to represent was a chimera. If the membership may have reached 1,000,000 at its greatest extent, only a minority was drawn to it for ideological reasons. Thousands of members were officials or army officers who had joined only to safeguard their careers, whilst thousands more were *campesinos* or shopkeepers who had done so to protect their livelihoods, the provinces with the highest membership all being strongholds of *latifundismo* or precarious tenancy.

For all that, however, the consequences were dramatic. Whether it was in the encouragement of the wholesale denunciation of *caciquista* abuses in the immediate aftermath of the coup, the orchestration of campaigns of popular support, or the staging of enormous parades and rallies, Primo was effectively creating a public opinion that had simply not existed in 1923. Also important here was the manner in which the dictator put his real *bonhomie* to good use in an endless stream of broadcasts, *communiqués*, articles, interviews and speeches in which flights of the most torrid patriotic rhetoric were commingled with a homely and intimate manner that gave him an air of simplicity and accessibility. Not satisfied with all this, Primo also sought direct contact with the populace, regularly strolling through the streets and chatting with passersby, and encouraging the dispatch of suggestions and complaints of all sorts to his office. In however artificial a sense, in short, the age of oligarchy was giving way to an age of the masses.

The Policies of Dictatorship

In terms of its structures, then, *primoderiverismo* gravely weakened the old order. Much the same is true of the social and economic policies that it followed, the dictatorship embarking on a process of construction and investment that greatly speeded up the changes that had already been eroding the foundations of the Restoration Monarchy. In many ways this was profoundly ironic. Primo was the embodiment of a tradition that was deeply religious, nationalistic, *españolista* and authoritarian, and came to power with the support of a monarchy desperate to defend its political position, a Catholic Church increasingly alarmed at the progress of secularization, and a bourgeoisie terrified by the rise of labour, whilst his only ideologues were representatives of traditionalism or Social Catholicism. Far from desiring modernization, the dictatorship therefore kicked against it, the starting point of its creed being the belief that since the eighteenth century Spain had been corrupted by a series of 'foreign' influences. Rationalism, liberalism, radicalism, anarchism, socialism, separatism, secularism and materialism had one by one been injected into the body politic, and for many years past had been poisoning the 'real' people of Spain. Now, however, all these influences were to be eradicated without mercy, and a new Spain created whose chief tenets would be the defence of the family, the maintenance of order, the pursuit of greatness, the unity of the Fatherland, and the triumph of Catholicism, the political, social and economic model adopted for this purpose being the corporatism increasingly advocated by Catholic thinkers as the only answer to the class struggle.

This creed permeated the regime from top to bottom. Thus, when in October 1925 Primo replaced the Military Directory that had in theory governed Spain since September 1923 with a new Civil Directory, four of its five civilian members were *mauristas* or Social Catholics who had become both enthusiastic proponents of the corporate state and leading lights in the UP. Setting aside the Ministers of War and Marine, who were loyal cronies of Primo with few ideas of their own, the other figure of note was Martínez Anido who brought his particularly acute sense of the army's 'mission' to the crucial post of the Ministry of the Interior. Meanwhile, the UP and the Somatén were rigidly centralized, and the former given control of local government. At the same time, too, significant efforts were made to reform Spain along corporatist lines. As early as March 1924 the new Municipal Statute incorporated a corporate franchise, this being replicated in the Provincial Statute of 1925; in November 1926 Spanish industry was reorganized on corporate lines through the establishment of the Organización Corporativa Nacional; and in October 1927, a rigged plebiscite led to the establishment of a hand-picked national assembly which went on to propose a new constitution whose centrepieces were the sovereignty of the state, and a *cortes* dominated by royal appointees and the representatives of cultural and professional bodies.

If Primo had been content simply to preside over social and economic stasis, this corporatist offensive might have secured the interests of Spanish property for some considerable time. However, the dictator had other plans, Spain's infrastructural backwardness being in his eyes both an embarrassment and a threat to national security. From all this, it followed that he was an enthusiastic proponent of government intervention in the economy, and all the more so as it seemed to offer a means of promoting social harmony. By the end of 1924 the dictator had therefore created a variety of new bodies – the Consejo de Trabajo, the Consejo de Economía Nacional, and the Comité Regulador de Producción Nacional – whose task it was to regulate almost every aspect of the economy, the whole edifice eventually being placed under the control of a new Ministry of National Economy.

However, for Primo, the state's role was not just limited to supervision and control. Thus, from early 1924, enterprises conforming to certain criteria relating to the employment of Spanish capital, labour and raw material were offered a variety of subsidies. Such largesse could operate in a wide variety of contexts, but the greatest rewards of this policy went to big business, and especially to such concerns as were in a position to finance the dictator's strategic aims. In the field of transport, for example, Primo was determined both to fill the many gaps in the railway system and to secure its general modernization. In consequence, under the terms of the Railway Statute of 1924, generous assistance was given to companies who were prepared to complete such strategic links as that between Burgos and the Mediterranean. Meanwhile, other companies were awarded extremely beneficial contracts for the construction of new trunk roads, the development of hydro-electric power, the construction of dams and reservoirs, the establishment of a modern telephone network, the initiation of a 'plantation economy' in Morocco, and the finance of the new state petrol monopoly, CAMPSA. Also assisted were agriculture and the car and aviation industries, whilst great efforts were made to encourage tourism, a key role here being played by the organization of a great Ibero-American exhibition in Seville in 1929. Buttressing government financial support were an extremely protectionist tariff policy and the imposition of *de facto* quotas on the employment of imported raw materials. All this, of course, was not devoid of a darker side – for example, in defiance of the statute of limitations promulgated in 1923, Primo, most of his ministers, and a considerable number of influential generals made huge profits from directorships that they were offered in favoured companies, whilst the ever-growing bureaucracy of state regulation provided boundless opportunities for corruption. Nevertheless, even taking into account the general boom of the 1920s, it cannot be denied that much was achieved. To 9,500 kilometres of new roads and 800 of new railways were added new city tram systems, a large number of dams and bridges, and a variety of significant harbour improvements, whilst Madrid, in particular, saw a great expansion of the metro, and the inauguration of the 'University City'. In line with all this activity there were significant increases in exports, industrial production, energy generation, and in the profits of big business. Meanwhile, further progress was ensured through the construction of large numbers of new schools and hospitals, the number of primary schools alone rising by some 8,000.

To achieve his economic goals, Primo was not afraid of confronting the social and institutional strata that formed his main power base. In order to increase revenue, for example, Primo embarked on a campaign, first, to ensure that the propertied classes declared their incomes in full, and, second, to extract more revenue from them. Success was far from complete – a plan for a progressive income tax, for example, was wrecked by fierce opposition from within the ranks of the regime – but sufficient progress was made for the annual yield of taxation to be raised by some 50 per cent. That said, however, the government's income remained far short of the tasks that were now imposed on it, the only way of balancing the budget therefore being to combine the issue of huge numbers of government bonds with financial sleight of hand – in particular, the transfer of much expenditure to a supplementary 'extraordinary budget' that was supposed to be financed from loan capital. Because the regime's activities were actually rather more cautious than has usually been assumed, a financial disaster was avoided, but the fact remains that, in financial terms, Primo's rule was highly shaky.

If the dictatorship's fiscal policies were not entirely successful, they do at least show a concern for interests other than those of the oligarchy. In this particular respect, the drive for development was not simply an end in itself, but also a means of restoring the social harmony dreamed of by Primo and his ideologues. Nor was prosperity the regime's only weapon in so far as this goal was concerned. In Italy and Germany, the emergence of authoritarian regimes was followed by the wholesale destruction of the labour movement. In Spain, by contrast, Primo sought rather to bend it to his own ends in line with the common army view, first, that the miserable inadequacy of Spain's conscripts made social reform needed on military grounds, and, second, that the moderate and disciplined Socialist movement was not an out-and-out enemy but rather a potential ally. Encouraged by the passive attitude of the Socialist leadership, Primo therefore ignored demands for all trade unions to be banned, and initiated contacts with the UGT almost immediately (the PSOE, by contrast, was a different matter, being left in no doubt that any excursions into the public domain would be treated with great severity). From the beginning of 1924, moreover, vigorous efforts were made to establish a system of 'mixed juries' to regulate hours, wages and conditions of work, twenty-nine sectors of industry eventually having the pyramidal structure of compulsory arbitration envisaged by the regime imposed upon them. Often bizarre and far from complete, the system nevertheless eventually covered perhaps 50 per cent of the industrial labour force. Thanks to a system of shop-floor elections which gave the union with the highest vote a monopoly of the seats, meanwhile, the UGT secured three quarters of the workers' representatives (also involved were the various Catholic unions, of whom the Sindicato Libre in particular had been much boosted by an influx of erstwhile *cenetistas* who either could not bring themselves to join the UGT, or lived in areas where its organization was non-existent).

For those workers represented in the system, the benefits of Primo's corporatism were considerable. With regard to wages, for example, in those areas where the arbitration machinery was particularly well-established, wages did not reflect the moderate fall experienced in the country as a whole. However, Primo's social policy was not restricted to the establishment of the arbitration boards or mixed juries that formed the centre-piece of the system. Thus, all sectors of the labour force benefited from the boom in public works, not to mention Primo's efforts to control the price of certain basic foodstuffs. Meanwhile, industrial action was never banned *per se*, the number of days' labour lost through strike action between 1924 and 1928 amounting to almost 3,750,000. At the same time, setting aside the issue of wages, conditions were being improved by a wide range of other government policies, Primo improving healthcare, providing generous family allowances, extending social insurance, ensuring that workers got at least one day off per week, regulating working conditions, planning the construction of cheap housing and attempting, somewhat ineffectually, to assist tenant farmers (in this respect it should also be pointed out that in 1928 Primo tried, albeit without success, to extend the *comités paritarios* to the landless labourers).

We now come to one of the great ironies of the dictatorship. In essence, the benevolent paternalism which the dictator's social policies embodied was supposed to protect the elites whom his rule in practice represented. Far from achieving stability, however, the politics of development could only deepen the problems faced by the old order. Spaniards were now better educated then ever before, illiteracy falling by over 8 per cent; travel had become much easier, thanks to better train services and the introduction of the motor-bus; the numbers engaged in agriculture declined very steeply, for the first time falling below 50 per cent of the population (by the mid-1920s, in fact, the regime was becoming seriously concerned about rural depopulation); and, above all, the proportion of the population that lived in towns and cities grew at a rate that was almost unprecedented, the 1920s seeing the population of Barcelona rise by 41 per cent. Alarming though the impact of this growth could be in certain areas – Madrid, Barcelona and Seville not only suffered appalling overcrowding, but became girded with a ring of miserable shanty towns – the cultural significance was even greater. Given the expansion of education and the rise of the service sector, for example, there at last emerged a modern middle class. Meanwhile, enormous changes swept the nation: the cinema exposed the country to an ethos and lifestyle that was as alien as it was exciting; the rapid growth of radio short-circuited *caciquista* techniques of news management; football increasingly provided an alternative to the bullfight; western-style clothing finally replaced traditional breeches and sandals; and an increasingly inadequate Church complained incessantly of falling attendances and sliding moral standards – not for nothing was the Catholic secret society known as the Opus Dei founded in Spain in 1928. In short, exactly as occurred in the 1960s, new habits and aspirations were being distilled that made further political turmoil extremely likely.

For the time being the regime was able to contain the growing tidal wave through a variety of propaganda means – the glorification of such events as the first non-stop flight across the South Atlantic, the stress that was placed upon Spain's special relationship with Spanish America, and the posturing efforts to secure the annexation of Tangier and acquire a permanent seat on the League of Nations' Security Council – but it is hard to see how Primo could have dominated the situation for more than a few years, and all the more so given the increasing unrest to which his rule was soon giving rise.

The Downfall of Dictatorship

As has already been noted, opposition to Primo had initially been muted. Catholic opinion was wildly enthusiastic, the Lliga and the Reformists sympathetic, the Republicans and Socialists more or less neutral, and the dynastic parties deeply split. As a result, the only overt opposition came from Santiago Alba, whose relatively advanced views had attracted such opprobrium that he had fled into exile in France, from where he kept up a constant stream of criticism. Rather than looking to the political world for the first signs of opposition to Primo, we must therefore turn to the intelligentsia. In this respect, the key was the highly prestigious Miguel de Unamuno. Alienated by the dictator's general air of philistinism, he was soon pouring scorn on the new regime. As he had only to open his mouth for various other intellectuals – amongst them Manuel Azaña, Gregorio Marañon and Ramón Pérez de Ayala – to follow suit, the result was a growing chorus of protest whose chief platforms were the review, *España*, and the Madrid Ateneo. Much irritated, on 22 February 1924 Primo responded by temporarily closing the Ateneo, and dismissing Unamuno from his post at the University of Salamanca. Needless to say, such methods were ineffectual. The attack on Spain's most prominent writer having given rise to great disquiet in the intellectual community, by the middle of 1924 it had become, at the very least, alienated from the regime. Primo's treatment of Unamuno having also caused a great stir amongst foreign writers and intellectuals, opposition became fashionable, and all the more so after Unamuno escaped to France amidst huge acclamation.

In Spain itself, all this ferment had little initial impact. Led by the gifted Manuel Azaña, in 1925 a number of Republican and Reformist intellectuals formed a new political party entitled Acción Republicana, whilst 1926 saw all the Republican parties join in a loose grouping known as

Alianza Republicana. Amongst the *turno* parties, meanwhile, certain *caciques* who had been hard-hit by Primo's 'iron surgery' began to show signs of restiveness, a good example being the erstwhile Minister of War, Alcalá Zamora. However, Republicans and Monarchists alike shrank from the idea of rebellion, whilst the masses showed no signs of taking action on their own account, an attempt on the part of Francesc Macià, the leader of Estat Catala, to raise Catalonia in revolt proving a complete fiasco. As so often before, in fact, the key factor was the army.

In so far as the army was concerned, the central issue was military reform. Determined to achieve progress on this front as much as on any other, Primo in consequence had to reduce the size of the officer corps. However, how the army was to be restructured without a major crisis was not apparent, and all the more so given the fact that most officers had at best given only tacit acquiescence to the coup. Meanwhile, there was also the problems of the very different views espoused by the *africanistas* and the *peninsulares*. Whilst both groups were agreed on the need to smash the anarchists and Catalans, the *africanistas* wanted victory in Morocco and promotion by merit; and the *peninsulares* withdrawal from Morocco and promotion by seniority. With Primo prone to acting in the most arbitrary and ill-considered fashion, it is therefore hardly surprising that large parts of the army were soon severely discontented.

As we have seen, discontent was initially centred on the Army of Africa. However, locked in a desperate struggle with the Moors, a long way from the centres of political power, and hated by the bulk of the army, this force was impotent. Meanwhile, of course, the *peninsulares* were delighted with developments, and all the more so as the involvement of large numbers of officers in the municipalities, ministries and corporate state provided them with fresh fields of employment. In this fashion the loyalty of the peninsular army's junior and middle-ranking officers was for the time being guaranteed, but amongst the high command things were very different. The army's most senior generals for the most part being closely connected to the political establishment, they were much alarmed at the growing evidence that Primo was aiming at a permanent dictatorship. Much annoyance was also caused by Primo's deliberate exclusion of all officers of a higher rank than brigadier from the Military Directory, abolition of the council of senior generals that had advised the government on defence matters, and attempts to block the advancement of men he regarded as being too liberal – Eduardo López de Ochoa, for example – or who had in some way incurred his enmity – such as Gonzalo Queipo de Llano. As a result, Aguilera resigned as president of the Supreme Council of War, and had soon forged an unholy alliance with such disgruntled *africanistas* as Cavalcanti and Berenguer in the hope of organizing a fresh *pronunciamiento*.

Nipped in the bud as this scheme was, Primo could at first feel reasonably safe. With the dramatic transformation of affairs in Morocco, however, matters became more serious. Much rewarded, the *africanistas* were entirely happy, of course, but discontent now flared up on the home front. In part the result of events in Morocco, this also stemmed from other factors. In the first place, having effectively abandoned his attack on *caciquismo*, Primo was beginning to reduce the numbers and influence of the 'government delegates', whilst, in the second, he had embarked upon a series of reforms that inevitably had an adverse effect on certain sectors of the officer corps. In brief, it was Primo's intention to create an army that, whilst much smaller, would be much better trained, equipped and organized, imbued with the tough fighting spirit shown in Morocco rather than the dead hand of *juntero* bureaucracy, stripped of the rivalries consequent upon its rigid division into arms of service, and, above all, possessed of no more officers than it actually needed. To achieve these aims, a whole series of measures were implemented over the period 1923–9. Military service was reduced to two years; large orders were placed for new rifles and machine-guns; recruitment to the officer corps was very severely restricted; considerable efforts were made to encourage early retirement; pay was increased for all officers up to the rank of brigadier; the general staff was abolished as a separate corps; a number of superfluous regiments were suppressed, particularly in the cavalry and artillery; the artillery, engineers and medical corps were all stripped of their jealously guarded right to promotion by seniority alone; a single military academy was established at Zaragoza for the induction of all new officers under the direction of Francisco Franco; and greater weight given to promotion by merit. Some of these measures were generally popular, whilst others were necessary or at least defensible. Nor can it be denied that they had some beneficial effects: for example, although the military budget was slightly smaller in 1929 than it had been in 1924, a much larger proportion was being spent on weaponry. Such improvements won Primo little credit, however, his credibility as a reformer being completely undermined by his constant interference with the mechanisms of promotion so as to exploit them for his own benefit. As a result the officer corps was soon seething with disaffection, with the *peninsulares* jealous at the advancement of the *africanistas*, the *cuerpos facultátivos* furious at the abolition of their privileges, the cavalry angry at the reduction in its strength, and a host of officers of all sorts bitterly resentful at the manner in which they had, or so they felt, been persecuted by Primo.

With both monarchist and republican opposition on the increase, it was not long before feelers were being put out to Primo's civilian opponents. It was at this time, for example, that masonry acquired such recruits as López de Ochoa and Queipo de Llano, whilst a number of officers also forged secret contacts with Alianza Republicana. Well aware of the growing ferment, in the course of 1925 Primo dismissed Weyler as Chief of the General Staff and arrested a few of the ringleaders, including López de Ochoa. However, so lenient was their treatment that the malcontents were undeterred, and by the beginning of 1926 a broadly based movement was afoot to restore a parliamentary regime. Headed by Aguilera and Weyler, the conspirators initially planned their revolt for April 1926, only to be forced to abandon operations at the last moment thanks to a variety of last-minute waverings. After two months of discussions that in theory secured still more support, it was agreed that the rising should take place on the night of 24–5 June. In the event, however, the whole affair was a fiasco: all the garrisons involved in the plot waiting for somebody else to move first, in the end nobody moved at all.

If Aguilera's rebellion had come only a few days later, it might have met with more success. Thus, 9 June had seen the promulgation of the decree abolishing the *cuerpos facultátivos*' right to promotion by merit. There was an immediate wave of protest, but Primo was initially most conciliatory, with the result that Aguilera completely failed to benefit. Very soon, however, it became clear that Primo's promises were not going to be honoured, and in early September the artillery officers of virtually every garrison in Spain therefore barricaded themselves into their barracks and declared themselves to be in revolt. However, the *cuerpos facultátivos* being much disliked, they received no support and in consequence had to surrender within a few days.

On this occasion retribution was not long in coming. Although only 63 officers were imprisoned, Primo seized upon the revolt as a perfect opportunity to break the artillery's *espirit de corps*, six regiments being abolished, large numbers of officers forced to retire, and the corps forced to accept the new norms for promotion. Yet all this was a pyrrhic victory. Resentment in the artillery remained very high, whilst it was also in large part won over to republicanism. At the same time, too, Primo made yet more personal enemies, as in the case of the *africanista* governor of Menorca, General Cabanellas, who was dismissed from his post at the end of July after being quite unfairly accused of sympathizing with the artillery. Still worse, Primo seems to have become convinced that he could act with impunity, in that it was not long before he had also picked fights with the navy and airforce. The decision to convoke a new constituent assembly having gained the cause of revolt new recruits, fresh plots could not be long delayed. In the course of 1928, indeed, Aguilera and the highly-respected Conservative, Sánchez Guerra, forged a fresh movement that gained the support of at least twenty different garrisons, whilst at the same time forging links with a variety of dynastic politicians and even the CNT. Eventually the rising was scheduled for 29 January 1929, but there was little agreement as to what its goals should be and even less confidence in the prospects of success, the result being that the only troops to revolt were the artillery regiment stationed in Ciudad Real, and the help of the masses limited to a four-day general strike in Alcoy. Once again, in fact, it seemed that Primo had triumphed.

By 1929, however, the regime was also under siege on another front. Hardly surprisingly, the dictatorship had witnessed a great expansion of higher education, the number of undergraduates doubling between 1923 and 1929. However, this proved a double-edged sword. Frequently progressive in outlook, the growing student community was confronted by a regime that was wholly reactionary. On top of this, meanwhile, Spain's students also found themselves facing such problems as over-crowded lecture theatres, inadequate libraries and sparse accommodation. Much encouraged by the defiance of such figures as Unamuno, the students therefore began to engage in sporadic outbreaks of unrest, in 1927 forming a new union known as the Federación Universitaria Escolar. However, the real explosion did not come till 1928, when it was discovered that Article Fifty-Three of a new University Law that was being introduced by the government allowed Catholic colleges to award their own decrees. The matter being one of consider-able sensitivity, the issue became the hub of an ever more daring assault on the regime that eventually saw the universities go on strike alto-gether.

Although the dictator was forced to capitulate on this issue, the ability of the opposition to overthrow his rule remains open to serious question. Even now few officers were prepared to take the risk of actually leading a revolt. Alba, Sánchez Guerra and their ilk were half-hearted, divided and short of followers. Alianza Republicana claimed to have 200,000 supporters organized into 500 local committees, but was convulsed by suspicions that the unscrupulous Lerroux was angling for a deal with Primo, the upshot being the formation outside its ranks of a new Republican Radical Socialist Party under Marcelino Domingo and Alvaro de Albornoz. Unwilling either to jeopardize the benefits of the last few years or to fight for what they perceived as the cause of bourgeois revolution, the Socialists did not break with the regime until the summer of 1929, and even then remained deeply suspicious of an alliance with a bourgeoisie whom they perceived as being determined to exploit the labour movement. Much weakened, the CNT was as divided as the UGT, the newly-established Federación Anarquista Ibérica – a militant Anar-chist secret society dedicated to ensuring that Spanish anarchism did not slide into mere syndicalism – being fiercely opposed to any notion of collaboration with the bourgeoisie. The Communists were so weak as to be utterly irrelevant. Last but not least, regionalism was not much of a threat either, the Basques and Catalans alike being absorbed in a variety of internal quarrels.

In whichever direction one looks, in short, there was no credible threat, and all the more so as the various foci of opposition was often as opposed to one another as they were to Primo. If the latter's days were clearly numbered, one must therefore look not to the strength of the opposition, but rather to the dictator's growing isolation. The *peninsulares* having already been dealt with, we need first to look at Alfonso XIII. Despite the major role that he had played in the coup, the king had never been satisfied with the dictator. Whereas Alfonso had dreamed of playing a major role in the regeneration of Spain, he had in fact been sidelined. Realizing that any challenge to Primo must also be a challenge to himself, he had therefore sought to distance himself from the dictator, cultivate his links with the army, and press for a return to some sort of constitutional government. Offered some hope in this last respect by Primo's convocation of a national assembly, the king was soon disappointed, for in September 1929 the dictator rejected the draft constitution it had elaborated, insult being added to injury by the fact that he had done so on the grounds that it handed the lion's share of power to the monarch.

If Primo's star was waning in the court, things were not much better amongst the bourgeoisie. Although the unrest in the propertied classes has often been attributed to the onset of the economic troubles that we shall examine below, in fact the dictatorship's policies were causing alarm from a much earlier date. In the first place, whilst Primo favoured the interests of property, the latter were so diverse that it was impossible to formulate an economic policy that favoured all of them at once. For example, whilst Primo's protectionism favoured primary concerns, it did not help secondary ones. Equally, if Primo's trade agreements favoured Spanish exporters – a primarily agrarian group – they were hamstrung by the artificially inflated value of the peseta. Yet another contradiction, meanwhile, was to be found in Primo's interventionism which tended heavily to favour large concerns at the expense of smaller ones. Add to all this Primo's betrayal of the cultural interests of the Catalan bourgeoisie, his interest in social reform, efforts to increase taxation, and protection of the working classes, and it will be appreciated that from as early as 1925–6 industry and commerce were showing signs of growing disquiet. Although it was in fact rather less severely affected by most of the factors outlined above, many sectors of agriculture were also restive, the abortive attempt to extend the *comités paritarios* to the countryside leading to much fury.

Another group that was no longer to be counted on was the Social

Catholics of the PSP and ACNP. Disillusioned by the failure of the dictatorship to follow its prescriptions, an abstentionist minority of the PSP under Angel Ossorio had in fact been opposing the regime since as early as 1924. For the time being such opposition remained minuscule, the representatives of Social Catholicism for the most part throwing themselves heart and soul into the formation of UP, but it was not long before serious concerns had begun to emerge. Ironically, these centred on Primo's establishment of a corporate state, the favour that was shown to the UGT putting the Catholic unions supported by Ossorio and his friends under heavy pressure and causing much alarm at what the effect might be on their peasant equivalents should the *comités paritarios* ever be extended to the countryside. Surrender in the university crisis having caused further dismay, political Catholicism was clearly looking for a new champion.

By the summer of 1929, then, as witness the failure of the Seville exhibition to attract the patronage of the propertied classes and the torpor that now characterized both UP and the *somatén*, relations between Primo and his original power base had become increasingly strained, the only friends that he had left being the *africanistas*. In this situation he was unfortunately hit by fresh troubles. After six years of comparative prosperity, Spain suddenly experienced a serious economic crisis that stemmed not, as has often been supposed, from the onset of the Great Depression (for in fact industrial and agricultural production remained very high throughout 1929), but rather from the inflated value of the *peseta*. In brief, the latter slid dramatically on the foreign markets, Primo being left with no option but to cancel the Extraordinary Budget and thereby to reveal the full fragility of the regime's finances.

Quite clearly, the dictatorship was now in crisis, further embarrassment being caused by the fact that those arrested in connection with the revolt of January 1929 were either found not guilty altogether or treated in the most lenient fashion possible. With the king demanding change, the dictator sought frantically to find some compromise solution, bringing forward a series of plans based, variously, on the convocation of new elections under the terms of the draft constitution of 1929, the holding of a plebiscite and the appointment of a new government. However, neither the king nor anyone else were impressed: no one would have anything to do with Primo's search for a political solution, whilst the lack of business confidence was driven home by the complete failure of a massive loan which the Minister of Finance, Calvo Sotelo, floated on the domestic market in December 1929.

The failure of his efforts to stem the slide in the value of the *peseta* soon forcing Calvo Sotelo to resign, Primo was deprived of the support of one of his most loyal civilian collaborators at the same time as he was assailed by yet more bad news. On the one hand, concrete reports began to emerge of a fresh military conspiracy under the leadership of the governor of Cádiz, General Goded, there being considerable circumstantial evidence to suggest that the plot was backed by the king. On the other, with student unrest fuelled by the cuts in government expenditure presaged by the disappearance of the Extraordinary Budget, the universities once again went on strike. Convinced that he was about to be dismissed, on the night of 25–6 January Primo therefore penned an open letter to the senior commanders of the army, navy and security forces asking for a declaration of support, and promising to resign immediately if it should become clear that he had lost their confidence. Needless to say, the answers were distinctly lukewarm, virtually the only officer fully to support Primo being the *africanista*, Sanjurjo. On 28 January, meanwhile, Alfonso received a message to the effect not only that a coup was imminent, but that it might even be directed at the monarchy. Faced by such a threat, Alfonso effectively demanded that Primo resign immediately. Depressed and unwell, the dictator surrendered. Going into exile in France the next day, within two months he was dead.

The Lessons of Dictatorship

The dictatorship of Miguel Primo de Rivera, then, was an abject failure even on its own terms. Of the three goals that the general had originally set himself, only one – the solution of the Moroccan problem – had been resolved, and then in a fashion diametrically opposed to that which Primo had intended. As for the other two, 'order' may have been restored in a temporary sense, but the basic tensions that had produced the turmoil of 1918–23 remained entirely unresolved; meanwhile, far from being eradicated, *caciquismo* had rather been absorbed into the structure of the dictatorship. If, more generally, the aim had been to curb a movement towards democracy, the dictatorship had actually made matters worse, the accelerated rate of urbanization, greater degree of political mobilization, improved communications and better education that it brought all reducing the oligarchy's scope for manipulation and manoeuvre, the very considerable improvements in Spain's infrastructure that formed Primo's most positive achievement therefore proving very much a double-edged sword.

Ruminating on the reasons for his downfall in the short time left to him before his death, the general decided that he had in many respects fallen between two stools. Thus, whilst repressing constitutionalism, he had yet left his political opponents considerable freedom of action; henceforward, as he remarked, 'Freedom ... ought always to be accompanied by Civil Guards'. The message was not to go unforgotten by a future dictator, a future dictator, moreover, who was to make certain that intrigue was never to be allowed to undermine his position in the manner that it had affected that of Primo. In other respects, however, there was much to emulate: whether it was in the attempt to instil society with the values of the army in society, the formation of a national patriotic movement, the use of the language of the religious crusade, or the demonization of liberalism, anarchism, socialism, communism and separatism, the dictatorship foreshadowed that of Francisco Franco. Whilst paving the way for the coming of the second republic, meanwhile, it also provided an object lesson in how it might be destroyed.

14

The Republic Implanted

Challenge and Failure

Just over a year after the fall of Primo de Rivera, Spain became a republic. With the provisional government that was established dominated by a coalition of Socialists and left-Republicans, it appeared that radical change would at last become reality. Herein, however, lay the rub. To retain the support of the Left, the Second Republic needed very much to make good its promise, and yet in doing so it could not but alienate the Right. Caught in an impossible dilemma made worse by a pitiless economic crisis, the new regime was to end by satisfying absolutely no one. Within two years the cause of reform had therefore collapsed, the only question being whether it would still be possible to save the Republic.

Dictablanda

The downfall of Primo did not mark the end of dictatorship *per se*. So far as the king was concerned, however, 1923–30 had now to be erased as quickly as possible, the only hope being to pretend that the constitution had merely been suspended. Desperate to restore the old order, the king chose the moderate General Berenguer as the dictator's replacement (one of Primo's earliest military opponents, the erstwhile High Commissioner of Morocco was by allegiance a *romanonista*). Meanwhile, the latter appointed a cabinet drawn largely from unrepentant Conservatives, announced that the constitution would be restored, issued a general amnesty, lifted the ban on the CNT, relaxed many of Primo's most draconian measures, restored the *ayuntamientos* and *diputaciones* of 1923, replaced many *upetista* civil governors with representatives of the old order, and drew up plans for the election of a new *cortes*. Spain, in short, was no longer a *dictadura* but a *dictablanda*.

In a number of respects, however, these plans were seriously flawed. Inextricably linked with Anual, Berenguer inspired little confidence even amongst the army, let alone public opinion as a whole, whilst he was also notoriously lacking in dynamism. Moreover, for him to have had any hope of success, a new *cortes* was needed straightaway. Yet nothing of the sort occurred. Whilst generally loyal to the monarchy, the Conservatives and Liberals wanted time to reconstitute their battered *cacicatos*. Unable to proceed in consequence, Berenguer's good faith was immediately called into question, but in fact his chances of success had always been fairly limited. Bitterly angry at the manner in which it had been stabbed in the back by Primo, the Lliga, which was still headed by Cambó, refused overtly to back the monarchy, whilst the Reformists declared for the cause of a constituent *cortes*, if not for that of a republic. Even the dynastic parties, moreover, were not wholly united in Berenguer's defence. A few of their chieftains openly proclaimed their conversion to republicanism – the most important examples were the leading Cordobese *cacique*, Niceto Alcalá Zamora, and Antonio Maura's younger son, Miguel; others – most notably, Sánchez Guerra – formed a new reformist movement known as the Constitutionalists; and still others simply stayed on the sidelines altogether. Even when the *turno* parties did actively work for the restoration of the old order, moreover, the divisions of the pre-1923 era continued to get in the way. At the same time, politics had moved on: Spain had entered an age of mass mobilization which rendered *ad hoc* committees of notables utterly inadequate. In both the *turno* parties sporadic attempts were made at modernization, but these were at best ineffectual, whilst they were often sabotaged by the savage feuding that everywhere broke out between those *cacicatos* that had supported the dictator and those that had been persecuted by him.

The disarray of the dynastic parties should not be taken to mean that the monarchy was lacking in defenders. On the contrary, if many members of UP deserted Primo's legacy for the Liberals or Conservatives or even the Republicans, others organized themselves into a variety of right-wing movements that trumpeted the principles of dictatorship and corporatism and threw themselves into a propaganda campaign that secured much attention amongst those elements of the bourgeoisie who were inclined to view a republic as being synonymous with social unrest. If some of their leaders, the most prominent of whom was the dictator's charismatic son, José Antonio, were in practice indifferent to the monarchy – Alfonso had, after all, effectively sacked Primo – the end result was nevertheless to concentrate the propertied mind upon implications of the situation from which it might otherwise have been distracted.

Such authoritarian movements were not the monarchy's only allies. Over the past thirty years the Catholic Church had developed an impressive array of lay organizations whose basic aim was the defence of the Church and the propagation of the principles of Catholicism. The most obvious example here is the league of 5,000 peasant syndicates and cooperatives known as the Confederación Nacional Católica Agraria, but others include the network of Catholic workers' syndicates that had been established under the aegis of the Marqués de Comillas; the highly elitist ACNP; women's groups such as Acción Católica de la Mujer; and single issue pressure groups as the Asociación Católica de Represión de la Blasfemia. Grouped together in a loose umbrella organization known as Acción Católica and possessed of a highly influential press, this multifarious movement now lent its full weight to the revitalization of monarchism, whilst the clergy also sounded warnings of impending cataclysm. In action too, meanwhile, were the various secular organizations which brought together members of the propertied classes – ladies' circles, chambers of commerce, social clubs and charitable associations.

Impressive though the efforts of these groups were – mass meetings abounded, for example, whilst Alfonso was bombarded with enormous petitions of support – such were the odds against which the royalists were having to battle that the issue was never really in doubt. Stimulated by the university strikes, the Republican movement had definitely been emerging from the doldrums. Thus, the various parties which made it up all began to show signs of renewed vigour, whilst their ranks were joined by several new arrivals in the form of the Radical Socialists and Acció Catalana (the first, as we have seen, had emerged from the split within the Radicals occasioned by growing mistrust of Lerroux, whilst the second was the product of a minor rebellion within the Lliga). If the republican movement had remained deeply divided – the Catalans were detested by many *españolista* republicans, for example – and utterly unequal to the task of toppling Primo, the restoration of a reasonable degree of political liberty provided it with fresh impetus. Helped by the impressive campaign mounted by Alianza Republicana, branches of one party or another, for example, were founded in many provincial towns with no Republican tradition, whilst still further organizations emerged in the form of Acció Republicana de Catalunya, the conservative group known as Derecha Republicana founded by Miguel Maura, and a Galician autonomist movement known as the Organización Republicana Gallega Autónoma.

If the republican movement was rapidly growing in size and momentum, it was also moving into areas to which it had hitherto paid little attention. On its right wing Maura was openly proclaiming that he had only become a republican in order to protect the interests of the establishment, and Lerroux that the republic should disarm the Left and conciliate the interests of property and industry. However, many of its other elements were now displaying signs of radicalism, such groups as Acción Republicana and the Radical Socialists loudly proclaiming the need for land reform, improvements in education, better welfare services and the guarantee of the right to work. Under the influence of Francesc Maciá in particular, meanwhile, Catalan republicanism had also very much moved to the Left, the Lliga having been completely discredited by its association with the dictatorship.

As yet somewhat aloof from the republican movement – so much so, in fact, that the authorities initially believed that they were going to remain loyal – were the Socialists, the latter's attempts to cut their links with the dictatorship having by no means reflected a *rappprochement* with the bourgeois opponents of the monarchy. Whilst a small faction headed by the leading moderates, Indalecio Prieto and Fernando de los Ríos, were convinced that it was the primary duty of the Socialist movement to establish parliamentary democracy, in so far as the leaders of the PSOE and the UGT, Julián Besteiro and Francisco Largo Caballero, were concerned, the bourgeoisie were to be left to make their revolution unaided. However, this line was to prove untenable. Not only were Prieto and De Los Ríos developing ever closer links with the republican movement, but Spain was in the grip of an unstoppable process of change from which the Socialist movement simply could not remain aloof. Thanks to Primo, in fact, public opinion was beginning to make itself felt in an unprecedented manner. More literate and better informed than ever before, the vast majority of Spaniards who were not direct beneficiaries of the old order were revelling in their new-found freedom and becoming bolder and bolder in their demands. Already boosted by this development – membership of the PSOE, for example, had more than doubled in the previous two years – the Socialists faced the choice of becoming more actively involved in the political process or simply being sidelined.

As if all this was not enough, the Socialist rank and file was also being radicalized by the Great Depression. First to suffer was agriculture. In the countryside of Andalucía, for example, falling prices and dwindling markets caused many great estates to let much land go out of cultivation, whilst many tenant farmers fell behind with the rent and were consequently evicted from their holdings, matters not being helped by the fact that 1930 witnessed a serious drought. As yet the Depression's effects were less severe in industry, but even so the curtailment of Primo's infrastructural projects affected certain sectors of the economy very deeply, whilst town and countryside alike were affected by a sharp rise in food prices. The result was serious trouble: revivified by their emergence from clandestinity, the Communists and CNT led a series of major strikes in a variety of towns and cities, whilst Andalucía witnessed numerous bread riots and other acts of violence. Despite the growing effervescence, the UGT at first condemned the strike movement, but there were limits to what the leadership could do, and all the more so as the UGT was for the first time beginning to secure large numbers of recruits from amongst the agricultural proletariat. With the CNT rapidly expanding and beginning to take recruits from the UGT and the Communists making modest progress in their bridgeheads in Bilbao and Seville, a real danger emerged that the Socialists would be marginalized. As a result the UGT also began to take part in the strike movement and even to express support for an alliance with the Republicans. Continuing to regard the latter as a squabbling collection of chiefs with few Indians to their name, Besteiro remained obdurate, but by the summer Largo Caballero – an opportunist whose chief guide was the immediate interests of the UGT – had come round to the idea of helping to bring down the monarchy.

If the forces opposed to Alfonso XIII were gathering strength, they were not yet united. However, the Republicans realized the need for political unity all too well, and it was not long before they had convened a conference of *catalanistas* and *españolistas* alike at San Sebastián. Held on 17 August 1930, this was beyond doubt the key moment in the fall of Alfonso XIII. Thus, in exchange for promises that the Republic would address the autonomy issue, the Catalans agreed to take part in a general revolutionary movement, the forces represented at San Sebastián also electing a revolutionary committee that would organize a coup against the regime and take over the reins of government, it being decided that the head of this body should be Niceto Alcalá Zamora. Represented at the meeting in an unofficial capacity by Prieto and De Los Ríos and offered three posts in the provisional government that would be established following the revolution, on 16 October the Socialists also joined up, the assumption being that the UGT would support the coming rebellion with a general strike.

By rebellion, of course, what was meant was a coup, there being general agreement that anything else was far too risky. The dictatorship having left the army riven with discontents of all sorts, the idea of a *pronunciamiento* was hardly far-fetched. Desperate to restore order, Berenguer was favouring officers who had been alienated by Primo and reversing many of his more arbitrary decisions, but all this was a case of 'too little, too late'. Meanwhile, a mixture of pique and personal ambition had won over a number of officers to the cause of republicanism: taking the three best-known examples, General Gonzalo Queipo de Llano was an old enemy of Primo who regarded himself as having been persecuted by him; Ramón Franco a disgraced one-time hero (the first man to fly the South Atlantic, in 1929 he had been expelled from the airforce after an attempt at the world seaplane record ended in a major scandal); and Fermín Galán an embittered *africanista* whose failure to obtain promotion had led him to become obsessed with misty dreams of heading a revolution.

Plans for a *pronunciamiento* were soon well advanced but in fact a series of *contretemps* ensured that the autumn came and went without one even being attempted. Frustrated and angry, Franco and Galán at length decided that they could wait no longer. Whilst the former took over the military airfield at Cuatro Vientos outside Madrid, on 12 December Galán raised his regiment in revolt and marched on Zaragoza (he was stationed at Jaca). Over the next few days scattered disturbances occurred in sympathy elsewhere, but the whole affair was a *débâcle*, Galán being surrounded, forced to surrender and executed by firing squad, whilst Franco commandeered a plane and fled abroad. Such was the chaos that the revolutionary committee ought by rights to have been thoroughly discredited, but in fact Alfonso's victory was distinctly pyrrhic: Galán's execution was a major blunder that laid the king open to charges of being a 'man of blood', whilst those members of the revolutionary committee who were arrested were fêted as popular heroes. Meanwhile, nothing could disguise the facts that significant sections of the army and police had failed to move a muscle, that the persecution of the conspirators had been more than somewhat half-hearted, and that those conspirators who were arrested were effectively allowed to carry on plotting from their prison cells. At the same time there was no let up in the general unrest: in January 1931, for example, there was a fresh upsurge in student protest, whilst a number of prominent intellectuals formed themselves into the self-styled Agrupación al Servicio de la República. Increasingly alarmed, Berenguer clamped down on civil liberty and initiated a purge of the officer corps, only for the Republicans, Socialists, Reformists and Constitutionalists all to announce that they would in consequence boycott the general elections to which he was still committed. Left with the prospect of conducting polls that would have been a charade even by Spanish standards, on 14 February the general tendered his resignation.

Persuaded that this was the only hope of avoiding a revolution, the king now agreed, first, that the new *cortes* should be a constituent assembly, and, second, that its election would be preceded by the choice of new *ayuntamientos* and *diputaciones*. The Conservatives, the Liberals and the Lliga all being in favour of this solution, on 18 February a government of monarchical union was duly established under Admiral Juan Bautista Aznar. With the forces of progress also back on board, the country was immediately plunged into a vibrant electoral campaign, it having been agreed that new *ayuntamientos* should be selected on Sunday 12 April. Conscious of how much was at stake, all the forces in the monarchist camp threw themselves into the struggle with the utmost ferocity, but their every effort was matched by that of the opposition whilst they were fighting in the most disadvantageous circumstances. Thus, 20 March saw the beginning of the trial of the 'provisional government', the problem being that the revolutionary leaders succeeded in putting the monarchy in the dock, and ended up with such nominal sentences that they were promptly released on the grounds of time served. With the campaign also marred by the employment of excessive force against a major student demonstration in Madrid, the outlook was hardly encouraging.

Meanwhile, the Republic's prospects had been immeasurably strengthened by the fact that the Anarchists had for the time being decided to abandon apoliticism. Thus, the CNT had a strong interest in securing the release of the many militants languishing in jail, whilst its most dominant figure, Angel Pestaña, was a 'pure' syndicalist who was much influenced by the example of his late friend and colleague, Salvador Seguí. Despite the opposition of the FAI, after much soul-searching the CNT therefore resolved to take part in the elections. By no means all the rank and file were prepared to follow such a course, but in some areas, at least, there seems little doubt that the Anarchist vote was a factor of considerable significance.

Although the full results of the elections were never published, the general picture is clear enough. In terms of the number of councillors, the monarchists gained an overwhelming majority. Otherwise, however, the opposition were triumphant. Forty-five provincial capitals out of fifty-two had fallen to the Republicans and Socialists, whilst they had also captured many other towns. The game being up, on 13 April Aznar resigned. Told by the forces of order that they would not fight, Alfonso quickly realized that he, too, would have to go, and by sunset on 14 April the king was heading into exile, Spain having once again become a republic.

The Provisional Government

The new government that was established at the birth of the Second Republic was in a difficult position. Having come to power in the face of much right-wing hysteria, it had obviously to conciliate the forces of reaction. That said, however, having come to power on the back of a demand for change that was all but unstoppable, it had also to satisfy the forces of progress, matters not being made any easier by the fact that it was hardly a united force. Consisting as it did of two representatives of Derecha Republicana (Alcalá Zamora and Maura), two Radicals (Lerroux and Martínez Barrio), two Radical Socialists (Albornoz and Domingo), three Socialists (Largo Caballero, De Los Ríos and Prieto), and one representative each of Acción Republicana, the ORGA and Acció Catalana (Azaña, Santiago Casares Quiroga, and Nicolau d'Olwer), it could not hope to maintain a real degree of stability. Thus,

Alcalá Zamora and Maura were Catholic conservatives who had changed sides because they believed that a republic was the only way of preventing revolution; Lerroux was an old-guard republican whose long-standing tendencies towards *españolismo*, patriotic bombast and social conservatism could not but be reinforced by the fact that the Radicals were being infiltrated by large numbers of refugees from the old order; and Largo was a Socialist whose essential reformism had never prevented him from responding to outbursts of rank-and-file radicalism. Caught in the middle were Azaña, Martínez Barrio, Albornoz, Domingo, Casares Quiroga, D'Olwer, Prieto and De Los Ríos whose political views were all more or less centrist. To complicate the situation still further, meanwhile, Largo and Prieto detested one another; the Socialists were rightly convinced that the Radical Socialists had adopted the title 'socialist' for no better reason than to poach their electorate; whilst Lerroux was mistrusted by all and sundry on account of his reputation for personal corruption, and at the same time resentful of his failure to obtain the premiership.

Within its very first hours of life, in fact, the many dilemmas facing the new regime had begun to make themselves felt. On the whole 14 April had been a good-humoured day, but even so there were signs that at least some elements of the Left wanted immediate vengeance. At the same time, too, certain elements on the fringes of the republican movement, of whom the most prominent was Ramón Franco, were advancing their interests by means of a campaign of the most blatant demagoguery. More problematically still, in Barcelona the proclamation of the republic had not gone entirely according to plan. The dominant force in Catalonia was now a recently formed amalgam of most of the left-catalanist parties known as the Esquerra headed by Francesc Macià – as might have been expected, the Lliga had been trounced on 12 April, whilst Cambó had gone into exile in France. Rather than simply proclaiming the republic, meanwhile, Macià had declared Catalonia to be a sovereign state that would seek membership of an entirely hypothetical Iberian federation. A reflection of differences in the interpretation of the Pact of San Sebastián and the fact that the only Catalan minister in the government came not from the Esquerra but Acció Republicana, which had for a variety of reasons remained outside its ranks, this action caused fury among the more *españolista* members of the government. Determined to restore Macià to order, the cabinet therefore dispatched a high-level delegation to Barcelona, and it was eventually agreed that, in exchange for a provisional government – the so-called Generalitat – and the right to draw up a statute of autonomy, Catalonia would wait until the latter had been formally approved by the *cortes*, the deal being sealed by a triumphal visit to Barcelona on the part of Alcalá Zamora.

Whilst some forces were seeking to radicalize the government, others were seeking to check its operations, if not to overthrow it altogether. Thus, the Right was by no means inclined to surrender without a fight. Under the leadership of the Jesuit-run newspaper, *El Debate*, and the ACNP, a large part of conservative opinion began to think in terms of how to manipulate the new situation from within, but for many diehards the only option remained that of confrontation. In this respect, moreover, they were much stimulated by the attitude of the Archbishop of Toledo, Cardinal Segura. A particularly combative figure who loathed all aspects of modernism and was convinced that the Church should control civic life, Segura was a protégé of Alfonso XIII, and had therefore been plunged into despair by the coming of the Republic, which he interpreted as the precursor of a Communist apocalypse. Despite the fact that the Church's official attitude was to counsel obedience, on 1 May he therefore issued a pastoral letter which reminded Catholics that Alfonso XIII had been a devout believer and good friend to the Church and instructed them to pray for divine help and stand firm against revolution. Encouraged by this attitude, the editor of the conservative daily, *ABC*, Juan Ignacio Luca de Tena, mobilized a group of well-connected malcontents and concocted a plan to destabilize the republic, regain the support of the army, and establish a monarchist movement.

On Sunday 10 May Madrid witnessed the first meeting of the resultant Círculo Monárquico Independiente. A number of those who attended the meeting behaved in an extremely provocative manner, thereby succeeding in attracting the attentions of a hostile crowd. Not surprisingly, the result was an ugly confrontation, and within a short space of time angry crowds were attacking the headquarters of *ABC* and setting fire to a number of churches. With most ministers unwilling to protect either the Church or a newspaper that had shown itself to be one of the Republic's most ruthless enemies, the government was slow to take action, but by dawn the next day it had had to agree to deploy the Guardia Civil. Order was soon restored, the disturbances having in reality been fairly limited in their extent, but even so the implications were profound. Enormous strains had been placed on cabinet unity (Minister of the Interior as he was, at one point Maura had threatened resignation); the Republic had blackened itself in the eyes of the Left by defending the Church; and the Right had been presented with a scare-story that it was to continue to capitalize on throughout the coming years.

To suggest, however, that the disturbances of 10–11 May were in any way decisive is excessive. Far more important were the provisional government's efforts to ensure that it presided over a state that was far more than just a monarchy without a monarch. Thus, in the field of agriculture, especially, reform was already well underway, and all the more so given the fact that the new Minister of Labour was Francisco Largo Caballero. Thus, the UGT having in recent months begun to make increasing inroads amongst the *braceros* of Andalucía and elsewhere (established in 1930, its Federación Nacional de Trabajadores de la Tierra had within a year enrolled over 90,000 members in Andalucía alone), it was therefore very much in Largo's interest to ensure that the momentum was maintained. From 28 April onwards the Ministry of Labour was in consequence the source of a series of decrees that bade fair to transform the structure of Spanish agriculture. The Law of Municipal Boundaries, for example, prohibited the hiring of any labour by an estate until work had been found for every single labourer in the municipality in which it was situated, whilst on 9 May Largo extended the existing system of arbitration boards to the countryside, thereby ensuring that disputes over wages and conditions were likely to be settled in favour of the workers rather than the employers (it will be remembered that each jury was chaired by an appointee of the government, which in the current situation effectively meant an official of the FNTT). Other measures that were introduced included decrees that improved the rights of tenant farmers; authorized municipalities to compel landowners to cultivate untilled land and give work to unemployed labourers; extended the eight-hour day to the countryside; and established a network of local labour exchanges. Last but not least, a special commission was established to begin work on a bill of agrarian reform that would allow for a measure of land redistribution.

Turning now to the question of Church–state relations, the general tone was set by announcements to the effect that the government intended to secularize education, healthcare, and the burial of the dead; legalize divorce; establish full religious liberty; end the state's support for the Church; and reduce both the power and the number of the religious orders. Nor was all this allowed to remain simply a matter of intent: as in the case of agriculture, a series of decrees had soon not only put much of this programme into practice, but also made it clear that the Church could expect the new regime to act in a manner that was generally vindictive and hostile.

In so far as the army was concerned, meanwhile, the lead was taken by Manuel Azaña, who had become Minister of War on the grounds of a long-standing interest in military affairs, his basic objectives being, first, to make the army more effective, and, second, to ensure that it was democtratized and brought to accept a completely new vision of its place in politics and society. It being obvious that a greater share of the military budget needed to be devoted to training and armament, the first priority was to tackle the perennial problem of the size of the officer corps. Thus, in 1931 Spain was burdened with 21,576 officers, when even the top-heavy structures that had been given to the army provided less than 15,000 posts. Very few officers having refused to take the new oath of allegiance that had been demanded of them following the advent of the Republic, Azaña had no option but to introduce yet another scheme of early retirement, and all the more so as he had also decided to halve the number of divisions. Whilst clearing the way for the army's re-equipment, Azaña at the same time proceeded with its democratization. At the simplest level this required the 'republicanization' of the high command – Goded and Ramón Franco, for example, were both given prominent posts – but Azaña also embarked upon a series of structural changes that were in one way or another designed to reduce the possibil-ity of a military coup, and in general to cut the army's pretensions down to size. Thus, the period of first-line military service was reduced from two years to one; the non-commissioned officers were flattered by improvements in their pay and conditions; the artillery and engineers were promised a greater share of promotions to the *generalato*; *africa-nismo* was discouraged by such means as the suppression of the general military academy of Zaragoza, a freeze on recruitment to the Foreign Legion, and the establishment of a special tribunal to review all promo-tions that had been granted on the grounds of merit; the ranks of lieutenant general and captain general were abolished; the army was deprived of all influence in local government and the administration of justice (notable casualties here were the military governors, the captains general, and the Law of Jurisdictions). Also noteworthy here are the efforts that were made to ensure that the army did not again get out of hand in Morocco, which was once more given a civilian High Commis-sioner.

Moderate though it may have been, there can therefore be no doubt that the provisional government was a genuinely reformist body. Whether it was in the area of the army, the Church or the land, a variety of measures were very quickly put into place to address the most immediate areas of contention, whilst the way was opened for Catalonia and other regions to negotiate a new relationship with Madrid. As yet, however, the Republic had not been given due form by the elaboration of a constitution. Many issues, in short, remained to be resolved.

The Constituent Cortes

Given the problems thrown up by the municipal elections, the formula-tion of a new political order was no easy task, large parts of the countryside remaining in the hands of the old order. Appointing new civil governors and provincial *diputaciones* though the government did, it therefore had no option but to order fresh elections in a large number of municipalities where *caciquista* manipulation had been especially blatant. Despite the massive victory for the Republicans and Socialists that resulted, however, the basic problem remained. Determined to protect their interests, many *caciques* had found new homes in the ranks of such groups as the Radicals or the Derecha Liberal, such a course of action being facilitated by the fact that the Republican right was well aware of its inability to attract mass support and therefore only too happy to accept the help of the propertied classes.

As more and more *caciques* turned to republicanism, so the prospects of a thorough-going reform began to diminish. Yet the need for real progress was becoming ever more pressing. Thus, although the CNT's *seguista* leadership opposed any action that would disrupt the new regime, from the very beginning anarchism was being pushed into a position of open hostility by such FAI militants as Buenaventuri Durruti and Francisco Ascaso. Charismatic figures who had made a name for themselves as revolutionary crusaders during the years of the *dictadura*, at rally after rally they denounced the provisional government, excoriated the Republic's labour decrees, and encouraged the rank and file to entertain expectations of the most utopian nature. With the UGT growing rapidly in power, the Socialists openly hostile and the economic situation continuing to deteriorate, such rhetoric could not but elicit a considerable response. From the beginning of May onwards strike action mushroomed, whilst the initially tiny FAI began to gain thousands of new members and even to think in terms of seizing control of the entire CNT, Pestaña and his moderate fellows only maintaining their positions with the greatest difficulty.

The CNT was not, of course, the only representative of the revolutionary Left. Thus, number no more than 1,000 members though it did in 1931, the Communists had responded to the coming of the Republic with such violence that by March 1932 they had increased their strength twelvefold and built up a sizeable union movement entitled the Confederación General del Trabajo Unitaria. Meanwhile, in Catalonia a group of Communist dissidents headed by the noted Marxist thinker, Joaquín Maurín, had established a rival movement known as the Bloc Obrer i Camperol. Dwarfed by the Anarchists and Socialists alike though these groups were, the fact remained that their very existence served as a spur to radicalization.

When Spain went to the polls to elect the constituent *cortes*, she therefore did so against a background of growing working-class militancy. If the Republic was to retain any credibility, it was therefore essential that the new assembly should be one capable of implementing a suitably radical agenda. This, however, was not the case, and that despite the fact that the Right remained in a state of utter disarray. Whereas its only hope was unity, it fought the elections on the basis of a common message – the idea that the 'Communist' Republic was the harbinger of mass murder, universal slavery and free love – trumpeted by several different forces. At the national level, true, there was but one force of any importance, this being the alliance founded by the editor of *El Debate*, Angel Herrera, to defend 'religion, country, order, family and property' under the title Acción Nacional. However, attract the support of large numbers of monarchists though AN did, Herrera's failure explicitly to affirm the monarchical principle ensured that it was challenged by a variety of die-hards who stood for election as monarchists or independents. Also in the lists were a variety of right-radical groups who were bent either on defending the interests of property by establishing an authoritarian state or on creating a new order based on the doctrines of national syndicalism, the Lliga, the Carlists and the Basque Nationalists, of whom the last two had resolved their long-standing internal differences and forged an alliance with one another (for all their desire for autonomy, the Basque Nationalists remained a deeply Catholic force that was largely dominated by the local clergy, and, what is more, one that was treated with the utmost hostility by the Republican authorities).

Not only was the Right badly split, meanwhile – in many areas candidates affiliated with Acción Nacional were opposed by Carlists, neo-fascists, independents or regionalists – but it was operating at an even greater disadvantage than in April 1931. Setting aside the fact that many local notables had by now switched their support to the Radicals or the Derecha Republicana, the events of 10–11 May had led to the suspension of some of its chief publications and the arrest of a number of militant activists. Nor were matters helped by changes in the electoral system, the government having divided the entire country into large multi-member constituencies and decreed that any list that received over 40 per cent of the vote in a constituency should be given 80 per cent of the seats, the aim being both to hit the *caciques* and take advantage of the relative unity that prevailed in the ranks of its supporters.

With the Right in general harassed and bullied by the local authorities, the wonder is not so much that the Republican–Socialist coalition triumphed in the elections of 28 June 1931, but that the Right succeeded in electing as many deputies as it did. Thus, compared with 385 government deputies – 113 Socialists, eighty-nine Radicals, fifty Radical Socialists, forty-three *esquerristas*, twenty-four *azañistas*, twenty-three representatives of Derecha Republicana, sixteen Galician regionalists, and twenty-seven other assorted Republicans – the Right was represented by twenty-four 'Agrarians', the vast majority of them supporters of Acción Nacional; seven Basque Nationalists; five Carlists; three *lligistas*; two Reformists; and a small number of independents, the only area where it had obtained any success being Vizcaya, Guipúzcoa and Navarre, where the Carlists, the PNV and a handful of Catholic independents had come together as the Coalición Vasco-Navarrista and secured a clear majority of the popular vote.

If 28 June had been a triumph for republicanism, it had nevertheless thrown up a situation of considerable instability. Thus, the elections had deepened the divisions that already existed in the San Sebastián coalition – the Socialists and the Radical Socialists, for example, had been dismayed by Lerroux's very strong showing – and yet the provisional government had *faut de mieux* to be confirmed in office. How long the latter could survive, however, was a moot point, the debate on the new constitution soon revealing the fragility of its position. Even on secular matters – the powers of the president, the relationship between state and region, the organization of the *cortes*, the question of female suffrage, the status of private property, the rights of labour – the governing coalition was deeply divided, the basic split being between the Radicals and Derecha Liberal on the one hand and the Socialists and Radical Socialists on the other. However, whilst most of these matters were settled by some sort of compromise, this was simply not possible when it came to the Catholic Church. Devout Catholics as they were, Alcalá Zamora and Maura could not accept Article Twenty-Six of the draft constitution presented to the *cortes*, for this in brief promised to end the subsidy that had hitherto been paid by the state to the Church, abolish the latter's immunity from taxation, subject the religious orders to a much greater degree of regulation, dissolve the Jesuits, and bar the Church from commerce, industry and education. No sooner had it been passed, therefore, than the two ministers resigned, the Republic in consequence being faced by its first cabinet crisis.

The departure of Derecha Liberal tended to strengthen the forces of progress. Having quickly made a considerable name for himself, Manuel Azaña was chosen to take over as prime minister, whilst the constitution acquired a more progressive caste than might otherwise have been the case. Finally passed on 9 December 1931, the new document declared Spain to be 'a republic of workers of all categories ... marked by a federative tendency that allows for the autonomy of municipalities and regions'. The legislative power – a unicameral *cortes* elected by universal suffrage – was deemed to be supreme, though the president was given a variety of powers designed to allow him to fulfil some of the functions that might otherwise have fallen to a second chamber. All the basic civil liberties were guaranteed, whilst a tribunal of constitutional guarantees was established to ensure that the constitution was respected and rule on clashes between president and *cortes* and *cortes* and region. Property was deemed in certain circumstances to be liable to expropriation for purposes of social utility. And, last but not least, Church and state were formally separated, and the army stripped of much of its power, the disappearance of the Captain Generalcies and Law of Jurisdictions being effectively confirmed. In short, Spain had – in theory – at last been democtratized.

The Reformist Bienio

The Republic's reformist gloss was confirmed by the events that followed the passage of the constitution. Admittedly the cause of conservative republicanism received a fillip in the form of the election of Alcalá Zamora to the post of President, but the task of government now became monopolized by the San Sebastián coalition's most progressive elements. Thus, ever growing differences had been emerging between Lerroux and the rest of the cabinet: distrusted by all and sundry on account of his corruption and opportunism, the Radical leader was furious at the facts, first, that it was Azaña who had replaced Alcalá Zamora as premier, and, second, that the *cortes* had resolved to serve out a full four-year term rather than submitting itself to fresh elections. Whereas Azaña believed that an alliance with the Socialists was essential, meanwhile, Lerroux wanted to eject them from the government. No sooner had Alcalá Zamora been elected President, therefore, than conflict erupted, only for Lerroux to be defeated and the Radicals driven from power. For the time being the latter's deputies continued on occasion to support the government in the *cortes*, but the fact remained that the regime was now very much one of the Centre-Left.

So important is the figure of Manuel Azaña for an understanding of the next two years that we must at this point say something of his character and background. Born in Alcalá de Henares in 1880 to a prosperous liberal family, he was orphaned at an early age and, like most young boys of his social class, received a strict Catholic education. Genuinely brilliant, at twenty he secured a doctorate of law, whereupon he set about carving out a reputation as a writer. Eventually forced to seek work as a government functionary after his family fell upon hard times, he nevertheless retained his contacts with the intellectual world, in 1913 being elected Secretary of the Ateneo. By this time, too, his political views had increasingly settled into an anti-clerical determination to modernize Spain. Provided with useful targets for his biting invective, first, by the pro-German leanings of the establishment during the First World War, and, second, the struggle in Morocco, he was by 1923 a figure of some prominence. Hitherto a Reformist, his position was further radicalized by the dictatorship, the end result being his conversion to Republicanism.

Confirmed as prime minister in December 1931, Manuel Azaña now set about addressing the major problems still facing the Republic, the new prime minister having defined these as the Church, the regions and the land. Taking the position of the Church first of all, this was regularized by a series of measures that translated Article Twenty-Six and the other relevant passages of the constitution from principle to reality. Thus, on 23 January 1932 Spain's 3,600 Jesuits were given precisely ten days to abandon their communities, whilst the order's property was immediately nationalized and its various educational establishments closed down, the same period also witnessing the issue of legislation legalizing divorce and secularizing the cemeteries. The subsidy to be paid to the Church in 1932 was more than halved, whilst in 1933 it would be ended altogether. Finally, October saw the beginning of debate on a new Law of Congregations that placed strict limitations on the activities of such few religious orders as were allowed to remain in existence and, in particular, banned them from any involvement in education (in a new development it also nationalized the property not just of the Jesuits, but of the whole of the Church). Hand in hand with all this went a sustained attempt to make good the numerous deficiencies in the state sector that had resulted from decades of over-reliance on the Church. Thus, some 7,000 new primary schools were opened, the many new teachers that were needed being found by raising teaching salaries and greatly expanding teacher training.

Rather more complicated than the question of the Church was that of the regions. Taking Catalonia first of all, the early summer of 1931 had seen the elaboration of a draft statute of autonomy that would have given Catalonia freedom in virtually everything but defence, international commerce and foreign policy. Known as the 'Statute of Nuria', this was submitted, first, to the approval of Catalonia's 1,063 *ayuntamientos*, and, second, to a popular plebiscite. Both of these tests having been being passed without a hiccup, on 13 August the statute was presented to the *cortes*. However, the Catalans had few friends in the government, and it was therefore not until May 1932 that discussion of the question began, such being the filibustering engaged in not just by the Agrarians but also some of the more right-wing Republicans that progress was extremely slow.

What would have happened had matters followed the natural course of events it is difficult to say, but in August 1932 the Republic was suddenly rocked by an attempted coup. A small group of monarchist generals had been plotting insurrection ever since the previous summer, and in the spring of 1932 they secured a number of new recruits, of whom the most prominent was the monarchy's last commander of the Guardia Civil, General Sanjurjo. A renowned *africanista*, Sanjurjo had initially accepted the Republic, but he had quickly become much alarmed, and all the more so when he was in February 1932 replaced by the Republican, Miguel Cabanellas. Nor was he alone in his disaffection: as men of order, a number of generals who had opposed Primo de Rivera and accepted the Republic with equanimity – the most prominent example was the new chief of the General Staff, General Goded – were also becoming increasingly alarmed. Egged on in their disaffection by a variety of representatives of the old order, of whom the most important was Melquíades Alvarez, not to mention the fact that Goded and two of his intimates were dismissed following a public altercation at a review in Madrid, Goded and his circle therefore themselves turned to conspiracy. Boosted by the fact that he was able to secure the support of the Carlists, Lerroux and the Italians alike, Sanjurjo had soon succeeded in uniting the various strands of conspiracy under his leadership, and on 10 August he duly seized control of Seville. As might have been expected, however, the whole affair went wrong: the government had known of the plot well in advance; the vast majority of the army and police remained loyal; and such were the divisions amongst the conspirators that some of them were deliberately kept in the dark as to the date of the rising. Apart from in Madrid, where an attempt was made to storm the War Ministry, there was therefore no effort to follow Seville's lead, the result being that the whole affair collapsed, Sanjurjo eventually being arrested in an attempt to flee to Portugal.

Failure that it was, the *sanjurjada* nonetheless proved a key factor in the resolution of the Catalan problem. Thus, the many Republican and Socialist deputies who had been failing to turn up at important divisions or remaining silent in the face of Agrarian sabotage being persuaded that they needed the Esquerra, the statute was finally approved by a large majority. Even then difficulties continued, however. As amended by the *cortes*, the statute was much less generous than its original, whilst those powers that were granted to the Generalitat were not handed over immediately but rather reserved for transfer at some unspecified point in the future. To be fair, the process was initiated relatively quickly, but even so a year later only public health, poor relief and local government had formally passed under Catalan control, whilst the Generalitat also remained starved of revenue, its relationship with Madrid therefore continuing to be marked by much tension.

In the other areas affected by the regionalist problem, meanwhile, progress had been even more limited. Taking Galicia first of all, the local regionalist movement was neither strong nor united – composed as it was of Republicans who happened to be Galicians, the ORGA was opposed by many gallegists – whilst Galicia had in any case become a bastion of the Radicals. A regionalist conference was held in La Coruña in June

1931, but a draft statute was only agreed upon with great difficulty, and it was not until December 1932 that it was submitted to Galicia's *ayuntamientos*. Despite a strong victory for autonomy, further delays ensued – once again, the fruit of latent *españolista* tendencies in the cabinet – the result being that the Azaña government came and went without any change in Galicia's status.

Meanwhile, things were much the same in the Basque country. Thus, the politics of Bilbao had long been dominated by bitter rivalry between the Socialists and the nationalist PNV, whilst the forces of progress in general were inclined to regard the latter as inveterate foes of the Republic and all it stood for. That said, so long as the institutions that resulted were not monopolized by forces hostile to its ideals, the Republican government was by no means opposed to the principle of autonomy, the new *diputaciones* that it had appointed in the Basque country and Navarre in fact being instructed to draw up an appropriate statute. If the intention was to pre-empt the PNV, the move was a failure, however: no sooner had the Republic been proclaimed than the nationalists had elaborated a statute and presented it to a general conference of the region's municipalities that was held at the Navarrese town of Estella on 14 June. At this point, however, the scheme ran into trouble, the fact being that both Alava and Navarre were dominated by the Carlists, the latter being happy with neither the idea of a single Basque homeland nor the prospect of rule from Bilbao which this necessarily implied, and inclined to envisage decentralization solely in terms of the old *fueros* of each individual province. Only one thing made the PNV's programme acceptable, and that was the fact that it laid down that the new Basque government should be given control of Church–state relations, the Estella conference therefore agreeing to accept the statute.

All this was neither here nor there, however. Always suspect in the eyes of Republicans and Socialists on account of the fact that it was centred on the municipality, and therefore on a unit whose electoral credibility was open to serious doubt, the process which reached its culmination at Estella was wrecked altogether by the new constitution, the latter reserving Church–state relations to the central government. That said, however, the matter was not dead: indeed, on 28 June the provincial *diputaciones* accepted the Estella statute – minus, of course, the crucial clauses on Church–state relations – as the basis on which it might be obtained. At last waking up to the fact that it could still secure a real measure of success, the nationalists abandoned their earlier maximalism and joined the *diputaciones* in their deliberations. By June 1932 a new statute was ready for approval, but at this point the process once again ran into difficulties. Baulked of their aims with regard to the Church, the Carlists had decided to have nothing more to do with the process, the result being that Navarre backed out. The statute having been drafted to cover all four of the provinces concerned, it had now to be amended. In theory this should have been an easy task, but matters were complicated by the fact that the Socialists and Republicans had effectively decided to eradicate the PNV as a political force. Negotiations were therefore delayed, whilst the authorities launched a campaign of harassment designed to discredit the PNV and force it into a posture of open opposition, the result being that the necessary plebiscite was not held until November 1933.

If progress on the autonomy question was singularly unimpressive, that with regard to agrarian reform was downright dismal. Spurred on by clear evidence that many civil governors and *ayuntamientos* were colluding with landowners to sabotage Largo's labour decrees, the provisional government had in fact established a special commission to consider the subject in May 1931, but no sooner had this body reported than it became clear that the issue was one which raised many difficulties. Thus, although all the leaders of the Republican coalition paid lip service to the need for reform, many of them were distinctly lukewarm on the matter. Alcalá Zamora, Maura and Lerroux were all opposed to land redistribution, whilst the Radical Socialists were for the most part little interested in reform except to the extent that it could be used as one more means of attacking the hated symbols of the past. As such, it was only with much difficulty that agreement was secured on the form that reform should take, whilst it was not until May 1932 that the *cortes* began consideration of the issue. Due to a combination of Agrarian obstruction, lack of interest amongst many government supporters, and the fact that many of the bill's provisions conflicted with conditions on the ground, progress was very slow even then, and it was once again only the revolt of General Sanjurjo that broke the impasse.

Did the Law of Agrarian Reform constitute the sort of measure that was needed if the economic power of the old elite was ever to be broken, however? On paper, certainly, its provisions seemed radical enough. In brief, no fewer than thirteen different categories of land were declared to be liable for expropriation, the overall quantity involved being quite considerable. Yet all was not as it seemed. In the first place, non-arable land and land that was directly cultivated by its owners was not subject to seizure at all. In the second, only a few categories of land – estates over which the owner's family had exercised seigneurial jurisdiction, or were continually leased out or badly farmed – could be taken in their entirety. In the third, the nine categories of land that remained were only subject to expropriation over a certain maximum that was defined not in overall terms but in those of the amount of land owned in each municipality. And, in the fourth place, no account was taken of the problem posed by different members of the same family owning land in the same district. As can be imagined, what all this amounted to was a bureaucratic labyrinth which afforded landowners every opportunity to minimize their losses. Still worse, the whole project was rendered immensely costly and time-consuming, the fact that the vast majority of the property that could be taken was deemed to be open to indemnification swelling the budget required by the reform still further. Conscious of this difficulty, the government also introduced a bill that for the first time established a general income tax, but the issue was one of such sensitivity that the rates – themselves very low – came into effect at so high a level that almost no money was raised by the new measure, the Azaña administration there-fore being placed in a position that was near impossible.

Deficient as it was, the Law of Agrarian Reform only tackled the problems of the *braceros*. For the thousands of small tenant farmers who were more characteristic of large parts of Spain, the central issue was not access to the land, but the terms on which they were permitted to farm it. Given that many smallholders were natural supporters of the Republic, it might have been thought that the government would have rushed to assist them, but in point of fact it was not until July 1933 that a bill was introduced to tackle the problem of leases and even then the opportunity was squandered. Aided by exhaustion, indifference and, in the Radical case, downright complicity, the Agrarians once again subjected the measure to a barrage of amendment, the government eventually falling before the bill could be passed. Still pending, meanwhile, were the recovery of the large areas of common land that had been illegally alienated during the nineteenth century, the establishment of cheap rural credit, and the amelioration of the particular problems that beset the tenant farmers of Galicia and Catalonia. Setting aside the manner of how the various measures that introduced by the Azaña government were implemented, in short, the achievements of the reformist *bienio* in the crucial field of agriculture were very limited.

The Gathering Storm

True though it is that the Republican regime was remarkably moderate in its approach to the social and political reform which it espoused, not to mention the fact that its measures were generally susceptible to a con-siderable degree of dilution, it was from the start subjected to a tirade of hatred and defamation which it could have done nothing to avoid. First target here was naturally enough the measures which it took to implant and defend itself, in which respect it has to be said that the Republic proved extraordinarily adept at laying itself open to charges that it was betraying its principles. Whether it was in the appointment of the new *diputaciones*, the revision of the results of the municipal elections, the spate of legislation by decree that marked the first few months of the life of the Republic, or the administrative pressure that marred the elections to the constituent *cortes*, the fact was that, however hypocritical the Right may have been in pointing it out, Spain's situation was hardly that of a genuine democracy. Also catastrophic was the pursuit of 'responsibilities'. Whilst few ministers wanted to drive the matter to extremes, the rank and file of the Socialists and Radical Socialists were determined to exact revenge and make good their claim to be revolutionary, the deputies of the two parties in consequence forcing the establishment of a parliamentary commission whose task it would be to hunt down all those implicated in the crimes of the dictatorship and the monarchy. Given considerable power, the new commission proceeded to arrest sixteen of Primo's ministers, and recommend that the king be stripped of all his estates and titles and sentenced to perpetual banishment. Given that all over the country Republican and Socialist militants were engaging in a variety of petty acts of persecution and harassment, the result was that the Republic was made to appear both vindictive and hypocritical (as the Right was quick to point out, the Socialists' collaboration with Primo was conveniently ignored).

By threatening the Republic, meanwhile, the Right were able to score a further series of propaganda victories. Let us take, for example, the case of Cardinal Segura. Having temporarily left Spain for consultations with Rome in the wake of the events of early May, Segura repeated his defiance in a private note to the government whilst at the same time hatching a plot designed to secure the Church's property against expropriation. Re-entering Spain on 13 June, the Cardinal was therefore arrested and expelled. Increasingly regarded as an embarrassment by the Vatican though he was – genuinely anxious to preserve some form of *modus vivendi* with the new regime, the latter had by September pressured Segura into proffering his resignation – the Cardinal could in consequence be portrayed as a martyr, the image of persecution that he represented being strengthened by the fact that the government also expelled the Bishop of Vitoria. In much the same way howls of outrage were provoked by the measures that the Provisional Government took against the Right in the wake of the disturbances of 10–11 May. To remain inert, however, would have been fatal, and all the more so as the Republic was under attack not just from the Right but also from the Communists and the FAI. On 20 October 1931 debate therefore began on a new 'Law for the Defence of the Republic' which empowered the government to repress any action that might be held to threaten the security of the regime. At about the same time, meanwhile, there also appeared the Guardia de Asalto, a new paramilitary police force that was even more heavily armed than the Guardia Civil and in theory marked by absolute loyalty to the Republic.

The response of the Right to these measures being to claim that the Republic had become a dictatorship, we come here to the distortion that was to be one of the most crucial weapons in its destabilization of the Republic. However unfair the Right was, so many hostages had been left to fortune that it was presented with a multiplicity of targets. Much vaunted though it was, for example, Azaña's reform of the army could not in the short term be said to have produced any great military benefit. As officers were effectively allowed to retire on full pay, by the end of 1931 some 8,200 had opted for retirement, but, gratifying as this was, the fact remained that there would be no reduction in the size of the pay bill for a very long time to come. Although military expenditure actually rose dramatically in the period 1931–3, the army therefore did not receive the new weapons it had been promised. A few new planes were bought for the air force, true, but critics of the government could therefore represent Azaña's entire policy as a deliberate attempt to destroy Spain's military power.

Even more telling, however, were the failures in agrarian policy. For example, slow to aid the small proprietor and tenant, the new regime in some respects actually threatened them. Thus, the various decrees issued by Largo Caballero greatly increased the labour costs of peasants used to taking on a few extra hands at harvest time, whilst seemingly giving rise to the possibility that the humblest of smallholdings would have to find work for large numbers of unemployed labourers. At the same time, although the Law of Agrarian Reform was clearly aimed at the large landowner, a mixture of clumsy drafting and cunning amendment ensured that it affected many medium and small proprietors, many of whom did not even live in areas characterized by *latifundismo*. Meanwhile, in those parts of Spain where small-scale peasant agriculture existed side-by-side with latifundist monoculture, the peasantry began to find themselves threatened by the same unrest that was plaguing their richer neighbours. Indeed, in some respects they were even more vulnerable: hungry *braceros* could often bully smallholdings into giving them work far more easily than they could large estates. The result was predictable: hitherto isolated and despised, the *caciques* were able to build a false community of interests between large and small proprietor, landowner and tenant.

Weight was lent to claims that the government intended to ruin Spanish agriculture by a combination of mismanagement and misfortune. In December 1931, the agriculture portfolio had been given to Marcelino Domingo. Notoriously incompetent, he was, as the Right were quick to point out, almost completely ignorant of agricultural issues. However, he was too proud to admit failure and in consequence resisted every effort to shift him to another post. Had Domingo been Spain's leading agronomist, however, he would still have been unable to get around such basic difficulties as the fact that Republican policy emphasized the need to keep as much land as possible in cultivation when the economic situation dictated a cut in production. Meanwhile, matters were not made any easier by the tricks engaged in by agricultural interests, and all the more so as these sometimes backfired, as when efforts into bamboozling Domingo into raising the minimum price of wheat led him rather to authorize large imports.

If the government was allegedly ruining Spanish agriculture, it was also bent on the destruction of religion. Whether or not this was actually true is beside the point. 'Spain', Azaña famously thundered, 'has ceased to be Catholic'; the Church was denied state support, barred from education, and threatened with the loss of its property; immense difficulties were placed in the way of catechesis; leading bishops were arrested and exiled; churches were burned; popular religious festivals were banned or otherwise interfered with; Catholic newspapers were shut down; and priests and ordinary church-goers threatened or abused. What more could the government's enemies want, and all the more so as Azaña's claims were, to say the least, highly exaggerated?

When all else failed, there was always the weapon of simple invective. In this respect, the figure of Azaña himself was a godsend. A shy man who hid behind a facade of arrogance and disdain and was inclined to be over-mordant in his rhetoric, he was possessed of a sallow and mottled complexion, protuberant eyes, a fleshy face and a receding hairline, the general impression being that of a frog. Meanwhile, the fact that he had been forced to seek work as a minor bureaucrat was a useful means of eliding his very solid reputation as an essayist and translator. As spite, as a friend once put it, had not ceased to be Catholic, he was therefore ruthlessly belittled and caricatured, the general impression that was created being that he was a mixture of incompetent, tyrant and sexual pervert.

Thanks to this barrage of misinformation, invective and hatred, the cause of the Right was much invigorated and lent a popular character which it had hitherto lacked. By the end of 1931, however, the enemies of the Republic had begun to divide into those elements who were prepared to work for their objectives by legal means, and those who were rather inclined to overthrow the Republic by force. Taking the Carlists first of all, the collapse of their plan for a 'Vaticanist Gibraltar' in the Basque provinces and Navarre led them to settle ever more firmly into a policy of conspiracy. A *modus vivendi* was established with the Alfonsists; the movement was given a much tighter structure and purged of the remnants of the divisions that had plagued its activities since the 1880s; and, with many conservatives rallying to a cause which they now identified with political salvation, Carlist organization was rapidly extended to parts of the country in which it had never had a foothold. Such expansion was sometimes fairly nominal, but of the general health of Carlism there could be no doubt: the number of militants in its northern and eastern heartlands multiplied dramatically; numerous youth and women's sections were founded; and a start was made on the organization of a militia known as the *requetés*. With the Carlists on the march, meanwhile, the Alfonsists had founded a new political movement as a front for the organization of rebellion. Originally known as Acción Española and headed by the erstwhile *maurista*, Antonio Goicoechea, this had initially affiliated with Acción Nacional, but had nonetheless lent wholehearted support to the *sanjurjada*. Disgusted with the direction taken by AN thereafter, by the end of 1932 Goicoechea had decided to go it alone, the movement that he headed now being entitled Renovación Española. Insignificant in numbers and organization, RE was yet a major threat in that the close links that it developed with the aristocracy gave it access not only to considerable funds, but also to the possibility of financial sabotage, the flight of capital that had been underway since 1931 in consequence continuing unabated.

The 'catastrophist' Right was not just limited to the Carlists and a rump of die-hard Alfonsists, however. As we have seen, the *dictablanda* had witnessed the emergence of a number of groups that looked not to an old-fashioned monarchy tricked out in the guise of a corporate state, but rather to a wholly new model of political organization. We come here to Spanish fascism, even if the only groups worthy of the name were initially handfuls of enthusiasts who had attached themselves to the obscure figures of Ramiro Ledesma Ramos and Onésimo Redondo, of whom the former was a would-be intellectual who spent his free time hanging around the student bars of Madrid, and the latter an official of a Catholic sugar-beet syndicate based in Valladolid. Starting from very different positions – Ledesma was violently anti-clerical and opposed to the old order, and Redondo a devout Catholic with strong links with the landed oligarchy – the two fell under the influence of Ernesto Giménez Caballero, a maverick writer who had become a great admirer of Mussolini. Obtaining a handful of adherents, in March 1931 Ledesma founded a paper called *El Conquista del Estado* in which he mixed condemnation of *caciquismo* and the Catholic Church with calls for the establishment of a state based on what he called national syndicalism. National syndicalism, meanwhile, was also the central theme of Onésimo Redondo, who in June 1931 founded a group known as the Juntas Castellanas de Actuación Hispánica. Neither Ledesma nor Redondo being at all successful –

their only supporters were a few right-wing students – the two were drawn ever closer together, and in October 1931 they joined forces to form Spain's first fascist party in the form of the Juntas de Ofensiva Nacional Sindicalista.

Had the JONS remained the only proponent of fascism in Spain, it is probable that the doctrine would have sunk without trace. Unwilling to secure the patronage of the oligarchy – Ledesma remained resolutely anti-clerical, refused to have anything to do with the *sanjurjada*, and based his propaganda on an attempt to win over the anarchists – the JONS got nowhere. Only in 1933 did the situation take a turn for the better. Miguel Primo de Rivera had had a son named José Antonio, a charming and modest young man who had played no part in the dictatorship, and had only been drawn into politics at all when he was invited to take on the post of Secretary General of one of the various authoritarian leagues founded to defend the monarchy in 1930. As such his baptism of fire was very much that of a reactionary conservative, but it was not long before he had become dissatisfied with his co-religionists. Thus, always disgusted at the manner in which his father had been betrayed by the monarchy, the army and the oligarchy, he at the same time became convinced that only a genuine revolution could save Spain from her ills. By the beginning of 1933 he had therefore become converted to fascism. José Antonio Primo de Rivera being a far more credible figure than Ledesma and Redondo, financial support was soon forthcoming from a number of different sources, and on 29 October 1933 the so-called Falange Española was duly launched at a 2,000-strong rally in Madrid.

For all the charisma of José Antonio, however, fascism did not make much of an impact, this being largely the work of José María Gil Robles. Born in 1898, Gil Robles was the devoutly Catholic son of a leading Carlist intellectual. A leading light of the PSP and ACNP and close friend of Angel Herrera, he had had no difficulty in securing election to the *cortes* and becoming president of Acción Nacional. Quickly renamed Acción Popular, the movement now experienced a process of rapid change. Initially a loose umbrella organization – adherents were allowed to keep their own counsel on the form of government which Spain should ultimately enjoy and be members of other political organizations – it soon became a party in its own right, complete with workers', women's and youth wings entitled Acción Obrerista, Asociación Femenina de Acción Popular and Juventud de Acción Popular. There being no formal programme, many would-be rebels remained in its ranks, but, being absolutely committed to the conquest of power by legal means, Gil Robles was most unhappy with this situation. In August 1932, moreover, his fears proved all too justified: many leading members of AP being involved in the *sanjurjada*, it was subjected to a sharp period of repression, whilst being forced to witness the rapid passage of the Law of Agrarian Reform and the Catalan statute. At a stormy meeting its followers were therefore duly forced to accept the principle of legality, Acción Popular being some months later renamed the Confederación Española de Derechas Autonomas.

Legalist though he may have been, Gil Robles was no democrat. A restoration may not have been vital to him (though not to many *cedistas*, all that was required of them being that they should renounce violence), but he still rejected all notion of political pluralism. Much influenced by Hitler and Mussolini, what he stood for was essentially the corporate state. Were he to come power, the Republic itself might survive, but democracy would be overthrown, the trade unions destroyed, social reform reversed, and regional autonomy abolished. In an attempt to woo the lower classes and obfuscate the blatant sectionalism for which the CEDA actually stood, much was made of Catholic social teaching, but this was, as we shall see, a mere figleaf. For the vast majority of its members, in fact, all that mattered was a return to 1931 (hence the fact that the CEDA cannot really be called 'fascist').

The End of the Bienio

The formation of the CEDA certainly did not put an end to conspiratorial activity. In the army, for example, Azaña's reforms had proved utterly counterproductive. For technical reasons that we need not go into here, promotion had become slower than ever, whilst many *africanistas* found that they were suddenly reduced in rank; meanwhile, the bulk of the officers who took early retirement were precisely the sort of men who might have been most expected to sympathize with the Republic (by contrast, almost all the *africanistas* stayed on). To professional concern, meanwhile, were added the passage of the Catalan statute, the continued labour unrest, and the growing hostility evoked by the Guardia Civil. In consequence, the failure of the *sanjurjada* did little to discourage conspiratorial activity, the only difference being that its leaders resolved that they must henceforward be better organized, to which end there appeared a new secret society known as the Unión Militar Española. Conscious of his reactionary views and great prestige amongst the *africanistas*, the conspirators meanwhile tried hard to win the support of the erstwhile hero of the Moroccan Wars and commandant of the Zaragoza academy, Francisco Franco (dismayed though he had been by the fall of dictatorship and monarchy alike, the latter had thus far kept aloof). Fearing that they would meet fierce opposition, the standard bearers of revolt also established strong links with the Carlists and Alfonsists and got in touch with Mussolini. Meanwhile, Rome was also visited by emissaries of the Carlists and RE, both whom remained resolved on rebellion. That said, however, the bulk of the Republic's opponents were as yet content to give Gil Robles the benefit of the doubt, the chance that he needed to prove the value of his approach in fact being none too distant.

The opportunity which Gil Robles was so soon to be afforded was bound up with a number of factors. Let us begin with the impact of the Great Depression. As has often been remarked, this event affected Spain less severely than many other countries. Thus, the fall in production *per capita* amounted to no more than 16 per cent, whilst gross national income actually registered a slight increase. As for unemployment, a maximum of 12.8 per cent compares very favourably to the sort of percentages experienced elsewhere. In some areas, indeed, and particularly those primarily serving the domestic market, business may even have profited from the cataclysm: in Catalonia, for example, the fall in the price of raw cotton cut production costs and reduced retail prices, thereby stimulating a growth in demand. Yet, for all this good fortune, Spain did not escape unscathed. Exports collapsed, whilst the hole in the domestic market left by the end of Primo's infrastructural projects remained unfilled. As a result by 1933 many parts of the economy were in serious trouble. Nor was a widespread slump the only effect of the depression. As the Latin American countries ran into difficulties so they blocked further Spanish immigration whilst at the same time adopting a range of policies that persuaded a number of previous immigrants to return home. Within Spain, meanwhile, falling employment opportunities in the towns and cities imposed a deceleration in the rate of urbanization which deepened the recession in the construction industry. Many workers who had already left the *campo* in the meantime coming to the conclusion that it was in their best interests to return home, the problem of rural over-population was distinctly accentuated.

However serious its effects, the Depression was not the only cause of the trouble. Some of Spain's problems could in part be put down to structural causes – the death rate had been steadily decreasing, for example – whilst others were linked with the political situation, many *latifundistas* deliberately taking land out of production as a means of averting expropriation or reasserting their dominance. Meanwhile, the coming of the Republic was also accompanied by a wholesale flight of capital that had further reduced inward investment and dragged down the value of the *peseta*. In any assessment of the Republic's economic problems, government mismanagement must also be taken into account. Mention has already been made of the mistakes of Marcelino Domingo, but in some respects the Republic's first Minister of Finance, Indalecio Prieto, is almost equally worthy of censure. Rightly critical of the chronic inefficiency of Spain's railways, Prieto believed that the way forward lay in the trunk road and heavy lorry, the disproportionate reduction in railway building that resulted making matters infinitely worse for iron and steel than might otherwise have been the case. For another example of the sort of disruption caused by more or less well-meaning attempts at reform, meanwhile, one has only to look at the Law of Municipal Boundaries. Thus, intended to protect *braceros* from the use of 'blackleg' labour, the measure struck very heavily at the many areas – Galicia and the more mountainous parts of Andalucía – where seasonal migration was essential.

Whatever may have been the precise reason, the reformist *bienio* was in consequence characterized by widespread misery. Setting aside the various structural initiatives pursued under the guise of agrarian reform, some help was forthcoming in the shape of public works programmes and the like, but a number of factors ensured that the Republic's response to the crisis would be ineffectual in the extreme. Thus, unwilling to tax the rich too heavily for fear of stirring up revolt, the hands of the government were tied by its absolute devotion to the financial orthodoxy of the day, there being no place in this for currency, price, investment, import and export controls, deficit financing, or what would soon be called Keynesianism. No financial expert, Prieto was obsessed with the need to rectify the mistakes of the dictatorship and restore faith in the economy. Great efforts were therefore made to restore the gold standard; interest rates raised to stimulate investment; the Bank of Spain compelled to prop up the *peseta*; and public expenditure kept at the lowest possible level. Switched though Prieto was to the Ministry of Public Works in 1931, his policies were little changed by his successor, Jaime Carner, the result being that relatively little money was made available to alleviate the crisis. In 1933, for example, the fund that had been established to subsidize unemployment benefit received less than half of 1 per cent of the national budget, whilst the body set up to administer the agrarian reform bill – the Instituto de Reforma Agraria – received only 50,000,000 *pesetas* a year.

To understand the impact which all this had on the chances of achieving the sort of fundamental reforms of which the lower classes had been dreaming in 1931, it is only necessary to look at agriculture. Emergency settlements aside – in the autumn of 1932 Azaña had temporarily settled some 40,000 landless labourers on a variety of properties in Extremadura, Andalucía and New Castile – by the end of the *bienio reformista* less than one thousand families had been assisted by the Instituto de Reforma Agraria. Whilst an immense amount of preparatory work was needed before a single acre of ground could be redistributed, the fact was that the Instituto simply did not have enough money.

Moreover, even those families which it did manage to settle faced many problems, including the absence of cheap credit and the fact that many of them had been settled on poor quality scrubland with which almost nothing could be done. In short, the whole affair was little short of a disaster.

To say that all of this constituted a great disappointment would be an understatement. In this respect, matters were rendered still worse by the fact that the new regime was little more sensitive than its predecessors in matters of law and order. Thus, in Seville artillery was deployed against anarchist strikers in July 1931, whilst the government made no attempt to reform the hated Civil Guard and continued to have frequent recourse to the military authorities. Astonishingly enough, a considerable portion of the CNT remained loyal to the relatively moderate 'pure syndicalism' personified by Angel Pestaña, the summer of 1931 therefore witnessing a violent debate within the ranks of the anarchist movement as to whether or not it was still possible to accept the Republic. Reduced to its essentials, the heart of this debate was a struggle over the nature of the CNT, Pestaña and his followers believing that it should transform itself into a reformist trade-union movement, and the rival *faistas* that it should remain committed to revolution by general strike. In the circumstances, however, there could only be one victor, and all the more so as it was becoming quite clear that the Socialists were openly exploiting their control of the Ministry of Labour to undermine the CNT. Known as the *treintistas* from the manifesto which thirty of its leaders had signed in August 1931, Pestaña's faction was therefore quickly expelled from all positions of power. The result was a major split, Pestaña eventually establishing a rival union movement known as the Sindicatos de Oposición. For some time the confusion continued, but the fact was that by the autumn of 1931 the anarchist movement was effectively at war with the Republic.

As autumn wore on so the tension increased still further. The government made liberal use of the Law for the Defence of the Republic to suspend anarchist newspapers and syndicates, ban meetings and demonstrations, close down union offices, and arrest leading militants. Still worse, the police showed no signs of any relaxation in their attitude, there being many instances in which they opened fire on unarmed crowds. Convinced that an all-out attempt to destroy them was underway, the *faistas* responded by organizing a further series of strikes and demonstrations, the result of which was still more violence. Most famous of the various incidents which occurred is that the massacre of four *civiles* at the village of Castilblanco on 1 January 1932, but there were also a string of others, most of which were the work of the forces of order. In all of this the hands of the revolutionaries were far from clean, but the fact was that police brutality seemed to have become worse than ever.

The events surrounding Castilblanco gave rise to an immense political furore. For the Right, the massacre of the Civil Guards – indeed, the whole chain of labour disturbances – provided them with yet more material for their campaign of defamation, whilst they were also not above exploiting the repression to drive a wedge between the Republicans and the Socialists. Less cynically, many bourgeois liberals displayed genuine dismay at the Republic's failure to control the police, and all the more so as General Sanjurjo, at this point still commander of the Civil Guard, adopted an utterly uncompromising position. However, the greatest outrage of all was produced amongst the Socialists. The unsophisticated labourers who made up the vast bulk of the membership of the FNTT – the agricultural section of the UGT – had inevitably been drawn into the unrest of the autumn and winter: indeed, Castilblanco was not an anarchist stronghold, but rather a Socialist one. To retain any credibility, the PSOE therefore could not but mount a noisy protest. For the time being, dislike of the Anarchists and their own deep-seated reformism kept the Socialist leadership solidly committed to participation in the government, but the coalition was quite clearly beginning to come under serious pressure.

However, if the Socialists were restive, the situation was not yet critical enough to produce any change of policy. On the contrary, when the FAI sought to capitalize on the growing unrest by organizing a revolutionary insurrection in central Catalonia in late January, the UGT refused point-blank to lend it their support, the rebels therefore being suppressed without difficulty. The repression was milder than normal – the authorities had evidently taken note of the protests of the previous month – but even so 110 *cenetistas* were deported to the isolated Spanish possessions on the west coast of Africa. Devastating a blow though this was – the deportees included almost the entire leadership of the FAI – unrest continued: for example, the coming of spring was marked by a variety of strikes and terrorist attacks in the province of Cádiz, whilst Caceres and Ciudad Real both saw angry FNTT militants set upon local mayors who had failed to support the demands of the workers. In Extremadura, in particular, meanwhile, groups of labourers repeatedly engaged in attempts to occupy parts of the great estates (the problem was particularly prominent in this region because of the prevalence of the group known as the *yunteros* – landless labourers who owned oxen and ploughs and were therefore well placed to take advantage of schemes of land redistribution). Last but not least, the Communists also took a hand, managing among other incidents to inspire a short-lived insurrection at Villa de Don Fadrique.

Although the autumn of 1932 witnessed a slight improvement in the attitude of the Republican authorities in the shape of Azaña's temporary settlement of substantial numbers of settlers on certain private estates, the beginning of 1933 was marked by a fresh catastrophe in the field of public order. Thanks in part to the return of most of the CNT militants who had been deported to Africa, a new anarchist revolt spread across large parts of Catalonia, the Levante and Andalucía. In most instances, the police were quickly able to restore order, but in the village of Casa Viejas a small group of militants barricaded themselves in a private house. After a fierce battle, most of the occupants were either burned to death or shot down as they tried to escape. Having dealt with the chief pocket of resistance, the police – a mixture of *civiles* and *asaltos* – conducted a random search of the town and arrested a dozen men who were then executed in cold blood in circumstances that suggested a deliberate attempt to incriminate them in the gunfight.

The twenty-two victims of Casas Viejas were not the only casualties of the massacre, the affair provoking a storm of unparalleled magnitude. Whilst the Right once again made hay, the Socialists were forced to confront the problems posed by their continued participation in government. Even as it was, it had been proving hard to hold the line against the growing anger of their rank and file. Modest enough as they were, the advances won by the Republic in the countryside were by the autumn of 1932 being whittled away by an employers' offensive that in many places amounted to a virtual lock-out, whilst it was becoming increasingly clear that little enough could be looked for from the Law of Agrarian Reform. At congresses held in October 1932, the PSOE and the UGT had ratified the policy of continued participation in the government, but unrest continued: as well as isolated acts of violence, there were major strikes amongst the miners of Asturias and the farmworkers of Salamanca, whilst it was only with the greatest difficulty that a similar action was avoided on the UGT-controlled railways. In this context Casas Viejas came as a veritable thunderclap. On 30 January 1933, too, Hitler came to power in Germany, reformism thus being cast as an accomplice in the rise of fascism. Reassured by the fact that the commission of enquiry established to investigate Casas Viejas eventually cleared Azaña of allegations of complicity, the PSOE still did not break away, but the only rationale for the arrangement was now that of keeping the Radicals out of power.

If the loyalty of the PSOE was increasingly shaky by the spring of 1933, that of Azaña's other chief allies was not much to be relied on either. Thus, the Radical Socialists had never been a very solid grouping, their members including genuine social reformers, demagogues intent on poaching support from the Socialists, and conservative republicans who had only joined the party as a result of personal quarrels with Lerroux, whilst they were now in a state of complete disarray. A faction on the right having begun to agitate against alliance with the PSOE, a series of disputes broke out which saw the Radical Socialists fragment into not two but three different factions, the fact being that the government was increasingly in tatters. What finally finished off Azaña, however, was rather the activities of the President. A vain and irresponsible figure who was deeply resentful of Azaña, Alcalá Zamora was anxious both to find a more tractable prime minister and to impose a brake upon anti-clericalism and social reform. Seizing upon the predictably unfavourable results that were produced by the partial municipal elections called on 26 April 1933 to replace the survivors of the 29,804 councillors who had been elected unopposed in the contest of April 1931 as a pretext, in early June he therefore announced that the country had lost confidence in the government. As the president had expected, Azaña promptly resigned, whereupon the president's natural ally, Lerroux, was summoned to form a new ministry. The Radical leader proving unable to form a cabinet, the old administration was restored to power, but, impelled by a further wave of unrest, Largo was now openly hinting at a breach with the government, whilst on 3 September Azaña was hit by a further hammer blow. As laid down by the constitution, on that date Spain's 50,000 town councillors voted to select the fifteen members of the Tribunal of Constitutional Guarantees who were deemed to represent the various regions of the country. Thanks in part to clashes between different elements of the coalition, the government won only five of the seats at issue. For a brief moment, the prime minister attempted to brazen things out, but it was useless: on 8 September 1933 Azaña was forced to surrender.

A Chronicle of Failure

For all the hopes that its coming had inspired, then, the Republic had failed to live up to expectations. Social and economic reform had proved halting and ineffectual; the regional problem had only been partially resolved; civil rights were frequently abused; the modernization of the army and security forces had been stymied; and both militarism and *caciquismo* were continuing to thrive. Indeed, even the Church had managed to survive the Republican–Socialist offensive remarkably well, the Jesuits and other religious orders having frequently been able to evade its legislation. Had Azaña been allowed to remain in power, matters just might have improved – by the summer of 1933 he had at last realized that the only hope was to satisfy the expectations aroused by the Republic. Yet, even so, it is difficult to see how Azaña could have lasted for very long, the fact being that the Republic was caught between the revolutionary devil and the reactionary deep blue sea.

What, then, rendered the *bienio reformista* so disappointing? Misfortune, incompetence, irresponsibility, shortsightedness, and sheer malevolence all played their part in this respect – one thinks here of the infantile revolutionism of the FAI, the form that was given to agrarian reform, the failure to anticipate Keynesianism, the unfavourable economic circumstances into which the Republic was born, and the violent antipathy of the Right. At the heart of the issue, however, lay something far more fundamental. In essence, April 1931 marked the triumph of Spanish liberalism, but contained within this doctrine were a series of beliefs – most notably, the freedom of property – that militated against social justice. Thus, social reform did not come about in Spain because the bourgeoisie was weak, but rather because it was divided. In 1931 as much as in 1810, 1854 and 1868, educated and even propertied circles were strongly in favour of reform. What was missing, however, was consensus as to the form that reform should take. Amongst a tiny handful of lawyers and intellectuals, there was from the start a belief that it was necessary to abandon the fundamental tenets of liberalism in favour of social democracy, but amongst most bourgeois politicians attitudes were very different. Whilst lip service was generally paid to the need for social reform, many elements of the Republican coalition did so in a spirit of mere demagogy. For others, meanwhile, social justice was a matter of secondary importance that was effectively pushed aside by the far more congenial problems associated with the Church and the army. When the Socialists persisted in forging ahead with the issue, the revolutionary coalition fell to pieces. Support for social reform gradually increased, but most Republicans settled into a conservatism that made the survival of a reformist administration a physical impossibility. Without such a regime, however, all was lost.

15

The Republic Beleaguered

Two Black Years

If the period 1931–3 had been the *bienio reformista*, for the forces of progress 1933–5 was the *bienio negro* – two black years in which reform was halted, the Left provoked into a catastrophic uprising, and the anti-democratic Right admitted to a share of power under the vociferous and provocative Gil Robles. Convinced that enough was enough, the forces that remained true to the spirit of 1931 set aside the divisions that had led to their downfall and came together in a desperate attempt to remedy the situation. When fresh general elections were convoked in February 1936, they were therefore ready to do battle. Grouped in a grand alliance known as the Popular Front, they triumphed at the polls and at once proceeded to implement a somewhat radicalized version of the Republic's original agenda. No sooner had the Popular Front won the elections, however, than right-wing legalism collapsed: determined to preserve its privileges, the oligarchy switched its support to the proponents of insurrection. Preparations for revolt soon being in full swing, for the next few months a desperate battle raged for the loyalty of the forces that would decide the outcome of the rising. Despite some very obvious disadvantages, in this respect the Popular Front actually did rather well, the result being that the long-heralded coup brought neither victory nor defeat, but rather civil war.

The Hour of Lerroux

Far more so than Gil Robles, the most effective agent in the counter-revolution was the Radical leader, Alejandro Lerroux. The 'grand old man' of republicanism, he could be elevated to the premiership in good conscience by a president desperate to slow down change and rid himself of the intractable Azaña, despite the fact that he was corrupt, opportunistic, and happy to govern with the support of the Right, thereby affording Gil Robles a degree of influence which he would never otherwise have achieved. The origins of this situation lie in the aftermath of the fall of the Azaña government. With Azaña out of the way, Lerroux was immediately invited to form a new government. The Radical leader succeeded in putting together a coalition which included representatives of most elements of Republican opinion, but, knowing that he would fix the elections, the president refused him a dissolution. Forced to face a *cortes* still dominated by the Socialists, Lerroux attempted to extract a vote of confidence by claiming that the only alternative was new elections presided over by himself. However, more progressive Republicans were already worried at Lerroux's efforts to court the Right, the new cabinet having been quick, for example, to suspend the law of municipal boundaries. In consequence, the PSOE was joined by Acción Republicana, the Esquerra, and the centre and left of the old Radical Socialists. Lerroux being crushed, fresh polls became inevitable, and these were duly convoked for 19 November under the aegis of a caretaker cabinet headed by Lerroux's deputy, Diego Martínez Barrio (the latter enjoying a reputation for considerable honesty, Alcalá Zamora appears to have hoped that his appointment would ensure that the elections were fair).

In taking such a line, the president displayed a certain prescience, the elections producing a dramatic turnaround. The *azañistas* and left and centrist Radical Socialists having refused to participate in a government that did not include the PSOE, the latter might have gone into the polls in alliance with their old partners. However, disillusioned, angry and over-confident, except in the case of a few branches associated with Prieto the Socialists decided against such a course. As a result the Left-Republicans and the Socialists went into the campaign not as allies but as political opponents, matters being made still worse by the fact that the *azañistas* and the various factions into which the Radical Socialists had split often fought each other as well as the Radicals and the PSOE. As might have been expected, the campaign was also marked by an immense effort on the part of the CEDA which made much use of the techniques of Nazi Germany and Fascist Italy and proved quite prepared to fashion local electoral pacts with the Carlists, Renovación Española, and the Radicals alike. Combined with the effects of a divided opposition, female emancipation, an electoral law that favoured coalitions, and the fact that few anarchists were now prepared to vote, all this paid off most handsomely, the final result producing 117 *cedistas* and 104 Radicals compared with fifty-eight Socialists, twenty-two *esquerristas*, and fourteen left-Republicans of various types (i.e. *azañistas*, left-Radical Socialists, *orgistas* and the like). As the Right could also muster twenty-nine Agrarians – now a separate party in their own right dominated by erstwhile Liberals – twenty-four *lligistas*, twenty-one Carlists, fourteen *goicoechistas* and a variety of conservative independents, the defeat of reform was virtually total, even if there had actually been little shift in public opinion (indeed, it has been estimated that the Left actually obtained some 30,000 more votes than the Right).

Such was the atmosphere of violence engendered by the campaign that the auguries for the future were anything but good: apocalyptic language aside, there were numerous complaints of bribery and intimidation as well as at least fourteen deaths. Within the ranks of the Socialists, too, there was a further lurch in the direction of the revolutionary bolshevism that had appeared in the summer of 1933. Thus, swayed by the flattering terms in which he was being spoken of by many militants, Largo now began to advocate revolution as the only means of securing concrete gains for the working classes. In this, moreover, he was supported by powerful elements of the Socialist movement, both the 50,000-strong Socialist Youth Federation (FJSE) and the 445,000 members of the FNTT having become increasingly unhappy.

Dramatic though Largo Caballero's language may have been, however, it needs to be treated with great circumspection. Despite his pleasure at being described as 'the Spanish Lenin' and desire to retain the confidence of the rank and file, the deeply cautious Socialist leader remained most unwilling to jeopardize the safety of the machine over which he presided. Thus, Largo's rhetoric was not a call to arms, but rather a desperate effort to force Alcalá Zamora to call fresh elections in which the Socialists could join with the Left-Republicans in repairing the damage. Absolutely no measures were taken actually to prepare for revolution, whilst Largo conspicuously failed to respond to a *faista* insurrection launched in December in Aragón by a Durruti convinced that the formation of an all-bourgeois government would persuade the masses to rally to his lead.

Whilst the Socialists and Anarchists were behaving in this ineffectual fashion, Gil Robles was showing more prudence than might have been expected. Well aware of the divisions that beset the Right, the CEDA leader realized that, as a fresh dictatorship would not be supported by the army, the only result of the formation of an all right-wing government would be new elections in which the Socialists, Left-Republicans and Left-Catalanists would not only come together once more, but also very likely be joined by the more principled elements of the Radicals. That being the case, it was for the time being much safer to defer to Lerroux, and all the more so as the latter was only too happy to accept the CEDA as the power behind the throne.

This position being accepted *faut de mieux* by RE, the Carlists and the Agrarians, there was nothing to prevent Lerroux from forming a cabinet. Inevitably the result – eight Radicals, one Agrarian, one member of the old Derecha Liberal (differences between Maura and Alcalá Zamora had led to this splitting into the Partido Progresista and the Partido

Republicano Conservador), one Reformist and two independents – was very much a right-of-centre enterprise. In view of the price being insisted on by Gil Robles for his support, this was just as well, his demands including a revision of the Laws of Congregations and Agrarian Reform, the abolition of much of Largo's work as Minister of Labour, and the amnesty of all those involved in the *sanjurjada*.

Whilst trying to disguise his actions, Lerroux hastened to comply. For example, the ban on clerical involvement in education and the sale of ecclesiastical property were immediately suspended, whilst the CEDA was allowed to introduce a bill that reinstated state support of the clergy. As for agriculture, the Instituto de Reforma Agraria was left more or less unmolested – it is in fact the case that it distributed almost twice as much land in the first nine months of 1934 than had been the case in the course of its entire life hitherto – as were the labourers who had been temporarily given plots of land in the autumn of 1932. That said, however, the future was distinctly bleak, the crucial Law of Municipal Boundaries being formally abolished and the Guardia Civil heavily reinforced.

The *bienio negro* should not be examined solely at the level of government decrees, however. Throughout the previous two years, the actual implementation of reform had very much depended on the attitude of the bureaucracy, provincial governors, *diputaciones*, *ayuntamientos*, and mixed juries. No sooner had Azaña fallen from power, however, than large numbers of civil governors were replaced, as were many officials, mayors, councillors, and chairmen of mixed juries, the new men invariably being drawn from the old oligarchy and its supporters. Except in Catalonia, which was largely protected by its statute of autonomy, the result was that the forces of reaction were allowed to run amok. Thus, at least 50 per cent of the wage rises achieved since 1931 were clawed back, whilst the workers and their representatives were subjected to a series of brutal reprisals and other acts of harassment.

It was not, of course, just in the areas of the Church and agriculture that the new reality made its impact felt. With the Radicals and their allies deeply hostile to any real notion of regional autonomy, problems were inevitable in these areas as well. In this respect Galicia and the Basque provinces were particularly vulnerable given that in neither case had autonomy been agreed. Taking Galicia first of all, the statute of autonomy that was in preparation had still not been submitted to a plebiscite by the time that the reformist *bienio* came to an end, the regionalist movement thereupon deciding to suspend operations and wait for better days. 5 November 1933, meanwhile, had witnessed a plebiscite on the new statute of Basque autonomy negotiated in the wake of the Navarrese secession of the previous year. Yet despite being an overwhelming victory for the nationalist cause, the vote was undermined by the fact that

Spanish-speaking Alava had returned a very different result from its more northern neighbours, the percentage of the electorate who had voted 'yes' having amounted to only 46 per cent. Reinforced though it was by victory in the general elections – the PNV took twelve of the fifteen seats on offer in Vizcaya and Guipúzcoa – the nationalist position was therefore very much open to challenge, and all the more so as suspicions were rife that the triumph of 5 November had in part been the result of systematic ballot-rigging. No sooner had the statute been presented to parliament, then, than agitation began for the exclusion of Alava. After a prolonged controversy, it was eventually agreed that a new plebiscite should be held in Alava, but even then a combination of concerted filibustering and bad luck ensured that progress was extremely slow, the statute still not having been ratified by the time that fresh elections were called in 1936.

If the Basque statute was delayed, it was in part because of the serious crisis that soon gripped relations between Madrid and Barcelona. Thus, on 12 April 1934 the Generalitat passed a Catalan law of agrarian reform. The product, first, of the assumption of the leadership by the left-leaning Lluis Companys following the death of Maciá in December 1933, and, second, of the emergence of a sudden threat to the party in the form of the Alianza Obrera (see below), this was designed to give the *rabassaires* the right to purchase the land that they farmed. Relations between the Radicals and the Esquerra had never been very good, Lerroux having continued to delay the transfer of powers to Barcelona. Now headed by Ricardo Samper – at the end of April 1934 Lerroux had resigned as a result of attempts by Alcalá Zamora to restrict the amnesty that was being granted to the rebels of 1932 – the government therefore objected to the law and referred it to the Tribunal of Constitutional Guarantees. Dominated, as we have seen, by the Right, the tribunal resolved that the new law abrogated the Catalan statute's reservation of matters relating to the law of contract to the state, and added a series of riders that bade fair to paralyse the Catalan administration altogether. There followed a well-orchestrated show of defiance, and Samper eventually agreed to accept the principle of the law in exchange for significant modifications in its content. No sooner had the deal been announced, however, than it was wrecked by Gil Robles, the latter proclaiming that he would bring down the government unless it not only rejected the law but further restricted the powers of the Generalitat. Small wonder, then, that the Esquerra became as obsessed as the Socialists with the prospect of the CEDA entering the government.

The Esquerra were not the only representatives of bourgeois liberalism troubled by the direction which events were taking, the *azañistas*, left and centre of Radical Socialists and the ORGA all having been horrified by the election results. Reduced to a mere twelve deputies, these groups had no option but to come together, and in February 1934 they therefore established a new party headed by Azaña known as Izquierda Republicana. Meanwhile, important changes were also affecting the Radicals. Hitherto Lerroux's chief lieutenant, Martínez Barrio was too principled to be happy with the situation, and in early February he therefore declared himself to be totally opposed to CEDA participation in government. Already dissatisfied with his behaviour, Gil Robles responded by threatening to bring down the government unless Martínez Barrio was removed from his post as Minister of War. Knowing that he was certain to be sacked, the latter decided to resign and join the right wing of the Radical Socialists in forming a new party known as Unión Republicana.

By the summer of 1934, moreover, the ranks of the political centre had been reinforced by the PNV. Initially very much a party of the Right, the Basque nationalists were being forced further and further to the left. Always genuinely interested in social reform, their leader, José Antonio de Aguirre, had already formed a loose alliance with the Esquerra and the ORGA as a means of advancing the cause of autonomy, whilst the abandonment of the concept of a 'vaticanist Gibraltar' was a tacit rejection of the theocratic ambitions of the PNV's founders. Angered by the Carlists' sabotage of the autonomy process and the government's treatment of the Catalans, the nationalists were now given still further motive for a move to the Centre by the fact that Samper chose the summer of 1934 to launch an assault on the *concierto económico*. Temporarily setting aside their differences with the PNV, the local left-Republicans and Socialists joined with them in a campaign of protest whose culmination was the election of a special commission to negotiate with the government. To this, however, the authorities objected, and the result was a fierce confrontation which resulted in many arrests. Though a deal was eventually agreed, by the early autumn the PNV was therefore squarely in the camp of reform.

Important though this stiffening of the Centre was, it was always clear that the most crucial issue in the struggle to protect the gains of 1931–3 was going to be the response of organized labour. All the more was this the case given, first, that the Centre's position in some respects remained distinctly ambiguous – at the very same time that the Esquerra was squaring up for a fight with the government, for example, it was also adopting an ever tougher line with regard to the CNT – and, second, that the defection of Martínez Barrio had left the Radicals more at the mercy of the CEDA than ever. With the anarchists divided, beaten and exhausted, the main protagonist was inevitably the PSOE, the latter currently being under great pressure. Thus, from as early as February 1933 the

Catalan Bloc Obrer i Camperol had been pressing for a general alliance against fascism in the hope that this would bolshevize the proletariat. Equally isolated, meanwhile, the tiny Catalan Socialist party (the Unió Socialista de Catalunya) had come up with a similar idea, the result being that by December 1933 the two organizations had come together to form the so-called Alianza Obrera or Alliance of Labour. Beleaguered as it was, the Catalan workforce responded with considerable enthusiasm. By the end of 1933, in fact, the Unió de Rabassaires – Catalonia's leading agricultural union – and the local representatives of both the UGT and the *treintista* Sindicatos de Oposición had all rallied to the Alianza. The CNT remained aloof, admittedly, but even so the alarm felt by the Esquerra was considerable – hence the hasty move to the Left described above – whilst Largo unsurprisingly came to the conclusion that the PSOE would once again be outflanked and therefore redoubled his revolutionary rhetoric.

By December 1933, then, the Socialist movement had been confirmed in a stance that was strongly revolutionary. With even the utterly social-democratic Prieto openly calling for the overthrow of the government, many officials and union leaders who opposed a revolutionary policy were replaced by *caballeristas*. Amongst the casualties was Julián Besteiro, whilst Largo himself now united the post of Secretary General of the UGT with that of President of the PSOE. Meanwhile, a revolutionary committee was established and orders issued to establish an armed militia, the Socialist movement also applying for admission to the Alianza Obrera. Yet the Socialists' conversion to revolution still cannot be taken at face value. Some elements were undoubtedly perfectly genuine, but this was not the case of either Prieto or Largo, of whom the former was chiefly interested in forcing Alcalá Zamora into granting fresh elections, and the latter in keeping control of the rank and file and taking over the whole of the Spanish labour movement. Meanwhile, whatever the pronouncements of their leaders, many local officials remained profoundly sceptical. As a result, preparations for revolution proved at best desultory and at worst downright farcical: the Socialist militia secured no more than a few hundred members, most of whom not only remained unarmed, but showed little enthusiasm or commitment. As for the Alianza Obrera, this to all intents and purposes remained a dead letter, the Socialists' desire to use it as a vehicle to establish their hegemony causing a considerable part of its supporters to decamp.

Half-hearted as they were, the Socialists' preparations were further disrupted by the increasing number of strikes being engaged in by the UGT. Had Largo been genuine in his rhetoric, it might have been thought that he would have seized upon the effervescence as a springboard for revolution, but not even the general strike embarked upon by the FNTT on 5 June could persuade him to do anything of the sort. On the contrary, indeed, Communist offers of help were rejected, and the FNTT told that it could expect no support from the rest of the UGT. Not surprisingly, then, the strike was utterly crushed. For no gain at all, thousands of militants were beaten up, imprisoned or deported; hundreds of union premises occupied by the police or closed down; the Socialist press censored or suppressed; and the Socialist voice in local government eroded still further, many PSOE town councillors being replaced by government nominees. Also lost, meanwhile, was much of what little weaponry the Socialists had managed to amass.

Realizing, perhaps, that Largo's bluff had been called, that section of the Socialist movement associated with Prieto drew back from the idea of revolution, and began rather to investigate the possibility of reviving the Republican–Socialist unity of 1931–3. However, fear revolution though he did, Largo could not turn back. Whilst the FJSE, in particular, continued to engage in strident demands for revolt, fascism was clearly on the march: an object lesson in its horrors having been afforded by the recent suppression of the Social Democrats in Vienna, the CEDA was becoming ever more fascistic in its style, whilst in February 1934 the Falange and the JONS had fused to form the Falange Española y de las JONS. In the countryside in particular, meanwhile, a process of whole-sale intimidation was underway: crowds were repeatedly fired upon; black-leg labour and the army used to ensure that the great estates continued to be worked as normal; and large numbers of 'trouble-makers' excluded even from what little work was available. With Falangist gunmen already taking potshots at Socialist militants, confrontation was inevitable, the only question being when it would finally erupt.

Red October

In so far as Gil Robles was concerned, the labour unrest of December 1933–June 1934 was a godsend in that it had inflicted terrible damage on the Left. Knowing that many Radicals were as eager as he was for the showdown that he considered inevitable, Gil Robles therefore decided that the time was ripe to press for a share in government. Unless a number of basic conditions were satisfied, he declaimed, the CEDA would seize power, his enraptured audiences being assured that revolution and separatism would then be smashed post-haste. No sooner had the *cortes* reassembled on 1 October, moreover, than the CEDA leader provoked a crisis by denouncing the compromise solution that had been offered to the Catalans. Left with no hope of maintaining his position, Samper immediately resigned, the task of government being handed to Lerroux who promptly announced the formation of a new cabinet that included the names of three *cedistas*.

So far as the Centre and Left were concerned, the CEDA appointments came as a bolt from the blue, it having been generally expected that Alcalá Zamora, who was known to loathe Gil Robles, would call fresh elections. As a result the CEDA leader's plans worked even better than he expected. Thus, whilst Azaña and Martínez Barrio registered ineffectual verbal protests, the Socialists and the Esquerra turned to armed revolt. Aided by the new police force he had been allowed to establish under Azaña and the green-shirted nationalist youth movement known as the *escamots*, Companys barricaded himself inside his presidential palace, whilst an incredulous Largo hastily ordered a general strike. Acting more or less spontaneously, meanwhile, a number of irregular bands armed themselves with such weapons as they could and launched a series of attacks on the police and other targets. The result, however, was a débâcle. Support for the strike was patchy even amongst the UGT – the FNTT, for example, was too disorganized, exhausted and demoralized to attempt anything – whilst the anarchists generally remained aloof. As for the attempts at armed insurrection, these were almost everywhere a complete failure: fierce gun battles took place in a variety of places, but those workers who had armed themselves were quickly rounded up, whilst Companys surrendered after a single night of token resistance. A few scattered demonstrations aside, in short, most of Spain was quickly back to normal.

Only in Asturias was the picture any different. Just as the Basque provinces and Navarre had been the one part of Spain where the Carlists had had ready access to arms in 1833, so Asturias was the one part of Spain where the same could be said of the Left in 1934. A major centre of the Spanish arms industry, the factories round Oviedo were full of weapons, just as the region's numerous coal mines were well equipped with dynamite. Add to this the fact that one of the few arms shipments actually to have reached the Socialists in 1934 had been landed in Asturias, and it will be seen that the region was uniquely favoured. However, it was not just the question of armaments that made Asturias a particularly likely trouble spot. Also important was the fact that the workforce was far more united than in most other parts of Spain, the combination of working conditions that were particularly unpleasant, economic difficulties that were particularly severe, employers who were particularly stubborn, and local leaders who were particularly pragmatic having ensured that the Alianza Obrera had acquired a strength that was lacking elsewhere. Thoroughly unionized and the veterans of many bitter strikes, the miners were therefore readier to do battle than any other section of the proletariat.

At all events, they went into action with considerable effect. Quickly suppressing the police units stationed in their home towns, the miners bore down on Oviedo, whose defenders were quickly confined to a small area in the centre of the city. With Gijón also in revolt and the province's arms factories all in the hands of the insurgents, within a matter of days the whole region had been transformed into a *de facto* soviet republic. At best the revolutionaries were living on borrowed time, however: a large force of troops was soon advancing on them from León, whilst six battalions of Moors and foreign legionaries were hastily dispatched by sea from Morocco, effective command of the operation being given to Francisco Franco, who had just been appointed special adviser to the Minister of War. Resistance was fierce, but too many of the militia were tied down in the siege of Oviedo, whilst they were both outnumbered and outclassed. One by one, then, the bastions of the rebellion were recaptured, and by 18 October all was over, though not before the government had lost over 1,000 casualties. Though no more than fifty murders and executions had taken place in the insurgent zone, the aftermath was grim indeed. Encouraged by Franco to behave with the utmost ferocity, the security forces shot many prisoners in cold blood, whilst rape and murder were also commonplace, those officers who attempted to restrain the violence – most notably, the Chief of the General Staff, Eduardo López de Ochoa – being openly defied. Tales of the savagery have in all probability grown in the telling, but even so there can be little doubt that what occurred in Asturias was chilling indeed, total civilian casualties amounting to at least 4,000.

Before moving on, one other point is worth making with regard to the fighting in Asturias. Often ignored, the military history of the insurrection is actually of crucial importance. That some of the militia fought heroically there can be no doubt, but their efforts can nevertheless be seen to have been distinctly flawed. The forces holding the passes that led to León, for example, were ultimately forced to disperse for want of food, whilst many militiamen displayed a tendency to waste their ammunition and panic under fire. There had, too, been serious splits between different sections of the movement – according to the anarchists, CNT-dominated Gijón had been deliberately deprived of arms – whilst the rebels' failure to take Oviedo was distinctly embarrassing in view of the fact that its defenders amounted to fewer than 2,000 men. In short, what was probably the most well-armed, militant and united proletariat in Spain had proved a paper tiger, the idea that revolution had anything much to offer in terms of the defeat of counter-revolution having therefore been opened to serious question.

As far as Gil Robles was concerned, October 1934 could not have been more satisfactory. Giving rise to lurid tales of wholesale red terror, it at the same time facilitated an all-out assault on the forces of progress. Whilst Lerroux did what he could to moderate the repression, at least 30,000 left-wingers were soon in prison, including Largo and a large part of the executives of the PSOE, UGT and FJSE alike. Also incarcerated were not only Companys and his fellow ministers, but also Manuel Azaña, who had happened to be attending a funeral in Barcelona at the time of the insurrection. Still others, such as Prieto, were in exile, in which respect they could consider themselves fortunate, many of those who were detained being subjected to the most horrific tortures. Meanwhile, the premises of the various labour movements were closed by the hundred, many newspapers suspended, the *ayuntamientos* and mixed juries subjected to yet another purge, and the strictest censorship imposed on all and sundry. As for Catalonia, the statute of autonomy was suspended for six months, the *rabassaires* law declared null and void, the Esquerra ejected from both local government and the civil service, and the University of Barcelona placed under government control, Companys and his fellows eventually being sentenced to ten years' imprisonment (accused of complicity, Azaña had at length to be released for want of evidence).

Swingeing as all this was, the Carlists and Alfonsists, in particular, were demanding still more draconian measures, including in some cases mass executions. Much as he sympathized, however, Gil Robles would not go too far for fear of forcing Lerroux to resign and giving Alcalá Zamora the opportunity to call fresh elections. For a time he did toy with the idea of a military coup, but he had no wish to risk being sidelined by some general, whilst it was in any case quite clear that much of the army would never have gone along with such an idea, the result being that Lerroux was for the time being left to enjoy the trappings of power (the belief that a coup was abandoned for fear of popular resistance is clearly wishful thinking: after all, the labour movement had just been shown to be militarily helpless).

The importance of October 1934 is almost impossible to underestimate. At the very least, Left and Right had had their worst fears confirmed about their opponents. For the former, the savage repression which it engendered was proof positive of the terrible fate that awaited them should the Right ever achieve power. For the latter, meanwhile, Asturias showed all too clearly that the goal of the Left was indeed a 'Bolshevik' revolution, the lurid version of events propagated by its spokesmen in the meantime conspiring to paint events in the worst possible colours. For neither side, in short, was co-habitation any longer an option. Conflict was for a time postponed by both sides' belief that they could win the fresh elections that would sooner or later have to be called, but, once these had taken place, the loser would have no option but to turn to violence.

This is not to say, however, that the Centre-Left had turned its back on the democratic process, nor still less that it was devoted to revolution *per se*. Whilst some of the militants who took up arms in October 1934 may have been fighting for the new Jerusalem, Largo and Companys were clearly reluctant rebels whose only concern was to force Alcalá Zamora to call new elections. As for charges that they were acting in defiance of the will of the electorate and trying to throw out a government whose only crime was that it was conservative rather than reformist, this is so much dross: not only did the elections of November 1933 prove nothing at all, but the CEDA was bent on overthrowing democracy and wreaking the most terrible vengeance against all those who had in any way offended the interests that it represented. If Lerroux really was dreaming, as has sometimes been argued, of uniting centrist opinion – the right of the PSOE, the successors of Acción Republicana and the Radical Social-ists, and the Radicals – in a great coalition that could alternate in power with the CEDA, then he was living in a fool's paradise.

Darkness

If, as is sometimes claimed, October 1934 killed the hopes of Gil Robles that he could secure power by legal means, then he was not aware of it. With the Left in disarray, the chances of success in fact seemed greater than ever, and all the more so as thousands of voters who had hitherto supported the Radicals were persuaded by the horror stories emanating from Asturias to switch to the CEDA. Eager to accelerate this develop-ment, Gil Robles lambasted the Radicals for their supposed weakness in tackling the revolution, continued to use the most strident rhetoric, and did nothing to restrain the ever wilder ranting of the *japistas*. At the same time, too, every effort was made to ensure that the government continued to follow a *cedista* agenda, several ministers who were deemed to be too liberal being forced to resign.

With the CEDA in power, meanwhile, Spain was also treated to a display of the realities of its social policy. Ferocious in its denunciation of marxism, liberalism and separatism, the CEDA's rhetoric had also exu-ded a more positive note based on the principles of Social Catholicism. Thus, the selfishness of the propertied classes was regularly denounced and much reference made to the need to ensure the right to work, encourage the extension of smallholding, and protect the rights of the tenant farmer. With the Ministries of Agriculture and Labour both amongst the three posts taken up by the CEDA, it was now ideally placed to put its ideas into practice, but nothing of any substance transpired. The CEDA's first Minister of Agriculture, Manuel Giménez Fernández – an attractive figure who was perhaps the only man in the entire CEDA who took its rhetoric seriously in this respect – was absolutely committed to the principles of Social Catholicism, true enough, the few months for which he was in office seeing him, first, extend the tenure of the temporary settlers of the autumn of 1932; second, seek to introduce a new lease law; and, third, attempt to accelerate the progress of agrarian reform by making more land available to such groups as the *yunteros*. However, labelled the 'white Bolshevik', Giménez Fernández was impeded at every turn, the measures that he espoused being either shelved or amended beyond all recognition. If all this was not bad enough, meanwhile, the Minister of Labour, José Oriol Anguera de Sojo, proceeded effectively to wreck the system of mixed juries by packing them with officials of such organizations as the CEDA's own Acción Obrerista, the result being that wages continued to plunge dramatically.

For a variety of reasons, even the rhetoric of reform was soon set aside. Not only were many of his followers chafing at the bit, but the immensely personable José Antonio Primo de Rivera was offering Gil Robles' followers the possibility of immediate victory. Even more troublingly in view of the manner in which they had extended their influence far beyond their traditional heartlands, the Carlists had recently ousted their relatively prudent leadership in favour of a much tougher group that did not intend just to pay lip service to insurrection, but actually to put the policy into practice. Still worse in some ways, meanwhile, were the activities of the dictatorship's erstwhile Minister of Finance, José Calvo Sotelo. A deputy of RE and very much its *eminence gris*, he was now putting himself forward as the leader of a kind of super-CEDA – a *bloque hispano-nacional* – that would unite the entire Right in a grand alliance. Increasingly concerned, early in 1935 Gil Robles therefore provoked a reshuffle of which the upshot was the departure of Giménez Fernández, an increase in the number of CEDA ministers from three to five, and his own entrance into the cabinet as Minister of War.

With Social Catholicism in full retreat, the counter-revolution proceeded to accelerate still further. Nowhere was this development more visible than in the countryside. Thus, Giménez Fernández's law on rural leases contained a loophole which permitted landlords to rid themselves of virtually any tenant on the pretext that they henceforward intended to cultivate the land themselves. This, needless to say, was now exploited to the full, the new Minister of Agriculture refusing pointblank to check such excesses. In Extremadura and New Castile, meanwhile, the squatters who had been granted an extension in their tenure by Giménez Fernández were all thrown off the land. At the same time, whilst land redistribution was not halted altogether, a new law of Agrarian Reform was put through that effectively rendered its predecessor null and void.

Whilst further restricting the progress of agrarian reform, the CEDA also blocked changes in other areas. Of these the most important was that of finance. Thus, determined to do something to ameliorate the Republic's fiscal situation, Lerroux appointed the noted *albista* banker, Joaquín Chapaprieta, Minister of Finance, and ordered him to produce a plan of reform. For the most part the resultant document proposed a mixture of financial retrenchment, greater efficiency and a reduction in the national debt, but it also spoke of reducing fraud and tax evasion. The result, of course, was a storm of protest, the Right denying that there was any problem in this respect and insisting that Chapaprieta's targets should be met entirely by cuts in expenditure. As such institutions as the army and the Guardia Civil were 'ring-fenced', moreover, the brunt of the burden was allowed to fall on education, health, poor relief and agrarian reform – the construction of new state schools was virtually halted, for example, another casualty being the state-sponsored travelling art exhibitions and dramatic ensembles that had been established in the course of the reformist *bienio* in an attempt to bring a little culture to the more remote parts of the country. Also badly hit, meanwhile, were the lower ranks of the civil service which saw not only reductions in pay but also many redundancies, these job cuts having the added advantage of facilitating a purge of the numerous fresh appointments that had been made in the period 1931–3 in an attempt to republicanize the administration.

If all this added to the anger of the Left and Centre, the most alarming feature of the new government was undoubtedly Gil Robles himself. Having insisted that he be appointed Minister of War, he immediately applied himself to securing the full support of the army. Thus, many of Azaña's reforms were significantly revised, whilst money was found to speed up the production of munitions, supply the troops with steel helmets, and buy a number of pieces of medium and heavy artillery (a category of weapon of which the army had hitherto been wholly deficient). Meanwhile, bribery was accompanied by reorganization: whilst known counter-revolutionaries were appointed to senior posts – the most notable example is Franco, who was made Chief of the General Staff – liberals and leftists were shifted to less sensitive jobs or placed on the list of supernumeraries. Demands were also made for the *civiles* and *asaltos* to be placed under the authority of the Ministry of War rather than that of the Interior, but in this respect Gil Robles was unsuccessful, even Lerroux being unable to stomach the concentration of so much power in the hands of a man who was so clearly equivocal in his views of the Republic.

In September 1935 Lerroux embarked upon a cabinet reshuffle

demanded by plans to save money by combining a number of ministries, but this caused such ructions that he had to step down in favour of Chapaprieta. Retaining the Ministry of Finance in his own hands, the latter proceeded to form a new cabinet consisting, apart from himself, of three Radicals, three *cedistas*, one *lligista* and one Agrarian (Lerroux was compensated for his demotion with the Ministry of Foreign Affairs). With Gil Robles still in command at the Ministry of War, a general process of reaction well underway, and yet another moderate – the respected Manuel Portela Valladares – excluded from the cabinet, all seemed rosy in the CEDA's garden.

In fact, however, serious trouble was brewing. Pride of place in this respect is often given to the successive scandals that proceeded to rock the Radical Party in the form of the so-called *straperlo* and Nombela affairs. Peripherally implicated in both of these issues, Lerroux was forced to resign from the cabinet, but in itself this was not a real problem, there being no reason why the Centre–Right alliance should not have served out its electoral mandate. What really provoked the crisis that erupted in the winter of 1935, by contrast, was rather the fact that, impelled by pressure from below, Gil Robles decided that the time had come to seize supreme power, the obvious weapon to hand in this respect being the new budget that was about to be introduced by Chapaprieta. Containing as it did a number of tax increases to which the Right objected very strongly, the CEDA therefore effectively talked it out. As Gil Robles had planned, on 9 December Chapaprieta resigned in disgust, but at this point things began to go wrong. Convinced that the Republic of April 1931 was in real danger, Alcalá Zamora rejected Gil Robles' demands that he be granted the power to form an all-CEDA administration that could preside over general elections of his own making, and chose rather the compromise solution of a cabinet headed by Portela Valladares and formed entirely of conservative Republicans. Allowed to function only because the *cortes* was not in session and the CEDA's sympathizers in the *generalato* unwilling to risk a coup, within three weeks this had collapsed on account of its realization that it could not govern without Gil Robles. Portela being left with no option but to secure a dissolution, the fresh elections so much desired by the Left and Centre were finally announced on 30 December.

Towards the Popular Front

Had the political situation been the same as that which prevailed in November 1933, Gil Robles need not have feared this prospect. In the succeeding two years, however, matters had changed dramatically.

Deeply divided in the previous contest, the forces of the Left and Centre had perforce been driven into one another's arms, whilst the anarchists now had a strong interest in securing a friendlier regime. Whilst revolutionary feeling remained very strong in parts of the Left, a working alliance was therefore established that ensured that the forthcoming elections would at least be fought on reasonably equal terms. To understand the origins of this unity we need to return to the aftermath of October 1934. Taking the Centre first of all, there can be no doubt that it was filled with genuine fear. Themselves the object of much persecution, Azaña and Martínez Barrio had therefore soon negotiated an alliance. Recognizing that it was essential that they obtained the support of the Socialists, they also agreed that the left-Republicans should press for an amnesty and adopt a much more positive attitude towards social reform, their message of reconciliation being driven home in a series of mass meetings of which one is reputed to have been the largest in the history of the world.

Obtaining an alliance with the Socialists proved difficult, however. Believing that the Left could neither carry out a revolution, nor win a general election on its own, Prieto was eager to respond to the Republicans' overtures, but many moderates were inclined rather to follow Julián Besteiro in continuing to reject any notion of taking part in a bourgeois cabinet. As for the *caballeristas*, meanwhile, they were continuing to advocate a revolutionary strategy, their views being fuelled by bitter memories of such events as Casas Viejas, and the fact that Asturias had become the centre of a powerful myth that grossly exaggerated the achievements of the revolutionaries. For Largo in particular, however, matters were more complex. Setting aside the fact that his dislike of Prieto made opposing him was almost a matter of principle, the Communists had been doing everything they could to claim the credit for the revolution in Asturias and blame its failure on the Socialists. Backed by the Comintern, they were also able to distribute much aid to the families of the militants who had been imprisoned, the result being that they secured a considerable increase in membership. Still worse, it was becoming clear that, under cover of promoting the establishment of a united front against fascism, they were angling at the *de facto* conquest of the entire Socialist movement. With many left wingers attracted by the notion of a single 'bolshevik' party that could defeat fascism and secure the triumph of the revolution, Largo realized that to play the revolutionary remained essential. Otherwise he stood to lose much support: not only were large parts of the working classes experiencing real misery, but the siren voices of the Communists were being joined by those of both the *pestañistas*, who were now organized into the so-called Syndicalist Party, and the Bloc Obrer i Camperol, which was in the process of merging with another dissident Communist group to form the largely Catalan Partido Obrero de Unificación Marxista.

Had matters been left to run their course it is probable that victory would have gone to the *caballeristas*. However, in the summer of 1935 Stalin's fears of a German attack on Russia led the Communist movement to abandon the revolutionary stance which it had maintained ever since its formation and adopt a policy based on the alliance of all forces of the Left and Centre against fascism. In Spanish terms, this meant that Prieto suddenly gained the support of, first, the Communists, and, then, most of the Socialist Left, the latter being convinced that they had no option but to follow the Communist lead. Suspicious of the Communists and Republicans alike, Largo at first refused to budge, but by early November it was clear that elections could not be far off. Approached by Azaña with a formal proposal for an electoral alliance, the PSOE president was finally forced to agree to negotiations, Izquierda Republicana, Unión Republicana, the PSOE, the UGT, the FJSE, the Communist Party, the Syndicalist Party and the POUM signing the agreement establishing the pact known as the Popular Front on 15 January 1936. A similar deal having been arranged in Catalonia in the form of the Front d'Esquerres, Gil Robles had a real fight on his hands.

Victory and Defeat

The elections of February 1936 are beyond doubt the decisive moment in the history of twentieth-century Spain. Conscious of their importance, the Right certainly threw itself into action with the utmost vigour, its inflammatory propaganda being fuelled by plentiful campaign funds, careful study of the methods of Hitler and Mussolini, and the support of the Catholic Church. Where persuasion failed, meanwhile, coercion and bribery were used instead: intimidation and vote-buying were general, whilst a number of provinces saw alliances with the new Partido Centrista that Portela Valladares had formed from a heterogeneous collection of conservative Republicans in the faint hope of forming an alternative basis for Centre–Right rule that gave the Right access to the full power of the government machine.

Campaign hard though the Right may have done, its efforts were more than matched by the efforts of the Popular Front, whose manifesto centred on the acceleration of social reform, the release of political prisoners, the abolition of all restrictions on trade unions, and the defence of the Republic against fascism. Sometimes face an uphill struggle though it did, the Popular Front enjoyed one important advantage. Whereas in 1933 the anarchists had withdrawn from the electoral process, the situation was now very different. Desperate both to free the thousands of militants who were still in prison and to protect the CNT against further repression, the Anarchists had good reason to support the Popular Front. At the same time, meanwhile, they also reasoned that a confrontation with 'fascism' was now certain, the only question being whether it would take place as a result of a right-wing victory at the polls, or a right-wing coup organized in response to a Popular Front victory. It being preferable to have the extra time implied in the latter option – the CNT, after all, was still all but unarmed – the leadership therefore agreed not to discourage their followers from voting.

Important though the support of the anarchists may have been, still more so was the fact that the Popular Front achieved a measure of unity that far outstripped that of its opponents. Thus, quickly establishing a central committee, it was able to ensure that in no electoral district was the electorate presented with more than a single list of candidates. On the Right, by contrast, hopes of a grand 'National Counter-Revolutionary Front' came to naught, the local representatives of the CEDA, RE and the Carlists therefore being left to make such arrangements as they could, not only with one another, but also with the *portelistas*, Radicals, Agrarians, Liberal Democrats and the followers of Alcalá Zamora and Maura. As neither the PNV nor the Falange would bow to the considerable pressure to which they were subjected to persuade them to ally themselves with the mainstream parties of the Right, unity would never have been total at the best of times, but, even if this failure is set aside, the results were disappointing. Thus, only in eight electoral districts were opponents of the Popular Front offered a single slate of candidates. Variants on the situation were manifold, but the general picture is one of the formation not only of 'official' candidatures, but also of dissident ones made up of groups who had for one reason or another been excluded from the main anti-revolutionary alliance or who felt that they had in some way been cheated of their just deserts. A heterogeneous collection of *centristas*, Radicals, conservative Republicans, die-hard Carlists and Alfonsists, and even dissident *cedistas*, such slates had little chance of picking up many votes, but a very considerable one of ruining the Right's chances of victory.

The conditions under which the contest was fought make it quite impossible to draw any safe conclusions from the results which came in after the polls closed on 16 February. All that is really clear is that the Popular Front won a solid victory, and that it did so because it had regained not only the unity which the Left and Centre had lost in 1933, but also the support of the anarchists. What is more it did so in conditions which make it difficult to argue that the Right had somehow been cheated of victory. The scale of the latter's defeat was somewhat accentuated in the course of the days that succeeded 16 February by a certain degree of fraud: as the electoral results were not formally scrutinized for four days, the triumphant forces of the Left were in a number of places able to indulge in a bit of ballot-stuffing of their own, whilst the second round of voting necessary in those electoral districts which had not produced a clear result on 16 February was held under the aegis of the new administration. Much the same is true, meanwhile, of the long debates held by the new assembly as to the validity of the credentials of those members who had eventually been challenged in the aftermath of the elections. However, the importance of these factors has been greatly over-stated – run-off elections were only necessary in five constituencies, for example, and changes in the deputies elected in another ten. Thanks to the Republic's curious electoral system, of course, the Popular Front received far more seats than its probable share of the vote suggested should theoretically be the case, but this was but just compensation for the wholesale efforts of the Right to interfere in the electoral process. Given that perhaps 500,000 of the Right's votes went either to the PNV or to conservative Republicans and the like, the Popular Front had probably secured a remarkable triumph (for the record, the Popular Front and Front d'Esquerres were eventually accorded 271 seats, the CEDA eighty-six, RE and the Carlists twenty-two, other conservatives and members of the Centre-Right sixty, and the PNV nine).

Whatever the precise result, the Right was horrified. Victory had been assumed to be certain, whilst its rhetoric had been so violent that there was a general feeling that apocalypse was nigh. The result was pandemonium. Still Chief of the General Staff, General Franco was convinced that the Popular Front was a creature of the Comintern designed to bolshevize Spain by the back door, and at the request of Gil Robles he at once sought to get Portela Valladares to agree to stay in power and declare a state of war. Unsuccessful in this respect, Franco actually tried to organize a revolt, but the considerable support that he received was insufficient to persuade him that success was likely, the result being that in the late afternoon of 19 February 1936 power passed into the hands of a somewhat reluctant Manuel Azaña (according to normal practice, Portela Valladares should not have resigned immediately, but instead waited until he lost the inevitable vote of confidence in the *cortes*).

Pre-guerra

In view of the terror that gripped the Right, it is somewhat ironic to note that the government that now assumed power did not contain a single Leftist of any sort. Whilst Prieto continued to favour PSOE participation in the cabinet, Largo's attitude was very different. Determined never again to share power with bourgeois liberals and convinced that Prieto was motivated by little other than vanity and ambition, so far as he was concerned the Popular Front had been little more than an electoral pact whose victory had been very largely brought about by the labours of the PSOE, and, in particular, himself. The ninety Socialist deputies would support the government in its implementation of the programme agreed prior to the elections, true, but they would not seek any representation in its ranks. Instead, the PSOE would wait until the government had worn itself out and then capitalize on the consequent disillusion of the working classes to form an all-Socialist administration, presumably through the medium of fresh elections. In the meantime, rather than joining the cabinet, Largo Caballero would concentrate on prosecuting the feud that had erupted with Prieto in the course of the negotiations that had led to the formation of the Popular Front (determined to 'bolshevize' the PSOE, Largo and several of his followers had resigned from its executive in the hope of forcing elections that would drive out the *prietistas*). This happy scheme might well, of course, be disrupted by some sort of right-wing coup, but this prospect did not dismay Largo at all: his head being filled with misty images of October 1934, he was convinced that the working classes would be more than a match for any such attack. Despite the fact that the resignation of the *caballeristas* had left him in full control of the party (the *besteiristas* had long since lost what little influence they had ever possessed), Prieto knew full well that he could not force his policy through in the face of Largo's opposition – the latter, after all, remained solidly entrenched in the UGT, whilst his followers dominated the FJSE and had a substantial degree of influence in the party. Even had this not been the case, moreover, neither Azaña nor Martínez Barrio desired the participation of the Socialists in the government, and to this end had ensured that the latter were given a share in the Popular Front's electoral lists that bore little relation to the actual strength of their support. In consequence the new cabinet was drawn entirely from Izquierda and Unión Republicana, the former having nine seats and the latter three.

It has often been argued that the failure of the Socialists to join the government was fatal to the Popular Front's survival. This, however, is a moot point. Whilst it is possible that Prieto would have brought greater energy and decision to the administration, and, further, that reform would have been speeded up, the presence of Socialists in the government would without any doubt have facilitated the organization of a coup whilst stripping the government of much of the considerable military support which it as yet retained. As a coup was coming anyway, the only difference that their presence could have made related to the chances of stifling the rebellion at birth, in which respect it is unlikely to have made much of a difference, the whole issue being really only of secondary importance.

That a coup was coming there can be no doubt, the Right not only refusing to accept the legitimacy of its defeat but also being gripped by collective panic. Whilst large numbers of the rich fled the country, the supporters of the CEDA began either to form their own militias or to transfer their support to an exultant and belligerent Falange (the switch could just as easily have been to the Carlists, but fascism was very much *a la moda*). With much support also coming in from the followers of RE, the tiny force that the Falange had constituted in February 1936 therefore experienced a period of rapid growth. Also helpful, meanwhile, was a considerable increase in the amount of financial support that it had been receiving from wealthy members of the oligarchy. So badly hit was RE by all this that it was forced virtually to dissolve itself, whilst it soon became clear that the CEDA was only awaiting a coup to go the same way.

If the Falange and the Carlists were growing in appeal, it was because they were overtly determined to overthrow the regime. However, given that neither movement was likely to be able to achieve anything on its own, the decisive question remained the attitude of the army. In so far as this body was concerned, indeed, preparations for a coup had already begun. Thus, at a meeting that took place in Madrid on 8 March attended by such generals as Franco, Fanjul and Mola, it had been agreed that a revolt should be organized under the titular leadership of General Sanjurjo, who was living in exile in Lisbon. Other than that, however, no details were settled, those present in consequence embarking on two quite different schemes. Thus, whilst Fanjul began work on an old-style *pronunciamiento* in Madrid, the much more reflective General Mola set about forming a broader movement that would draw in every garrison in the Peninsula, the Army of Africa, the Falange and the Carlists.

Whatever the government did, then, it faced the near certainty of a rising, the only question now being the latter's chances of success in which respect the crucial issue was above all the attitude of the armed forces and police as a whole. In so far as this was concerned, there was still a great deal to play for. Since the revolt in Asturias, the strength of the UME had grown enormously, whilst a variety of links had been established between disaffected elements of the officer corps and the more militant elements of the Right. That said, however, there was still a long way to go before the bulk of the armed forces could be depended on in the event of a coup – hence the failure of the attempt to annul the elections by force of arms. Much, then, depended on the events of the next few months, the great tragedy for the Republic being that almost everything conspired to make matters as black as possible.

Well to the fore in this respect were the activities of the working classes and their representatives. No sooner had the results started to come in, in fact, than a variety of groups began to vent their desire for revenge.

Churches, police posts, prisons and party offices were attacked, and landowners and industrialists threatened or intimidated, whilst excited street demonstrations were legion. Having been radicalized not just by repression but months of heavy rain that had brought work to a stand-still, latifundist Spain went up in flames. Thus, strikes and land occupations quickly became widespread, whilst the *braceros* in many cases simply requisitioned crops, animals and agricultural implements, or forced the great estates to give them work, frantic attempts at resistance by the owners, who had themselves been hard-hit by the downpours, only making matters worse. Whilst all this was going on in the country-side, meanwhile, every other sector of the economy was also coming under serious pressure. Thus, thanks in part to spiralling unemployment – the period January–June saw the number of workers who had been laid off in Catalonia rise by one-third, for example – strikes abounded on all sides. And in town and country alike, the atmosphere grew ever more violent: carried away by euphoria, the workers adopted an attitude that was as menacing as it was provocative, whilst at the same time launching a determined assault on such groups as Catholic trade unions.

If matters on the ground were distinctly volatile, the situation was not helped by the workers' leaders. Within the CNT, for example, the total failure of the insurrectionary tactics of 1931–3 had not affected the dominance of the FAI in the slightest, the result being that the CNT congress that was organized following the victory of the Popular Front not only effectively committed it to an anarchist revolution, but for good measure declared its goal to be the collectivization of the land and the establishment of libertarian communism. Also agreed was the formation of an armed militia, but significantly enough the *raison d'être* of this force was declared to be the defence of the CNT against reaction, the fact being that the FAI had no plans actually for proceeding to a revolution which even the most extreme *faistas* now recognized would be futile.

If the position of the anarchist leadership is at least understandable, that of the Socialists, or, at least, the *caballeristas*, is downright culpable. Whilst glorying in his nickname of 'the Spanish Lenin', employing the most violent rhetoric and engaging in a ferocious struggle with Prieto for control of the PSOE, Largo in fact had no desire to turn his words into reality. Thus, not only did he reject proposals emanating from the POUM – the only left-wing movement genuinely in favour of overthrowing bourgeois democracy in the spring of 1936 – for an immediate revolu-tion, but he also in practice sought to restrain rank-and-file militancy. What he was rather doing was playing politics, his policy being aimed, first, at avoiding the perils of a Spanish 1917 by scaring Azaña into ceding power to the Socialists; second, at protecting the Socialists' power base; and, third, at absorbing the anarchists, Communists and POUM alike.

Needless to say, however, the Right was utterly blind to these nuances, its fears being encouraged by the fact that, whilst the anarchists in effect rejected Largo's blandishments pointblank, the Communists did not. On the contrary, as eager to take over the Socialists as Largo was eager to take over everyone else – they were, after all, still a minority force – they had already merged their trade union movement with the UGT, and now succeeded in persuading the naive and irresponsible leaders of the FJSE to join forces with its much smaller Communist counterpart and form a new movement known as the Juventudes Socialistas Unificadas. Catalonia witnessing a similar Socialist–Communist merger in the form of the Partit Socialista Unificat de Catalunya, the Right therefore seemed to have good reason to be frightened.

Calls for a Spanish revolution may have been little more than sound and fury, but they yet created a climate that was highly favourable to the conspirators. In this process, however, the parties and trade unions of the Left were not the only culprits. Whilst all the spokesmen of the Right did everything that they could to paint a picture of a Spain that was on the brink of the abyss, the Falange in particular had immediately launched a campaign of terror that could not but encourage a military coup. Beyond the ranks of the Falange, meanwhile, an attempt was made to revive the Sindicato Libre, the gunmen which these employed only adding to the general mayhem. With the number of terrorist incidents escalating by the day – for the Left responded with many shootings of their own, whilst at the same time engaging in occasional bouts of fratricidal strife – more and more officers began to regard the restoration of order as their duty and in consequence pay heed to the UME.

The level of violence was beyond any doubt much exaggerated but it was not the only issue raising tension in the officer corps. Thus, the victory of the Popular Front was a triumph not just for social justice but also regional autonomy. In Catalonia, the Basque country and Galicia, for example, the elections of February 1936 had caused much excitement, whilst demands for autonomy also began to be heard from regions in which it had hitherto had little or no tradition such as Aragón, Old Castile, Asturias, Valencia, the Canaries, the Balearics and Andalucía. Even if some of these may have reflected attempts on the part of local elites to save themselves from a progressive government in Madrid, it therefore really did seem as if the unity of the fatherland was in danger. As for the government, meanwhile, it could easily be accused of collusion. Short of inviting Gil Robles to join the cabinet, outlawing the trade unions, and engaging in wholesale repression, there was probably nothing that it could have done to forestall the coming crisis.

That said, in so far as the Right was concerned, the Popular Front's conduct proceeded to go from bad to worse. Thus, no sooner had it come to power than it released thousands of leftist prisoners; ordered the reinstatement of all those workers who had been dismissed from their jobs in the wake of October 1934; imposed a freeze on the eviction of tenant farmers; rescinded many evictions; resumed control of the estates of those who had been involved in the *sanjurjada*; dismissed the conservative figures who had been appointed to the chair of many mixed juries; reinstated many of the decrees of Largo Caballero; restored the autonomy of the Generalitat; resumed moves towards ratification of the Basque statute; sanctioned a referendum in Galicia (which proceeded to go in favour of autonomy by an overwhelming margin); resumed the wholesale construction of secular schools; and forced the Church to give up its role in teaching. Having thus overturned the *bienio negro*, it also set about extending change still further. In the countryside, for example, the Civil Guard was ordered to adopt an attitude of restraint, whilst many land seizures were legitimized. Meanwhile, a series of decrees made much more land available for expropriation and streamlined the organization of the Instituto de Reforma Agraria, whilst from May onwards the *cortes* was presented with a series of new measures that would have reinstated the general lease law lost in 1933, further extended the land available for expropriation, and imposed a surcharge on all major landowners.

Revolution or no revolution, there can be no doubt that this programme inflicted considerable pain on the industrial and land-owning oligarchy – labour costs are estimated to have risen in parts of the south by as much as 300 per cent, whilst the Instituto de Reforma Agraria distributed more land in the period March–July 1936 than in the whole of its previous history. Insult was added to injury, meanwhile, by the fact that the Republic served notice that it had no intention of ignoring right-wing destabilization. Thus, the Falange was banned and the Carlists and the JAP subjected to the strictest surveillance, the many arrests that followed including that of José Antonio, whilst an end was made of the indiscriminate issue of firearms licences to Rightists that had characterized the *bienio negro*, and tight restrictions imposed on the export of currency.

If the government adopted a firm line with regard to the Right, it was no less vigilant with regard to the army. Mistakes were made, certainly, a good example being the dispatch of Mola to the Carlist stronghold of Pamplona, but all the key posts in the military hierarchy were given to men whose politics were believed to be beyond reproach, whilst known malcontents were placed under surveillance and either left without a command or packed off to remote outposts in which they could do little harm (thus, Fanjul found himself out of work, Franco in the Canaries, and Goded in the Balearics). News of Fanjul's plot soon reaching the authorities, moreover, most of the ringleaders were arrested and a

number of other officers transferred to other posts or suspended altogether. Beyond that, however, little could be done other than to praise the
army's loyalty in the hope of winning it over through sheer flattery.

Of this, however, there was little hope: with the officer corps being
widely accused of cowardice by the Right, the Left making serious
attempts to subvert the loyalty of the rank and file, such senior officers as
López de Ochoa being arrested for nothing more than the fact that they
had helped to suppress the Asturian rising, and all that the military held
dear seemingly in very real danger, even the free-thinking freemasons,
Queipo de Llano and Cabanellas (commanders, respectively, of the
border guards and the Zaragoza military district) both began to toy with
the idea of a coup. Indeed, by the end of March alone, the UME had
probably secured the support of something like half the officers on the
active list, not to mention another 1,800 who were either in the reserve or
had retired altogether.

With matters in this state there occurred a political crisis that is often
argued to have been decisive in settling the fate of the Republic. Alcalá
Zamora being universally distrusted, it was a matter of common consent
that he should be removed, and on 7 April he was therefore voted out of
office. Azaña being elected president in his stead, the intention was that
the premiership should now go to Prieto, but such a move was blocked by
the *caballeristas*, and the scheme therefore proved a non-starter. However, why this has always been the subject of such lamentation amongst
historians sympathetic to the cause of the Second Republic is something
of a puzzle. That Prieto intended to accelerate reform there is no doubt –
amongst other things he intended to reduce the power of the Guardia
Civil – but he was so hated by the Left that his chances of calming the
working classes were very slim. As for the Right, it regarded him with just
as much loathing as Largo or Azaña, whilst the implementation of his
plan to reform the *civiles* would have hastened the coup and driven even
more officers into the insurrectionary camp than would otherwise have
been the case. With Prieto himself a diabetic who was subject to fits of
depression, the idea that he might somehow have rescued the Republic
appears far-fetched indeed.

Although the accession of Azaña to the presidency may have helped
inflame tensions on the Right, the whole affair is little more than an
irrelevance. For all that Santiago Casares Quiroga – the *azañista* who
actually became prime minister – was a sick man of mediocre ability, by
May 1936 not only was a coup certain, but the sort of vigorous action
whose want is so often criticized would have been counter-productive. As
an example, arming the workers would simply have stoked the fires of
labour unrest and alienated many of those officers who as yet remained
aloof from the conspiracy, whilst doing little to increase the regime's

chances of survival (as Astarias had shown, even the most determined and well-armed workers could not prevail unaided). By the same token, the government could only take action against those officers whose conduct was too overt to ignore, in which respect Casares Quiroga was in fact no less vigilant than Azaña, investigating a number of officers in the Foreign Legion, raiding Mola's headquarters and launching a series of arms searches in Navarre.

Such actions making little difference other than further to inflame feelings in the army, the movement to overthrow the Popular Front gathered pace by the day. With the humiliation of Fanjul and the so-called 'junta of generals' which he had established in Madrid, the focal point was now very much the tall and bespectacled figure of Emilio Mola. A prominent *africanista* who had published a highly critical analysis of Azaña's reforms, with the help of the UME 'the director' had no difficulty in securing the support of the Army of Africa, winning over adherents in every garrison in the Peninsula, and making contact with the Right. Getting the support of the Carlists and the Falange proved harder than expected – both tried to insist on a variety of guarantees – but eventually they were lined up with the conspiracy, considerable support for which was also obtained from what was left of both the CEDA and RE. Within the ranks of the army the cautious Franco remained aloof, but Mola did gain the support of Queipo de Llano and Cabanellas, both of whom had been much alarmed by the removal of Alcalá Zamora.

So what, then, was agreed? In military terms the plan was simple. In brief, the garrisons of metropolitan Spain's eight military districts, Morocco, the Canaries and the Balearics were all to rise simultaneously with the support of the police, the rest of the armed forces, the Carlists, the Falange and such other armed civilians as might rally to the cause, the general expectation being that the fighting would be over in a matter of hours. In political terms, however, matters were more difficult. Whereas the generals and the UME – who were, after all, very much a mixed bag – wanted to keep the objective as vague as possible so as to maximize military support for the coup, the Carlists, Alfonsists and Falangists all wanted to impose their own ideas on the movement, still more difficulties being thrown up by such questions as the relationship of the party militias with the military command. The generals themselves being deeply divided as to what they wanted, there was eventually no option but to resort to the vaguest of compromises, all that was agreed being that Sanjurjo would head a 1923-style 'directory' that would restore order and suppress the forces of the Left and Centre.

By the beginning of July Mola judged that the movement was as ready as it was ever likely to be. If Franco still remained on the sidelines, it was assumed that the outbreak of a rising would force him to throw in his lot with the rebels, to which end a British plane had been chartered to pick up the general from the Canaries and get him to Morocco to take command of the Army of Africa. Apart from Mola, Goded, Queipo de Llano and Cabanellas, few senior officers were actively committed to the coup, but so many of the middle and junior ranks could be relied upon that it was assumed that any die-hards would quickly be overthrown. The leadership of the Carlists in particular were proving remarkably stubborn in adhering to their proscriptions for the aftermath of the coup, but there were encouraging signs that the rank and file would rally to the army come what may, the Carlist organization in Navarre being in a state of open revolt on the issue. As for José Antonio, meanwhile, so far was he from insisting on a falangist revolution that he was now castigating Mola for procrastination (for various reasons, target dates of 30 June, and 10 July had had successively to be abandoned).

In reality, however, matters were very far from being cut and dried. In many garrisons it was by no means clear that revolt was certain, many officers remaining either an unknown quantity or absolutely loyal to the government, whilst attempts were being mounted to infiltrate the UME and establish a rival Unión Militar de Republicanos Anti-Fascistas. Communications within the conspiracy were also problematic, there being no guarantee either that all its members would act on cue or that one element or another would not launch some premature strike that would jeopardize the whole edifice. As for the various right-wing militias, they remained ill-armed and poorly trained. For the ever-cautious Franco, all this was simply too much, and all the more so as he was less aware of the deficiencies of the workers' militias than many of his fellows, the result being that on 12 July he informed Mola that he would not be joining the insurgents. Absolutely furious, Mola asked Sanjurjo to take Franco's place at the head of the Army of Africa, but privately he was in despair: without 'Miss Canary Isles', as he scornfully called him, the rebellion was unlikely to get anywhere.

Even at this late stage, then, there was no guarantee that a rising would not simply have fizzled out in the same manner as the *sanjurjada*. What changed this situation were the events of the night of 12–13 July. From their seats in the *cortes* Calvo Sotelo and Gil Robles had for weeks been whipping up hostility to the Popular Front. Exaggerated in the extreme, their language had provoked angry protests, and it was not long before Calvo Sotelo paid the price. On 12 July the spiral of assassinations and counter-assassinations that had been raging ever since the elections claimed a fresh victim in the person of a leftist captain of the *asaltos* named José Castillo. The second such officer to die in this fashion in a matter of days, his co-religionists at the barracks at which he was stationed were incensed. Assembling a number of JSU gunmen, they eventually resolved on the murder of either Gil Robles or Calvo Sotelo. The former chancing not to be at home, the latter was taken from his flat, shot in the back of the head, and dumped at the gates of one of Madrid's largest cemeteries.

Long cited by apologists of the military rising as the last straw that led to rebellion, the murder of Calvo Sotelo was obviously no such thing. That said, however, so shocking were the circumstances of his death that many officers who had previously remained loyal, or, at least, uncommitted, now became convinced that action was indeed necessary. Amongst them was a terrified Franco, who was convinced that such a fate could befall him too and in consequence promised Mola his full support. Realizing that it was now or never, Mola responded by ordering his forces to go into action on 18 July. In the meantime, much of Spain was in uproar: not only were the funerals of Castillo and Calvo Sotelo accompanied by massive demonstrations and yet more violence, but Gil Robles made an inflammatory speech in which he laid the blame for all Spain's ills on the government, asserted that democracy had completely broken down, and announced that Spain could expect her liberation forthwith. Warned that trouble was afoot in Morocco in particular, on 17 July Casares Quiroga ordered a number of the destroyers stationed at Cartagena to take post in the Straits of Gibraltar and instructed the commander of the Spanish forces at Melilla to arrest a number of his subordinates. The latter, however, were too quick for him: mobilizing a number of troops, they kidnapped the general concerned – Manuel Romerales quinto – proclaimed Franco commander of the Army of Africa, declared martial law, instigated a general round-up of all known liberals and leftists, and occupied all the key public buildings and military installations. Within a few hours, moreover, their example had been followed by all the other garrisons in the protectorate. In an alliance that was to be typical of the next few days, the local representatives of the airforce, the *asaltos*, and the trade unions fought back bravely, but by dawn on 18 July it was all over. Though nobody realized it as yet, the first battle of the Spanish Civil War had been fought and won.

The Gates of Hell

As the last few shots sputtered in Melilla in the small hours of 18 July 1936, Spain hovered on the very brink of catastrophe, there being three possible outcomes of the situation that had now emerged. The first, of course, was that the rising might achieve the rapid, total and uncompromising effect that had been achieved in Melilla (within a matter of hours Romerales, the mayor, the acting high commissioner of Morocco, and a variety of officers, officials, policemen, trade unionists and political militants of one sort or another had all been shot). The second, meanwhile, was that the rising would go off at half-cock and quickly fall apart. As for the third, and by far the most terrible, Spain might end up divided into two armed camps that would have no option but to fight it out in a prolonged civil war. To the surprise of almost all concerned, it was this last option which prevailed: far from being settled in a few days, the conflict was to drag on for almost one thousand.

Given the efforts that had been made to subvert the armed forces and the police since February 1936, the advantages which the Right had enjoyed in organizing its civilian volunteers, and the utter inadequacy of the various left-wing militias, even the very best of whom were untrained, few in number, and armed with nothing other than a handful of pistols, shotguns and sticks of dynamite, this might at first sight seem somewhat surprising. However, a number of factors rendered complete success extremely unlikely. Setting aside the fact that the Falangist and Carlist militias were themselves less than spectacular as a fighting force – having seen its role mainly in terms of street fighting, for example, the former had never really sought much in the way of military training – not even the fate of Calvo Sotelo was enough to render rebellion universal. Committed Communists, Socialists or even *azañistas* might have been relatively few and far between in the armed forces as a whole, but the air force was imbued with a strongly progressive tradition; the navy possessed of a lower deck radicalized enough to challenge the lead of a largely rebellious officer corps; and the army deeply divided, the preponderance of *africanismo* amongst the conspirators being inclined to ensure the loyalty of many *junteros*, gunners and engineers.

As some of the conspirators knew all too well, in fact, the strategy that they had been pursuing since February 1936 had been as much of a failure as anything propounded by Gil Robles. Tragically for Spain, however, if too few officers had been won over to the rebellion to guarantee victory, enough had joined it to stave off defeat. If this was the case, it was largely the fault of the Spanish Left, the latter having done everything it could to play into the hands of the conspirators. By advocating – or in many cases pretending to advocate – revolution, they had done nothing to curb the understandable excitement that had swept the working classes in the wake of the Popular Front's victory, whilst in effect fighting the battles of the Right. In defence of their actions, it is certainly possible to argue that they greatly strengthened popular resistance to the coup. The trouble with such arguments, however, is the fact that they ignore not only the greater impetus that was given to the conspirators by the revolutionary threat, but also the absolute inability of the people to prevail against them except when they fought in the company of elements of the armed forces. In short, Spain was about to be plunged into a holocaust for which the responsibility lies first with the Right's refusal to accept even a modicum of reform; second, the posturing and hegemonism that characterized the Spanish labour movement; and only third the failings of the unfortunate Republican politicians who have been so excoriated by apologists of the Left and Right alike.

16

The Republic Overthrown

The Great Paradox

The uprising of 17 July 1936 ushered a great irony. Thus, although the rebels were to claim that they had risen to prevent revolution, few sections of the Left were actively committed to a revolution, and even fewer were possessed of much chance of success. In the aftermath of the rising, however, matters were very different, those areas of the country where the rising had failed seeing doors open that had hitherto been barred. Long postponed, a Leftist assault on the glaring inequities of Spanish society therefore finally began, the only problem being that it did so in circumstances in which it was both unlikely to prevail and all but certain to wreck the hopes of the reformist cause as a whole.

The Longest Weekend

Premature though it may have been, the Moroccan revolt was soon seconded elsewhere. At dawn on Saturday 18 July Franco declared martial law in the Canary Islands, and set off by air for Morocco. In Córdoba, Cádiz, Algeciras and Jérez, too, the army, Guardia Civil, Carlists and Falange joined the rising and quickly took control. Resistance was often fierce, however – the *asaltos* on the whole stayed loyal – and in Málaga a rising by some junior officers was defeated altogether, whilst Seville was only secured due to the fact that Queipo de Llano succeeded in single-handedly deposing the Captain General and persuading the garrison and the police to follow his lead, the gallant fight put up by some of the city's workers making no difference whatsoever.

What, meanwhile, was the response of the government? Deciding, quite rightly, first, that arming the workers would provoke insurrection throughout the country; second, that such a decision would lead to revolution; and, third, that it would not even guarantee the defeat of the rebels, Casares Quiroga refused to do anything of the sort. Instead, no sooner had news of the Melilla revolt broken, than frantic efforts were made to confine the rebellion to Morocco, maintain order amongst the populace, and overawe the Army of Africa through aerial and naval bombardment. Meanwhile, the navy's battle squadron was sent from El Ferrol to join the warships already dispatched to the Moroccan coast. As the rising spread, moreover, the commanders involved were declared to have been dismissed and their soldiers ordered not to obey them, whilst troops were mobilized to restore order and a number of known malcontents placed under arrest.

By midnight on 18 July, however, it had become all too clear that this strategy had failed, Casares Quiroga therefore quickly resigning in favour of the moderate Martínez Barrio, the aim now being some sort of accommodation with the rebels through the formation of a centrist government of some sort. However, in the early morning of Sunday 19 July the garrisons of Barcelona, Gijón, Oviedo, Albacete, Toledo, Guadalajara, Caceres, Salamanca, Segovia, Avila, Zamora, Palencia, Valladolid, Burgos, Vitoria, San Sebastián, Pamplona, Zaragoza, Huesca, Jaca, Teruel, Valencia, Ibiza and Majorca all rebelled, this example being followed by some forces in Madrid and the officers of most of the ships in the navy. As before, however, the rebels found that victory was not going to be easy. It being high summer, many soldiers were on leave, the result being that everything hung on the *asaltos* and *civiles*. Wherever these joined the uprising, all was well, but elsewhere the rebels faced a difficult task that was not made any easier by the fact that Martínez Barrio had now been left with no option but to arm the people (to the extent that he could: in those places where the military and police were solidly in favour of the rebellion, of course, no arms were forthcoming). How great a difference this actually made is a moot point, but in Barcelona the columns of troops who tried to take over the city were shot to pieces and eventually forced to surrender, the numerous prisoners including General Goded, who had flown to Barcelona to take command. In San Sebastián, Gijón, Madrid, Valencia and Mahón, meanwhile, the rebels were so intimidated that they hastily barricaded themselves into a variety of strongholds to await relief. However, only in Andalucía was there much prospect of help, and even there matters were complicated by the fact that the crews of most of the warships in and around the Straits had overthrown their officers and declared for the government. The sailors proving poor hands at managing a fleet, a few troops from the Army of Africa were got across to Algeciras and Cádiz, whilst such few aircraft as were available were used to fly a handful more to Seville, but even so matters were clearly hanging in the balance.

Hopes of compromise having failed, on the evening of 19 July Martínez Barrio therefore resigned in favour of a new cabinet dedicated to military victory headed by the *azanista*, José Giral. Meanwhile, with their cause in serious trouble, both Franco and Mola decided to seek help from abroad, the obvious place to turn being Hitler and Mussolini. Within a matter of days help was on the way: whilst a number of bomber-transports flew direct to Morocco, a variety of fighters and maintenance supplies were dispatched by sea, along with the requisite mechanics. Meanwhile, similar requests were emanating from Madrid, the Republic having quickly turned to the Popular Front government that had recently been established in France under Léon Blum.

For the next few days, however, the war would have to be waged entirely with such resources as the two sides already had. The result was further stalemate. Thus, 20 July saw León and Granada fall in the face of ineffectual popular resistance, as well as a series of risings in Galicia in defiance of the military authorities, who in this instance had remained firm in their allegiance. Loyal police and workers did what they could, but in this case they quickly succumbed, along with the crews of various ships that had stayed at El Ferrol, all of which had managed to over-whelm their officers. However, risings at Almería and Cartagena were crushed, as were the ones that had taken place the previous day in Mahón and Madrid, whilst the rebels' titular leader, General Sanjurjo, was killed when the plane that had been sent to pick him up from Portugal crashed on take-off.

After three days of fighting, in short, the honours remained about even. The situation was as yet very confused, but the rising may be said to have triumphed in Morocco, western Andalucía, Galicia, northern Extrem-adura, Old Castile, Navarre and Aragón. A number of isolated strongholds aside, meanwhile, the Cantabrian littoral, Catalonia, the Levante, New Castile, southern Extremadura and eastern Andalucía were all in the hands of the government, along with the cities of Madrid, Barcelona, Bilbao and Valencia. So much for the geographical division of Spain, but what did all this mean in terms of resources? In brief, the government had the majority of the population, the enormous gold reserves of the Bank of Spain, and the bulk of Spain's manufacturing industry, mineral resources and export crops, the only real advantage that had fallen to the rebels, or, to use their own name, Nationalists, being a rather greater share of the food supply.

All things being equal, then, it appeared that the Republic ought to come out on top if it should come to a long war, though the division of its territory into two separate zones was rather unhelpful. In so far as the short term was concerned, meanwhile, it could boast control of a large preponderance of Spain's 260,000 motor vehicles, 275,000 of her 500,000 rifles and carbines, 1,500 of her 4,500 machine guns, 400 of her 1,000 pieces of artillery, fifty of her sixty-five armoured vehicles, 300 of her 400 naval, military and civil aircraft, and twenty-seven of her thirty-one battleships, cruisers, destroyers and submarines. That said, however, not counting the large numbers of conscripts on summer leave, the rebels had ended up with a notional 91,000 men out of the 159,000 soldiers and policemen who were actually under arms, whilst many of the government's share either could not be counted on – the Guardia Civil concerned often went over to the Nationalists at the first opportunity – or had been shattered in unsuccessful attempts at rebellion. Even if this disparity was offset by the fact that some of the forces in the insurgent zone had been destroyed in attempts to resist the coup, the Republicans had relatively few of the army's combat units, the Nationalist advantage being augmented still further by the support of the veteran Army of Africa. As for officers, the Republic could rely on no more than 2,000 of the 15,400 officers on active service in the army, the air force and the security forces, the majority even of these being older men employed on the staff or in second-line units. In the navy, meanwhile, the situation was still worse: out of 243 officers of the rank of captain and above, no more than twenty-four were still loyal.

To conclude, then, though seriously disadvantaged, the Republic was not defenceless, whilst the Nationalists appeared to be in real trouble. Thus, in northern Spain Mola was desperately short of ammunition and open to attack from several different directions at once, whilst many of the Nationalist enclaves dotted around Republican Spain were undoubtedly open to being overwhelmed. Thanks in large part once again to the Left, however, within a very few days the opportunity had gone beyond recall, the Republic thereafter being committed to a defensive struggle in which it could at best hope to avoid defeat.

The Two Spains

The division of Spain prefigured by the events of the rising had soon more or less been formalized. From Burgos, Pamplona and Seville on the one hand, and Madrid, Barcelona and Bilbao on the other, hastily organized 'columns' of troops, police and militia drove off in the direction of the nearest enemy. At the same time, 'mopping up' operations continued on both sides, the Republicans putting paid to Nationalist outposts in Alcalá de Henares, Guadalajara, Sigüenza, Gijón, Albacete, Valencia, and San Sebastián, and the Nationalists to Republican ones in a host of *pueblos* in Galicia and western Andalucía. Nationalist garrisons still held out in Granada, Oviedo, and the *alcázar* of Toledo – the fortress that dominates the city to this day – but by the end of July the country had been divided into two different zones.

If the front lines remained distinctly permeable, this was just as well given the events that now unfolded. Taking the Nationalists first of all, no sooner had the rebels taken power than they set about the physical extermination of all the forces of progress. Having first summarily executed anyone who had physically opposed them, they immediately proceeded to arrest anyone who was in any way associated with left-republicanism, socialism, anarchism or communism, and very often their families as well, the victims also including many people whose only crime was to fail to meet the social norm. Torture was frequent, conditions intolerable, legal process minimal, and punishment exemplary: lengthy prison sentences were commonplace and execution routine, the number of those who had been shot by the end of 1936 probably amounting to at least 50,000.

Horrific as these events were, they were undoubtedly of great importance in the growing unity that was the second chief characteristic of Nationalist Spain, imbuing it as they did with a strong vested interest in victory at all costs. Even had this not been the case, however, there was little chance of the rebel cause being seriously disrupted by internal disputes. Support for the Falange and the Carlists alike had soared, whilst the military situation had given them much power, but neither force was in any condition to press its views upon the generals, and all the more so as their militias were rapidly losing their autonomy (see below). Even if this had not been the case, the Falange was headed by figures of the second rank – under arrest since March, José Antonio had had the misfortune to be in a prison that ended up in the republican zone whilst Onésimo Redondo had been killed in a skirmish in the first days of the fighting – and the Carlists deeply divided. With both the Falange and the Carlists also becoming more and more diluted by large numbers of erstwhile *cedistas* and Alfonsists and desperate refugees from forces as disparate as the Radicals, the Basque nationalists and the Anarchists, the army was in consequence able to do as it liked.

With power in the hands of the generals, 24 August saw the organization of a six-man military junta under the presidency of the erstwhile republican, Miguel Cabanellas. Meanwhile, the third characteristic of Nationalist Spain was being established by the forthright support that the Catholic Church had almost everywhere lent to the uprising (the only exception was to be found in the Basque provinces). Driven both by a desire to secure the Church's interests in the new Spain and to put an end to its persecution under the Republic, the clergy eulogized the rebellion, invoked divine intervention on its behalf, served with the Nationalist forces as chaplains, and in some cases played an active part in the repression. As for the military authorities, meanwhile, they rushed to welcome the Church's advances. Thus, the local commanders treated the clergy with great respect, attended mass on a regular basis, distributed religious insignia among their men, declared war on blasphemy, imposed a strict moral censorship, and allowed the

Republic's anti-religious legislation to fall by the wayside. With the Carlists and even the Falange happy to fall into line, the Nationalist cause in consequence became a veritable crusade.

At the same time, of course, an effective army was quick to appear. Though arms, uniforms and equipment were initially in short supply, the Nationalists' human resources were mobilized with some effect. Thus, those conscripts who had been on leave were compelled to return to their regiments; large numbers of reservists were called up in accordance with the existing laws of military service; and the thousands of Falangist and Carlist volunteers were formed into regular units commanded by regular officers. All these forces, meanwhile, were given a modicum of training, whilst the greatest efforts were made to ensure that the best possible use was made of the Nationalists' scanty resources (rather than hoarding the copious stocks of ammunition which had been amassed in Morocco, for example, at the earliest possible opportunity Franco sent large quantities of it to Mola, whose reserves were at one point down to less than ten rounds per man). With the labour force subjected to the strictest discipline and the first steps taken in the mobilization of the economy for total war, Nationalist Spain was truly on the march.

In the Republican zone, by contrast, the very opposite was the case. Thus, no sooner had the decision been taken to arm the people – in practice, the various labour movements – than the revolution finally became a reality, the state – and, for that matter, the Generalitat – immediately being supplanted by that of a complex network of local committees whose composition generally reflected the balance of political forces in the towns in which they were established. The result was the utmost confusion. Absolutely chimerical hitherto, for example, the Left's militias now became a reality. Armed with weapons distributed by the government, captured from the insurgents, or simply commandeered from the army and police, thousands of young men and women had soon been enrolled in one or other of the various 'red' militias, and all the more so as the new militiamen were offered the generous wage of ten pesetas a day. Hastily organized into *ad hoc* 'columns', many of them had soon left for the front, but some were kept back by their own leaders, whilst many more were having much too much fun roaring up and down the streets in commandeered cars and trucks, swaggering about draped in bandannas and bandoleers, and flirting with the thousands of young women for whom the war had come as a liberating experience. Thousands of weapons, then, were wasted, whilst the forces who were sent to the front were often armed with a hotch-potch of arms for which it was impossible to find adequate munitions. Artillery pieces, too, were dragged off to the front in ones and twos rather than being massed in larger batteries, whilst the Republic's pool of motor vehicles was squandered by the conversion of hundreds of trucks into improvised armoured vehicles that turned out to be death traps. Wasteful of weapons and *matériel* as they were meanwhile, the militias were also damaging in another sense. Aware that they could get far higher pay in the militia, many soldiers deserted to their ranks. In the same way, when the government tried to start calling up its reservists on 28 July – a move, incidentally, that was greeted with howls of protest from the anarchists – many men chose not to appear.

The seeming reluctance of so many of the militia actually to leave for the front was not helped by a general conviction that the Nationalists were powerless, but the trouble went far deeper than that. Thus, many workers stayed away from work for days or even weeks on end, whilst those who did appear were loud in their demands for higher wages and shorter hours and unregenerate in their absenteeism and pilfering. Equally, recruitment to the militia quickly fell off, whilst fewer and fewer men actually left for the front. Union membership soared, certainly, but attendance at meetings was very low, whilst there was a often marked reluctance to volunteer for auxiliary service. Amongst a hardcore of militants, doubtless, there was enthusiasm aplenty, but otherwise the picture was profoundly depressing.

Revolution was accompanied by terror. With arms distributed wholesale, a savage onslaught against all those who were associated with the *status quo* was inevitable. Nothing like as terrible as was generally claimed by the insurgents, there is no doubt that the situation was quite terrible enough. Setting aside those who were executed at the hands of the state authorities after formal trials – most notably, José Antonio – first to suffer were some of those captured in the aftermath of the fighting, a number of prisoners being massacred in cold blood. However, the killing was not just restricted to those directly involved in the uprising. In most of republican Spain bands of armed men were soon engaging in a reign of terror, whether on a freelance basis or as the private *chekas* of various parties and trade unions. Needless to say, many Catholic schools, convents and places of worship were soon in flames, whilst thousands of priests and religious were seized by the revolutionaries. Any representative of the Right was also fair game, however, as, indeed, was any member of the propertied classes in general. Nor did the humble escape, such victims including Catholic trade unionists and *caciquista* 'trusties'. As in Nationalist Spain, meanwhile, arrest all too often meant death, the numbers of those murdered without trial, executed after the briefest of hearings, or killed in prison massacres provoked by enemy air raids, probably amounted to at least 50,000, including nearly 7,000 priests and religious.

If the 'terror' was greatly exaggerated by the Nationalists – the vast majority of the Republican leadership was dismayed by what was taking place and did its best to restrain the *chekas* – Republican Spain was nevertheless soon in the grip of a genuine social transformation. That said, conditions varied enormously from one region to another. The newspapers, clubs and party offices of the Right were universally requisitioned, along with most large hotels, many ecclesiastical buildings, and the property of those who had supported the insurrection, whilst the churches were closed, but otherwise the situation was at its most extreme in those areas that were dominated by the CNT and the POUM. Thus, in Barcelona, almost every economic activity was collectivized, whilst the city famously acquired an aspect that was uniquely proletarian. In much of Aragón and Andalucía, meanwhile, *latifundios* and smallholdings alike were pooled in large-scale collectives and farmed according to the principles of libertarian communism. In such areas, money was often either abolished altogether or replaced by a system of coupons; wages paid in accordance with family size; the population fed in communal soup-kitchens; craftsmen, mechanics and agricultural specialists forced to work for the collective in exchange for their food; animals, vehicles, implements and machines held in common; and intensive efforts made to politicize the populace. Last but not least, efforts were soon being made to establish the sort of federal organization which the anarchists had always envisaged: in Catalonia, for example, there emerged an 'economic council' whose task was to coordinate the work of Catalan industry, whilst Aragón acquired a *de facto* regional government known as the Consejo de Aragón.

Impressive as this activity was, however, it was by no means replicated throughout Republican Spain. Indeed, even in those areas where the anarchists were strongest, the picture was distinctly patchy. Barcelona, for example, was collectivized, whereas the Catalan countryside was not. Similarly, in the liberated areas of Aragón, collectivization was often limited to the estates of those who had joined the uprising, or to those peasants who were willing to join such schemes voluntarily. Meanwhile, such qualifications are still more apparent elsewhere. In many areas – New Castile, for example – the land was for the most part either divided amongst the peasantry and farmed on a cooperative basis or exploited by the revolutionary authorities on precisely the same basis as before. There were other pockets of extreme revolution – Gijón and Málaga, for example – but these were countered by others that were positively reactionary, a good example being Vizcaya, where the Basque Nationalists did everything that they could to keep social change to a minimum.

If economic change was partial, for many Spanish women the uprising represented a moment of exciting opportunity. Often enjoying far more personal freedom than had been usual, they began to emerge from their customary subservience. All the more was this the case, meanwhile, as the vibrant poster art of Republican Spain frequently adopted female images. On one level, of course, this was a play upon female vulnerability and pathos; on another a metaphor for the heroism of the Spanish people as a whole; and on still another a hint that life at the front would be fun in more senses than one. Nor was the idea even specifically a progressive one, for had not 1808 produced such female heroines as Agustina Aragón? The result is that we should not go too far in this respect. All over Republican Spain women joined the militias, or, more often, flung themselves into a variety of ancillary work, but from the earliest days it was made clear that women were firstly to be 'home-front' heroines. Such stereotyping was allowed to go largely unchallenged even by the handful of women who were prominent in Republican politics, the increasingly famous Communist leader, Dolores Ibarruri, going so far as to decry the very concept of feminism. Very few women actually went to the front, meanwhile, whilst those that did soon found that the treatment that they received in the trenches differed little from that which they received in their home towns. As time passed, moreover, traditional roles reasserted themselves still further, the few women who had reached the trenches eventually being sent home on the pretext that they were infecting many soldiers with venereal disease.

That said, however, the image of the *miliciana* nonetheless remained a liberating one, just as the struggle could not but continue to enhance their position. Thus, women became involved in a wide variety of war work. Most typically, this involved such stereotypical tasks as nursing and the care of soldiers, orphans and refugees, but a minority also became involved in the military administration, the trade unions, the bureaucracy, the civil defence forces, and the machinery of propaganda, the progressive nature of Republican Spain creating openings that were generally absent elsewhere. As a good example, one might cite the Milicias de la Cultura, the latter being a force of volunteers whose task it was to combat illiteracy amongst the common soldiers whilst at the same time boosting their political and cultural awareness. To some extent, there were also fresh opportunities for paid employment, whilst even the domestic round acquired wider horizons given the tough conditions faced by most housewives, feminist historians having argued that the war encouraged a new sense of sisterhood.

If women were becoming more self-conscious, they were also becoming more organized. In some cases this was the product of little more than an attempt to mobilize women as cannon-fodder, the Communist-dominated Asociación de Mujeres Antifascistas being a good example of a woman's organization that remained completely uninterested in the advancement of women *per se*. Rather more interesting is the Anarchist group known as the Mujeres Libres as this not only stemmed from growing resentment amongst female anarchists of the condescension, harassment and derision which they met at the hands of their male colleagues, but was also disowned by the leadership of the CNT, and that despite – or because of – the fact that by 1938 it had acquired a membership of some 30,000. Meanwhile, not only were women becoming more organized, but they were also making genuine conquests. In November 1936 Spain gained her first woman minister in the person of the leading anarchist, Federica Montseny. Appointed to the health portfolio, the new arrival was quick to legalize abortion, though in reality few women seem to have been willing or able to avail themselves of the measure. Rather more important, then, are the real efforts that were made to further female education and training, there being no doubt that the war witnessed a significant fall in female illiteracy.

The March of the Army of Africa

Within a very short time, then, two very different social and political systems had emerged in Spain, of which the first was characterized by central control, political unity and ideological reaction, and the second by their very antithesis. Whatever the merits or demerits of the two Spains, however, what mattered in the summer of 1936 was their ability to measure up to the demands of modern war, in which respect there was – however unfortunately – absolutely no contest. In the immediate aftermath of the uprising, the initiative very much lay with the Republicans. The Nationalist footholds in western Andalucía were too weak to engage in more than the most limited offensive action, whilst the advance on Madrid which was the only attack that Mola had been able to launch had quickly ground to a halt. Temporarily, then, the Republicans were safe from attack, but they proved utterly incapable of making any progress. Thus, in Aragón, Castile and Andalucía alike their columns were checked the moment that they ran into serious resistance. Capable of overwhelming isolated groups of Rightists and Civil Guards, the militias could not make the slightest impression on troops who were properly dug in and willing to put up a fight. In Aragón in particular, meanwhile, the problems were worsened by differences between the POUM, the CNT, and the PSUC, none of which were prepared to cooperate with one another, the result being that Mola was able to hold his ground without difficulty.

In the interior of the Republican zone, the situation was if anything even more embarrassing. Most of the Nationalist supporters that were still holding out in its depths were quickly starved into surrender or overwhelmed, but in Oviedo and Toledo the forces concerned were well-ensconced and possessed of fair stocks of food and munitions. With blatant disregard for their real value, considerable Republican forces had soon been amassed against both these targets, but in neither case was the slightest progress made, and that despite the fact that the defences had soon been reduced to piles of rubble.

Whilst the Republicans were squandering time and resources in this fashion, the balance was tilting ever more heavily against them. Trapped in Morocco, Franco was greatly assisted by the rapid arrival of the thirty bomber-transports that had been dispatched by Hitler and Mussolini. Whilst some of these frightened off the Republican fleet and opened the way for seaborne traffic, the rest flew 12,000 men to Seville. As early as 2 August these measures had allowed the dispatch of two columns of Moors and Foreign Legionaries in the direction of Mola's positions in southern Extremadura. No more than 2,000-strong, supported by only a few light field pieces, and possessed of little air support, the two columns had by 11 August advanced some 100 miles to the town of Mérida. Mola's southernmost troops being only a few miles further on, the Nationalist zone had in consequence been united, but one more matter remained to be effected before Franco's troops could embark upon the advance of Madrid that was the next phase of his plan. Thus, twenty-five miles to the west Badajoz was garrisoned by a considerable enemy force, and on 14 August the Nationalists therefore launched themselves against its walls. Well-protected as they were, the defenders put up a brave fight, but the Foreign Legion were soon inside the city, there following a well-publicized massacre. Whilst all this was going on, meanwhile, other troops from the Army of Africa – again, no more than a few hundred – were occupying the whole of western Andalucía, the village militias who were the only loyalist forces in the area being able to do nothing to impede their progress.

In the space of less than a fortnight, then, at the head of only a few thousand men, Franco had 'liberated' hundreds of square miles of territory, united Nationalist Spain, and relieved Mola, and that despite the fact that he had received comparatively little in the way of foreign aid. Nor did matters get any better for the government. Not only did a variety of factors ensure that French help was limited to a handful of aircraft and a few other arms, but heavy counterattacks in the Córdoba and Mérida sectors alike both proved to be complete failures – the infantry and artillery were poorly coordinated, whilst such airpower as the republicans could muster was wasted in pinprick raids against such towns as Salamanca. Still worse, the government was quite unable to make the best use of its resources: ignoring the increasingly pressing danger on the Madrid front, the Generalitat threw away several thousand men in a futile effort to invade rebel Mallorca.

Whilst the republican war effort was proceeding in this ineffectual fashion, yet more telling blows were reigning down upon it. Thus, whilst an ill-defended Guipúzcoa was overrun by Nationalist forces intent on isolating the Cantabrian littoral from the French border, Oviedo was relieved and Sigüenza recaptured. Once again, no foreign elements were engaged on the Nationalist side other than a few aircraft, whilst the troops involved had on the whole not even come from the Army of Africa. Despite these victories, the north of Spain was hardly the focus of attention. In the Tagus valley the *alcázar* of Toledo was still holding out in a siege which had acquired epic status. More to the point, however, Franco now launched a 'knock-out blow' against Madrid. Advancing across yet more Republican-held territory, by 3 September his troops had reached Talavera. Once again, the campaign was painful to behold. Though no more than 5,000 troops were available, sufficient trucks and buses had been commandeered for the entire force to be motorized, whilst the number of planes that had been received from Germany and Italy had risen to at least ninety. As a result, the much larger Republican forces were repeatedly outflanked, and their counterattacks beaten off with heavy losses. By the end of September, indeed, the Nationalists had relieved Toledo. Some days were lost in this operation – a factor that is often counted as being of some importance – but October saw the Nationalists on the march again, their forces having now received not only many fresh troops, but also a number of German and Italian tanks and close-support weapons. However, progress was now much slower. Much more numerous than their assailants, the defenders had constructed many fortifications, whilst they had also received a number of Russian armoured cars, tanks and aircraft of their own (see below), the latter being used to launch a series of ferocious counterattacks. Nevertheless, by the first week of November the Nationalists had reached the southern outskirts of the capital, the scene now being set for the battle of Madrid.

Behind the Lines

Needless to say, the fighting had a considerable effect on the politics of both sides. Let us begin with the Nationalists. At the beginning of the war, the effective leader of the rebellion had been General Mola (in punishment for his excessive caution, Franco had even been excluded from the junta appointed to head the uprising). Very soon, however, the situation had been transformed. Thus, setting aside his stunning victories, Franco had quickly established a monopoly of German and Italian aid, whilst his known monarchism held far greater appeal than the crypto-republicanism of Queipo de Llano, Cabanellas and Mola, the result being that his fellow generals had no option but to allow his considerable ambition free play. As a result, Franco had no difficulty in having himself elected first commander-in-chief and then premier, the sleight of hand of his friends having within a matter of hours ensured that it was put about that he had actually been made head of state, which role he now simply assumed.

In the Nationalist zone, then, the early autumn saw the emergence of a dictator of a particularly ruthless cast. In its Republican counterpart, by contrast, divisions were intensified. Whilst the regime was given a more proletarian flavour – on 4 September the discredited Giral government gave way to a PSOE-dominated coalition headed by Largo – unity was another matter. Horrified by military defeat and the high profile of the CNT and the POUM alike, Largo was now minded to militarize the militia, restore the authority of the state, and establish a command economy (industrial production had fallen dramatically, whilst the cities were already experiencing severe food shortages). There being no place in any of this for utopian experimentation, the political future looked rocky indeed.

As far as the Socialist left was concerned, Largo's sudden change of heart was little short of treason, and yet there was little that they could do to alter matters. Not only was logic implacably opposed to their continued maximalism, but they were in a minority in the government, the new prime minister being supported by the liberals, the *prietistas*, and, most importantly, the Communists, the PCE regarding the revolution as a complete disaster. So important did this latter force become that we must examine its position in more detail. Very much the weakest of the main proletarian movements in July 1936, the party was threatened with complete eclipse, whilst the Comintern's current line required the very opposite of what was happening. That said, however, it also quickly became apparent that a major opportunity was at hand. Considerable elements of the Republican population being not only opposed to revolution, but deprived of all protection, opposing the revolution would bring the party a mass base, whilst at the same time eliminating the Communists' various rivals on the Left.

By the time that the so-called 'government of victory' was formed in September 1936, the Communists had already secured a considerable degree of success. Losing no opportunity to decry the revolution, proclaim that the war was being fought in defence of democracy, defend the principle of private property, and protect individual peasants and members of the bourgeoisie, the party at the same time made a determined effort to show that military discipline was the key to victory. Entitled the Fifth Regiment, the party militia was therefore from the beginning given the best training possible, dressed in military fashion and placed at the disposition of the high command, the party in the meantime doing everything that it could to talk up the results. At the same time, the Communists also tried hard not to lose their links with the proletariat. Nationalization of all major industries and a greater degree of workers' participation in management were stressed, for example, whilst the Republic of the future was portrayed as a people's state in which democracy was to be accompanied by social justice. By the summer of 1937, the PCE and PSUC could therefore claim 387,000 members. Impressive as this figure was, however, it by no means told the full story, the fact being that the Communists had attracted the support of many figures in the administration and military hierarchy, and were able to use their influence to ensure that their nominees secured a variety of vital positions. Aided by the facts, first, that a variety of 'fellow travellers' in the PSOE could be relied upon to follow the party line at all times, and, second, that Stalin sent not just arms, but also a large number of military advisers, the result was that the Communists came to wield an influence that far outweighed their actual strength.

The conversion of Largo and rise of the Communists were inextricably linked to the Republic's international isolation and shortage of arms. With every advance, the Nationalists were seizing more and more of the weapons that had been inherited from the pre-war army, whilst the production and supply of fresh armaments faced tremendous difficulties. Yet support from outside was minimal. Governed by a regime with strong Republican sympathies, Mexico was doing what little it could to help, true, but Britain and France had adopted a policy of non-intervention, whilst German and Italian aid was now beginning to pour into Nationalist Spain in a positive flood. Determined to increase Communist influence, Stalin, admittedly, was dispatching large shipments of arms, whilst the Comintern, as we shall see, had quickly initiated various other forms of help. However, Stalin's support was clearly postulated on the absence of revolution – indeed, was designed to secure such a position – whilst the fact was that he was also far away, France remaining by far the most obvious source of aid. As a result the defeat of the revolution became doubly vital, being at one and the same time the only means by which Stalin could be kept on side and Paris persuaded to reverse its position.

As a result of these pressures the autumn of 1936 was a time of significant change. Many areas – eastern Aragón, Catalonia and the Cantabrian littoral – remained outside the government's control, but in central, eastern and southeastern Spain its writ began increasingly to be re-imposed. Energetic moves were made to end the repression, expropriation of the land was placed under the control of the Institute of Agrarian Reform, collectivization was halted, and the *asaltos* and border guards greatly expanded so as to create a shock-force that could crush the revolution. Largo being as yet unwilling to do away with the revolutionary committees, however, it was in the armed forces that change was greatest. Aided by the fact that, outside Catalonia, where a 'Central Anti-Fascist Militia Committee' had stepped into the breach, none of their parent organizations had the capacity to maintain them in the field, the government was able to subordinate the militias to the state in exchange for the sinews of war. As early as 28 September, indeed, Largo announced that they were to be merged with the regulars in a new 'People's Army of the Republic', sweetened though the pill was by the adoption of the red star and clenched fist salute and the creation of a corps of political commissars.

Even where the central government was helpless, revolution was on the retreat. In Catalonia, for example, Lluis Companys was even less sympathetic to the revolution than Largo, whilst he could rely on the enthusiastic support of the PSUC. By the end of November, then, the Generalitat had suppressed the *chekas*, re-established a regular police force, dissolved the local committees, codified collectivization, subjected industry to a considerable decree of government intervention, ordered the militarization of the militias, and set up a regular army of its own. Rewarded for its loyalty with the ratification of the long-delayed statute of autonomy, meanwhile, the PNV was able to take complete control of the government of Vizcaya, though, exactly as was the case in Catalonia, this success was only achieved with the assistance of the Communists and their fellow travellers. As in Catalonia, too, a new army and police force was immediately established, control of the latter effectively being monopolized by the PNV.

The militarization of the militias proved to be a long and difficult process. Yet progress was by no means unimpressive. Not only was a formal general staff established, but the Ministry of War assumed complete control of matters of pay and supply, whilst the militias began to be organized into proper units. With the new army in receipt of at least some arms, including large numbers of Russian-crewed armoured vehicles and aircraft of a sort that often outclassed the German and Italian material being received by the Nationalists, Franco had a real fight on his hands.

Battle for the Capital

Grouped together on the southern edge of Madrid, the Nationalist forces whose task it was to rush the defences never had much chance of success. Numbering only some 10,000 men, they were supported by all the German and Italian war material that had yet reached the front, but this amounted to no more than forty-five light tanks, fifteen 37mm anti-tank guns, twenty-six 65 mm infantry guns, and a handful of 20 mm anti-aircraft guns. Also available were a number of Spanish armoured cars, fifty-two pieces of artillery, most of them light, and well over 100 aircraft. Facing them in the front line, however, were about 13,000 Republican militia, supported by forty-five guns and all the much better Russian armour and aircraft. With the Republicans also ensconced in strong defensive positions – for Madrid is situated on a bluff high above the river Manzanares – the battle looked likely to be grim indeed.

Needless to say, such detachment is easy sixty years after the event. In the Madrid of November 1936 it would have been impossible. For all the boasts of the Left that Madrid would prove the grave of fascism, the Nationalists appeared invincible, matters not being helped by the fact that on 6 November the government abandoned the capital for Valencia, leaving the city in the hands of a junta of defence headed by General José Miaja. The city was clogged with refugees, many of the defenders demoralized and exhausted, the authorities in a state of complete confusion, and the Nationalists possessed of an excellent plan which essentially called for their troops to outflank the Republican forces and take them in the rear. However, at the very moment that the Nationalists launched their assault in the early morning of 7 November, they were thrown into confusion by a sudden Republican counterattack. In the course of the fighting, meanwhile, a copy of the Nationalists' plan was captured, the night of 7 November in consequence witnessing frantic efforts to reinforce the most threatened sector of the defences. To all intents and purposes the Nationalists had now lost the battle. Given the superior reserves of the Republicans, their only hope had been to seize the city immediately. Denied a quick victory, they were now locked into a struggle of attrition from which they were unlikely to emerge victorious. Bomb and shell the city though they might, the increasingly depleted and exhausted Nationalists could make little progress. Still worse, their attempt to outflank the city simply pulled them deeper and deeper into a salient in which they could be attacked from all sides by the ever more numerous defenders, who had rapidly been reinforced by the first troops of the new army and a great deal of fresh artillery. Desperate to relieve the pressure, meanwhile, the Republicans were also launching repeated attacks on the Nationalist flanks, the result being that many of the insurgents' few reserves had to be deployed to protect their communications. Deprived of all superiority, the attackers finally reached the positions that they had been supposed to reach on the first day of the battle on 17 November, but more than that they could not do. Disappointed and angry, by 23 November even Franco had been forced to give up.

Dramatic as it was, the Nationalist assault on Madrid quickly spawned a variety of myths, not least because the Communists were eager to make as much capital out of what had taken place as possible, and the rebels to explain away their defeat. Most of them too silly to waste any time upon, it is, however, necessary to examine the question of the foreign volunteers who arrived in the capital at a crucial point in the fighting on 8 November. The first of the famous International Brigades, these troops were the work of the Comintern. Thus, amongst other things it had decided to organize a force of foreign volunteers as a demonstration of the Popular Front in action and means of subverting the revolution, the vast majority of those who went being rank-and-file Communists. Not ready for action in any strength until the very eve of the assault on Madrid, in the event only one small brigade could be rushed to the city. Even these few hundred men, moreover, were neither well-armed, nor well-equipped, nor well-trained. Encourage the battered defenders though their arrival may have done, to claim that they saved the city is therefore ridiculous – indeed, they were at first not even sent to the most crucial sector of the front. Just before the end of the battle a second brigade arrived, to be sure, but this was of much the same stamp as the first, and was in any case not much engaged.

Over the next couple of months three more International Brigades were organized at the base which had been established for them in Albacete, the number of troops that they could put into the line eventually amounting to something over 10,000 men. Dominated throughout by the Communists, they were for propaganda purposes for the next two years employed as shock troops and in consequence played a leading role in almost all the major battles of the war. On the whole possessed of a distinguished record, they therefore suffered casualties at a rate that far outstripped the average of the Popular Army as a whole, some 86 per cent of the 35,000 men who enlisted in their ranks being either killed or wounded. Brave though they were, however, the reality was very different to the heroic image perpetrated by the Communists: no better officered, armed, trained or equipped than the rest of the Popular Army, their performance was marred by exactly the same defects.

Whilst the foreign aid received by the Republic was thus acquiring physical shape, a parallel development was taking place in Nationalist Spain. Thus far the relatively few Germans and Italians who had arrived in Spain had notionally operated as part of the Spanish Foreign Legion. By the end of October, however, the Germans had determined to form an independent air corps, the result being the emergence of the famous Condor Legion. Augmented by anti-aircraft, searchlight, communication and workshop units, expanded to a strength of around 100 planes, and periodically supplied with the latest German fighters and bombers, this force thereafter enjoyed an entirely separate existence (by contrast, the

German tanks continued to fight with the Foreign Legion). Meanwhile, the ever vainglorious Mussolini was also determined that his forces should be organized on an independent basis, the consequence being, first, that the Condor Legion acquired an Italian counterpart known as the *Aviazzione Legionaria*, and, second, the arrival of a large expeditionary force known as the Corpo di Truppe Voluntarie, the total number of Italian troops serving in Spain at any given time eventually amounting to some 50,000.

The German and Italian aid extended to Franco was not just restricted to these forces, however. At sea, for example, both Hitler and Mussolini were quick to dispatch warships to assist the Nationalists. Thus the heavy cruisers, *Deutschland* and *Admiral Scheer*, were sent to the Straits of Gibraltar, whilst Italian submarines and destroyers were soon preying on merchant ships attempting to reach such ports as Valencia and Barcelona. Meanwhile, other warships escorted Italian ships bound for Franco and on occasion even bombarded the Republican coast (as did the *Deutschland* when it was bombed in May 1937). Contributing as it did to the Republican's ever worsening logistical problems, all this was vital to Franco's eventual victory. In addition, however, Germany and Italy also continued to supply the Nationalists with armaments and supplies of every description. Aircraft, rifles, machine guns, artillery pieces, anti-tank guns, anti-aircraft guns and ammunition all arrived in abundance, as did all the other paraphernalia of modern war, Italy even going so far as to turn a number of warships over to the Nationalists. It is important, however, that this aid is not exaggerated. Whilst certainly more extensive than anything received by the Republicans, Germany was only in the early stages of rearmament and Italy possessed of an arms industry that was at best mediocre, the result being that much of the weaponry that was sent left much to be desired. Thus, relatively few tanks were available, and those which did arrive were hopelessly outclassed by their Russian counterparts, whilst the bulk of the artillery consisted of a variety of antiquated models dating from the First World War and even earlier.

Convoyed across the Mediterranean in the face of a hostile navy of considerable power, the amount of aid available from Russia was never likely to match that supplied by Hitler and Mussolini, and all the more so as Stalin had good reason not to send too much in view of the constant accusations that Spain was in the grip of a Communist revolution. Paid for at enormous cost, moreover – in October 1936 well over half the Spanish gold reserve was sent to Russia in order to finance the purchase of arms – the *matériel* that was obtained did not even represent value for money. Whilst by no means insignificant in quantity, the weaponry involved was often very poor. The armour, certainly, was always superior to its German and Italian counterparts; the aircraft only surpassed in the latter half of the war; and the best of the artillery and small arms on a par with those received by the Nationalists. However, much of the material was not Russian at all, but rather oddments that had been taken in the course of the Russian Civil War. In at least some cases completely unserviceable, it was also heterogeneous in the extreme. Much the same is true, meanwhile, of the many weapons that were acquired on the black market, such countries as Poland being delighted to earn much needed foreign exchange by selling the Republicans such things as exorbitantly priced consignments of useless First World War tanks.

Having experienced their first real test in the attempt to storm Madrid, the two war machines were soon engaged in a further series of battles. Their gamble having been defeated, the Nationalists had been left in a very exposed position. No sooner had they abandoned their original offensive, then, than they launched a series of attacks west of the city that were designed to secure their communications. Known as the battle of Boadilla, the result was a grim slogging match that by 9 January 1937 had cost the Republic a broad swathe of territory. The Nationalist rear having thus been secured, Franco was able to implement the next phase of his strategy, which was to isolate Madrid from the rest of Republican Spain and force it to surrender. Taking advantage of Madrid's isolation – its only lifeline was the Valencia highway – Franco amassed a powerful striking force and on 6 February struck out eastwards for the river Jarama. At first progress was swift, but the Republicans outnumbered their attackers, whilst they were also well dug-in. In fierce fighting, Franco was therefore checked, and by 24 February the battle was over, Madrid having once again been saved.

With the battle of the Jarama still in progress, attention now briefly shifted to the southernmost extremity of the front. Protected by mountains to the west and north, the province of Málaga constituted an isolated enclave that projected deep into Nationalist territory. Defended only by 12,000 ill-armed and disorganized militia, wracked by political divisions and almost impossible to reinforce, the zone was vulnerable in the extreme. Nearby, meanwhile, were the steadily growing forces of the CTV, whose commanders were itching to show what they could do. Franco having given his consent, on 3 February the attack began with the support of almost fifty Italian aircraft. Hopelessly outclassed, the defence collapsed, and by 8 February the capital had fallen. Desperate to reach safety, thousands of refugees fled towards Almería, only to be mercilessly bombed and shelled. Behind them, meanwhile, the *limpieza* got to work with a vengeance, the number of executions amounting to at least 5,000 in 1937 alone.

Despite all this, however, Franco's chief goal remained Madrid.

Ignoring airy Italian dreams of blitzkrieg-style offensives that would have seen drives either northeastwards from Málaga towards Valencia, or southeastwards from Teruel to the sea, he therefore opted for an offensive to the northeast of the capital in the Guadalajara sector. We come here to a question that has occasioned much criticism of Franco as a military commander. Thus, what the Italians were proposing were offensives in depth that might in theory have ended resistance in a matter of weeks. In advocating such a course they had a strong vested interest – largely motorized as it was, the CTV would inevitably have played a leading role – but the fact remains that their ideas seemed to make sense. Why, then, did Franco not accede to them? According to his increasingly angry and frustrated allies – for the Germans were as interested as the Italians in such a strategy – the answer was that he was unimaginative and over-cautious, whilst it has also been claimed that Franco wanted the longest war possible on the grounds that this would inflict the utmost degree of punishment upon the enemy. Yet, calculating and merciless as he was, Franco also had common sense on his side. Whilst he certainly did not wish to give his allies the sort of role to which they aspired, blitzkrieg-style attacks were simply not a feasible option at this point except where the enemy was already broken or in a state of utter disarray (as had been the case with Málaga). Neither Germany nor Italy being able to supply the requisite military technology, talk of affording sufficient time for the utter eradication of the revolution therefore appears rather as a diplomatic blind which should not be taken at face value.

Franco's caution was soon borne out. Sent to the Madrid front as the lynchpin of the new offensive, the Italians struck southwestwards towards Guadalajara, and quickly drove a salient deep into Republican territory. However, entirely reliant on wheeled transport, the CTV was largely confined to the few highways that traverse the region, the result being that the march was slowed down by a series of traffic jams. Short of supplies, inadequately clothed, and operating in the most dismal weather, which amongst other things deprived them of air support, the Italian soldiers became more and more demoralized – a number had been tricked into going to Spain, whilst the rest had only joined up to escape the desperate economic situation that prevailed at home. By 10 March, then, the CTV had come to a standstill, the result being that the Republicans were able to launch a devastating counterattack with some of the best forces in the Popular Army. No sooner had they done so than the deficiencies in the CTV's armament were cruelly exposed, and within a matter of days it was therefore in headlong retreat.

Crisis on the Homefront

If the battles round Madrid had shown anything, it was that the centralisation of authority on the one hand and militarization of the militias on the other had brought enormous dividends. Thus, Franco had mostly been able to concentrate his slender resources upon the Madrid front and thereby suck the nascent Popular Army into a costly struggle which it could not refuse. Meanwhile, Russian aid and the militarization of the militias had enabled the Republic to check the Nationalists, and build the sort of war machine that was its only hope of survival. In neither case, however, had the two policies been carried through to fruition, the result being that the spring of 1937 was in both zones marked by political crisis.

Let us begin with the Nationalists. Ensconced in the bishop's palace at Salamanca, guarded by a specially uniformed bodyguard and lauded to the skies by his propaganda machine, Franco had by early 1937 acquired a pre-eminence which seemed unshakeable. Thus, the civil and military administration was dominated by loyal nominees, and the Church positively fawning in its subservience, whilst Calvo Sotelo, Sanjurjo and Primo de Rivera were dead and Gil Robles in exile. For all that, however, Franco did not feel entirely secure. Mola, Queipo de Llano and the monarchist commander of the airforce, General Kindelán, were restive; the Alfonsists, the Falangists and the Carlists by no means happy with the direction that events had taken; and the Germans and Italians inclined to be extremely critical. At the same time, relations between the Falange and the Carlists were far from cordial, whilst neither were even united in themselves, in both groups opinion being divided between ultras who wished to defend their respective programmes at all costs and temporizers who were happy to collaborate with the military authorities.

Faced by a series of incidents of which the most dramatic was the expulsion of the rebarbative Carlist leader, Manuel Fal Conde, on what amounted to a charge of conspiracy, Franco hit upon the idea of political unification, the plan being that the Falangists, Carlists, Alfonsists and *cedistas* should be brought together in a single movement answerable only to himself, other obvious advantages being that the machinery of government could be tightened up, and greater control imposed on the Carlist and Falangist militia. Once resolved upon, the matter did not take long to arrange. Presented with an ideal head of the new movement in the person of his capable and intelligent brother-in-law, Ramón Serrano Suñer, a much-admired *japista* and friend of José Antonio, who had been caught in the Republican zone and just escaped from Madrid, Franco simply threw open the possibility of a merger and waited for it to become clear that the Carlists and Falangists would never agree to take such action, whilst at the same time doing all that he could to foment the struggle for control of the Falange which had erupted between supporters and opponents of its new head, Manuel Hedilla. Franco being enabled in this fashion to play the role of honest broker, on 18 April the formation of the catch-all Falange Española Tradicionalista y de las Juntas de Ofensiva Nacional Sindicalista was therefore announced by decree. As for resistance, it was almost non-existent. Hedilla, true, proved obstreperous and had to be imprisoned, but otherwise almost no voices were raised in protest, the fact being that few Carlists or Falangists were wedded to ideological purity or willing to forego participation in the structures of the new movement, the general air of complacency being increased by rumours that the Germans had been encouraging Hedilla to launch a coup.

Whilst Nationalist Spain was unified with relative ease, the same was not the case with its Republican counterpart. By the end of 1936 the revolution was much curbed, New Castile and the Levant having in large part been forced to accept the authority of the government and allow their militias to be incorporated in the Popular Army. Meanwhile, in Catalonia, too, the Generalitat had to a large extent ended the situation of dual power that it had been forced to tolerate since the uprising. In Aragón, especially, however, anarchism continued to reign unchecked, whilst the Catalan industrial belt remained very much dominated by collectivization. And, as for the northern zone, it was all but out of control of the government altogether, the only redeeming feature of the situation being that in Vizcaya the Basque Nationalists and the Communists had reduced the revolution to a non-event. Whilst the Nationalists concentrated on Madrid, the remaining bastions of revolution could more or less be ignored, but the implications of Guadalajara made this all but impossible: hardly had the guns fallen silent, indeed, than Franco had launched a fresh campaign which called forth a response not just from the forces of the capital, but also from those of Catalonia and Aragón.

Even had this not been the case, the winter of 1936–7 made it very clear that the Republic was facing economic disaster. It is but fair to point out that this was not necessarily the fault of collectivization *per se*, transport difficulties, lack of capital, shortages of fuel and raw materials, and lack of skilled management all combining to ensure that the difficulties faced by the revolutionaries were immense. In the case of agriculture, in particular, meanwhile, the weather had been unfavourable, and labour badly hit by military service. Yet certain facts cannot be gainsaid. By the autumn of 1936 food prices had already risen dramatically whilst many commodities were in short supply, the inflationary spiral having been worsened still further by the wholesale emission of tokens, vouchers, coupons and paper money of all sorts.

Whatever the responsibility of the revolutionary movement may have been, the growing economic difficulties were pretext enough for the government to intensify its offensive. Even before the battle of Madrid an important goal had been secured in this respect in that, on 4 November, the unremitting Nationalist advance had persuaded the anarchists to accept four posts in the government. Meanwhile, supported by the Communists and the Republicans, Largo – a rather vain individual who had been touched to the quick by the government's flight to Valencia – was able to proceed with the next step of counter-revolution without let or hindrance. Thus, December saw a general move to sweep away the revolutionary committees, re-establish the traditional machinery of government, end the power of the *chekas*, and tighten the control of the Ministry of War over the remaining militias. Whilst the writ of the central government still did not reach as far as Catalonia, there, too, the revolution was in full retreat, the PSUC forcing a cabinet reshuffle that led to the exclusion of the POUM, the abolition of the committees of supply that had hitherto controlled the distribution of food to the populace, and an increase in the power of the Generalitat with regard to both taxation and industry. In Catalonia and the rest of Republican Spain alike, meanwhile, all attempts at further collectivization were firmly blocked.

The situation in the Republican zone did not, of course, change overnight. Many of the revolutionary committees refused to dissolve themselves, just as many militia columns tried to ignore militarization. Yet the power of the revolutionary left was as clearly on the wane as that of the Communist Party was on the increase. In this respect, the advantages that it had derived from a vigorously counter-revolutionary domestic policy and the arrival of Russian arms had been swelled by its appropriation of most of the credit for the defence of Madrid (apart from anything else, the junta formed on the eve of the assault had quickly fallen under its sway). Needless to say, this brought a flood of fresh recruits, including still more leading army officers, whilst at the same time exposing the forces of the revolution to further denigration (it was, for example, claimed that the militias who held the Aragón front had not lifted a finger to help the capital). Whilst the ground was being cut from under the feet of the revolution in this fashion, a complex sub-plot was also beginning to emerge. Thus far, Largo's interests had largely coincided with those of the Communists, but it was not long before a gap had begun to emerge between the two. Jealous of the Communists' appropriation of the defence of Madrid, Largo came increasingly to resent the patronizing behaviour of the Russian military advisers. Even more alarming, perhaps, was the fact that the Communists were beginning to attract many converts from the PSOE and its sister organizations, and were pressing for it to merge with the PCE. Last but not least, they had also launched a campaign to disgrace Largo's most loyal military adviser, Colonel José Asensio Torrado. Goaded beyond endurance, the premier finally flew into a rage at a meeting with the Russian ambassador and the distinctly pro-Communist Foreign Minister, Julio Alvarez del Vayo, only to find that the Communists effectively declared war on him as well.

So complex is the situation that now prevailed that it almost defies description. Largo, the Communists, the Esquerra, the right wing of the PSOE and the remnants of left-republicanism were all agreed on the necessity of crushing the revolution, but the first two were bitterly at odds with one another, the third the object of the united dislike of the other four, and the fourth at war with the first. In the revolutionary camp, meanwhile, the anarchists, left-wing socialists and the POUM were all opposed to the policies of the government and the Generalitat, whilst in many instances being deeply opposed to each other's blueprint for the new Spain. The *dénouement* is well known. Amidst a climate of increasing tension, which saw several murders and outbreaks of fighting, the government, Generalitat and Communists continued with their efforts to destroy the revolution. Success was at best mixed. A mutiny on the part of the anarchist 'Iron Column' was crushed without difficulty, whilst the state was able to take control of the Franco-Spanish frontier. However, an attempt to force the surrender of all those arms still held on the home front in Catalonia was defeated. At length on 3 May 1937 a relatively minor dispute over control of the telephone exchange in Barcelona sparked off the inevitable explosion. Flinging up barricades, large numbers of the CNT and the POUM sprang to arms, there following a confused struggle which eventually cost some 500 lives. Within five days the rising had been put down, however. With it died the revolution, the last remnants of trade-union power and the militia system now being firmly swept away. Thus, a strict deadline was set for the surrender of all weapons, the control patrols and revolutionary committees were finally dissolved, the revolutionary tribunals purged and placed under the control of regular judges, the industrial collectives were subjected to tighter control than ever, and the last of the militias turned into regular troops. Collectivization in the countryside was allowed to survive for a little longer so as to ensure that the harvest was brought in, but, after months of vilification in the press, in August the Consejo de Aragón was dissolved and many collectives occupied by Communist-led troops who had been brought to the region to take part in the impending assault on Zaragoza (see below). Perhaps two-thirds of the collectives – essentially those where there was no evidence that force had been employed in their establishment – were allowed to survive, but many even of these lost part of their land to the original owners, whilst the rest disappeared altogether.

By August 1937, then, the revolution was dead. Also broken, however, were Largo, the POUM and the Generalitat. Taking Largo first of all, the premier was at loggerheads with his former allies. Determined to break the PCE's control of the army, the Socialist leader had dissolved the Communist-controlled junta that still ruled Madrid and demoted several leading Communist generals, and was now proposing to switch the main Republican military effort to Extremadura. Hurling the blame for what had happened in Catalonia at the premier, the Communists therefore walked out of the cabinet. Their example being followed by virtually all the other ministers apart from the four anarchists and two loyal Socialists, Largo was placed in an impossible position. For a brief moment he essayed resistance, but fears of losing Russian aid proved too much, and on 18 May the Socialist leader surrendered, being replaced by the erstwhile Minister of Finance, Juan Negrín.

Turning now to the POUM, the Communists had long since desired its elimination, the rising therefore coming as a godsend in that Nin and Maurín could be accused of treason. So long as he was prime minister, Largo refused to go along with such attacks, but, once he was gone, the POUM's enemies had a free hand. Masterminded by senior representatives of the Comintern and the Soviet secret police, a plot was hatched to prove that the POUM was linked to a Nationalist spy ring that had just been unmasked in Catalonia, whilst the government that had succeeded that of Largo was quickly persuaded to make the POUM illegal, order the arrest of its leading militants, and place its militias under reliable commanders. Nin, meanwhile, was tortured in an effort to get him to admit the ludicrous charges that had been laid against him (Maurín would doubtless have got the same treatment, but for the fact that he had been caught on the wrong side of the lines and imprisoned by the Nationalists). Refusing to give way, he was eventually killed, the show trial that had been organized to deal with his followers in consequence falling flat (the few men brought to trial were only convicted of rebellion rather than collaboration). Nevertheless, things were quite bad enough: many party militants were either murdered or held in prison for a considerable time.

Last of the casualties of the 'May Days' was the cause of Catalan autonomy. With its territory flooded by police loyal to the Valencia government, the freedom of manoeuvre open to the Generalitat was obviously circumscribed, and all the more so as it was in June remodelled so as to exclude the CNT. Still worse, Companys had been forced to agree that the central government should resume responsibility for defence and public order, the independent army that he had been trying to form henceforth being absorbed into the Popular Army, and, as a new 'Army of the East', placed under yet another convert to Communism, General

Pozas. Meanwhile, of course, the PSUC was also very much in the ascendant. The final seal on the situation was not imposed until the autumn of 1937, when the government moved *en bloc* from Valencia to Barcelona, but the fact was that Catalan autonomy was as dead as the Spanish revolution.

So much for a bare outline of the events that took place in the *retaguardia* in the period November 1936–May 1937. What, however, are we to make of them? Whilst the subordination of Carlists, Falangists and Alfonsists alike to the will of General Franco was beneficial to the insurgent cause, the destruction of the revolution is regularly claimed to have sounded the death-knell of the Second Republic in that the people were deprived of the will to resist, and the Popular Army condemned to fight a war which maximized the advantages of its opponents. Such arguments, however, are very difficult to substantiate. Notwithstanding the assault on the Left, the Republic remained infinitely more progressive than at any other point in its history. Land reform was continued, rents frozen, welfare and health-care services improved, and enormous efforts devoted to improving education, whilst there was clearly a strong perception that all this remained worth fighting for, Franco only winning the war after a long, hard fight. As for the idea that there was an alternative to the sort of war that the revolution's enemies were espousing, this is simply laughable: setting aside the need for foreign aid, the militias had already been shown to be useless, whilst dreams of some sort of proletarian guerrilla war were utterly ephemeral. Like it or not, in short, a disciplined regular army, and all that this entailed, was the only hope.

Turning Point

If anything was needed to legitimize the destruction of the revolution, it was the military events of 1937. Shifting the balance irrevocably in favour of the Nationalists, these made it all the more essential for the Republic to maximize the value of its remaining resources in the hope that changing international circumstances would somehow bring better days. To understand this development, it is necessary to return to the battle of Guadalajara, the fact being that this led to a major reassessment of Nationalist strategy. Whereas the aim had hitherto been to win the war by means of a great decisive battle, it was now clear that such a goal was beyond Franco's grasp, the result being that the focus of the struggle shifted from Madrid to the territory that the Republicans continued to hold in northern Spain. Isolated from the rest of the Republican zone and preoccupied with a variety of internal problems, this was too ill-armed and politically divided to be able to contribute much to the war. However, possessed as it was of Spain's greatest resources of coal and iron ore, of her most important war industries, and of a large population, the mere fact that it was still in Republican hands constituted a considerable boon. By the same token, of course, the Cantabrian littoral also now became a prime target for the Nationalists. No sooner had Guadalajara ended, then, than Franco turned north.

In taking this option, Franco in theory faced a task of considerable magnitude – the northern zone was protected by a range of high mountains and supported by war industries that could produce arms of all sorts. Given the fact that the coastline was some 300 miles long, moreover, the overstretched Nationalist navy had not been able to prevent the arrival of a fair amount of foreign weaponry. In fact, however, the zone was at Franco's mercy. As conservative as ever, the Basque Nationalists were loathed by most of their allies, just as they themselves hated the Left. One result being that Vizcaya sent little iron ore to Asturias, and Asturias little coal to Vizcaya, industrial production had therefore fallen to a fraction of its full potential. Commanded by a weak nonentity, the Republican 'Army of the North' meanwhile existed on paper alone, the civil authorities in the three provinces doing all that they could to ensure that they retained control of their own forces. Even had greater desire existed to switch resources from one province to another, meanwhile, it was difficult to do so, lateral communication depending on a single narrow-gauge railway. Short of decent airfields, possessed of relatively few aircraft, and within easy reach of the Nationalist air bases, the whole zone was also uniquely vulnerable to aerial attack, whilst its forces were poorly trained, undisciplined, badly led, low in morale, and ensconced behind defence works that were incomplete and ill planned.

In short, Franco was set for fresh victories. At all events on 31 March Vizcaya was hit by 35,000 men, 216 guns, 100 tanks, and 140 aircraft, only the difficult terrain, the prolonged drizzle typical of the region, and the caution of the Nationalist high command ensuring that the campaign did not become a rout. Some of the defenders fought bravely enough, but even so by the end of April the Nationalists were within twenty miles of Bilbao. Amongst their gains, of course, was the smouldering wreckage of the town of Guernica which on 26 April was heavily bombed by the Condor Legion in an attempt to spread panic and block the retreat of a large force of troops who were heading for the town from the east. Stiffened by better defences, resistance now became much tougher, and it was therefore not until early June that the Nationalists were in a position to attack Bilbao. Once that was the case, however, the issue could not be long delayed: pulverized by bombs and shells, by 19 June those of the surviving defenders who did not choose to give themselves up – as at least 10,000 Basque nationalist troops did – had evacuated the city. In all, some 30,000 men had been killed, wounded or taken prisoner, whilst the scale of the victory was reinforced by the fact that the PNV had taken active steps to prevent the implementation of a scorched-earth policy. With the way apparently open for the immediate conquest of the rest of northern Spain, the Nationalists could afford to be distinctly exultant.

The fall of Santander and Asturias was not to take place quite so quickly, however. In so far as the Valencia government was concerned, the attack on Vizcaya was not especially inclined to stir it into precipitate action: not only was the PNV prone to adopt airs that were very much above its station, but it was rightly regarded with much distrust. Disinclination to assist the Basques was in the meantime fostered by military realities in that it was impossible to get anything more than a few aircraft to Bilbao. Yet Franco clearly could not be allowed to take control of all the resources of Vizcaya, the result being that in May and June Segovia and Huesca witnessed the first in a long series of diversionary offensives designed to take some of the pressure off the northern front. On 6 July, meanwhile, these relatively minor operations were followed by a much bigger attack in the vicinity of Madrid known as the battle of Brunete.

The biggest Republican offensive of the war thus far, Brunete displayed the merits and demerits of the Popular Army to perfection. Brilliantly planned and conceived, the attack was pressed home with much courage and succeeded in driving a salient deep into the Nationalist positions. However, possessed of a largely improvised officer corps, the Republicans had little idea of how to manoeuvre under fire and were in consequence held up by the tiny garrisons of such villages as Quijorna. Meanwhile, in part because it was found all but impossible to coordinate their movements with those of the infantry, the army's tanks were not used to good effect, whilst the artillery lacked the reserves of ammunition that it needed. At the same time, the 'mixed brigade' that formed the basis of Republican military organization tended to split the army's tanks and artillery up into 'penny packets' and in consequence to dilute their power still further. As for the Republic's aircraft, their pilots could neither hold off their enemy counterparts, nor deliver adequate close support. As a result, the front was soon stabilized, Franco then throwing in thousands of reinforcements in an attempt to inflict as many Republican casualties as possible. When the battle finally came to an end twenty days after it began, there can be no doubt as to who was the victor. Though they had gained a few miles of territory, the Republicans had lost over 20,000 men and wasted much precious *matériel*.

Given the Republic's logistical troubles, such losses simply could not be endured, and all the more so as the offensive did no more than delay the Nationalist assault on Santander by a few days. Launched on 14 August, indeed, it broke through almost immediately, the Nationalist forces in consequence reaching the port in a matter of days. Cut off in the eastern part of the province and unwilling to fight on, meanwhile, the remnants of the PNV forces surrendered *en masse*. By 1 September all was over. At a cost of less than 3,000 casualties, the Nationalists had eliminated at least 45,000 Republican troops, whilst at the same time capturing a quantity of arms, equipment and ammunition that was even greater than that collected in Vizcaya, and putting an end to the embarrassing failure of Basque Catholicism to line up with their 'crusade'.

At virtually the same time as the Nationalists were occupying Santander, meanwhile, the Republicans had embarked on another costly offensive. Quiescent and thinly held, the Aragón front was an obvious target, and all the more so as Zaragoza lay only a short way behind the lines. Meanwhile, as we have seen, concentrating troops in the area also offered a means of crushing one of the last bastions of the revolution. On 24 August 80,000 troops therefore went into action on a wide front. In the immediate vicinity of Zaragoza in particular much progress was made, but once again the attack had soon bogged down. In part this was because of the heroic resistance put up by the garrison of the village of Belchite, but the Popular Army also displayed the same deficiencies as it had at Brunete. Fought to a standstill, indeed, the Republicans were soon being ejected from many of their gains. As a result when the fighting finally died down in the middle of October, all that the Republicans had to show for their efforts was a few square miles of barren steppe. Casualties, by contrast, had been very heavy, whilst the Republic had consumed much of its limited reserves of munitions.

As if all this was not bad enough, the offensive had not even brought any succour to Asturias. Thus, with the fighting in Aragón still at its height, on 1 September the Nationalists attacked. Assisted by heavy rain and the mountainous terrain, the 50,000 defenders fought bravely, but their position soon became untenable, and they eventually disintegrated into little more than a mob of fugitives. On 21 October, indeed, the Nationalists marched into Gijón, the many Republican troops who had not been able to escape by sea being forced to surrender. Along with many of their Basque and *santanderino* predecessors, large numbers had soon been pressed into Franco's service, the Nationalists also again making good use of the copious amounts of war material that they had seized. In addition, of course, a large force of troops was now available for service elsewhere. Above all, however, the rebels now had the industrial base that they had hitherto lacked: quickly mobilized in the service of the Nationalist cause, the northern zone was soon producing large quantities of new weapons as well as funding the purchase of yet more material from Germany and Italy. Unless some *deus ex machina* came to the rescue in short, the Republic was doomed.

To Resist is to Conquer

By the time that Gijón fell, the Republican government had for some five months been in the hands of the Socialist academic, Juan Negrín. Much vilified by anti-Communist writers, the new prime minister was a rather more complex figure than many of his detractors have allowed. Thus, the scion of a prosperous bourgeois family who was very much on the right of the Socialist party, he was in full agreement with the need to end the revolution, whilst he was slow to recognize just how far the Communists had been able to dominate the army and security forces, and extremely foolish in the extent of his contempt for Largo, whose personal mediocrity blinded Negrín to the need to give him his backing in May 1937. That said, however, Negrín was no mere Comintern cat's paw. Prepared to sup with the devil for the sake of winning the war, he was a sincere democrat who had as little time for Communist hegemonism as he did for left-wing revolution, whilst he soon became increasingly resentful of the pretensions of the PCE and its Russian advisers. Whether he could actually have broken away from them is a moot point – the deeply divided PSOE was hardly an effective power base – but for the remainder of the war he did all he could to restrict their influence and secure the British and French support that was the only hope of shattering their grip.

Genuine though he was in his intention to challenge the Communists, Negrín was facing an uphill task. Unwilling and unable to join the Left, he was also estranged from Largo (not that the latter could have offered him much support: in the summer and autumn of 1937 he was stripped of his remaining positions of influence, and eventually silenced altogether). Meanwhile, Communist influence was greater than ever. Nearly half the Popular Army were members either of the PCE, the PSUC or the JSU, whilst Communist representation at the rank of battalion commander and above was even higher: over two-thirds of the mixed brigades had Communist commanders, whilst prominent converts included such generals as Pozas, Miaja, and the commander of the airforce, Hidalgo de Cisneros. The erstwhile militia leaders, Lister, González and Modesto, were all divisional commanders; Communists peppered the general staff, the war ministry, and, especially, the political commissariat; and the International Brigades and the air force were essentially Communist preserves, many of the latter's pilots actually being Russian. At the same time, meanwhile, the Communists had also built up an impressive array of nominally independent civilian organizations whose aim was to put pressure on the government and augment its profile, whilst they were also clearly still angling for the unification of the PCE and the PSOE.

Whilst Negrín killed off the pressure for Socialist and Communist unification, the most prominent figure in the resistance was rather his long-term friend and ally, Prieto. Thus, appointed Minister of Defence, Prieto lost no time in banning all party propaganda from the armed forces; engineering the removal of many Communists from the upper echelons of the political commissariat; ending the administrative independence of the International Brigades (which were in any case becoming more and more Spanish, the supply of foreign volunteers having begun increasingly to diminish); transferring many Communist staff officers to less sensitive posts; and trying to ensure that the new secret police force known as the SIM that was being forced upon the Republic by the Russians did not immediately fall under Communist control. Realizing that the Communists were in consequence out to get him, in the early winter Prieto decided to secure his position by means of a major military victory, the obvious target being the Nationalist bastion of Teruel, which was almost surrounded, lightly garrisoned, and difficult to defend. Entrusted to the non-Communist Republican, Juan Hernández Saravia, the assault began on 15 December. Aided by the fact that, as Prieto had hoped, the Nationalist air force was grounded by inclement weather, 100,000 Republican troops surrounded the Nationalist garrison and occupied a large expanse of territory. However, hopes that such a shock had been administered to the Nationalists that they could be forced to accept a compromise peace – the sub-text of the whole operation – were soon dashed. Though taken by surprise – he had actually been massing his forces for a fresh offensive against Guadalajara – Franco quickly launched a massive counter-offensive. Hampered by a prolonged blizzard, the relief forces did not reach the city in time – after a Stalingrad-like struggle the garrison surrendered – but even so the Nationalist advance continued, the increasingly exhausted Republicans not only being driven back, but also losing large amounts of territory that they had held at the start of the battle. With Teruel itself reconquered, by 23 February the battle was over, Republican casualties numbering some 54,000.

The year nineteen thirty-eight therefore found the Republic in a situation that was increasingly desperate. Setting aside the terrible losses in the North, Brunete, Belchite and Teruel had between them stripped the Republic of much of its stock of arms and munitions, whilst living conditions were now downright desperate. The Republican navy having shown itself to be utterly incapable of protecting the beleaguered shipping lanes that led to Valencia and Barcelona, food was very scarce. The winter had been bitterly cold throughout, and, with fuel for heating limited, the civilian population in consequence suffered terribly. Cold and malnourished, they also began to suffer from disease. Meanwhile, in many instances they also had to endure the direct attention of the

Nationalists. Heavily bombed in the course of the Nationalist assault in November 1936, Madrid had thereafter been constantly shelled, whilst the Italians were now making repeated raids on Barcelona. Despite efforts to maintain popular enthusiasm, morale was therefore clearly in decline. At the front, perhaps, things were better, but even so there was a general air of wrangling and mistrust. With the SIM in addition busily turning the Republican zone into a police state, the situation could not have been more dispiriting.

In the Nationalist zone, by contrast, the material situation of the populace was much better. Except for a few commodities, food was not in short supply, whilst there were also reasonable supplies of tobacco and other luxuries. Meanwhile, thanks to a combination of partiality in the realms of high finance and the increasing likelihood of victory, the rebel *peseta* remained reasonably stable, the consequence being that inflation did not become a significant factor until 1938, by the end of which year prices had risen by an average of 40 per cent since 1936. For the wealthy, indeed, life was positively comfortable, the ease with which the Nationalists were able to obtain cheap credit ensuring that no attempt was made to conscript their capital. Other than the presence of large numbers of men in uniform, and periodic brawls between Spanish soldiers on the one hand and Moors, Germans and Italians on the other, there was in fact a general air of normality that was not much belied by a few rather half-hearted attempts to encourage a measure of austerity. As for overt political conflict, it was minimal. Within the FET y de las JONS, a number of die-hard Falangists, Carlists and Alfonsists continued to grumble, whilst thwarted ambition combined with a measure of ideological conviction to ensure that a number of generals – most notably, Queipo de Llano and the prominent *africanista*, Juan Yagüe – engaged in occasional criticism of Franco, but the community of interest that bound the Nationalist camp together was simply too strong for anything very much to happen, convenient though it probably was that Mola had been killed in an air crash in June 1937. A few malcontents were imprisoned or exiled, certainly, but otherwise all was quiet.

What sort of Spain was being built by Franco and his supporters, however? According to the Nationalist propaganda machine, Franco stood for the construction of a new Spain based on not just order but also social justice. Central to this populist message was the continued espousal of syndicalism on the part of the FET y de las JONS, in whose leadership a large number of 'old shirts' continued to be prominent. In March 1938, moreover, a new 'labour charter' was promulgated that amongst other things promised a minimum wage, social security, controls on the working day, guaranteed holidays, and even a degree of agrarian reform. Needless to say, however, the reality was very different.

The 'movement', as it was commonly known, quickly assumed monstrous proportions, but it was slow to develop any form of syndical organization to replace the old trade unions, all of which had naturally been banned. Also quick to go were the mixed juries, the 'labour magistracies' that replaced them being nothing more than tools of the oligarchy. Meanwhile, wages not only remained extremely low, but failed to keep up with inflation, the situation of many households being rendered still worse by the absence of their menfolk at the front (such families did receive allowances, but these were so small as to be utterly derisory). With strike action outlawed, the position of the working classes was therefore grim indeed. Aside from the defence of the social order, in fact, the chief concern of the regime was the mobilization of the populace for war. Rallies and parades abounded, whilst children were conscripted into a uniformed youth movement and women encouraged to join either the Sección Feminina of the FET y de las JONS or the separate social welfare agency known as the Auxilio Social (indeed, from October 1937 they were in theory obliged to offer themselves for at least six months' national service). As in the Republican zone, some qualified as nurses, whilst still others engaged in such activities as knitting socks or becoming a soldier's 'godmother'. Meanwhile, all sections of the population were under constant pressure to contribute to the many collections that were held to raise money.

In terms of its political and economic organization, meanwhile, Nationalist Spain was characterized by constant stress on national unity and extensive state intervention in the economy. Basque and Catalan autonomy were officially outlawed, and every effort made to eradicate every vestige of separate identity once the provinces concerned were actually occupied. All authority, meanwhile, was centred in the hands of Franco himself, the *caudillo*, as he became known, monopolizing the legislative and executive power and boasting of his determination to create a totalitarian state. As for the economy, a host of controls and regulations of all sorts had soon been imposed, whilst such bodies as the Servicio Nacional del Trigo, the Servicio Nacional de Reforma Económica Social de la Tierra and the 'vertical syndicates' theoretically set up in all branches of the economy by the Labour Charter all served to reinforce the power of the regime, whilst at the same time providing employment for the ever-growing ranks of the FET y de las JONS.

In much of this, of course, there was a strong hint of Nazi Germany and Fascist Italy, both of which the Nationalists often shadowed. As the war progressed, for example, the anti-Semitism that had always been a standard part of the rhetoric of the Spanish Right underwent a marked increase in intensity. For a variety of reasons, however, too close an alignment with the regimes of Hitler and Mussolini was discouraged.

Violently opposed to any form of radicalism, Franco was in any case deeply aware that the Church was unhappy with many aspects of fascism, and, further, that its populist rhetoric was hardly likely to appeal to the propertied classes. In order to escape from these contradictions, the most convoluted efforts were made to distance the Nationalist regime from any open comparison with fascism. Repeated attempts, for example, were made to praise and flatter the aristocracy, whilst the propagandists of the regime never ceased to maintain that the FET y de las JONS was based on principles that were authentically and quintessentially Spanish – hence the constant efforts that were made to associate the regime with the *reconquista* and the 'golden age'. In all this, meanwhile, Franco was greatly assisted by his religious policy, the hierarchy being flattered and conciliated, the Republic's anti-clerical laws swept aside, and Catholicism's social, cultural and educational influence restored to a position that it had not enjoyed for generations.

The extent to which the Nationalist authorities were successful in turning their war into a popular crusade is a moot point. In terms of overt political and military involvement and social and cultural conformity, their success was considerable. Thus, some 300,000 men joined the various militias alone, whilst still other volunteers were to be found in the Foreign Legion and the regular army. As for the FET y de las JONS, it eventually attaining a strength of some 900,000 members. Overt religious devotion, too, revived, whilst there seems to have been little difficulty in raising patriotic donations. In itself, however, all this means little. Thus, thousands of progressive Spaniards attended mass, joined the Falange, or enlisted in the armed forces for no other reason than survival. Moreover, conformity by no means equated to repentance: not only did anarchist cells survive in the ranks of the Falange, but many men went to the front with the deliberate intention of defecting at the first possible opportunity. Meanwhile, there was much resistance, guerrilla bands emerging in many parts of Spain. The more absurd simplicities of the Nationalists and their apologists may therefore safely be ignored, but, for all that, large parts of the population were prepared to go along with Franco, conformity being rendered all the easier because the savagery of the repression was limited by practicalities. Executions continued throughout the war, the number of prisoners and slave labourers ran into hundreds of thousands, and a concerted effort was made to rid the bureaucracy, the universities, the teaching profession, the judiciary and the municipalities of anyone who did not share the *mores* of Nationalist Spain. Conditions in the increasingly overcrowded gaols, meanwhile, can best be described as terrible. To kill or imprison all those implicated in some way or other with the cause of his opponents was impossible even for Franco, however. Thus, as time went on, large numbers of prisoners-of-war were absorbed into the ranks of the army, whilst those who had done no more than simply vote for Socialist or Republican candidates were generally allowed to go free. Whilst no one could be certain that they were safe – aside from anything else, 1937 saw the establishment of a powerful secret police – survival therefore ceased to be entirely impossible.

Before moving on from this survey of Nationalist Spain, it is worth examining the situation in Spanish Morocco. A vital source of manpower – something over 60,000 Moors enlisted with the Nationalist forces in the course of the war – it has often been argued that the Republic should have done more to whip up discontent with Spanish rule. Yet to have done so would have alienated both France and Russia, whilst it is unclear how much effect such a policy would have had, the policy that Franco followed being subtle in the extreme. Thus, the support of the Caliph was obtained through flattery, that of the tiny westernized elite through a mixture of manipulation, concession, and vague promises of reform, and that of the hill tribes through downright bribery. With the economy of the protectorate thrown into considerable confusion by the war – the price of the imports on which the populace increasingly depended soared – recruitment on the whole proved easy enough, especially given the ease with which the Republicans could be represented as godless infidels. As casualties mounted, so enthusiasm declined, substantial numbers of volunteers having to be obtained from the equally impoverished French zone. Occasional riots and other outbreaks of violence aside, however, the trouble never got out of hand, the general impression being that attempts to whip up an insurrection would in reality have been fruitless.

Whatever the true picture of Nationalist Spain and Spanish Morocco may have been, the spring of 1938 found Franco in a most favourable position. Financed by a mixture of credit, patriotic donations and the export of minerals and agricultural products, large quantities of German and Italian war materials were continuing to arrive in the country. Much of this equipment remained obsolescent, but many of the aircraft were now much better than before, whilst small numbers of such ultra-modern weapons as the German 88mm anti-aircraft gun had also begun to appear. Large quantities of weapons and equipment had been acquired on the battlefield – one-third of the tank force now consisted of the Russian T26 – whilst as many as 400 factories were engaged in some form of war production. Unlike the Republic, the Nationalists were also experiencing few difficulties in making purchases on the open market, large quantities of oil and wheeled transport being acquired from such companies as Texaco, Ford and Chrysler. Only 200,000-strong at the end of 1936, Franco's forces had therefore risen to over twice that figure, whilst the *ad hoc* military organization of the early days had at last been replaced by a formal structure of brigades, divisions and corps. Inside Spain, the CTV, the Aviazzione Legionaria and the Condor Legion were all ready to do Franco's bidding, whilst Italian ships and aircraft continued to intervene in the conflict with little let or hindrance. And in the wider world countless officials, bankers, politicians and army officers were in one way or another all but overtly aiding the Nationalists. Weary, battered and aided only by the Soviet Union, a flow of foreign volunteers that had slowed to a trickle, and an 'aid to Spain' movement whose efforts were but a fraction of what was needed, the Republic was facing a task that was harder than ever.

Before very long, meanwhile, the position had worsened still further. The unwonted loss of the Nationalist cruiser, *Baleares*, to a rare sortie from Cartagena on 6 March was rather offset by the fact that the skeletal rebel navy had since 1936 been joined not only by two cruisers and two minelayers that had been under construction in El Ferrol, but also four destroyers and two submarines that had been provided by Italy. In any case, 9 March saw events of much greater importance begin to unfold on the Aragón front. Profiting from the exhaustion of the Republican forces after Teruel, Franco launched a new offensive. Crushed by a hurricane bombardment, the defenders collapsed almost immediately, the Republicans thereafter being utterly incapable of stopping the flood. With the enemy fleeing in despair, the Nationalists were at last able to engage in the sort of blitzkrieg operations which the Italians had always advocated. No sooner had the line been shored up in one place than it therefore collapsed somewhere else, whilst the Republican air force was driven from the skies, and the movements of the Republicans further disrupted by bombing, communication difficulties and breakdowns in the supply of food and munitions. Many units were cut off and captured, whilst others were all but annihilated. Frantic efforts were made to stem the rout by the execution of scapegoats, the appointment of new commanders, the dispatch of reinforcements, and the arrest of malcontents of all sorts, but nothing did any good: having occupied the whole of Aragón and a broad swathe of western Catalonia, on 15 April the leading Nationalist troops reached the Mediterranean coast at Vinaroz. The Republic, in short, had been cut in two.

As the Republican forces dissolved in rout, so a fresh crisis erupted in Barcelona. Determined to get rid of Prieto, the Communists had for some time been accusing him of defeatism, in which respect it is but fair to say that the Minister of Defence was by now so demoralized that he had openly begun to advocate surrender. Organizing angry demonstrations to demand Prieto's resignation, the Communists also put it about that Stalin was only prepared to send more aid to Spain if he went. Negrín himself having decided that Prieto could not remain at his post, he therefore demanded his resignation.

In itself the fall of Prieto had little effect, but, for all that, events now took something of a turn for the better. Deciding for a variety of reasons to follow up their arrival at Vinaroz with a drive on Valencia rather than the more obvious target of Barcelona, the Nationalists made only slow progress, eventually being brought to a halt a few miles north of their objective. Whilst the Republican forces in central Spain were thus absorbing the attentions of the Nationalists, the government was making good the damage inflicted upon the forces of Catalonia in March and April. In this respect, it was greatly assisted by developments on the diplomatic front. Much shaken by the *anschluss*, France had adopted a more relaxed attitude with regard to non-intervention. As a result large quantities of arms began to enter Catalonia, Negrín being sufficiently encouraged to launch a bid to force Franco to the negotiating table, with which goal in mind on 1 May he announced the conditions on which he would accept a peace settlement. Very reasonable though these were, they were rejected out of hand, Negrín therefore proceeding to the next element of his strategy. Thus, having built up a powerful force in Catalonia, like Prieto before him he sought to bludgeon the Nationalists into coming to terms, on the night of 24–5 July 80,000 Republican troops therefore beginning to cross the river Ebro – then the front line in this sector – between Cherta and Mequinenza.

Thus began the most terrible battle of the war. Rapidly overwhelming the thin defending forces, the Republicans had soon occupied a major bridgehead. As so often before, however, initial success was followed by stalemate, this time at the town of Gandesa. Faced by determined resistance – typically enough, Franco had rushed reinforcements to the sector – the Republicans suffered heavy casualties and were brought to a halt. Digging in, they were then subjected to a ferocious counter-offensive designed, first, to restore Franco's faltering prestige, and, second, to wreck them beyond repair. However, the Republicans were not only better armed than ever before but also favoured by the mountainous terrain, whilst they also displayed a degree of heroism that utterly belies many of the claims made with regard to the destruction of the revolution. Victory therefore took over three months, the last Republican troops not being withdrawn until 16 November.

Endgame

Once again, the results were catastrophic. Casualties were about equal, whilst the Republicans had managed to save most of their guns and other heavy equipment. Only in terms of aircraft, in fact, were the Republicans clearly the loser, having lost well over 100 bombers and fighters for no more than 40 of their opponents. At the very least, however, this was a bad bargain, for whereas Franco's losses could easily be replaced, the same could not be said for those of the Republic. Although Catalonia was still capable of producing large quantities of munitions, production was increasingly being disrupted by shortages of raw materials and the earlier Nationalist capture of many of the hydroelectric plants on which the region depended. Meanwhile, Catalonia had never produced much in the way of actual weaponry, the bulk of this having always had to come from abroad. Thanks to British pressure, the French frontier had again been closed, however, whilst the Munich agreement had caused Stalin to rein in the supply of Russian arms. After much negotiation, true, it was agreed that 10,000 Italian troops should withdraw from Spain in exchange for a similar withdrawal on the part of the 12,000 foreign volunteers who still remained in the Popular Army, but even this was not much of a gain, the Italians who were withdrawn being ordinary infantrymen of no particular value whereas the International Brigaders were all hardened veterans.

In short, the military position of Catalonia was downright desperate. Nor were matters made any easier by its politics. Ever since the government had moved to Catalonia, the Generalitat had been complaining bitterly about the manner in which Catalan autonomy had increasingly become a mere fiction. Determined to put an end to this situation, in the very midst of the battle of the Ebro Negrín had faced Companys with the choice of complete capitulation or accepting the task of heading the Republican government. His bluff called, Companys duly climbed down, whereupon Negrín imposed still tighter controls. Meanwhile, rumours of treason were rife and personal disputes of all sorts manifold, the population in the meantime having to endure both the onset of another winter and a further series of air attacks.

In these circumstances, Franco was hardly likely to pay any attention to Negrín's ever more pathetic suggestions of a compromise peace. On the contrary, indeed, on 23 December the full force of the Nationalist armies was flung against Catalonia. Only in numbers of men did the Republicans equal the enemy, the Nationalists' superiority in artillery and aircraft being extremely marked. The campaign was not quite a walk-over – for the first two weeks, indeed, the Nationalists made little progress – but gradually their superior firepower began to tell, and on 3 January they finally broke through. Within a matter of days the whole of Republican forces were fleeing in panic or laying down their arms, whilst fast-moving Nationalist columns sliced through their ranks in the direction of Tarragona and Barcelona. Desperate attempts on the part of the Communists to rally the defenders had no more effect than the arrival of a few more arms from France, Paris having been panicked into once more opening the frontier. Heavily bombed, meanwhile, Barcelona was in a state of turmoil, whilst there were no proper positions from which it could have been defended even had it been possible to rally the ragged mobs of unarmed men to which the Catalan forces had been reduced. On 23 January the government therefore fled to Gerona, the Nationalists rolling in to the city three days later. No sooner had they done so than they embarked on a *limpieza* of truly apocalyptic proportions, all those Republicans who could do so in the meantime embarking on a desperate flight for the French frontier. To the accompaniment of a few brave rearguard actions, one last meeting of what remained of the *cortes* at Figueras and another fruitless offer of peace negotiations, some 460,000 men, women and children flooded across the French frontier into what was to prove a miserable exile. One by one, meanwhile, the border crossings were occupied, and by 10 February it was all over, the scale of the defeat being worsened still further by a revolt that led to the surrender of Menorca.

With the Republican government soon back in such territory as remained to the loyalists, the policy of resisting to conquer might yet have continued for a while longer. The international community, true, was now openly coming out in favour of the Nationalists – Britain and France, for example, formally recognized Franco on 27 February – whilst Madrid had been reduced to near starvation. Moreover, the Republicans were not only short of food, but also almost entirely bereft of industry, their manufacturing potential having been almost entirely concentrated in Catalonia. Yet, whilst aircraft, in particular, were in short supply, it seemed that something might yet be done. The four field armies that held the central zone still had 500,000 men under arms, whilst they had been afforded a considerable period of rest and recuperation and even possessed a record of military victory: on 5 January 1939 a major offensive in the area of Pozoblanco had occupied more enemy territory than any other Republican attack of the war and inflicted severe casualties on the Nationalist forces. At the same time, secret diplomatic contacts had revealed that Franco would not offer even the slightest concessions to the Republicans, whilst on 13 February the generalissimo had issued a decree that made it clear that the repression would be savage indeed. Though even the Communists made it plain that they would not oppose surrender, Negrín determined to fight on to the bitter end.

The commanders in the central zone had other ideas, however. Dominated by officers of the old army, of whom the few who had become Communists – most notably Miaja, who was the overall commander – had only done so out of opportunism, they were jealous of such figures as Modesto, convinced that Franco was only proving obdurate because of the Communist complexion of the regime, and sceptical of the chances of their troops putting up much of a fight. Thus emerged one of the most tragic episodes of the war. Under the leadership of Colonel Segismundo Casado, a plot was hatched to overthrow the government, arrest all those in favour of resistance, and deliver the remaining loyalist territory to the Nationalists. Also involved in the plot were a variety of dissident Anarchists and Socialists, the most prominent being Julián Besteiro. Although Franco remained totally obdurate, on 5 March Casado duly seized control of Madrid, being joined in his revolt by Miaja, the fleet, and parts of the garrisons of Valencia, Murcia and Cartagena (the latter also witnessed an uprising on the part of the local 'fifth column'). Deciding that the game was up, Negrín and his allies all fled by air. However, elements of the Republican forces were still opposed to surrender, the result being a confused struggle which eventually saw Casado triumph and the fleet set sail for French-controlled Bizerta. Resuming his negotiations with Franco, the rebel leader discovered that the only terms on offer remained unconditional surrender. All that was left, therefore, was to gain as much time as possible for those in danger to escape or go into hiding, but the Nationalists knew perfectly well what was afoot, and on 26 March they finally went into action. It was the end. Everywhere the Republican forces collapsed, whilst Cartagena, Alicante and Valencia were besieged with frantic refugees, the last pockets of Republican territory being occupied on 31 March.

Into the Posguerra

Thus ended the Spanish Civil War. Not counting the many thousands who died in the post-war repression or the ravages of disease and malnutrition, some 400,000 people had been killed: 200,000 on the battlefield, 100,000 in the Nationalist *limpieza*, 60,000 in the 'terror', and 40,000 in air raids and the like. If physical damage was more plentiful than overwhelming, meanwhile – only a few small places had suffered real devastation, whilst infrastructural damage had only attained serious proportions on the railways – the total cost of the war was still some 30,000,000,000 *pesetas*.

Why, though, had the war taken so long to win? Given the conventional picture of a powerful Franco supported by all the resources of two mighty war machines, and a defenceless Republic cheated and betrayed at every turn, it might have been thought that victory ought to have come far more rapidly than it did. In answer, it is usually claimed either that Franco deliberately postponed the defeat of his opponents, or that the Republic was sustained by the fervour and heroism of its inhabitants. However, neither argument is particularly satisfactory. Whilst Franco may have missed certain chances, there is little real evidence that he deliberately lengthened the war. Equally, the undoubted courage of many of those who fought for the Republic was of limited value in a military context, whilst in any case co-existing with a rather more varied pattern of behaviour than has often been admitted. At the simplest level the chief factors that delayed the Nationalist victory were, first, the fact that the balance of technology was rather less favourable to Franco than has sometimes been imagined; and second, that the Republic turned its back on the militias and organized a regular army. Constantly sapped though the Republic was by the baneful effects of the revolution, the political rivalries that divided the loyalist forces, the deficiencies of the scheme of military organization which it adopted, and the problems that it met in actually building the new armed forces which its situation required, the war could hardly be otherwise than long and drawn out. In the event, the British and French relief forces of which its leaders dreamed never materialized, but the policy still came close to success: had the Munich crisis led to the war that was generally expected, for example, the fortunes of the Republic might have been very different. None of this is to say, of course, that the foreign intervention was unimportant, nor still less that Franco received far more help than did his opponents. Mere quantity is not everything, however: whereas the Nationalists invariably maximized the impact of what they were sent, the Republicans just as invariably squandered it, or at the very least proved unable to make use of it effectively.

At the close of this long survey, it is obviously worth asking how the civil war fits in with the wider picture that we have gradually built up in the course of the past 385 pages. In this respect, simplistic concepts of a 'war of the two Spains' are not really of very much help, and all the more so if the latter are defined in narrow ideological terms. Nor, indeed, was civil war in any sense an inevitable development, the only reason why such a conflict broke out being that, despite all the advantages that it was offered, the conspiracy to overthrow the Republic failed to win the support of a large enough proportion of the armed forces. What was inevitable was a major crisis, however. Ever since the days of the *cortes* of Cádiz, a situation had been developing in which a total lack of social justice was allowed to coincide with – indeed, was perpetuated by – a striking level of economic backwardness. If a variety of solutions had been offered as a means of remedying this situation, the implication of all of them was that the hold of the social and economic groups who had gradually come to dominate society and politics alike was unlikely to remain unchallenged. The more that time went by, meanwhile, the more the crisis deepened, the result being that, when it finally came, the explosion was one of unparalleled magnitude. Albeit with some difficulty, the old order emerged from the crisis more or less unscathed. Whether it would be able to do so from the peace was another matter altogether.

Glossary

afrancesado	Literally, 'frenchified one'; supporter of Joseph Bonaparte.
afrancesamiento	Literally 'frenchification'; sympathy with/attempt to implement French models, especially those of the Napoleonic empire.
africanista	Literally 'africanist'; officer of the Army of Africa/ colonialists.
agraviado	Literally 'the aggrieved'; proto-Carlist rebel, 1826.
agraviados, guerra de los	Literally 'war of the aggrieved'; neo-Carlist revolt, 1826.
albista	Supporter of/pertaining to Santiago Alba.
alcalde	Mayor.
anti-autoritarios	Supporters of Bakunin in the Spanish section of the First International.
antiguo régimen	*Ancien régime*; old order.
apostolicismo	Ultramontane Catholicism.
apostólico	Ultramontane Catholic.
armas generales	Literally 'general arms'; the infantry and cavalry of the Spanish army.
asalto	Assault Guard.
audiencia	Provincial high court.
autonomista	Autonomist; regional nationalist.
autoritarios	Supporters of Marx and Engels in the Spanish section of the First International.
ayacucho	Clique of officer-corps veterans of the wars of Spanish-American independence associated with Baldomero Espartero.
ayuntamiento	Town hall; town council; municipality.
azañista	Follower of Manuel Azaña.
baldios	That portion of the common lands used as grazing land.
barrios bajos	Literally 'low quarters'; the popular districts and slums in the southern half of the old city of Madrid.
benévolo	Right-wing Federal Republican, 1870–3.
besteirista	Right-wing Socialist associated with Julián Besteiro.

bienes nacionales	Literally 'national properties'; property expropriated from the Church, the municipalities; or, more rarely, political opponents.
bienio	Two-year period.
bracero	Day labourer (agricultural only).
caballerista	Left-wing socialist associated with Francisco Largo Caballero.
cacicato	Sphere of influence pertaining to a *cacique*.
cacique	Landowner or other local notable possessed of sufficient economic power to be able to exert political influence in his locality.
caciquismo	Term used to describe the corruption, fraud and electoral manipulation characteristic of Spanish constitutionalism in the period 1810–1923.
calamar	Right-wing *progresista*, 1870–3.
camarilla	Court faction with the ear of the monarch.
campesino	Literally 'countryman'; in practice, a generic term used to describe all those sectors of the rural lower classes engaged in agriculture.
campo	Countryside.
canalla	Scum; mob.
carabiniero	Border Guard.
carnaval	Literally 'carnival'; the feast of Shrove Tuesday.
caudillo	Literally 'ruler'; the formal title adopted by Francisco Franco.
cedista	Member of the CEDA.
cenetista	Member of the CNT.
centralista	Member of Alonso Martínez's Partido Centralista.
chancilleria	High court.
charte	Literally 'charter'; French constitution of 1814.
cheka	Militia patrols engaged in 'Red Terror', 1936.
cimbrio	Left-wing demócrata, 1870–3.
ciudad condal	Literally 'the city of the counts'; Barcelona.
civil	Civil Guard.
clero y culto	Literally, 'clergy and liturgy'; the subvention paid by the Spanish state to the Church under the terms of the concordat of 1851.
comerciante	Merchant.
concierto económico	Literally 'economic agreement'; the agreement regulating the fiscal privileges that were the last surviving portion of the historic rights of the Basque provinces.
conjunción	Literally 'conjunction'; Republican-Socialist alliance, 1909.
consumos	Indirect taxes levied on foodstuffs at municipal level.

contribución única	Literally 'the single contribution'; new system of taxation introduced by the *cortes* of Cádiz.
convento	Friary, convent, monastery.
corbata	Supporter of eighteenth-century faction associated with the military aristocracy.
corrida	Bullfight.
cortes	Parliament.
cortijo	Complex of barns, granaries, and living accommodation that constituted the headquarters of a *latifundio*.
costista	Follower of Joaquín Costa.
criollo	American-born European inhabitant of Spanish America.
cristino	Supporter of María Cristina and Isabel II, 1833–9.
cuerpos facultátivos	Literally 'qualified/privileged arms'; the artillery, engineers and other technical services of the Spanish army.
demócrata	Supporter of the Partido Progresista–Demócrata, 1849–73.
derechos de puertas	Internal customs dues levied on market produce.
desamortización	Expropriation and/or sale of entailed land.
desamortizador	Disamortizer; disamortizing.
desastre, el	Literally 'the disaster'; i.e. 1898.
dictablanda	Literally 'soft rule'; pun on *dictadura* used to describe the regime of General Berenguer.
dictadura	Dictatorship.
diputación provincial	Provincial council.
doceañista	Literally 'man of 1812'; a veteran of the *cortes* of Cádiz.
doctrinario	Right-wing Moderado.
enchufismo	Literally 'being plugged in'; nepotism.
españolista	Castilian centralist; anti-regionalist Catalan.
esquerrista	Member of the Esquerra Republicana de Catalunya.
exaltado	Literally 'exalted one'; radical liberal, 1820–54.
extremeño	Inhabitant of/pertaining to Extremadura.
fabricante	Manufacturer.
faista	Member of/pertaining to the FAI.
fernandino	Supporter of Fernando VII.
fijo	Permanent employee of a *latifundio*.
fin de siglo	Turn-of-the-century.
forero	Galician rentier.
forista	Galician landlord.
franquismo	Francoism.
franquista	Supporter of/pertaining to Francisco Franco.
fronterizo	Left-wing *unionista*, 1870–3.
fueros	Traditional rights/privileges/codes of justice.

gaditano	Inhabitant of/pertaining to Cádiz.
gamacista	Client/follower of Germán Gamazo.
generalato	All army officers of the rank of brigadier and above.
generalitat	Autonomous government of Catalonia.
gloriosa, la	Literally 'the glorious'; revolution of 1868.
goicoechista	Supporter of Antonio Goicoechea.
golilla	Supporter of eighteenth-century faction associated with the civilian bureaucracy.
grandeza	Aristocracy.
grandeza de servicio	Literally 'aristocracy of service'; aristocrats awarded titles in recognition of particular acts of service to the throne.
hacendado	Landowner.
huerta	Irrigated area devoted to fruit, market gardening, etc.
ilustrado	Literally 'enlightened one'; eighteenth-century intellectual/man of letters.
independiente	Literally 'independent'; man of means.
internacionalista	Spanish supporter of the First International.
intransigente	Left-wing Federal Republican, 1870–3.
isabelino	Supporter of Isabel II.
isturizta	Client/follower of Francisco Javier Isturiz.
japista	Member of the JAP.
jefe político	Literally 'political head'; provincial governor.
jerezano	Inhabitant of/pertaining to Jérez.
jornalero	Day labourer.
josefino	Supporter of/pertaining to Joseph Bonaparte.
junta	Committee of government or administration.
juntero	Any member of a junta; more specifically, the officers involved in the protest movement of 1917 and after.
labrador	Landowner; prosperous tenant farmer.
latifundio	Great landed estate.
lerrouxista	Supporter of Alejandro Lerroux.
leva	Forced levy of convicts, vagabonds, etc, to fill the ranks of the army.
limpieza	Literally 'clean-up'; purge, liquidation of political opponents.
lligista	Member of the Lliga Regionalista de Catalunya.
madrileño	Inhabitant of/pertaining to Madrid.
maja	Feminine of *majo*.
majo	Literally 'fellow, lad, chap'; colloquial term used to describe the lower classes of Madrid.
malagueño	Inhabitant of/pertaining to Málaga.
malhechor	Literally 'evil doer'; criminal, bandit.
mancomunidad	Partial statute of autonomy received by Catalonia in 1914.

mando único	Literally 'single command'; the unification of all political and military authority.
maurista	Follower of Antonio Maura.
mayorazgos	Estate held in perpetuity – i.e. in entail – by the Church or a noble house.
meseta	The high plateau of Central Spain.
Mesta	Powerful sheep-owners' corporation abolished by the Liberals.
minifundio	Smallholding of too small a size to support a family.
ministro-regente	Literally 'Prime-minister-Regent'; i.e. Espartero.
moderado	Supporter of the Partido Monárquico Constitucional, 1834–73.
moderantismo	Literally 'moderatism'; term used to describe the doctrines and positions associated with the *moderados*.
monista	Supporter of Alejandro Mon.
monja de las llagas, la	Literally, 'nun of the wounds'; nickname of Sor Patrocinio.
murciano	Literally, Murcian; also non-Catalan migrant to Barcelona.
narvaisita	Supporter of Ramón Narváez.
oficialidad de complemento	Reserve officer corps.
orgista	Member of the Organización Regionalista Gallega Autónoma.
pablista	Supporter of Pablo Iglesias in PSOE.
partida	Guerrilla band.
paseo	Literally 'stroll, walk'; in Spanish Civil War euphemism for murder/execution.
paviada	Revolt of General Pavia, January 1874.
peninsulares	Literally 'men of the Peninsula'; officers who remained in Spain rather than serving in Morocco, 1909–26; also Spaniards resident in Spanish America prior to independence.
pestañista	Supporter of Angel Pestaña in CNT.
petimetre	I.e. *petit maitre*; ironic late-eighteenth-century nickname used to lampoon fashionable young men who had adopted French fashions and mannerisms.
pidalista	Supporter of Pedro Pidal.
pistolero	Gunman.
plaza de toros	Bullring.
populacho	Literally 'the mob'; the lower classes.
posibilista	Literally 'possibilist'; supporter of Emilio Castelar.
polaco	Literally Pole; supporter of Luis Sartorius.
pretendiente	Office-seeker.
prietista	Supporter of Indalecio Prieto.

primoderiverista	Supporter of/pertaining to Miguel Primo de Rivera.
progresismo	Literally 'progressivism'; term used to describe the doctrines and positions associated with the *progresistas*.
progresista	Supporter of the Partido Progresista, 1834–73.
pronunciamiento	Literally 'pronouncement'; military rebellion.
propios	That portion of the common lands rented out by municipalities to tenant farmers.
pudiente	Local notable; *cacique*.
pueblo	Literally 'people'; town or village.
purificación	Purification, purge.
puritano	Left-wing Moderado, 1841–54.
puro	Left-wing *progresista*, 1854–6; also right-wing *unionistas*, 1870–3.
quinta	Conscript; levy of conscripts.
rabassair	Catalan tenant farmer.
real	Basic unit of Spanish currency prior to 1870.
real sitio	Literally 'royal place'; term applied to the towns of Aranjuez, La Granja and El Escorial.
regidor perpetuo	Hereditary town councillor for life.
reina gobernadora	Literally 'Queen-Governor'; i.e. María Cristina.
renovación	Literally 'renovation'; reform, renewal.
renovador	Literally 'renovator'; most commonly, an opponent of the constitution of 1812.
requeté	Carlist militiaman or guerrilla band.
resellado	Progresista supporter of Unión Liberal.
retaguardia	Home front.
retraimiento	Boycott of parliament.
rey deseado, el	Literally, 'the desired one'; i.e. Fernando VII.
reyes, los	The king and queen.
riverista	Supporter of Nicolás Rivero.
saneamiento	Literally, 'clean up'; purification.
sanjurjada	Revolt headed by General Sanjurjo, August 1932.
santanderino	Inhabitant of/pertaining to Santander.
seguista	Supporter of Salvador Seguí and/or the position which he espoused.
señor	Feudal lord.
señorialismo	Spanish feudal system.
señorio	Feudal fief.
servil	Opponent of the Constitution of 1812.
sexenio	Six-year period.
silvelista	Supporter of Francisco Silvela.
solidaritista	Supporter of Solidaritat Catalana.
somatén	Catalan homeguard (later special constable).
sorteo	Ballot for military service.

straperlo	Gambling device associated with notorious 1935 scandal.
tío pepe	Literally 'Uncle Joe'; common alias.
titulado	Titled member of the nobility.
treintista	CNT moderate, 1931–6.
trienio	Three-year period.
turno	Turn.
turno pacífico	Literally 'pacific alternation'; term used to describe the political system of the Restoration Monarchy, 1875–1923.
ugetista	Member of the UGT.
unionista	Supporter of Unión Liberal.
upetista	Supporter of Unión Patriótica.
vallesoletano	Inhabitant of/pertaining to Valladolid.
veintista	Participant in the revolution of 1820.
vicalvaristas	Participant in the military coup of 1854.
vicalvarada	Military coup of 1854.
vilumista	Neo-absolutist *moderado*, 1843–5.
Voto de Santiago	A levy on grain imposed on the lands of the crown of Castile payable to the archbishopric of Santiago.
yuntero	Tenant farmer owning his own mules and agricultural implements.
zarzuela	Comic opera.
zorrillista	Supporter of Manuel Ruiz Zorrilla.

Select Bibliography

1 General

M. Artola, *La Burguesía Revolucionaria, 1808–1874* (Madrid, 1990).

G. Brenan, *The Spanish Labyrinth: an Account of the Social and Political Background of the Civil War* (Cambridge, 1943).

R. Carr, *Spain, 1808–1975* (Oxford, 1982).

E. Fernández de Pinedo et al., *Centralismo, Ilustración y Agonia del Antiguo Régimen, 1715–1833* (Barcelona, 1980).

J. García Delgado (ed.), *La Crisis de la Restauración: España entre la Primera Guerra Mundial y la Segunda República* (Madrid, 1986).

—— (ed.), *España entre dos Siglos, 1875–1931: Continuidad y Cambio* (Madrid, 1991).

P. Malerbe et al., *La Crisis del Estado: Dictadura, República, Guerra, 1923–1939* (Barcelona, 1981).

M. Martínez Cuadrado, *Restauración y Crisis de la Monarquía, 1874–1931* (Madrid, 1991).

S. Payne (ed.), *Politics and Society in Twentieth-Century Spain* (New York, 1976).

M. Tuñón de Lara (ed.), *La Crisis del Estado Español, 1898–1936* (Madrid, 1978).

2 Thematic

2.1 The economy

L. Alonso, *Comercio Colonial y Crisis del Antiguo Régimen en Galicia, 1778–1818* (La Coruña, 1986).

J. Fontana, *El Comercio Libre entre España y América Latina, 1765–1824* (Madrid, 1987).

R. J. Harrison, *An Economic History of Modern Spain* (Manchester, 1978).

J. Nadal, *El Fracaso de la Revolución Industrial en España, 1814–1913* (Barcelona, 1975).

—— et al. (eds), *La Economía Española en el Siglo XX: una Perspectiva Histórica* (Barcelona, 1987).

J. Palafox, *Atraso Económico y Democracia: la Segunda República y la Economía Española, 1892–1936* (Barcelona, 1991).

D. Ringrose, *Spain, Europe and the 'Spanish miracle', 1700–1900* (Cambridge, 1996).

N. Sánchez-Albornoz (ed.), *The Economic Modernization of Spain, 1830–1930* (New York, 1987).

G. Tortella, *Banking, Railroads and Industry in Spain, 1829–1874* (New York, 1977).

——, *El Desarrollo de la España Contemporánea: Historia Económica de los Siglos XIX y XX* (Madrid, 1994).

—— and J. Palafox, 'Banking and industry in Spain, 1918–1936', *JEEH* (1984), pp. 81–111.

—— et al., *Revolución Burguesa, Oligarquía y Constitucionalismo, 1834–1923* (Barcelona, 1993).

M. Tuñon de Lara et al. (eds), *Crisis del Antíguo Régimen e Industrialización en la España del Siglo XIX* (Madrid, 1977).

2.2   Society

J. Aisa and V. M. Arbolea, *Historia de la Unión General de Trabajadores (UGT), 1888–1931* (Bilbao, 1974).

J. Andrés-Gallego, 'El movimiento agrario confesional de principios del siglo XX', *Hispania* (1981), pp. 155–95.

A. Barrio, *El Anarquismo en Gijón: Industrialización y Movimiento Obrero* (Oviedo, 1982).

——, *Anarquismo y Anarcosindicalismo en Asturias, 1890–1936* (Madrid, 1988).

A. Bernal, *La Propiedad de la Tierra y las Luchas Agrarias Andaluzas* (Barcelona, 1974).

A. Calero, *Historia del Movimiento Obrero en Granada, 1909–1936* (Madrid, 1973).

——, *Movimientos Sociales en Andalucía, 1820–1936* (Madrid, 1979).

J. Caro, *Introducción a una Historia Contemporánea de Anti-Clericalismo Español* (Madrid, 1980).

L. Castells, *Modernización y Dinámica Política en la Sociedad Guipúzcoana de la Restauración, 1876–1915* (Madrid, 1987).

J. Castillo, *El Sindicalismo Amarillo en España* (Madrid, 1977).

——, *Proprietarios Muy Pobres: sobre la Subordinación Política del Pequeño Campesino en España – la Confederación Nacional Católico-Agraria, 1917–1943* (Madrid, 1979).

L. Charnon Deutsch and J. Labanyi (eds), *Culture and Gender in Nineteenth-Century Spain* (Oxford, 1995).

J. Connelly Ullmann, 'The warp and the woof of parliamentary politics in Spain, 1808–1939: anti-clericalism versus neo-catholicism', *ESR* (1983), pp. 145–76.

J. Cruz, *Gentlemen, Bourgeois and Revolutionaries: Political Change and*

Cultural Persistance among the Spanish Dominant Groups, 1750–1850 (Cambridge, 1996).

P. Fernández Albaladejo, *La Crisis del Antiguo Régimen en Guipúzcoa, 1766–1833: Cambio Económico e Historia* (Madrid, 1975).

V. Fernández Benítez, *Carlismo y Rebeldia Campesina: un Estudio sobre la Conflictividad Social en Cantabria durante la Crisis Final del Antiguo Régimen* (Madrid, 1988).

——, *Burguesia y Revolución Liberal: Santander, 1812–1840* (Santander, 1989).

J. García Nieto, *El Sindicalismo Cristiano en España* (Bilbao, 1960).

H. Graham and J. Labanyi (eds), *Spanish Cultural Studies: an Introduction – the Struggle for Modernity* (Oxford, 1995).

P. Heywood, *Marxism and the Failure of Organised Socialism in Spain, 1879–1936* (Cambridge, 1990).

T. Kaplan, 'The social base of nineteenth-century Andalusian anarchism in Jérez de la Frontera', *JIH* (1975), pp. 47–70.

——, *Origenes Sociales del Anarquismo en Andalucía: Capitalismo Agrario y Lucha de Clases en la Provincia de Cádiz, 1868–1903* (Barcelona, 1977).

L. Lorente Toledo, *Poder y Miseria: Oligarcas y Campesinos en la España Señorial, 1760–1868* (Madrid, 1994).

B. Martin, *The Agony of Modernization: Labour and Industrialization in Spain* (Ithaca, New York, 1990).

J. Martínez Alier, *Labourers and Landowners in Southern Spain* (London, 1971).

S. de Moxo, *La Disolución del Régimen Señorial en España* (Madrid, 1965).

X. Paniagua and J. Piqueras, *Trabajadores sin Revolución: la Clase Obrera Valenciana, 1868–1936* (Madrid, 1973).

A. Perinat and M. Marrades, *Mujer, Prensa y Sociedad en España, 1800–1939* (Madrid, 1980).

P. Radcliff, 'Elite women workers and collective action: the cigarette makers of Gijón, 1890–1930', *JSH* (1993), pp. 85–108.

A. Shubert, *The Road to Revolution: the Coal Miners of Asturias, 1860–1934* (Urbana-Champaign, Illinois, 1987).

——, *A Social History of Modern Spain* (London, 1992).

M. Tuñon de Lara, *El Movimiento Obrero en la Historia de España* (Madrid, 1972).

C. Winston, *Workers and the Right in Spain, 1900–1930* (Princeton, New Jersey, 1985).

2.3   Politics

V. Alba, *The Communist Party in Spain* (New Brunswick, New Jersey, 1983).

F. Arias, *El Republicanismo Malagueño durante la Restauración, 1875–1923* (Córdoba, 1985).

M. Artola, *Partidos y Programas Políticos, 1808–1936* (Madrid, 1974).

A. Balcells, *Catalan Nationalism Past and Present* (London, 1996).

A. de Blas, *Tradición Republicana y Nacionalismo Español, 1876–1930* (Madrid, 1991).

R. M. Blinkhorn, 'Spain: the "Spanish problem" and the imperial myth', *JCH* (1980), pp. 5–25.

M. Bookchin, *The Spanish Anarchists: the Heroic Years* (New York, 1977).

C. de Castro, *La Revolución Liberal y los Municipios Españoles, 1812–1868* (Madrid, 1979).

S. Christie, *We, the Anarchists! A Study of the Iberian Anarchist Federation, 1927–1937* (Hastings, 1996).

M. Duncan, 'Spanish anarchism refracted: theme and image in the millenarian and revisionist literature', *JCH* (1988), pp. 323–46.

A. Fernández Domínguez, *Leyes Electorales Españolas de Diputados a Cortes en el Siglo XIX: Estudio Histórico y Jurídico-Político* (Madrid, 1992).

J. Fusi, *Política Obrera en el País Vasco, 1880–1923* (Madrid, 1975).

J. Gil, *Conservadores Subversivos: la Derecha Autoritaria Alfonsina, 1913–1936* (Madrid, 1994).

J. Gómez Casas, *Historia de la FAI* (Bilbao, 1977).

R. Kern, *Red Years, Black Years: a Political History of Spanish Anarchism, 1911–1937* (Philadelphia, 1978).

F. Lannon and P. Preston (eds), *Elites and Power in Twentieth-Century Spain* (Oxford, 1990).

M. Martínez Cuadrado, *Elecciones y Partidos Políticos de España, 1868–1931* (Madrid, 1969).

R. Nuñez, 'Patria y ejército desde la ideología anarquista', *Hispania* (1991), pp. 589–643.

S. Payne, 'Catalan and Basque nationalism', *JCH* (1971), pp. 15–51.

——, *Basque Nationalism* (Reno, Nevada, 1975).

——, 'Spanish conservatism, 1834–1923', *JCH* (1978), pp. 765–89.

——, 'Nationalism, regionalism and micro-nationalism in Spain', *JCH* (1991), pp. 479–92.

A. Peiro and B. Pinilla, *Nacionalismo y Regionalismo en Aragón, 1868–1942* (Zaragoza, 1981).

J. S. Pérez Garzón, *Milicia Nacional y Revolución Burguesa: el Protótipo Madrileño, 1808–1874* (Madrid, 1978).

O. Ruiz Manjón, *El Partido Republicano Radical, 1908–1936* (Madrid, 1976).

J. Tusell, *Oligarquía y Caciquismo en Andalucía, 1890–1923* (Barcelona, 1976).

—— (ed.), *Estudios sobre la Derecha Española Contemporánea* (Madrid, 1993).

2.4 The army and matters military

M. Ballbé, *Orden Público y Militarismo en la España Constitucional, 1812–1983* (Madrid, 1983).

R. Bañón and T. Barker (eds), *Armed Forces and Society in Spain Past and Present* (New York, 1988).

C. Boyd, *Praetorian Politics in Liberal Spain* (Chapel Hill, North Carolina, 1979).

G. Cardona, *El Poder Militar en España Contemporánea hasta la Guerra Civil* (Madrid, 1983).

J. Cepeda, *El Ejército en la Política Española, 1787–1843: Conspiraciones y Pronunciamientos en los Comienzos de la España Liberal* (Madrid, 1990).

E. Christiansen, *The Origins of Military Power in Spain, 1800–1854* (Oxford, 1967).

F. Fernández Bastarreche, *El Ejército Español en el Siglo XIX* (Madrid, 1978).

D. Headrick, *Ejército y Política en España, 1866–1898* (Madrid, 1981).

S. Payne, *Politics and the Military in Modern Spain* (Stanford, California, 1967).

C. Seco, *Militarismo y Civilismo en la España Contemporánea* (Madrid, 1984).

2.5   The Church

A. Botti, *Cielo y Dinero: el Nacionalcatolicismo en España, 1881–1975* (Madrid, 1992).

W. Callahan, *Church, Politics and Society in Spain, 1750–1874* (Cambridge, Massachusetts, 1984).

J. Castells, *Las Asociaciones Religiosas en la España Contemporánea, 1767–1965* (Madrid, 1973).

R. García Villoslada (ed.), *Historia de la Iglesia en España, V: la España Contemporánea* (Madrid, 1979).

F. Lannon, *Persecution, Privilege and Prophecy: the Catholic Church in Spain, 1875–1975* (Oxford, 1987).

S. Payne, *Spanish Catholicism: a Historical Overview* (Madison, Wisconsin, 1973).

3   Chronological

3.1   The revolutionary and Napoleonic era

D. Alexander, *Rod of Iron: French Counter-Insurgency Policy in Aragón during the Peninsular War* (Wilmington, Delaware, 1985).

F. Andújar, *Los Militares en la España del siglo XVIII* (Granada, 1991).

M. Ardit, *Revolución Liberal y Revuelta Campesina: un Ensayo sobre la Desintegración del Régimen Feudal en el País Valenciano, 1793–1840* (Barcelona, 1977).

M. Arriazu (ed.), *Estudios sobre Cortes de Cádiz* (Pamplona, 1967).

M. Artola, *Los Orígenes de la España Contemporánea* (Madrid, 1959).

——, *Los Afrancesados* (Madrid, 1976).

J. Aymes, *La Guerra de la Independencia en España, 1808–1814* (Madrid, 1975).

R. Bayod, *El Reino de Aragón durante el Reino Intruso de los Napoleón* (Zaragoza, 1979).

A. Berkeley (ed.), *New Lights on the Peninsular War: International Congress on the Iberian Peninsula, 1780–1840* (Lisbon, 1991).

A. Bernal, *La Lucha por la Tierra en la Crisis del Antiguo Régimen* (Madrid, 1979).

R. Blanco, *Rey, Cortes y Fuerza Armada en los Orígenes de la España Liberal, 1808–1823* (Madrid, 1988).

F. Carantoña, *La Guerra de la Independencia en Asturias* (Oviedo, 1983).

——, *Revolución Liberal y Crisis de las Instituciones Tradicionales Asturianas* (Gijón, 1989).

P. Casado, *Las Fuerzas Armadas en el Inicio del Constucionalismo Español* (Madrid, 1982).

P. Chavarri, *Las Elecciones a las Cortes Generales y Extraordinarias, 1810–1813* (Madrid, 1988).

N. Cruz, *Valencia Napoleónica* (Valencia, 1968).

J. Cuenca, *La Iglesia Española ante la Revolución Liberal* (Madrid, 1971).

M. Diz, *El Manifiesto de 1814* (Pamplona, 1967).

C. Esdaile, 'Wellington and the Spanish army, 1812: the revolt of General Ballesteros', *CREP* (1987), pp. 93–108.

——, *The Spanish Army in the Peninsular War* (Manchester, 1988).

——, 'Heroes or villains? The Spanish guerrillas in the Peninsular War', *HT*, XXXVIII, no. 4 (April, 1988), pp. 29–35.

——, 'The Marqués de la Romana and the Peninsular War: a case-study in Spanish civil-military relations, *CREP* (1993), pp. 366–74.

——, *The Duke of Wellington and the Command of the Spanish Army, 1812–14* (London, 1990).

A. Espinar, *Málaga durante la Primera Etapa Liberal, 1812–1814* (Málaga, 1994).

J. Fisher, 'Commerce and imperial decline: Spanish trade with Spanish America, 1797–1820', *JLAS* (1998), pp. 459–79.

I. Fletcher (ed.), *The Peninsular War: Aspects of the Struggle for the Iberian Peninsula* (Staplehurst, 1998).

P. García Gutiérrez, *La Ciudad de León en la Guerra de la Independencia* (León, 1991).

M. Gómez Bajo, *La Guerra de la Independencia en Astorga, 1808–1814* (Astorga, 1986).

R. Guirao and L. Sorando, *El Alto Aragón en la Guerra de la Independencia* (Zaragoza, 1995).

E. Hamilton, 'War and inflation in Spain, 1780–1800', *QJE* (1944), pp. 36–77.

B. Hamnett, *La Política Española en una Epoca Revolucionaria* (México City, 1985).

J. Harbron, *Trafalgar and the Spanish Navy* (London, 1988).

R. Herr, *The Eighteenth-Century Revolution in Spain* (Princeton, 1958).

——, *Rural Change and Royal Finances in Spain at the End of the Old Régime* (Berkeley, California, 1989).

H. Lafoz, *La Guerra de la Independencia en Aragón: del Motín de Aranjuez a la Capitulación de Zaragoza* (Zaragoza, 1996).

A. Laspra, *Intervencionismo y Revolución: Asturias y Gran Bretaña durante la Guerra de la Independencia, 1808–1813* (Oviedo, 1992).

J. Longares, *La Ideología Religiosa del Liberalismo Español, 1814–1843* (Córdoba, 1979).

M. López Pérez and I. Lara, *Entre la Guerra y la Paz: Jaén, 1808–1814* (Granada, 1993).

L. Lorente, *Agitación Urbana y Crisis Económica durante la Guerra de la Independencia, 1808–1814* (Cuenca, 1993).

G. Lovett, *Napoleon and the Birth of Modern Spain* (Princeton, 1965).

J. Lynch, *Bourbon Spain, 1700–1808* (Oxford, 1989).

F. Marti, *El Proceso del Escorial* (Pamplona, 1965).

——, *El Motín de Aranjuez* (Pamplona, 1972).

E. Martínez Quinteiro, *Los Grupos Liberales antes de las Cortes de Cádiz* (Madrid, 1977).

A. Martínez de Velasco, *La Formación de la Junta Central* (Pamplona, 1972).

M. Mercader, *Catalunya i l'Imperi Napoleònic* (Montserrat, 1978).

J. Mercader, *José Bonaparte, Rey de España* (Madrid, 1971–83).

F. Miranda, *La Guerra de la Independencia en Navarra: la Acción del Estado* (Pamplona, 1977).

P. Molas (ed.), *La España de Carlos IV* (Madrid, 1991).

A. Moliner, 'La peculiaridad de la revolución española de 1808', *Hispania* (1987), pp. 632–46.

M. Morán, *Poder y Gobierno en las Cortes de Cádiz* (Pamplona, 1986).

——, *Revolución y Reforma Religiosa en las Cortes de Cádiz* (Madrid, 1994).

I. Morant, *El Declive del Señorio: los Dominios del Ducado de Gandía, 1705–1837* (Valencia, 1984).

M. Moreno, *Sevilla Napoléonica* (Seville, 1995).

C. Oman, *A History of the Peninsular War* (Oxford, 1902–30).

E. la Parra, *La Alianza de Godoy con los Revolucionarios* (Madrid, 1992).

R. Rodríguez Garraza, *Tensiones de Navarra con la Administración Central, 1778–1808* (Pamplona, 1974).

C. Seco, *Godoy: el Hombre y el Político* (Madrid, 1978).

F. Suárez Verdeguer, *Las Tendencias Políticas durante la Guerra de la Independencia* (Zaragoza, 1959).

——, *Conservadores, Innovadores y Renovadores en las Postrimerías del Antiguo Régimen* (Pamplona, 1965).

J. Tone, *The Fatal Knot: the Guerrilla War in Navarre and the Defeat of Napoleon* (Chapel Hill, North Carolina, 1994).

3.2   The First Restoration

T. Anna, *Spain and the Loss of America* (Lincoln, Nebraska, 1983).

J. Comellas, *Los Primeros Pronunciamientos en España, 1814–1820* (Madrid, 1958).

M. Costeloe, *Response to Revolution: Imperial Spain and the Spanish-American Revolutions, 1810–1840* (Cambridge, 1986).

E. Díaz Lobón, *Granada durante la Crisis del Antiguo Régimen, 1814–1820* (Granada, 1982).

J. Fontana, *La Quiebra de la Monarquía Absoluta, 1814–1820: la Crisis del Antiguo Régimen en España* (Barcelona, 1971).

E. González López, *Entre el Antiguo y el Nuevo Régimen: Absolutistas y Liberales – el Reinado de Fernando VII en Galicia* (La Coruña, 1980).

J. Lynch, *The Spanish-American Revolutions, 1808–1826* (London, 1973).

C. Maqueda, 'La restauración de Fernando VII y el reclutamiento militar', *RHM*, no. 62 (January, 1987), pp. 71–92.

M. Marliani, *El Reinado de Fernando VII* (Madrid, 1986).

F. Marti, *Iglesia y Estado en el Reinado de Fernando VII* (Pamplona, 1994).

A. Monente, 'La conspiración de Lacy', *Hispania* (1977), pp. 601–21.

M. Pintos, *La Política de Fernando VII entre 1814 y 1820* (Pamplona, 1958).

D. Pennell, 'State power in a chronically weak state: Spanish coastguards as pirates, 1814–50', *EHQ* (1995), pp. 353–80.

M. Ramos, *La Conspiración del Triangulo* (Seville, 1970).

E. Resnick, 'The failure of absolutism in Spain, 1814–1820', *IS*, (1975), pp. 75–81.

M. Sánchez Gómez, *Sociedad y Política en Cantabria durante el Reinado de Fernando VII: Revolución Liberal y Reacción Absolutista* (Santander, 1989).

3.3   The Trenio Liberal, 1820–1823

J. Brinas, *La Desamortización Eclesiástica en el País Valenciano durante el Trienio Constitucional* (Valencia, 1978).

B. Buldaín, 'La junta provisional de 1820: instalación y atribuciones', *RHC* (1982), pp. 39–63.

——, 'La implantación del nuevo régimen en 1820', *CIH* (1989), pp. 73–9.

J. Comellas, *Los Realistas en el Trienio Constitucional, 1820–1823* (Pamplona, 1958).

——, *El Trienio Constitucional* (Madrid, 1963).

V. Conejero, *El Trienio Constitucional en Alicante y la Segunda Represión contra los Liberales* (Alicante, 1983).

G. Feliu, *La Clerecia Catalana durant el Trienio Liberal* (Barcelona, 1972).

A. Gil, *Las Sociedades Patrióticas, 1820–1823: las Libertades de Expresión en el Origen de los Partidos Políticos* (Madrid, 1975).

——, *El Trienio Liberal* (Madrid, 1980).

J. del Moral, *Hacienda y Sociedad en el Trienio Constitucional, 1820–1823* (Madrid, 1975).

P. Peguenaute, *Represión Política en el Reinado de Fernando VII: las Comisiones Militares, 1824–1825* (Pamplona, 1974).

M. Revuelta, *Política Religiosa de los Liberales en el Siglo XIX: el Trienio Constitucional* (Madrid, 1973).

R. del Río, *Orígenes de la Guerra Carlista en Navarra, 1820–1824* (Pamplona, 1987).

J. Rodríguez Gordillo, *Las Proclamas Realistas de 1822* (Seville, 1969).

J. Ruíz Alemán, *El Levantamiento Realista de Orihuela en 1822* (Murcia, 1970).
J. Torras, *Liberalismo y Rebeldía Campesina, 1820–23* (Barcelona, 1976).
I. Zavala, *Masones, Comuneros y Carbonarios* (Madrid, 1971).

3.4　*Liberalism enthroned, 1823–1839*

M. Asensio, *El Carlismo en la Provincia de Ciudad Real, 1833–1876* (Ciudad Real, 1987).
F. Asín, *Aproximación al Carlismo Aragonés durante la Guerra de los Siete Años* (Zaragoza, 1983).
F. Asín and A. Bullón, *Carlismo y Sociedad* (Zaragoza, 1987).
J. Barreiro, *El Carlismo Gallego* (Santiago de Compostela, 1976).
A. Bullón, *La Primera Guerra Carlista* (Madrid, 1992).
I. Burdiel, *La Política de los Notables Moderados y Avanzados durante el Régimen del Estatuto Real, 1834–6* (Valencia, 1987).
I. Castells, *La Utopia Insureccional del Liberalismo: Torrijos y las Conspiraciones Liberales de la Década Ominosa* (Barcelona, 1989).
M. Castroviejo, *Aproximación Sociológica al Carlismo Gallego: la Primera Guerra Carlista en la Provincia de Lugo* (Madrid, 1977).
J. Clemente, *Los Orígenes del Carlismo* (Madrid, 1979).
——, *Las Guerras Carlistas* (Madrid, 1986).
J. Extramiana, *Historia de las Guerras Carlistas* (San Sebastián, 1979).
F. Fernández Segado, 'Las bases vertebradoras de la constitución de 1837', *Hispania* (1987), pp. 679–744.
J. Fontana, *Hacienda y Estado en la Crisis Final del Antiguo Régimen Español* (Madrid, 1973).
——, *La Revolución Liberal: Política y Hacienda, 1833–45* (Madrid, 1977).
F. García Villarubia, *Aproximación al Carlismo Andaluz en la Guerra de los Siete Años, 1833–40* (Madrid, 1979).
R. Herr, 'El significado de la desamortización en España', *MC*, no. 131 (December, 1974), pp. 55–94.
P. Janke, *Mendizábal y la Instauración de la Monarquía Constitucional en España, 1790–1853* (Madrid, 1974).
J. Longares, *Política y Religión en Barcelona, 1833–1843* (Madrid, 1976).
——, *La Divulgación de la Cultura Liberal, 1833–1843* (Córdoba, 1979).
C. Marichal, *La Revolución Liberal y los Primeros Partidos Políticos en España, 1834–1844* (Madrid, 1980).
J. Millán, *Realismo y Carlismo en el Sur del País Valenciano* (Alicante, 1982).
M. Mina, *Fueros y Revolución Liberal en Navarra* (Madrid, 1981).
A. Moliner, *Joaquín María López y el Partido Progresista, 1834–1843* (Alicante, 1988).
E. Olcina, *El Carlismo y las Autonomias Regionales* (Madrid, 1974).
J. Pan, *Carlistas y Liberales en Navarra, 1833–1839* (Pamplona, 1990).
M. Revuelta, *La Exclaustración, 1833–1840* (Madrid, 1976).
R. Rodríguez Garraza, *Navarra de Reino a Provincia, 1828–1841* (Pamplona, 1968).

G. Rueda, *La Desamortización de Mendizábal y Espartero en España* (Madrid, 1986).

M. Sánchez Gómez, *El Primer Carlismo Montañes: Aspectos Sociales y Localización Geográfica* (Santander, 1985).

F. Suárez Verdeguer, *Los Agraviados de Cataluña* (Pamplona, 1972).

F. Tomàs, *El Marco Político de la Desamortización en España* (Barcelona, 1971).

——, 'Recientes investigaciones sobre la desamortización: intento de síntesis', *MC*, no. 131 (December, 1974), pp. 95–160.

J. Torras, *La Guerra de los Agraviados* (Barcelona, 1967).

J. de Urquijo, 'Represión y disidencia durante la primera guerra carlista', *Hispania* (1985), pp. 131–86.

3.5 Isabeline liberalism, 1839–1868

C. Almuiña, 'El antimonarquismo de los Progresistas, 1864–65: Antonio Cánovas del Castillo y la ley de prensa del 29 de junio de 1864', *CIH* (1979), pp. 5–34.

J. Azagra, 'El motín de la milicia en Valencia el 6 de abril de 1856', *Hispania* (1974), pp. 442–62.

S. Cabeza, *Los Sucesos de 1848 en España* (Madrid, 1981).

F. Cánovas, *El Partido Moderado* (Madrid, 1982).

——, *El Moderantismo y la Constitución de 1845* (Madrid, 1985).

J. Comellas, *Los Moderados en el Poder, 1844–1854* (Madrid, 1970).

N. Durán, *La Unión Liberal y la Modernización de la España Isabelina: una Convivencia Frustrada, 1854–1868* (Madrid, 1979).

A. Eiras, *El Partido Demócrata Español* (Madrid, 1961).

——, *Sociedades Secretas Republicanas en el Reinado de Isabel II* (Madrid, 1962).

M. Espadas, *Baldomero Espartero* (Ciudad Real, 1985).

A. Fernández García, 'Enfermedad y sociedad: la epidemia de cólera de 1865 en Madrid', *CIH* (1979), pp. 155–86.

J. Gil, *Krausistas y Liberales* (Madrid, 1975).

D. Headrick, 'Spain and the Revolutions of 1848', *ESR* (1976), pp. 197–223.

V. Kiernan, *The Revolution of 1854 in Spanish History* (Oxford, 1966).

A. Laguna, 'José María Orense, ideólogo del Partido Demócrata Español', *Hispania* (1984), pp. 343–68.

C. Lida, *Agitaciones Populares y Toma de Consciencia durante el Bienio Constitucional, 1854–1856* (Madrid, 1969).

D. López Garrido, *La Guardia Civil y los Orígenes del Estado Centralista* (Barcelona, 1982).

J. Maluquer, *El Socialismo en España, 1833–1868* (Barcelona, 1979).

J. Marcuello, 'Sistema constitucional, práctica parlamentaria y alternativas conservadoras en el liberalismo isabelino', *Hispania* (1993), pp. 237–76.

J. del Moral, *Gasto Público y Expansión Económica en España, 1845–1865: Hacienda y Política en la España de Moderados y Progresistas* (Madrid, 1979).

J. Ollero, *El General Espartero, Logroñes de Adopción: Consideraciones en Torno a su Epoca y su Dimensión Política y Humana* (Zaragoza, 1993).

J. Pabón, *Narváez y su Epoca* (Madrid, 1983).

F. Paredes, *Pascual Madoz, 1805–1870: Libertad y Progreso en la Monarquía Isabelina* (Pamplona, 1982).

V. Pinilla, 'La conflictividad social en Zaragoza durante el bienio progresista', *Hispania* (1984), pp. 583–600.

——, *Conflictividad Social y Revuelta Política en Zaragoza, 1854–1856* (Zaragoza, 1985).

M. Puga, *El Matrimonio de Isabel II* (Pamplona, 1964).

M. Rodríguez, 'Espartero y las relaciones comerciales hispano-británicas, 1840–1843', *Hispania* (1985), pp. 323–61.

N. Rosenblatt, 'The Concordat of 1851 and its relation to moderate liberalism in Spain', *IS* (1978), pp. 30–9.

J. de Urquijo, 'La milicia como instrumento de presión política en el bienio progresista', *Hispania* (1981), pp. 17–46.

——, '1854: revolución y elecciones en Vizcaya', *Hispania* (1982), pp. 565–606.

——, *La Revolución de 1854 en Madrid* (Madrid, 1984).

——, 'La revolución de 1854 en Zamora', *Hispania* (1991), pp. 245–86.

3.6   The Sexenio Revolucionario, 1868–1874

J. Andrés-Gallego, 'Las juntas revolucionarias de 1868: una interpretación', *BRAH* (1979), pp. 39–86.

E. Arias, 'Expectativas y limitaciones de la democracia en la Sevilla del sexenio, 1868–1874', *ETF* (1990), pp. 65–84.

J. Aróstegui, *El Carlismo Alavés y la Guerra Civil de 1870–1876* (Vitoria, 1970).

J. Catalinas, *La Primera República: Reformismo y Revolución Social* (Madrid, 1973).

J. Donézar, *La Constitución de 1869 y la Revolución Burguesa* (Madrid, 1985).

J. Fernández Rua, *1873: la Primera República* (Madrid, 1975).

V. Garmendia, *La Segunda Guerra Carlista, 1872–1876* (Madrid, 1976).

V. Gascón, *La Revolución del 68 en Valencia y su Reino* (Castellón, 1978).

A. Gil, *La Revolución de 1868 en el Alto Aragón* (Zaragoza, 1980).

R. Grabalosa, *Carlins i Liberals: la Darrera Guerra Carlina a Catalunya* (Barcelona, 1971).

G. Harper, 'El rey intruso: the accession of Amadeo of Savoy', *IS* (1977), pp. 33–41.

C. Hennessy, *The Federal Republic in Spain: Pi y Margall and the Federal Republican Movement, 1868–1874* (Oxford, 1962).

J. Hernando, 'Madrid, 1868: la fiesta revolucionaria', *Ayeres*, (1991), pp. 25–8.

M. Izard, *Manufactureros, Industriales y Revolucionarios* (Barcelona, 1979).

J. Lacomba, *La I República: el Trasfondo de una Revolución Fallecida* (Madrid, 1973).

C. Lida and I. Zavala (eds), *La Revolución de 1868: Historia, Pensamiento, Literatura* (New York, 1970).

C. Llorca, *Emilio Castelar, Precursor de la Democracia Cristiana* (Madrid, 1966).

M. López Cordón, *La Revolución de 1868 y la I República* (Madrid, 1976).

F. Marti, *La Cuestión Religiosa en la Revolución de 1868–1874* (Madrid, 1989).

J. Millán-Chivite, *Revolucionarios, Reformistas y Reaccionarios: Aproximación a un Estudio de la Generación de 1868* (Seville, 1979).

J. Nadal, *La Revolución de 1868 en Gerona: la Actuación de la Junta Revolucionaria Provincial* (Gerona, 1971).

E. Oliver, *Castelar y el Periodo Revolucionario Español, 1868–1874* (Madrid, 1971).

R. Oliver, *Así Cayó Isabel II* (Madrid, 1986).

P. Parrilla, *El Cantonalismo Gadítano* (Cádiz, 1983).

R. Serrano, *El Sexenio Revolucionario en Valladolid: Cuestiones Sociales, 1868–1874* (Valladolid, 1986).

——, *La Revolución de 1868 en Castilla y León* (Valladolid, 1992).

R. Vallverdú, *El Tercer Carlisme a les Comarques Meridionals de Catalunya, 1872–1876* (Montserrat, 1997).

J. Vilar, *El Sexenio Democrático y el Cantón Murciano* (Murcia, 1983).

—— and P. Egea, 'Mineria y sociedad en el distrito de Cartagena durante el sexenio democrático, 1866–1874', *Hispania* (1982), pp. 607–54.

J. Villanueva, *Alcañiz, 1868–1874: entre la Legalidad Septembrina y la Insurrección Carlista en el Bajo Aragón* (Teruel, 1987).

3.7 The Restoration Monarchy, I: Cánovas and Sagasta

E. Alvarez Conde, 'El pensamiento político canovista', *REP* (1977), pp. 233–95.

E. Beck, 'The Martínez Campos government of 1879: Spain's last chance in Cuba', *HAHR* (1976), pp. 268–89.

——, *A Time of Triumph and of Sorrow: Spanish Politics during the Reign of Alfonso XII, 1874–1885* (Carbondale, Illinois, 1979).

S. Ben-Ami, 'Basque nationalism between archaism and modernity', *JCH* (1991), pp. 493–521.

R. M. Blinkhorn, 'Ideology and schism in Spanish traditionalism, 1876–1931', *IS* (1972), pp. 16–24.

J. Chandler, 'The self-destructive nature of the Spanish Restoration', *IS* (1973), pp. 65–72.

J. Comellas, *Cánovas del Castillo* (Madrid, 1997).

J. Connelly Ullman, *The Tragic Week: a Study of Anti-Clericalism in Spain, 1875–1912* (Cambridge, Massachusetts, 1968).

J. Corcuera, *Orígenes, Ideología y Organización del Nacionalismo Vasco, 1876–1904* (Madrid, 1979).

J. Durán, *Agrarismo y Movilización Campesina en el País Gallego, 1875–1912* (Madrid, 1977).

A. Elorza and M. Ralle, *La Formación del PSOE* (Barcelona, 1989).

G. Esenwein, *Anarchist Ideology and the Working-Class Movement in Spain, 1868–1898* (Berkeley, California, 1989).

M. Espadas, *Alfonso XII y los Orígenes de la Restauración* (Madrid, 1975).

M. Fernández Almagro, *Cánovas: su Vida y su Política* (Madrid, 1972).

J. García Delgado (ed.), *La España de la Restauración: Política, Economía, Legislación y Cultura* (Madrid, 1985).

L. Gómez Llorente, *Aproximación a la Historia del Socialismo Español hasta 1921* (Madrid, 1972).

V. Gómez Mier (ed.), *La Restauración Monarquica de 1875 y la España de la Restauración* (San Lorenzo del Escorial, 1978).

R. Gutiérrez Lloret, 'Restauración y republicanismo: élites locales y representación política en Alicante, 1875–1895', *ETF* (1990), pp. 119–29.

R. J. Harrison, 'Big business and the rise of Basque nationalism', *ESR* (1977), pp. 371–91.

A. Jiménez-Landi, *La Institución Libre de Enseñanza y su Ambiente* (Madrid, 1973–87).

R. Kern, *Liberals, Reformers and Caciques in Restoration Spain, 1875–1909* (Albuquerque, New Mexico, 1974).

——, 'Catastrophe and regeneration as themes of political criticism in the Bourbon restoration, 1877–1885', *IS* (1974), pp. 29–33.

C. Lida, *La Mano Negra: Anarquismo Agrario en Andalucía* (Algorta, 1992).

F. Márquez Santos, 'La logia madrileña 'Fraternidad Ibérica' durante la Restauración', *Hispania* (1985), pp. 363–82.

F. Marti, *Política Religiosa de la Restauración, 1875–1931* (Madrid, 1991).

M. Marti, 'Las diputaciones provinciales en la trama caciquil: un ejemplo castellonense durante los primeros años de la restauración', *Hispania* (1991), pp. 993–1041.

R. Núñez Florencio, 'El presupuesto de la paz: una polémica entre civiles y militares en la España finisecular', *Hispania* (1989) pp. 197–234.

——, *Militarismo y Anti-Militarismo en España, 1888–1906* (Madrid, 1990).

A. Ollero, 'Sagasta y su proyecto político', *Berceo*, no. 104 (January, 1983), pp. 83–102.

M. Ollero, 'La tolerancia religiosa en la constitución de 1876: análisis de la campaña de protesta', *ETF*, pp. 107–21.

M. Pérez Picasso, *Oligarquía Urbana y Campesinado en Murcia, 1875–1902* (Murcia, 1979).

J. Peset, 'El Real Consejo de Instrucción pública y la restauración canovista', *Hispania* (1988), pp. 989–1030.

J. Piqueras, 'Los inicios del partido socialista obrero español en Valencia', *Hispania* (1981), pp. 621–36.

J. Real, *El Carlismo Vasco, 1876–1900* (Madrid, 1985).

J. Real, *Partidos, Elecciones y Bloques de Poder en el País Vasco, 1876–1923* (Bilbao, 1991).

C. Robles, *Insurrección o Legalidad: los Católicos y la Restauración* (Madrid, 1988).

A. Rodríguez González, 'El conflicto de Melilla en 1893', *Hispania* (1989), pp. 235–66.

A. Ruiz Salvador, *El Ateneo Científico, Literario y Artístico de Madrid, 1835–1885* (London, 1971).

L. Sánchez Agesta, *La Constitución de 1876 y el Estado de la Restauración* (Madrid, 1985).

J. Termes, *Anarquismo y Sindicalismo en España: la Primera Internacional, 1864–1881* (Barcelona, 1972).

J. Varela, *Los Amigos Políticos: Partidos, Elecciones y Caciquismo en la Restauración, 1875–1900* (Madrid, 1977).

C. Velasco, 'Cánovas del Castillo y la articulación del estado nacional', *CEICE* (1978), pp. 61–97.

3.8   The Restoration Monarchy, II: 1898

J. Andrés-Gallego, 'La última evolución política de Castelar', *Hispania* (1970), pp. 385–93.

——, 'Los grupos políticos del 98', *Hispania* (1978), pp. 121–46.

S. Balfour, 'Riot, regeneration and reaction: Spain in the aftermath of the 1898 disaster', *HJ* (June, 1995), pp. 405–23.

——, *The End of the Spanish Empire, 1898–1923* (Oxford, 1997).

C. Blanco, *Juventud del 98* (Madrid, 1970).

J. Figuero and C. Santa Cecilia (eds), *La España del Desastre* (Barcelona, 1997).

J. Fusi and A. Niño (eds), *Vísperas del 98: Orígenes y Antecedentes de la Crisis del 98* (Madrid, 1997).

R. J. Harrison, 'Catalan business and the loss of Cuba, 1898–1914', *EcHR* (1974), pp. 431–41.

——, 'The beginnings of social legislation in Spain, 1900–1919', *IS* (1974), pp. 3–8.

——, 'The regenerationist movement in Spain after the disaster of 1898', *ESR* (1979), pp. 1–27.

——, 'Financial reconstruction in Spain after the loss of the last colonies', *JEEH* (1980), pp. 317–49.

E. Inman, *La Crisis Intellectual del 98* (Madrid, 1976).

J. Maurice and C. Serrano, *J. Costa: Crisis de la Restauración y Populismo (1875–1911)* (Madrid, 1977).

R. Pérez de la Dehesa, *El Pensamiento de Costa y su Influencia en el 98* (Madrid, 1966).

C. Robles, 'Reformas políticas y pacificación militar en Cuba', *Hispania* (1992), pp. 173–224.

S. Salaün and C. Serrano (eds), *1900 en España* (Madrid, 1991).

M. Sánchez Mantero, 'El europeismo-progresismo fluctuante de los escritores del noventa y ocho entre el "desastre" y la gran guerra, 1898–1814', *RHC* (1991), pp. 65–92.

C. Serrano, *Final del Imperio: España, 1895–1898* (Madrid, 1984).

J. Smith, *The Spanish-American War: Conflict in the Caribbean and the Pacific, 1895–1902* (London, 1994).

J. Varela, 'Aftermath of splendid disaster: Spanish politics before and after the Spanish-American War of 1898', *JCH* (1980), pp. 317–44.

3.9 The Restoration Monarchy, III: Alfonso XIII

J. Alvarez Junco, *Periodismo y Política en el Madrid del Fín del Siglo: el Primer Lerrouxismo* (Madrid, 1983).

——, *El Emperador del Paralelo: Lerroux y la Demagogia Popular* (Madrid, 1990).

O. Alzaga, *La Primera Democracia Cristiana en España* (Barcelona, 1973).

J. Andrés-Gallego, 'La crisis del partido liberal, 1903–1907', *Hispania* (1975), pp. 391–428.

A. Balcells, *El Sindicalisme a Barcelona, 1916–1923* (Barcelona, 1965).

M. Cabrera, *Santiago Alba: un Programa de Reforma Económica en la España del Primer Tercio del Siglo XIX* (Madrid, 1989).

J. Chandler, 'Spain and her Moroccan protectorate, 1898–1927', *JCH* (1975), pp. 301–22.

——, 'The responsibilities for Anual', *IS* (1977), pp. 68–75.

A. Comalada, *España: el Ocaso de un Parlamento, 1921–1923* (Barcelona, 1985).

J. de la Cueva, 'The stick and the candle: clericals and anti-clericals in northern Spain, 1898–1913', *EHQ* (1996), pp. 241–65.

A. Delgado, '¿Problema agrario andaluz o cuestión nacional? El mito del "trienio bolchevique" en Andalucía, 1918–1920', *CHC* (1991), pp. 97–124.

C. Ehrlich, '*Per Catalunya i l'Espanya gran*: Catalan regionalism on the offensive, 1911–1919', *EHQ* (1998), pp. 189–217.

S. Forner, *Canalejas y el Partido Liberal Democrático* (Madrid, 1993).

J. Gárate, 'Los militares españoles ante la Gran Guerra', *Hispania* (1985), pp. 579–614.

F. Gómez Ochoa, 'La alianza Maura-Cambó de 1921: una experiencia de reformismo conservador durante el reinado de Alfonso XIII', *RHC* (1991), pp. 93–108.

M. González Hernández, *Ciudadanía y Acción: el Conservadurismo Maurista, 1907–1923* (Madrid, 1990).

——, *El Universo Conservador de Antonio Maura: Biografía y Proyecto de Estado* (Madrid, 1997).

G. Gortazar, *Alfonso XIII, Hombre de Negocios: Persistencia del Antiguo Régimen, Modernización Económica y Crisis Política, 1902–1931* (Madrid, 1986).

R. J. Harrison, 'The failure of economic reconstitution in Spain, 1916–23', *ESR* (1983), pp. 63–88.

F. Luengo, *La Crisis de la Restauración: Partidos, Elecciones y Conflictividad Social en Guipúzcoa, 1917–1923* (Bilbao, 1991).

J. Macarro, *Conflictos Sociales en la Ciudad de Sevilla en los Años 1918–1920* (Córdoba, 1984).

J. Marín, *Santiago Alba y la Crisis de la Restauración, 1913–1930* (Madrid, 1990).

A. Más, *La Formación de la Consciencia Africanista del Ejército Español, 1909–1926* (Madrid, 1988).

G. Meeker, *The Revolutionary Left in Spain, 1914–1923* (Stanford, California, 1974).

J. Pabón, *Cambó* (Barcelona, 1952–69).

R. Pennell, 'The responsibility for Anual: the failure of Spanish policy in the Moroccan Protectorate, 1912–21', *ESR* (1982), pp. 67–86.

R. Punset, 'Maura y el maurismo: perspectiva histórica de la revolución desde arriba', *Sistema*, no. 33 (November, 1979), pp. 129–41.

F. Romero, 'Spain and the First World War: the structural crisis of the liberal monarchy', *EHQ* (1995), pp. 555–82.

J. Romero-Maura, *La 'Rosa del Fuego': el Obrerismo Barcelonés de 1899 a 1909* (Madrid, 1989).

J. Ruiz Sánchez, 'Los católicos sevillanos ante el reinado de Alfonso XIII: entre la tradición y el progreso', *ETF* (1990), pp. 131–41.

C. Seco, *Alfonso XIII y la Crisis de la Restauración* (Madrid, 1979).

A. Smith, 'Anarchism, the general strike and the Barcelona labour movement, 1899–1914', *EHQ* (1997), pp. 5–40.

M. Suárez Cortina, *El Reformismo en España: Republicanos y Reformistas bajo la Monarquía de Alfonso XIII* (Madrid, 1986).

T. Trice, *Spanish Liberalism in Crisis: a Study of the Liberal Party during Spain's Parliamentary Collapse, 1913–1923* (New York, 1991).

J. Tusell, 'Para la sociologia política de la España contemporánea: el impacto de la ley de 1907 en el comportamiento electoral', *Hispania* (1970), pp. 571–630.

C. M. Winston, 'The proletarian Carlist road to fascism: *sindicalismo libre*', *JCH* (1982), pp. 557–85.

3.10 *Dictadura* and *dictablanda*

F. Alía Miranda, *Ciudad Real durante la Dictadura de Primo de Rivera* (Ciudad Real, 1986).

L. Alvarez Rey, *Sevilla durante la Dictadura de Primo de Rivera: la Unión Patriótica, 1923–1930* (Seville, 1987).

J. Andrés Gallego, *El Socialismo durante la Dictadura, 1923–1930* (Madrid, 1977).

S. Ben-Ami, 'The dictatorship of Primo de Rivera: a political reassessment, *JCH* (1977), pp. 65–84.

——, *Fascism from Above: the Dictatorship of Primo de Rivera in Spain, 1923–1930* (Oxford, 1983).

S. Fleming and A. Fleming, 'Primo de Rivera and Spain's Moroccan problem, 1923–27', *JCH* (1977), pp. 85–99.

G. García Queipo de Llano, *Los Intelectuales y la Dictadura de Primo de Rivera* (Madrid, 1988).

J. Gómez Navarro, *El Régimen de Primo de Rivera* (Madrid, 1991).

—— et al., 'Aproximación al estudio de las elites políticas en la dictadura de Primo de Rivera', *CEICE* (1979), pp. 183–208.

M. González Calbet, *La Dictadura de Primo de Rivera: el Directorio Militar* (Madrid, 1987).

R. Martínez Segarra, 'Grupos económicos en el Somatén', *CEICE* (1979), pp. 209–23.

C. Navajas, *Ejército, Estado y Sociedad en España, 1923–1930* (Logroño, 1991).

——, 'La ideología corporativa de Miguel Primo de Rivera, 1905–1919', *Hispania* (1993), pp. 617–49.

J. Palomares, *Nuevos Políticos para un Nuevo Caciquismo: la Dictadura de Primo de Rivera en Valladolid* (Valladolid, 1993).

E. Pérez Romero, *La Provincia de Soria durante la Dictadura de Primo de Rivera, 1923–1930* (Soria, 1983).

F. Puell, 'La cuestión artillera', *Hispania*, XLVII (1987), pp. 279–308.

F. del Rey, 'El capitalismo catalán y Primo de Rivera: en torno de un golpe de estado', *Hispania* (1988), pp. 289–307.

O. Ruiz Manjón, 'La dictadura de Primo de Rivera y la consolidación del entimiento republicano en España: una interpretación del Partido Radical', in *RHC* (1982), pp. 167–77.

M. Tuñón de Lara, 'En torno a la dictadura de Primo de Rivera', *CEICE* (1979), pp. 9–35.

J. Tusell, *La Crisis del Caciquismo Andaluz, 1923–1931* (Madrid, 1977).

——, *Radiografía de un Golpe de Estado: el Ascenso al Poder del General Primo de Rivera* (Madrid, 1987).

—— and G. García Queipo de Llano, 'La dictadura de Primo de Rivera como régimen político: un intento de interpretación', *CEICE* (1979), pp. 37–63.

3.11   Republic and civil war

R. Abella, *La Vida Cotidiana durante la Guerra Civil* (Barcelona, 1973–75).

M. Ackelsberg, *Free Women of Spain: Anarchism and the Struggle for the Emancipation of Women* (Bloomington, Indiana, 1991).

F. Aguado, *La Revolución de Octubre de 1934* (Madrid, 1972).

V. Alba and S. Schwartz, *Spanish Marxism versus Soviet Communism* (New Brunswick, New Jersey, 1988).

M. Alexander and H. Graham (eds), *The French and Spanish Popular Fronts: Comparative Perspectives* (Cambridge, 1989).

A. Alfonso, *Los Partidos Políticos y la Autonomía en Galicia, 1931–1936* (Madrid, 1976).

F. Alía, *La Guerra Civil en Retaguardia: Conflicto y Revolución en la Provincia de Ciudad Real, 1936–1939* (Ciudad Real, 1994).

M. Alpert, 'The Spanish Republican Army, 1936–1939', *IS* (1973), pp. 26–32.

——, *La Reforma Militar de Azaña, 1931–1933* (Madrid, 1982).

——, *El Ejército Republicano en la Guerra Civil* (Madrid, 1989).

G. Alvarez Chillida, 'Nación, tradición e imperio en la extrema derecha española durante la década de 1930', *Hispania* (1982), pp. 999–1030.

L. Alvarez Rey, *La Derecha en la Segunda República: Sevilla, 1931–1936* (Seville, 1993).

J. Avilés, *Los Republicanos de Izquierda, 1930–1936* (Madrid, 1983).

——, *La Izquierda Burguesa en la II República* (Madrid, 1985).

A. Aviv and I. Aviv, 'Ideology and political patronage: workers and working-class movements in Republican Madrid, 1931–34', *ESR* (1981), pp. 487–515.

—— and ——, 'The Madrid working class, the Spanish Socialist Party and the collapse of the Second Republic, 1934–1936', *JCH* (1981), pp. 229–50.

A. Balcells, *Crisis Económica y Agitación Social en Cataluña, 1930–1936* (Barcelona, 1971).

M. Barras, *Acció Catalana, 1922–1936* (Barcelona, 1984).

S. Ben-Ami, *The Origins of the Second Republic in Spain* (Oxford, 1978).

——, 'The forerunners of Spanish fascism: Unión Patriótica and Union Monárquica', *ESR* (1979), pp. 49–79.

J. Beramendi and R. Máiz (eds), *Los Nacionalismos en la España de la II República* (Madrid, 1991).

W. Bernecker, *Colectividades y Revolución Social: el Anarquismo en la Guerra Civil, 1936–1939* (Barcelona, 1982).

M. Bizcarrondo, *Araquistaín y la Crisis Socialista en la II República – Leviatán, 1934–1936* (Madrid, 1975).

R. M. Blinkhorn, '"The Basque Ulster": Navarre and the Basque autonomy question under the Second Spanish Republic', *HJ*, (1974), pp. 595–613.

——, *Carlism and Crisis in Spain, 1931–1939* (Cambridge, 1975).

—— (ed.), *Spain in Conflict: Democracy and its Enemies* (London, 1986).

B. Bolloten, *The Spanish Civil War: Revolution and Counter-Revolution* (Chapel Hill, North Carolina, 1994).

T. Borras, *Ramiro Ledesma Ramos* (Madrid, 1971).

A. Bosch, *Ugetistas y Libertarios: Guerra Civil y Revolución en el País Valenciano, 1936–1939* (Valencia, 1983).

C. Boyd, ' "Responsibilities" and the Second Spanish Republic, 1931–6', *EHQ* (1984), pp. 151–82.

J. Brademas, *Anarcosindicalismo y Revolución en España 1930–1937* (Barcelona, 1974).

G. Brey and J. Maurice, *Historia y Leyenda de Casas Viejas* (Madrid, 1976).

P. Broué and E. Témime, *The Revolution and Civil War in Spain* (London, 1972).

M. Cabrera, *La Patronal ante la II República: Organizaciones y Estrategía, 1931–1936* (Madrid, 1983).

R. Carr (ed.), *The Republic and the Civil War in Spain* (London, 1971).

——, *The Spanish Tragedy: the Civil War in Perspective* (London, 1977).

J. Casanova, *Anarquismo y Revolución en la Sociedad Rural Aragonesa, 1936–38* (Madrid, 1985), pp. 177–219.

——, 'Anarchism and revolution in the Spanish Civil War: the case of Aragón', *EHQ* (1987), pp. 430–52.

—— et al., *El Pasado Oculto: Fascismo y Violencia en Aragón, 1936–1939* (Madrid, 1992).

A. Checa, *Prensa y Partidos Políticos durante la II República* (Salamanca, 1989).

R. Chueca, *El Fascismo en los Comienzos del Régimen de Franco: un Estudio sobre FET y de las JONS* (Madrid, 1983).

J. Cifuentes and P. Maluenda, *El Asalto a la República: los Orígenes del Franquismo en Zaragoza, 1936–39* (Zaragoza, 1995).

C. Cobb, *Los Milicianos de la Cultura* (Bilbao, 1995).

J. Coverdale, *Italian Intervention in the Spanish Civil War* (Princeton, New Jersey, 1975).

W. Christian, *Visionaries: the Spanish Republic and the Reign of Christ* (Berkeley, 1996).

M. Cruells, *De les Milícies a l'Exercit Popular a Catalunya* (Barcelona, 1974).

——, *El Separatisme Català durant la Guerra Civil* (Barcelona, 1975).

R. Cruz, *El Partido Comunista de España en la II República* (Madrid, 1987).

A. Durgan, *B.O.C., 1930–1936: el Bloque Obrero y Camperol* (Barcelona, 1996).

C. Ealham, 'Anarchism and illegality in Barcelona, 1931–7', *ContEH* (1995), pp. 133–51.

A. Egido, 'La hispanidad en el pensamiento reaccionario español de los años treinta', *Hispania* (1993), pp. 651–73.

S. Ellwood, *Spanish Fascism in the Franco Era: Falange Española de las Jons, 1936–76* (London, 1987).

——, *Franco* (London, 1994).

V. Enders, 'Nationalism and feminism: the Sección Femenina of the Falange', *HEI* (1992), pp. 673–80.

S. Fleming, 'Spanish Morocco and the alzamiento nacional, 1936–1939: the military, economic and political mobilisation of a protectorate', *JCH* (1983), pp. 27–42.

D. Foard, 'The forgotten falangist: Ernesto Giménez Caballero', *JCH* (1975), pp. 3–18.

J. Fontana et al., *La II República: una Esperanza Frustrada* (Valencia, 1987).

R. Fraser, *Blood of Spain: the Experience of Civil War, 1931–1939* (London, 1979).

J. Fusi, *El Problema Vasco en la II República* (Madrid, 1979).

——, *Franco: a Biography* (London, 1987).

V. Gabarda, *Els Afusellaments al País Valencià, 1938–1956* (Valencia, 1993).

A. García, *La Iglesia Español y el 18 de Julio* (Barcelona, 1977).

J. García Delgado (ed.), *La II República Española: Bienio Rectificador y Frente Popular, 1934–1936* (Madrid, 1988).

P. García i Jordán, *Els Catòlics Catalans i la Segona República, 1931–1936* (Montserrat, 1986).

R. Garriga, *El Cardenal Segura y el Nacional-Catolicismo* (Barcelona, 1977).

——, *Ramón Franco, el Hermano Maldito: Apogeo y Decadencia de una Familia* (Barcelona, 1978).

I. Gibson, *The Assassination of Federico García Lorca* (London, 1979).

——, *La Noche que Mataron a Calvo Sotelo* (Barcelona, 1982).

J. Gil, 'La opinión pública ante las reformas hacendistas de Joaquín Chapaprieta', *Hispania* (1987), pp. 1001–21.

——, *La Segunda República* (Madrid, 1989).

M. Gimeno, *Revolució, Guerra i Repressió al Pallars, 1936–1939* (Barcelona, 1989).

A. Girona, *Guerra i Revolució al País Valencià* (Valencia, 1986).

H. Graham, *Socialism and War: the Spanish Socialist Party in Power and Crisis, 1936–1939* (Cambridge, 1991).

J. de la Granja and C. Garitaonandia (eds), *Gernika: 50 años después – Nacionalismo, República, Guerra Civil* (San Sebastián, 1987).

R. J. Harrison, 'The inter-war depression and the Spanish economy', *JEEH* (1983), pp. 295–321.

J. Hernández Andreu, *Depresión Económica en España, 1925–1934: Crisis Mundial antes de la Guerra Civil Española* (Madrid, 1980).

A. Hernández Lafuente, *Autonomía e Integración en la Segunda República* (Madrid, 1980).

I. Herreros, *Mitología de la Cruzada de Franco: el Alcazar de Toledo* (Madrid, 1995).

M. Ivern, *Esquerra Republicana de Catalunya, 1931–1936* (Montserrat, 1989).

G. Jackson, *The Spanish Republic and Civil War, 1931–1939* (Princeton, New Jersey, 1965).

—— and A. Centelles, *Catalunya Republicana i Revolucionaria* (Barcelona, 1982).

E. Jardí, *Francesc Macià, President de Catalunya* (Montserrat, 1981).

R. Jensen, 'Jose Millán Astray and the Nationalist "crusade" in Spain', *JCH* (1992), pp. 425–48.

V. Johnston, *Legions of Babel: the International Brigades in the Spanish Civil War* (Harrisburg, Pennsylvania, 1967).

S. Juliá, *Orígenes del Frente Popular en España, 1934–1936* (Madrid, 1979).

——, *Madrid, 1931–1934: de la Fiesta Popular a la Lucha de Clases* (Madrid, 1984).

T. Kaplan, 'Spanish anarchism and women's liberation', *JCH* (1971), pp. 101–10.

G. Kelsey, *Anarchosyndicalism, Libertarian Communism and the State: the CNT in Zaragoza, 1930–1937* (Dordrecht, 1991).

A. López Fernández, *El General Miaja, Defensor de Madrid* (Madrid, 1975).

A. López López, *El Boicot de la Derecha de las Reformas de la Segunda República: la Minoria Agraria, el Rechazo Constitucional y la Cuestión de la Tierra* (Madrid, 1984).

M. López Martínez, 'Cambio y represión: la conjunción negativa – la destitución de los ayuntamientos republicano-socialistas [en] Granada, 1933–1936', *RHC* (1995), pp. 119–44.

R. Low, *La Pasionaria: the Spanish Firebrand* (London, 1992).

J. Macarro, 'Causas de la radicalización socialista en la II República', *RHC* (1982), pp. 178–224.

——, *La Utopia Revolucionaria: Sevilla en la Segunda República* (Seville, 1985).

M. de Madariaga, 'The intervention of Moroccan troops in the Spanish Civil War: a reconsideration', *EHQ* (1992), pp. 67–98.

E. Malefakis, *Agrarian Reform and Peasant Revolution in Spain: Origins of the Civil War* (New Haven, Connecticutt, 1970).

S. Mangini, *Memories of Resistance: Women's Voices from the Spanish Civil War* (New Haven, Connecticutt, 1995).

J. Martín y Ramos, *Els Orígens del Partit Socialista Unificat de Catalunya, 1930–1936* (Barcelona, 1977).

J. Martínez Leal, *República y Guerra Civil en Cartagena, 1931–1939* (Murcia, 1993).

F. de Meer, *La Constitución de la II República* (Pamplona, 1978).

J. de Mesa, *El Regreso de las Legiones: Voluntarios Italianos en la Guerra Civil Española* (Granada, 1994).

J. Mintz, *The Anarchists of Casas Viejas* (Chicago, 1992).

P. Monteath, 'Guernica reconsidered: fifty years of evidence', *WS* (1987), pp. 79–104.

J. Montero, *La CEDA: el Catolicismo Social y Político en la II República* (Madrid, 1977).

R. Morodo, *Los Orígenes Ideológicos del Franquismo: Acción Española* (Madrid, 1985).

A. Nadal, *Guerra Civil en Málaga* (Málaga, 1984).

M. Nash, '*Milicianas* and home-front heroines: images of women in revolutionary Spain, 1936–1939', *HEI* (1989), pp. 235–44.

——, 'Women in war: *milicianas* and armed combat in revolutionary Spain, 1936–1939, *IHR* (1993), pp. 269–82.

——, *Defying Male Civilization: Women in the Spanish Civil War* (Denver, Colorado, 1995).

C. Navajas, 'La revisión azañista de la legislación militar dictatorial: la memoria de la comisión Sastre', *Hispania*, (1991), pp. 287–313.

G. Ojeda (ed.), *Octubre 1934* (Madrid, 1984).

J. Ordovas and M. Montero, *Historia de la Asociación Católica Nacional de Propagandistas* (Pamplona, 1993).

S. de Pablo, *Alava y la Autonomía Vasca durante la Segunda República* (Vitoria, 1985).

M. Pastor, *Los Orígenes del Fascismo en España* (Madrid, 1975).

S. Payne, *Falange: a History of Spanish Fascism* (Stanford, California, 1961).

——, *The Spanish Revolution* (London, 1970).

——, *The Franco Régime, 1936–1975* (Madison, Wisconsin, 1987).

——, 'Political violence during the Spanish Second Republic', *JCH* (1990), pp. 269–88.

——, *Spain's First Democracy: the Second Republic, 1931–1936* (Madison, Wisconsin, 1993).

A. Paz, *Durruti* (Madrid, 1978).

J. Peirats, *Anarchists in the Spanish Revolution* (Toronto, 1977).

E. Pons, *Guerrillas Españolas, 1936–1960* (Barcelona, 1977).

J. Pons and J. Solé, *Anarquía i República a la Cerdanya, 1936–1939: el 'Cojo de Málaga' i els Fets de Bellver* (Monserrat, 1991).

E. Portuondo, *La Segunda República: Reforma, Fascismo y Revolución* (Madrid, 1981).

P. Preston, 'Alfonsine monarchism and the coming of the Spanish Civil War', *JCH* (1972), pp. 89–98.

——, 'The struggle against fascism in Spain: *Leviatán* and the contradictions of the Socialist Left, 1934–6', *ESR* (1979), pp. 81–103.

——, *The Coming of the Spanish Civil War: Reform, Reaction and Revolution in the Second Republic, 1931–1936* (London, 1979).

—— (ed.), *Revolution and War in Spain, 1931–1939* (London, 1984).

——, *Franco: a Biography* (London, 1993).

—— and H. Graham, *The Popular Front in Europe* (London, 1987).

—— and A. L. Mackenzie (eds), *The Republic Besieged: Civil War in Spain 1936–1939* (Edinburgh, 1996).

R. Proctor, *Hitler's Luftwaffe in the Spanish Civil War* (Westport, Connecticutt, 1983).

H. Raguer i Suñer, *La Unió Democràtica i el seu Temps* (Montserrat, 1976).

M. Ramírez (ed.), *Estudios sobre la II República Española* (Madrid, 1975).

G. Redondo, *Historia de la Iglesia en España, 1931–1939* (Madrid, 1993).

A. Reig, *Ideología e Historia: sobre la Represión Franquista y la Guerra Civil* (Torrejón de Ardoz, 1986).

——, *Violencia y Terror: Estudios sobre la Guerra Civil Española* (Torrejón de Ardoz, 1990).

V. Richards, *Lessons of the Spanish Revolution, 1936–1939* (London, 1972).

R. Richardson, *Comintern Army: the International Brigades and the Spanish Civil War* (Kentucky, 1982).

R. Robinson, *The Origins of Franco's Spain: the Right, the Republic and the Revolution, 1931–1936* (Newton Abbot, 1970).

L. Romero, *Por qué y como mataron a Calvo Sotelo* (Barcelona, 1982).

R. Salas, *Historia del Ejército Popular de la República* (Madrid, 1973).

R. Sánchez López, *Mujer Española, una Sombra de Destino en lo Universal: Trayectoria Histórica de Sección Feminina de Falange, 1934–1977* (Murcia, 1990).

M. Seidman, 'Work and revolution: workers' control in Barcelona in the Spanish Civil War, 1936–38', *JCH* (July, 1982), pp. 409–33.

——, 'The unOrwellian Barcelona', *EHQ* (1990), pp. 163–80.

——, 'Individualisms in Madrid during the Spanish Civil War', *JMH* (1996), pp. 63–83.

V. Serrano and J. San Luciano (eds), *Azaña* (Madrid, 1980).

A. Shubert, 'Revolution in self-defence: the radicalisation of the Asturian coalminers, 1921–34', *SH* (1982), pp. 265–82.

J. Solé, *La Repressió a la Reraguardia de Catalunya, 1936–1939* (Montserrat, 1989–90).

H. Southworth, *Guernica! Guernica! A Study of Journalism, Diplomacy, Propaganda, and History* (Berkeley, California, 1977).

M. Suárez Cortina, *El Fascismo en Asturias, 1931–1937* (Oviedo, 1981).

R. Tamames, *La República. La Era de Franco* (Madrid, 1988).

M. Termens, *Revolució i Guerra Civil a Igualada, 1936–1939* (Montserrat, 1991).

G. Thomas and M. Morgan Witts, *The Day Guernica Died* (London, 1975).

H. Thomas, 'The hero in the empty room: José Antonio and Spanish Fascism', *JCH* (1966), pp. 174–82.

——, *The Spanish Civil War* (London, 1977).

J. Thomas, *Falange, Guerra Civil, Franquisme: FET y de las JONS de Barcelona en els Primers Anys del Régimen Franquista* (Madrid, 1992).

J. Tusell, *Las Elecciones del Frente Popular en España* (Madrid, 1971).

——, *Franco en la Guerra Civil: una Biografía Política* (Barcelona, 1992).

—— and G. García Queipo de Llano, *Los Intelectuales y la República* (Madrid, 1990).

M. Valdés, *De la Falange al Movimiento, 1936–1952* (Madrid, 1994).

S. Varela, *Partidos y Parlamento en la Segunda República* (Madrid, 1978).

S. Vilar, *La Naturaleza del Franquismo* (Barcelona, 1977).

A. Viñas, 'Gold, the Soviet Union and the Spanish Civil War', *ESR* (1979), pp. 105–28.

——, *Guerra, Dinero, Dictadura: Ayuda Fascista y Autarquía en la España de Franco* (Barcelona, 1984).

R. Viñas, *La Formación de las Juventudes Socialistas Unificadas, 1934–1936* (Madrid, 1978).

M. Vincent, *Catholicism in the Second Spanish Republic: Catholicism in Salamanca, 1930–1936* (Oxford, 1996).

R. Whealey, 'How Franco financed his war – reconsidered', *JCH* (1977), pp. 133–52.

——, *Hitler and Spain: the Nazi Role in the Spanish Civil War* (Lexington, Kentucky, 1989).

4 Abbreviations

AHR	–	American Historical Review
BRAH	–	Boletín de la Real Academia de Historia
BUM	–	Boletín de la Universidad de Madrid
CEICE	–	Cuadernos Económicos de Información Comercial Española
CHC	–	Cuadernos de Historia Contemporánea
CIH	–	Cuadernos de Investigación Histórica
ContEH	–	Continental European History
CREP	–	Consortium on Revolutionary Europe Proceedings
EcHR	–	Economic History Review
EHQ	–	European History Quarterly
EM	–	España Moderna
ESR	–	European Studies Review
ETF	–	Espacio, Tiempo y Forma

HAHR	–	Hispanic American Historical Review
HEI	–	History of European Ideas
HJ	–	Historical Journal
HT	–	History Today
IHR	–	International History Review
IS	–	Iberian Studies
JCH	–	Journal of Contemporary History
JEEH	–	Journal of European Economic History
JIH	–	Journal of Interdisciplinary History
JLAS	–	Journal of Latin-American Studies
JSH	–	Journal of Social History
MC	–	Moneda y Crédito
QJE	–	Quarterly Journal of Economics
REP	–	Revista de Estudios Políticos
RHC	–	Revista de Historia Contemporánea
RHM	–	Revista de Historia Militar
SH	–	Social History
WS	–	War and Society

Index

Page numbers in bold type refer to main or detailed references